Principles of Cost Accountancy

Principles of
Cost Accountancy
A Managerial Perspective

Fifth Edition

ALAN PIZZEY BSc (Econ.), FCCA, ACIS, MBIM
Principal Lecturer in Accounting, Trent Polytechnic

based on previous editions by
C. I. Buyers, CA, FCMA and G. A. Holmes, FCA

CASSELL

Cassell Educational Ltd: Artillery House, Artillery Row, Westminster, London, SW1P 1RT

British Library Cataloguing in Publication Data

Pizzey, Alan
    Principles of cost accountancy:
    a managerial perspective. —5th ed.
    1. Cost accounting
    I. Title II. Buyers, C.I.
    657′.42   HF5686.C8

ISBN   0-304-31371-8

Typeset by Macmillan India Ltd, Bangalore 25
Printed in Great Britain by Mackays of Chatham Ltd

Contents

Contents

Preface

The original textbook *Principles of Cost Accountancy* by C. I. Buyers and C. A. Holmes was well respected and proved to be very useful to student and teacher alike. I have used the book in both these capacities and can vouch for its excellence. Accordingly, I feel privileged to have been asked to rewrite the book and to continue the tradition associated with it. I have tried to maintain the features of the original work, which I found most useful in the past, yet update and broaden the coverage for a new generation of students.

The purpose of this edition is to give a thorough introduction of the subject to students commencing their studies in cost and management accounting. Costing, however, is not an end in itself but a tool to be used by the accountant in assisting management. Therefore, I have written the book with a managerial perspective, laying the emphasis on the application of cost accounting principles to management accounting. The use of costs in planning and control is a natural progression from the techniques of cost finding and application and itself leads into decision making and evaluation. For this reason, sections on decision making in the short and long term and on the evaluation of performance have been added. Because management concerns people, the chapter on behavioural aspects of budgetary control is particularly significant to this work.

I hope that this book will be welcomed by both teachers and students on courses leading to the early stages of the professional accounting examinations, on foundation courses in accounting, on undergraduate courses covering cost accounting – perhaps as part of a business studies degree, and on BTEC and SCOTBEC courses. It seems unfortunate that textbooks seem to be written for specific courses or levels, it is my intention that the managerial perspective incorporated within this book will introduce more advanced topics to students, so that they will find the book helpful beyond the early stages of their accounting education. The discussion of rules for decision making and the mixture of current theory with a practical approach will, I trust, establish the book as a companion volume to *Accounting and Finance: A Firm Foundation*.

In response to comment from students and teachers, relevant exercises have been included at the end of each chapter, with solutions provided as an appendix. Further review questions are also added at the end of each chapter. A special lecturers' manual, which accompanies this book, contains the solutions to these exercises. Thus students can check their own progress and teachers can use the manual on their courses, adding some of their own favourite examples if they wish to, by setting work from the review questions to test students' progress.

I would like to thank Brian Howlett for his helpful comments on the original text, Deborah Fox for editorial expertise, Simon Lake for encouragement and organisational assistance, and not least my patient secretary for all the work entailed in the preparation of this book.

A. V. Pizzey
1986

To Barbara, Jonathan and Joscelin
without whose forbearance and encouragement
this book would never have been completed

Section I
Cost Finding

1

Introduction to Cost Accounting – Its Place in the Management System

In one sense all the figures produced by the accounting system for a particular business are of interest to managers at one level or another. A narrower definition of management accounting might describe it as the application of accounting techniques to provide information that will help management. The role of management is to plan the business in the long and short term, to take decisions, to communicate those plans and decisions to other managers or operatives who must translate them into action, to control operations, and finally to analyse and evaluate the results. As a member of the management team, the management accountant must use all his skills to assist in these tasks, whether those skills are derived from the principles of financial accounting, cost accounting, quantitative methods, economics, or behavioural science.

A cost is 'the amount of expenditure (actual or notional) incurred on or attributable to a specific thing or activity' (Institute of Cost and Management Accountants); and cost accounting is the system whereby the management accountant identifies, ascertains, records, classifies, allots and presents cost data. Costing is an analysis to allocate cost to products or services or time periods, so that the costs of various activities undertaken by a business are disclosed, and can be set against revenue to reveal the profitability of these activities. Each business has its objectives and costs are the resources used up to achieve those objectives. The cost accountant organises the system that records and measures such resources, and provides firm information to management on which further decisions can be based with confidence.

It is difficult to select the appropriate amount to be charged as a cost. Suppose a builder uses up a tonne of sand on a job, how is the cost of that resource to be defined? Can it be counted as the price paid for the sand when it was bought six months previously (historic cost – say £25), or as what must be spent today to buy more sand (replacement cost – say £30), or as the expenditure that could be avoided by using the sand for an alternative purpose (opportunity cost – say £28)? No doubt other definitions of cost could be used.

From the outset cost accounting must be recognised as a service to management, existing only because it fulfils a requirement for information and because managers are willing to meet the expense of providing the information they use. Cost information should only be produced if it provides a benefit deemed to be worth more than its cost, and with a view to the effect the information will have on the people to whom it is provided. It is a well-established principle among management accountants that costing should provide information that is relevant to the needs of its recipients, which can be easily understood and assimilated by them, provided at an appropriate time, which renders the information useful, at a cost that is less than the benefit to be derived from the information.

Management Accounting and Financial Accounting

The major difference between these two is a matter of attitude and approach, but the details can be summarised as follows:

1. *Users.* A wide spectrum of persons, from shareholders and creditors to customers and the Inland Revenue, use financial accounts, which are public documents, whereas management accounts are prepared for management purposes only and, as such, are of a confidential nature.
2. *Legal Rules.* Financial accounts are drafted in accordance with the provisions of the Companies Acts and Statements of Standard Accounting Practice, whereas the management accountant drafts his statement in a form that he considers will best suit the circumstances and the recipient.
3. *Time and Purpose.* Financial accounts usually report on past events, showing what has happened on a historic basis as a matter of stewardship, but management accounts often deal with future events that are planned to happen; or if they are produced after the event, the time-lag between statement and event is a short one. The purpose of management accounts is to assist in planning operations, and to control by comparing actual events with the plan.
4. *Analysis.* Financial accounts reveal the results for the business as a whole, whereas management accounts seek to break down the business into its constituent parts and report on each part. Financial accounts are usually stated in monetary terms, but a management statement may be expressed in terms of volume or standard hours as well as in monetary terms because it is tailored to fit a particular purpose.

Cost Control

The primary aim of a commercial concern is to make a profit. Yet profit does not arise automatically in the course of business: it is the excess (if any) of selling price over cost. As, in practice, selling price is usually influenced by the competition of rival concerns or products, as well as by the strength of consumer demand and a host of other market conditions beyond the producer's control, it follows that any success he may have in selling his goods or services profitably is likely to depend upon his ability to control his costs, and upon the extent to which he can keep them below the selling price imposed upon him by competition. This operation can be expressed in the formula:

$$\text{Selling price} - \left\{ \text{Production cost} + \text{Distribution cost} + \text{Selling cost} + \text{Administration cost} \right\} = \text{Profit (Loss)}$$

Cost control has been defined as the regulation by executive action of the costs of operating an undertaking, particularly where such action is guided by cost accounting. It covers the control of material usage and material prices; of wages cost, separating the effect of efficiency from rates of pay; of maintenance and service costs; and of all other items of indirect expenditure.

   The first stage in cost control is the setting of standards or targets of performance against which the actual costs can be measured. A yardstick commonly used in this comparison is the cost record of a previous period. This is reliable, however, only when prices and methods remain unchanged, the volume of production is constant and the proportion of sales of various products does not change substantially from period to period. Moreover, as such a comparison disregards the standard of efficiency attained in the earlier period, there is a risk of an indifferent current record seeming to be good only because it is compared with one that is even worse. A better, and more modern, plan is to compare actual performance with a pre-determined budget or standard, expertly drawn up to show what expenditure *should be* incurred, or what a product ought to cost under conditions of high efficiency. This is the method of budgetary control and standard costing, which will be described in chapters 9 and 10. *The second stage* is to analyse costs to show managers exactly where and why costs are being incurred. *The third stage* is to compare actual cost with planned cost, which, if necessary, will generate remedial action.

Costing as a Basis for Estimating

Although selling prices are frequently regulated by conditions beyond the supplier's control, this is not always entirely so. In some businesses, and for contract and jobbing work, for example, firms are commonly invited to submit quotations or estimates for the supply of specified goods or services. When this happens, the supplier will quote a price based upon the formula:

$$\text{Production cost} + \text{Distribution cost} + \text{Selling cost} + \text{Administration cost} + \text{Profit} = \text{Selling price}$$

Recourse to cost records will give the estimator useful information about the cost of previous jobs of a similar kind and other statistical details that will facilitate the drawing up of a trustworthy estimate. Some costs are not specific to a job, and the development of reliable bases for the absorption of overhead costs will improve the accuracy of tenders and estimates. The amount he will include for profit will be determined with due regard to the custom of his trade and to any relevant special factors, such as the state of his order book.

Once a customer has accepted a quotation this determines the selling price of the goods regardless of the costs subsequently incurred. The actual costs will, however, be recorded, and for the purpose of contrast will be compared with the estimate on which the quotation was based.

Costing as a Basis for Operating Policy

Almost every decision made by management has repercussions upon cost, and it is a function of the cost accountant to show the probable financial effect of alternative courses of action. Thus, he may be called upon to prepare a statement comparing the cost of buying a particular service from an outside supplier with that of providing it internally, in order to assist management in deciding upon the best policy to adopt. When such a policy decision has been made, the cost accountant will trace the actual results and provide data comparing them with those anticipated. In the presentation of information of this type the cost accountant has great scope for the exercise of ingenuity and skill, particularly as the average manager is not a trained accountant and needs clear, concise statements that he can readily understand.

Advantages of Costing

In addition to fulfilling the objectives referred to above, a costing system will provide the following benefits to management:

(a)   The relative profitability of various activities will be revealed, and management thus given the opportunity to review them and to consider the elimination or modification of those from which little or no advantage is derived.

(b)   The disclosure of unprofitable or excessively costly operations may lead to the development of new or improved methods, the reduction of waste and greater economy in the use of resources.

(c)   Cost accounts will reveal the cause of any increase or decrease in the profit shown in the financial accounts.

(d)   Since an adequate system of material and wages accounting is a prerequisite of a sound system of costing, some control over these items of expenditure will be ensured.

(e)   Management will be informed of the unabsorbed overhead expenditure that arises when plant is not employed to capacity and will be able to modify its policy accordingly.

(f)   Information will be forthcoming to enable management to compare the probable results of alternative courses of action e.g. as to whether it is more profitable to produce a component or to buy it from a manufacturer who specialises in its production.

(g)   When the various concerns in a particular industry agree to record their costs uniformly and to submit their results to a trade association or to an independent public accountant, information of the utmost value to the members of the industry can be exchanged without prejudice to the interests of the individual members concerned.

(h)   Where running contracts provide for the adjustment of an agreed price in the event of a change in costs, the records of an efficient costing system can be employed to facilitate the acceptance of a new price by customers.

Costing does, of course, have some disadvantages. It can be expensive to operate, time-consuming for managers to raise basic data, and at times so complex as to be difficult for managers to understand and use. It may be operated in an inflexible and unsympathetic manner. Most of these drawbacks can be avoided if the costing system is well designed and administered in an atmosphere of teamwork and co-operation.

Applications of Costing

While cost accounting is generally looked upon as a feature of manufacturing concerns, its applications are in fact much wider. For example, the principles of cost accounting are applied successfully in the wholesale and retail trades, in road transport undertakings, and in farming. Costing not only provides the facts from which policy decisions can be made, but the basic principles of costing can be applied alike to the transactions of large and small undertakings and even to those of individuals.

Designing a System of Cost Accounts (see Chapter 19)

The keynotes of a good system of cost accounts are simplicity and common sense. The simple record and the clear form of control that can be easily understood by all concerned, are always more effective than the over-complicated system that provides a mass of information, the significance of which is only vaguely understood by those to whom it is presented. Simple systems are usually cheap, and produce data in good time for it to be relevant.

Before a costing system is installed, therefore, a great deal of consideration is called for, and much planning needed. In particular, the business must be studied in detail to find out exactly what information is required and to ensure that the obtainable results will justify the cost of the additional staff and records involved. Clearly, the design of a system of cost accounts, and the details of the methods to be employed, will vary widely according to the individual features of each concern. Whatever the nature or size of the undertaking, the system must, above all, be designed to suit it precisely and be as straightforward as possible. If this is done the time and money devoted to it will be a profitable investment.

Cost accounting systems are designed to ascertain two major types of cost: the total cost of each of the various activities and functions of a business and the cost per unit of each of the concern's products and services. Every division of activity or function that the cost accountant wishes to cost separately is regarded as a *cost centre*, and the unit of product or service chosen as the unit for costing purposes, is known as a *cost unit*.

The Cost Centre

Whilst the main aim of every trading undertaking is the production and/or distribution of either a product or a service, it is normally possible to identify many subsidiary activities and functions within a concern. Thus, in a manufacturing business the activities of production, selling, administration, research, and so on are readily apparent, and each of these main functions consists of various distinct activities. For instance, it is possible to distinguish between a department stamping metal blanks, one machining them, and another assembling them; all departments undertaking production activities. Such analysis may be taken further to distinguish the activities of one individual machine from those of another. This is what the cost accountant does. He sets up cost centres to enable him to ascertain the costs he needs to know, and he is careful to design the costing system so that it produces the degree of detail he needs.

The degree of detail required is not the same in every business. For instance, whilst in a jobbing engineering works the operating cost of a particular machine (or of a group of like machines) may be important and hence give rise to a separate cost centre, it is rarely necessary to analyse the costs of process or production line manufacture to such a degree. Each individual process or production line therefore frequently forms one cost centre regardless of the number of machines it contains.

To keep the cost accounting system as simple as possible, identical or similar machines are frequently grouped together to form one cost centre. Since one of the main reasons for obtaining the costs of each centre of activity separately is the need for cost control, it is necessary to separate costs for which different individuals are responsible. A single cost centre should not, therefore, include elements controllable by more than one manager. For instance, two sections each consisting of ten identical machines should not form one cost centre if they are supervised by separate foremen.

So far the concept of the cost centre has been considered only in relation to the production function, but it is equally important in relation to the others. Thus, in a large organisation it is necessary to distinguish between selling costs that are the responsibility of one area manager, and those for which another is responsible; and between the costs of different methods of advertising and sales promotion, and so on. Similarly, it may be important to accumulate distribution costs in a manner that will facilitate the comparison of the relative profitability of selling in various parts of the world.

Another important class of activity is that which, although it forms no part of the main activities of production, selling and distribution, nevertheless serves those engaged therein. Payroll preparation, for instance, is not part of the main activities of production, selling and distribution, yet it is essential to the proper running of the business. Again, without proper maintenance, plant eventually comes to a standstill, and, unless transport is provided, goods lie uncollected. It is apparent, therefore, that service activities of this nature are of the utmost practical importance. Moreover, they involve heavy costs, which must be as efficiently ascertained and controlled as those of production. It follows that many of the cost centres set up are service cost centres. In practice, it is quite common to find the following:

Service	To which are charged:
Building service	The cost of providing accommodation for the period e.g. rent (or a charge for depreciation in lieu), rates, insurance, security, fire prevention, cleaning, lighting, heating, maintenance, and ventilation.
Equipment service	The cost of providing any service that relates to plant, machinery, fixtures, tools, jigs, and other equipment for the period e.g. depreciation, inspection of equipment, plant maintenance, insurance, and power supply.
Materials service	The cost of providing any service in respect of materials used by an undertaking e.g. handling, inspection, material control, purchasing, receiving, stocktaking, storage, transporting, and weighing.
Personnel (including payroll)	The cost of providing any service in respect of employees e.g. personnel office, welfare, canteen, wages, office and timekeeping, first-aid and training.
Power house	The cost of producing the concern's own power.
Production	The cost of providing any service to the production activities of the undertaking e.g. general clerical work, production control, and work study.

As the requirements of individual concerns differ, it is not possible to lay down general rules as to the cost centres that should be set up in particular circumstances. However, some idea of those that might be provided in a medium-sized engineering company may be gained from the accounts code outlined later in this chapter.

The Cost Unit

We have seen how the cost accountant accumulates costs by sections of activity termed cost centres, but it is not enough to know the total cost of each of these functions. Admittedly this offers some measure of control, for one can budget the cost to be incurred before the event and later compare the actual result with the budget. A significant indicator, however, is the cost per unit of activity. Thus, whilst it may be helpful to know that the power house cost £16 100, as against a budget of £16 000, a clearer picture might be gained from the statement that the cost per unit produced was 70p in the year concerned, compared with a budget and outside purchase cost of 75p.

All sorts of cost units are adopted – the criterion for adoption being the applicability of a particular cost unit to the circumstances under consideration. Thus, the hospital accountant may ascertain the cost per patient-day or out-patient visit, whilst a local authority accountant might be more concerned with costs per passenger-mile of the authority's transport service, the cost per mile of street cleaning, and so on. A factory accountant, on the other hand, might be concerned with the cost of annealing a tonne of steel or the storage cost per tonne of materials.

So far, most of the cost units considered have measured the cost of some service, but product costs are also expressed in this manner. Thus, a builder usually regards each individual job or contract as a separate cost unit, and the brick manufacturer expresses the cost of his output as so much per batch of 1000 bricks. In other cases, unit costs may be expressed in dozens or hundreds or in terms of weight, length, area, or volume.

Primary Costs

Any cost, whether it be that of a job or other unit of product or of a process or of an activity, is composed of one or more of the three *elements of cost* (or primary costs) i.e. material cost, wages, and expense.

Material Cost is the cost of commodities purchased by an undertaking from an outside supplier. Commodities are all kinds of goods and merchandise, except immovable property, such as land.

Wages is the term used to denote the cost of remunerating (by wages, salaries, commission, bonuses etc.) the employees of an undertaking. It is not, as in common parlance, confined to the weekly pay of manual workers. It refers only to the cost of remunerating the undertaking's own employees and not those of other businesses or of persons working on their own account.

Expense is a specialised term used in costing to signify the cost of services provided to an undertaking, and the notional cost of the use of owned assets. The word should not be confused with the commonly used expressions 'expenses' and 'expenditure', which may include payments for wages and outlay upon the purchase of goods and services of all kinds.

It will be seen that these three terms embrace the cost of the materials bought, the remuneration of labour, the cost of outside services employed, and also depreciation and interest.

The process of grouping costs according to their common characteristics is known as *cost classification*. The division into the primary costs, referred to above, is one form of classification. Others are the allotment of costs to cost centres and cost units.

Cost Classification

Costs may be classified in logical groups according to their nature and a number of other characteristics such as: function, relation to the product, type of cost, behaviour, controllability and normality.

Function

Costs can be classified according to the purpose for which they are incurred e.g. manufacturing, selling and distribution, administration, research and development. In this way management can see the relative importance of the various functions of the business for total cost.

   Functional classification leads to the grouping of costs according to broad divisions of activity:

(a)   Production or manufacturing cost: the cost of the sequence of operations, which begins with supplying materials, labour and services and ends with primary packing of the product. When there is no primary packing, as with a railway locomotive, the production cost is, naturally, confined to the cost of producing the article.
(b)   Selling cost: the cost of seeking to create and stimulate demand and of securing orders e.g. advertising, debt collection, estimating, representation cost in respect of salesmen's and travellers' salaries, expenses etc.
(c)   Distribution cost: the cost of the sequence of operations, which begins with making the packed product available for despatch, and ends with making the reconditioned returned empty package, if any, available for re-use. It thus includes all costs from the time the product has received its primary packing and been taken into the warehouse, including the cost of packing the product into secondary containers, its loading into vehicles and carriage to the customer. Also, where applicable, the terms 'distribution cost' includes the cost of receiving returned empty containers and of reconditioning them and putting them into store to await re-use.
(d)   Administration cost: the cost of formulating the policy, directing the organisation, and controlling the operations of an undertaking, which is not related directly to a production, selling, distribution, or research or development activity or function.

Ignoring for the time being the costs of research and development:

$$\frac{\text{Production}}{\text{cost}} + \frac{\text{Selling}}{\text{cost}} + \frac{\text{Distribution}}{\text{cost}} + \frac{\text{Administration}}{\text{cost}} = \frac{\text{Total}}{\text{cost}}$$

If direct costs are separated and shown together as prime cost, we get:

$$\frac{\text{Prime}}{\text{cost}} + \frac{\text{Production}}{\text{overheads}} + \frac{\text{Selling}}{\text{overheads}} + \frac{\text{Distribution}}{\text{overheads}} + \frac{\text{Administration}}{\text{overheads}} = \frac{\text{Total}}{\text{cost}}$$

In addition to the direct manufacturing activities, most businesses have service divisions, which give rise to costs such as building, equipment, materials, personnel, and production services.

Relation to the Product

Costs are classified as direct costs and indirect costs or overheads, according to how closely the cost can be related to cost units e.g. direct labour works on the product whilst indirect labour provides services to the manufacturing function.

Type

Costs are classified according to the purpose for which the cost is incurred e.g. materials, labour, expense.

Behaviour

Costs can be classified according to how they behave, i.e. fixed, semi-variable and variable costs. This classification is important in decision making when a particular cost may not behave in a normal, expected way in certain circumstances. Costs that do not change as a result of a decision are not relevant to that decision, which should be made only in the light of relevant costs.

Fixed Costs such as rent, rates or salaries remain the same during the short term and do not vary when the volume of production increases or decreases. The standing expenses for a period are sometimes referred to as 'committed' costs because they have been incurred in advance of production and will not be affected by the volume of activity. In the long run no cost is fixed as all costs can change if the time scale is long enough.

Variable Costs vary in direct proportion to the volume of output e.g. if the timber used to make a coffee table costs £5 for each table, the cost will be nil if no tables are produced, £50 for ten tables and £5000 for a thousand tables.

Semi-variable Costs vary in sympathy with, but not in proportion to, the volume of output. They sometimes have a fixed element combined to a variable element in their make-up e.g. one foreman can supervise ten men, but if production increases and twelve men are employed, a second foreman will be needed and the cost of supervision will increase. This is known as a *stepped cost*.

Controllability

Costs can be classified according to whether their amount can be influenced by management, i.e. they are controllable, or whether the level of the cost is determined by factors outside the business. Obviously it would be wrong to hold a manager responsible for the escalation of a cost that was outside his control. Where management has the power to determine how much will be incurred under a certain cost heading, such costs are referred to as *discretionary* or *managed costs* e.g. the managers decide how much they wish to spend on selling expenses or development costs as a result of policy decisions taken when future activity is planned.

Normality

Costs can be analysed as normal if they amount to what is expected within the budget or plan, or abnormal if they exceed budget levels. Clearly it is advantageous to identify abnormal costs at an early stage so that remedial action can be planned.

The appropriate cost classification to be made in a business will depend on the circumstances and on the purpose for which the costs are being made. Cost analysis for control purposes to compare actual costs with a budget will probably require classification into function, type, controllability and normality; costing for decision making requires cost behaviour as a primary classification; and costing for purposes of valuing a stock of work-in-progress will require classification as to function and type.

Capital and Revenue Expenditure

It is most important to distinguish between capital and revenue expenditure. Capital expenditure is that incurred in acquiring, extending or improving assets of a permanent nature that are to be used to carry on the business or increase its earning capacity. It includes the purchase of buildings, plant, motor vehicles etc. Revenue expenditure is that incurred in the day-to-day operations of the business. It embraces material cost, wages and expenses, and includes, of course, the cost of maintaining the buildings and plant in an efficient state. Revenue expenditure must be charged at once as a cost of the period in which it is incurred, but capital expenditure can be spread over the life of the fixed assets concerned as depreciation.

Cost Codes

In classifying costs it is convenient to use abbreviations to signify particular cost classifications. This involves the preparation and use of a cost code, which is a series of alphabetical and/or numerical symbols each of which represents a descriptive title in a cost classification.

Alphabetical symbols have the advantage that they may be formed into a mnemonic code, after this fashion:

S	Sales
SA	Sales – Advertising
SAL	Sales – Advertising – London Area
SAN	Sales – Advertising – Northern Area
SAS	Sales – Advertising – Scotland
SM	Sales – Management
SR	Sales – Representation
SRL	Sales – Representation – London Area
SRN	Sales – Representation – Northern Area
SRS	Sales – Representation – Scotland

Not all classifications can be readily coded in a mnemonic form. For instance, in the above code, Market Research cannot be coded SM or SR, for these codes have already been allocated, and the use of either SMR or SRM would suggest either Sales Management for an area the name of which begins with R, or Sales Representation for an area the name of which begins with M.

Mixed codes can be usefully employed to exploit the ability of computers to print at high speed, or display direct to a clerk, though most codes are entirely numerical.

Numerical codes may be built up in a number of ways, the most elementary being the allotment of a series of numbers to classifications without any attempt to group like classifications. More usual, are codes built around numerical suffixes, each of which represents some main classification. For example, a code of three digits might be built up with the suffix 7 representing Distribution, 75 being External Transport and

751	Drivers' wages
752	Petrol and oil
753	Licences
754	Insurance (of motor vehicles)
755	Maintenance (of motor vehicles)
756	Depreciation (of motor vehicles) etc.

Where necessary, a code of this type can be broken into sections separated by hyphens or oblique strokes for ease of working.

Obviously, in designing an accounts code one must have in mind the particular circumstances of the business concerned e.g. its size, its organisational structure and the methods used in the manufacture of its products. All accounts codes fulfil somewhat similar needs: in an integrated cost and financial accounting system, they provide, for instance, for the recording of assets and liabilities, and of costs. Since these costs may be grouped into five main classes – production, service department, selling, distribution, and administration costs – it is a simple matter to design a skeleton system, on the following basic plan, which will be adopted throughout the remainder of this book.

Accounts Codes	Group of Accounts
100–199	Assets
200–299	Liabilities
300–399	*Spare*
400–499	Production costs
500–599	Service department costs
600–699	Selling costs
700–799	Distribution costs
800–899	Administration costs
900–999	Operating statements, Profit and loss accounts etc.

Control (or Summary) Accounts

Error tracing in a large integrated accounting system would be rather like looking for the proverbial needle in a haystack were it not for the use of special control accounts, which by summarising the entries in a group of accounts provide a system of sectional balancing.

The control accounts used in financial book-keeping in connection with the sectional balancing of debtors and creditors ledgers are similar in character to those used to control cost records, such as those in respect of distribution costs or records of assets like stock and work-in-progress. Throughout the remainder of this book, the existence of a system of control accounts is assumed.

Accounting Periods

In any accounting system it is necessary to account for income and expenditure over definite periods of time. Financial accounts are always made up annually, though in many cases they are also prepared to cover shorter periods such as a month, a quarter, or a half-year. For the purpose of cost control, however, a year is much too long a period to wait for information, and cost accounts must therefore be prepared weekly, monthly, or for four-weekly or other convenient periods. The actual period chosen depends upon several factors. Firstly, it should be sufficiently short to ensure that excess costs are traced before serious losses have been incurred. Secondly, it should be long enough to permit a reasonable degree of average to enter into the picture and to prevent an excessive volume of clerical work. Thirdly, for purposes of comparison, all periods should represent as nearly as practicable the same amount of working time. Last, but by no means least, the delay should be short enough to ensure that managers are still interested in that costing period when the cost statement is delivered to them.

Generally, any costing period of more than a month may be ruled out as too long. There is, unfortunately, no period that is entirely satisfactory, but one of the following is generally adopted:

The Calendar Month. This is a suitable length of time, but as it may vary from 20 to 23 full working days its use as a costing period makes comparison between the results of one month and another difficult.

The Week. Weekly cost control statements are excellent from the aspect of comparison, and they reveal losses quickly, yet the week is too short a period in which to obtain a reasonable averaging of costs. The preparation of weekly figures imposes a burden upon the accounts and cost offices, but the employment of an unduly large clerical staff may be avoided by the application of computerisation to costing.

The Four-weekly Period. Many companies now divide the year into 13 four-weekly periods for cost control purposes. Each period is of the same duration except where statutory holidays occur. As book-keeping records and statements are usually still dealt with on a monthly basis, the adoption of four-weekly costing periods necessitates the splitting of the day-book and cash book entries at the end of each month as well as at the period ends. All things considered, however, the four-weekly period is generally regarded as the best alternative for most businesses.

Costing Methods

The costing methods to be employed in a particular business are determined with due regard to the unit of cost used. The principal methods are as follows:

Job Costing. This is the method used to cost single orders or contracts. It is applicable to bridge construction, structural steel work, shipbuilding and jobbing engineering, to name but a few examples. The principle is to charge each unit or job with the actual cost of materials, wages, and expense incurred, and to add thereto an equitable proportion of the overhead of the business. Where job costing is used in connection with large contracts it is sometimes referred to as *contract costing*.

Batch Costing. The principles of batch costing are the same as those for job costing, but this method is used to cost a group of identical products that maintains its identity throughout one or more stages of production. The cost unit is the *batch*. This method is employed for costing boots and shoes, nuts and bolts, and many other commodities that are manufactured in distinct batches.

Process Costing. This method is used in industries where there is a continuous output of one or more products. The cost is stated in terms of the unit of output, and for control purposes or for the ascertainment of by-product costs, it is often necessary to calculate the cost per unit at each stage of production. Process costing is used in the mining and chemical industries, by gas and electricity undertakings, brickworks etc. Typical units of cost are the tonne of coal raised, the 100 litres of liquid produced and the 1000 bricks made. In process costing all the appropriate costs are charged against the particular product or stage of production and, at the end of a suitable period, the total cost is divided by the number of units produced to obtain the cost per unit. The term *single* or *output costing* is often used to denote the costing of units of output in businesses in which only one product is manufactured e.g. a brickworks or coal-mine.

Standard Costing and Budgetary Control

Standard costing connotes the setting up of definite standards or targets of performance in advance of the costing period and the expression of these standards in monetary terms. The standards are set to cover material usage and price, labour and machine time and rates, the methods to be employed, the amount of the overhead expenditure, and the rate at which it is to be absorbed. Actual performances are recorded in total and measured against these standards, the differences being extracted to show where corrective action is needed. It will be appreciated that where ordinary job or process cost methods are used, the cost will vary every time it is calculated because of the changing factors that operate from period to period. A standard cost, on the other hand, is pre-determined and cannot vary. This is because variations are extracted as they occur and charged direct to variance accounts.

Closely allied to standard costing is the principle of *budgetary control*. Whilst standard costing applies the principle of pre-determined standards to each process or operation, budgetary control emphasises the application of standards in the form of pre-determined budgets to the control of total expenditure on materials and wages and to the control of the overhead.

Marginal Costing

Job costing, batch costing and process costing each have as their aim the ascertainment of the total cost of producing, distributing, and selling a specific type of cost unit. Marginal costing, on the other hand, considers the fixed and the variable elements of cost separately, and aims to demonstrate the effect upon unit costs of changes in volume, or of the fixed and variable elements of cost. Emphasis is placed, not upon net profit as the excess of selling price over total cost of producing, distributing, and selling (including apportioned or absorbed overheads), but upon the excess of selling price over the variable costs, which is termed the margin or contribution. No attempt is made to allocate or apportion fixed overheads to individual cost centres or units of cost as in full absorption costing. The total of the fixed overheads is simply deducted from the aggregate of the contributions made by the various products to give the net profit of the period.

SEMINAR EXERCISES

1.1   A transport contractor has approached you with a request that you explain to him how cost accounting would help to improve the management of his business. The contractor's fleet consists of 18 vehicles: 7 are large vehicles used for long-distance work, and the remainder are medium-sized vehicles employed on more local journeys. Some, but not all, maintenance and repair work is undertaken by the company itself, and there is a thriving administration and selling department.

Required:

Outline the information which you think a cost accounting system should provide for the business.   (25 marks)

1.2   Spark Stores PLC owns 60 shops in the UK, which sell a range of electrical goods. The company has three regional warehouses in which it accumulates stocks of goods, and then delivers them to the shops in its own fleet of vans. There is a head office in London for central management and administrative functions.

Required:

(a)   Discuss the cost information that would most help the management of Spark Stores PLC to plan and make decisions, and to control and evaluate activities.
                                                                         (16 marks)

(b)   Suggest cost classifications suitable for this business.   (6 marks)

                                                                    (Total 22 marks)

2

The Costing Treatment of Materials

There are two major aspects to the costing treatment of materials: the system whereby their purchase, storage and usage is organised, controlled and documented; and the selection of an appropriate basis on which to charge the materials to the production process.

MATERIAL CONTROL

Material control is the system that ensures the provision of the required quantity of material of the required quality at the required time with the minimum amount of capital tied up. It covers the following functions:

1. Stock control.
2. Scheduling of requirements.
3. Purchasing.
4. Receiving and inspecting.
5. Storing and issuing.

If a cost accounting system is to be fully effective, there must be a proper system for the control of material from the time a requisition to purchase is made until the material is issued to production. Material represents an important asset and is often the largest single item of cost per unit of production; accordingly, the success or failure of a concern may be influenced by efficient material purchasing, storage and utilisation. It follows that the costing system must be organised so as to facilitate the efficient operation of the functions of buying, storing, and issuing material.

Where materials are not systematically controlled, excess stocks of some items are likely to occur with a consequent unnecessary tying up of capital and loss through obsolescence and deterioration. At the same time, shortages of other materials may arise just when they are urgently needed, and production will then be delayed. Furthermore, haphazard buying and lack of control is bound to result in the purchase of material of too good or too poor a quality for the purpose for which it is intended, and also in the carrying of a greater variety of stocks than is required. The purchasing of material is a highly specialised function. By ordering the right quantity and quality of material at the most favourable price, and by ensuring that it arrives at the right time, the efficient buyer is able to make a valuable contribution to the success of a business.

Efficient material control cuts out losses and forms of waste that otherwise tend to pass unnoticed. Thus, incoming material should be checked against orders to ensure that the correct quantity and quality have been received. Theft, breakage, deterioration, and the use of excessive floor space can be reduced to a minimum by proper controls, and much avoidable idle time in the factory will be cut out if materials are available to meet the demands of the production staff. Finally, and most important to the cost accountant, it is impossible to produce reliable costing information if the records of material issues are unsatisfactory. It should be remembered that a cost statement cannot be more accurate than the information on which it is based.

Requirements of a System of Material Control

The major requirements of a satisfactory system of material control are:

1. Co-ordination between the departments involved in the buying, receiving, inspection, and storage of materials and in accounting for them.
2. Centralisation of purchasing under the authority of a competent buyer to eliminate buying by unauthorised or unskilled personnel.
3. The planning and programming of material requirements.
4. Material standardisation and simplification.
5. The proper classification and, where applicable, coding of materials.
6. The use of standard forms for orders, requisitions, etc., upon which written and signed instructions are given; a system of authorisation.
7. Control by budget of material and equipment purchases. (Budgetary control is considered in detail in Chapter 9.)
8. The operation of internal check to ensure that all transactions involving materials and equipment are checked by reliable and independent officials.
9. The storage of all materials in well planned and properly designated stores, subject to adequate safeguards and supervision.
10. The operation of efficient stock control procedures and records.
11. Adequate records to control materials during production and the quantities manufactured for stock.
12. Regular reports to management upon purchases of materials, issues, stocks, and in particular obsolete stocks, returns to suppliers, spoilage and waste, etc.

Stock records are often held on computer, either mainframe or micro, which allows instant access by Visual Display Unit, constant updating, and the facility to draw off a printed copy of the stock sheets at regular intervals.

STOCK CONTROL

The materials purchased by a concern may be classified either as stock items that are taken into store and held until required, or as direct deliveries to the point of consumption. The control of those materials that are stock items is known as *stock control*. Items delivered direct are also part of the stocks of the organisation and should be rigorously controlled as they are outside the direct influence of the central stores. The function of stock control is to protect the materials in stock and to obtain the maximum stock turnover consistent with the maintenance of sufficient stocks to meet all requirements. Stock turnover is the ratio the cost of the materials used per annum bears to the average stock of raw materials.

The Economic Order Quantity (EOQ)

The quantity to be held in stock will influence the decision as to how much to buy and how often purchases are to be made. These three items – stock, order and buying frequency –

are joined together as part of a decision that must trade off the benefits of holding large stocks against the costs incurred in holding large stocks. Some of these factors cannot be easily expressed in quantitative terms.

The costs of holding large stocks are:

1. Interest payable on funds borrowed to finance the stock.
2. The costs of operating a large store e.g. rent, rates, light and heat (or refrigeration and air-conditioning), insurance, spoilage (deterioration), spillage, protection, pilferage, and labour costs.
3. Obsolescence, or the danger that items held in stock for a long period will become outdated, and therefore of no further use in the production processes.
4. Downward price fluctuations, which give competitors who buy later a cost advantage.

Against these costs must be set the advantages of holding large stocks:

1. Large stock holding capacity enables a business to place large orders, which can be used to negotiate favourable trade discounts with suppliers. The trick, in practice, is to place a large order at a favourable price, and then to negotiate with the supplier that you will 'call off' parts of the order in succeeding periods, thereby reducing the funds tied up in stock.
2. A large stock acts as a safety margin and protects a business from disruption to its production activities which is consequent upon a 'stock out' (the lost goodwill when delivery dates are not met) and the cost of buying small amounts at short notice.
3. The quality and/or colour of materials or components will remain constant over a long period if they are drawn from a single batch delivered at one point in time.
4. Large stocks will act as a hedge against inflation in a period of rising prices, giving the business a cost advantage over its rivals.
5. Ordering, accounting and inspection costs will be reduced if larger orders are placed at less frequent intervals. This advantage is of dubious validity, since a large order will require the attention of a senior, well-paid buyer if mistakes are to be avoided, which will have a long-term influence on costs.

These advantages and disadvantages loosely demonstrate the balance between holding (or carrying) cost and ordering cost. As the order quantity increases, so stock carrying cost will

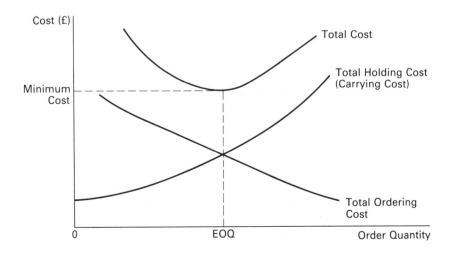

rise, but with larger orders, the ordering cost will fall as there are fewer orders placed. The optimum situation is to calculate an economic order quantity that will balance holding cost against ordering cost, thereby keeping total cost to a minimum. The EOQ occurs at the point where the total cost is at a minimum and ordering costs equals holding cost. The EOQ can be calculated by using the formula:

$$EOQ = \sqrt{\frac{2AP}{S}}$$

A = Annual usage in units; P = Purchasing cost per order; and S = Stock holding cost of one unit for a year.

Obviously, to compute the holding cost of one unit of stock for a year, when perhaps a thousand different lines are held in stock, and to derive a purchasing cost per order require a certain amount of cost allocation, which may invalidate the practical application of the formula. Note that the stock out costs, and other advantages of holding large stocks have been ignored in the formula. The reasoning behind the formula is:

Holding cost = Average stock (Quantity ordered ÷ 2) × Holding cost per unit

Ordering cost = (Annual usage ÷ Quantity ordered) × Cost of placing each order

EOQ is found where holding cost equals ordering cost, i.e.

$$\frac{Q}{2} \times S = \frac{A}{Q} \times P$$

which translates as:

$$Q^2 \times S = 2A \times P$$

$$Q^2 = \frac{2AP}{S}$$

$$Q = \sqrt{\frac{2AP}{S}}$$

Maximum and Minimum Stocks

Once management has determined the quantity of each material that it is economic to hold in stock, some form of control must be initiated to ensure that the stocks do not depart seriously from these quantities. Under the 'maximum and minimum' stock system normally used for this purpose definite maximum and minimum levels are set for each item of stock. The minimum stock is the lowest level to which the inventory should be allowed to fall. It is the cushion stock determined by management that allows some margin of safety. The maximum stock is the upper level of the inventory and the quantity that must not be exceeded without specific authority from management. Between these two quantities a further level is set, known as the *re-order point*. This is the level to which the stock is normally allowed to fall before an order for further supplies is placed. It is the sum of the minimum stock and the usage expected to occur in the re-order period, i.e. the lead time between the sending of an order and the receipt of the goods. In determining the maximum stock it is necessary to take into account a further factor: the re-order quantity or *economic order quantity*. This amount is the optimum or best possible quantity to buy having regard to the particular circumstances of each case or, in other words, the normal order level. Maximum stock may be calculated as follows:

$$\text{Maximum stock} = \text{Re-order level} + \text{Re-order quantity} - \text{Minimum usage during re-order period}$$

The following example will make the position clear:

Normal usage (units)	500 per day
Minimum usage	300 per day
Maximum usage	650 per day
Economic order quantity	75 000
Re-order period – lead time	25 to 30 days
Minimum level	
(10 days at normal usage)	5 000

Re-order level = Normal usage × Normal lead time + Minimum level

= (500 × 30) + 5000 = 20 000

Maximum level = Re-order level + Economic order quantity − Minimum quantity used in re-order period

= 20 000 + 75 000 − (300 × 25) = 87 500

This determines the maximum storage space required for this material.

$$\text{Average level} = \frac{\text{Maximum} + \text{Minimum}}{2} = \frac{92\,500}{2} = 46\,250$$

It will be seen from the above that stocks will fall below minimum if usage after the placement of an order is above average, or if the lead time is longer than expected. Stock will not be exhausted, however, so long as the maximum usage and maximum re-order period are not exceeded. Maximum usage during the lead time would cause an extra 4500 units (30 days × 150 units) to be consumed. It is therefore an important duty of the purchasing office (or sometimes that of the production control department) to 'chase' supplies and so ensure that delivery promises are kept.

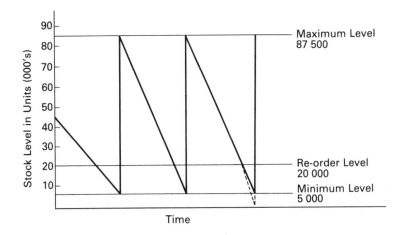

The normal pattern of stock holding can be illustrated as above, using the figures from the preceding example. The dotted line shows what would happen if in the third sequence in the cycle of usage/ordering/receiving, the factory stepped up production from normal usage to maximum usage during the lead time. The safety margin is large enough to cope with the change in the demand rate by the plant.

Maximum, minimum, and re-order levels are not static. They must be varied to suit changing circumstances. Thus, alterations will take place if the usage of certain materials is increased or decreased, if the re-order period changes, or if, in the light of a review of capital available, it is decided that the overall inventory must be increased or decreased. Management wishing to adopt a more prudent stock control system will calculate on the basis of maximum usage and lead time to increase their safety margin.

Stock turnover calculated on these figures would be:

$$\frac{\text{Normal usage in units}}{\text{Average stock in units}}$$

Assuming 250 working days in a year (50 five-day weeks) normal usage would be $500 \times 250 = 125\,000$ units. Therefore stockturn under normal conditions would be 2.7 times or, alternatively, expressed in working days:

$$\frac{\text{Average stock}}{\text{Normal usage}} \times \frac{250}{1} = \frac{46\,250}{125\,000} \times \frac{250}{1} = 92.5 \text{ working days}$$

This calculation can also be made using the cost of average stock and normal usage, and is often based on 365 calendar days.

Perpetual Inventory System

Stock control is effected by means of *perpetual inventory records* kept by the stock control department for each material stocked. The perpetual inventory record, where not computerised, may be maintained in loose-leaf or card form and frequently shows:

1. Description of the material.
2. Code number, component or part number.
3. Location in the stores.
4. Unit of measurement, e.g. kilogram, litre, tonne, etc.
5. Quantity:
   (a) received
   (b) issued
   (c) ordered but not yet received
   (d) appropriated but not yet issued
   (e) balance in stock.

6. Re-ordering arrangements:
   (a) maximum and minimum stocks
   (b) re-order level, quantity, and delivery time
   (c) delivery schedules, where appropriate.

STOCK RECORD CARD

Description: Steel Eye Bolts
Code: EB 76
Drawing: B 7124
Maximum: 1175   Re-order Level: 400
Minimum: 200   Re-order Quantity: 800

Date 19—	On Order				On Hand				Allocated			Free Stock
	Ref.	Ordered	Rec'd	Bal.	Ref.	Rec'd	Issued	Bal.	Job No.	Qty	Bal.	
Jan. 1								500				500
3					R17		50	450				450
15									G117	100	100	350
16	P142	800		800								1150
20									G132	250	350	900
31					R19		100	350	R19	−100	250	
Feb. 7	P142		800		X62	800		1150				
14					R28		250	900	R28	−250	0	
20									G142	400	400	500

Stock Record Card for Use in Stock Control

A typical *stock record card* is illustrated. This information could be shown on a computer print-out, or be available on screen at the touch of a button. Details of the entries are as follows:

19—
Jan.
1   Opening balance and free stock. These are identical as no allocations have been made to jobs.
3   Issue of 50 bolts against Stores Requisition R17. This stock had not previously been allocated.
15   Allocation of 100 bolts to Job G117. This brings the balance of unallocated stock down to 350, which is below the re-order level, and a fresh order must be placed.
16   Order placed for re-order quantity of 800. Note that the free stock balance is increased by the quantity on order as the latter will be scheduled to arrive before the minimum or cushion stock is exhausted and may be allocated to future production.
20   Allocation of 250 bolts against Job G132.
31   Issue of 100 bolts previously allocated against Job G117. Note that the stock on hand and allocated balances are reduced, but that free stock is unaffected.

Feb.
7   Receipt of 800 bolts on order, the goods received note reference being X62. Stock on hand is increased, but free stock remains unchanged as this was included when the order was placed.
14   Issue of 250 bolts previously allocated against order G132. The allocated balance is reduced to nil and the stock on hand and free stock are identical.
20   Allocation of 400 bolts against order G142. At this date there is a physical balance of 900 bolts in stock. 400 are specifically allocated and 500 are still available for other jobs.

As the purpose of the perpetual inventory record is the control of stocks from day to day, it is essential that it be kept up to date. It is primarily intended as an aid to material control, but if value columns are added it can also be used for cost accounting purposes.

Some difficulty arises where the supplier's unit of measurement is not suitable for the daily issue of materials. As the number of issues is very much greater than the number of receipts, it is normal to convert each receipt of material into the unit of issue. Liquids, for example, may be purchased by the tonne and issued by litres, but the stock records will show all transactions in terms of litres.

In order to ensure accuracy of perpetual inventory records, physical stocks should be checked systematically under a system referred to as *continuous stocktaking*, whereby:

1.   A few items are checked each day.
2.   All items are checked within some definite period, such as three or six months.
3.   The checking is carried out by staff having no other responsibility for either stock records or the stocks themselves.
4.   All differences are recorded on an appropriate report form, the entries providing the basis upon which the perpetual inventory record and the stores control account in the cost ledger are adjusted.

The physical check is frequently made at the time each order for fresh supplies is made out. Stocks are at a low level at this point and the checking of both quantity and condition is facilitated. It is useful to find the true physical stock at this stage in order to make a realistic order, and to hasten supplies if necessary.

The main causes of difference between physical stock and the perpetual inventory are as follows:

1.   The entry of incorrect quantities in the records.
2.   The making of postings to the wrong stock account.
3.   Errors of addition and subtraction.
4.   Over or under issue.
5.   Losses on breaking bulk.
6.   Variations of weight caused by drying, or the absorption of moisture.
7.   Theft.

The first three items can normally be traced by comparing the bin card and stock record. The others are often more difficult and the auditor must investigate the counting or weighing methods, including the conversion factors when goods are weighed, instead of being counted.

The maintenance of satisfactory perpetual inventory records obviates the need for the physical checking of all stocks at the year end. As long as each stock has been checked at some time during the three or six months before the close of the year, any discrepancies have been adjusted, and the system is found to be working properly, the balances on the perpetual inventory records may be accepted as stock on hand. This avoids the dislocation of production, which arises when all the stocks are checked at one time. It also provides stock figures for monthly or four-weekly accounts that could not normally be prepared satisfactorily without this information. In addition, a sound perpetual inventory system, coupled with a continuous stores audit, reveals stock losses much earlier than an annual stocktaking, and as the work is carried out systematically and without undue haste, the figures are generally more reliable.

Physical Stocktaking

Most businesses that do not maintain a perpetual inventory such as that described above, undertake a physical stocktaking at least annually at the end of their financial year. The methods they employ vary according to the nature and the volume of the stock held, but, where practicable, the stocktaking should be carried out at a weekend when the stock is stationary and a special staff can be detailed for the task.

Raw Material and Finished Stocks. The quantity of each item will be counted, weighed, or otherwise determined by a stores clerk who will attach a stocktaking ticket on which he has specified the item and entered the amount held. Other members of the firm's staff who are not normally connected with stock will then go round the stores, check each item, and initial the tickets. When all the stock has been taken, two or three senior officers will make a tour of each store to ensure that each item of stock has been physically checked and is covered by a ticket. At the same time they should make a few test checks to verify the accuracy of the entries made. After this the tickets will be collected and held for subsequent pricing. As a precautionary measure, the tickets should be printed with serial numbers, and when the tickets are collected the numbers should be examined to ensure that all tickets used are accounted for.

As the physical stock includes only items actually on the premises at the year end, care must be taken to see that the purchases for the year include only items that have been received up to the last day of the year. If, for example, a firm's year ends on 31 December, and goods invoiced by a supplier on 29 December are not received until 2 January, the invoice should be put through the books in January. Alternatively, if the invoice is included in the December purchases, the goods in transit must be included in the stock. Similarly, any goods despatched to a customer near the year end must be invoiced as on the exact day of despatch, and the invoice included in the appropriate financial year. It is important to establish a correct 'cut off point'.

Work-in-Progress. The physical check of work-in-progress is often difficult, because it involves the checking of each job on the shop floor and the detailing on the stocktaking tickets of the amount of work already carried out on each item. Where there are suitable costing records, however, it is usually only necessary to verify the existence of each job or batch of material and to include this in the stock at the total cost to date according to the work-in-progress ledger.

PURCHASING AND THE RECEIPT OF MATERIALS

Whilst there is room for considerable variation in practice, the important steps in connection with the purchase and receipt of materials are as follows:

1. Initiation of the purchase procedure by means of a purchase requisition.
2. Preparation of the purchase order and its despatch to the supplier.
3. Receipt of the materials; raising a goods received note.
4. Inspection or testing of the materials; acceptance into stores.
5. Notification to the supplier in respect of defects, rejects, etc. – request for a credit note from him.
6. Passing of the bill for payment; on receipt of the invoice it is checked against the order and the goods received note.
7. Entry in financial and cost books.
8. Payment of the account when it appears on the supplier's statement providing the appropriate period of credit has expired.

Purchase Requisition

The *purchase requisition* is the formal instruction to the buying department to purchase goods. It is prepared by the person requiring the goods, who must state the quantity of each article required, a description of the goods including quality, specification, etc., the account to be charged and, where appropriate, the name of the supplier and the point of delivery. Two copies will normally be prepared, one for the buying department and the second for retention in the originator's file.

1 PURCHASING DEPARTMENT COPY	**PURCHASE REQUISITION**	No. 46789 Date ....

Please purchase for:
.........................Department   Production Order No. ..

Item No.	Quantity	Description of Articles	Charge Account

Special Instructions:

Required by ....   To be delivered at ....

Signed by.....................................

FOR USE OF PURCHASING DEPARTMENT ONLY Purchase Order No............. Supplier .... Delivery Date.................... PFI	(*Signature of person authorised to sign requisitions*) Approved by: ....

Purchase requisitions in respect of regular stocks will be prepared by the stock control department and authorised by the production controller or in smaller companies by the departmental or works manager. Requisitions involving capital expenditure or maintenance material will normally be prepared under the authority of the chief engineer. Different individuals will normally be responsible for different classes of expenditure and it is therefore important that each person's responsibility is clearly defined. The buyer must not accept any requisition that is not properly authorised. For example, if the chief engineer has authority to incur capital expenditure not exceeding £5000 on any item, any requisition for a greater amount might require the signature of the managing director.

The Purchasing Department

Purchasing, or buying, is a specialist activity frequently carried on by a separate department under the control of a purchasing officer or buyer. Economical buying is the aim of any enterprise, but the cheapest material offered is not necessarily the most effective. Better materials may prove to be more economical in the long run; they may be less wasteful or their use may result in the production of a superior product. The effect of inferior material upon machinery must also be borne in mind. Inaccurately finished material may cause hold-ups that could be avoided by the use of a slightly more expensive material, and the cost of such a hold-up, where a whole production line is disrupted, may be considerable. On the other hand, material of a quality superior to that needed should not be bought where a cheaper grade is adequate for the purpose for which it is intended. The important rule is to buy the right quality at the right price. The buyer should make his purchases from dependable sources of supply and maintain ethical standards in his dealings with suppliers. Co-operation with suppliers' representatives is essential, and the buyer should be particularly interested in the possibilities of using new products to advantage. The buying department is able to add together the requisitions of several departments, and can thus place a large order after negotiating a favourable trade discount with the supplier.

The purchasing officer will in all his activities carry out the policy of his organisation with regard to buying. The policy of some concerns is to purchase on a bargain basis, though this is almost entirely confined to staple commodities and the major materials of process industries. Whilst this method offers large profits on buying, it is outside the province of the purchasing officer to gamble on the commodity markets. When such risks are taken, it is usual to find buying under the control of a purchasing director, skilled in dealing in futures on the international commodity markets.

In certain industries, contracts for considerable amounts representing future requirements are given to suppliers. For instance, a car manufacturer may contract ahead for the supply of tyres and sparking plugs for a year's requirements at a time. This system has the advantage that it avoids the carrying of large stocks – in fact, some manufacturers are able to carry almost no stock at all, relying entirely upon continuity of supply and service. It has the added advantage that the supplier, by obtaining a regular and secure market for his product, is able to quote particularly favourable terms.

It is usual for the buyer to be given wide discretion as to the choice of supplier. There are cases, however, where his freedom is restricted, for example, where there are interconnected companies, or where purchases have to be made from firms that are good customers, and when a particular brand of material is specified. Where articles have not previously been purchased, it is usual to obtain three or four alternative quotations. For regular supplies this is not necessary, provided occasional check quotations are obtained, and it is generally advantageous to cultivate regular and dependable sources of supply.

Purchase Order

The form used for ordering supplies is known as the *purchase order*, and it is normal for a business to specify that no goods will be accepted unless such an official order has been placed. This prevents individuals from giving verbal orders to travellers without written records passing through the normal channels. The purchase order is prepared from the specification included in the purchase requisition and is signed by the buyer. It will contain the name and address of the purchaser, the name of the supplier, the date of the order, terms, prices, and delivery instructions; and if special materials, components, or equipment are ordered, reference will be made to drawings, blueprints, or detailed specifications. The buyer must make his requirements absolutely clear, and frequently refers to the standard specifications published by the British Standards Institution, which are now universally accepted.

1—Supplier's Copy				
				Order No. 14621
PARK PRODUCTS LTD, ST ALBANS			FOR OFFICE USE ONLY	
			Dept	
PURCHASE ORDER			PR No.	
To...			Date..............	
PLEASE SUPPLY, in accordance with conditions set out on back of this order:				
Quantity	Description		Code	£
Please quote order number on all advice notes and invoices				
To be delivered at.............................		For PARK PRODUCTS LTD		
on....................19..				
PF2			Buyer	

In an integrated system where accounting and costing records are produced together, the order and a number of copies will be printed together. The original order will be despatched to the supplier and copies will be sent to the goods receiving department, the inspection department when required, to the requisitioning department and to the accounts department for checking against the invoice when it arrives. Two copies may be retained by the purchasing department. The first will be used for the entry of purchase record cards and then be filed under the supplier's name for subsequent reference when the relative invoices are passed. The second or follow-up copy will be filed by delivery date, and will be used to check progress on the order to ensure that delivery promises are adhered to.

The purchasing department will also maintain for each class of goods a record of all quotations received. The records will state the prices, delivery times, discount and general terms quoted by the various suppliers, and will provide a sound basis for the selection of the particular supplier in respect of future orders. Purchase record cards will be kept to record details of each order placed, showing the names of the suppliers, the date the order was placed, dates of receipt of goods and notes regarding the quality of the goods, reasons why particular goods were rejected, etc. (See question 2.2 at the end of this chapter.)

Receipt of Materials

All incoming materials should be received by a goods receiving department, which will unpack them and verify their quantity and condition. The quantity is checked against the copy purchase order and the supplier's advice note which is normally sent with the goods, and a *goods received note* is prepared. This shows the date, supplier's name, purchase order number, quantity, and description of the goods, their condition on arrival and details of returnable packing material, and it is signed by the checker. A single goods received note will normally detail all the items received in a particular consignment, but in some cases clerical procedures are simplified by the use of a separate note for each item. The particular procedure to be adopted depends upon the type of goods received and the general stores organisation. Goods received notes are normally prepared in triplicate, the top copy going to the purchasing department, the second copy accompanying the goods to the department or stores to which they are sent, and the third being retained in the goods receiving department. Where technical or laboratory inspection is necessary the goods are passed to a separate inspection section, which will provide a quality report either on the goods received note or separately. In either case the report is forwarded to the purchasing department.

To Inspection Department, then to Stores or Department receiving goods **GOODS RECEIVED NOTE**			GRN No. 99889 Date Received Purchase Order No. Advice Note No. Account No.
Received via	No. of Boxes	Gross Weight	
Quantity	Description (*Enter one item only*)		
INSPECTION			Received into Stores by:
Quantity Passed	Quantity Rejected	Inspector	
Reason for Rejection: PF3		Date	Date

Stores Copy of a Goods Received Note

If invoices are checked in the accounts department rather than the purchasing department, a copy of each goods received note should be routed there. Where the goods received are not of the type ordered, are not in accordance with the specification, are damaged, or are incorrect in quantity, it is usual to inform the suppliers, requesting a credit note from them to set off against all or part of the invoice that they are about to despatch.

The unsatisfactory materials may be returned to the suppliers immediately, or they may be held pending their instructions.

Approval of Invoices

When invoices are received from suppliers, the purchasing department will check that the description of the goods and prices agree with the purchase order. The quantities will be verified from the goods received note and reference will be made to inspection or test reports as required. Some businesses separate this task from the buying department as a matter of internal check, and site their invoice department as part of the accounting department. It is normal to impress invoices with a rubber stamp in which each individual who takes part in the passing of an invoice will insert his initials. The purchasing department staff will sign for quantity, quality, and price, and will normally enter the appropriate ledger code number. Each invoice should be checked for verification of extensions and additions, and will then be passed for payment by an authorised official.

In some businesses it is the practice to send purchase invoices to the stores, departmental managers or other appropriate officials for checking. This is not advisable as there is a tendency to authorise invoices from memory without actually checking that the particulars are correct. An exception arises in respect of certain invoices for new plant or maintenance work where the technical nature of the invoice is such that the purchase department is not competent to verify the amounts charged. Invoices of this nature are normally sent to the chief engineer for signature before being passed for payment.

Many buying and storage routines are computerised, allowing instant access to bin totals, or details of orders placed. However, these electronic wonders are only possible if accurate information is fed into the system, and that information is usually derived from a system of prime documents such as is described above.

STORES AND STOREKEEPING

Storekeeping

Good organisation of the stores is a noteworthy feature of a well-run business and a suitably trained and experienced person, well versed in the principles of good housekeeping in the factory, should be in charge of each store.

Types of Stocks

Goods in store fall under the following broad classifications:

1. Raw material.
2. Components.
3. Consumable stores, e.g. fuel, oil, or stationery.
4. Work-in-progress.
5. Finished goods (warehouses).
6. Tools, patterns, and plant maintenance supplies.

They may also be subdivided into those stores from which issues are continuous, e.g. of flour in a bakery, and those from which issues are intermittent.

Raw Material may be stored in bulk or otherwise. Examples of specially constructed bulk stores are silos for grain and bunkers for coal. Frequently, however, bulk storage is provided in stockyards, and it is common practice to store such commodities as rough castings and rolled steel sections in such yards. Materials that are unsuitable for outdoor storage are generally stored in specially constructed storehouses. Two examples of specialised bulk stores are the bonded warehouse in which dutiable goods, such as tobacco or spirits, are stored under the supervision and control of HM Customs and Excise, pending payment of duty, and a refrigerated store for fruit picked in season at a jam factory.

In general, such stores should be sited with regard

(a)   to access by road and/or rail;
(b)   to proximity to the department or departments to be supplied.

These rules, whilst of general application, are particularly important in connection with the storage of heavy and bulky materials.

Components are the separate pieces entering into a complete product. They may be classified broadly into those made on the premises and those bought out; and also into those that are standard stock and those made to special order for a particular job. The combination of two or more components is known as a sub-assembly.

Stores Systems

Whatever system of storage is adopted there must be 'a place for everything and everything in its place' if the stores are to operate efficiently. There are certain basic precepts with regard to stores organisation and layout, and a number of the more important of these are mentioned below.

Floor space is expensive and must be used to the best advantage. It is therefore necessary to build upwards, to stack materials wherever possible, using stacking trucks with forked tables that can be raised by power. Where stacking is not feasible, bins or shelves must be provided. Metal racks take up less space than wooden ones, and a further saving of space can be made by the use of close-packed racks, the sections of which slide on a system of rollers and rails, those in front moving from side to side and leaving a gap in the row through which those in the rear can be reached.

Receipts into stores, and issues from stores, should take place at separate entrances or windows, and all stores and stockyards should be under the control of and accessible to authorised personnel, and should be locked when not in use.

The items stored should be classified and coded under distinctive alphabetical and numerical symbols. The classification should be so designed that individual items can easily be located and suitable mnemonics can sometimes be adopted. The advantages to be gained from the use of a satisfactory materials code are:

1.   The reduction of clerical effort, as a symbol can be more quickly written or typed than a detailed description.
2.   Ambiguity is avoided as a particular code can refer only to one item or to one particular size of item.
3.   Coding facilitates the tracing of particular materials in a card index or price list, and assists in the sorting of information into categories.
4.   Coding is an essential feature of computerised stock control systems.

Pre-packaging into the amounts usually required facilitates issue, and where materials are subject to depreciation, deterioration or obsolescence, they should be stored in such a way that the oldest material can be used up first.

The importance of accurate weighing, counting, and measuring cannot be over-emphasised. The production control section must be able to plan the manufacturing operations in full confidence that the physical stocks agree with the records. Serious delays are inevitable if shortages are discovered just when materials are required for use. In some businesses it is the practice to notify the stores some time in advance of material requirements to enable the storeman to check that all items are available. This gives extra work and is unnecessary if accuracy is maintained in the physical counting of stores and in the clerical records.

Protection of Stored Materials

Attention must be paid to the proper protection of particular types of material against certain risks, the major risks being:

1. Fire e.g. with petrol and explosives.
2. Rust and corrosion e.g. of castings and forgings.
3. Deterioration e.g. of rubber.
4. Evaporation e.g. of volatile liquids.
5. Dust e.g. on stationery.
6. Theft e.g. of valuable metals such as gold and platinum.
7. The effects of weather e.g. heat, cold, and moisture affecting timber, liquids and deliquescent substances.

Central and Departmental Stores

While it is ideal from the control point of view to have one central store receiving and issuing all materials, this is not a practical proposition unless the physical layout of the works is so designed that every department would be within easy reach of such a store. When decentralised stores are unavoidable, control over all the stores should still be centralised. The advantages of central stores are:

1. The overall capital tied up is reduced, as separate departmental stores may each hold stocks of common items.
2. Bulk buying is facilitated as purchase requisitions are made out by the concern as a unit and not on a departmental basis.
3. The consequent improvement of layout results in an overall saving of storage space.
4. The smaller overall staff needed brings easier supervision.
5. Centralisation of records is possible, with a consequent reduction in clerical cost.
6. Stock may be checked with greater ease.
7. Control and protection are facilitated on a central site.

There are the following disadvantages:

1. It may be necessary to move small quantities of stores over considerable distances when it would be less costly to ask suppliers to deliver direct.

2.   Stores cannot be issued so promptly when they have to come from a distance. It is uneconomical to send a person or a truck with a single item, and requirements must be notified in advance so that efficient truck utilisation can be planned.
3.   Heavy or bulky stores should be received direct at the department from which the issue will take place so that subsequent handling is avoided as far as possible.

A useful compromise is the *imprest system* under which all materials are held in bulk in a central store. A number of decentralised stores exist, each drawing their supplies from the central store. In general, each sub-store is given as a commencing stock sufficient supplies for a little more than the re-stocking period. At the end of each week or other suitable period the sub-store passes all its requisitions to the central store, which reimburses it for these issues and thereby restores the stock of each material to its imprest level. The control over sub-stores is excellent as over-issues will not be reimbursed and the storeman will have to explain any discrepancies. This system combines the advantages of centralised buying with the benefits of having stock conveniently available at several issuing points. It does, however, lead to the proliferation of paperwork and checking by the personnel involved.

Bin Cards

In most organisations the storekeeper maintains a quantity stock record of each material, such records being known as *bin cards*. Where a stock ledger is maintained in the accounts department and stock records are kept in the production control department, bin cards are sometimes dispensed with on the grounds that they represent a needless duplication and that the storekeeper should not be burdened with clerical work. A reasonably efficient stores staff is, however, quite capable of undertaking simple clerical work and the running record provided by the bin card enables the storeman to exercise a measure of control over the stores for which he is responsible.

		BIN CARD						
Maximum			Material Code					
Minimum			Bin No.					
Order Level			Description:					
RECEIPTS			ISSUES			BALANCE	AUDIT	
Date	GR No.	Qty	Date	Req. No.	Qty	Qty	Date	Initials
SF1								

A bin card is attached to the bin, drawer or shelf in or on which each individual material is stored, and it provides a running record of receipts and issues in the simplest possible form. An entry will be made at the time of each receipt or issue and the new balance will normally be extended. Where the storeman initiates purchase requisitions, the maximum and minimum stock will be shown on the bin card together with re-order level and quantity. The storeman must make a note whenever a stock reaches re-order level so that he can prepare the necessary purchase requisition as soon as he has the available time to do so. Productive staff should not be kept waiting for material while records are prepared, but it is good practice to record the outgoing material on each bin card at the time it is removed from the bin. Where there is no central stores record, a stock ledger sometimes takes the place of the bin cards in the stores. In this case the storeman has all the records in one place at his desk and generally makes the entries from the requisitions at quiet times.

Receipt of Material into Store

After incoming materials have been checked by the goods receiving department they are passed to the appropriate store, together with two copies of the relative goods received note. Acknowledgment of receipt is given by the storeman, who signs one of the copies and returns it to the goods receiving department. Having done this he places the material in the appropriate bin or on the appropriate shelf and makes the necessary entries on the bin card. The details are recorded in the stock ledger from another copy of the goods received note sent to the accounts department or cost office.

Issues from Stores

If stock records are to be accurate, precautions must be taken to ensure that no material leaves the stores without due authorisation and without a proper record being made. Authority for issue is given by means of a *materials requisition*.

MATERIALS REQUISITION				Account No.		
To			Store	Order No.		
Quantity	Unit	Description		Code	Cost Office	
					Rate	Amount
						£
Signature		Date	Cost Centre	Issued by:	Entered Stock Records	

The materials requisition (or stores requisition) details the items required, showing quantity, description, code or part number and the cost centre or job to be charged. It authorises the cost office to charge the particular job, and the departmental work-in-progress account, or the appropriate cost centre and overhead control account with the value of the goods and to pass a corresponding credit to the stock account. Requisitions are normally prepared in triplicate, the top copy being passed to the store while the duplicate is retained by the department receiving the goods. The storekeeper records the entry on the appropriate bin card at the time of issue and passes the requisition to the stock record clerks. The third copy of the requisition goes to the cost office, where it will be priced and form the voucher for the appropriate accounting entry.

Copies of the standard material specifications are held in the production office and store, and shortly before the materials are required a requisition is prepared quoting the specification number and quantity to be issued. In a standard costing system each item is pre-costed so that the standard cost of the complete specification can be entered as one figure each time an issue takes place.

Where a standard article is manufactured, material quantities are normally pre-determined, and the requisition is prepared for the exact amount of materials required to complete the job. Should any further material be required, it will be necessary to prepare an *excess materials requisition*, which automatically draws attention to the excess usage and normally shows the reason under a suitable coding system.

Where production methods are standardised, material requistions are frequently pre-printed as part of the paperwork set used for production control purposes. Pre-printed requistions save time on the shop floor and are clearer and more reliable than their handwritten counterparts; in addition, they state clearly the correct amount of material to be issued for each order.

Where material is issued in excess of requirements the balance is returned to the stores together with a *materials return note*, which is similar to a materials requisition, but normally printed in a different colour. Details will be entered on the bin card and the materials return note will be sent to the cost office, where the appropriate entries will be made.

Wherever possible, the transfer of materials from one job to another should be avoided because of the risk of omitting to make the necessary records. Where such transfers are permitted, however, a *materials transfer note* showing the job numbers to be debited and credited will be prepared and passed direct to the cost office for the appropriate adjustment in the work-in-progress ledger to be made.

Alternatives to Detailed Stores Accounting

No business that handles materials can be run efficiently without material control, but the system must be designed to suit the business concerned. There are cases in which detailed stores accounting can be modified or even be dispensed with. In a continuous process industry materials are often delivered in bulk to the point of use, and regular checks of quantities are made to ensure that purchase requisitions are prepared when replenishment becomes necessary. Where large quantities are used, the materials may be scheduled with the supplier for regular daily or weekly deliveries according to a definite programme. At the end of each suitable period stocks will be ascertained by direct measurement, or by the use of quantity-level markings on the bin or in the case of liquids by dipping the tank. The actual usage will be obtained from the formula:

Materials used = Opening stock + Materials purchased − Closing stock

Where, however, the same bulk material is issued to more than one process, it is normally necessary to record the issues to each.

In some cases material usage may be determined from machine output without a detailed record of input, but it is then necessary to keep a separate record of scrapped articles and to exercise strict control of total usage. Detailed records will normally be dispensed with in the case of material of small value where the extent of any loss cannot be large. For example, while the use of major materials in a jobbing engineering shop must be recorded, detailed records might be cut out for bolts, nuts, washers, cotter pins, oils, jointing materials etc. and these will be charged out on an established basis. Cases like this must be approached with common sense. After all the relevant facts have been considered a decision must be made as to whether the controls are likely to cost more than they save.

PRODUCTION PLANNING AND CONTROL

In any well-organised factory the functions of production control and material control are so inter-related and co-ordinated with costing that any failure in their operation will be reflected in the costing system. Production control in fact embraces material control, and is the system that covers the regulation of materials and the production facilities in such a way that the required quantity of goods of the required quality is produced at the required time by the cheapest and best method. Production control covers the following functions:

1. *Advance Planning of Production.* This involves the determination of the economic production quantity, the quality, and quantities of materials, the methods to be employed, and labour and plant requirements.
2. *Routing.* This covers the study of each order to determine the individual operations required and the type of machines or productive facilities to be employed. Operation layouts will be prepared detailing the manufacture of each component, sub-assembly and final assembly.
3. *Scheduling.* This involves the programming of each operation and the loading of the machines so that the raw material and each component and sub-assembly are available at the required time, and that a satisfactory balance of work is available for each machine.
4. *Issue of the Production Order.* This puts into operation the production plans, the drawing of materials and the movement and control of the job at every stage of manufacture. The movement and control functions are generally known as *progressing* and in so far as they control the quantities achieved at each stage of production they are vital to costing.

Production orders are issued in many forms according to the requirements of the particular business, and a complex job may be broken down into a number of separate orders issued to different departments as required. For standardised production it is normal to prepare a master layout and to produce duplicated action and progress copies of the production order together with material requisitions, job cards, identity tags, job completed notes, despatch record cards, etc. A system of this type greatly facilitates standard costing, as a product cost sheet can be prepared from the same master layout as the production records. The job can then be costed from standard data before production begins, and the cost office is thereafter interested only in any variancies (i.e. deviations) from the pre-determined cost.

MATERIAL COST

In most cases the purchase price of a material is directly obtained from the supplier's invoice. The basic price may need to be adjusted. Statement of Standard Accounting Practice (SSAP) 9 defines cost for stock purposes as all expenditure incurred in the normal course of business to bring the material to its present location and condition. This includes the purchase price plus any import duties payable, transport or handling costs, less trade discounts negotiated with the supplier.

Discounts

Trade Discount is an allowance made from the full invoice price to a customer who buys goods in the ordinary course of trade, e.g. a wholesaler may invoice goods to a retailer at the retail selling price less a discount of $33\frac{1}{3}\%$, which represents the retailer's gross profit.

A *Quantity Discount* is a similar reduction in price given to a purchaser who buys in large quantities. The deduction of both trade and quantity discounts is made on the invoice and only the net figure is entered in accounting and stock records.

Cash Discount is an allowance made by the supplier when the purchaser pays his account at once or within the period of credit allowed. Purchases are recorded gross with the cash discount treated as income when the account is paid.

Transport Costs

The price charged by the supplier may or may not include the cost of air, sea, or land transport, and other storage or delivery costs. Where the purchaser has to pay separately for carriage and other costs in respect of incoming materials the charges should, where practicable, be regarded as part of the purchase price of the material concerned. Where, however, it proves impossible or unprofitable to analyse into its separate components an item of carriage relating to several materials, it may be necessary to regard this expenditure as an item of overhead.

Other costs incurred by a business in connection with the receipt and inspection of materials are normally regarded as overheads, as also is the cost of storage when a long period is involved e.g. in the timber trade. These overheads are sometimes absorbed as part of the production cost of each job, but where the figures are large they may be included separately in the product costs at a rate per tonne or per thousand units etc. These items are sometimes covered by inflating the stock prices, but this course is not normally adopted because of the difficulty of apportioning the costs to individual stocks.

Boxes, Bags, and Other Containers

Any charge made by the supplier for non-returnable containers should be included as part of the purchase price. Where a charge is made for returnable containers, and the full sum is refundable on their return, container stock accounts will have to be maintained to record the arrival and return of the containers, but no 'cost' entries will be necessary. However, where the amount refundable upon the safe return of the container is less than that charged originally, the difference between these amounts is in effect a part of the purchase price and should be treated as such.

Pricing Material Issues

There are a number of factors to be taken into account in pricing the materials issued to production. Where purchase prices are constant over a long period and the quantities purchased do not vary to any extent, there is little difficulty. In practice, however, it is found that prices do fluctuate partly through changes in the value of money e.g. inflation, partly through changes in world commodity prices, partly through buying from alternative sources, and partly because of differences in quantity discounts. Under these circumstances it is clear that there may be a number of identical articles in a bin all bought at different prices. When one of these articles is issued, it is necessary to consider the price at which it should be charged to production. There are a number of methods of pricing materials, each having particular advantages and disadvantages, which must be understood if the most suitable method is to be used in particular circumstances. The more important methods are as follows:

1. Specific price.
2. First-in-first-out price   (FIFO).
3. Last-in-first-out price   (LIFO).
4. Simple average price.
5. Weighted average price.
6. Standard price.
7. Market price (replacement price).
8. Inflated price.
9. Base stock.

In current practice, methods 2, 5, and 6 are most often used.

Specific Price

This is the price actually paid for the material bought. This method of pricing can be used only for particular items of material that can be separately identified when they are in stock or which are ordered for, and issued to, particular jobs, the requisitions being priced at the exact cost recorded on the appropriate stores card. The method may also be used where particular batches of material are readily identifiable even though issues are made to a number of different jobs. For example, in the steel industry it is normal to buy a batch of material called a cast and for control purposes to maintain the identity of each cast. The original cost per tonne of each cast is known and the material may be charged out at this price each time it is issued.

   This system is somewhat awkward for general use, but it is frequently employed where non-standard products have to be purchased to meet a particular customer's specification. Some undertakings use this method to price issues of materials they do not normally stock, although adopting some other method to price materials in regular use.

First-In-First-Out Price (FIFO)

This is the price paid for the material first taken into the stock from which the material to be priced could have been drawn. This method assumes that the materials are used up in the same sequence as they were purchased, i.e. that the older materials have been used up first. Whereas this is essential in the case of materials that deteriorate, it does not necessarily follow that all stocks are used up in chronological order, but for pricing purposes it is assumed that the items longest in stock are used up first. FIFO is most suitable for use where the material is of comparatively high value and not in frequent demand. It is also appropriate where there are relatively few changes of purchase price, or where the ratio of the number of issues to the number of receipts is not large.

Example

A company makes the following purchases of a commodity:

		£
3 January	1000 kg at 25p	250.00
8 March	500 kg at 27.5p	137.50
4 May	800 kg at 30p	240.00
		£627.50

Issues are made as follows:

10 January	400 kg
15 February	400 kg
12 March	400 kg
15 April	200 kg
6 May	600 kg

The stores ledger account will be as follows:

RECEIVED					ISSUED					BALANCE
Date	Invoice No.	Quan- tity	Price	Value	Date	Req. No.	Quantity	Price	Value	Quantity
19— Jan. 3	J1476	kg 1000	£ 0.250	£ 250 000	19—		kg	kg	£	£	kg 1000
					Jan. 10	B119	400	0.250	100 000	600
					Feb. 15	B291	400	0.250	100 000	200
Mar. 8	J2124	500	0.275	137 500						700
					Mar. 12	B388	400 200	0.250	50 000	
							200	0.275	65 000	300
					Apr. 15	B476	200	0.275	55 000	100
May 4	J3617	800	0.300	240 000						900
					May 6	B592	600 100	0.275	27 500	
							500	0.300	150 000	300

The following points should be noted:

1. The balance on the account is 300 kg at 30p = £90.
2. A number of major companies employ not two figures after the decimal point (i.e. pence) but three (i.e. tenths of a penny) for stores purposes.

3. After each batch of material has been exhausted, a line is drawn across both the received and issued sides. The first price after the last line on the received side is the one applicable until that batch is exhausted. Thereafter, it will be ruled off and the next price taken. This has the additional advantage that when balancing the account only items below the last line need be considered.
4. The running quantity balance is necessary where the stores ledger is used for perpetual inventory purposes. It is not, however, necessary to evaluate the balance after each issue.

Advantages of the FIFO method of pricing are:

1. The price is based on cost, and hence no profits or losses arise solely by reason of the method of pricing.
2. The price is based on actual records, used systematically, and not upon an estimate.
3. The resulting stock balance usually respresents a fair commercial valuation of stock.
4. The method is based on the sound principle that older material will be used up first.

However, where a large number of purchases are made at different prices and unit prices therefore have to be calculated frequently, the method proves both troublesome and expensive in operation. Also, where price fluctuations are large, a substantial difference may occur in the price at which material is charged to two similar jobs started on the same day. During a period of inflation, issues based on earlier pre-inflation prices will not represent the replacement cost of the material used, so that profit may be overstated.

Last-In-First-Out Price (LIFO)

This is the price paid for the material last taken into the stock from which the material to be priced could have been drawn. LIFO is sometimes employed in an attempt to ascertain the profit that would have been earned were it not for material price changes during the period under review. The use of LIFO is advocated by those who follow the principle that cost should be related as closely as possible to current price levels.

Where material is valued on the LIFO method the costs are calculated on a basis that approximates to replacement cost. This has considerable advantages in a period of rising prices as it puts sales and cost of sales on the same footing, and automatically eliminates the windfall profit (or holding gain) that would otherwise be shown, e.g., in the wire drawing industry prices are fixed by national agreement and are amended whenever the cost of raw material is increased. Assuming that rod is purchased at £400 per tonne and conversion costs average £300 per tonne, a selling price of £750 will show a net profit of £50 per tonne. If, after some time, rod prices increase to £440 per tonne and selling prices to £790, the net profit will still be £50 per tonne. On the FIFO basis, however, until existing stocks are exhausted material will continue to be charged out at £400 and for a limited period the cost per tonne will be shown to be £700 compared with the new selling price of £790, i.e. a profit of £90 will be computed. On the LIFO basis the material will be priced at £440 per tonne on the first delivery after the increase and violent fluctuations in profit will be avoided.

Where materials are not purchased regularly LIFO fails to give the full benefits that would arise from the use of replacement costs. In practice it is not, however, easy to obtain all the replacement costs as prices change, and LIFO has the advantage of simplicity in that reference need be made only to the last receipt on the stores ledger to obtain the price.

Example

Assuming the same purchases and receipts as were taken for the previous example, the stores ledger account will be as follows:

RECEIVED					ISSUED					BALANCE	
Date	Invoice	Quan-tity	Price	Value	Date	Req. No.	Quantity	Price	Value	Qnty	Price
19—		kg	£	£	19—		kg	kg	£	£	kg	£
Jan. 3	J1476	1000	0.250	250 000							1000	0.250
					Jan. 10	B119		400	0.250	100 000	600	0.250
					Feb. 15	B291		400	0.250	100 000	200	0.250
Mar. 8	J2124	500	0.275	137 500							200	0.250
											500	0.275
											200	0.250
					Mar. 12	B388		400	0.275	110 000	100	0.275
					Apr. 15	B476	200	100 0.275	27 500	100	0.250
								100 0.250	25 000		
May 4	J3617	800	0.300	240 000							100	0.250
											800	0.300
					May 6	B592		600	0.300	180 000	100	0.250
											200	0.300

Advocates of this plan claim that the profits disclosed tend to be more stable, year by year, and that the resulting accounting information is thus a better guide to the management. On the other hand, the plan has certain disadvantages:

1. LIFO, as with the FIFO price, involves considerable clerical work.
2. Stock values are determined by the prices of the oldest lots on hand; these prices may be entirely out of line with current replacement prices. A false working capital position is thus shown in the balance sheet. If stock falls below the opening balance sheet level, the system will charge out some material at last year's very low prices, thus overstating the profit.
3. Whilst the LIFO method of valuation shows the stock in hand at cost, it does so as the cost of the oldest material still in stock, and where price levels are falling it may be necessary to write off substantial amounts to reduce the value of stock shown to the current market value.
4. Stock based on LIFO is not acceptable in accounts laid before the Inland Revenue.
5. As in the case of FIFO, a substantial difference may be shown in the cost of two jobs solely because the stores for one happened to be drawn a few minutes before those for the other.

LIFO was stated to be a non-acceptable basis for stock valuation in SSAP 9, but it was subsequently given legal validity by the Companies Act 1981 (now The Companies Act 1985).

Simple Average Price

This price is calculated by dividing the total of the prices of the materials in the stock from which the material to be priced could have been drawn, by the number of prices used in that total. Very little can be said in favour of this method, as it pays no regard to the relative quantities held at each price. There might, for instance, be 100 items in stock at 25p each, and 10 000 at 15p, yet an issue of 5000 would be made at the simple average of 25p and 15p, i.e. at 20p each.

Weighted Average Price

This price is calculated by dividing the total cost of material in the stock from which the material to be priced could have been drawn, by the total quantity of materials in that stock. Whereas the simple average price is suitable for use only when the prices of the various consignments vary very little – otherwise it tends to give absurd results – the weighted average price can be used even where the prices of successive deliveries differ, because the weighting evens out the effect of these variations in price.

Example

If we use again the figures of the previous examples, the stores ledger account will be as follows:

RECEIVED					ISSUED					BALANCE
Date	Invoice No.	Qnty	Price	Value	Date	Req. No.	Qnty	Price	Value	Quantity
19—		kg	£	£	19—		kg	£	£	kg
Jan. 3	J1476	1000	0.25000	250 000						1000
					Jan. 10	B119	400	0.25000	100 000	600
					Feb. 15	B291	400	0.25000	100 000	200
Mar. 8	J2124	500	0.27500	137 500						700
					Mar. 12	B388	400	0.26786	107 144	300
					Apr. 15	B476	200	0.26786	53 572	100
May 4	J3617	800	0.30000	240 000						900
					May 6	B592	600	0.29643	177 858	300
					Jun. 30	Balance	300	0.29642	88 926	
		2300		627 500			2300		627 500	
										300
July 1	Balance	300	0.29642							

The prices are calculated as follows:

	£		£
200 at £0.25000	50.000	100 at £0.26786	26.786
500 at 0.27500	137.500	800 at 0.30000	240.000
700	£187.500	900	£266.786

£187.5 ÷ 700 = £0.26786.   £266.786 ÷ 900 = £0.29643.

It will be seen that the balance at the end of the half-year has been taken out at the price of £0.29642 to square the account.

The use of this method is not limited to materials of stable price as is the simple average method. The basis of the price calculation is a simple one involving only the division of the total value of the material in stock by the quantity in stock. Other advantages of the method are that the need to calculate a new price arises only with each new receipt of stock, and so all issues then are taken at this price until the next lot of material is received.

As with the FIFO and LIFO methods, the weighted average price method calls for many calculations. To avoid errors in the pricing of issues and stock balances, the price per unit must be carried to a sufficient number of decimal places to ensure accuracy to the nearest penny. Another disadvantage of the method is that excessively high (or low) prices for material paid in the past are reflected in the average for a considerable time after the expensive (or inexpensive) material has been used.

Stock records showing issues at weighted average price give a fair indication of stock values that can be used in the financial accounts. The weighted average method, when applied to opening and closing stocks, gives a profit figure in between the two extremes achieved by FIFO and LIFO, although it is fair to say that it may use a figure for stock valuation that has not in fact been paid for the stock.

Standard Price

Under this method a pre-determined price is fixed for each material normally held in stock. The standard price is set for a definite period such as a year, and takes into account the probable trend of prices over that period. In setting standards it is normal to round off the figures to a reasonable degree in order to simplify the pricing of requisitions and to reduce the possibility of errors, e.g., if in a rising market a commodity has been purchased in the last three months at 37p, 37.6p, and 39p it would be reasonable to set the standard at 40p. The standard price will take into account normal quantity discounts and the cost of carriage inwards and should reflect the price the buyer expects to pay in the forthcoming period.

When standard prices are used, the difference between the actual and standard cost of each purchase is written off to a *materials price variance account*. In practice each invoice is re-priced at the standard price and the difference is taken out in the purchase analysis as follows:

	£	
Invoice for 100 articles at 41.3p	41.30	
Standard cost – 100 articles at 40p	40.00	

	£	£
The book-keeping entry will be:		
Raw material stock account	Dr. 40.00	
Materials price variance account	1.30	
To purchase ledger control account		41.30

The stock record will be entered with 100 at 40p.

Example

Again using the receipts and issues of the previous examples, the stores ledger account will be as follows:

			Standard Price – £0.280		Unit – kilogram	
RECEIVED			ISSUED			BALANCE
Date	Invoice No.	Quantity	Date	Req. No.	Quantity	Quantity
19—		kg	19—		kg	kg
Jan. 3	J1476	1000				1000
			Jan. 10	B119	400	600
			Feb. 15	B291	400	200
Mar. 8	J2124	500				700
			Mar. 12	B388	400	300
			Apr. 15	B476	200	100
May 4	J3617	800				900
			May 6	B592	600	300

Note that in this case it is unnecessary to record values in the stores ledger. As every entry is priced at standard cost, the value in stock at any time is simply the product of the balance and the standard price.

There will be a favourable price variance of £16.50 computed as follows:

19—			Actual Cost	Standard Cost
			£	£
January	3	1000 kg	250.00	280.00
March	8	500 kg	137.50	140.00
May	4	800 kg	240.00	224.00
			£627.50	644.00
				627.50
				£16.50

Whilst this method is used mainly in connection with standard costing it can be employed in practically any other system. It has the following advantages:

1. It is simple to use, although where the stock comprises a wide variety of materials of different sizes and weights, the setting of standards takes considerable time.
2. Comparison of actual prices and standard prices provides a check on the purchasing department.
3. The effect of price variations is eliminated from the job or process costs, and satisfactory comparisons can therefore be made.

In times of inflation however, or where there are considerable fluctuations in the cost of the commodity concerned, it may be difficult to fix standard prices.

Replacement Price

This is the price at which, at the date of consumption, material could be bought identical with that being consumed. Replacement price is used when it is desired to reflect current price conditions in costs. While this may be very desirable for a particular purpose, it is, in practice, difficult to obtain current costs for each item in stock; and even where revised price lists are available, the work of revaluing the complete inventory every time a change takes place is particularly onerous. This method is most suitable for businesses that buy large quantities of materials well in advance of requirements in order to obtain cheap prices, the benefit of which will not be passed on to the customer.

Inflated Price

Issues of material may be charged at inflated prices under any of the normal pricing methods. This is done in order to charge the user of the material with any particular losses or charges that are known to have occurred. For example, inevitable losses may arise from evaporation or the breaking of bulk, and these can be taken into account in the costing records by charging all issues at a price in excess of cost. Similarly, when it is desired to cover particular handling or storage charges in the cost of material issued, issue prices will be increased to cover this factor.

Whilst an inflated price is rarely entirely accurate, its use does approximately recover the full cost of the material concerned. The following example makes the position clear.

RECEIVED					ISSUED				
Date	Invoice No.	Qnty	Price	Value	Date	Req. No.	Qnty	Price	Value
19—		litres		£	19—		litres		£
Jan. 7	1236	1000	20p	200.00					
					Jan. 10	71	200	22.5p	42.50
					20	94	400	22.5p	85.00
					Feb. 8	116	200	21.25p	42.50
					28	Balance	140	20p	28.00
					28	Loss	60		2.00
		1000		200.00			1000		200.00
Mar. 1	Balance	140	20p	28.00					

It will be observed that a physical stocktaking on 28 February revealed a balance of 140 litres to carry down, and a loss of 60 litres. By inflating the price of the material, charging it out at 21.25p per litre instead of at the cost price of 20p, the normal losses through evaporation and upon issue have been taken into account. It will be seen that only the sum of £2 remains to be written off to the costing profit and loss account, representing losses in excess of those anticipated when the inflated price was fixed.

Base Stock Method

This method is still used by certain industries, although as a result of its rejection by the Inland Revenue and by SSAP 9 it is becoming less common. It assumes that a definite minimum weight or volume of material must be maintained at all times as a fixed asset of the company, and it is the practice to value this at the same amount every year regardless of price fluctuations. The inventory in excess of base stock is normally valued at the lower of cost and market values. The advantage of this method is that it reduces fluctuations in annual profits that would otherwise appear as a result of price changes.

Choice of Method

Before leaving the subject of the pricing of material issues it is useful to sum up the various factors that influence the choice of method. Firstly, it must be appreciated that from the point of view of price the methods can be grouped under three headings:

1.   *Valuation at original cost*, including FIFO and the average methods.
2.   *Valuation at market price*, including LIFO.
3.   *Valuation at fixed prices*, including *standard price*.

In a period of falling prices it is conservative to value on the FIFO or average method, as the older or more expensive items are then absorbed into cost first and the less expensive items are left in stock. This brings the inventory reasonably into line with the value that will be used for financial accounting purposes.

In a period of rising prices, the pricing methods based on cost tend to show inflationary profits which appear to be highly satisfactory, but may nevertheless conceal factory losses and inefficient production. There is a definite argument for extracting separately the amount of windfall profit made when price rises occur. The pricing methods based on market value maintain a balance between material cost and selling price, but as the stock balances include goods at the earliest prices the inventory is considerably undervalued.

The standard cost method can be operated satisfactorily in either a rising or a falling market as price fluctuations are automatically segregated into variance accounts. The variances may be written off at the times of purchase or be held in suspense and charged to the profit and loss account in the period of issue.

Other factors affecting the choice of method are:

1.   The nature of the business.
2.   The relative number of issues compared with receipts.
3.   The frequency with which prices change.
4.   The proportion that raw material bears to total cost.
5.   The necessity for maintaining uniformity within an industry.

It will be appreciated that no hard and fast rules can be laid down regarding pricing methods – this is just another of the many instances where the cost accountant must weigh up the facts carefully, and by the exercise of sound judgement and common sense arrive at the most satisfactory all-round solution. A consistent approach must be followed, using the same method, once selected, each year.

Work-in-Progress, Component and Finished Goods Stocks

Up to the present in this chapter stock records and pricing methods have been considered mainly from the point of view of purchased material. Most companies have stores containing partly manufactured and finished goods and the treatment of these must not be overlooked.

The *work-in-progress store* contains partly manufactured goods. The term normally relates to a store in which the output of one department or operation is held pending its transfer to the next department or operation. In many instances the material is held for only a few days or hours and it is then quite normal practice to dispense with stock records and to leave the material under the control of the 'progress' staff. There are cases, however, where a work-in-progress store holds definite quantities of stock in a semi-finished condition, and requisitions fresh supplies as required. In a standard costing system the partly manufactured goods are taken into stock at standard cost, comprising direct material cost, direct wages and production overheads, and all cost differences are written off. In batch costing each batch is required to be taken into stock at the actual cost of that batch, and as this will vary with each batch, it is necessary to price each issue by one of the methods explained earlier in this chapter.

The *component store* contains finished parts and sub-assemblies that are held for final assembly into the finished product. Stock records are necessary because the stock of each component must be maintained at the correct level. Components will be ordered by the production control department when the re-order level is reached and, as in the case of part-finished stocks, these will be entered in the stock ledger at cost of production. Again, issues will be made at FIFO, LIFO, average price, or as required.

The *finished goods store* contains finished articles ready for despatch, and the stock records will be similar to those of components.

Work-in-progress will be on the shop floor at the time a valuation is required and the figures for this purpose must be obtained from the cost records. In a jobbing shop it is customary to keep a job record in which all materials, labour and overheads expended on each job will be charged. As the jobs are completed and transferred to finished stock, the manufacturing account will be credited and the cost transferred to the appropriate finished stock account or, where the goods are for immediate despatch, to the cost of sales account. It will be appreciated that the balancing of a work-in-progress ledger may be a fairly heavy task, and where the totals are required promptly for monthly or four-weekly accounts, it is necessary to keep one or more total work-in-progress control accounts in the cost ledger. The totals of all the debits and credits to individual jobs will be entered in the control accounts and the balances of these will be used for the monthly accounts.

Whilst the monthly profit and loss account will normally incorporate the stocks and work-in-progress at the values at which they are shown in the inventory, it must be remembered that this may not be suitable for the annual financial accounts. The stock in the financial accounts is normally shown at cost or market value, whichever is lower, and the inventory values may have to be adjusted to this basis. It is advantageous to be able to use the same valuation basis for both the monthly and the annual accounts, and it may be said that the FIFO and weighted average methods are normally acceptable for financial purposes, apart from any reductions required to reduce the cost to market value.

Reports on Materials

The cost office must provide suitable reports regarding material costs to each level of management. Where possible, details of excess material usage should be provided for the departmental foremen and managers and, when the latter are responsible for their own departmental stores, they should also receive reports showing any deficiencies that come to light from the stores audit. In many industries, particularly those of a process nature, useful reports can be provided to compare material inputs and outputs and to show up the percentage losses that have occurred at each stage. If possible, all reports should show values as well as weights, as the presentation of figures in monetary terms puts the facts into a more impressive and more easily understood form.

Management at higher levels should be presented with details of excess material usage in a summarised form, with separate departmental totals. Where standard pricing techniques are in force, further reports should be prepared to show the excess cost or saving through price variances, and it is helpful to break these down to show how much is due to changes in the market and how much to incorrect buying policies.

Reports should be prepared at regular intervals to show the total value of stock held by each department or in each store, and the figures should be compared with those in previous periods to reveal the movements that have taken place in the total inventory. Where budgetary control is in operation, stocks will be compared with the budgeted levels and operating statements prepared to show the material usages, and in particular excess usages, in respect of each department. Slow-moving stocks must be identified, perhaps by the calculation of a stockturn statistic. This figure would show the number of times usage covers the average stock held. Where slow-moving stocks exist, efforts to buy more must be relaxed, and eventually a decision as to whether the items should be stocked or sold off must be made.

SEMINAR EXERCISES

2.1 In a store, a stock of component 437Q is maintained on a stock record card. The following receipts and issues take place during the months of October, November and December.

Date	Invoice	Receipts	Requisition	Issues
4 October	10/417	1800 at £1	–	–
10 October	–	–	D127	1000
25 October	10/649	1600 at £1.20	–	–
1 November	–	–	D460	1000
20 November	–	–	D512	1000
6 December	12/131	1400 at £1.60	–	–
20 December	–	–	D720	1000

The opening stock on 1 October was 200 units; value £1 each.

Required:

Write up a stock record card for component 437Q on the basis of FIFO, LIFO, and weighted average cost.
Show clearly the cost of components charged to production in the quarter.

(20 marks)

2.2 Draft a flow chart to illustrate the system for requisitioning, purchasing, receiving and paying for materials. (20 marks)

2.3 (a) Explain the term *economic order quantity* (EOQ), and demonstrate its connection with the re-order level. (6 marks)

(b) From the data given below calculate for component 967:

(i) re-order level
(ii) minimum stock level
(iii) re-order quantity
(iv) average stock held under normal conditions.

Component 967

Maximum storage space available:	64 000 units
Normal consumption per week:	3 200 units
Maximum consumption per week:	4 000 units

Estimated lead time from order to delivery: three weeks (maximum)
two weeks (normal) (8 marks)

(c) From the data given below calculate for component 967 the optimum number of orders to be placed each year and the EOQ. The options available are to place one, two, three, four, five, or six orders per annum.

> Annual usage of component 967: 18 000 units
> Unit cost: £4.80
> Cost of placing an order: £30
> Stock holding cost as a percentage of average stock: 1%.

Use a schedule or the EOQ formula. (8 marks)

(Total 22 marks)

REVIEW QUESTIONS

2.1 (a) Outline a suitable system for collecting the material cost of each job in a manufacturing company employing historic job costing. (8 marks)

(b) AYE PLC manufactures a range of products from one basic material. In October the opening stock of the material was 1650 kg and, at the end of the month, a physical count revealed a stock of 1900 kg, which was 250 kg less than that shown by the inventory records. Except for the returns to the supplier shown below, all material recorded as being issued from store was consumed by production.

The material costs £5 per kilogram. At the beginning of October the amount owing to creditors for supplies of this material was £13 800 and during the month AYE PLC paid these creditors £37 200 and returned £1600 of faulty material. At the end of the month the amount owing to the creditors concerned was £15 000.

The company operates an historic batch costing system fully integrated with the financial accounts.

Required:

(i) Calculate the value of material issued to production during October and record the month's transactions for the material in a stores account showing both quantities and value. You should clearly indicate the account into which (or from which) the corresponding entry should be posted. (9 marks)

(ii) Briefly consider the possible reasons for the stock loss revealed by the physical count. (5 marks)

(Total 22 marks)

2.2 At the beginning of May the opening stock of a particular component was 540 units; total value £2160.

During the month the following supplies were received:

> 8 May 600 units; total value £2700
> 15 May 600 units; total value £3300
> 22 May 600 units; total value £3600

There is a standard carriage charge included in the above amounts, of £200 per delivery, for transporting the components to the factory. The invoice for the goods received on 22 May had not been received by the end of the month.

Shown below are the issues from store during May:

2 May	500 units	17 May	500 units
9 May	150 units	23 May	120 units
16 May	500 units	28 May	130 units

The components issued on 9 May were used in the general plant maintenance programme and those issued on 23 May were incorporated into plant and equipment being constructed by the company's engineers to mechanise part of the manufacturing process. All other issues were made direct to production for inclusion in the output of the company's products, the issue on 28 May made in order to replace components damaged by incorrect handling.

On 21 May 40 units were returned to store from production and, at the end of the month, the closing stock was 400 units.

Required:

(a) Record the month's transactions in a stores account for this component indicating very clearly the account into which (or from which) the corresponding entry should be posted. You should assume the company operates an historic batch costing system, fully integrated with the financial accounts, and uses a first-in-first-out method of pricing material issues.   (17 marks)

(b) Briefly contrast the effects of using FIFO with the LIFO method of pricing material issues from store.   (5 marks)

(Total 22 marks)

2.3 The Managing Director of the Direct Desk Company Limited, manufacturing desks of a standard size, asks you as the recently appointed works accountant to investigate the material control procedures operating in the factory. You have arranged for a physical stock count of raw materials and finished goods to take place at the beginning and end of May. The results of this stocktaking and other data relevant to the consumption of material during May are shown below.

Physical Stocktaking	Opening Stock at Beginning of May	Closing Stock at End of May
Desks	730	925
Raw materials:		
Timber	4000 square metres	5500 square metres
Varnish	1600 litres	700 litres
Other Data		
Sales: 4600 desks		
	Timber	*Varnish*
Works manager's estimate of material consumption per unit, including an allowance for normal waste	3 square metres	0.47 litres

	Timber	Varnish
Purchase price of opening stock	£3.40 per square metre	£1.20 per litre
Purchases of materials:		
6 May	12 500 square metres at £3.50 per square metre	400 litres at £1.10 per litre
20 May	7000 square metres at £3.70 per square metre	1800 litres at £1.30 per litre
Value of material issued to production:		
13 May	£28 000	£1200
27 May	£36 400	£1550

The value of material issued to production has been obtained by using the following methods of pricing material issues:

Timber – LIFO
Varnish – FIFO.

Required:

(a) Write up a stock record card for timber and for varnish disclosing any differences arising between the book stock and the physical count.

(10 marks)

(b) Compare actual consumption for each material with estimated consumption.

(4 marks)

(c) List possible reasons for differences disclosed in (b).   (8 marks)

(Total 22 marks)

3

The Costing Treatment of Labour

As with materials, labour costing may be divided into two linked sections: first, the system whereby labour cost is recorded and payment is made, and second, the use made of labour costs in the firm.

Personnel Records and Payroll

Duties connected with the engagement, discharge, and transfer of labour are normally carried out by a separate employment or personnel department to which requisitions for new employees are sent, as necessary, by the production departments. Requisitions for new personnel are made on a prescribed form and specify the number of workers of each grade and sex required. On receiving such a requisition the employment officer will consult any records he may have of persons available for employment, apply to the local Jobcentre, advertise, or take such other action as will enable him to fill the vacancies. On engaging a newcomer, the employment officer will make out an *employee's record card*. This will show full personal details of the employee, particulars of previous employment, medical category, and wage rate on engagement. Normally spaces are also provided for the employee's clock number, the subsequent recording of transfers and promotions, wage rate amendments, details of attendance, merit and conduct reports, sickness and accidents and the date and reason for leaving.

The clock number allotted to an employee upon engagement is normally retained by him throughout his period of service and acts as a quick means of reference. It is usually shown on clock cards, time sheets, payroll, and tool issue records. In certain trades the clock number is referred to as a check-number, ticket-number or simply as an employee-number. Frequently the clock number is in two parts, the first being a prefix to designate the department to which the employee is allocated, and the second giving the permanent identity number by which the employee will be known, e.g., the number 91472 might indicate that the employee is allocated to department 9, and that his personal identity number is 1472. If an employee is transferred from one department to another only the prefix of his clock number will be altered.

The scheme of numbering employees will depend upon the circumstances of each organisation, but a full list of clock numbers will be maintained by the employment department.

As each new employee is engaged, the employment department will receive his National Insurance document and, where applicable, an income tax form. These will be passed to the wages department together with a new engagement form on which will be shown particulars of the new employee, including his clock number and commencing wage rate. Similarly, the employment department will notify the wages department of any discharges, transfers or changes in the rates of pay of existing employees.

Front

EMPLOYEE'S RECORD CARD	Surname: Christian Names:			Clock No.
Engagement Particulars	**Employment Record**			
Home Address:	Date	Department	Grade	Employment
Date Employed Date of Birth Married/Single Height Weight General Physique Category				
Previous Employment:	**WAGE RATE RECORD**			
	Date	Rate	Particulars	Date	Rate	Particulars
References:						
Notes:						

Back

TIMEKEEPING AND MERIT						TRAINING, PROGRESS AND CONDUCT	
Year	Days Lost		Overtime Hours	Lost Time Hours	Merit & Notes	Date	Particulars
	Sickness	Other					
Date left: Reason for Leaving: General Remarks:							

Wage rates for manual workers are normally determined by national agreement between the appropriate trade union and employers' federation. In some industries e.g. the hotel and catering industry, the Department of Employment sets up wages councils empowered to lay down the terms and conditions of employment and to prescribe compulsory minimum wage scales. These councils are the subject of political controversy and may soon disappear. The wages and salaries of management and clerical staff, and the wages of employees not covered by formal agreements or statutory requirements, are determined by individual employers, with regard to the nature and responsibility of the work involved and to the level of wages prevailing locally. Whatever the method adopted, the employment officer should have standard rates for each grade of his company's employees to obviate inequalities between workers of similar grades and proficiency. It is, of course, essential as a matter of internal control that the employment records are maintained outside the wages department.

Labour Turnover

The personnel or employment department must endeavour to keep labour turnover at a minimum. Labour turnover is normally measured as the ratio of the number of persons leaving in a period to the average number on the payroll e.g. if 200 persons leave a company in a year and the average number on the payroll is 1000, labour turnover will be expressed as 20 % per annum. It must be noted that all persons who leave must be included whether they leave voluntarily or are dismissed, irrespective of whether they are replaced.

Some authorities calculate labour turnover in accordance with the formula:

$$\frac{\text{New engagements} + \text{Persons leaving}}{\text{Average number on payroll}}$$

This formula provides for the inclusion of two persons in the numerator where the person leaving is replaced, and of only one where the number of workers is being reduced. The first formula is generally more satisfactory as management is primarily concerned with the loss of labour after money has been spent on training. It will be appreciated that the training and education of labour and the procedures of advertising for and selecting replacements can be very costly. In some companies workers are given a training course, which may last anything from a week to several months, and even after this period of training the new workers will probably not be as dexterous as their colleagues and may cause considerable scrap and faulty work, which is a further cost of labour turnover. Bearing this in mind, a company must concentrate on keeping its trained workers and for this reason frequently provides canteens, welfare facilities, and other amenities to maintain good relations with them.

Every business should prepare periodic labour turnover statistics either in the form of graphs or as monthly statements. It is imperative that labour turnover be analysed by cause, distinguishing the avoidable from the unavoidable, and showing whether workers are leaving through dissatisfaction or are being dismissed because of unsuitability or bad selection. The personnel officer must investigate the reasons why workers leave, and rectify any avoidable causes of labour dissatisfaction and unrest.

A study of the reasons for labour turnover will normally indicate the lines on which management should proceed to reduce its incidence. Labour turnover will be minimised if departmental managers give reasonably long notice of their requirements and future lay-offs. This information enables the employment department to arrange transfers of workers within the business and the shedding of labour through retirement etc. Again, it may be possible to accept unprofitable work for short periods in order to retain skilled workers, or to hold in reserve special jobs to be undertaken only when a surplus of labour arises. In some companies it is the policy to keep the whole labour force operating on a three- or four-day week rather than to lose permanently a proportion of the workers through temporary redundancy.

Within the costing system a separate account should be set up to record the cost of training. This will be charged with the wages of learners during periods of instruction, the wages and salaries of instructors, the cost of materials and facilities set aside for training, and special allowances for training granted within the framework of incentive schemes. From these figures average costs per worker trained can be ascertained. Where appropriate, differential costs can be brought out for the training of different classes of labour.

LABOUR TURNOVER REPORT				
				August, 19—
	This Month	Last Month	Year to Date	
			This Year	Last Year
Average labour force	900	900	800	700
Number of separations	27	22	114	81
Labour turnover %	3.0	2.4	14.2	11.6
Reason for Leaving:				
(a) Voluntary:				
Higher wages	5	4	22	9
Better prospects	3	2	9	7
Unhappy at job	2	3	14	10
Conditions of work	2	1	7	8
Distance to travel	1	–	2	3
Retirement and death	1	–	5	4
Marriage	—	2	6	5
Other reasons	1	–	3	2
TOTAL	15	12	68	48
%	1.7	1.3	8.5	6.9
(b) Dismissals:				
Insubordination	2	2	9	10
Incompetence	5	4	20	12
Health	1	–	4	2
Redundancy	2	1	6	2
Absenteeism	1	–	1	1
Timekeeping	1	2	4	4
Other reasons	–	1	2	2
TOTAL	12	10	46	33
%	1.3	1.1	5.7	4.7

Note: High labour turnover mainly due to wage rates below average for this area. Best quality of labour cannot be obtained at present rates – hence large number of dismissals for incompetence.

The personnel department will normally maintain detailed records of overtime and shift work. As overtime is paid for at higher rates than normal daywork, most workers are willing to take advantage of opportunities to undertake it, and the overtime habit develops. To combat this all overtime working should be properly authorised – the departmental manager preparing a list of overtime workers and passing it to the personnel department, and the timekeepers, permitting only the sanctioned time to be booked on the time cards. Thus overtime working can be strictly controlled. The personnel department has a duty to ensure that regulations are not infringed, and to maintain a check on overtime they should submit to top management a weekly report showing the number of normal and overtime hours worked in each department. Similar records will be kept of the number of times each worker is late or absent and the total amount of time lost. Regular reports should be sent to departmental managers so that disciplinary action can be taken in the cases of persistent offenders.

Attendance Records

The simplest form of attendance record is a manual register, which each employee signs on arrival and departure, noting his times in and out. Whilst the fact that entries progress in time sequence gives some protection against irregularity, this form of record is subject to considerable abuse by employees. Arising from this system, however, is a time register device which permits an employee to sign the exposed portion of a paper tape, and to state his time of arrival or departure before pulling a handle that moves the written portion of the tape out of sight under an enclosed housing. The next employee being unable to see the previous time entered will tend to record his own time honestly. A further variation of this system is an autographic time register in which the pulling of the lever automatically stamps the correct time opposite the signature of the employee. The disadvantages of manual registers and autographic time registers are the hold-ups that occur when each worker has to sign his name in turn, and the amount of clerical work involved in the posting of entries to individual attendance records. A careful balance must be maintained between the need to record punctual attendance and a cheap and socially acceptable system.

Time Recording Clocks

Time recording clocks are now widely used in businesses, whereby a worker records all his time for a week on a clock card bearing his name.

Two racks known as the *In* and *Out* racks are normally provided. The *In* rack is on the factory side of the clock and this contains the cards of all workers who are inside the factory. The *Out* rack, which is on the other side of the clock, holds the cards of all workers who are not in the factory. In general, provision is made for the printing of the day of the week and of the hour and minute of arrival and departure in the morning and the afternoon. Some machines print particulars of late arrival or overtime in red, the changeover from black to red being made automatically at pre-determined times.

A timekeeper will be in charge of the clocks to ensure that workers do not stamp each other's cards and that no worker enters or leaves the premises without the time being properly recorded. Where workers leave for a special purpose during the course of the day, they should present a properly authorised pass-out slip to the timekeeper or gatehouse security personnel. On the reproduced clock card illustrated overleaf, times after 12 noon are shown by a line under the hour figure. The insertion of the card in a suitable 'time recorder' produces the record in the right position, all movements from day to day and column to column being automatic. Late arrival, early departure, and overtime records

No. 4329

No. .... *73* ....

Name ...... *H. Johnson* ....

Week Ending...... *6th April*

IBM UNITED KINGDOM LTD

INTERNATIONAL TIME RECORDING DIVISION

	MORNING		AFTERNOON		EVENING		Total
	IN	OUT	IN	OUT	IN	OUT	
	8 00	12 00	1 00	5 00			8
	8 00	12 02	12 59	5 33			8½
	7 59	12 01	1 00	5 31			8½
	7 58	12 00	12 57	5 32	6 00	8 30	11
	8 10	12 02	12 59	5 30			8¼
							44¼

ORDINARY TIME	Hours	Rate	£
OVERTIME			
Less National Insurance ...			
Other Deductions ...			
		Net Wages	

Clock Card reproduced by courtesy of IBM United Kingdom Limited

(underlined in the illustration) are shown in red to assist the time office and also to give a silent reproof in appropriate cases. The worker has been penalised to the extent of a quarter of an hour for lateness on Friday morning. The summary at the foot of the card will be completed on the following lines, assuming a $42\frac{1}{2}$ hour week, an hourly rate of £3.50, and an overtime rate of time and a quarter:

		£
Ordinary time, $41\frac{3}{4}$ hours at £3.50		146.13
Overtime $3\frac{1}{8}$ hours		10.94
		157.07
Less National Insurance and		
Other deductions say		31.14
		125.93

The $3\frac{1}{8}$ hours overtime are arrived at by adding $\frac{1}{4}$ of $2\frac{1}{2}$ hours to the $2\frac{1}{2}$ hours overtime worked on Thursday.

It is best to instal time recording clocks at the factory gate, rather than in each department. This latter practice is costly and implies that the employee will not be paid for time spent preparing for work and getting to his work station. Time recording clocks have the advantage of producing a definite, unchallengeable record. Where a worker has clocked in after starting time, there can be no argument. In addition, such clocks provide a record of each worker's time in a form suitable for payroll purposes, with clear figures that can readily be extended and totalled at the end of the week. From the point of view of internal check, mechanical time recording leaves considerably fewer loopholes for fraud than other methods.

Outside Workers

Where workers are sent out to customers' premises they frequently report to the works both at starting time and at finishing time, and no difficulty then arises regarding their time booking. Where they proceed direct to the site it is customary for them to complete a daily time sheet and to send it to their foreman or manager who will certify that payment may be made. While any system of this nature is open to abuse it is customary to employ an outside foreman who visits the workers on site to check their attendance and also to keep in touch with the general progress of the work. Where a considerable number of employees are engaged at a building or other site, it is normal to instal time clocks and for the time cards to be initialled by the site foreman and sent up to head office at the end of each week.

Some difficulty arises where casual labour is engaged by the foreman at an outside site and, for the purpose of internal check, a head office clerk should attend to pay these workers. When this is not practicable the foreman may be issued with a petty cash float from which to make the payments. It should be arranged, however, that some person other than the foreman completes the record of casual worker employment.

Outside workers must not be confused with *outworkers*, a term that refers to employees in certain industries, such as knitwear, who work in their own homes. Outworkers are issued with definite amounts of material, which are recorded, and they are required to produce a corresponding quantity of finished goods. As goods are finished they are handed in to the store, where they are inspected and piece-work tickets are issued. The payment for outwork is normally included with the employee's wages at the end of the week, but where payment is made direct, special arrangements are necessary.

Payroll Routine

The calculation of an employee's remuneration varies according to the basis on which he is paid. The main bases are:

1. *Time or day rate wages*, where the employee is paid a fixed hourly or weekly rate irrespective of the amount of work he produces.
2. *Piece-work*, where the employee is paid a fixed rate per unit or piece produced irrespective of the time taken.
3. *Premium or bonus schemes*, where the employee is paid at a fixed hourly rate and receives in addition a bonus related to the amount of work he produces.

We have already seen how each worker's time is recorded on his arrival at, and departure from, the factory. It is normal for the timekeeper to compute the number of hours worked daily and weekly by each employee and to enter ordinary and overtime hours in the spaces provided on the clock cards. At the end of each week the clock cards are passed to the wages department where the calculation of the hours is checked and the figures entered on the payroll. Overtime is usually better paid than ordinary day work, normally being calculated on some such basis as time-and-a-half or double time. In the simplest type of payroll the workers' names and clock numbers are entered down the left-hand side of a sheet together with hourly rates of pay. The ordinary time and overtime are entered and extended at the hourly rate to give the gross wages from which certain statutory and voluntary deductions have to be made to arrive at the net amount payable. Computer packages are now available to process the payroll data. The following are the main deductions found in practice:

Income Tax Pay-As-You-Earn. The employer is under a statutory obligation to deduct income tax from the pay of all employees whose earnings are sufficient to incur liability. Weekly and monthly tax tables are provided by the Inland Revenue and a code number is issued for each employee. A simple calculation computes the amount of tax to be deducted.

National Insurance. Contributions payable under the National Insurance Acts are paid partly by the employer and partly by the employee. The employees proportion is deducted from their pay, and paid over to the Department of Health and Social Security(DHSS) by the employer.

Charities and Welfare Schemes. Many businesses have a scheme for collecting a few pence a week from each employee for payment to local charities. Similarly, deductions are sometimes made to cover employees' subscriptions to recreation clubs, and for annual outings, etc. In all these cases the employee signs a form of authority for the deduction to be made from his wages until further notice is given.

Contributory Pension Schemes. Where an employee agrees to become a member of a contributory pension scheme, his contribution will be met by weekly deductions from wages.

Overalls, Tools etc. Where a firm obtains tools or overalls for employees at preferential terms, the cost of these will normally be deducted from wages at a regular weekly rate. Certain amounts may be added to the wage earned to cover such items as subsistence payments, 'dirty money' for working in poor conditions etc.

The total of the deductions less additions is subtracted from gross wages to arrive at the net amount payable to the employee.

Once the net wages have been calculated, pay slips will be prepared to detail this calculation for each worker – his ordinary wages, overtime wages, any bonus or piece-work earnings, and all the deductions that have been made from gross wages to arrive at the net figure. The pay slip details may be prepared on the wages envelope or on a separate slip.

The separate preparation of the payroll, the tax deduction record, and the pay slip may be avoided by the use of a peg board, which holds the three documents in alignment and allows them to be written simultaneously by the use of carbons. The pay slip is thus a complete copy of the entry on the payroll. Alternatively a computer package may be used to make the calculations and produce the required documents.

Preparation of Wage Packets

Once the payroll has been completed, a coin and notes analysis should be prepared so that the cashier can advise the bank in advance of the exact requirements in terms of £5 notes, £1 coins, 50p pieces and bronze. Where the payroll is large, the preparation of the wage packets will be carried out by a number of officials and the coin and note analysis should be

Example of a wage sheet

and the other two documents that can be produced at the same time if a carbon is used.

1. Bottom copy – sheet of pay slips to go into each pay envelope – perforated for tearing.

Employees' Pay slips

HOURS		RATE		WAGES				PAYE					DEDUCTIONS					Name & Number
Day	O/Time	Pay	O/Time	Bonus	Sick	Allow-ances	Gross	Gross to date	Free pay	Taxable pay	Tax to date	Tax	Tax	N.I.	Holiday –Sports	Total	NET	

2. Middle copy – Wage sheet or payroll – totals of certain columns provide figures for posting into the cost accounts as shown.

Wage Sheet for Week Ending............ Costing Week No.............

HOURS	RATE		WAGES				PAYE					DEDUCTIONS						Employer's NI
Day O/Time	Pay	O/Time	Bonus	Sick	Allow-ances	Gross	Gross to date	Free pay	Taxable pay	Tax to date	Tax	Tax	N.I.	Holiday –Sports	Total	NET	Name & Number	
	Debit work-in-progress account.	Debit Factory Overheads account.	Debit Factory Overheads account.	Debit Factory Overheads account.	Debit Factory Overheads account.							Credit creditor account.	Credit creditor account.	Credit creditor account.	Credit cash.			Debit factory overheads account, and credit National Insurance as a creditor.

3. Top copy – Tax deduction card for each employee.

Personal Tax Deduction Card

Rate of pay............ Tax code............ N.I. ....

Name
Clock Number
Department

Tax Week	RATE		WAGES				PAYE					DEDUCTIONS				
	Pay	O/Time	Bonus	Sick	Allow-ances	Gross	Gross to date	Free pay	Taxable pay	Tax to date	Tax	Tax	N.I.	Holiday –Sports	Total	NET

1

sectionalised in such a way that each official can be given the exact cash for his own section. Payment by cheque avoids this time-consuming activity, and employers are now actively encouraging its introduction.

After completion of the payroll details, a cheque will be drawn to cover the exact requirements and this will be presented to the bank on the morning during which the wages are made up. As advance notice of the detailed requirements will have been given to the bank, it will already have the money made up in the required form. The cash will be checked on receipt and the cashier will subdivide it into sections, one or more of which will be dealt with by each separate payroll cashier.

Where transparent window-envelopes are used, the notes should be fanned out so that they can be counted without opening the envelope, and the coins should be placed in front of the notes where they will be visible. When the time arrives for the actual pay out of wages, the paying officer should be provided with a form on which to record the details of unclaimed pay envelopes: this should be signed by the paying officer and the foreman or other witness. On completion of the pay out this form will be returned to the cashier, together with the unclaimed wages. Proper precautions should be taken to ensure that a person who calculates the wages for one section of the payroll does not also make up the pay packets for that section.

Payment of Wages

From the point of view of internal check it is desirable for the pay out to be witnessed by the foreman or some other responsible person who is able to identify each worker. In some organisations the workers are marshalled in clock number order and the pay out is made at the timekeeper's window. Where matters are properly organised little waiting time occurs. As it is generally stipulated that wages must be checked and discrepancies reported immediately, a space should be provided in which workers can check their pay packets. Where window-envelopes are used, the workers must check the money and notify any discrepancies before the envelope is opened.

As it is not normally practicable for the employee to sign his name when he receives his wages, the clock card is very often used as a receipt. Details of the pay are shown on the cards, which are normally handed out personally by the foreman on the previous day. Where the figures are disputed, adjustments can be made before the pay packets are made up. As the foreman himself hands the cards to the workers he can ensure that they get into the right hands and so minimise the chance of wages being given to wrong workers. Where adjustments have to be made after the payroll has been completed, a certified list will normally be prepared by the chief wages clerk and the items will be dealt with through petty cash or through a special wages 'float'. Any such adjustments will be made in the following week's payroll, and petty cash or the float will be reimbursed from the proceeds of the next wages cheque.

A mobile trolley is sometimes used to enable the paying officer to pass from bench to bench and pay the workers whilst they are at work. This enables payment to be made with the least possible interruption of work.

Internal Check – Wages

Internal check is the system of dividing up work in such a way that no one person deals completely with any transaction, so that fraud could be committed only by the collusion of two or more persons. As the opportunities for fraud arise more frequently in connection with wages than in any other class of transaction, certain definite safeguards should be enforced. These may be summarised as follows:

1. The system of recording time of arrival and departure should be carefully controlled. Time clocks should be installed and the recording of time adequately supervised.
2. Where piece-work and bonus systems are in operation, the quantities produced should be certified by a competent inspector and records should be signed by the foreman responsible. Extra allowances and payments for lost time should be recorded on forms provided for the purpose, which should be signed by a responsible official.
3. Piece-work rates should be clearly laid down and the terms of bonus schemes defined in writing so that no doubt can exist as to the method of payment.
4. All overtime should be properly authorised and the form of authority should be passed to the wages department for verification of overtime bookings.
5. Standard wage rates' schedules should be prepared. All alterations in wage rates should be made out on proper forms and be approved by a responsible official.
6. The clerks who prepare wages sheets should not take part in the make-up of the wages envelopes. Where this is unavoidable, no clerk should know in advance which section of the payroll he will be required to make up.
7. All wages and bonus calculations should be worked out by one clerk and be checked by another, and the totalling and cross addition of the sheets should be checked.
8. The wages sheets should often be scrutinised by the personnel officer or works manager to guard against the inclusion of 'dummy' workers on the payroll.
9. There should be a satisfactory system for ensuring that all workers are identified before they are handed their wage packets.
10. Wages should not be handed to any person other than the worker concerned except on production of a signed request made out on an authorised form, and this should only be permitted in exceptional cases e.g. disablement or sickness.

Accounting for Wages

For costing purposes it is important to know how much of the total wages bill is incurred by each separate function of the business. It is usual to arrange the payroll in such a way that all workers in each cost centre are together, and to provide for the extraction of separate cost centre sub-totals. Frequently these cost centre sub-totals are carried to the last sheet of the payroll where they are summarised in order to ascertain grand totals for gross and net wages, pay-as-you-earn, National Insurance (each share separately), overtime premium, and so on. The payroll summary or wage sheet acts as a form of journal voucher crediting cash and debiting the appropriate labour cost headings.

REMUNERATION AND INCENTIVES

The term *remuneration* is used to cover the total monetary earnings of employees and thus includes hourly wages, payment by results and other financial incentives. Incentives are arrangements of a financial or non-financial nature made to stimulate human effort and effectiveness.

Management must continuously endeavour to improve labour effectiveness and so reduce labour cost. Whilst management can increase efficiency by providing improved equipment, by the adoption of better methods and by more effective utilisation of plant, the most important contribution must come from labour. Accordingly, every system of remuneration should be so designed as to encourage the individual worker to do his best. The payment of low wage rates may seem to give rise to low labour costs, but this is not generally the case because high wages tend to attract the best workers, and the application of incentives gives an added encouragement to increase output.

Management must aim at the reduction of the unit cost of every commodity produced or service rendered, and it can further this aim by encouraging speedier production and so increasing output and lowering overheads per unit. In formulating a scheme for payment by results, management is often willing to pay the worker a constant wage per unit produced even though production is increased substantially. Whilst no saving in wages thus accrues to the management, the latter does gain the benefits of reduced overheads and greater production.

Example

Workers are paid £120 per week and fixed overheads per employee are £50 per week. The suggestion is made to change to a system of payment by results (£1 per unit) and it is expected that production will increase by 50%.

	Time Work	Payment by Results
Weekly production per worker	100	150
	£	£
Wages cost	120	150
Overheads per worker per week (assumed to be fixed)	50	50
	170	200
Cost per unit	£1.7	£1.33

Under the system of payment by results the worker has received 25% higher wages and management has saved 37p per item produced, or 22%. The system therefore benefits both employer and employee. In some incentive schemes of the premium bonus type the labour saving is shared between employer and employee in a pre-determined ratio, whilst management still gets the benefit of reduced overheads.

The attitude of workers to different methods of remuneration is of paramount importance. Many workers oppose incentive schemes on the ground that increased labour efficiency will give rise to redundancy. Efforts on the part of management to introduce incentive schemes, therefore, tend to be more successful at times when there is scope for further output from the existing labour force. Increased productivity at a time of high unemployment is seen as a means of preserving jobs, by undercutting competitors. Care should be taken to ensure that wages cannot rise to such an extent that the workers are able to earn sufficient for their needs without achieving the desired level of efficiency. When high wages can be too easily earned the workers may work hard for two or three days and then, having already earned a good bonus, slack off for the remainder of the week or even stay away. Alternatively, they may not produce at maximum efficiency for fear that rates will be cut if wages are allowed to become too high.

It is usually essential to relate remuneration to time and production, and for the wages policy to be so devised that the different types and grades of labour are suitably paid for their skill, ability and experience. Mere provision of an incentive scheme is not, however, a substitute for good management. If an employer is to gain full benefit from his employees' efforts he must, by good management, create mutual trust and contentment. Yet good management must go further than this, for an incentive scheme that is based upon the employees' ability to produce is likely to rebound upon the heads of management unless conditions are so organised that employees are not hindered by lack of production facilities, material or work. In fact, one of the great benefits of remuneration schemes based upon output is that such schemes virtually compel management to put its own house in order.

Whilst overtime is sometimes unavoidable, sound principles dictate that an employee should receive adequate remuneration without having to work an excessive number of hours; in other words, an employee has a right to adequate leisure as well as to a reasonable remuneration.

Principles Applicable to all Incentive Schemes

The following general principles apply to all incentive schemes:

1. The reward should be related to the effort involved and should be just and fair to both employer and employee. The additional earnings offered to the workers should be sufficiently high to provide an inducement to greater effort.
2. Payment should be made as soon as possible after the work is completed, for workers are more inclined to strive for a bonus payable within a week than for one in which the benefit is delayed for a longer period.
3. The general principles of any proposed scheme, and the methods to be employed in determining the standards, should be agreed upon in advance with the workers or their elected representatives.
4. The scheme should be clearly defined and intelligible to the workers. Steps should be taken to see that it is fully understood and not likely to be misinterpreted.
5. The scheme should provide for worthwhile and attainable objectives, with standards of performance not beyond the capabilities of the average worker.
6. No limit should be placed upon the amount of individual earnings.
7. The scheme should be reasonably permanent and not be changed without first obtaining the workers' agreement.
8. The employee's earnings should not be affected by matters beyond his control. He should, for example, be compensated for breakdowns and other hold-ups for which he is not responsible.
9. Rates of payment by result should not be fixed until after the job has been properly assessed: once piece rates or time allowances have been determined and agreed they should not be altered unless conditions change or new methods are introduced.
10. The scheme should be coupled with a sound routine of inspection to ensure that workers are paid only for good production. There should also be adequate controls to minimise the possibility of false bookings of time or quantity.
11. The system should be capable of operation without excessive clerical work.
12. The scheme should facilitate supervision and assist in production control. If possible, it should provide a basis for budgetary control and standard costing.

13. The main aim of the scheme should be to influence the workers' morale. Every effort should therefore be made to promote their understanding of the scheme and their support of it.
14. The scheme must take account of any relevant national or local trade agreements.

Indirect Incentives

Whilst an employee is primarily interested in the size of his pay packet, he is nevertheless influenced by indirect incentives of the kind that provide an atmosphere in which direct monetary incentives have the greatest chance of success. Confidence in the ability of management and of its sincerity and fair-mindedness is in itself a most important indirect incentive. In addition, the provision of canteens, recreation facilities, suggestion bonus schemes, and accident prevention plans all assist in maintaining the workers' morale.

Many cases arise where the nature of the work is such that the offer of direct incentives is impracticable because of the absence of definite standards of performance. In some such cases indirect workers are paid bonuses that are related to the incentive earnings of the direct workers whom they serve or supervise. In others, the position is met by merit pay, annual bonuses, profit-sharing schemes, in lieu bonuses, etc. Many concerns provide incentives in the form of pension schemes, long-service awards, suggestion awards, and good timekeeping bonuses. Whatever the scheme, the objective is to retain the services of the good worker and to induce him to serve his employer diligently and to the best of his ability.

Initiation of Incentive Schemes

The following are the more important points to be considered before instituting a scheme of payment by results:

1. The scheme should be applied to one section of the works at a time, the first application being made in a department where labour relations are known to be satisfactory and there are good prospects of success.
2. A new scheme should not be applied until sufficient orders and materials are available to allow for considerable increase in output. Workers are disheartened if, as soon as they start earning good bonuses, there is not enough work to enable them to take advantage of the new arrangement. In some cases it is preferable to let the labour force run down to a comparatively low level before the start. This can normally be achieved by natural wastage.
3. Methods, machine speeds and work routing should be studied in detail, and any possible improvements made before each operation is timed.
4. Each job and operation should be considered by a competent work study engineer who should establish standard methods and times.
5. A simple explanation of the scheme should be compiled and copies passed to the workers or their representatives. This should normally contain the guarantee that standard times will not be altered no matter how much bonus is earned, unless methods or conditions are changed.
6. Suitable time sheets, piece-work tickets, lost time cards, extra allowance tickets, etc. must be designed and the wages staff instructed in the method of calculating the bonus.

7. The scheme should be operated on a short trial basis before its official start.
8. When the scheme is commenced the work study staff should be available to assist and encourage the workers to attain the speeds called for in their standards.

REMUNERATION SYSTEMS

Remuneration schemes may be considered under three main headings: Time Rates; Piece Rates; and Premium Bonus Systems. Payment of time rates may be at ordinary levels or at high wage levels.

Time Rates at Ordinary Levels

Under this plan labour is paid for the time worked irrespective of the volume of production during that time. Payment may be based upon the hour, the day, or the week, or it may be at a fixed salary rate. Payment at time rate is easily understood and requires a minimum of clerical work. It is generally adopted in the following cases:

1. Where the services rendered cannot be measured with sufficient accuracy to form the basis of payment by results. Indirect workers and office staff are generally paid on a time basis.
2. Where a considerable degree of skill is needed and quality of output is of first importance.
3. Where the speed of production is governed by the time in process or machine speed over which the operator himself has little or no control. This happens in process industries such as chemical engineering and oil refining, as well as on assembly lines where the flow of work is regulated by the speed of the conveyor belt.
4. For learners.
5. Where the probable gain of increased production is insufficient to warrant the cost of operating a scheme of payment by results.

A time basis of remuneration may also be employed in conjunction with some other system of incentive that offers a satisfactory remuneration to employees, or where the current level of production is considered by management to be satisfactory; though whether a time basis is in fact appropriate in these cases is open to debate.

Where time rates are paid at ordinary levels, earnings remain fixed regardless of output. The employer thus obtains the benefit of such savings as arise from increased efficiency and there is a proportionate reduction in the cost per unit produced.

Payment on a time basis has the following advantages:

1. The system is easily understood.
2. It requires a minimum of clerical work, and therefore has a lower wages office cost than a more complicated scheme.
3. As a worker has no financial incentive to hurry jobs he tends to concentrate on quality. Time work is thus most suitable where a high degree of craft skill is called for.

A disadvantage of payment on a time basis is that it provides no financial incentive to increase production, because the inefficient worker receives the same wages as the efficient one. Also, whilst there may be a general desire on the part of the worker to give a full day's work, the collective result is an output less – and often very much less – than that obtainable where an incentive scheme is in force.

Time Rates at High Wage Levels

Under this system the employee is remunerated at time rate, i.e. by the hour, day, week, or other agreed period of time, but the time rate is appreciably higher than that normally paid in the industry or district.

This system is as simple and cheap in operation as that of the ordinary level time rate basis. It provides an incentive because the management that pays high wage rates also demands a high level of performance and efficiency. The best workers are attracted to the concern paying the high rates and, once employed, they make a special effort to guard against dismissal through failure to attain the required standards. This method is universal in its application, but to obtain the best results it calls for a considerable degree of management control. It is particularly suitable where a high standard of quality is as important as the quantity of work produced.

The effect on labour cost of paying time rates at high levels is that whilst the total wages cost is greater than under normal time rates, the incentive effect of high time rates is such that production is greater, or of superior quality, and the wages cost per article is generally lower than under normal time rates. Moreover, where overheads are high, an employer may benefit from the use of high time rates even where the wages cost per article is greater than that under normal time work, because of the consequent reduction in the overhead costs per article produced.

Piece Rates

Under a basic piece rate system an operator is paid a fixed sum per unit produced, regardless of the time taken. The main systems of piece rate payment are: straight piece rates; piece-work with guaranteed day rate; and differential piece rates.

Straight Piece Rates

Remuneration is measured as a fixed sum per unit produced regardless of the time taken to produce it. Alternatively, under what may be termed the piece-time rate, or standard hour plan or standard time system, a pre-determined time is set for each specified operation, the operator being paid at a fixed time rate for the number of standard hours of work he produces. The difference between these two schemes is shown in the following examples:

Piece Rate Basis	Piece-time Basis
Piece rate: 12p per piece	Piece-time for 12 pieces: 1 hour
Pieces produced: 15	Standard rate per hour: 144p
Remuneration: $12 \times 15 = 180$p	If 12 pieces are made in 48 minutes, 144p will be paid, i.e. the operator will receive one hour's pay for only 48 minutes work, which is equivalent to 180p per hour

Piece-work or the piece-time system may be applied either to the whole of a worker's wages or to only a proportion known as his basic wage. In the latter case the balance or cost of living element is paid for on a time work basis.

Straight piece rates can be applied only where the work is of a sufficiently repetitive nature to allow the setting of definite piece rates. It may be used to speed up the rate of production or to retain employees who would otherwise be attracted away by higher remuneration obtainable elsewhere.

Straight piece rates have the following advantages:

1. Simplicity.
2. They provide a strong incentive because remuneration is in direct ratio to the worker's effort.
3. High production rates are obtained with a consequent reduction of overheads per unit.
4. Costing is simplified because the exact cost of labour for each unit throughout the range of output is known in advance.
5. The piece-time rate system has the advantage that the very careful time study necessary for its working provides a sound basis for production control and standard costing. Also, it enables different time rates to be fixed for workers having different lengths of service, whilst the standard time for the job remains constant.

Straight piece rates have certain disadvantages:

1. The setting of piece rates or standard times involves a considerable amount of work at the outset and also during the operation of the scheme. As unduly high rates are difficult to cut, care must be taken to establish fair rates in the first instance. Revisions must be made whenever the method or machine speed is altered.
2. A rigid system of inspection is necessary to ensure that quality standards are maintained and that quantity bookings are correct.
3. Workers tend to consider that lateness and absenteeism are permissible on the ground that they are the only losers. As an idle machine represents a loss to the employer, lateness and absenteeism must be dealt with as a disciplinary matter.
4. As a uniform rate is paid regardless of quantity, there is no special incentive for exceptional effort. Similarly, no particular penalty is imposed for sub-standard effort.
5. The worker's remuneration is not secured and may fall below that of a worker paid on a time basis. This may happen either through the worker's own fault or because of the inefficiency of his employer or fellow workers. For this reason remuneration at straight piece rates has generally been superseded by piece rates with a guaranteed day rate.

Piece Rates with Guaranteed Day Rate

Under this method the operator receives the straight piece rate for the number of pieces he produces, provided that his total remuneration is greater than his earnings on a time rate basis. When the piece rate earnings fall below this level the time rate earnings are paid instead. An alternative form of the method is the guaranteed time rate (per hour, day, or week) plus a piece rate payment for output above a stated minimum.

In any system in which time-work rates are guaranteed it is normally preferable to view the earnings on a weekly basis before paying the guaranteed minimum. Where each job is separately considered, workers may work exceptionally hard on the first job and so ensure high piece-work earnings, and then slack off for the succeeding job, knowing that their time rate will apply. Again, the comparison of weekly piece-work earnings with guaranteed day work, averages out discrepancies such as arise when the work undertaken comprises easy jobs and more difficult ones.

Labour cost per piece decreases with increasing production until piece-rate earnings exceed the guarantee; thereafter, the labour cost per piece remains constant.

Piece rates with a guaranteed day rate have advantages similar to those attributable to straight piece rates. In addition, they avoid insecurity by providing a guaranteed minimum and the worker is not unduly penalised when his piece-work earnings are low through circumstances beyond his control.

Disadvantages of piece rates with a guaranteed day rate are similar to those of straight piece rates except that the cause of insecurity of the worker and trade union disapproval are avoided. They have, however, the additional disadvantage that the guaranteed minimum removes the incentive to improve upon comparatively low rates of production.

Differential Piece Rates

Under differential piece rate schemes, earnings vary at different stages within the range of output: sometimes they vary proportionally more than, sometimes proportionally less than, and sometimes in proportion to, output. All such schemes aim at maximum production by giving an additional incentive to increase output just at the stage at which the worker would otherwise begin to feel that further effort was not worth while. Differential piece-work systems are also valuable as a means of encouraging learners. Rates are increased in steps as an incentive to the learner first of all to reach the average worker's standard and, later, to attain the higher standards achievable by him as a highly skilled worker. This standard is known as *high task*.

Under the 'Taylor' system there are two rates: a low one for output below high task, and a higher rate, which applies to the total output once the high task threshold has been exceeded. This simple system encourages workers to reach and exceed a high production target. The 'Merrick' system uses three rates instead of two: a basic rate is paid up to the point at which production reaches 83 % of high task (or standard production) when piece rates are increased by 10 % for total production, and at high task, 120 % of the basic rate is paid for all pieces that the operative has produced up to and beyond that point. This puts a higher rate of pay within the grasp of less efficient workers, thus motivating them whilst the best operatives can earn even higher rewards. The 'Gantt' system pays a guaranteed time rate for performance below standard, with a stepped bonus when standard performance is reached, and a higher rate still on total output when standard is exceeded. Again, the less skilled are encouraged and the efficient rewarded.

Premium Bonus Systems

Study of remuneration in relation to time and output has led to the introduction of premium bonus schemes. These are similar to the piece-time system to the extent that a time allowance is made for the job; they differ from the piece-work system only in the manner in which the 'bonus' arising from the saving of time is shared between the employer and the employee.

Features common to most premium bonus systems are:

1. Time rate is usually guaranteed.
2. The employee's remuneration per hour increases with production, but not in proportion to it.
3. Wages cost per unit reduces as efficiency increases.

4. As savings are shared between employer and employee, the employer has the incentive to improve methods and equipment and so facilitate an increase in production.
5. As the worker's remuneration does not normally increase in proportion to production, incorrect rate-fixing will not have such expensive consequences as it would with straight piece-work.

All premium bonus systems suffer from the common objection on the part of employees to share savings with their employer. Such plans depend for their success upon the setting of accurate time standards. Under the 'Halsey' scheme if the job is completed in less than the standard time, the operator is paid for half of the time saved, and the employer benefits by the other half.

$$\text{Earnings} = \text{Time rate} \times (\text{Time taken} + \text{Half time saved})$$

The premium percentage can be varied from 50%.

Job Evaluation

This is the calculation of the labour value of each occupation with regard to the amount of training, skill, physical and mental effort, responsibility, and danger involved. Each characteristic is given a definite points value and the total of all the points shows the relative worth of each different occupation. Basic wages are then set in accordance with the relative points values.

Merit Rating

Whilst job evaluation seeks to establish a basic rate for each job, merit rating aims at determining the relative worth of each worker. Where the nature of the work is such that it is impracticable to install a direct incentive scheme, many of the benefits of such a scheme may, nevertheless, be obtained by scientific merit rating; and where the operator has little control over the speed of production this may in fact yield better results than direct incentives.

Under a simple scheme workers might be rated under the following headings: Quantity of Work; Quality of Work; General Ability; Knowledge of Work; Co-operation; Attendance; Personal Characteristics. Points might be awarded under each of these seven headings, as follows: Excellent 5; Very Good 4; Good 3, Mediocre 2; Poor 1; Very Poor 0. The maximum points obtainable would be 35, and merit payments might be made to workers on the following lines:

Points	Pence per Hour
30–35	120
25–29	90
20–24	60
15–19	30
Below 15	Nil

Under a merit rating scheme each worker is rated separately by two individuals at monthly or quarterly intervals, and the merit money is paid for all hours worked until the next rating takes place. The worker should be told where he is losing points so that he can try to improve his rating. Merit ratings are normally prepared by the foreman and by the works manager, personnel officer, or some other senior official.

Advantages of merit rating are that:

1. Workers have a definite incentive to improve in all the qualities highlighted by the scheme.
2. Discipline is assisted as any insubordination is likely to affect the person's next rating.
3. The careful study of workers and the qualities required of them leads to a better all-round understanding.
4. The system can be operated without standard times or detailed clerical records, and is particularly suitable for maintenance department workers.

A disadvantage is that unless the rating is scientifically applied and strictly fair the scheme can lead to dissatisfaction on the ground of favouritism.

Group or Collective Schemes

Under this heading fall various systems of payment by results that are applied collectively to a group of workers, as distinct from individual bonus systems, which are applied to the production of each worker. The amount produced by a team of workers is measured and the bonus payable on that production is calculated. The computed bonus can then be shared equally, or between workers of differing skills in differing specified proportions, the latter commonly being based on the individual time rates, although agreed percentage allocations may be used.

Group bonus schemes may be employed:

1. Where individual output cannot be measured, but that of a group of workers can e.g. on a production line.
2. Where output depends less upon the efforts of particular individuals, and more upon the combined efforts of a group, a department, or even of the whole undertaking.
3. Where the management wishes to encourage a team spirit.

Bonus Systems for Indirect Workers and Staff

Incentive schemes may be introduced for indirect workers either to increase the efficiency of the services they provide to direct labour, or to induce foremen and supervisory staff to increase departmental efficiency and so reduce costs. Also, when bonuses are given to direct workers it may be necessary to make some equivalent payment to indirect workers to prevent labour unrest.

As the output of indirect workers is generally difficult to measure, it is frequently necessary to group indirect workers, e.g. internal transport workers, inspectors, etc. with the group of direct workers with which they are directly associated, and to base their bonus upon the output of those direct workers. In a system of this type, however, due attention must be given to the relationship between the numbers of direct and indirect workers. The problems of providing a bonus system for indirect workers who provide a general service, such as sweeping up, canteen and storekeeping, is frequently more difficult, and the bonus must necessarily be determined on a much wider basis. Thus it may take the form of a bonus based on the output of the plant as a whole, or of individual merit rating in the form of a high time rate.

Incentives for staff generally take a non-monetary form, such as the issue of luncheon vouchers, the provision of longer holidays than those given to works employees, and pension schemes. Even where a monetary incentive is given it tends to take the form of a Christmas or half-yearly bonus. The interval between payments is then so long that much of the incentive is lost and the bonus tends to be regarded as a part of the employee's salary.

Monetary incentives for staff are sometimes used, e.g. foremen are sometimes paid a weekly bonus based upon:

(a) Output of the department for which the foreman is responsible.
(b) Hours saved, or the standard hours of work produced by the workers under the foreman's supervision.
(c) Savings in expenditure against that budgeted.
(d) Product quality.
(e) Reduction of waste or scrap.
(f) Reduction of labour turnover.
(g) Maintenance of promised deliveries.

Profit Sharing and Co-partnership

Profit-sharing schemes are schemes in which there is an agreement between the employer and the workers whereby they are paid, in addition to wages, a pre-determined share of the profits of the undertaking.

Co-partnership or co-ownership confers upon employees the opportunity to share in the capital of the business and to receive the part of the profits that accrue to their share of ownership. Thus, employees may be given a loan to enable them to buy the company's shares; or "employees' shares" may be given to workers. Alternatively, a block of shares may be reserved for employees who are given certain privileges in regard to their purchase. In some instances, the employees are free to deal with the shares in a normal way; in others, the shares are regarded as "employees' shares" subject to conditions or restrictions.

Both profit-sharing and co-partnership schemes recognise that an employee contributes towards the profit of the undertaking he serves. By conferring upon him the opportunity to share in the profits, and possibly to have a share in the capital of a business, the aim is to give him an interest in the undertaking and its fortunes. Many schemes provide for a minimum period of service as a condition of participation, and this tends to reduce labour turnover.

Advantages of such schemes are that employees who own shares in a company may be expected to take a keen interest in its activities. If this happens, labour relations are improved and this tends to reduce labour turnover.

Disadvantages of both profit-sharing and co-partnership schemes are that:

1. Lazy and indifferent workers share equally with the hard-working and efficient ones.
2. The additional earnings received under most plans are comparatively small.
3. The rewards are too long deferred.
4. Trade unions do not favour the principle.
5. There may be a certain amount of distrust of the declared profits.
6. Profits are not primarily the workers' concern and may be reduced by bad management and indifferent plant.
7. Co-partnership schemes suffer from the economic disadvantage that an employee who is also a shareholder has 'too many eggs in one basket'. Thus, in a depression, at the

very time when he is in danger of losing his employment, the value of his shares will have fallen owing to the adverse conditions affecting his industry.

Non-monetary Incentives

The range of non monetary incentives is extremely wide. Their aim is to make the employment attractive as well as lucrative to the employee. Non-monetary benefits may be provided free, or there may be a partial contribution by the employees. Typical of the non-monetary benefits found in industry are:

Educational: Day-release classes; training schools for employees; scholarships or self-education subsidies.
Health: Works doctors, nurse and trained first-aid staff; dental service.
General: Sports and recreation facilities; canteens; financial or other assistance in respect of housing; subsidised sick and benevolent funds; contributory savings funds.

Pension schemes and holidays with pay schemes may be regarded as partly financial and partly non-monetary incentives, but in either case they are becoming an accepted part of employment conditions and are thus losing their incentive effect. Awards for long service may be either monetary or non-monetary. The main difference between the two is that monetary incentives are directed mainly to short-term achievement, and non-monetary incentives look to the future, the aim being to attract the best class of worker and, by encouraging a spirit of loyalty, to reduce labour turnover and to build up a happy, healthy staff.

Learners

Where standard times are properly drawn up to allow the skilled and competent worker to earn only a reasonable bonus, it follows that learners will be unlikely to make any additional earnings during their initial few weeks of work. This is particularly unfortunate where workers are transferred from jobs on which they have already been augmenting their incomes by bonuses. The problem can be met by the introduction of suitable learning allowances, the amounts of which will reduce week by week until the worker is sufficiently trained, when they will cease. The actual amounts of the allowances will be determined by work study but in a job which takes five weeks to learn they might be as follows:

Learners' Allowance – Percentage of Standard Time

Week 1	50%
Week 2	40%
Week 3	30%
Week 4	20%
Week 5	10%

The learners' allowances will be added to standard hours and the learners' earnings calculated on the total hours thus obtained.

A similar system is sometimes employed when apprentices are engaged upon incentive work. Some authorities contend that apprentices should not be put on bonus until their time has expired, but others consider it worth while to give them the opportunity to increase their earnings by improved production. Under the bonus schemes based on standard time the apprentice will work to the normal times but be paid at his apprenticeship rate. To enable him to meet the standard times he will be given an apprentice allowance, possibly on the lines of 50% for a first-year apprentice, 40% for a second-year apprentice and so on.

Idle Time

In most incentive schemes arrangements are made to compensate workers for time lost through matters beyond their control, such as a power failure, mechanical breakdown, shortage of material, and lack of orders. It is normal to pay time-work rates for these hold-ups and to exclude this time from the calculation of the bonus. Idle time is generally booked separately and treated as an overhead in cost accounts.

The Changing Pattern

There is a current trend growing away from incentive schemes towards time rates. This is caused by the growing realisation that many factors beyond the control of the individual worker have a direct effect upon the output in terms of which incentives are measured. With the advent of increasing automation the machine sets the pace, and subject to keeping the plant in operation, which is the concern of the maintenance person, the operator has little or no control over production. Similarly, the prevalence of mass production lines and complex process units, both of which require a planned output during a given period of time and call for a concerted effort from everyone concerned, has created a situation in which the performance of the individual worker can no longer be measured in terms that can be related to earnings. In circumstances such as these the industries concerned have reverted to time rates and, by cutting out the disputes that sometimes arise in connection with incentives, have improved labour relations and reduced labour turnover.

TIME BOOKING AND LABOUR REPORTS

Payroll is analysed for control purposes under cost centres and there may be several categories of wages in each of these. Wages that can be allocated to a cost centre are direct in relation to that cost centre but only the wages incurred on actual production are direct in relation to the unit of cost. With standard costing the cost of jobs and other cost units is pre-determined and it is often unnecessary to allocate the actual wages to the cost units, but with job, process, and other historical costing methods, the actual costs incurred have to be allocated and apportioned to the cost units and it is necessary to maintain special records in order to obtain such wages allocations.

Each productive worker may be engaged on several jobs every day and, in order that the correct allocations may be made, he must record carefully the time he spends on each job and any time during which he is idle or engaged on cleaning up or other work, that is indirect in relation to the cost units. Wages that are indirect in relation to the cost units are absorbed as part of the overheads. It is not necessary for the indirect workers to record their time in detail. As the absorption of the overheads may be related to the time spent by the direct workers on the job or the labour cost of the job, it follows that a large part of the total cost ascertained is dependent upon time bookings and that accuracy in these is essential.

Time Sheets

These may be completed on a daily or weekly basis. The routine with weekly time sheets is the same as that for daily time sheets except that the worker enters all the particulars of work carried out for a complete week on one sheet. The disadvantage of inaccuracy tends to be more serious as some workers attempt to fill up their time sheets for two or three days together and, in practice, cases arise where, owing to forgetfulness, no time at all is booked to certain orders. Weekly time sheets should be used only where the number of jobs worked on in a week is small and strict supervision is available to ensure accuracy. The form of the weekly time sheet can be identical to that of the daily time sheet, or it can be prepared with separate columns for each day. The latter is very suitable where workers are regularly engaged on only a few jobs as it obviates the necessity of repeating the narrative each time work is performed, and all entries against each job can be totalled before their extension by the cost office.

WEEKLY TIME SHEET		Name							Clock No.		
		Dept or Cost centre							Week ending		
Order No. or Code	Description of Work	Time Taken						Hours	Rate	Cost
		Mon.	Tues.	Wed.	Thur.	Fri.	Sat.			
										£
	Total									
	Signed (Worker)						Foreman	Calculations	Entered Summary	

Job Ticket

Under this system a separate job ticket is prepared for each operation to be carried out on every order. Job tickets are normally 'pre-printed' from standard layout sheets. The basic information remains unchanged every time manufacture take place and the issue of a job ticket is an instruction to the worker as well as a means of booking his time.

Job tickets are generally issued from the foreman's office, a clerk marking the time of issue. On completion of each job the worker returns the card to the office, where the time finished is entered and the card for the next job issued to him. When a worker is idle or engaged on non-productive work, an *idle time card* or *labour transfer form* will be issued to ensure that the total recorded time balances with the attendance clock cards.

JOB TICKET		Index No.		Description of Part		Order No.			
Priority		Quantity Ordered		Date Required		Departments		Goods from Last Operation	
Op. No.		Description of Operation		Tools Required		M/c. No.	Cost Centre	Entered Prod. Control	
Special Instructions									
Operator's Name		Clock No.		Made		Scrap		Good	Passed by
Started	Finished		Time Taken	Rate		Cost	Calculations		Entered Summary
Date	Time	Date	Time			£			

IDLE TIME CARD	Name		Clock No.		Normal Code		

	Particulars	Reason Code	Time		Hours	Rate	Cost
			Start	Finish			
Reason Code							£
1. No Work							
2. No Instructions							
3. No Setting							
4. No Materials							
5. No Machine							
6. No Tools							
7. Breakdown							
8. Accident							
9. Others	Signed	Date	Calculations		Entered Summary		

The advantages and disadvantages of job tickets may be summarised as follows:

Advantages:

(a) As the job or order number and particulars are printed on the ticket, this information is bound to be recorded correctly.

(b) As the starting and finishing times are normally entered by a clerk in the office, there is little danger of inaccuracy in the booking.

(c)   The amount of writing to be done by the worker is negligible.
(d)   The information is clear and legible and in a form suitable for cost office analysis.
(e)   The system provides a very useful link-up between production control, and costing.

Disadvantages:

(a)   Where workers perform several jobs every day the amount of paperwork can become heavy.
(b)   The foreman cannot see at a glance how much work each person has performed in a day.
(c)   The failure to book idle time and intervals between jobs often makes reconciliation with the time cards very difficult.
(d)   The system tends to be inflexible where numerous last-minute alterations occur in the method of manufacture.

Job Cards Following Each Job Through the Works

Under this system a job card in the form of an operation layout is prepared in advance. Details of all the operations are shown and the first person enters his clock number and time taken against the appropriate section of the work, and every person who subsequently performs an operation will similarly enter his clock number and time taken.

JOB CARD	Description of Job		Quantity	Works Order No.
	Slotted Bolt SB1321		144	A1712

Op. No.	Particulars	Clock No.	Date	Time Start	Time Finish	Hours	Rate	Cost
								£ ·
1	Turn C/L							
2	Thread Roll 5 mm							
3	Mill Flats							
4	Drill							
5	Remove rags							
6	Inspect							
7	Pack							
8								
9								
10								
	Total							

Material Required	Date Started	Date Finished	Passed Inspection
	Signed (Foreman)		Entered Costing

The advantages of this type of card are:

(a)   As all the labour cost for each job is already on one card the preparation of further wages analysis is obviated.
(b)   The job card is useful for control purposes – where a cost is excessive it can be seen at a glance which operation or worker was responsible.

The disadvantages are:

(a)   Where jobs are in progress for a long time it may be several weeks before details of the first operations are received in the cost office, and it is then practically impossible to reconcile the time bookings with the payroll hours.
(b)   Where workers enter their own times there is a tendency to understate the time taken.

Wages Analysis

The cost office must analyse the figures and charge each job or other unit of cost with the appropriate amount of wages. Methods vary according to the circumstances of each case and the equipment available, but the system must be designed to produce the required information accurately and with the minimum of clerical labour. Time booking records provide columns for entry of total hours, rate per hour, and wages cost. The cost office will deduct starting time from finishing time and insert the net time against each entry on the time sheet. Against this will be shown the worker's hourly rate, and the product of hours and rate will be entered in the wages cost column, which will be totalled.

In a small jobbing business in which only a few jobs are in progress at any one time the wages chargeable to each job can be listed on analysis sheets. A separate column is provided for each job and the job number is entered at the top. The clock numbers of the workers are inserted down the left-hand side and the wages costs from each time sheet are entered in the appropriate columns. At the end of the week all the columns are added and the grand total should agree with the total wages of the productive workers shown on the payroll. Where the time taken on each job is required as well as the money value, separate 'hours' columns will be incorporated in the wages analysis. In all but the smallest concerns the wages analysis will be by cost centres to correspond with the payroll. The totals from the wages analysis will be debited to the individual job accounts in the job or work-in-progress ledger, whilst at the same time the total productive wages is posted to the debit of the job ledger control account. Lost time will be transferred to the appropriate cost centre code and will subsequently be incorporated in the overheads.

When the job card follows the work through the factory, all the labour entries for the job will be on the card when it reaches the cost office. The hours must be extended at the appropriate wage rates to obtain the cost per operation, and the total labour cost will be debited to the job ledger.

Maintenance and Capital Work

Labour analysis used in connection with productive work can also be applied to maintenance and work of a capital nature carried out by the firm's own employees. In a maintenance department the individual workers complete daily or weekly time sheets to show the time they have spent on each particular job or standing order number. To ensure that the records are as accurate as possible, the time sheets should be checked and initialled by the maintenance foreman or by the foreman of the department for which the work is carried out, and subsequently passed to the cost office for analysis, to produce totals for each job carried out. While it is normally necessary to cost capital and exceptional work on a specific job basis, minor work such as routine repairs is normally classified under standing order numbers and charged against the appropriate departments and cost centres. When idle time occurs, the maintenance workers will book their time to an idle time standing order number; the wages cost will be extracted and debited to the appropriate cost centre account as already explained. In cases where holiday pay is received by direct workers, the amount may be charged to production by means of an inflated hourly rate and is therefore treated as a direct cost.

Overtime premiums, however, are usually treated as overheads and are thus absorbed to all jobs in the department. It would be wrong to charge extra labour costs to certain jobs merely because of the time of day at which they were completed. As an exception, overtime may be charged to a specific job if the reason for the overtime worked can be attributed directly to that job.

LABOUR REPORTS

The prompt presentation of clear and well-designed reports is an essential feature of cost accounting. Each report should provide definite information in the most practical manner and too much detail should be avoided. It must be remembered that reports are prepared to assist the executive members of the staff who are not accountants and who cannot spend time analysing figures. Any analysis should be made by the cost office so that any unessential detail is suppressed. Reports must be varied according to the level of management to which they are presented and should be prepared at regular daily, weekly, monthly, or other pre-determined intervals. The essential features of good reporting are as follows:

1. The report should be headed with a clear and descriptive title and should show the date or period covered.
2. The form of the report should be simple and suitable for the level of management for which it is intended. The report may be made up either as a figured statement or in graphical form.
3. The maximum use should be made of comparisons, either with standards or with previous periods. Comparisons emphasise the exceptions and show at once where abnormalities have occurred.
4. Information should be selected by the cost office so that the salient points are brought out without unnecessary detail.
5. The report should answer questions known to exist in the minds of management and should be drawn up in a way that will lead to action where this is required.
6. Reports should be presented as soon as possible after the close of the period concerned. A daily report should be presented on the following day, a weekly report in the following week, and a monthly one within a week or ten days from the end of the month.
7. Reasonable accuracy is essential. One inaccurate report casts doubt on all other reports. At the same time it must be remembered that excessive accuracy is expensive both in time and money, and should never be an excuse for delayed presentation.
8. Every report prepared by the cost office should accentuate cost control.

Payroll Reports

The payroll is normally laid out with separate sections and totals for each cost centre and with sub-totals for productive and non-productive wages. The comparison of the labour costs in each section with the pre-determined standards of performance and wage rates provides the most satisfactory report, but a simple statement showing the breakdown of departmental wages compared with previous averages is most helpful to management. In some cases the wages can be related to output as a cost per tonne, cost per 1000 cubic metres etc. The actual form of the report must depend on the circumstances of each case. Similar reports can be prepared for the higher executives but much of the detail will be eliminated and it might be suitable to show, in summarised form, only the total direct and indirect labour in each department and the cost per tonne etc. where applicable.

Information regarding wages week by week can be presented very suitably in the form of a graph, showing trends and summarising a situation. In the example shown, it will be seen that while the labour cost has fallen since week 4 there has been an upward trend over the last six weeks without a commensurate increase in output. The graph of cost per tonne shows a marked increase and it is quite clear that labour costs must be reduced or output be increased.

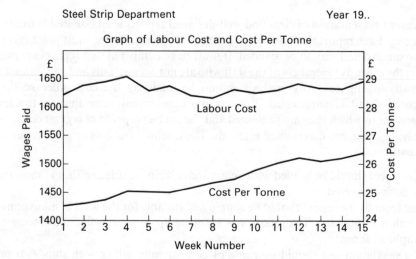

It is often helpful to depict two factors on one graph using different vertical axes, so that a comparison can be made. Comparison with the cost for the same period in a previous year or the average cost to date this year is helpful when management evaluate these figures.

Labour Efficiency Reports

Where a properly constituted incentive scheme is in operation it is possible to measure the efficiency of individual workers against the pre-set standards, and foremen find it useful to have reports on the performance of each of their workers or of their assembly line. Individual labour performance reports are normally prepared daily or weekly and may show the standard hours of work done, the actual hours on production, and the ratio of the two as an efficiency percentage. Where under an incentive scheme a worker performs one-and-a-half standard hours of work in a clock hour when working at incentive speed, his labour efficiency would normally appear as 150%, i.e. 50% above day work rates, but for presentation purposes it is preferable to adjust the figures so that incentive or high task level is shown at 100% and day work as $66\frac{2}{3}\%$. An example of a *daily efficiency report* for a department with three assembly lines is shown below. It will be observed from this that the production-line efficiency is the ratio that the actual rate of production per hour bears to the standard rate. Lost time is excluded from the production time in calculating labour efficiency. Note, also, that this is a cost statement that is not expressed in monetary terms.

DAILY PRODUCT AND EFFICIENCY REPORT								
Department: Tin Box Assembly							23 April 19. . .	
Line	Production Line	Production	Total Hours	Rate per Hour	Standard Rate per Hour	Production Line Efficiency %	Lost Time Hours	Labour Efficiency %
1	2.5 Kilo Toffee Tins	6000	8	750	700	107	.50	114
2	500 Gram Biscuit Tins	4200	8	525	800	66	1.00	75
3	3 Litre Paint Tins	2400	3	800	1000	80	—	80
3	2 Litre Paint Tins	3000	4	750	1000	75	.70	91
3	1 Litre Paint Tins	1200	1	1200	1200	100	.10	111
4	Rd Cornered Tins	3400	8	426	500	85	1.00	97
Notes: Line 2: Breakdown on seaming machine – 1 hour. 3 Trainees on this assembly line.								

Departmental labour efficiency is often presented in the form of a graph from which the trend can be seen. This is particularly useful at the commencement of an incentive scheme where management must strive to bring the general level of performance up to the standards set by work study.

Job and Process Reports

Detailed analysis of the labour costs of individual jobs or processes may be required showing the labour cost of particular operations, grades, or types of labour. Where jobs or batches of work are completed at regular intervals it is useful to compare the labour cost per unit, or per thousand, each time the particular job is undertaken and so obtain some measure of the increase or decrease in labour efficiency. In process industries the labour cost per unit of output will be reported each week, but as labour is only one of a number of costs it is normal to incorporate the wages figure in a process cost statement.

Productivity

Productivity for a group of workers or a department can be measured by comparing actual production against the amount that was intended to have been produced. Where a range of products is made, the work to be completed can be expressed in terms of standard hours.

Example

In a knitwear factory the 8000 garments produced in a four-week month are the equivalent of 3800 standard hours of work – an allowance of $28\frac{1}{2}$ minutes for each garment. If the work were completed by 20 operatives working a 40-hour week (3200 hours) the average time per garment is 24 minutes, and the labour cost per garment has fallen as a result of this efficiency. Productivity can be measured as:

$$\frac{3800}{3200} \times \frac{100}{1} = 118\%$$

Alternatively, if the same team produce 8400 garments in the same time in the next month, their productivity can be said to have increased by 5% over that period:

$$\frac{8400}{8000} \times \frac{100}{1} = 105\%$$

If, for example, a planned task is estimated to take 28 000 hours and the labour force concerned is considered to be 90% efficient, the labour time actually required for its completion will be:

$$28\,000 \times \frac{10}{9} = 31\,111 \text{ hours}$$

Overtime and Idle Time Reports

As the payment of overtime calls for careful control, the cost office normally prepares weekly reports to show the overtime cost. The report, as presented to the foreman, may show the overtime earnings of each person and should, as a minimum, give the amount for each cost centre. Overtime reports for higher management will normally show the total overtime wages paid in respect of each department, with suitable comparisons for previous periods.

The illustrations given here show two weekly overtime reports suitable for presentation to different levels of management. The first report, which is intended for the departmental foreman, shows the daily and weekly overtime hours and the weekly cost for each worker in the department. Comparative figures may be shown if required, but they are generally omitted when so much other detail is included. The same details in total form are given in the second report which has been prepared for the information of the chief engineer, and this report also incorporates the other departments or cost centres for which he is responsible. If the report were intended for use by the managing director, only departmental totals would be shown, with both overtime and lost time included on one sheet. These reports exemplify how the amount of detail varies according to the level of management for which the report is intended. In practice, each report would include such explanatory notes as would be necessary for its proper understanding.

Weekly idle time reports should also be prepared for each department, giving an analysis of time lost under different headings. It is most important to segregate idle time arising from shortage of orders from that which occurs as a result of machine breakdowns or departmental inefficiency. Again, summaries showing the total idle time in each department should be prepared for the works manager.

WEEKLY OVERTIME REPORT   Maintenance   Week ended...............19....

Section and Name	Actual Hours on Overtime								Extra Hours	Total Cost
	Mon.	Tues.	Wed.	Thur.	Fri.	Sat.	Sun.	Total		
										£
Engineers:										
J. B. Smith	—	2	—	4	—	4	—	10	5	17.40
P. Faulkner	—	2	—	4	—	4	—	10	5	17.40
J. Clegg	—	2	—	2	—	4	—	8	4	14.32
P. Thomson	—	2	—	2	—	4	—	8	4	15.76
Sub-Total	—	8	—	12	—	16	—	36	18	£64.88
										£
Electricians:										
P. Turnbull	—	2	—	—	—	8	8	18	13	28.60
J. George	—	2	—	—	—	4	—	6	3	14.86
			*			*		*		
Grand Total	—	26	—	40	—	72	16	154	94	£108.34

Weekly Overtime Report for Departmental Foreman (*Detail omitted for purposes of illustration)

WEEKLY OVERTIME REPORT   Maintenance & Technical   Week ended.............19.....

Section	Actual Hours on Overtime								Extra Hours	Total Cost	Average Cost This Year
	Mon.	Tues.	Wed.	Thur.	Fri.	Sat.	Sun.	Total			
										£	£
Maintenance:											
Engineers	—	8	—	12	—	16	—	36	18	64.88	61.80
Electricians	—	4	—	6	—	24	8	42	28	84.46	64.90
Joiners	—	6	—	8	—	16	—	30	18	66.68	61.86
Labourers	—	8	—	14	—	16	8	46	24	75.28	74.80
Development	—	2	—	2	—	8	—	12	6	50.80	55.48
Boiler House	6	6	6	6	6	6	4	40	12	78.80	80.30
Power House	—	2	—	—	—	4	—	6	3	25.46	24.56
Total	6	36	6	48	6	90	20	212	109	£446.36	£179.70

Weekly Overtime Report for Chief Engineer

Budgetary Control Statements

Where budgetary control is in operation, departmental operating statements will be prepared at the end of each month or four-week period. These will show a comparison of the standard and actual material cost, wages and expense, and will bring out all excess costs as variances. An example of an operating statement and more complete details are given in Chapter 9.

Summary

Summarising the position; reports to the foreman should be presented at short intervals – daily or weekly – and should contain detail down to the performance and earnings of each person. Departmental superintendents will normally receive reports showing the performance of individual cost centres. Complete details of any particular cost centre will be provided as required. The works manager will be given weekly wages analysis statements, performance statements, and overtime and idle time statements, which will normally be in the form of departmental totals. At Board level, reports will be condensed into profit and loss accounts, summary operating statements, four-week departmental wages totals, etc. Much, however, depends upon the size of the business, and where the managing director is in daily contact with the works he may call for detailed weekly reports. There is no definite form for the preparation of labour reports, so the cost accountant must design these himself and be prepared to adjust or completely revise them to suit changed circumstances.

SEMINAR EXERCISES

3.1   Shown below is one week's basic payroll data for the assembly department of Tiptree Timber Products Limited, a manufacturer of a range of domestic furniture.

	Direct Workers	*Indirect Workers*
Total attendance time	1600 hours	1350 hours
Basic hourly rate of pay	£2–50	£1–50
Overtime hours worked	100 hours	40 hours
Shift premium	£180	£70
Group Bonus	£190	£90
Employees' deductions:		
Income tax	£470	£200
National Insurance	£150	£70
Employer's contributions:		
National Insurance	£250	£110

Overtime, paid at basic time rate plus one half, is used as an inducement to increase the factory output. However, 20% of the overtime shown above, for both direct and indirect workers, was incurred at the specific request of a special customer who requires, and is paying for, a particular batch of coffee tables to be completed quickly.

Analysis of the direct workers' time from returned work tickets shows:

Productive time		1390 hours
Non-productive time:	Waiting for Materials	50 hours
	Machine Breakdown	40 hours
	Idle Time	45 hours
	Waiting for Instructions	75 hours

Required:

(a)   Write up the assembly department's wages, work-in-progress and production overhead control accounts, and other relevant accounts.   (14 marks)

(b) Explain the reasons for, and effect on product cost of, your treatment of the following items:

    (i) Employer's National Insurance Contributions
    (ii) Group Bonus
    (iii) Overtime Earnings.   (8 marks)

         (Total 22 marks)

3.2 (a) Describe what you understand by the term *labour turnover* and list its cost implications.   (7 marks)

(b) Makers PLC have recognised a rising trend of labour turnover for the last six costing periods. Calculate a labour turnover figure from the data below and state what further information you would need before you could make a useful report to management.

	Average Number of Employees	Number of Leavers	
Period 1	2000	120	
2	2400	240	
3	2200	200	
4	2000	200	
5	2000	220	
6	2000	260	(7 marks)

(c) List the reasons for high labour turnover in a business.   (8 marks)

         (Total 22 marks)

3.3 Kegworth Kats Limited produce racing catamarans.

(a) Shown below is a summary of one week's payroll data for the Moulding Department, for manufacturing two different types of hull: the 'Puss Cat' and the 'Go Cat'.

	Direct Workers	Indirect Workers
Hours Worked:		
Ordinary time	7200 hours	1600 hours
Overtime	1260 hours	160 hours
Basic hourly rate of pay	£7.20	£4.20
Net wages paid	£54 215	£6015
Analysis of direct workers' time:		
Productive time:		
Puss Cat 480 units	4800 hours	
Go Cat 150 units	2250 hours	
Non-productive down time (hours paid for when no production was achieved)	1410 hours	

The Moulding Department employs 180 direct and 40 indirect operatives. All operatives are paid at hourly time rates. Overtime, which is regularly worked to meet budgeted production targets, is paid at time rate plus one third.

Required:

Construct the Moulding Department's wages control account for the previous week **clearly** indicating the accounts into which the corresponding entries would be posted.   (10 marks)

(b) The works manager of Kegworth Kats is considering introducing a piece-work incentive scheme for the direct workers in the Moulding Department. A work study expert considers that the operation to produce a Puss Cat should be performed, under normal conditions, by one operative in 8 hours; for a Go Cat the corresponding time is 12 hours. Unavoidable non-productive down time is expected to remain at approximately 20% of productive time.

The works manager suggests that direct operatives should be paid a piece rate of £80 for each Puss Cat produced; £125 for each Go Cat produced, and non-productive time should be paid at £5 per hour.

You have been asked to appraise the above scheme. It should be assumed that the previous week's payroll data shown in (a) above represents an average week in the Moulding Department.

Required:

(i) Examine the effect of the proposed scheme on the labour costs in the Moulding Department. Any assumptions you consider necessary should be clearly stated. (10 marks)

(ii) Briefly discuss any additional considerations that would need to be thoroughly examined before the feasibility of the proposed incentive scheme could be finally assessed. (5 marks)

(Total 25 marks)

4

The Costing Treatment of Overheads

WHAT ARE OVERHEADS?

Expenses are defined as the cost of services provided to an undertaking and the notional cost of the use of owned assets. Like materials cost and wages, expenses may be either the direct or indirect cost of a particular cost centre or cost unit. Direct expense is that which can be attributed to a cost centre or cost unit, and indirect expense that which cannot. These indirect costs, whether of materials, labour, or expense not closely related to a cost unit, are termed *overheads*. The prime cost of a product comprises direct material cost, direct wages and direct expenses, i.e. all costs that are connected specifically to a particular cost unit. Overheads, however, must be apportioned and absorbed on an arbitrary basis. In practice most items of expense are direct in relation to some cost centre, but indirect as regards the product. Such costs as rent and rates, heating and lighting, insurance and depreciation are often allocated to the appropriate department, the total costs of which are then apportioned to other cost centres before being absorbed as overhead to the cost of units produced. Such costs are direct costs of the first cost centre, but indirect costs of others, e.g. factory rent may be divided between the power house that makes no products, and two production departments. The power house is an indirect cost centre, and, as such, its overheads must be, in turn, apportioned to the production departments, where eventually they are absorbed into the total cost of each cost unit produced. A royalty payable for a licence to manufacture a product is a direct expense of the product, and transport charges payable to a coach company for transporting workmen to the site of an outside job is a direct expense of the contract concerned. The difficulty of costing overhead expense is in designing a system that will apportion overheads fairly and logically to cost centres, then divide indirect cost centre overheads to production departments and then absorb the overheads allotted to production cost centres to cost units or products as they pass through the cost centres. The objective of this prolonged and sometimes expensive exercise is to find the full absorbed cost of each product and show management how that cost is built up as the product passes from one department to another.

Cost accountants must not lose sight of the fact that their purpose is to provide useful data for managers. A true cost will be helpful when prices are set, or jobs are tendered for, but misallocation of overheads can lead to prices that sell products at a loss, or that are so high as to price the company out of its market. An arbitrary allocation of overheads to a department will not help the manager to control his costs, and if he is unable to influence overhead costs, he cannot be held responsible for them. Managers should be charged for the services they use, so that the system contains an incentive to economise and reduce costs. Comparison of actual cost to budgeted or intended cost may also act as an incentive.

Rent

The rent payable by a manufacturer or trader who does not own his premises is obviously a cost to be taken into account in computing the cost of providing his building accommodation, and should be apportioned to the factory, sales office, warehouse, and general office as an indirect cost of production, selling, distribution, administration, etc. Unless the owner-occupier of premises includes a similar charge his costs will fail to take into account the fact that, in his capacity of owner, he has forfeited the right to receive rent by occupying the premises himself. His costs will not therefore be comparable with those of a manufacturer who rents his accommodation, although capital is tied up to pay for the buildings.

Comparability in this connection is important where a producer is a member of a group of companies, where a concern has several factories producing a similar article, or where information is to be exchanged with other manufacturers as part of a uniform costing scheme. The argument that because the product costs of two manufacturers are computed on different bases, they will charge different selling prices, is largely fallacious. A producer normally charges what the market will bear, and the market will bear neither more nor less solely because of the different basis of computation. However, if cost is the basis of a price tendered for a job under competitive conditions, overheads attributed on false bases may overprice or underprice the work, resulting in either a failure to gain work, or the acceptance of contracts at prices that do not cover the true cost of the job.

Some cost accountants include as a building service cost a notional rent, or rent-charge equivalent to the rent the owner-occupier would otherwise have to pay, the corresponding credit being to profit and loss account. Other cost accountants, however, feel that where premises are owned it is sufficient to include in lieu of rent only the cost of repairs, maintenance and depreciation of the building. This divergence of opinion is also apparent in the question of interest of capital.

A similar position arises in connection with machinery. If, for instance, a concern leases vehicles, plant, or a computer, it is appropriate that the hire charge should be treated as a cost. One might argue that a concern that owns similar equipment ought to charge a notional hire charge for its use, but there is less support for this contention than exists in connection with rent-charges in respect of buildings. Most cost accountants seem content to regard depreciation, maintenance and repairs as a sufficient measure of the cost of employing an owned machine. A recent standard accounting practice has ruled that the hire charge on certain leased assets should be treated partly as a capital repayment and partly as interest on a notional borrowed amount, and that assets on long leases should be depreciated as though they were owned by the company using them.

Taxation

In the past, when rates of taxation were low, it was easy to accept as a matter of principle that taxation was an appropriation of profit and not a charge deductible in arriving at it. However, increased rates of direct taxation have left reduced margins of profit available for rewarding capital, and brought into prominence the question of whether direct taxation, such as corporation tax, should really be excluded from costs.

Value added tax is in certain circumstances included in the costs of a purchaser. This might suggest that it is equally proper to include in costs corporation tax on the grounds that there is no logical reason to exclude from costs one type of taxation while including the other. Despite this, it is almost universal in this country to regard direct taxation as an appropriation and not to include it in costs.

Where cost information is presented with regard to alternative choices (e.g. the cost of making a component, or of buying it externally), the question of direct taxation may frequently be disregarded entirely, since the alternative choice which produces the greater profit before tax will also produce the greater profit after tax. Yet this will not always be the case, and it is proper to take into account any taxation consequences of the alternative courses, e.g. the capital allowances available upon the purchase of an item of machinery in comparison with the rent otherwise deductible.

Depreciation

Depreciation is the diminution in the value of a fixed asset due to use and/or the lapse of time. In its primary meaning the word depreciation is used to denote loss of value that arises through wear and tear or some other form of material deterioration, or the effluxion of time. When it occurs it does so irrespective of whether any record of it is made in cost or financial accounts. Moreover, it happens in spite of any day-to-day repairs and maintenance that are carried out.

When the accountant speaks of depreciation he often refers not to this actual and inevitable diminution in value, but rather to the arbitrary amount he will be charging as an expense in his accounts to cover the depreciation that he expects to arise, or to spread the cost of the asset over the period of its useful economic life. The adequacy of this amount will depend upon the skill and care with which the depreciation and the working life are estimated.

The assessment of future depreciation can seldom be made with mathematical accuracy because one cannot foresee the future. When a premium of £1000 is paid for a ten-year lease, it is certain that the whole of the amount of the premium will cease to exist as an asset at the end of the term of the lease, so £100 a year can accurately be written off as depreciation. Depreciation arising from wear and tear, however, can only be estimated and the accuracy of the estimate will vary according to the skill and experience of the estimator. Thus, an engineer can give an authoritative opinion that the life of a particular machine will be a stated number of years, provided that it will be worked under normal conditions and be effectively maintained, but he cannot do more than state what he believes to be probable in the light of the facts known to him at the time. Yet wear and tear is not the only contingency that may cause a reduction in the value of an asset. The ultimate record of a machine that appeared at the outset to have a reasonably certain working life of a given number of years may prove to be very different from that foretold when the machine was new.

Obsolescence means that a machine in otherwise good working order is reduced in value either because demand for what it can produce falls, or because competition from new, more efficient machines renders it uneconomic to use.

Clearly depreciation is an overhead expense, and should be divided fairly so that it can be properly charged to the cost of each unit made by the machine concerned. There may be a number of machines in a workshop or department, some of which lie idle for part of the time. It is customary for the total depreciation of fixed assets used in the cost centre to be charged as an overhead and absorbed to production by an appropriate method.

The amount of depreciation chargeable to a particular time period can be calculated by the application of several alternative methods. The 'straight line' method divides the cost net of expected scrap value by the number of years of the economic life of the asset, thus charging each time period with the same amount irrespective of use.

The 'production hour' method divides cost less expected scrap value by the number of hours of work expected from the machine during its life, and applies the resulting rate to the hours worked in each costing period, thus relating the depreciation charge to activity rather than the passage of time. The 'reducing balance' method writes off a constant percentage from a gradually reducing capital cost, thereby charging more as depreciation in the early years of the life of the asset, and less in the later years.*

Replacement Values

If a business is to remain in existence it must have sufficient funds available to replace its plant, buildings, and other fixed assets when those currently employed are worn out or become obsolete. It is often contended, therefore, that depreciation charges should be based on replacement values rather than historic cost, and that unless a business makes a profit after charging depreciation computed in this way it cannot be said to be operating profitably. The arguments in favour of basing depreciation charges on replacement values are that:

(a)   Where costs are used to determine selling prices, or to measure their equity, full provision should be made for the replacement of the assets used.

(b)   Unless replacement values are used for this purpose, the depreciation charge made in respect of identical machines having identical lives will differ if they are purchased (in a time of changing prices) at different prices.

Against this it may be argued that the use of replacement values is a departure from actual cost, and if adjustments are made in this case similar adjustments will probably be necessary in connection with stocks and other assets in periods of changing money values.

The general opinion appears to be that whilst the present method of accounting is not entirely satisfactory in times of changing price levels, no alternative recommends itself sufficiently to warrant its universal adoption.

Reassessment of Working Life and Residual Value

Where possible, arrangements should be made for the reassessment of the working life and residual value of each asset at intervals during its working life, depreciation being recalculated on the basis of any revision found to be necessary. This should assist in avoiding any serious miscalculation of depreciation.

Acquisition of New Assets

Practice amongst financial accountants differs with regard to the charge for depreciation in the year of acquisition. Some charge a full year's depreciation on every asset owned at the end of the accounting period, while others charge a full year's depreciation on assets owned

---

* For a further discussion of depreciation methods see *Accounting and Finance – A Firm Foundation*, Chapter 6, by A. V. Pizzey.

throughout the year and only the appropriate fraction of a year's depreciation on those acquired during the year. The latter method, whilst involving more calculations, produces a charge for depreciation that is acceptable to the cost accountant as a measure of the services provided by the assets in question, whereas the former does not.

Costs to be Capitalised

On the purchase of a fixed asset it is considered good accounting practice to charge as part of the cost of the asset, not only its net invoice price, but also acquisition and installation expenses e.g. the cost of estate agent's, surveyor's, solicitor's and architect's fees, and similar costs in connection with buildings; the cost of preparing foundations for and installing plant or equipment, together with any transport costs incurred; and the cost of delivering lorries etc. together with the cost of painting and signwriting.

The depreciation charge, by whatever method it is computed, is based on the total capitalised cost of the asset and not merely on its net cost.

Relation of Depreciation to Use

Accountants generally recognise the need to increase depreciation charges in periods in which there is excessive overtime, or in which additional shifts are worked, because such unusual activity tends to decrease the probable working life of assets (measured in years) below that originally estimated. The production hour and production unit methods are designed to take such changes into account automatically, but if other methods are employed, an adjustment will be needed to accelerate the depreciation.

Physical deterioration is undoubtedly increased by use, but it is not necessarily appropriate to increase depreciation charges in exact proportion to usage, for the normal depreciation charge is intended to take account of deterioration caused by wear and tear and that arising from obsolescence or the effluxion of time, which are not increased with greater use. Wear and tear may, however, increase faster than increases in use at high outputs, especially where there is round-the-clock working with little opportunity to attend to routine maintenance. Everything depends upon the circumstances.

A logical corollary to this would appear to be that periods of less than average use ought to be charged with less depreciation than those of normal activity, but many accountants view this suggestion with disfavour on the grounds that lack of use may be evidence of pending obsolescence. There is no doubt that the element of depreciation attributable to the effluxion of time ought to be charged in any event.

Obviously where double- or treble-shift working is normal, this will be borne in mind when assessing the working life of assets for the purpose of computing normal depreciation. No question of accelerating this charge then arises unless unusual extra-shift working occurs.

Assets Retained in Use After Being Fully Depreciated

Where an asset is retained in use after it has been entirely written off, as will happen with any method of depreciation except the reducing balance method if the estimated working life of the asset is exceeded, the cost accountant faces a difficult problem. If he ceases to charge depreciation his costs will include only part of the cost (e.g. the cost of maintenance) of providing the service the asset produces. The costs will be less than those he prepared previously, and less than those he will prepare when the asset is replaced. They will be of little use, therefore, for purposes of comparison.

One alternative is to continue to charge the same amount of depreciation as was charged before. This will provide comparable costs but leaves the cost accountant with the problem of disposing of the excess depreciation. To credit it against overhead does not solve the problem and it is probably best either to transfer it to a reserve for plant obsolescence or to credit it to the profit and loss account as miscellaneous income. Any excess 'provision' is, from the viewpoint of financial accounting, a reserve and not a provision.

Yet the very fact that an asset is still in use after the end of its estimated working life is evidence that its life was previously underestimated. One consequence of this is that the depreciation charge has in the past been too great. To continue to use such an inflated rate may be inadvisable, particularly where costs are used either to fix, or to measure the suitability of, selling prices. The policy favoured by SSAP 12 is to revalue the asset, and depreciate this new value over what is now considered to be the remaining life of the asset.

Assets Retired Prematurely

Not infrequently the converse of what has just been considered occurs, and as a matter of policy an asset is taken out of use before the end of its useful life. Usually this will mean that a loss will occur on its realisation – the depreciation written off being insufficient to reduce it to its present second-hand value. In so far as such a loss is unconnected with the amount of use made of the asset and results from an outside factor, it is hardly a fair charge against any particular product or department, and is best written off against profits generally. Losses of this nature should be written off immediately.

Fixed Asset Register

It is usual to maintain only one asset account in the general ledger for each main class of asset e.g. freeholds, leaseholds, plant and machinery, cars and vans, and so on; and to keep any detailed records required in the form of *fixed asset registers* controlled by the appropriate asset account in the *general ledger*.

A typical *plant register* makes provision for the recording of:

1. The cost, description, serial number and date of purchase of the machine, together with the name of its maker and invoice reference.
2. The estimated life of the machine and its residual value.
3. The method by which depreciation is to be provided and the amount written off each period.
4. Any additions to the machine and any changes in the depreciation charge caused by these changes.
5. The location of the machine and
6. Details of disposal, together with the loss or gain arising from this.

It is frequently useful to record in addition:

7. Details of the maintenance cost each period and of significant overhauls.
8. Information regarding the capital allowances granted for taxation purposes.

Registers for other classes of fixed asset will be designed to suit their individual purpose. Whether the information is recorded as a written record in a plant register or on a computer file accessed by print-out or visual display unit, the data needed remain the same.

If no fixed asset register is maintained it will be necessary to consult original records every time an asset is disposed of in order that the necessary adjustments can be made to the cost and aggregate depreciation-to-date figures disclosed in the financial accounts, and in order that the appropriate balancing allowance or charge can be computed for taxation purposes.

PLANT REGISTER	Description					Location	Serial No.	
	Maker							
	Invoice Reference						Date purchased	

Year	Cost and Add'ns	Depreciation	Written-down Value	Repairs & Mainten-ance	Notes			£
	£	£	£	£		Original Cost		
						Installation etc.		
						Total		
						Less Residual Value		
						Net Capital Cost		
						Estimated Life		
						Annual Dep'n.— Straight Line		
						Disposal Date:		
						Written-down Value Net Proceeds	£	
						Gain/Loss		

General Remarks

A fixed asset register is of great assistance to the cost accountant when he is ascertaining the depreciation charge to be made to each separate cost centre, for, as stated previously, the general ledger normally contains only one account for each main class of asset in the works, the balance on which is not otherwise divisible between cost centres.

It is desirable to number each item of plant and equipment conspicuously in order that it can be identified with the corresponding asset record. One system often used is to allocate to each machine a code number, the first section of which provides information regarding the cost centre in which the machine is employed, and the second section is the 'personal' identity number of the machine. For instance, 413/599 might be used to indicate machine 599 which is employed in cost centre 413 i.e. Department A, Machine Group 3. Observe how the asset code is tied in with the accounts code discussed in Chapter 1.

Production, Selling, Distribution and Administration Overheads

It is usual to classify and separately accumulate production, selling, and distribution overheads; since whereas the former applies to the goods produced during the period, the selling and distribution overheads apply only to the goods sold and distributed during the period. Thus whilst it is proper to take into account production overhead when valuing finished stocks, no element of selling or distribution cost should be added in pricing goods that remain unsold and undistributed. This means that the cost accountant must try to relate production overheads to cost units, but that selling and administration overheads are best charged direct to the costing profit and loss account.

The following are the main items included in production, selling, and distribution overheads respectively:

Production Overheads

Factory rent (or a charge in lieu where the building is owner-occupied), rates, and insurance of the building.
Power and fuel.
Salaries of foremen, supervisors etc.
Remuneration of technical directors.
Wages of gatemen, patrolmen, night watchmen, factory clerks, timekeepers, inspectors, storekeepers, toolroom staff etc.
Idle time.
Lighting and heating the works.
Depreciation and maintenance of tools, plant, machinery, land, and factory buildings.
Indirect materials used in production.
Oil, waste, and factory supplies.
Works stationery, telephones etc.
Cost of production control and progress departments, work study etc.

Selling Overheads

Salaries, commission and travelling expenses of sales, and technical representatives, and sales managers.
Advertising.
Catalogues, price lists etc.
Rent, rates, maintenance, and insurance of showrooms and sales offices.
Selling department salaries, stationery etc.
Bad debts and collection charges.
Legal costs in connection with salesmen's agreements etc.
Telephones and postages connected with selling.
Cash discounts allowed.

Distribution Overheads

Packing materials.
Carriage and freight outwards.
Rent, rates, depreciation, and insurance of warehouses.
Depreciation and running costs of delivery vans.
Wages of packers, van drivers etc.

Administration Overheads is frequently regarded as a further class of overhead and accumulated separately, though some accountants apportion administration costs between the primary activities of the business: production, selling, and distribution. The main overhead accounts are:

Rent, rates, and insurance of general offices; their lighting, heating, and cleaning.
Office salaries, including salaries of administrative directors.
Depreciation of office buildings, furniture, machinery etc.
Bank charges.
Hire of office machinery.
Audit fees.
Office telephone and postages.
Printing and stationery.

More complex organisations require more detailed analysis. Once the overheads are identified and their costs accumulated in the appropriate overhead account, the next problem is to relate them in the first instance to the appropriate department or cost centre and, in the second instance, to the cost units passing through those centres.

RELATING PRODUCTION OVERHEADS TO DEPARTMENTS AND COST UNITS

Early cost accountants recognised that there were many costs that were difficult or even impossible to allocate specifically to one particular job or product. These costs they termed 'overheads', and beyond realising that overheads were as much a part of the costs of the business as the so-called direct costs, they probably had little idea of their scientific disposal. Generally they attempted to spread them over production on some arbitrary basis. Popular methods included their absorption as a percentage of direct wages, or of direct material cost, or of prime cost. None of these methods was *universally* satisfactory and occasionally they gave quite astounding results as will be seen from the following example:

Example

A manufacturer found that his production costs for an accounting period (Year 10) had been as follows:

		£
Direct wages		800 000
Direct material cost		200 000
		1 000 000
Production overheads		1 600 000
	Total cost	£2 600 000

The direct costs of Job 112 undertaken during Year 11 were:

		£
Direct wages		800
Direct material cost		30 000

The job consisted of the erection of a prefabricated building.

According to which of the three methods of overhead absorption the manufacturer adopts, the 'cost' of Job 112 will be shown to be:

	Method 1	*Method* 2	*Method* 3
	Percentage of Direct Wages	Percentage of Direct Material Cost	Percentage of Prime Cost
	$\dfrac{1\,600\,000}{800\,000} \times 100$	$\dfrac{1\,600\,000}{200\,000} \times 100$	$\dfrac{1\,600\,000}{1\,000\,000} \times 100$
	$= 200\%$	$= 800\%$	$= 160\%$

Cost of Job 112:	£	£	£
Direct wages	800	800	800
Direct material cost	30 000	30 000	30 000
Production overheads	1 600	240 000	49 280
	£32 400	£270 800	£80 080

Note: obviously the results shown in this deliberately exaggerated example bear no resemblance to one another, and cannot each provide a reasonable approach to the truth – assuming even that there is such a thing as a 'true cost'. However, it is not suggested that these methods *never* give reasonable results and that there are no circumstances in which they might properly be employed.

The rates for the absorption of the overheads were set at the beginning of the year, and based on a previous year's figures. These rates are estimates and may well be wrong if last year's figures do not reflect the conditions experienced this year. Therefore it is not uncommon that the amount charged out to jobs does not coincide with the cost incurred. In this case any unabsorbed cost is charged direct to costing profit and loss account, and if more is absorbed than is incurred, a credit to profit and loss account is the result. In book-keeping terms the correct entries are to debit the factory account (known as work-in-progress or manufacturing account) and credit the overheads account. If overhead absorption rates are set at the start of each year and based on expected budgeted activity, then if budget levels are exceeded, or not achieved, the consequent over- or under-absorption of overheads, written off to profit and loss, acts as a reminder to management of the effect of departures from budget. A pre-set rate allows all jobs to be charged overheads on the same basis and avoids confusing fluctuations caused by increased seasonal activity, or short-term cost movements.

Computation of Pre-determined Overhead Absorption Rates

Since overhead must be absorbed upon some definite basis, the first requirement in fixing an overhead absorption rate is to determine the basis of absorption. The bases most commonly employed by undertakings using the simple blanket, or general factory, rate of absorption are:

1. A direct labour hour rate.
2. A cost unit rate – if it is possible to absorb the overheads of the business fairly on this basis.
3. A direct wages percentage rate, where direct wages reasonably signify the use made of production facilities.

It is then necessary to budget two factors:

1. The overhead to be incurred in the forthcoming period (normally a year); and
2. The quantity of the 'base' in that period.

Thus, if a direct labour hour rate is to be employed, it is necessary to budget the number of direct labour hours that will be worked in the period and the production overhead for that period.

Example

The Ivanhoe Manufacturing Company Limited absorbs production overheads by means of a general works overhead rate per direct labour hour. The production manager estimates that his men will work 127 500 hours in the year ending 31 December. After studying the accounts for the preceding year, and bearing in mind the changed volume of activity planned and any other changes in circumstances, the accountant budgets that the production overheads that will be incurred in that year are as follows:

Production Overhead Budget for the Year 19–

	£
Indirect labour – cleaners, timekeepers, inspectors, production control and planning, work study, etc. and supervision	123 500
Indirect materal – oil and grease etc.	24 500
Rent, rates, and depreciation of building	10 000
Depreciation and maintenance of machinery	35 000
Light, heat, power and water	29 500
Printing, stationery, and telephone	1 100
Idle time	2 500
National Insurance	18 000
Overtime	10 900
	£255 000

Pre-determined overhead absorption rate for production overheads:

$$\frac{£255\,000}{127\,500} = £2 \text{ per direct labour hour}$$

Some small and medium-sized undertakings employ the accounts of the immediate past period, *without adjustment*, as the basis of the 'budget' for overheads for the ensuing period. This will provide satisfactory results only if both total overheads and the quantity of the base of absorption remain unchanged, or if, fortuitously, both change in the same proportion.

Example

The accounts of the Seascale Manufacturing Co. Ltd provided the following information regarding the year ended 31 December, 19—:

	£
Direct wages	231 800
General works overheads	139 080
Net profit	20 120

3
5
9
4
8

On the basis of this, general works overheads were absorbed during the following year by means of wages percentage rate of:

$$\frac{139\,080}{231\,800} \times 100 = 60\%$$

Direct wages that following year were actually only £150 000 so, of the general works overhead incurred (£105 080), only £90 000 was absorbed, leaving an under-absorption of £15 080. In proportion to the net profit of a concern of this size, such an under-absorption could prove disastrous.

Had the directors been able to foresee the fall in volume and to adjust the figures on which they based their rate of absorption, the position might have been more like this:

Since it is estimated that volume in the second year will only be 75 % of that in 19—, and since wage rates are expected to increase by 5 %, a reasonable estimate of the direct wages to be incurred might be:

$$£231\,800 \times \frac{75}{100} \times \frac{105}{100} = \text{(say) } £182\,542$$

and since general works overheads are one-half fixed, and one-half variable, and are unaffected by changing price levels, they might reasonably be expected to be:

$$\frac{£139\,080}{2} + \left(\frac{£139\,080}{2} \times \frac{75}{100} \right) = £121\,695$$

This would give a wages percentage rate of:

$$\frac{£121\,695}{£182\,542} \times \frac{100}{1} = 66\tfrac{2}{3}\%$$

Even on this basis – the estimation it must be realised is relatively poor – there is an under-absorption, though it is now only £5080.

Overheads Account

	£		£
Cost incurred		* Cost absorbed	
	105 080		100 000
		Costing p/l	5 080
	———		———
	£105 080		£105 080

Work-in-Progress Account

	£		£
Direct materials	–		
Direct labour	–		
Factory overheads	100 000		

* $66\frac{2}{3}$% of £150 000 = £100 000

Treatment of Particular Types of Cost

Certain particular types of cost are a source of difficulty in all types of undertaking – whether simple or highly developed. Generally the problem is whether they should be charged as direct or indirect costs; and the problem is usually much the same whatever the size of the organisation and whether it adopts a single general factory overhead rate, or separate departmental rates as described below. Typical costs providing this type of problem are:

Idle or Lost Time. The wages paid for time during which productive workers are not usefully employed cannot be charged to any particular job and should be incorporated in production overhead so that its cost is spread over production generally. In departmental businesses it is usual to record separately the cost of idle time in each department in order that regular reports can be prepared to reveal the extent of the loss by department and the cause.

Overtime and Shift Premiums. Where in a jobbing business it is necessary to incur the additional costs of overtime or shift premiums in order to increase output, the premium element should be separated from direct wages and treated as a production overhead. This has the effect of spreading the additional cost of overtime or shift working over all production instead of penalising the particular work in which it occurred. On the other hand, where overtime is worked to meet the requirements of a particular customer, the additional cost is a proper charge to the job concerned and is accordingly excluded from production overhead.

The treatment of overtime and shift premiums in the case of a processing industry presents certain difficulties. That which is caused by the inefficiency of the process should be regarded as a direct cost of the process, as should that which arises from some peculiarity of the process (e.g. a need for continual supervision), which entails night working as a normal practice. It may be best, however, not to include in process costs any overtime and shift premiums that arise fortuitously and not as a result of inefficiency, as their inclusion would make the costs difficult to compare. Typical of the costs here referred to are the overtime premium paid to workers (having a 40-hour week) completing the fourth batch of a product, production of each batch of which occupied 11 hours. For some purposes it would be proper to include the full wages, including overtime premium, as part of the cost of the last batch. This would be so when there is doubt as to whether that batch is profitable to produce at all, but in normal circumstances where it is desirable to compare the cost of one batch with that of another it is best to regard the premium as a production overhead.

National Insurance. It is generally most convenient to regard the employer's share of National Insurance contributions of employees engaged on jobbing work as a production overhead. When a contractor's employees tend to remain on one job for many weeks at a time, it is possible to treat the contributions as a direct charge to the contract concerned. In the case of process workers, too, it is frequently possible to charge National Insurance contributions direct to the process. It is always possible to employ an inflated direct wage rate so as to absorb the contributions, but such a course is generally regarded as an unnecessary refinement.

Holiday Pay. Most employees are entitled to statutory holidays such as August Bank Holiday, Christmas Day and Boxing Day, and also to a paid summer holiday. The appropriate fraction of a year's cost may be charged direct to the contract or process each week. Alternatively, the amount may be charged to production overhead. Again there is the opportunity to employ an inflated rate of direct wages to absorb both the normal weekly wages and the appropriate part of holiday pay.

Apprentices. During their period of training the time of apprentices engaged upon productive work should normally be charged to the appropriate job, though this procedure admittedly gives rise to a number of difficulties. Apprentices generally take more time than skilled operatives to perform a given task and they are likely to cause more scrap. On the other hand, they are paid a lower rate per hour. The wages of workers under full-time training who cannot normally make any real contribution to production should be treated as a production overhead. It is extremely difficult in either of these cases to ensure equality of the costs of jobs produced by trained operatives with those produced by apprentices or trainees.

Attendance Bonuses. Sometimes workers who perform the full number of shifts in a working week, or who lose no time over a stated period, are entitled to an attendance bonus. As such bonuses are effectively part of their wages, they are sometimes regarded as direct and charged by means of an inflated direct wages rate. The alternative is to treat them as a production overhead. In process or contracting industries they may properly be charged direct to the process or contract concerned.

Setting-Up Cost. Where setting-up is completed by specialist setters their wages are normally treated as a production overhead. On the other hand, where an operator sets his own machine, his time is rarely separated into setting-up time and operating time – it is all regarded as part of the direct cost of the job. The cost of setting-up has a considerable effect upon unit costs as is shown by the example on page 149.

Compensatory Payments. Where workers receive a compensatory payment based upon their length of service at the time of their redundancy, this payment cannot be said to be a cost of production and should be charged separately to the profit and loss account.

Similarly, payments made in lieu of bonus to operators unable to work owing to a major machine breakdown cannot be regarded as a normal consequence of production and should be charged to the profit and loss account and not to production overhead.

Costs Sometimes Charged Directly and Sometimes Indirectly. Care must be taken where the same type of cost is charged directly in certain circumstances and indirectly in others, to ensure that a definite policy is laid down and followed. Obviously, where a pre-determined rate of absorption is employed, the budget must be drawn up in accordance with this general policy, and any departure from this in recording the actual costs incurred will affect the overheads under- or over-absorbed. A typical cost that may be charged directly or indirectly is overtime premiums.

Inspection. Where inspectors are engaged full-time in connection with a particular process, inspection costs are normally regarded as a direct cost of that process. Where, however, the inspection staff is engaged in a wide variety of work it will not normally be practicable to allocate inspection costs to jobs, and the cost will be included in production overheads.

Drawing Office Costs. Where drawing office costs are heavy, draughtsmen may be required to book their time to individual jobs. Their wages will then be included as a direct cost of the jobs concerned. In many instances, however, the drawing office is regarded as providing a general service to the undertaking as a whole, and its cost is treated as a production overhead.

Material Carriage, Handling, and Storage. The cost of bringing material to the factory is frequently regarded as part of the cost of the material itself, though it may not be possible to treat it as such where a carriage charge covers a large number of individual materials. The only solution is to charge any carriage inwards that cannot be charged as a material cost to production overhead.

Where a blanket rate is used to absorb general factory overheads, any costs incurred in the inspection, storage, and internal transportation of materials are regarded as production overheads. In so far as the costs of storage and materials' handling bear little or no relation to the number of direct labour hours worked, their absorption as parts of the general overhead by means of a method based on time in process does not necessarily provide accurate costs, but the only alternative is to adopt separate rates for this purpose.

Scrap and Rectification. The treatment of scrap and rectification is considered in detail in Chapters 5 and 7. It is sufficient to state here that whilst abnormal scrap is not regarded as a cost but charged direct to the profit and loss account, normal scrap may be treated as a production overhead or as a part of the direct cost of a job or process according to circumstances.

Maintenance of Plant and Factory Buildings. The costs of maintaining and cleaning plant and factory buildings will be included as part of production overheads, and this is so whether the work is performed by outside contractors or by the concern's own workmen.

In order that certain accounting years may not be unduly burdened with maintenance, a maintenance provision may be set up to which the estimated cost of the liability for future maintenance is credited. Yet it is a matter of policy whether any attempt should be made to equalise overhead absorption rates between one year and another by such means.

Installation of New Machinery. Expenditure upon the installation of new machinery should be treated as part of the cost of the machine and will affect costs directly only in so far as the work is completed by the concern's own workmen or materials are used ex stock, when the costs will be charged to a job account in the same way as it would be if work were done for a customer. Most accountants accept that it is proper to include, as part of the cost of such work, an element in respect of production overheads. It would not be appropriate, however, to make any addition on account of distribution or selling costs, which will not of course be incurred, or of profit.

Where machinery is moved from one location in the plant to another, it is considered proper *either* to write off the original installation costs and to charge those incurred on re-installation to 'capital,' or to leave the original installation costs charged to the asset account and to write off those of re-installation to 'revenue.' Where the previous installation cost is unknown, the new installation costs should always be written off to production overheads. It is not correct to permit a double capitalisation of installation costs.

Cases sometimes arise where expenditure is incurred in preparing a site for the installation of new plant, and the project is abandoned before the plant is installed. Such expenditure neither gives rise to an asset, nor is it a normal cost of production. It should therefore neither be capitalised nor charged to production overheads, but treated as a direct charge to the profit and loss account.

Dismantling of Plant. Dismantling costs should be charged to the account of the asset dismantled, and set off against any salvage or compensation moneys or sale proceeds received. The final gain or loss on realisation should be transferred direct to the profit and loss account.

Services. Where production overheads are absorbed by means of a blanket rate, the costs of services such as the provision of power, steam, gas or compressed air are not separately ascertained but treated as items of production overheads.

Research and Development. The cost of research specially undertaken, in order that a particular job may be satisfactorily completed, may be regarded either as a direct cost of that job, in which case it will be charged to it, or as the price paid to acquire knowledge that will be of general advantage, in which case it may be charged to production overhead. Research directed at the improvement of methods and of current products may be treated as a production overhead and spread over production generally, but that directed towards the discovery or development of new methods, products, or processes may have little connection with current production and should be charged directly to the profit and loss account.

Advertising. Normal advertising in trade journals, periodicals, and newspapers; by poster, radio, or television; and the cost of publicity literature and samples, are normally written off as a selling overhead at the time they are incurred.

Expenditure on advertising of a more permanent nature, such as an illuminated sign or the extensive campaigning required to launch a new product, may be temporarily capitalised and written off over a short term of years.

Royalties. Royalties of an incidental or general nature may be treated as part of selling overhead, but those paid for the use of patents or the right to market particular products are normally charged direct.

Carriage Outwards. Where carriage outwards forms the basis of a separate charge to the customer or its cost is heavy in relation to the value of the goods despatched, it should be treated as a direct expense of the order concerned. The cost of sea or air transport on goods charged c.i.f. should always be regarded as a direct cost.

In other cases, carriage outwards should be treated as a distribution overhead. Where a business sells standard lines it may be possible to allocate it to specific products or product groups. Otherwise carriage must be apportioned over output on some more general basis. In any event it is frequently necessary to provide management with information regarding the cost of carriage on particular lines or lot sizes, or to specific destinations.

Losses of Finished Stock. Whilst abnormal losses of finished goods are normally written off direct to the profit and loss account, normal losses such as those caused by handling, breaking bulk, evaporation, and other natural causes should be regarded as distribution overhead.

Packing Materials. A distinction is drawn between primary packing and other packing, i.e. between the cartons and bags in which goods are packed for sale, and the packing material necessary to protect them during transit. The former is a cost of production, and the latter a distribution cost.

Value Added Tax. Normally, value added tax on inputs will be accumulated in one account, for recovery in due course from Customs and Excise. Only where input tax is, for one reason or another, unrecoverable should VAT be treated for all purposes as part of the total cost of the material or expense to which it relates.

ABSORPTION AND APPORTIONMENT OF OVERHEADS IN MORE COMPLEX CIRCUMSTANCES

The simple method of absorbing production overheads by means of a single blanket absorption rate may prove satisfactory where a concern produces only one product, or where all its products pass through the same processing steps, spending a similar proportion of their total time in each step. It is not suitable either where the business has several separate departments, each of which produces a distinct product, or where the operations carried out on each product require a different combination of facilities and there is therefore a diversity of production. Two examples will illustrate the problem involved.

Example 1

Elmo Tools PLC has two main lines: a patent three-bladed electrician's screwdriver having a plastic handle, produced on mass-production lines for sale through chain stores; and a range of micrometers noted for their high accuracy. The department producing screwdrivers is highly mechanised though much of its labour is only semi-skilled. The micrometer department, on the other hand, has a highly skilled labour force and is rather less mechanised, although it employs relatively expensive high-accuracy measuring devices to ensure the accurate calibration of the instruments produced.

It will be apparent that there are the following outstanding differences between the products:

	Screwdriver	Micrometer
Selling price per article	Low	Relatively high
Quantities produced	Great	Small
Machinery employed	High value – automatic	High value – precision
Type of labour	Semi-skilled	Highly skilled
Electric power consumed	High	Low
Maintenance of machinery	Routine preventive maintenance – fairly constant	Variable
Inspection labour costs	Low	High

It would obviously be unfair to apply the same rate of production overhead to the production of each department in these circumstances, unless, by coincidence, a separate computation of the rate applicable to each showed this to be proper.

Example 2

The Red, White, and Blue Press, a small printing business employs seven presses of three distinct types: four capable of printing only one colour at a time, two capable of printing in two colours on the same run, and one 'Perfector' machine capable of printing both sides of a sheet simultaneously. Production overheads, including depreciation, amount to £20 000 in a four-week period of 160 working hours.

One could use this information to compute a single rate for the absorption of production overheads per machine-hour as follows:

$$\frac{\text{Production overheads per four-week period}}{\text{Machine-hours per period}} = \frac{£20\,000}{160 \times 7}$$

$$= £17.86 \text{ per machine-hour}$$

However, since the machines operate at approximately the same speed, this would charge a single-colour job with the same overhead as one in two colours or one printed on both sides. Since two-colour and Perfector machines cost more to buy and occupy rather more floor space than single-colour machines, this is obviously inequitable. Furthermore, since even in the absence of separate machine rates for costing purposes, the estimator will place a higher value on the time of a two-colour machine than he does on that of one that prints in one colour when he prices a job for a potential customer, costs based on such a single rate will be quite incomparable with the estimates. So one main function of cost accounting – that of comparing actual costs with those estimated – will remain unfulfilled. If an estimator did base his prices on a single rate for all machines, his prices for two-colour work would be the same as those for single-colour work – the former being too low and the latter too high. It is likely in consequence that the concern would be swamped with orders for work to be executed on two-colour and Perfector machines, but would lose most orders for work to be executed on single-colour presses because its quotations for such work were too high.

If costs are to be useful to management the cost accountant must compute separately the cost of operating each class of machine. Assuming he finds in a four-week period in which each machine works 160 hours that costs are:

	£
Single-colour (4 machines)	9 600
Two-colour (2 machines)	7 200
Perfector (1 machine)	3 200
	£20 000

the individual machine-hour rates he computes will be as follows:

	£
Single colour	$15.0 [£9600 \div (4 \times 160)]$
Two-colour	$22.5 [£7200 \div (2 \times 160)]$
Perfector	$20.0 [£3200 \div 160]$

and by employing them he will ensure that the charge to each individual job represents a fair estimate of the cost of providing the facilities employed in its execution.

Cost Centres

Cost centres are generally named after some person or his function, some item of equipment, or some location, or a group of these. In appropriate circumstances they bear the name of a process or operation. Thus examples are:

Persons or their functions:
Welfare officer.
Production control.
Items of equipment of groups of these:
Tower crane.
No. 2 Shaper.
Locations:
Edmonton main factory block.
Central Scottish sales area.
Processes:
Machining.
Silver plating.
Services:
Canteen.
Power house.

There can be no definition of the size of a cost centre; of how many people a section must employ before it can be considered one; or even of the level of supervision involved. Cost centres may be large or small; their costs may be heavy or light; they may employ one person or a hundred, be under the control of a single employee, or be the personal responsibility of the managing director. Cost centres simply serve the purpose of providing convenient 'pegs' on which to 'hang' costs so that the resulting information may prove most useful to management.

Thus, to take but one example: if a company has a fleet of a hundred lorries, it may be quite content to know the total running cost, and not to analyse this in any way. The whole fleet may then be regarded as a *single cost centre*. However, a more enlightened management may insist on knowing the comparative costs and performances of the various makes and types of vehicle used. Each class of vehicle would then be made a separate cost centre. Many cost accountants would consider it an unnecessary complication to carry the analysis still further, but it would be possible to treat each vehicle as a separate cost centre so that the running cost of each separate lorry could be reported to the transport manager. Analysis costs money, and the cost accountant must maintain a proper balance between the level of detail provided to managers and the cost-effectiveness of the system that he operates.

Cost centres can be divided into those which relate to the main purposes of the business: production, selling, and distribution; and those which merely provide a service to these functions and play no part themselves in altering the product physically, or in its sale or distribution. These are known as *service cost centres*, and are discussed below.

The former include:

Production Cost Centres to which are charged the costs of all production materials, labour, and services involved in producing the product with its primary packing (if any), including the cost of production management.

Selling Cost Centres to which are charged the costs of:
1. Advertising and publicity, including sample distribution and gift schemes.
2. Salesmen and sales agents, sales clerical department, and sales management.
3. Estimating.
4. Debt collection.
5. Product maintenance and the cost of giving service to customers under a guarantee or otherwise.
6. Market research.

Distribution Cost Centres to which are charged costs such as those of:
1. Warehousing finished products.
2. Packing goods in secondary containers and container costs e.g. storage and reconditioning of returned empties.
3. Despatching e.g. labelling and loading packages.
4. Transport of products to customers.
5. Managerial and clerical costs of distribution.

Administration Cost Centres to which are charged costs such as those of:
1. Directors' remuneration and expenses.
2. General management.
3. Cost and financial accounting, and internal audit.
4. Secretarial and legal activities.

Service Cost Centres

Basically it is possible to identify five main service functions that are likely to be found in almost every undertaking: Building Services; Equipment Services; Material Services; Personnel Services; Production Services. Each may conveniently form one or more cost centres. Once the direct cost of each of these service functions has been ascertained, it is possible to arrange for its apportionment between the centres it serves as a first step in the computation of the overhead absorption rate appropriate to each of the production cost centres.

Accumulation of Costs by Cost Centre

The cost accountant terms each of the separate functions of the business in respect of which he accumulates costs a *cost centre*. In the cases referred to above, 'screwdrivers', 'micrometers' and 'single-colour presses', 'two-colour presses', and 'Perfector presses' might represent the cost centres set up in respect of production departments, though other cost centres would exist in connection with other types of activity. Furthermore, whilst the accumulation of costs by function is an important step in the absorption of overhead, this is not its sole aim. Any system of cost centres must take into account the information needs of management.

The managers of concerns of different types need dissimilar information. Thus, the requirements of the managing director of a retail department store manifestly differ from those of the managing director of an engineering company. Similarly, the information needed in connection with a jobbing trade is quite unlike that called for in mass-production. Again, the management of a large group of companies manufacturing a wide range of products needs information of a different class from that appropriate to the head of a small family business.

It is the duty of the cost accountant to set up a system that will enable him to satisfy the day-to-day needs of his management, whilst at the same time ensuring that he can occasionally supply less frequently requested data without undue difficulty. He will need to balance the increased speed with which *ad hoc* reports can be prepared under a more complex system – and the consequent decrease in their cost – against the additional cost and the extra burden imposed by such a system. It is the function of the cost accountant to provide management with the information it desires, though circumstances may arise in which it is proper for him to endeavour to convince management that it has wider needs than it realises. Where the cost accountant has a progressive management, his task will be fulfilled more simply if he is able to assess the likely subjects of future interest and to predict the questions that management will ask at some later date. It would be wrong, however, to compile a mass of information the significance of which would be appreciated by the managers of an advanced undertaking, but lost on his own. There can be no standard list of cost centres suitable for every possible business, and those needed by a particular concern are likely to vary from year to year.

Many smaller undertakings, the managements of which are not satisfied that they have need of cost control information on the grounds that they already have the whole business 'at their fingertips', employ relatively simple departmental cost accounting systems, thus gaining the advantages to be derived from the computation and application of separate departmental or machine-hour rates, but they do not set up cost centres for control purposes. There are several production overhead accounts – one for each 'department' – and a similar number of production overhead absorbed accounts. Instead of items of production overhead passing automatically to the single overhead account, it will now be necessary to allocate those items that relate specifically to a particular department to that department, and to apportion each of the remainder on an appropriate basis. The bases of apportionment that are most frequently adopted are shown in the table on page 112.

Accounting for Overheads

The procedure in accounting for overheads 'departmentally' is as follows:

1. Record all costs incurred in the appropriate cost centres ledger control accounts (in total), at the same time posting items in detail to the relative cost centre accounts.
2. Costs that are capable of direct allocation to cost units (e.g. product direct wages and direct materials) are transferred to work-in-progress, the entries being: debit work-in-progress ledger control (in total) and job accounts individually if job costing is appropriate; and credit the production cost centres ledger control (in total) and the cost centres ledger accounts (in detail). Any balance remaining on the production cost centres ledger control represents production costs that are indirect in relation to the product, i.e. it represents production overheads.
3. Service cost centre costs are then apportioned to the main activity cost centres i.e. to production, selling, distribution, and administration cost centres. Costs of administration cost centres may then either be apportioned to production, selling, and distribution. Some overhead expenses can be apportioned direct to cost centres e.g. rent divided on the basis of floor area.
4. The costs remaining on each production cost centre account are then applied (as production overheads) to the jobs upon which it is engaged or to the cost units passing through the cost centre, by means of a selected absorption rate. Work-in-progress ledger control account is debited with the total production overheads absorbed (whilst the various job accounts are debited individually) and a production overhead absorbed account is credited therewith.
5. Where production overheads are absorbed by means of a pre-determined rate, the production overheads absorbed are unlikely to match exactly that incurred, but if a separate production overhead absorbed account is maintained for each cost centre it will be possible to obtain details of any under- or over-absorption, cost centre by cost centre, simply by comparing the balance on each cost centre account with that on the corresponding overhead absorbed account. Where such an analysis is required when only one overhead absorbed account is kept, it will be necessary to work from basic documents.
6. Selling and distribution overheads at this stage remain debited to their appropriate cost centre accounts. Their final disposition is discussed later in this chapter.

Before this procedure is illustrated it is necessary to consider the types of cost that fall within each of the main service centre classifications, and also to state the alternative bases upon which their apportionment may be made.

Building Services

Typical of the costs charged to building services are:

(a) Rent, charges in lieu of rent, depreciation, rates, and insurance of buildings.
(b) Lighting and heating: electricity, gas, coke, oil; fuel storage, handling, stoking, etc.; maintenance of boilers, pipes, wiring, and similar equipment; provision of hot and cold water for washing purposes.
(c) Cleaning of floors, walls, yards etc.; cleaning of windows, light shades, and reflectors.
(d) Maintenance of buildings whether carried out by the concern's own workers or by outside contractors.
(e) Fire prevention, internal policing and watching, including the provision of burglar alarms and fire-fighting equipment.

(f) Provision of clocks and time recording devices; provision of telephone service (as against the charge for calls that is dealt with departmentally).

(g) Building management: salaries of personnel engaged on building management; fees of architects, estate agents, surveyors etc. in so far as they are not capitalisable.

Where several independent buildings exist, each will normally be regarded as a separate cost centre. For a single-storey building of uniform height, building service costs are usually apportioned according to effective floor area.

Example

Acme Manufacturing PLC has two main buildings. The budgeted building service cost of the smaller building is £194 400 p.a. This building houses only three cost centres:

	Area square metres
Assembly Centre B1	16 000
Machine Group 16	6 000
Sales statistics	3 920
	25 920
Stairs, corridors, lifts etc.	4 080
	30 000

$$\text{Cost per square metre of effective floor area} = \frac{£194\,400}{25\,920} = £7.50 \text{ per square metre p.a.}$$

Apportionment:	£ *per annum*
Assembly Centre B1 – 16 000 at £7.50	120 000
Machine Group 16 – 6000 at £7.50	45 000
Sales statistics – 3920 at £7.50	29 400
	£194 400

The above amounts must be added to the budgets for costs allocated direct to the cost centres concerned in order that the relative pre-determined overhead absorption rate for each centre can be computed.

Apportionment on a straightforward effective floor area basis is not necessarily appropriate for multi-storey buildings, the different floor levels of which do not have the same occupational value, nor is it appropriate where all activities do not need the same working height. In the former case it is possible to weight floor areas to take into account the differing floor values, and in the latter case to apportion according to cubic capacity instead of area.

Example

Bilo PLC occupies a three-storey building in the centre of a town. The ground floor is used by the sales department, partly as showrooms and partly as a district sales office. The first floor is occupied by the area accounts office, and the second floor by a local sub-store under the control of the distribution manager.

The annual running cost of the building is £500 000. The effective floor area of the various levels is not identical: that of the ground floor is 10 000 square metres; that of the first floor 8000 square metres, and that of the second floor 6000 square metres. It is accepted that the value of the floors decreases with height in the ratio 5:4:3. Apportion the annual cost of the building between administration, selling, and distribution.

		Weighted Floor Area	Apportionment
Ground floor (selling)	5 ×10 000	50 000 (50%)	250 000
First floor (administration)	4 × 8 000	32 000 (32%)	160 000
Second floor (distribution)	3 × 6 000	18 000 (18%)	90 000
		100 000	£500 000

Where individual building services are treated as separate cost centres, some other basis of apportionment may be employed. For instance, where lighting is regarded as a separate function, its cost may be apportioned to cost centres according to either the number of lamps in each centre, or their estimated total electricity consumption.

Equipment Services

Typical of the costs regarded as equipment service costs are the costs of:

(a)   Depreciation and maintenance of the firm's equipment.
(b)   Inspection and testing of tools, machines, belting etc.
(c)   Charges for equipment hired from contractors and for maintenance of such equipment in running order.
(d)   Power supply for operating equipment e.g. steam, gas, water, electricity, or compressed air.
(e)   Tool and jig storage.
(f)   Plant record service, including records relating to the condition of equipment and to ensure that preventive maintenance is carried out.
(g)   Plant or Equipment Engineer's Department.
(h)   Research, design, and development of equipment (in certain circumstances).

Depreciation and maintenance of equipment are generally allocated specifically to cost centres on the basis of an analysis of information contained in the plant register. The cost of power, etc. consumed may be allocated direct where separate meters are available to measure the consumption of individual cost centres. In the absence of meters the consumption of each cost centre can be estimated on the basis of the horse-power rating of motors etc. and their normal usage. Other costs may be apportioned on a direct labour hour basis, or according to estimates of tool usage.

Material Services

Costs commonly accumulated under the heading of material services include those of:

(a)   Material control.
(b)   Purchasing, receiving, weighing, inspection, and storage of materials.

(c) Material handling.
(d) Stocktaking.
(e) Research, design, and development in regard to materials.

Where the services provided can be timed and expressed in terms of labour-hours, material service costs can be apportioned on that basis. Generally, this is not possible, however, and then some basis such as material cost; weight; the number of requisitions handled, etc., must be employed, although none of these is likely to be entirely equitable. The difficulty of handling components worth hundreds of pounds may be far less than that of handling a pound's worth of a cheap bulky material such as sand. Again, the cost of issuing 100 gems of a total weight of less than 28 grams, but which need to be counted and measured separately, is likely to be far greater than that of issuing a few bags of cement; and so on.

If, however, the value of the materials issued does present a fair measure of the service provided by the receiving, storekeeping, and material handling function, it is possible to absorb the cost of the service by applying a material cost percentage rate specially for this purpose; and this method is frequently adopted even where it is known not to be entirely equitable, since it is the only feasible way of apportioning such costs.

Example

The material services budget of Lion PLC for the year 19— is as follows:

	£
Material control	9 500
Purchasing	32 500
Receiving and weighing	10 800
Inspection (on receipt)	6 500
Handling	23 000
Storekeeping	125 000
Stocktaking and stores audit	14 500
	£221 800

Material service costs are to be absorbed by applying a material cost percentage rate. Budgeted material issues for the year are £27 725 000.

Material cost percentage rate to absorb material service costs:

$$\frac{\text{Material service costs}}{\text{Material issues}} \times 100 = \frac{£221\ 800}{£27\ 725\ 000} \times \frac{100}{1} = 0.8\%.$$

Personnel Services

The type of service cost relating to personnel services includes:

(a) Personnel management: selection and grading of employees, interviewing, advertising for personnel, and the keeping of employee records.
(b) Training.
(c) Canteen and similar facilities.
(d) Timekeeping, the computation of wages, payroll preparation, and the payment of wages.
(e) First aid, medical and dental services.

Apportionment on the basis of the number of personnel employed is frequently equitable, though not always. There may, for instance, be circumstances in which such a method would unfairly burden one centre to the advantage of another. This would be the case where the personnel of some department receive bonuses that involve the compilation of additional records and considerable calculations, whilst the members of another department are paid a 'straight time' wage. It would be unfair, too, where training costs are much higher in one department than another, as in an airline, where it is far more expensive to train air-crew than ground staff.

Production Services

Many production costs that are indirect in relation to the product are capable of allocation direct to a production cost centre as costs within its control. Such costs are not production service costs, this term being reserved for the costs of service departments concerned with production, as against the costs of the production departments themselves. Typical production service costs are those relating to:

(a)   Production control, planning and progressing; production records.
(b)   Rate fixing and work study.
(c)   Production research.
(d)   Development e.g. the cost of operating an experimental installation before beginning normal production by a new or improved technique.

Sometimes a single cost centre is set up for all production services, but it is quite possible to provide a separate centre for each separate service e.g. work study.

Where it is feasible to estimate the cost of services supplied to individual cost centres, as when records are maintained of the time expended upon work studies for individual centres, direct allocation of some costs to production cost centres may be possible. Generally, however, it is necessary to apportion production service costs either on the basis of technical estimates of the services provided to each section, or on a direct labour-hour or machine-hour basis.

Bases of Apportionment

The following table amplifies what has already been stated with regard to the bases of apportionment commonly used in connection with overhead costs other than those bases concerned solely with selling and distribution. Where several bases are stated the most common or most appropriate basis is listed first.

Bases of Apportionment

Canteen	Number of employees. Total wages.	Unless the extent to which the canteen is used varies greatly between departments.
Caretaking	Area of floor space. Value of buildings.	
Charitable subscriptions and donations	Number of Employees. Total wages.	Unless treated as a 'non-costing' item.

Cleaning:		
Buildings	Area of floor space.	Unless inequitable.
Windows	Area of windows.	
Depreciation:		
Buildings	Area of floor space.	
	Cubic capacity.	
	Value.	
Plant and machinery	Cost or written-down value.	Details of actual cost obtainable from an analysis of plant register.
Vehicles	Cost or written-down value.	Details of actual cost obtainable from an analysis of vehicle register.
Design	Chargeable man-hours.	Allocated per time sheets.
Drawing office	Number of drawings made.	
	Chargeable man-hours.	Allocated per time sheets.
Electric lighting	Area of floor space.	Unless separate meters are provided.
	Estimates of consumption based on wattage of lamps.	
	Number of lamps.	
Electric power	Kilowatt hours of plant.	Unless separate meters are provided.
Fire prevention	Area of buildings.	Possibly weighted where fire risk varies in different processes.
	Cubic capacity of buildings.	
	Value of buildings, stock, etc.	
	Estimated usage.	Unless separate meters are provided.
Goods transport	Tonne miles operated.	
	Miles run.	
	100 cubic metres of materials transported.	
	Litres of liquid transported.	
	Value of goods transported.	
Heating	Area of floor space.	The heat consumption of processes requiring heat – as distinct from the mere heating of buildings – should be separately metered and charged direct to the process concerned.
	Cubic capacity of building.	
Holiday pay	Total wages.	Unless accumulated on the payroll itself on a cost centre basis.
House magazine	Number of personnel employed.	Unless used also for external publicity.
Idle time		Should always to be accumulated by cost centres; otherwise the information is useless for cost control.
Inspection	1000 parts.	
	Value of items inspected.	
Insurance:		
Accident	Total wages.	Unless the probability of accident is greater in some departments than in others, when weighting must be resorted to.
	Number of employees.	

Buildings	Area of floor space. Cubic metres capacity. Value of building.	
Employers' liability	Total wages. Number of employees.	
Loss of profits	Treated as an administration cost and apportioned therewith.	More frequently regarded as a non- costing item.
Plant & machinery	Value.	
Vehicles	Number. Value.	Unless separately recorded.
Jigs, tools & fixtures	Machine operating hours. Chargeable man-hours required to produce particular tools, etc.	
Lighting	Area of floor space. Number of lamps. Wattage of lamps.	
Maintenance: Buildings	Area of floor space. Value of building (amongst a group).	Maintenance costs are usually recorded separately, building by building, and apportionment amongst buildings is not usually required.
Plant & machinery	Value of machinery.	Normally recorded separately, machine by machine.
Vehicles	Value of vehicles.	Normally recorded separately, vehicle by vehicle.
Material handling	Number of requisitions handled. 100 cubic metres of materials handled. Number of employees served. Value of materials handled.	
Material storage	100 cubic metres of materials handled. Value of materials stored. Number of requisitions handled.	
Medical, dental, and first-aid	Number of employees. Total wages.	Unless medical examination is confined to certain trades or grades.
National Insurance	Number of Employees. Total wages.	Usually allocated specifically to cost centres.
Oil and grease	Estimated usage.	Machine-hours operated or transport-miles run may assist in the making of the estimate. Generally, there is a direct charge to the centres using the materials.
Passenger transport	Number of passenger-miles	
Pattern-making	Chargeable man-hours employed. Number of patterns made.	Per time sheets.
Pensions	Total wages. Number of employees.	Unless allocated direct to cost centres.
Personnel department	Number of employees. Total wages.	

Planning and progress	Machine operating hours. Direct labour hours.	
Power	Kilowatt hours of plant. Machine operating hours.	Frequently separately metered.
Production control	Machine operating hours. Direct labour hours.	
Profit-sharing payments	Number of employees. Total wages.	Unless treated as a 'non-costing' item.
Purchasing	Value of materials. Number of orders placed.	
Rates	Area of floor space. Cubic metres capacity of building. Value of particular buildings or floors therein.	
Recreation	Number of employees. Total wages.	
Rent or equivalent rent charge	Area of floor space. Cubic metres capacity of building. Value of particular buildings or floors therein.	
Storage	Number of requisitions handled. 100 cubic metres of material stored. Litres of liquid stored. Value of materials stored.	
Superannuation	Total wages. Number of employees.	Usually allocated direct to cost centres.
Supervision	Number of employees. Total wages.	Unless some centres require far more supervision than is apparent from a consideration of the personnel employed or their total remuneration.
Telephone: Calls	Number of calls made.	Unless records of the actual cost of each call are maintained and used as the basis of direct charges.
Provision of instruments	Number of stations.	
Time office	Number of employees. Total wages.	
Training	Number of trainees.	Unless the cost of training is sufficiently high to justify the separate recording of the cost of training individuals or groups.
Transport	Number of vehicle-operating hours.	
Ventilation	Area of floor space. Cubic metre capacity.	Unless made necessary by some particular process.
Wages department	Number of employees. Total wages.	Unless the partial application of bonus schemes etc., make the cost of paying certain personnel far greater than that of paying others.

Washrooms etc	Number of employees.
	Total wages.
Watching and patrolling	Area of floor space.
	Value of buildings, stocks, etc.
Window cleaning & maintenance	Area of windows.
Work study	Number of studies made.
	Number of employees served.
	Number of chargeable man-hours occupied by the studies.

Note: The degree of analysis suggested by this apportionment table is only feasible in large businesses, and even then the cost involved in such analysis may not be exceeded by the value to management of the full cost information produced. Apportionment based on faulty logic as to what is fair in certain circumstances may produce misleading costs.

Example

Engineering Products PLC is divided for costing purposes into the following four departments, each of which is regarded as a cost centre:

> A. Machine shop
> B. Plate and welding shop
> C. Assembly shop
> D. Maintenance department

Production overheads for a month were as follows:

Building services:	£	£
Rent and rates	2 400	
Depreciation of buildings	700	
Electric light	500	
Maintenance of buildings	1 300	
Insurance of buildings	700	
		5 600

Equipment services:	£	£
Electric power	3 000	
Depreciation of equipment (reducing-balance basis)	2 100	
Insurance of equipment	900	
		6 000

Production services:		
Supervision salaries	20 000	
Works clerks' salaries	10 000	
Inspection	5 000	
General expenses	800	
		35 800

Material services:		
Central stores	4 000	
Insurance of stock	400	
		4 400

Personnel services:		
Timekeepers	5 000	
Canteen and welfare	2 500	
Insurance – employers' liability ˙	900	
		8 400

Miscellaneous:		
National Insurance (A, £780; B, £520; C, £1040; D, £260)	2 600	
Packing materials (Dept. C)	1 000	
		3 600

The following additional information is available:

	A	B	C	D	Total
Total wages	£30 000	£20 000	£40 000	£10 000	£100 000
Number of personnel	40	20	$47\frac{1}{2}$	$7\frac{1}{2}$	115
Area (square metres)	10 000	5 000	15 000	2 000	32 000
Written-down value of equipment	£40 000	£25 000	£10 000	£15 000	£90 000
Average stock	£20 000	£10 000	£5 000	£5 000	£40 000
Material consumed	£100 000	£40 000	£30 000	£20 000	£190 000
Effective kilowattage of equipment	150	20	30	20	220
Chargeable hours of maintenance service	1000	1500	500	—	3000

Maintenance materials are stored in the maintenance department. It is estimated that the inspectors spend their time as follows:

Department A:	50%
Department B:	20%
Department C:	30%

All machines are used for approximately the same percentage of total time. It is estimated that the cost of electricity for plating and welding is £500 per period.

Maintenance materials were used as follows: Department A, £10 000; Department B, £8000; Department C, £2000.

Required:

Show the allotment of production overheads to the three production departments. Do not forget maintenance department wages.

It will be observed that expenditure is allotted first to all four departments, and that maintenance costs are then allotted according to the work performed for each production department. This is a relatively simple case as there is only one service department. The more complex problems that arise where there are several service departments are considered in the following pages.

COST ALLOTMENT SHEET						
Production				Period ended...........19.....		
	Basis	A	B	C	D	Total
		£	£	£	£	£
Building Services	Area	1 750	870	2 630	350	5 600
Equipment Services:						
Power	Effective kilowattage	1 700	230	340	230	2 500
	Specific		500			500
Depreciation & Insurance of Equipment	Written-down value	1 330	830	340	500	3 000
Production Services:						
Works Clerks' Salaries and General Expenses	Total Wages	3 240	2 160	4 320	1 080	10 800
Supervision Salaries	Number of Personnel	6 960	3 480	8 260	1 300	20 000
Inspection	Specific	2 500	1 000	1 500	—	5 000

	Basis	A £	B £	C £	D £	Total £
Material Services:						
Central Stores	Material Consumed	2 350	940	710	–	4 000
Insurance of Stock	Average Stock	200	100	50	50	400
Personnel Services:						
Timekeepers, Canteen and Welfare	Number of Personnel	2 610	1 300	3 100	490	7 500
Employers' Liability	Total Wages	270	180	360	90	900
Maintenance						
Wages	–	–	–	–	10 000	10 000
Materials	–	–	–	–	20 000	20 000
Miscellaneous:						
National Insurance	Specific	780	520	1 040	260	2 600
Packing Materials	Specific	–	–	1 000	–	1 000
Departmental Totals before Apportionment of Service Department Costs		£23 690	12 110	23 650	34 350	93 800
Apportionment and Allocation of Costs of Department D:						
Material (Specific)		10 000	8 000	2 000	20 000	–
Wages and Overheads (Chargeable Hours)		4 780	7 180	2 390	14 350	–
Costs incurred		£38 470	£27 290	£28 040	£0	£93 800

To take this example a stage further, assume that budgeted overheads for the three production departments were A: £40 000; B: £256 000 and C: £30 400, and that these costs were absorbed to production on the basis of a rate for each direct labour-hour. The hours expected to be worked in each department were:

A 40 operatives × 40 hours × 4 weeks = 6400 hours ÷ £40 000 = £6.25 per hour
B 20 operatives × 40 hours × 4 weeks = 3200 hours ÷ £25 600 = £8.00 per hour
C 47½ operatives × 40 hours × 4 weeks = 7600 hours ÷ £30 400 = £4.00 per hour

The actual hours worked in each department were: *A* 6600 hours, *B* 3000 hours and *C* 7500 hours. The overhead accounts for the three departments would appear as follows:

Department A Overhead Account

	£		£
Overhead cost incurred	38 470	Work-in-progress: A overhead absorbed (6600 × £6.25)	41 250
Costing p/l overhead over-absorbed	2 780		
	£41 250		£41 250

Department B Overhead Account

	£		£
Overhead cost incurred	27 290	Work-in-progress: B overhead absorbed (3000 × £8)	24 000
		Costing p/l overhead under-absorbed	3 290
	£27 290		£27 290

Department C Overhead Account

	£		£
Overhead cost incurred	28 040	Work-in-progress: C overhead absorbed (7500 × £4)	30 000
Costing p/l overhead over-absorbed	1 960		
	£30 000		£30 000

Reciprocal Service Costs

The apportionment of service department costs presents, in practice, certain difficulties, which have not so far been considered, for many service centres provide services to other service centres. For example, when a concern produces its own electricity, the power house will provide the building service centre with current for heating and lighting, whilst that centre will provide the power house with building accommodation. Any apportionment of power house costs to the building services cost centre will serve to increase the costs of that centre and hence add to the costs of the power house. If this additional cost is then apportioned to the centres consuming electricity, it too will increase the cost of building services, and hence the cost of those services to the power house. This goes on *ad infinitum*, the adjustments gradually decreasing in amount, as in the illustrated example below. It will be obvious why the method used is sometimes referred to as the vicious circle or continued allotment method.

Suppose in the example above that there were five departments:

A	Machine shop	Overheads incurred	£33 690
B	Plate and welding shop	Overheads incurred	£20 110
C	Assembly shop	Overheads incurred	£25 600
D	Maintenance department	Overheads incurred	£14 350
E	Power house	Overheads incurred	£17 640

This arrangement gives three production departments and two service departments, each of which use the services of the other. It is necessary to make an assessment of the proportion of maintenance and power house services rendered to other departments as follows:

D	Maintenance	A:	40%
		B:	30%
		C:	20%
		E:	10%
E	Power house	A:	35%
		B:	25%
		C:	25%
		D:	15%

An apportionment based on continued allotment can be made:

	A £	B £	C £	D £	E £
Cost incurred	33 690	20 110	25 600	14 350	17 640
Power house re-allocated	6 174	4 410	4 410	2 646	(17 640)
Maintenance re-allocated	6 797	5 099	3 400	(16 996)	1 700
Power house re-allocated	595	425	425	255	(1 700)
Maintenance re-allocated	102	77	51	(255)	25
Power house re-allocated	11	7	7	–	(25)
Costs to be absorbed by Production Departments	£47 369	£30 128	£33 893	–	–

Note:　At the last allocation the maintenance department was ignored, being considered too small an amount, and the power house cost was apportioned to the production departments on the basis of 35/85; 25/85 and 25/85 respectively.

A similar apportionment can be made by algebraic means using simultaneous equations:

> Let X = Total overheads of power house
> Let Y = Total overheads of maintenance department

The two equations can be formulated as follows:

$$X = £17\,640 + .1Y$$
$$Y = £14\,350 + .15X$$

These formulae can be re-arranged and multiplied out to eliminate the decimals. Thus four further formulae are derived:

(i) $10X - Y$ $= £176\,400$
(ii) $-1.5X + 10Y = £143\,500$
(iii) $100X - 10Y = £1\,764\,000$　　　Equation (i) multiplied by 10
(iv) $98.5X$ $= £1\,907\,500$　　　Equation (ii) added to (iii)
Therefore X $= £19\,365$

> 35% of X should be allocated to A = £6778
> 25% of X should be allocated to B = £4841
> 25% of X should be allocated to C = £4841

Now that X is known, Y can be calculated by substitution:

$$10 \times £19\,365 - Y = £176\,400$$
$$£193\,650 - £176\,400 = Y$$
$$£17\,250 = Y$$

> 40% of Y should be allocated to A = £6900
> 30% of Y should be allocated to B = £5175
> 20% of Y should be allocated to C = £3450

	A £	B £	C £
Cost incurred	33 690	20 110	25 600
Power house	6 778	4 841	4 841
Maintenance	6 900	5 175	3 450
	£47 368	£30 126	£33 891

Slight differences from the first solution are caused by rounding. If more than two service departments are involved the algebra becomes more complicated.

Further analysis reveals:

		£
Department A	Cost incurred – below budget	1530
	Hours worked – above budget (200 × £6.25)	1250
	Total over-absorbed	£2780
Department B	Cost incurred – in excess of budget	1690
	Hours worked – below budget (200 × £8)	1600
	Total under-absorbed	£3290
Department C	Cost incurred – below budget	2360
	Hours worked below budget (100 × £4)	(400)
	Total over-absorbed	£1960

Cost Accounting—A Complete Example

In practice the apportionment of service department costs is not always put through the accounts; any information is transmitted by memorandum. Where, however, there is a fully integrated cost and financial accounting system and such apportionments are recorded in the accounts, the records will appear somewhat as shown in the following illustration.

Example

Albert's Limited, a medium-sized engineering company, operates a system of budgetary control as a result of which it employs pre-determined rates of cost apportionment and overhead absorption. In the month ending 30 June 19—, the following transactions took place:

(1) Materials were issued as follows:

	£
Production	324 000
Selling	200
Distribution	2 000
Administration	500
Building services	400
Equipment services	250
Material services	400
Personnel services	100
Production services	3 000
	£330 850

(2) The payroll analysis disclosed that the wages earned were:

	£
Production	276 000
Selling	9 000
Distribution	5 000
Administration	5 000

	£
Building services	500
Equipment services	3 000
Material services	4 000
Personnel services	2 200
Production services	5 000
	£309 700

(3)   Expense was allocated as follows:

	£
Production	2 500
Selling	2 800
Distribution	2 800
Administration	2 500
Building services	5 000
Equipment services	9 250
Material services	600
Personnel services	2 500
Production services	500
	£28 450

(4)   Product direct costs transferable to work-in-progress during the period were:

	£
Material cost	299 000
Wages	265 000
Expense	100
	£564 100

(5)   Building service costs are apportioned on the basis of floor area; the pre-determined apportionment rate being 10p per square metre.
The floor area occupied by the various departments is as follows:

	square metres
Production	29 000
Selling	13 000
Distribution	3 000
Administration	4 000
Building services	0
Equipment services	3 000
Material services	3 000
Personnel services	4 000
Production services	4 000

(6)   Equipment service costs are, so far as possible, allocated direct to other centres. Equipment maintenance service is charged at 25p per chargeable man-hour.

	Depreciation Power, Insurance etc.	Equipment Maintenance – Chargeable Man-hours
Production	8000	9000
Selling	1000	2600
Distribution	800	2400

	Depreciation Power, Insurance etc.	Equipment Maintenance – Chargeable Man-hours
Administration	100	400
Building services	50	20
Material services	100	–
Personnel services	50	40
Production services	450	400

(7) Material service costs are apportioned by employing a pre-determined rate of 4% of material cost.

(8) The pre-determined rate of apportionment applicable to personnel service costs is 5% of total wages.

(9) Production service costs are apportioned to production cost centres at the rate of 5p per labour-hour. Employees of those centres worked 198 000 labour-hours in the period.

(10) Production overheads are absorbed by means of separate cost centre hourly rates as follows:

	£
Machine Centre 1	1.50 per machine-hour
Machine Centre 2	0.75 per machine-hour
Assembly	0.25 per direct labour-hour.

The following information is supplied with regard to the period in question:

Machine Centre 1 worked 28 000 machine-hours
Machine Centre 2 worked 40 000 machine-hours
Assembly worked 48 000 direct labour-hours.

(11) Selling, distribution, and administration costs are to be charged direct to the profit and loss account.

(12) Under- or over-apportioned costs and under- or over-absorbed overheads are to be charged to the profit and loss account of the period.

(13) Work-in-progress at the beginning of the period was £156 000, whilst the production cost of production completed during the period was £659 000. The opening stock of finished products was £323 000, and the production cost of those sold £645 000. Sales for the period were £710 100.

Required:

(i) A statement in columnar form showing the allotment of primary costs for the period to production, selling, distribution, and administration.

(ii) Summary accounts relating to the following cost centres:
    production; selling; distribution; administration; building services; equipment services; material services; personnel services; production services;
    together with the following additional accounts:
    work-in-progress; finished goods stock; production cost of sales; sales; production overhead absorbed.
    These accounts may be in abbreviated 'T' account form, showing only those details essential to their understanding.

(iii) Statement of profit or loss for the period.

(i)

SUMMARY OF COSTS ALLOTTED (Period ended 30 June 19—)									
Costs	Cost Centres								
	Production	Selling	Distribution	Administration	Building Services	Equipment Services	Material Services	Personnel Services	Production Services
Primary:	£	£	£	£	£	£	£	£	£
Material	324 000	200	2 000	500	400	250	400	100	3 000
Wages	276 000	9 000	5 000	5 000	500	3 000	4 000	2 200	5 000
Expense	2 500	2 800	2 800	2 500	5 000	9 250	600	2 500	500
	602 500								
Product Direct:									
Material	299 000 Cr.								
Wages	265 000 Cr.								
Expense	100 Cr.								
	38 400	12 000	9 800	8 000	5 900	12 500	5 000	4 800	8 500
Building Services:									
10p per square metre	2 900	1 300	300	400	6 300 Cr.	300	300	400	400
Equipment Services:									
Actual	8 000	1 000	800	100	50	10 550 Cr.	100	50	450
25p per equipment service man-hour	2 250	650	600	100	5	3 715 Cr.	–	10	100
Material Services:									
4% of material cost	12 960	8	80	20	16	10	16 / 5 234 Cr.	4	120
Personnel Services:									
5% of wages	13 800	450	250	250	25	150	200	110 / 5 485 Cr.	250
Production Services:									
5p per labour-hour	9 900								9 900 Cr.
	£88 210	£15 408	£11 830	£8870	£304 Cr.	£1 305 Cr.	£382	£111 Cr.	£80 Cr.
	Balances being indirect product costs of the main activities of the company.				Balances being service centre costs *over*/under apportioned.				

(ii)

Production

	£		£
Cost centre direct:		Work-in-progress:	
Material cost	324 000	Product direct material cost	299 000
Wages	276 000	Product direct wages	265 000
Expense	2 500	Product direct expense	100
		Balance being production overheads allocated to production cost centres c/d	38 400
	£602 500		£602 500

	£		£
Balance b/d	38 400	Balance c/d	88 210
Cost centre indirect:			
Building services	2 900		
Personnel services	3 800		
Equipment services (£8000			
+ £2250)	10 250		
Material services	12 960		
Production services	9 900		
	£88 210		£88 210
Balance b/d (production		Production overheads absorbed	84 000
overheads incurred)	88 210		
		p/l account – under-absorption	4 210
	£88 210		£88 210

Selling

	£		£
Direct:		p/l account	15 408
Material cost	200		
Wages	9 000		
Expense	2 800		
	12 000		
Indirect:			
Building services	1 300		
Personnel services	450		
Equipment services (£1000			
+ £650)	1 650		
Material services	8		
	£15 408		£15 408

Distribution

	£		£
Direct:		p/l account	11 830
Material cost	2 000		
Wages	5 000		
Expense	2 800		
	9 800		
Indirect:			
Building services	300		
Personnel services	250		
Equipment services (£800 +			
£600)	1 400		
Material services	80		
	£11 830		£11 830

Administration

	£		£
Direct:		p/l account	8 870
Material Cost	500		
Wages	5 000		
Expense	2 500		
	8 000		
Indirect:			
Building services	400		
Personnel services	250		
Equipment services (£100 + £100)	200		
Material services	20		
	£8 870		£8 870

Building Services

	£		£
Direct:		Apportioned to other centres	6 300
Material cost	400		
Wages	500		
Expense	5 000		
	5 900		
Indirect:			
Personnel services	25		
Equipment services (£50 + £5)	55		
Material services	16		
p/l account – over-apportionment	304		
	£6 300		£6 300

Equipment Services

	£		£
Direct:		Allocated to other centres	10 550
Material cost	250	Apportioned to other centres	3 715
Wages	3 000		
Expense	9 250		
	12 500		
Indirect:			
Building services	300		
Personnel services	150		
Material services	10		
p/l account – over-apportionment	1 305		
	£14 265		£14 265

Material Services

	£		£
Direct:		Apportioned to other centres	5218
Material cost	400	Contra – material services	16
Wages	4000	p/l account – under-apportionment	382
Expense	600		
	5000		
Indirect:			
Building services	300		
Personnel services	200		
Equipment services	100		
Contra – material services	16		
	£5616		£5616

Personnel Services

	£		£
Direct:		Apportioned to other centres	5375
Material cost	100	Contra – personnel services	110
Wages	2200		
Expense	2500		
	4800		
Indirect:			
Building services	400		
Equipment services (£50 + £10)	60		
Material services	4		
Contra – personnel services	110		
p/l account – over-apportionment	111		
	£5485		£5485

Production Services

	£		£
Direct:		Apportioned to production	
Material cost	3000	cost centres	9900
Wages	5000		
Expense	500		
	8500		
Indirect:			
Building services	400		
Personnel services	250		
Equipment services (£450 +			
£100)	550		
Material services	120		
p/l account – over-apportionment	80		
	£9900		£9900

Production Overhead Absorbed

	£		£
Balance c/d	84 000	Work-in-progress:	
		Mach. C. 1—28 000 hours at £1.50	42 000
		Mach. C. 2—40 000 hours at 75p	30 000
		Assembly—48 000 hours at 25p	12 000
	£84 000		£84 000
Production overheads	£84 000	Balance b/d	£84 000

Work-in-progress

	£		£
Balance b/f	156 000	Finished goods	659 000
Production (product direct costs)	564 100	Balance c/d	145 100
Production overheads absorbed	84 000		
	£804 100		£804 100
Balance b/d	145 100		

Finished Goods

	£		£
Balance b/f	323 000	Production cost of sales	645 000
Work-in-progress	659 000	Balance c/d	337 000
	£982 000		£982 000
Balance b/d	337 000		

Production Cost of Sales

	£		£
Finished goods	645 000	Trading account	645 000

Sales

	£		£
Trading account	710 000	Sundry debtors	710 100

Trading and Profit and Loss Account

for the month ended............19....

		£
Sales		710 100
Less production cost of sales		645 000
Gross profit		65 100

	£	
Selling costs	15 408	
Distribution costs	11 830	
Administration costs	8 870	
		36 108
		28 992

Less net over-apportionment and under-absorption of costs through variations from the budgets*		2 792
Net profit		£28 200

* The net over-apportionment and over-absorption of costs is made up as follows:

	Under £	Over £
Building services	–	304
Equipment services	–	1305
Personnel services	–	111
Material services	382	–
Production services	–	80
Production	4210	–
	4592	£1800
	1800	
	£2792	

Overhead Absorption Rates

This is a convenient point at which to summarise what has been said with regard to overhead absorption rates, to define each and provide an illustration of its application.

Direct Materials Cost Percentage Rate. An actual or pre-determined rate of overhead absorption, which is calculated by dividing the cost to be absorbed by the materials cost incurred, or expected to be incurred, and expressing the result as a percentage.

Example

Budgeted production overheads to be absorbed	£56 000
Material cost expected to be incurred	£280 000

$$\text{Material cost percentage rate} = \frac{56\,000}{280\,000} \times 100 = 20\%.$$

Thus if the material cost of Job 99 is £180, production overhead absorbed by that job will be 20% of £180, namely £36.

Direct Wages Percentage Rate. An actual or pre-determined rate of overhead absorption, which is calculated by dividing the cost to be absorbed by the wages expended, or expected to be expended, and expressing the result as a percentage.

Example

Budgeted overheads to be absorbed	£56 000
Wages expected to be incurred	£112 000

$$\text{Wages percentage rate} = \frac{56\,000}{112\,000} \times 100 = 50\%.$$

Thus if the wages incurred on Job 99 are £80, production overheads absorbed by that job will be 50% of £80, namely £40.

Prime Cost Percentage Rate. An actual or pre-determined rate of overhead absorption, which is calculated by dividing the cost to be absorbed by the prime cost incurred or expected to be incurred and expressing the result as a percentage.

Example

Overheads to be absorbed	£56 000
Prime cost	£336 000

$$\text{Prime cost percentage rate} = \frac{56\,000}{336\,000} \times 100 = 16.66\%.$$

Thus if the prime cost of Job 99 is £260, production overheads absorbed by that job will be 16.66% of £260 namely £43.3.

Labour-Hour Rate. An actual or pre-determined rate of overhead absorption, which is calculated by dividing the cost to be absorbed by the direct labour-hours expended or expected to be expended.

Example

Budgeted overheads to be absorbed	£56 000
Number of direct labour-hours	33 600

$$\text{Labour-hour rate} = \frac{£56\,000}{33\,600} = £1.66.$$

Thus if 36 direct labour-hours are spent on Job 99, production overheads absorbed by that job will be $36 \times £1.66 = £59.76$.

Machine-Hour Rate. An actual or pre-determined rate of overhead absorption, which is calculated by dividing the cost to be absorbed by the number of hours for which a machine or machines are operated or expected to be operated.

Example 1

Budgeted overheads to be absorbed	£56 000
Budgeted number of machine-hours	22 400

$$\text{Machine-hour rate} = \frac{£56\,000}{22\,400} = £2.50$$

Thus if Job 99 takes 12 machine-hours, production overheads absorbed by that job will be 12 × £2.50 = £30.

In some companies the costs of operating a machine are summarised for a period, say a year, and divided by the number of hours the machine is expected to work in a year, so that an hourly rate that can be used in pricing or estimating is computed.

Example 2

A machine costing £28 000, including installation costs of £400, has an anticipated life of five years, with a residual value of £500. It is to be depreciated on a straight-line basis. From this information and the following particulars compute a machine-hour rate:

	£
Cost p.a.	
Insurance	400
Rent and rates	1250
Repairs and maintenance	5500
Consumable stores	3000
Production services (apportioned)	2600

Power costs 15p per working hour.

The year contains 250 working days of 8 hours each, but it is anticipated that the machine will be idle 15% of this time. The machine-hour rate is to be computed on the basis of anticipated working hours.

Machine-Hour Rate Computation

Machine .... Period ending............................

	Per Annum	Per Working Hour
	£	£
Fixed costs:		
Depreciation	5 600	
Insurance	400	
Rent and rates and building service	1 250	
Repairs and maintenance	5 500	
Consumable stores	3 000	
Production services (apportioned)	2 600	
	18 350	10.79
Variable costs:		
Power	255	0.15
	£18 605	£10.94

Note: From the information given in the example, it is not possible to classify the costs concerned as variable or fixed in a more realistic manner. In practice a number of the costs shown as fixed would vary with the number of hours worked and, strictly, then should be shown as variable.

Cost Unit Rate. An actual or pre-determined rate of overhead absorption, which is calculated by dividing the cost to be absorbed by the number of cost units produced or expected to be produced.

Example

Budgeted overheads to be absorbed	£56 000
Expected number of units of production	28 000

$$\text{Cost unit rate} = \frac{£56\,000}{28\,000} = £2 \text{ per unit}$$

Whilst such a rate is frequently associated with standard costing, such a system is not essential to its use: many businesses absorb costs on the basis of a rate per tonne, rate per litre etc.

Where a single product is produced or products are basically similar, the cost unit rate is the simplest method of absorbing overhead. It is frequently possible to reduce even unlike products to some common factor by applying weights.

Relative Merits of Particular Bases of Absorption

It is proper to employ a *direct materials cost percentage rate* only where material cost forms the major part of total cost and where overheads tend to relate to material cost. This is rarely the case, except when the cost absorbed is connected with the handling of materials, and even then only when the prices paid for materials give a fair measure of the work involved in their handling. Since changes in material price are often unaccompanied by equivalent changes in overheads, this rate is likely to prove unsatisfactory in times of changing commodity prices. Is it fair to charge more overheads to a product that is constructed from expensive material? Despite this, a material cost percentage rate is sometimes used for the absorption of storage, receiving, purchasing, and handling costs in the absence of a more satisfactory alternative.

The direct wages percentage rate presents little difficulty as regards either calculation or application, and since it relates overhead absorption to labour time, albeit indirectly, it is preferable to the materials percentage method. It can properly be employed only when wages form the greater part of total cost and the wages paid give a fair indication of the time required to complete a particular job. This may be the case with either manual or machine operations, but is unlikely where workers differ in skill, age or sex, since the different classes will then receive dissimilar hourly rates. Is it fair to charge lower overheads to work completed by an apprentice than to a similar job completed by a qualified tradesman?

The wages percentage rate is perhaps more likely to be equitable when employed on a departmental or cost centre basis, than when used on a factory-wide one; since there is normally a greater similarity of wage rates within a small group than within a large one. Unless there is uniform efficiency and productivity throughout the section in question, the wages percentage rate is unlikely to provide satisfactory results where workers are remunerated on a piece-work basis; since the same use of facilities may be made by employees who produce differing outputs and hence receive differing remuneration.

It has already been stressed that the wages percentage rate is really suitable only when wages form the dominant part of total cost e.g. in a hand-operated or skill-oriented situation. If the method is used, where machine time rather than labour is the important factor, there is a danger that costs produced will fail to recognise the cost of machine time and exaggerate errors in labour-time booking since the wages percentage rate is likely to be relatively high – perhaps 100 to 300 % or more of direct wages.

The third type of percentage rate, the *prime cost percentage rate*, is also easy to compute and to apply since it is based upon data collected for other purposes. It can properly be used, however, only where prime cost gives a reasonable indication of time in process: this generally means that wages must be a function of time and that the ratio of material cost to wages must be constant from job to job and product to product. As circumstances in which this happens rarely occur, the use of the prime cost percentage rate usually results in an inequitable allotment of overhead.

Where most work is completed manually or upon machines having a low operating cost in relation to the cost of labour, the *labour-hour rate* is the most suitable rate to use since, as most production overheads vary according to time, labour-hours reflect their incidence most satisfactorily. Whilst the labour-hour rate does not suffer from the disadvantages of the wages percentage rate, as it is unaffected by factors such as skill and age, which cause variations in rates of pay, it is subject to the disadvantage that labour-time records have to be specially maintained, if they are not being kept for some other purpose. Where machinery forms the dominant element in production the labour-hour method is no more suitable than is the wages percentage rate.

In such cases, where the cost of using machinery forms an important element of overhead cost, machine time provides the most equitable basis for the absorption of overhead. *Machine-hour rates* are also appropriate for use when a worker or group of workers tends several machines, since in such circumstances accurate time booking against particular units of work is almost impossible. It is sometimes suggested that a disadvantage of the machine-time method is that the keeping of machine times will involve additional clerical work, but modern management is likely to require machine utilisation records for production control purposes in any event.

Cost unit rates, based on the standard labour or machine-hour content of the standard unit, are commonly employed as part of a system of standard costing and budgetary control, and such rates, or labour-hour and machine-hour rates, dependent upon which of these factors is the more important, form what are generally accepted to be the most scientific methods of absorbing production overhead.

Accounting for Selling and Distribution Costs

Up to the present it has been suggested that because of the difficulty of allotting them scientifically, selling and distribution costs should be treated as direct charges to the profit and loss account of the period during which they occur: no attempt is then made to allocate or apportion them to particular units sold or distributed on the grounds that an inaccurate apportionment is worse than useless. However, this does not mean that selling and distribution costs are never allocated or apportioned. A few concerns record in their cost accounts the allocation of selling and distribution costs to territories, products or order sizes, but it is more usual to add a fixed percentage for these costs for purposes of price fixing or estimating, and to confine detailed analysis to memorandum records. Recent years have, however, seen increased interest in the accounting for and control of selling and distribution costs.

Detailed Analysis of Selling and Distribution Costs

The type of information management requires regarding selling and distribution costs is that which will enable it to decide:

(a)   The territories in which it should endeavour to expand.
(b)   The type of customer it should seek (or occasionally avoid).
(c)   The minimum order size it should regard as acceptable.
(d)   The products it should push.
(e)   The distribution channels it should employ.
(f)   The salesmen to promote, encourage, train, rebuke, or drop.

The most common types of classification used in the analysis of selling and distribution costs are:

1.   Products or product groups.
2.   Sales territories.
3.   Channels of distribution (e.g. wholesale, retail, chain store etc.) in order to ensure an equitable price-structure.
4.   Order sizes (to assess whether savings on large orders warrant the allowance of quantity discounts etc.).
5.   Salesmen.
6.   Solicitation methods (e.g. advertisement, direct mail, salesman's call etc.).
7.   Delivery methods (e.g. road, rail, air, etc.).
8.   Customer or customer type (e.g. chemists, grocers, etc.).
9.   Warehouse or store.
10.   Credit terms (e.g. cash, credit and hire-purchase sales).

SEMINAR EXERCISES

4.1   The Carreau Company Limited are manufacturers of decorative tiles, operating three manufacturing processes in which tile blanks are produced, then decorated, and finished. The Company makes blanks for other manufacturers to use, and will decorate and finish blanks from other manufacturers.

The processes are highly mechanised, with energy supplied from a central power house and machine repair services provided by the maintenance department.

The overhead budgets of the production departments have been compiled by allocating the service departments on the following basis:

Power house	Blank making	45%
	Decorating	25%
	Finishing	20%
	Maintenance	10%
Maintenance	Blank making	40%
	Decorating	25%
	Finishing	20%
	Power house	15%

The overhead budgets for each four-week period are: £50000 for blank making, £25000 for decorating and £16000 for finishing. The overheads are absorbed to production on the basis of machine-hours, using as standard hours available: blank making 10000 hours, decorating 6000 hours and finishing 3000 hours.

During September, overheads incurred by the departments were:

Blank making	Decorating	Finishing	Power House	Maintenance
£28 300	£16 400	£15 700	£19 600	£12 700

Actual machine-hours worked by the departments were recorded as:

Blank making	Decorating	Finishing
9000	5420	3700

Required:

(a) Write up the overhead accounts for each of the production departments.

(16 marks)

(b) Prepare a simple statement to explain overheads over- or under-absorbed in each production department.

(6 marks)

Note: Absorption rates to be calculated to three decimal places.

(Total 22 marks)

4.2 A factory with three departments uses a single production overhead absorption rate expressed as a percentage of direct wages cost. It has been suggested that departmental overhead absorption rates would result in more accurate job costs. Set out below are the budgeted and actual data for the previous period, together with information relating to Job 2843.

Budgeted data

Department:	Direct Wages £000's	Direct Labour-Hours 000's	Machine-Hours 000's	Production Overheads £000's
Casting	50	20	80	240
Assembly	200	100	20	60
Finishing	50	50	–	150
	300	170	100	450

Actual data

Department:				
Casting	60	24	90	260
Assembly	160	90	28	56
Finishing	60	60	–	160
	280	174	118	476

During this period Job 2843 incurred actual costs and actual times in the departments as shown below:

Department:	Material £	Direct Wages £	Direct Labour-Hours	Machine-Hours
Casting	240	200	40	80
Assembly	120	120	80	20
Finishing	20	20	20	–

After adding production overheads to prime cost, one third is added to production cost for gross profit. This assumes that a reasonable profit is earned after deducting administration, selling and distribution costs.

Required:

(a)   Calculate the current overhead absorption rate and using that rate calculate the production overheads charged to Job 2843 and state the production cost, expected gross profit and price of this job.   (3 marks)

(b)   Comment on the suggestion that departmental overhead absorption rates would result in more accurate job costs, and compute such rates, briefly explaining your reason for each rate.   (7 marks)

(c)   Using the rates calculated in (b) above, show the overheads, by department and in total, that would apply to Job 2843.   (3 marks)

(d)   Show the over/under-absorption, by department and in total, for the period, using:
   (i)   the current rates in your answer to (a) above, and
   (ii)   your suggested rates to your answer to (b) above.   (9 marks)

(Total 22 marks)

4.3   Minim Limited manufactures two products at its small factory. Both products are passed through the Machine shop and the Assembly department. A canteen is also operated as a separate department. Next year's budget shows:

	Product A	Product B
Selling price (per unit)	£68	£75
Sales volume	1750 units	2750 units
Increase (decrease) in finished stocks	250 units	(250) units
Material cost (per unit)	£9	£6
Direct labour:	hours per unit	hours per unit
Machine shop (£4 per hour)	5	6
Assembly department		
(£3 per hour)	4	4
Machining:		
Machine shop	4	8
Assembly department	1	–

	Machine Shop £	Assembly Department £	Canteen £	Total £
Production overheads:				
Variable	28 000	9 000	–	37 000
Fixed	46 000	30 000	16 000	92 000
	£74 000	£39 000	£16 000	£129 000
Number of employees	30	18	2	
Floor area	8000 m²	2000 m²	2000 m²	

Required:

(a) Calculate an overhead absorption rate for each production department and the total budgeted cost per unit of each product; and briefly justify the methods of overhead absorption.   (20 marks)

(b) What will be the impact on budgeted profit, if, next year, the actual results are as predicted, except that sales and production of product A are 300 units higher than budget?   (5 marks)

                                                                          (Total 25 marks)

REVIEW QUESTIONS

4.1 Wollaton Weavers PLC are a large company in the clothing trade. The budget for next year reveals that the company operates three production and two service departments.

	Production £000's			Service £000's		Total £000's
	Weaving Dept	Proofing Dept	Finishing Dept	Personnel	Maintenance	
Direct materials	15 000	7 000	3 500	–	–	25 500
Direct wages	5 000	11 000	4 000			20 000
Indirect materials						
and wages	2 200	1 800	600	3 000	7 600	15 200
Power	10 400	2 000	400	200	1 600	14 600
Rent and rates						8 000
Factory administration and						
supervision						10 000
Machine insurance						2 400

Further data extracted from the budget:

Floor area (square metres)	6 000	13 500	3 000	6 000	1 500	30 000
Machine-hours	8 million	2 million	2 million	–	–	12 million
Direct labour-hours	5 900 000	8 850 000	2 950 000	–	–	17 700 000
Number of employees	450	3 000	300	50	150	3 950
Book value of plant	£4 million	£1 million	£1 million			£6 million

The maintenance department does not service the personnel department.

Required:

(a) Calculate suitable overhead absorption rates for the production departments.
                                                                          (18 marks)

(b) Comment on the suggestion that the company should use a single blanket absorption rate for overheads at the factory.   (7 marks)

                                                                          (Total 25 marks)

4.2 You have recently joined an industrial company as cost accountant. The company operates its own power generating plant as a service department, providing power, light and heat to all production departments.

The system for accounting for power plant costs is to apportion the costs incurred each month to the production departments on the basis of an engineer's estimate of their power consumption, made at the beginning of the year. This estimate is also the basis of the power cost apportionment in the budget.

It has been suggested that this system should be replaced by a two-part charge for power to production departments; the first part being an apportionment of the budgeted fixed cost of the generating plant, and the second a variable charge per unit used, derived from budgeted variable costs of the generator, when operated at standard efficiency.

Required:

In the light of your views on the reasons for charging out service department costs to production departments, comment on the present and proposed systems.

(18 marks)

4.3 Agricultural Engineering PLC is a manufacturing company operating three production departments. Shown below are next year's budgeted manufacturing costs, per unit, for each of the three lawn-mowers manufactured by the company.

	Hovver		Bovver		Super	
	£	£	£	£	£	£
	per unit	per unit	per unit	per unit	per unit	per unit
Direct materials		36.00		54		72.00
Direct wages:						
Machining department	15.00		12.00		21.00	
Assembly department	18.00		22.50		31.50	
Finishing department	9.00	42.00	4.50	39	3.00	55.50
Production overheads:						
Machining department	16.80		12.00		7.20	
Assembly department	9.00		11.25		15.75	
Finishing department	3.75	29.55	3.75	27	3.75	26.70
Total budgeted manufacturing cost per unit		£107.55		£120		£154.20

Prime costs are variable; production overhead contains both fixed and variable elements.

The company operates a full absorption costing system and next year's budgeted overhead absorption rates, based upon next year's budgeted overheads and activity, are:

Machining	Assembly	Finishing
£2.40 per machine-hour	50% of direct wages	£3.75 per unit

Next year's budgeted total direct wages for Assembly, analysed by product are:

Hovver	Bovver	Super
£237 600	£618 750	£220 500

Stocks of work-in-progress are not carried.

Required:

(a) Describe the circumstances in which it would be appropriate to use each of the absorption methods indicated in the question. (8 marks)

(b) Calculate next year's total budgeted overheads for each of the three departments in Agricultural Engineering PLC. (6 marks)

(c) Assume that next year the actual results are exactly as those predicted in the budget except that production of *Super* is 200 units higher than that budgeted and, as a consequence, the overheads over-absorbed in the three departments are:

Machining	Assembly	Finishing
£1260	£2520	£300

Analyse the overheads incurred in the machining and assembly departments between fixed and variable. (8 marks)

(Total 22 marks)

Section II
Cost Accounting Principles Applied

5
Job and Batch Costing

JOB COSTING

'Job costing is that form of specific order costing which applies where work is undertaken to customers' special requirements and each order is of comparatively short duration. The work is usually carried out within a factory or workshop and moves through processes and operations as a continuously identifiable unit.' (ICMA)

Job costing is used in businesses that perform work on specific jobs, orders, or contracts that can be identified throughout the various stages of production. A job cost system is thus one in which the costs incurred are allocated or apportioned to the job, which is the unit of cost. Job costing is usual in connection with machine tool manufacture, foundries, job printing, and general engineering, where each product is manufactured to the customer's requirements. It is also widely used for the costing of batches of similar articles such as shoes, or nuts and bolts, but when there is an element of standardisation in the product, standard costing should be used where possible. Job costing is a basic costing procedure and one that may be used in conjunction with other systems. For example, a business may manufacture machine tools specially to customers' requirements, and in doing so use standard parts and sub-assemblies that can be pre-costed: job costing will then be necessary only for the non-standard parts and for the final assembly details. Again, a business manufacturing standard lines may apply standard costing to its production operations but use job costing principles to ascertain the cost of toolroom and maintenance work, each job undertaken by such departments being regarded as a separate entity.

The main purpose of job costing is to determine the profit or loss made on each job and to be able to show the cost to date on stocks of work-in-progress at the end of an accounting period. Profit measurement serves as a check on the accuracy of the estimates on which prices have been quoted. Comparison of the job cost with the estimate or with the cost of similar jobs completed in the past helps to bring to light any inefficiencies that may have occurred in the course of production. Thus, job costing separates profitable jobs from unprofitable ones and provides a check on past estimates as well as a basis for estimating for similar work in the future. It is used to a considerable extent where government and other contracts are accepted on a *cost plus* basis (i.e. at a price based on an agreed cost + agreed percentage profit) or where quoted prices are subject to adjustment for subsequent changes in costs.

Job costing calls for the maintenance of adequate production control records. Each job must be given its individual works order number and the separate orders must be capable of identification at all stages of production.

Where customers' orders cover a number of different items, e.g. 12 different castings, these will normally be subdivided and issued to the works as a number of separate orders. Similarly, where an order for a very large quantity of parts is received, this should be split into separate batches so that job costs can be prepared without waiting for the completion of the entire order. Where orders are so split up, it is convenient to use one order number and to add an oblique stroke followed by 1, 2, 3 etc. to distinguish between the first, second, and other items on the customer's order, or between the first, second, or other batch in a large order. Every material requisition and time sheet entry must contain the appropriate works order number to ensure that the relative costs are charged to the right job.

As each order is put into production a *job cost sheet* (or job ledger account) will be prepared, and on this will be recorded the cost of material used, the labour and machine time taken, and any other costs attributable to the job. A copy of the works order may be sent to the cost office as an advice that the job is due to begin and that a cost sheet is to be prepared.

Job costing routine involves a considerable amount of recording and analysis, and in factory work it is essential to have reliable production control records. The system must clearly show materials issued to jobs, labour time expended on jobs and the appropriate absorption of overheads as jobs pass through the production cost centres. Each job must be planned in advance and a works order issued to all departments that will be engaged upon the job. Material requisitions will be prepared for all the materials required, and copies of the documents will normally be passed to the Stores in order that arrangements can be made to issue the materials as and when they are required. The progress department will arrange for the work to be moved from operation to operation and, where a batch of similar articles is being made, it will record the good production and scrap at each stage. As work is done in the factory, gangs or individual workers will book their time on time sheets, and these will be passed to the cost office daily or weekly for summarising and posting to the appropriate job cost sheets. On completion, the works copy of the order or other form of advice, e.g. a copy of the finished goods store receipt, will be sent to the cost office as an advice that the cost can be finalised, and where a batch of articles has been produced this form will show the quantity manufactured and the number scrapped at each stage of production.

Recording Materials Used

The method of recording receipts and issues of materials on material requisitions was explained in detail in Chapter 2. As stated, the issue of materials to a job from stock may be represented as follows:

Debit Job ledger control account (or Work-in-progress ledger control account)
Credit Material stock ledger control account

As the totals are posted to the control accounts, the individual items are debited to the appropriate job cost accounts and credited to the appropriate stock accounts. The totals of the balances on the individual accounts are reconciled with the control accounts periodically to verify the accuracy of the individual postings.

As material requisitions are received in the cost office they are priced, extended and, where necessary, coded. Each requisition shows the works order number to which the material is to be charged and the stock account that is to be credited. The method of proceeding from this stage will depend upon the quantity and relative value of the individual requisitions. Where the number is small they can be posted individually to the detailed accounts and the totals posted to the relative control accounts. In most cases,

Requisi-tion	Order Number:								
	P1946	P1971	P2011	P2012	P2013	P2018	P2020	P2021	Total
	£	£	£	£	£	£	£	£	£
S1711	7.642								7.642
S1801	3.181		2.917	2.917	2.917				11.932
S1756	13.461								13.461
S1911		11.213							11.213
S1912						2.518			2.518
S1913							3.720	3.720	7.440
S1940						3.666			3.666
Totals	£24.284	£11.213	£2.917	£2.917	£2.917	£6.184	£3.720	£3.720	£57.872

MATERIALS ANALYSIS BY JOB   23 January 19—

Requisi-tion	Material Code						
	A201	A202	A203	B209	C201	D201	Total
	£	£	£	£	£	£	£
S1711	7.642						7.642
S1801		11.932					11.932
S1756		13.461					13.461
S1911				11.213			11.213
S1912					2.518		2.518
S1913						7.440	7.440
S1940						3.666	3.666
Totals	£7.642	£25.393		£11.213	£2.518	£11.106	£57.872

STORES ISSUES ANALYSIS   23 January—

In General Ledger

Work-in-Progress Ledger Control

	£
Stock control	57.872

Material Stock Ledger Control

	£
Work-in-progress control	57.872

In Subsidiary Ledgers (Typical Accounts)

Job Ledger: Job P1946

	£
Materials	24.284

Material Stock Ledger: Stock Account A201

	£
Work-in-progress	7.642

Records for the Analysis of Material Requisitions and the Appropriate Ledger Entries

however, the number of issues is sufficiently large to warrant the preparation of daily or weekly summaries in the form illustrated and the totals of these will be posted to the individual accounts in the manner shown. Where the number of material requisitions is large the computerisation of the records facilitates this analysis.

Recording Wages

For the purpose of control, wages are analysed as direct and indirect by cost centres, but this is not sufficient for the purpose of job costing. The direct labour entries shown on the individual time sheets must be analysed by job number and the totals posted to the individual job cost accounts and to the appropriate control accounts in the general ledger. Only wages that are direct in relation to the cost unit are posted in this manner. The indirect wages are analysed and accumulated under overhead accounts.

When the time sheets or operation tickets are received in the cost office the wages rates will be entered and the time extended by the rate to obtain the labour cost. In principle each time sheet should be extended by the actual wage rate for the person concerned, but where varying amounts of bonus and overtime occur it is difficult to obtain exact rates. Under such circumstances an average rate may be used for each class of labour, any difference in the total being posted weekly to a 'wages adjustment account'.

The methods of allocating wages to each job are similar in principle to the material cost allocations referred to above. When the number of jobs is large, separate wages totals for each operation may be prepared. It is often convenient to post each item direct to a separate section of the job cost sheet and to total the entries when the job is completed, as illustrated. Whatever method is used, it is important to balance the total of the wages charged up through the costing system with the payroll.

The accounting entries are:

> *Debit* Job Ledger control account (or Work-in-progress ledger control account) and
> *Credit* Payroll account –

with the direct wages chargeable to jobs, whilst at the same time debiting the appropriate job cost accounts in the job ledger.

Direct Expenses

As far as possible expense should be allocated direct to individual jobs. Most items originate from invoices, and these should be charged direct to the job ledger control account (or work-in-progress ledger control account). At the same time each invoice should be marked with the number of the job to which the cost is to be allocated in order that a summary of the direct charges can be prepared and passed to the cost office for the entry of the individual items on the appropriate job cost sheets. Where direct expenses originate from some other source (e.g. the cash book) similar principles apply.

Overhead Expenditure

Overhead expenditure is allocated as far as possible to cost centres, and items which are not capable of direct allocation are apportioned in the manner described in Chapter 4. The

JOB COST SHEET				Order No.:		
Customer:				Quantity:		
Particulars:				Date:		

PAPER Quality	Quantity	Rate p.	Cost £	INK Weight	Rate p.	Cost £

ORIGINATION				PRINTING			FINISHING		
	Hours Rate	£		M/c. No. Hours Rate	£		Hours Rate	£
Artists						Cutting		
						Folding and Packing		
Camera								
Plates						**SUMMARY**		
								£
Retouching						Paper Ink Artists Camera Retouching Plate Preparation Printing Cutting Folding and Packing		
Plate Preparation						Production Cost		
Plates						Administration Selling		
						Total cost		

Job Cost Sheet for Use in the Printing Trade

different methods of absorbing overhead expenditure have already been discussed, and it is now only necessary to consider the figures that must be accumulated for the purpose of control and for the establishment of the absorption rates. When we come to the actual costing of each job, we must total the direct material cost, the direct wages, and the direct expense of the job. If separate departmental rates are employed, separate totals must be computed for each cost centre. Overhead is then applied as required. The direct materials, wages and expense, and the absorbed overhead in all centres are totalled to give the production cost. Unless they are regarded as direct charges to the profit and loss account of the period, each job must absorb, in addition to production overhead, part of the administration, selling and distribution overheads. The addition of these to production cost gives the total cost of the job. It is, however, unwise to absorb part of the selling and distribution costs to unfinished jobs as part of the calculation of stocks of work-in-progress.

Cost Accounting for Small Orders

In recent years considerable interest has been shown in techniques whereby administration, selling, and distribution costs are expressed in terms of output. For example, the cost of sales accounting might be expressed as the cost of keeping one live sales account for one year, or as a cost per hundred sales ledger entries. The emphasis thus laid upon the cost of recording work frequently leads to increased attention being paid to the relatively high administration costs (in the widest sense of the term) involved in executing small orders. One aspect of this problem is exemplified when an engineering concern receives orders of low value and finds that the cost of costing these is disproportionately high compared with the cost of production. Yet this is only one facet of a more general problem: administration costs connected with orders are not fully variable with size – there is an irreducible minimum below which they do not fall. This minimum administration cost represents the cost of receiving the order and either acknowledging or declining it. If the order is accepted, there follow the costs of issuing production orders, production control generally, cost accounting, sales invoicing and sales ledger accounting, the preparation of statements, the issue of despatch documents, etc. and all these costs contain a proportionately large fixed element. The problem is how to deal with this. Several alternatives exist. One is to ignore the problem, on the principle of 'taking the rough with the smooth', and this is undoubtedly the best course to adopt where only a comparatively few small orders are received, as it would involve additional complications and unwarranted costs to devise a special procedure for dealing with a few small orders, apart from the problem of fixing a dividing line between large and small jobs. Another possibility is to establish a policy of rejecting all orders below a prescribed minimum value, or of applying a minimum charge high enough to cover the unavoidable extra costs involved. This is not always possible however, as it may cut across the concern's policy of 'giving service' and so maintaining goodwill. The alternatives so far envisaged involve no change in procedures, but cases may arise in practice where the volume of small orders necessitates a departure from standard practice.

Where such activities can be isolated in a separate department, entirely different principles can be applied, normal cost and financial accounting practices and ordinary production and material control procedures being suitably modified. For instance, there might be a single *general jobbing account*, which might be charged with all wages, materials, and expenses in respect of small orders and credited with the value of any work-in-progress in hand at the end of the period, together with the selling price of jobs completed in the period. The balance on the account will represent the profit or loss for the period on small orders. Where such activities cannot be segregated and treated as a separate department, the use of a general jobbing account is less satisfactory, as it will generally be accompanied by a loss of control over both material and labour – the temptation being to charge to general jobbing any time and material that is inconvenient to charge elsewhere. In either case, since detailed cost accounting records are dispensed with, it will be necessary to fix an arbitrary selling price. Any attempt to fix prices accurately would necessitate detailed records, the cost of which is prohibitive.

Since management policy in relation to small orders demands a knowledge of the cost implications of their acceptance or refusal, and since conditions tend to vary from time to time, it is advisable to compute small order costs, if not as a matter of course, at least occasionally, whatever simplification of procedure is otherwise adopted.

BATCH COSTING

Batch costing is a modification of job costing. While job costing is concerned with the costing of jobs that are made to a customer's particular requirements, batch costing is used where standard articles are manufactured in definite batches and held in stock for sale to customers generally. In the boot and shoe industry it would, for example, be much too costly to manufacture a single pair of shoes to meet the requirements of one customer; instead, an order is put through periodically to manufacture, say, 1000 pairs of a particular size and style of shoe. The finished shoes are held in stock for sale on demand, normal stock control principles being applied so that when the re-order level is reached a fresh order is automatically placed. Just as each job has its order number, so each batch is given a definite order number and all materials issued are allocated to that number. Time sheets or job tickets are prepared by the direct workers to show the amount of time spent on each order. The costing of material requisitions and time sheets follows normal job costing principles and the overheads are absorbed on one of the bases already explained. When each order is completed, the cost sheet is totalled and the total cost divided by the quantity produced to show the cost per article or per dozen etc. as required.

Where the cost of setting-up prior to production is high, unit costs fall rapidly with increased batch size. The fixing of the latter requires careful thought, an effort being made to balance the cost advantages of longer runs with the cost and other disadvantages of larger stocks e.g. increased working capital requirements; increased risks of pilferage and obsolescence; greater storage space needs etc.

Example

Component 84X is made entirely in cost centre 76. Materials cost 16p per component, and each component takes 10 minutes to produce. The machine operator is paid £4 per hour, and the machine-hour rate is £1.50. The setting up of the machine to produce component 84X takes 2 hours 30 minutes.

On the basis of this information prepare cost sheets showing the production and setting-up costs, both in total and per component, assuming that a batch of (a) 100 components, and (b) 1000 components is produced.

(a) Cost Sheet for a Batch of 100 of Component 84X

		Cost of the Batch £	Cost per Unit £
Setting-up cost:			
Wages	2 hours 30 minutes at £4 per hour	10.00	
Machine-hours	2 hours 30 minutes at £1.50 per hour	3.75	
		13.75	0.137

Production cost:		£	
Material cost	100 at 16p	16.00	0.160
Wages	16 hours 40 minutes at £4 per hour	66.66	0.667
Machine-hours	16 hours 40 minutes at £1.50 per hour	25.00	0.250
		107.66	
	Total production and setting-up cost	£121.41	£1.214

(b) Cost Sheet for a Batch of 1000 of Component 84X

		Cost of the Batch £	Cost per Unit £
Setting-up cost:			
Wages	2 hours 30 minutes at £4 per hour	10.00	
Machine-hours	2 hours 30 minutes at £1.50 per hour	3.75	
		13.75	0.014
Production cost:		£	
Material cost	1000 at 16p	160.00	0.160
Wages	166 hours 40 minutes at £4 per hour	666.67	0.667
Machine-hours	166 hours 40 minutes at £1.50 per hour	250.00	0.250
		1076.67	
	Total production and setting-up cost	£1090.42	£1.091

COST ESTIMATING

In this chapter it has been shown how the job cost of each product is built up after the work has been completed. In many cases, however, it is necessary to estimate the cost of jobs in advance in order to be able to quote an appropriate selling price. The estimator, normally an engineer or technical assistant, must examine each job in detail and break it down into its component parts. From this analysis, material requirements are determined, and they will be priced at the price expected to rule at the time when the material will be required in order to obtain the estimated material cost. Similarly, the estimator must determine the number of hours of work in each category that must be carried out in each cost centre, and extend them at the wage rates expected to rule, in order to estimate the direct labour cost.

The estimator will rely on the cost accountant to provide him with overhead absorption rates, and he will normally use the same rates as are being employed by the cost accountant. Assuming that overhead is absorbed on a direct labour-hour or machine-hour basis, the estimator will calculate overhead from the estimated number of hours of work involved in each cost centre, and will add this to the direct material cost, direct wages and direct expense (if any) to obtain his estimated production cost. In a similar manner, he will be provided with a basis for the absorption of selling and distribution costs.

By following as far as possible the same methods as the cost department, the estimator not only ensures accuracy in his figures but also facilitates a comparison of the estimate with the final costs when these are subsequently prepared.

MAINTENANCE AND CAPITAL WORK

Where a business employs its own maintenance staff to undertake repairs or to construct new assets, it needs to know the cost of each such job completed, and to this end its costing routine will follow normal job-costing principles. At the same time the business will wish to know the proportion of the maintenance cost to charge to each cost centre and individual machine. In these circumstances *service orders* are often prepared in triplicate by the departmental manager responsible for any capital work or major repair. Each service order will contain clear instructions regarding the work to be carried out and be signed by a responsible official. The three copies will be passed to the maintenance department, which will allot a serial number and pass the top copy to the official responsible for carrying out the work. The second copy will be filed for reference and the third one sent to the cost office. All material requisitions for issues of material to jobs will contain the appropriate service order number and they will be priced and posted by the cost office to the job cost accounts bearing that reference. Each maintenance team, or in some cases each worker, will prepare a time sheet and stating against each service order the time taken. The cost office will allocate the wages to the orders from the time sheets. On completion of the work the two top copies of the service order will be sent to the cost office as a signal that the cost may be extended. Brief details of the cost will then be entered on the two copies of the service order and these will be returned to the originator and the maintenance department respectively to inform them of the cost of the work.

Minor repair jobs are sometimes carried out without a written service order, their cost being charged to cost centre *standing order numbers* i.e. cost codes within the cost centre, specially set apart for this purpose. In the simplest case each cost centre will have one maintenance standing order number, but several numbers can be provided if required. For example (61) might denote general plant repairs, (62) electrical repairs, (63) building repairs, and (64) fork-lift truck repairs. The standing order for electrical repairs in cost centre 12 would be shown as 12/62, building repairs 12/63 etc. Materials and wages will be charged to standing order numbers in the same manner as for service orders and at the end of each costing period the cost office will notify each cost centre foreman of the amounts charged against him under each heading.

Cost Office Copy		Order No.:
SERVICE ORDER		
From:		
Particulars of work to be carried out:	Charge to:	
	Machine No.:	
	Date required:	
	Date completed:	
	Chief Engineer:	
£	Signed	Date
Material Cost		
Wages		
Overheads	Authorised	Date
Total Cost	Estimated Cost: £	

Service Order Form: Front

Note: The ruling shown for the back appears only on the cost office copy of the service order form, and is used for accumulating the cost of the job.

MATERIAL COST				WAGES				
Date	Details	Rate £	Cost £	Date	Details	Hours	Rate £	Cost £
				OVERHEADS				
				Date	Details		Rate £	Cost £
	Total				Total			

Service Order Form: Back

The actual costing of the jobs will follow normal job-costing principles. Direct material and wages will be allocated to the appropriate service and standing orders and overheads will be added on one of the bases explained in the previous chapter. The simple wages percentage rate is frequently used for this purpose, but greater accuracy can be obtained by the use of labour- and machine-hour rates.

In the service order form illustrated, costing columns are ruled on the back of the cost office copy and this takes the place of a separate job cost sheet.

While under this service order routine each job is costed on completion, statements are frequently produced to show the cost to date on particular jobs at the end of each month. This is particularly valuable where the engineering department have estimated the cost in advance and are required to keep within this figure. In such a case the cost office will supply each month a statement showing the cumulative cost to date, broken down under suitable headings. From these figures the chief engineer can obtain some guidance as to whether the cost of any job is likely to exceed the authorised limit and can either take the necessary measures to cut down future costs or ask the Board for additional funds.

SCRAP AND RECTIFICATION

A number of references have already been made to scrap and rectification and the costing principles of each job have been discussed, but it is appropriate to consider these principles in more detail. Normal losses, such as inevitable offcuts, shreddage, turnings, and ends are always regarded as part of the cost of the job. Abnormal losses may occur because the ideal size or type of material is not available, because of faulty materials received from a supplier, or through bad workmanship. All costs incurred for a particular job or other cost unit should, strictly speaking, be charged to the job concerned. Thus, if abnormal losses occur, extra material will be issued and extra work performed, and as a result the cost of

	REJECT TICKET		
Worker's Name:	Assembly No.:		Order No.:
Particulars of Material Rejected:			SCRAP RECTIFY
Reason: Code:	Action to be taken:		PAY FOR NOT PAY FOR
			Disposed of by:
Signed: Date:	Signed: Date:		
Charge Account Quantity	Rate £	Cost £	Date

Reject Ticket in the Form of a Tie-on Label

the job will be higher than expected. Where the losses are charged in this manner it is difficult to ascertain precisely how much money is being lost as a result of scrap and to what this is due. When abnormal losses occur, and they can be recognised and evaluated, it is generally advisable to credit the job with the amount of the loss and to charge it to a departmental or cost centre scrap account. Unless abnormal scrap losses are identified to individual jobs, it will be impossible to measure the true profit made on a job and to disclose the extent of variance of actual costs from costs forecast when the job was estimated. It must be realised that the main purpose of any costing system is to control costs, and that only if management receives properly presented scrap reports will it be able to cost scrap and waste.

After each stage of production the manufactured article is normally inspected before it is passed to the next operation. Where the inspector rejects articles he shows the reason on a *reject ticket*, which is often in the form of a label attached to the faulty material. A carbon copy duplicate will generally be prepared for cost office use. The reject ticket will specify the articles rejected and the reason for rejection, and it will be returned with the goods to the department responsible. The rejected goods will be examined by the foreman of the department responsible or by one of the production engineers, who will decide whether rectification is possible and, if not, how the goods are to be disposed of. The action to be taken will be entered on both copies of the reject ticket, one copy of which will be sent to the cost office. In some cases the reject ticket is sent to the production control department, which arranges for the manufacture of replacements as required; in others the ticket may be used as direct authority to draw a replacement from the store.

The cost office will cost each reject ticket and prepare an analysis, firstly of the jobs to be credited and secondly of the cost centre to be debited, showing details of the separate cost under each main cause heading. The costing of scrap gives rise to some difficulty, as the cost increases after each operation has been carried out. This makes it necessary to take out a cumulative cost to date at the end of each operation. This can be seen from the following costing of steel strip.

Mild Steel Strip 12 mm × 3 mm		Weight in tonnes (end of process)	Opera- tion Cost £	Cost to date £	Cost per tonne to date £
Raw material – hot rolled strip 5.4 tonnes at £135 a tonne		5.4	729.00	729.00	135.0
Clean	5.4 tonnes × £4 per tonne	5.3	21.60	750.60	141.6
Anneal	5.3 tonnes × £5 per tonne	5.3	26.50	777.10	146.6
Roll	4 hours × £6 per hour	5.2	24.00	801.10	154.1
Slit	12 hours × £4 per hour	4.8	48.00	849.10	176.9
Cut lengths	16 hours × £5 per hour	4.7	80.00	929.10	197.7
Pack	4 hours × £2 per hour	4.7	8.00	937.10	199.4

It will be seen that if a tonne had to be scrapped after the rolling stage it would be necessary to charge £154 to scrap. If, however, the faults were not noticed until the strip was ready to be packed, or if the faults occurred at the cutting stage, the cost would have increased to £197.7 per tonne, or if the work of packing had been completed to such a stage that normal wages were paid to the packers, £199.4 per tonne.

The basic rule is that the cost of work normally lost in production (5.4 tonnes is reduced to 4.7 tonnes) is absorbed into the cost of 'good' production, but that scrap and rejected work is costed out as a separate item. The reject ticket provides a space in which the inspector will enter whether or not wages will be paid for the operation at which rejection took place, and the scrap must be costed accordingly.

If in the above example 1.2 tonnes had been rejected at the slitting stage the cost would have proceeded as follows:

		Weight in tonnes (end of process)	Opera- tion Cost £	Cost to date £	Cost per tonne to date £
Slit	12 hours × £4 per hour	4.8	48.00	849.10	176.9
Less: scrap –1.2 tonnes		1.2		212.28	
		3.6		636.82	176.9
Cut lengths	12 hours × £5 per hour	3.525	60.00	696.82	197.7
Pack	3 hours × £2 per hour	3.525	6.00	702.82	199.4

Thus £212.28 has been charged to scrap account and the final cost of the good strip is unaltered. If, on the other hand, we let the job bear the cost of the scrap, the costs would be as follows:

		Weight in tonnes (end of process)	Opera- tion Cost £	Cost to date £	Cost per tonne to date £
Slit	12 hours × £4 per hour	3.6	48.00	849.10	235.9
Cut lengths	12 hours × £5 per hour	3.525	60.00	909.10	257.9
Pack	3 hours × £2 per hour	3.525	6.00	915.10	259.6

As the profit margin on steel strip is small a loss would certainly be shown if the cost were taken at £259.6 and the impression might be gained that this was work of an unprofitable nature. If a true view of the profitability of this job is to be derived, the cost of scrap involved in its production must certainly be taken into consideration. Conversely, the scrap was produced in the slitting department and, as such, should be seen as an overhead cost of that cost centre, but is it fair to charge even a small proportion of that cost to other jobs through the absorption of cost centre overheads? In cases where the individual job is left to bear the cost of scrap, the saleable value of the scrap should, if possible, be deducted in the job cost. If in the above example the saleable value was £15, this would be deducted to make the final cost £900.10. In most cases, however, it is more satisfactory for control purposes to transfer all the cost of scrapped work to the appropriate cost centre scrap code and to credit that account with the sale proceeds of the faulty material. Care must be taken, however, that the particular liability of some jobs to produce more scrap than others is not lost sight of, though this information will be apparent from a study of the *scrap report*, which is in effect an analysis of all the reject tickets.

Where articles are job costed it is in practice often necessary to wait until each job is completed before calculating the scrap cost, and in some cases the actual calculation involves so much work that approximations have to be made.

Where scrap is stated to be due to faulty raw material supplied by an outside concern the cost office will price the reject ticket and report the loss to the buying department. While a supplier will not normally give credit in excess of the original cost of the raw material, it is important for the buyer to know what losses are occurring through the purchase of material from a particular supplier. If, for example, he has been trying to economise by buying cheaper material, the scrap costs may show this to be mistaken policy. Where the material is replaced by the supplier, or a credit note is given, the amount should be credited to the department against which the cost has been charged.

Rectification

Where the reject ticket contains instructions to rectify the faulty work, the actual cost of rectification will normally be excluded from the cost of the job and charged instead to the appropriate cost centre rectification account. The man who carries out the work will therefore book his time to the *rectification standing order number* and this will be costed and charged by the cost office to the required account. Any additional material required as a result of the rectification will similarly be charged to this account. In preparing rectification costs, overhead should normally be included and the work costed at the same rates as original work. If it is required to charge each job with the actual rectification costs incurred the wages and overheads will be debited to the job in the same manner as other work carried out.

Scrap in Stores

It was explained in an earlier chapter how normal wastage in Stores can be absorbed by inflating the rate at which the material is charged out. Where abnormal wastage and breakages occur these should normally be noted on reject tickets. The reject tickets will be treated for this purpose as material requisitions to credit the stock accounts, and the cost will be charged to the storekeeping cost centre. The segregation of scrap losses in this manner is important for the purpose of control as it shows management not only what losses are occurring, but also the places where they occur and the reasons.

Scrap Used for Other Purposes

Where articles are rejected for one purpose the material can sometimes be used for another, e.g. in tin-box manufacture if a biscuit tin is scrapped because of a faulty seam the good material can be cut out and used in the manufacture of round bottoms or lever rings. Some difficulty often occurs in determining the cost at which the transfer should be made from one job to another. A certain amount of the material and all the wages and overheads that have gone into the making of the biscuit tin will be lost, and on top of this there is the cost of cutting up the tin and further costs arising from the inevitable slowing down of the subsequent press work. In some cases the total cost of the faulty article is written off as scrap and any saving that can be made by using the article is regarded as a windfall profit. Where it is possible to put a reasonable market value or estimated value on the scrapped article the transfer can be made at this price. It is sometimes possible to deduct the additional costs applied to the faulty material from the normal cost of similar articles made by the prescribed methods and to transfer the material at this price. Methods vary according to the circumstances but the difference between the cumulative cost of the original article and the cost at which it is transferred should always be written off to the 'scrap account'.

Sales of Scrap Material

Normal offcuts, turning scrap, short ends, and faulty material, particularly certain non-ferrous metals, may have a considerable saleable value, which must be credited to the cost of each job. For example, in the case of the strip costing shown above, 0.6 tonnes out of the total 0.7 tonnes lost would be in the form of offcuts and damaged ends. If this had a value of, say, £25 in the scrap market it would be quite in order to deduct this from the total cost of the job. Where the value of the scrap is small in relation to the job cost it is normal to regard its sale as a windfall profit to the department, but a separate credit may be put through to the scrap account. Where the amount is large, it should be deducted from the cost of the job concerned or, where more appropriate, an average figure may be deducted from every job. Any charges for collecting the scrap will normally be offset against the proceeds so that the net amount only is credited.

Scrap Reports

Scrap and rectification reports should be prepared at frequent intervals and submitted to all levels of management, from the cost centre foreman to the works manager. The cost centre report is a simple statement showing the cost of scrap and rectification under a number of headings to exhibit the reasons therefor. A departmental manager will receive a report covering all cost centres under his control, while a consolidated report will be prepared for higher works management. A scrap code should be set up to assist in the analysis of the figures. Thus, code 1 might be faulty materials, code 2 faulty handling, code 3 faulty machining, and so on as required. A specimen report for submission to a departmental manager is illustrated.

Cause Code		Cleaning Shed	Anneal-ing	Rip-ping	Patent-ing	Wire Drawing	Total
	SCRAP REPORT Wire Mill Period 7 ended.....................						
	Scrap:	£	£	£	£	£	£
1	Faulty raw material					29	29
2	Incorrect material					70	70
3	Wrong tensile					20	20
4	Seams					40	40
5	Faulty manufacture		11	25	130	92	258
6	Faulty handling					5	5
7	Incorrect instructions		20				20
8	Other causes	2		3			5
	Rectification:						
1	Incorrect material					12	12
2	Tensile				10	85	95
3	Surface defects			10			10
4	Faulty manufacture	5	7		25	38	75
5	Other causes			5		7	12
	Total	£7	£38	£43	£165	£398	£651

Notes: XY Company have agreed to replace all faulty material (£29).
Heavy patenting scrap on 35-gauge wire for XL Company.

Scrap–Further Processing

One common decision to be taken on the shop floor is whether to sell scrap material at once, or, alternatively, to undertake further work on the material to enhance its saleability in the market. It must be stressed that the cost of the scrap up to the point of its rejection is completely irrelevant to this decision. The only costs and revenues to be taken into account are those that arise or change as a result of the decision, i.e. revenue is the difference between the scrap value and the enhanced value, and cost is the cost of the further operations on the material after the point of scrapping. The cost up to the point of scrapping will not change whether the scrap is sold at once or submitted to further processing, and therefore this cost is not relevant to the decision.

SEMINAR EXERCISES

5.1 The Oddjob Engineering Company manufactures heavy electrical plant and switchgear to customers' specific requirements. The costs associated with each job are recorded on a job cost card. The job card for job number 14–7–86 is shown below:

Job No.   14–7–86   *Customer*: Electrical Installations PLC
Date Commenced: 1 July
Expected Completion Date: 1 September   *Price*: £6500
Delivery Date: 1 October   *Invoice*: 12/148
Dated: 4 December

Description: Heavy Duty Electric Motor

Date	Ref.	Material		Labour			Overheads			Miscellaneous	
		Est. £2000		Est. £1800			Est. £900			Est. £60	
		Cost £	Cum. £	Hours	Cost £	Cum. £	DLH Cost £	Rate £2 Cum. £		Cost	Cum.
21/7	MR7/850	1820	1820								
24/7	MRN7/13	(520)	1300								
25/7	MR7/920	740	2040								
31/7	Labour Analysis			280	1120	1120	560	560			
14/8	MR8/65	317	2357								
31/8	Labour Analysis			160	640	1760	320	880			
15/9	Inv. 8374									530	530
24/9	Inv. 8961									60	590
30/9	Labour Analysis			100	500	2260	200	1080			

		£		
Summary:	Material	2357	Comment Inv. 8374–Component parts	
	Labour	2260	Inv. 8961–Special packing	
	Overheads	1080		
	Misc.	590		
	Total Cost	6287		
	Price	6500		
	Profit	£213		

Required:

(a) Comment on the costing system in operation at Oddjob Engineering.
(8 marks)

(b) Discuss the profitability of job No. 14–7–86.   (8 marks)

(c) Outline control action required on this job.   (6 marks)

(d) Suggest improvements in the design of the job card.   (3 marks)

(Total 25 marks)

6

Contract Costing

Contract costing follows the same principles as job costing, and is used by such businesses as builders and public works contractors to undertake work on a contract basis. The organisation of a contractor's business is such that most of his costs can be allocated direct to contracts. While the contract is basically the cost unit, it may, for the purpose of control, also be regarded as a locational cost centre, the site agent or supervisor being responsible for all expenditure incurred. The agent or 'clerk of the works' is responsible to a contracts manager, who will control several contracts. On large building sites there will be a strong management team with engineers and quantity surveyors, a raw materials store with a storekeeper and perhaps a separate wages office to deal with the labour force, who may live at the site or nearby. Whereas under other costing systems expenditure is normally allocated firstly to the cost centre and secondly to the individual job, the nature of contract work is such that the only allocation required is direct to the contract. Contracts are identified by name and/or number. Overheads are normally restricted to the head office and storage costs, and, as they tend to be small in relation to the direct costs, they are often absorbed on some such arbitrary basis as a percentage on prime cost. In some cases, however, separate cost centres are set up for specialised departments or for equipment (such as bulldozers and mobile cranes) which are then charged out to contracts by applying a machine-hour rate.

As the main purpose of the accounting system is to reveal the profit or loss of each contract, separate contract cost accounts are normally incorporated in the financial ledgers. The manufacturing account is divided into a number of accounts, one for each contract, often brought together by the maintenance of a contract account. Computerisation facilitates the analysis of costs to individual contracts and cost codes and the production of a contract account each month for managerial control purposes. The amount of work-in-progress recorded for each contract is totalled to produce a work-in-progress stock figure, which appears on the balance sheet. All direct costs are allocated direct to the contract, and head office overheads are applied at regular intervals. On completion, the contract price is credited (the corresponding debit being made to the contractee's personal account) and the final balance, which represents the profit or loss, is transferred to the profit and loss account. As management may call from time to time for the details of the cost of each contract, a cost account is often perpared with sub-totals for material costs, sub-contracting costs, wages, plant usage costs, etc.

Materials

Most of the materials are ordered for each specific contract and can therefore be allocated as a direct cost when the invoice is received and passed for payment. In some cases, however, certain items are held in a central store and requisitioned by the contract agent or quantity surveyor as required. The costing and allocation of these requisitions is straightforward, and while they are normally charged at cost on the first-in-first-out basis, an inflated figure is sometimes used in order to include the cost of storage and handling. Materials returned to store are credited to the contract account, as are those moved from one site to another, under the authority of a materials transfer note.

Where it is necessary to provide a detailed breakdown of the cost of each contract, the materials may be coded to represent different classifications. These may be according to the type of material e.g. bricks, timber, cement, tiles, fittings etc., or be related to the work undertaken e.g. foundations, structural steel work, building work, joinery, electrical work, or plumbing. On a large building contract of perhaps four or five years duration, costing £40 million, it is not uncommon for materials to be analysed under as many as 50 cost classifications. The aim should be to follow the form of the original estimate, so that in the event of an unsatisfactory profit margin the particular factors responsible can readily be ascertained.

Wages

All wages of workers engaged on a particular contract are allocated direct to that contract regardless of the nature of the work; the payroll is normally sectionalised by site to facilitate both the payment and allocation of the wages. Where information is required as to the separate cost of each trade or class of labour, the payroll for each contract will be sectionalised so as to provide separate sub-totals that will be posted individually to each contract cost account. The workers employed by small contractors frequently move from site to site and it is necessary to provide time sheets from which the allocations can be made. Workers on large sites are often divided into gangs, and the 'ganger', or foreman, completes a time sheet so that the wage cost of the gang can be allocated to the functions they have performed e.g. concreting, shifting materials, formwork etc. The wages of those head office and central stores workers who cannot be identified with any particular contract will be posted to 'indirect' cost centres. These costs will be totalled for absorption by contracts on an equitable basis.

Plant and Machinery

There are two different methods of charging the cost of plant, such as cement-mixers, earth-moving equipment, cranes and other machines, to the contracts on which they are used. In large contracts where the plant may be required for several years, it is often found convenient to charge the original cost of new plant or the written-down value of part-used plant direct to the contract. When the contract is completed, or the plant is no longer required, it may be sold at the site and the contract will be credited with the proceeds. Alternatively, if the plant is required for use on other contracts it will be revalued and an entry will be put through, crediting the contract account and debiting the plant and machinery account or the new contract to which the plant is sent. On long contracts, since it is customary for managerial purposes to calculate the profit monthly, a valuation of all plant and equipment must be made at regular intervals or adequate provision must be made for depreciation – the quantity surveyors prove helpful in this revaluation. Alternatively, a plant register showing monthly depreciation allocations can be used. The very nature of the work means that the working life of plant may suddenly be foreshortened, perhaps by an accident, so extreme prudence must be used when a forecast of economic life is made.

Where plant is sent to contract sites for only a short time, the revaluation method is not satisfactory, and it is usual to charge out the use of the plant on a daily or monthly basis. For this purpose all plant will come under the control of a plant manager who will be responsible for all plant costs. Separate machine-hour rates must be calculated for each type of machine and the plant department may be organised into cost centres, which may be based on the following:

Bulldozers
Tractors
Mobile cranes
Motor lorries
Compressors
Cement-mixers
General.

All costs will then be allocated as far as possible to the appropriate individual cost centre and any general expenditure apportioned. The total cost of each cost centre is then divided by the anticipated number of working hours of the machines therein in order to arrive at an hourly cost rate. The wages of the machine operator may either be included in this cost rate, or, where more appropriate, they may be charged direct to the contract.

The large contracting companies usually hive off plant transactions into one or more separate companies, which can charge contracts for the use of plant, and also trade outside the group. It is useful to send a site manager an invoice for plant used once a week or once a month, to remind him of the cost of plant at his disposal and encourage him to return it to the plant yard, rather than allow it to stand idle on the site.

Services

Some contractors maintain separate joinery and manufacturing shops in which materials are prefabricated for use on contract sites, e.g. doors, window-frames, partitions, and ornamental woodwork may be manufactured centrally and sent out complete to the site. In such cases normal job-costing principles are applied to these departments and their production is transferred to the contract at estimated market price. All specific costs will be allocated to the joinery and other shops and they will also be charged with a proportion of the general overheads of the business. If the size of these operations becomes significant it is usual to create a separate company or division to organise them.

Direct Expense

Many contractors are not sufficiently versatile to carry out all the work themselves and must therefore sub-contract part of this to specialists. Sub-contractors' charges appear in the main contract account as direct expense. Other direct expenses include architects' and consultants' fees, the hire of plant from outside firms, electricity, insurance, telephone charges, postage, and other general expense items if they are able to be allocated to particular contracts.

Overheads

While all expenditure is charged as far as possible to individual contracts, it is not practicable to allocate the costs of management, selling, head office, or central stores on this basis. These costs are normally small in relation to the direct costs and most contractors apportion them to contracts periodically, on an arbitrary basis e.g. per labour cost or turnover percentage. This is not an accurate method, as one contract may have heavy sub-contracting costs while others are carried out by the contractor's own labour force. Again, the relative costs of wages and materials may vary considerably from contract to contract, and in the case of overseas work the services provided by head office may be considerably less than those for local contracts. As an alternative method, general overheads may be absorbed in proportion to the number of labour-hours expended on each contract, while overheads relating to stores can be recovered by inflating the prices at which the materials are charged to the contracts.

Income

As each contract or part of a contract is completed an invoice for the price will be prepared and the amount credited to the contract cost account. The account will then be balanced to ascertain the net profit or loss and this will be transferred to the profit and loss account. In the case of large contracts it is customary for the contractee to make payments on account as the work reaches certain stages. The value of the work completed to date is certified by an architect and this amount is normally paid subject to a percentage deduction known as *retention money*. In some cases the value of the work certified is credited to the contract cost account, the contractee's account being debited. In other instances the information is shown only in memorandum form on the contract cost account until the work is completed. Much depends on the length of time involved in each contract and whether or not it is intended to take any part of the profit on the contract before completion.

PROFIT ON UNCOMPLETED CONTRACTS

Where a contract extends over a number of years the question arises as to whether part of the profit should be credited to the profit and loss account each year. To defer taking profit or loss until completion may distort the fair view of the company's activities disclosed by the profit and loss account, since profit on contracts completed during the year will be credited but no account will be taken for the profitable work completed but not yet handed over to the client. Statement of Standard Accounting Practice 9 (SSAP 9) therefore encourages the financial accountant to take credit for reasonably ascertained profit while contracts are in progress, and this practice is followed in more frequently produced cost accounts. A number of rules for the recognition of profit on contracts have been established:

1. Profit can only be taken on work covered by an architect's certificate. Work not certified as being satisfactorily completed should be carried forward at cost.
2. Where the outcome of the contract cannot reasonably be assessed it is prudent not to take up any profit to date. This is the case with contracts in the early stages of building when a final result cannot be forecast and work to date is carried forward at cost.

3. The profit, if any, should reflect the proportion of the work carried out at the accounting date, taking into account any known inequalities of profitability in the various stages of contract, and a prudent view of future events.
4. Any loss disclosed to date should be taken in full, and where it is suspected that a loss will eventually be made, prudence dictates that provision should be made for the whole loss as soon as it is recognised. Thus work-in-progress will be carried forward at cost, less attributable loss, an amount which equates to net realisable value. Large unprofitable contracts absorbing a considerable part of the company's capacity in the future should be charged with related future overheads when the provision for losses is calculated.
5. Work-in-progress on long-term jobs is carried forward at cost plus attributable profits taken to date, less any foreseeable losses provided for. Progress payments received and receivable are deducted from this figure.
6. Interest is not normally included as a cost to the contract unless sums borrowed can be identified to specific contracts.
7. No attributable profit should be taken until the outcome of the contract can be foreseen with a reasonable degree of certainty, the amount regarded as earned to date being that part which prudently reflects the work performed to date. There are several methods for injecting a measure of prudence into this calculation, but the method selected should be used consistently. These methods are demonstrated in the example below.

Example

Bingham Builders PLC are a firm of building contractors. In the present conditions of slack trade they have only four current contracts. Operating data for the four contracts for the three months ended 30 September 19— is as follows:

Contract	A	B	C	D
	£	£	£	£
Contract price	620 000	640 000	580 000	470 000
Value of work certified	570 000	310 000	240 000	32 000
Cash received from contractees	480 000	260 000	200 000	–
Work-in-progress at 1 July	437 450	176 458	53 814	–
Materials on site at 1 July	10 400	–	–	–
Costs incurred during the quarter:				
Materials	46 412	26 419	76 981	14 618
Labour	31 283	18 620	83 765	5 500
Overheads excluding depreciation	12 513	7 448	6 840	2 200
Plant: valuation at 1 July	83 465	51 214	37 450	–
valuation at 30 September	87 220	48 378	26 925	18 260
purchased during quarter	21 478	17 253	21 000	26 476
Cost of work not yet certified	3 458	4 970	3 871	1 534

During the quarter, materials costing £1000 were transferred from Contract C to Contract D. Contract A is nearing completion and the quantity surveyors estimate that a further £25 000 will be incurred to complete the job, and that any plant remaining on the site will be sold for £70 000 at completion. No further plant purchases are planned for this contract.

The work-in-progress figure for Contract A as at 1 July 19— includes an estimated profit of £26 480, but there is no profit brought forward for Contracts B and C. The plant valuation is the written-down value (wdv) at that date.

Required:

(a)   Prepare an operating statement to disclose the profit considered to be made by each contract in the quarter to 30 September 19—, and explain briefly to the contracts manager how you have arrived at the profit figure disclosed for each contract.

(b)   Write up a contract account for each contract.

OPERATING STATEMENT

Contract A

Nearing completion so it is feasible to estimate the final profit on the job and take an appropritate proportion of that amount to the profit and loss account.

	£	£
Price		620 000
Costs at 1 July (447 850 – 26 480)	421 370	
Costs incurred this quarter:		
Materials	46 412	
Labour	31 283	
Overheads	12 513	
Plant (83 465 + 21 478 – 87 220)	17 723	
Costs to completion	25 000	
Depreciation to completion (87 220 – 70 000)	17 220	
		571 521
Total estimated profit on the contract		£48 479

Formula to use:

$$\frac{Cash}{Certificate} \times \frac{Certificate}{Price} \times Total\ estimated\ profit$$

$\dfrac{480\,000}{570\,000} \times \dfrac{570\,000}{620\,000}$	$\times\ 48\,479 =$	37 532
Less profit taken last quarter		26 480
Profit to be taken this quarter		£11 052

Contract B

This contract is part way through its term, so if a profit is shown to date it is feasible to take a proportion of that profit, so long as the final profit on the job is expected to exceed the profit to be taken to date.

	£	£
Value of work certified		310 000
Cost of work certified:		
Cost to 30 June	176 458	

	£	£
Costs since 30 June:		
Materials	26 419	
Labour	18 620	
Overheads	7 448	
Depreciation		
(51 214 + 17 253 − 48 378)	20 089	
	249 034	
Less costs not certified	4 970	
		244 064
Estimated profit to date		£ 65 936

A formula is applied to this profit to reduce the amount taken to the profit and loss account for reasons of financial prudence.

$$\frac{2}{3} \times \frac{\text{Cash received}}{\text{Certificate}} \times \text{Estimate Profit}$$

$$\frac{2}{3} \times \frac{260\,000}{310\,000} \times 65\,936 = £36\,867$$

Contract C

	£	£
Value of work certified		240 000
Cost of work certified:		
Cost to 30 June	53 814	
Cost since 30 June:		
Materials (76 981 − 1000)	75 981	
Labour	83 765	
Overheads	6 840	
Depreciation	31 525	
(37 450 + 21 000 − 26 925)		
	251 925	
Less costs not certified	3 871	
		248 054
Loss to date		£ (8 054)

The full amount of this loss will be taken to the profit and loss account.

Contract D

	£	£
Value of work certified		32 000
Cost to date:		
Materials (14 618 + 1000)	15 618	
Labour	5 500	
Overheads	2 200	
Depreciation		
(26 476 − 18 260)	8 216	
Less costs not certified	(1 534)	30 000
Estimated profit to date		£ 2 000

Since this contract has recently started, it is too early to foresee the eventual result, so no profit is taken to the profit and loss account.

Contract Account

	A £	B £	C £	D £		A £	B £	C £	D £
Work-in-progress	437 450	176 458	53 814	–	Material to Contract D	–	–	1 000	–
Material stock b/d	10 400	–	–	–	Material stock c/f	–	–	–	–
Plant at wdv b/d	83 465	51 214	37 450	14 618	Plant at wdv c/f	87 220	48 378	26 926	18 260
Suppliers – materials	46 412	26 419	76 981	5 500	Loss to p/l account	–	–	8 054	–
Wages control	31 283	18 620	83 765	2 200	Work-in-progress c/f	566 833	285 901	243 871	31 534
Overheads	12 513	7 448	6 840	26 476					
Plant purchased	21 478	17 253	21 000	1 000					
Material from Contract C	–	–	–	–					
Profit to p/l account	11 052	36 867	–	–					
	£654 053	£334 279	£279 850	£49 794		£654 053	£334 279	£279 850	£49 794

	A £	B £	C £	D £
Material stock b/d	–	–	–	–
Plant at wdv b/d	87 220	48 378	26 925	18 260
Work-in-progress b/d	566 833	285 901	243 871	31 534

The work-in-progress figure is calculated as cost to date, plus profit to date, less loss to date for each contract. This figure will be shown in the balance sheet, and progress payments received to date will be deducted. The progress payments will be recorded as credits on the client's (contractee's) account, until the completion of the job, when the supplier is debited with the price, and contract account is credited.

Contract Account B

	£		£
Work-in-progress b/d	176 458	Plant at wdv c/f	48 378
Plant or wdv b/d	51 214	Balance – cost to date c/f	249 034
Materials b/d	26 419		
Wages	18 620		
Overheads	7 448		
Plant purchased	17 253		
	£ 297 412		£ 297 412
Cost to date b/d	249 034	Contractee account – value of work certified	310 000
p/l account: profit taken to date	36 867	Balance c/f – cost of work not certified	4 970
Balance c/f profit in suspense	29 069		
	£ 314 970		£ 314 970
Balance b/d – plant at wdv	48 378	Balance b/d – profit in suspense	29 069
Balance b/d – cost of work not certified	4 970		

An alternative method for dealing with payments on account, or progress payments, is to credit them to the contractee account and debit that account with the value of work certified. The corresponding credit for the value of work certified is posted to the contract account. The cost of work not yet certified is carried forward from the credit side of the contract account, thus leaving as a debit balance, profit to be taken to profit and loss account and profit in suspense to be carried forward. The example above restates the account for Contract B. This alternative method is not very satisfactory in that it fails to produce a work-in-progress figure. The original method would show a current asset in the balance sheet as follows:

Work-in-progress	£285 901	
Less payments on account	£260 000	£25 901

The alternative would show in the balance sheet the contractee account as a current asset debtor balance: ($£310 000 - £260 000) = £50 000$, and this would be offset by the credit balance profit in suspense, £29 069, and cost of work not yet certified, £4970 as stock of work-in-progress, overall a net asset balance of £25 901.

Payments on account are usually subject to retention, but if the certified amount net of retention has not been paid, the amount for payments on account received and receivable would be deducted from work-in-progress and the amount due, but not yet paid, would appear as a debtor. For example, in the case of Contract B above, suppose 10 % retention is allowed per the contract, a certificate of £310 000 should result in a receipt of £279 000 as a payment on account and this amount would be deducted on the balance sheet. However, only £260 000 has been received from the contractee, so the balance of £19 000 would be shown as a debtor.

Two methods of computing profit to be taken before completion of a contract have been shown in the example above, but they are not universally used in practice. They are merely ways in which a measure of prudence can be injected into the calculation. In some companies, after the estimated profit has been computed, a meeting is held, attended by the contracts manager, quantity surveyors, site agent, and accountant, to identify future difficulties likely to be experienced on the contract, and to agree provisions to be made against time penalties, rising material prices, the cost of rectification work and other hazards.

SEMINAR EXERCISES

6.1 (a) Sloane City Council has awarded a contract to Sloane Direct Labour Organisation (SDLO) to construct 50 council houses near the city centre. Work started at the site on 1 April 19–4 and was due for completion on 30 June 19–6. During the period to 31 March 19–5, the expenditure on the contract was as follows:

	£
Material issued from central stores	94 110
Material sent by suppliers direct to council house site	284 700
SDLO wages	184 930
Hired lorries, plant and machinery	61 490
Plant and machinery purchased on 1 April for specific use	130 000
Tools and consumable items	1 800
Rate Fund administration – apportioned	21 460

On 31 March 19–5, the stock of materials at the site amounted to £31 640 and there were amounts outstanding for SDLO wages, £4000, and for hired lorries, plant and machinery, £500.

SDLO revenue account has received on account the sum of £641 700, which represents the amount of certificate No. 1 issued by the city architects (Rate Fund) in respect of work completed to 31 March 19–5, after deducting 10% retention money for the Rate Fund. It is estimated that work costing £4000 is not covered by this certificate.

Also (1) the plant and machinery specifically purchased is to be depreciated at 20% straight line with no residual value, and (2) the SDLO only takes 2/3 of the profit on work certified to its revenue account.

Required:

(i) Prepare a contract account for the period to 31 March 19–5.

(8 marks)

(ii) Show your calculation of the SDLO profit to be taken to the credit of the SDLO's revenue account. (4 marks)

(iii) Calculate the work-in-progress. (3 marks)

(iv) Illustrate how the contract would appear in the balance sheet of SDLO, according to best accounting practice (3 marks)

(b) What rules should cost accountants observe when deciding the amount of profit to be taken on a contract according to the provisions of SSAP 9 on stocks and work-in-progress. (7 marks)

(Total 25 marks)

6.2 Midshire Contracting PLC is engaged in three building contracts at the end of the quarter dated 30 June 19—. The costing clerk has identified operating data for the three contracts, which is:

	A £	B £	C £
Contract price	300 000	360 000	560 000
Value of work certified	280 000	180 000	18 000
Cash received from contractees	250 000	150 000	–
Work-in-progress at 31 March	248 612	62 345	–
Costs incurred during the quarter:			
Materials	16 500	47 651	4 820
Labour	9 500	35 820	6 210
Overheads excluding depreciation	3 415	10 460	2 112
Plant: valuation 30 June	41 720	87 465	40 000
valuation 31 March	40 271	61 220	–
purchases during the quarter	2 958	37 000	41 678
Cost of work not yet certified	497	4 396	1 470

Contract A is nearing completion and the quantity surveyors estimate that a further £8600 will be incurred to complete the job, and that the plant on site will be sold for £38 000 when the job is finished. No further plant purchases are planned for this contract.

The work-in-progress figure for Contract A as at 31 March included an estimated profit of £14 850, but there is no profit brought forward for Contract B, or for Contract C, which commenced on 1 April.

The director and site agents are anxious to learn of the profitability of the current contracts.

Required:

Prepare an account for each contract with a brief memorandum explaining the profit disclosed. (18 marks)

6.3 Bildem PLC is a civil engineering company engaged in the construction of major building projects. Most of the contracts undertaken extend over a period of several years.

Shown below are the expenses incurred for the year ended 31 December 19–6, together with other operating details, for three of the contracts in which the company is currently engaged.

	Hospital £000's	Power Plant £000's	Dam £000's
Contract price	6000	15 300	18 000
Value of work certified by contractees' architects	3525	11 250	16 500
Cash received from contractees	3000	10 125	14 850
Work-in-progress at 1 Jan. 19–6	–	3 600	10 050
Cost incurred during the year:			
Materials	1650	2 400	1 575
Labour	1050	1 725	1 462
Other expenses, excluding depreciation	525	712	1 162
Plant and equipment:			
wdv 1 Jan. 19–6	450	1 200	1 050
wdv 31 Dec. 19–6	900	787	262
Purchases during the year	1087	600	187
Cost of work not yet certified	112	–	1 200

The agreed retention rate is 10% of the value of work certified by the contractees' architects.

The dam is nearing completion and the site manager estimates that costs, additional to those tabulated above of £637 000, will be incurred in order to complete the contract. He also considers that the plant and equipment on site will be worthless by the time the contract is complete.

The nature of the work undertaken by Bildem PLC is such that it may be regarded as reasonable for the company to include in its annual accounts a prudent estimate for profit attributable to that part of the work on each contract certified as complete at the end of each accounting year.

The opening stock of work-in-progress shown above includes an estimated profit of £1 725 000 for the dam, but none for the power plant as, at the beginning of the year, work on this project had only recently commenced.

The directors of Bildem PLC propose to incorporate into the company's profit and loss account for the year ended 31 December 19–6 the following amounts of profit/(loss) for each contract:

Hospital	Nil
Power Plant	£1 080 000
Dam	£3 600 000

Required:

(a) Do you agree with the proposed profit/(loss) figures for the three contracts? Support your argument with appropriate calculations and alternative amounts where necessary. (21 marks)

(b) Show relevant entries for each contract on the balance sheet of Bildem PLC as at 31 December 19–6, incorporating any revised profit figures. (6 marks)

(Total 27 marks)

REVIEW QUESTIONS

6.1   On 3 January 19–8 Wasp Construction PLC started work on the construction of an office block for a contracted price of £3 000 000 with completion promised by 31 March 19–9. Budgeted cost of the contract was £2 400 000. The construction company's financial year end was 31 October 19–8 and on that date the accounts appropriate to the contract contained the following balances:

	£000's
Materials issued to site	644
Materials returned from site	56
Wages paid	272
Own plant in use on site, at cost	384
Hire of plant and scaffolding	288
Supervisory staff: direct	44
indirect	48
Head office charges	252
Value of work certified to 31 October 19–8	1600
Cost of work completed but not yet certified	160
Cash received related to work certified	1320

Depreciation on own plant is to be provided at the rate of 12.5% p.a. on cost.

£8000 is owing for wages.

Estimated value of materials on site is £96 000.

No difficulties are envisaged during the remaining time to complete the contract.

Required:

(a)   Prepare the contract account for the period ended 31 October 19–8 showing the amount to be included in the construction company's profit and loss account.
(8 marks)

(b)   Explain the reason(s) for including the amount of profit to be shown in the profit and loss account. (5 marks)

(c)   Show extracts from construction company's balance sheet at 31 October 19–8 so far as the information provided will allow. (5 marks)

(Total 18 marks)

6.2   A. B. Construction PLC is currently undertaking three separate contracts to build a bank, an office and a library. Financial data for these contracts are:

	Bank £000's	Office £000's	Library £000's
Contract price	1600	1350	2200
Balances b/f on 1 January:			
Work-in-progress	–	380	740
Material stock	–	–	50
Plant at wdv	–	70	340
Wages accrued	–	(4)	–

	Bank £000's	Office £000's	Library £000's
Transactions during year:			
Material delivered to sites	80	198	360
Wages paid	40	94	220
Payments to sub-contractors	–	–	70
Salaries and direct expenses	12	40	50
Plant issued	180	30	–
Plant transferred	–	16	(16)
Balance c/f at 31 December:			
Material stock	(16)	–	–
Plant at wdv	(140)	–	(220)
Accrued wages	–	10	–
Sub-contractor pre-paid	–	–	(30)
Value of work certified at 31 December	170	780	1900
Cost of work not covered by a certificate	–	–	52
Payment on account received	153	702	1710

The work-in-progress b/f on the library includes £30 000 of profit taken in the profit and loss account up to 1 January. Administrative overheads amount to £72 000, arising from the running costs of departments providing services to all contracts, and are apportioned to contracts on the basis of wage cost incurred.

The library contract is scheduled for completion in three months and the quantity surveyors estimate that further costs of £276 000 will be incurred on top of those costs detailed above if it is to be completed on time.

Required:

(a)   Draft a contract account for each contract for the year to 31 December.

(18 marks)

(b)   Explain your reasons for computing the profit figures to be carried to the profit and loss account. (6 marks)

(Total 24 marks)

7

Process Costing

Job costing occurs in cases where production is carried out under specific orders, mainly to a particular customer's specification. The job acts as the cost unit, and to some extent the cost centre as well. Each unit can be readily identified and work on it costed direct to the job. There are, however, many instances where the identity of individual orders is lost in the general flow of production. This applies particularly to continuous and mass-production processes where identical units receive exactly the same treatment, and so incur the same costs, and to industries where a single product or a limited range of products is manufactured. In such cases the method known as *process costing* is used – costs are accumulated for each separate process or operation, and subsequently related to production quantities passing through the process to ascertain the unit cost. Some products may not pass through all processes, so that the cost of a completed unit will be the aggregate of cost added by each process used to produce the goods.

Process costing is employed in the oil, chemical, soap, and textile industries, in food manufacture, in paper-making, and in paint and ink manufacture, to name but a few applications. Its main characteristics are:

1. The setting-up of process cost centres and the accumulation of the material cost, wages, and overheads by these process cost centres.
2. The charging of the output of one process as the raw material of a subsequent process.
3. The collection of accurate production statistics for each process.
4. The averaging of the costs of all production in each process to derive a unit cost.
5. The segregation of the costs, where one product is split up into two or more different products or where by-products arise at some stage of the production.

Process costing may be applied either where a separate plant is set up for the production of a single product, or where particular production facilities are employed at different times to produce a variety of products. Where, as in mining or public utilities, there is a single product, the method is frequently termed *single* or *unit costing*, but this is merely another form of process costing.

In job costing all costs are allocated or apportioned primarily to cost centres and subsequently to individual jobs, each of which is regarded as a cost unit. Process costing is simpler, as unit costs can normally be obtained merely by dividing the cost of the process by the number of units produced. Paperwork is generally reduced to a minimum and as process costing lends itself readily to the techniques of standard costing, this should be used wherever possible.

The Relative Accuracy of Job and Process Costing

Job costs are identified and recorded separately, whereas the costs of a process are averaged out over the units of through-put, so at first glance it would seem that job costing is more accurate than process costing. However, both methods depend for their accuracy on material requisitions from stores to process and job, and the accuracy of the materials issue pricing system, labour analysis and overhead absorption techniques. With process costing, all operatives, direct and indirect, are charged to the process, but with job costing, indirect labour costs may only reach a job by means of overhead absorption rates. With process costing some overhead expenses can be allocated direct to processes, but with job costing they only influence the job cost through absorption.

Job costing is expensive in that it requires a considerable amount of paperwork and clerical effort to record the costs of each job, as they are incurred. However, such a record facilitates the accurate assessment of the cost of work-in-progress at the end of each costing period, and allows management to review the cost on a job to date at any point in time. With process costing, individual units of output cannot be identified, and as it is necessary to estimate how near to completion these units are at the end of a costing period, work-in-progress stocks for process costing can be inaccurate. The costing treatment of by- or joint products arising from a process may require an arbitrary apportionment of costs, which renders the cost data produced liable to inaccuracy.

Cost Centres

The division of a business into suitable cost centres is most important, though it is not possible to lay down any system of cost centres which will suit the needs of every concern; each case must be considered on its merits. Cost centres are set up primarily as an aid to the control of costs, so a separate cost centre is normally required for each main phase of production at which the output can be measured. A single cost centre may embrace a series of different operations through which the product passes on its way to completion, but where output and losses can be measured at different stages of production, it is preferable for the purpose of control to split the series of operations into a number of separate cost centres.

Service cost centres are set up in the same way as for job costing, separate centres usually being required for power house, building services, material services, personnel, maintenance, laboratory, inspection, and so on.

Cost Units

Costs may be expressed in terms of number, weight, volume, time, etc. and the cost unit adopted varies from industry to industry, and even from concern to concern. The following are examples:

Brick-making	1000 bricks made
Bolts, nuts, and rivets	Gross or 1000
Steel manufacture	Tonne
Steam production	1000 lb raised
Paint manufacture	Litre
Electricity undertakings	Kilowatt hour
Hospitals	Patient-day.

In the simplest case there is only one cost unit, but when the same production facilities are used in the manufacture of a number of different units, these must be separated into suitable product groups. For example, foundry costs are sometimes calculated as a single rate per tonne regardless of the size or complexity of the castings involved. This would clearly be inequitable in the case of a foundry that produced a range of castings, from large to small. As detailed job or batch costing often involves too much clerical work in jobbing foundries, it is usually preferable to separate castings into a number of groups according to weight and/or complexity and to treat each group as a distinct cost unit. As separate parts of the foundry are normally set aside for different grades of casting, the division of production into a number of groups is not difficult. Even where the same facilities are used throughout, it is usual to set up all the moulds for a batch of similar castings at one time, so the costs for each such batch can usually be channelled into the appropriate cost unit group. Similar principles apply in other industries, but in considering the desirability of analysing costs according to size, weight and/or complexity, it should be remembered that the practical problems involved in splitting the costs sometimes outweigh the advantages to be gained by so doing.

Direct Materials.   Where there is a central store, the charging of direct material issues to individual process cost centres follows the principles already outlined. Each issue is measured, then recorded on a material requisition, which summarises the issues of each material to particular centres during a specified period. The issues are priced and charged to the appropriate cost centres.

Where a store serves only one centre, the clerical work of recording each separate issue can generally be avoided by computing the total usage during a given period in accordance with the following formula:

$$\text{Consumption} = \text{Opening stock} + \text{Receipts} - \text{Closing stock}$$

This method can be applied, for instance, where a large quantity of coal is consumed by one particular process, and the coal stockyard is so laid out that the rapid estimation of stock is facilitated e.g. by the coal being stored in easily countable five-tonne lots. It is also suitable for use in connection with packing materials and items of small value, such as labels. For liquids, gases, etc. the flow of material can be recorded by integrating meters, readings of which are taken for costing purposes at appropriate intervals.

Technical estimates of consumption may be relied upon where the clerical work involved in separately recording issues from a general store is excessive in relation to the value of the information obtained. In a foundry, for example, instead of recording every separate issue of sand, it would be quite proper to estimate the consumption by each of the several process centres into which the foundry is divided. Again, where a single process is carried out for separate purposes on successive days, as in the preparation and freezing sections of frozen food manufacture, it is possible to estimate consumption by counting the number of containers or labels used and taking into account the loss in process.

In some industries it is known that certain chemical substances combine in definite proportions. In others, regular analytical tests of the product ensure uniformity of material content. By taking advantage of these facts it is often possible to determine material usage more conveniently and economically than by making numerous direct measurements.

If estimation is confined to the apportionment of a known total usage between several centres, no stock differences can arise. Where, however, the total usage is itself estimated, comparatively small differences will be disclosed by a comparison of the physical stock with the stock records. These must be written off to the profit and loss account after enquiries have been made to pinpoint their cause.

Somewhat conflicting considerations are involved in choosing a method of measuring material usage, and the cost accountant must give due weight to each. The main points to be borne in mind are as follows:

1. Unnecessary clerical effort wastes manpower and money; procedures should therefore be as simple as possible.
2. Stock control must not be lost: pilferage and losses through poor storekeeping must continue to be brought to the notice of management, and there must be no loss of efficiency through the keeping of excessive stocks, or allowing stocks to fall below the minimum level.
3. Excessive documentation is time-consuming. It may be better to provide, promptly, information which is 99 % accurate, rather than to delay presentation unduly in an endeavour to ensure 100 % accuracy. Simplification of procedures not only tends to reduce costs, it also enhances the value of the information presented to management. On the other hand, reasonable accuracy is essential.

Direct Wages.   All wages of workers engaged full-time on a process are allocated direct from the payroll analysis to the appropriate process cost centre and are normally also charged to a number of separate codes within that centre for the purpose of control. Where workers are engaged on more than one process, it is normally necessary for them to prepare time sheets so that the appropriate proportions of their gross wages can be allocated to each cost centre. Supervision, general service, and other labour applicable to more than one cost centre will be apportioned on the most satisfactory basis. The wages of workers for any time not usefully employed will normally be transferred to an idle time account and be included under the overheads of the process.

Where more than one product is manufactured in a particular process cost centre, for example, various sizes and shapes of fire brick, it is not normally necessary for individual workers to record the time they spend on each order. Instead, the time the cost centre is engaged on each order will be recorded and an hourly cost centre rate applied to ascertain the cost of each particular batch.

Direct Expenses.   Expenses such as depreciation, equipment rentals, maintenance charges, electricity, national insurance, etc. are allocated as far as possible from the purchase invoice or other voucher, direct to the cost centre concerned.

Overheads.   Overhead costs are apportioned to the individual cost centres on the most equitable bases. The apportioned overheads may be charged direct to the *process account* in the ledger or, alternatively, the figures may be absrbed on an hourly or per unit basis, any difference being written off to the *overhead absorption account*. The former method is preferable where there is continuous production of a single product; but where a variety of articles are manufactured by the same facilities it is more satisfactory to charge all the overheads to control accounts and to absorb it on a time basis.

SIGNIFICANT FEATURES OF PROCESS COSTING

There are five major difficulties which beset the cost accountant when dealing with process costing:

1. The correct treatment of waste and scrap.
2. Accounting for losses or gains in process.

3. Computing a correct value for stocks of work-in-progress at the end of a costing period.
4. Accounting for inter-process profits.
5. Producing meaningful costs for joint and by-products which may emerge from a process.

WASTE AND SCRAP

Example

In a jam factory four processes are operated, namely preparing, mixing, boiling, filling and packing. The preparing process generates waste, defined as discarded substances having no value. The mixing process, where sugar is added to the fruit, generates scrap, defined as discarded material which has some recovery value. The general rule is to merge the cost of waste into the cost of good production by means of the averaging process. Scrap receives a similar treatment, except that the costs of the process are reduced by the amount for which the scrap has been sold. Sometimes scrap material can be re-introduced into the process as raw material at a later period. In this case the credit and debit act as contra entries and are costed at the amount that would have been paid for the new material not now required. Where scrap generates reclamation costs, or requires further treatment, a separate account should be opened to monitor these costs for control purposes.

It is convenient to draft process accounts with columns for quantities alongside the costs, since it is the quantity produced that is to determine the average cost per unit, and form the input to the next process.

Preparing Process

	kg	£		kg	£
Material	6000	2000	Waste	500	–
Labour	–	400	Transfer to mixing process	5500	2600
Overheads	–	200			
	6000	£2600		6000	£2600

Cost per kg: £2600 ÷ 5500 kg = 47.2p
The waste is recorded, but as it has no scrap value its cost is merged with the cost of good production.

From the preparing process material is sent to the mixing process.

Mixing Process

	kg	£		kg	£
Transfer from preparing process	5500	2600	Scrap	500	50
Material (sugar)	500	200	Transfer to boiling process	5500	3500
Labour	–	500			
Overheads	–	250			
	6000	£3550		6000	£3550

500 kg of waste from the mixing process was scrapped and sold for 10p per kilogram

Cost per kilogram is £3500 ÷ 5500 kg	63.6p
Cost in previous process	47.2p
Cost per kilogram in this process (£900 ÷ 5500 kg)	16.4p

LOSSES AND GAINS IN PROCESS

When materials are processed they sometimes lose or even gain in volume as a result of the process. Engineers or chemists can calculate the amount that they expect to lose (normal wastage) or gain, and the rule is to merge the cost of normal losses into the cost of good production passed on to the next process or put into the stores. Any abnormal losses or gains must be brought to the attention of management and shown as separate charges or credits in the costing profit and loss account.

Continuing the example from the jam factory, the boiling process adds pectin to the mixture but it is expected to lose 10% of its weight from all the materials put through the process. The filling and packing process adds the cost of jars and cartons as material but expects to lose 5% of its weight from the through-put because of breakages.

Boiling Process

	kg	£		kg	£
Transfer from			Normal loss		
mixing process	5500	3500	(5800×0.1) (580×0.15)	580	87
Materials (pectin)	300	100	Actual quantity transferred to		
			filling process	5000	4131
Labour	–	400	Abnormal loss	220	182
Overheads	–	400			
	5800	£4400		5800	£4400

The normal loss quantity is sold for scrap at 15p per kilogram and has been credited to the process account. The balancing figure in the kilogram column, after normal waste and transfers are deducted, must be the amount of abnormal losses in the process. The costs are averaged over the volume that should have been produced, so that abnormal losses are credited to the process and debited to the abnormal loss account at full cost. Any income from scrap sales of abnormal loss quantities is credited to the abnormal loss account and thus the net cost is shown in the costing profit and loss account.

$$\frac{\text{Net cost}}{\text{Expected amount}} = \frac{£4400 - £87}{5800 \text{ kg} - 580 \text{ kg}} = \frac{£4313}{5220 \text{ kg}} = 82.6\text{p}$$

5000 kg transferred at 82.6p = £4131 (raised to accommodate rounding)
220 kg abnormal loss at 82.6p = £182

Abnormal Losses

	£		£
Boiling process	182	Scrap sales – Cash book	
		(220×0.15)	33
		p/l account	149
	182		182

Filling and Packing Process

	kg	£		kg	£
Transfer from			Normal loss – scrap sale		
boiling process	5000	4131	(5000×0.05) (250×0.3)	250	75
Materials	–	500	Actual quantity		
Labour	–	300	transferred to stores	4900	5319
Overheads	–	300			
		5231			
Abnormal gain	150	163			
	5150	£5394		5150	£5394

Clearly the balancing figure in the quantity column is a debit of 150 kg, so losses in process are less than was expected. This is termed an *abnormal gain*. If the process had worked properly, 250 kg of normal waste would have been sold as scrap. The net cost of the process is computed on the assumption of normal working, i.e. that these sales were made at 30p per kilogram.

$$\frac{\text{Net cost}}{\text{Expected amount}} = \frac{£5231 - £75}{5000 - 250 \text{ kg}} = \frac{£5156}{4750 \text{ kg}} = 108.5\text{p full cost}$$

The units transferred and the abnormal gain are costed at this amount:

4900 kg × £1.085 = £5316.5 (this amount has been rounded up in the above account)

The process account has been credited, however, with the sale of 250 scrap units, whereas in reality only 100 units have been scrapped, so the cash received is 100 × 30p = £30. The difference is accounted for in the abnormal gain account.

Abnormal Gain Account

	£		£
Scrap sales – amount		Filling process	163
foregone	45		
p/l account	118		
	£163		£163

Scrap Sales

	£		£
Filling and packing process:		Cash (100×0.3)	30
Scrap sales of normal loss	75	Abnormal gain – scrap	
		sales foregone (150×0.3)	45
	£75		£75

This example has been shown in the form of double entry accounts. The information could also be expressed as a costing statement.

Operating Statement – Jam Production		kg	£	Week ending..........Unit Cost	%
Preparing:	Material	6000	2000		
	Labour	–	400		
	Overheads	–	200		
	Waste	(500)	–		
Mixing:	Preparing	5500	2600	47.2p	43.5
	Material	500	200		
	Labour	–	500		
	Overheads	–	250		
	Scrap	(500)	(50)	16.4p	15.1
Boiling:	Mixing	5500	3500		
	Material	300	100		
	Labour	–	400		
	Overheads	–	400		
	Normal loss	(580)	(87)		
	Abnormal loss	(220)	(182)	19.0p	17.5
Filling:	Boiling	5000	4131		
	Material	–	500		
	Labour	–	300		
	Overheads	–	300		
	Normal loss	(250)	(75)		
	Abnormal gain	150	163	25.9p	23.9
Production transferred to stores		4900	£5319	108.5p	100

To take this example one stage further; let us suppose that the 100 kg lost through wastage in the filling process could be reconstituted, at a cost of 50p per kilogram, and sold to employees at 70p per kilogram. The decision as to whether to commit resources to this scheme must rest entirely on costs that are relevant to the scheme. The cost to date of the reconstituted scrap can play no part in the decision since it will not change as a result of that decision. Reconstitution for 50p per kilogram, to promote sales at 70p per kilogram, gives a surplus of 20p per kilogram, but the scrap sales revenue of 30p per kilogram is foregone under this scheme, so it would not pay to make the reconstitution unless the cost were to fall, or selling price were increased, or the scrap price were reduced.

STOCKS OF WORK-IN-PROCESS

At the end of a costing period there may be some cost units remaining in a process, which are not yet completed. The cost of these semi-finished units of work-in-progress must be credited to the process account for the current costing period, and carried forward at cost to the next period, when they will be completed. This credit and debit will affect the cost of completed units in both periods, but it is difficult to calculate the appropriate cost to be carried forward. As already stated, unit cost is an average, the costs of the process being divided by the number of units completed in the period. If the amount of stock of work-in-process is to be credited to cost for the period, an estimate must be made as to how much cost has been incurred on these semi-finished units up to this point. They may be complete for materials, which are drawn from stores when the units enter the process, but they may only be, say, 40% or 60% complete so far as labour costs and overheads are concerned. If 100 units are 40% complete for labour and overheads at the end of the period, the work undertaken on them up to that point is equivalent to the completion of 40 units, and work equivalent to that to make 60 units will be required in the next period before they can be transferred to the succeeding process or into the finished goods stores. This device of translating work-in-process to equivalent units of completed production facilitates the apportionment of process costs between production completed during a month and the stock of work-in-process carried forward. Sometimes the term 'effective units' is used instead of 'equivalent units'. The calculation is complicated by the fact that work-in-process may be more complete for one element of cost e.g. materials, than for another, say labour, or other process conversion costs.

Example

10 000 kg of material at £1 each are introduced into Process A during the month of June. By the end of the month 8000 units have been transferred to Process B, leaving a closing stock of 2000 units of one kilogram each. Clearly the process cost for materials is based on 10 000 effective units having been completed at £1 each, of which 2000 remain in stock. Labour and conversion costs for Process A during June amount to £18 000, but the closing stock of 2000 units is estimated to be 50% complete. Therefore, the £18 000 has been incurred to make 8000 finished units and 2000 half-finished units (= 1000 equivalent units), 9000 units in all.

$$\frac{£18\,000}{9000\ \text{units}} = £2\ \text{per unit.}$$

Thus goods transferred to Process B amount to 8000 units; material (£1) and labour and conversion costs (£2) total £3, multiplied together = £24 000.
The stock of work-in-process is equivalent to:

2000 units of materials at £1 each	£2000
1000 units labour and conversion	£2000
costs at £2 each	
	£4000

If the example is extended to Process B, more complicated circumstances can be included, as materials are added towards the end of the work. In June Process B has an opening stock of 3000 units, which are 40% complete for labour and conversion costs, but only 30% complete for materials, and which have been carried forward from May at £8500. During June 8000 units are introduced from Process A at £3 each and at the end of June a closing stock of 2000 units, which are 50% complete for materials and 80% complete for labour and conversion costs, remains. Throughout this month Process B has incurred material costs of £27 300 and labour and conversion costs of £37 600.

Equivalent Unit Calculation

	Units	Material	Labour and Conversion
Opening stock	3000		
Equivalent units to complete: 3000 × 70%		2100	
3000 × 60%			1800
Units introduced and completed:			
8000 less closing stock 2000	6000	6000	6000

	Units	Material	Labour and Conversion
Closing stock	2000		
Equivalent units of production to date:			
2000 × 50%		1000	
2000 × 80%			1600
Total equivalent units		9100	9400
Divide process cost by equivalent units		£27 300	£37 600
		9100	9400
		= £3	= £4

Closing stock is calculated as:

	£
2000 units (cost from Process A, £3)	6 000
1000 units of materials at £3	3 000
1600 units of labour and conversion costs × £4	6 400
	£15 400

The process account could be drafted as follows:

Process A

	Units	£		Units	£
Materials	10 000	10 000	Transfer to Process B	8 000	24 000
Labour conversion	–	18 000	Closing stock	2 000	4 000
	10 000	£28 000		10 000	£28 000

Process B

	Units	£		Units	£
Opening stock	3 000	8 500	Transferred to stores	9 000	82 000
Transferred from			Closing stock	2 000	15 400
Process A	8 000	24 000			
Materials	–	27 300			
Labour and conversion	–	37 600			
	11 000	£97 400		11 000	£97 400

The cost of completed production £82 000 is a balancing figure, but can be substantiated as follows:

	£
3000 units of opening stock cost b/f	8 500
Cost to complete:	
2100 units of material ×£3	6 300
1800 units of labour and conversion ×£4	7 200

	£
6000 units introduced and completed:	
Costs from Process A (6000 × £3)	18 000
Materials (6000 × £3)	18 000
Labour and conversion costs (6000 × £4)	24 000
	£82 000

This method relies heavily on a FIFO assumption that work-in-process at the beginning of the period will be completed before the end of the period, and that closing stocks are drawn from the units introduced during the period.

A complication occurs if normal and abnormal losses are experienced in the process. The general rule is to introduce them into the calculation of equivalent units, charging the costs apportioned to normal losses to the cost of completed units, and the cost of abnormal losses to the profit and loss account. The logic of this method is that losses are detected at the end of the process when completed production is inspected, so it is fair to merge the cost of normal losses into the cost of units transferred, but not fair to carry forward part of the cost of normal loss of one period in the cost of the stock of work-in-process. Suppose in the example above 600 units were expected as a normal loss, but abnormal losses of a further 300 units were incurred. At the beginning of June 3000 units were in process, and these, together with 6000 units introduced during the month, have been completed; in total, 9000 units. It is logical to assume that one third of losses, normal and abnormal (300 units) were derived from the opening stock and the remainder from work introduced during the month. This assumption influences the calculation of equivalent units.

Equivalent Unit Calculation

	Units	Material	Labour and Conversion
Opening stock completed	3000		
3000 – 300 × 70%		1890	
3000 – 300 × 60%			1620
Normal losses: 200 × 70%		140	
200 × 60%			120
Abnormal losses: 100 × 70%		70	
100 × 60%			60
Units introduced and completed	6000		
6000 – 600		5400	
6000 – 600			5400
Normal losses		400	
			400
Abnormal losses		200	
			200
Closing stock	2000		
2000 × 50%		1000	
2000 × 80%			1600
Total equivalent units		9100	9400

The units have been re-arranged but the total remains the same, so the cost per unit will also remain the same as in the previous part of the example: materials £3, and labour and conversion £4.

The process account would be drafted as follows:

Process B

	Units	£		Units	£
Opening stock	3 000	8 500	Normal loss	600	–
Transfer from Process A	8 000	24 000	Abnormal loss	300	2 928
Materials	–	27 300	Transfer to store	8 100	79 072
Labour and conversion	–	37 600			82 000
			Closing stock	2 000	15 400
	11 000	£97 400		11 000	£97 400

The costs of good and lost production (£82 000) must be divided by the 8400 units expected to be produced = £9.762 each, to calculate the cost of abnormal loss and goods transferred to the finished goods store.

The cost of units transferred to stores in the earlier example (£82 000) has now been divided between normal and abnormal losses and completed production, and the normal loss further apportioned to abnormal loss and good production.

As a variant on this example, suppose the inspection that rejects the lost production takes place before the end of the process. Assume that when the losses are recognised the process is at the halfway stage, so that lost units from those introduced in June are 50% complete, and the work performed on the opening stock rejected was sufficent only to process those units to the halfway stage (materials 30% complete up to 50% = 20% equivalence and labour and conversion 40% complete up to 50% = 10% equivalence).

Equivalent Unit Calculation

	Units	Material	Labour and Conversion
Opening stock completed	3000		
3000 – 300 × 70%		1 890	
3000 – 300 × 60%			1 620
Normal losses: 200 × 20%		40	
200 × 10%			20
Abnormal losses: 100 × 20%		20	
100 × 10%			10
Units introduced and completed	6000		
6000 – 600		5 400	
6000 – 600			5 400
Normal losses: 400 × 50%		200	
400 × 50%			200
Abnormal losses: 200 × 50%		100	
200 × 50%			100
Closing stock: 2000 × 50%	2000	1 000	
2000 × 80%			1 600
Total equivalent units		8 650	8 850
		£27 300	£37 600
		8 650	8 850
		= £3.156	= £4.249

Closing stock would be calculated as:

	£
2000 units from Process A at £3	6 000
1000 units of material at £3.156	3 156
1600 units of labour and conversion at £4.249	6 798
	£15 954

Closing stock now takes a larger proportion of the cost incurred because the lost production was rejected at an earlier stage.

Process B

	Units	£		Units	£
Opening stock	3 000	8 500	Normal loss	600	–
Transfer from Process A	8 000	24 000	Abnormal loss	300	2 909
Materials	–	27 300	Transfer to store	8 100	78 537
Labour and conversion	–	37 600	Closing stock	2 000	15 954
	11 000	£97 400		11 000	£97 400

The cost of good and lost production (£81 446) must be divided by the 8400 units expected to be produced = £9.696 each in order to calculate the cost of abnormal losses and goods transferred to the finished goods store.

INTER-PROCESS PROFITS

In some businesses it is the practice to charge the output of each process to the succeeding process at market value instead of at cost. By this means each process is charged with its input at current prices and no process obtains the benefit of savings, or has to bear the losses, caused by the efficiency or inefficiency of earlier processes. As each process must stand on its own feet the true profits or losses can be ascertained and appropriate action taken where the profit on any process is insufficient. In some cases it is difficult to find current prices for output, and there is a temptation to compute 'notional' prices. No benefit is gained by including a notional percentage profit on each process when it is impossible to ascertain market prices.

Inter-process profits have the disadvantage of complicating the costing records and should be avoided unless some definite benefit can be obtained from their use. It will be appreciated that such profits inflate the values of the stock of work-in-process appearing in the cost records, and it is therefore necessary to adjust all stock values down to cost when annual or monthly accounts are prepared. The procedure involved is demonstrated in the following example:

Process 1

	£		£
Materials	10 000	Stock c/d	7 000
Wages	4 000	Process 2 (transfers at	
Overheads	20 000	*market value*)	30 000
Profit (found to be 10%			
of the transfer price)	3 000		
	£37 000		£37 000
Stock b/d	700		

Process 2

	£		£
Process 1	30 000	Stock c/d	13 000
Wages	5 000	Finished stock (transfers at	
Overheads	10 000	*market value*)	40 000
Profit (found to be 20%			
of the transfer price)	8 000		
	£53 000		£53 000
Stock b/d	13 000		

One half of the finished stock has been sold during the period.

The adjustment required to bring stocks to cost is calculated as follows:

Reduction
£

Process 1 stock £7000:
 As the profit was taken only on the output, this stock is at cost.

Process 2 stock £13 000:
 This stock is valued at cost price for the process, which includes £30 000 of process 1

 material and £15 000 for conversion cost. $\dfrac{30\,000}{45\,000}$ of £13 000 or £8670 represents the

 proportion of process 1 material of which the profit element is 10%. The stock must
 therefore be reduced by. . . .   867

Finished stock £20 000:

 This stock includes process 2 profit of 20%, which must be eliminated i.e.

 $\dfrac{20}{120} \times £20\,000$.   4000

 £20 000 − £4000 leaves £16 000
 The balance of £16 000 is valued at process 2 cost price, which includes process 1

 material amounting to $\dfrac{30\,000}{45\,000}$ of £16 000 = £10 670. This figure includes 10% profit

 and must be reduced by. . .   1067
 | £5934 |

This procedure becomes more complex for each additional process, and added difficulties arise where there are opening as well as closing stocks. As already stated, the inclusion of inter-process profits is best avoided unless the benefits outweigh the added complications.

Example

The following information given regarding Medica Salts PLC for the month of May 19—, concerns one product in its range.

Process I
 10 000 kg of material, costing £6500, were put into process.
 Wages for the month were £9000.
 Direct expenses were £810 for the month, and £2340 was apportioned to the process as production overheads.

8000 kg were completed and transferred to process B and 2000 are still in process. On this work-in-process, all necessary material has been used, but it is considered to be only one-half complete as regards labour, expense, and overheads.

Process II

Wages for the month were £7040.

Direct expenses for the month were £1280 and £1408 was apportioned to the process as production overhead.

Two classes of material were added costing £6400: 2000 kg of A, which add to the quantity in process, and 500 kg of B, which do not affect the quantity in process.

3600 kg were lost in process and the remaining 6400 kg were transferred to the finished goods store.

Required:

Prepare a statement of process costs and one showing production in terms of quantity.

PROCESS COST STATEMENT

for the month of May 19—

	Process I		Process II		Total
	Total Cost	*Unit Cost*	*Total Cost*	*Unit Cost*	*Total Cost*
	£	£	£	£	£
Costs in Preceding Process:					
Transferred in			16 000	2.00	
Adjustment for Added Materials				−0.40	
				1.60	
Adjustment for Lost Units				0.90	
				2.50	
Costs in Current Process:					
Material	6 500	0.65	6 400	1.00	12 900
Wages	9 000	1.00	7 040	1.10	16 040
Expense	810	0.09	1 280	0.20	2 090
Overheads	2 340	0.26	1 408	0.22	3 748
Total Process Costs	£18 650	£2.00	£16 128	£2.52	£34 778
Cumulative Cost to be Accounted For	£18 650	£2.00	£32 128	£5.02	£34 778
Costs Accounted For:					
Transferred to:					
Process II	16 000	2.00	–	–	–
Finished Goods	–	–	32 128	5.02	32 128
Work-in-Process	2 650	1.325	–	–	2 650
	£18 650		£32 128		£34 778

Production Report – Quantities

	Process I	Process II
	kg	kg
Put into process or received from preceding process	10 000	8 000
Material Added	–	2 000
To be accounted for	10 000	10 000
Transferred to next process or to finished goods store	8 000	6 400
Work-in-Process, 31 May 19— (Complete as to material, but one-half complete otherwise)	2 000	–
Lost in Process	–	3 600
Total accounted for	10 000	10 000

Calculations:

1.   The addition of 2000 kg of material in process II makes the total to be accounted for 10 000 kg. Spreading £16 000 (process I costs) over 10 000 kg of material gives a cost in the preceding process equivalent to £1.60 per kg. The adjustment necessary is therefore a deduction of 40p per unit from the previous unit cost of £2.

2.   The reduction of the output of process II to 6400 kg makes it necessary to spread £16000 (costs in process I) over only 6400 kg of production and so gives a cost in preceding process of £2.50 per kg. The difference between £2.50 and £1.60 per kg represents the increase in unit cost due to the loss of 3600 kg.

3.   The unit cost of the work-in-process is computed as follows:

	per kg £
Material	0.650
Wages	0.500
Expense	0.045
Production overheads	0.130
	£1.325

Not infrequently the output of one process feeds more than one succeeding process, some of the partly completed product passing to one process and some to another for completion in different ways. A simple illustration of this occurs in the case of a fish packer who maintains one department for cleaning, filleting, etc. the fish, part of the output from which is frozen, whilst the remainder is tinned. In a simple case like this it is quite easy to show the costs of all three processes side by side, merely splitting the output of the first process between the others. This is illustrated in the example below. Often, however, one process feeds several others, and as it would be difficult to show the costs of all these on one sheet it is preferable to resort to the separate presentation of the costs of each process.

Example

Beaverbush PLC produces a proprietory hair tonic, under the trade name of 'Grey Mist', in two sizes: size A, which sells direct to hairdressers at 60p, and size B, which sells to retailers at 20p, to market at 32p. The factory has three processes: X, which produces the hair tonic; Y, which packs it into 60p bottles and Z which bottles it into 32p bottles. Part of the liquid hair tonic produced by process X passes from that process to process Y and part to process Z.

The following information is supplied with regard to the one-week period ended 28 February 19—:

Process X

1000 litres of liquid L costing £480, and 200 litres of liquid M costing £420 were mixed with 50 litres of liquid N costing £300. Wages for the period were £600, and overheads were £360.

50 litres were lost in process, 450 litres were transferred to process Y and 550 litres to process Z. The remaining 200 litres are complete but have not been passed to a bottling centre.

PROCESS COST STATEMENT – GREY MIST

for the one-week period ended 28 February 19—

	Process X		Process Y		Process Z	
	Total Cost	*Cost per Litre*	*Total Cost*	*Cost per Size A Bottle*	*Total Cost*	*Cost per Size B Bottle*
Costs in Preceding Process:	£	£	£	£	£	£
Cost per litre converted to cost per bottle			810	0.200	990	0.050
Costs in Current Process:						
Material:						
L	480	0.40				
M	420	0.35				
N	300	0.25				
Bottles and Labels			81	0.020	238	0.012
Secondary Containers			40	0.010	119	0.006
Wages	600	0.50	81	0.020	237	0.012
Overheads	360	0.30	162	0.040	396	0.020
	£2160	£1.80	£364	£0.090	£990	£0.050
Cumulative Cost to be Accounted For	£2160	£1.80	£1174	£0.290	£1980	£0.100
Costs Accounted For:						
Transfers to Process:						
Y	810					
Z	990					
Transfer to Finished Goods			1174		1980	
Work-in-Process	360					
	£2160		£1174		£1980	

Production Report

	Process X	Process Y	Process Z
	Litres	(bottles size A)	(bottles size B)
Put into Process	1250	4050	19 800
Transferred to: Process Y	450		
Process Z	550		
Finished Goods Store		4050	19 800
Lost in Process	50		
Work-in-Process (complete)	200		
Quantity accounted for	1250	4050	19 800

Note: There is no lost unit cost adjustment as the loss occurred in the first process.

Process Y:

Wages for the period were £81 and overheads were £162. Bottles and labels cost £81 and secondary containers £40.

One litre of liquid fills nine bottles of size A, and there was no loss in process. No work-in-process existed at either the beginning or end of the month.

Process Z:

Wages for the month were £237 and overheads were £396. Bottles and labels cost £238 and secondary containers £119.

One bottle size B holds one-quarter as much as one of size A. No loss in process occurred, and there was no work-in-process at either the beginning or the end of the period.

Required:

Prepare a statement showing the cost of each litre of 'Grey Mist' produced, and the production cost of each size of bottle, together with a table showing how the quantity of liquid put into process is accounted for.

JOINT AND BY-PRODUCT COSTING

In some industries the processing of a particular raw material gives rise to the production of several finished products of differing values. Increasing competition has compelled many businesses to consider products that were formerly regarded as waste and to seek an outlet for them either in their existing state, or after further processing. As the original material is passed through various processes before the split-off point occurs, the cost accountant is faced with the difficulty of apportioning the costs incurred between the individual products. There is generally no ideal solution to this problem and a number of different methods are used according to the value of the material involved, the amount of processing, and the relative values of the individual items. Products of the type referred to are known as *by-products* or *joint products*.

By-products

The term 'by-product' is used to cover residual material which is recovered incidentally from the production of a major product. By-products may be sold either in the condition in which they are extracted from the main product or they may undergo further processing to make them marketable. The following are examples:

1. Blast furnace slag may be used for the manufacture of building blocks, or it may be processed further and used in the manufacture of cement.
2. Fish bones and offal are used in the manufacture of oils and fertilisers.
3. In the meat trade the dressed carcase is regarded as the major product, the hides, tongues, liver, tripe, bones, grease, and tallow being regarded as by-products.
4. Waste timber may be used in the manufacture of rayon or it may be ground into powder for use in linoleum manufacture. Again, in the timber trade there is always a ready market for sawdust and firewood. All these products may be regarded as by-products.

Joint Products

The term 'joint product' is used where the split up of the original material results in the production of two or more products in such proportions and of such a nature that no single one of them can be regarded as the major product. The products are separated in the course of processing, each having a sufficiently high saleable value to merit recognition as a main product. The following are illustrations:

1. The distillation of oil results in the production of various grades of petrol, paraffin, fuel oil, and lubricants, all of which are joint products. Many minor products have also been developed by the petrochemicals industry and some of these reach proportions significant enough to warrant their also being regarded as joint products. It is not uncommon to have joint and by-products produced at a refinery.
2. Mining in which copper and silver are produced from the same ore.
3. The production of different grades of apples, flour, canned foods, tea, or tobacco from the original material supplied in bulk.
4. Where the steel industry manufactures coke in coking ovens this is regarded as the major product, much of the gas being used for heating purposes and the remainder being sold as a by-product. In such an instance the tar, benzol, etc. are also generally looked upon as by-products arising from the production of coke.

BY-PRODUCT ACCOUNTING

Of the several methods employed in accounting for by-products, none is entirely satisfactory. In practice, the most suitable of the methods described below must be chosen with due regard to all the relevant circumstances. The main methods are:

(a) Other income method.
(b) Total sales, less total costs.
(c) Total cost, less value of by-products.
(d) Apportionment of cost.

(a) *Other Income Method.* In this method, which can be applied only where the value of by-products is very small in relation to the main product, any sum realised from the sale of by-products is transferred to the profit and loss account as sundry income, being regarded as a windfall profit. The method is unsatisfactory where several main products are manufactured, as it does not reflect the individual credits applicable to each process nor is the credit reduced to take into account the share of any administration, selling and distribution costs applicable to the by-product sales.

(b) *Total Sales less Total Costs.* Under this method, which is very simple in operation, all the costs incurred on the major product and the by-products are accumulated, and their sum is deducted from the total sales of all the products. This is reasonably satisfactory where the value of the by-products is small in relation to the main product and where the by-products are marketed in the state in which they emerge from the main product.

(c) *Total Cost less Value of By-products.* There are several variations of this method, which is the most satisfactory one for general use. Under the simplest procedure all costs are charged to the main product, which is credited with the income arising from the sale of by-products.

Example

	£
Total production cost	10 000
Less sale of by-products	1 000
Net cost of main product	9 000
Add administration, selling and distribution overheads (7½% of £12 000)	900
Total cost of main product	9 900
Net profit	1 100
Selling price of main product	£11 000

This method may be varied by applying administration, selling and distribution costs separately to the by-products in the following manner:

	£	£
Total production cost		10 000
Less sale of by-products	1000	
Less administration, selling and distribution overheads (7½% of £1000) say	75	925
		9075
Add administration, selling and distribution overheads (7½% of £11 000)		825
Total cost of main product		9 900
Net profit		1 100
Selling price of main product		£11 000

Where further work on the by-products is necessary after the split-off point, the cost thereof will normally be subtracted from the revenue, before making the deduction from the cost of the main product as follows:

	£	£
Joint cost		15 000
Subsequent costs of main product		5 000
		20 000
Less sale of by-products	4000	
Less subsequent costs of by-products	1500	
	2500	
Less administration, selling and distribution overheads (5% of £4000)	200	2 300
Net cost of main product		17 700
Add administration, selling and distribution overheads (5% of £20 820) say		1 040
		18 740
Net profit		2 080
Selling price		£20 820

(d) *Apportionment of Cost.* While this method is used more in connection with joint products than with by-products, it is often applied where there are two or more main products as well as a number of minor by-products. The principle is to apportion the total cost up to the point where the split up occurs, between all the separate products that emerge at this stage. This method is explained in more detail below and is only suitable where there is a satisfactory basis for making the apportionments, and it is normally used where the value of the by products is relatively large.

The principle of by-product accounting is that, having set out to make a main product, a business finds that marketable waste arises at various stages. Whether or not this waste requires further processing, its production can be looked upon as only incidental. Where the by-products assume major significance they must normally be regarded as joint products and the costs must be apportioned in the most suitable manner.

JOINT PRODUCT ACCOUNTING

As joint product accounting covers circumstances in which no one product can be regarded as the major product, it is necessary to apportion the costs incurred so that the profit or loss on each product can be obtained. It is a relatively simple matter to allocate costs occurring after the point of separation specifically to the products concerned and it is only those joint costs that occur before separation which call for apportionment on an equitable basis. The following are the three main methods of making the apportionments:

(a) Apportionment by weight, measure, or quantity, or by some other physical property.
(b) Apportionment on the basis of eventual market values.
(c) Apportionment on the basis of market value at the point of separation.

Apportionment by Weight, Measure, or Quantity. Under this method the cost is apportioned according to the relative weight, volume, or quantity of each joint product obtained at the point where the split up occurs. Thus, if one tonne of processed material costing £7000 is divided into 1000 kg of product A, 500 kg of product B and 740 kg of product C, the cost will be apportioned as follows:

$$
\begin{aligned}
&&& \pounds \\
\text{Product A:} &\quad \frac{1000}{2240} \times \pounds7000 &=& 3130 \\[2mm]
\text{Product B:} &\quad \frac{500}{2240} \times \pounds7000 &=& 1560 \\[2mm]
\text{Product C:} &\quad \frac{740}{2240} \times \pounds7000 &=& 2310 \\[2mm]
&&& \overline{\underline{\pounds7000}}
\end{aligned}
$$

This method may be employed in cases such as a sawmill in which hardwood logs are sawn up and stacked for seasoning. While the longer and wider sections are regarded as more valuable than the short and narrow ones, it is virtually impossible to apportion the cost on a strictly accurate basis, and for want of a better method the apportionment may be made at an average rate per cubic metre of product regardless of dimensions. The method may also be used where such material as fruit is sorted into grades, and as it is impossible to apportion the costs accurately, the apportionment may be made in proportion to the weight of each grade obtained. While this method is not entirely satisfactory it has the virtue of simplicity, and where the same processes are applied to all products it is reasonable to apportion the cost at an average rate per unit. Cost must, however, be distinguished from selling price as, although identical costs are shown for various grades of the same product, higher prices will naturally be quoted for the better qualities.

This method may also be applied satisfactorily where a complex raw material such as coal or oil is separated into a number of different materials and varying weights of each are produced. The following example, covering the production of coke, coal gas, and other joint products from coal, illustrates the procedure:

	Average Yield per tonne of Coal (a) kg	Distribution of Waste (b) kg	Total (a) + (b) kg	Apportionment of Cost £
Coke	1540	80	1620	30.512
Gas	420	22	442	8.320
Benzole	25	1	26	0.488
Sulphate of ammonia	24	1	25	0.472
Tar	121	6	127	2.392
Loss (mainly water)	110	–	–	
	2240	110	2240	£42.184

The total cost of £42.184 represents the cost per tonne of coal used plus the cost of processing up to the point of separation. As the ovens are gas fired, part of the cost of gas will be re-charged as a process cost.

Apportionment on the Basis of Market Values. Under this method costs are apportioned between various joint products according to the total market value of each when they are eventually sold. This method of apportionment is an interesting departure from the normal concept of cost. In some industries e.g. glue manufacture, the processing costs are in fact lowest for the highest priced product. Against this, however, the purchase price of raw material normally reflects the relative proportions of high- and low-value products it contains, and it is reasonable to apportion a greater cost per unit to the more valuable than to the less valuable products. For example, certain ores contain varying quantities of copper, silver, and gold, and where the relative content of the most valuable elements is known to be large the ore will command a high price in the market. It would be wrong in such circumstances to apportion the price at a flat rate per kilogram of each product.

Example

After undergoing a number of processes each tonne of a certain raw material produces four joint products in the following quantities:

	Quantity kg	Unit Market Values £
Product A	100	5
Product B	400	1
Product C	200	2
Product D	50	8
Waste	50	1
Losses	200	–
	1000	

The total cumulative cost is £1000 per tonne of material processed and this will be apportioned as follows:

Product	Quantity kg	Unit Value £	Total Value £	Percentage of Total value	Apportionment of cost £
A	100	5	500	28.57	285.7
B	400	1	400	22.86	228.6
C	200	2	400	22.86	228.6
D	50	8	400	22.86	228.6
Waste	50	1	50	2.86	28.6
Losses	200	–	–	–	–
	1000		£1750	100	£1000

Where products emerge in an unmarketable state it may not be possible to determine a direct unit value, and in some cases this must be obtained by deducting from the final selling price all costs incurred subsequent to the point at which the split up occurs. This method apportions pre-separation-point costs on the basis of sales revenue, which is remote and not necessarily connected to these early costs.

The calculation shows the amount of joint cost incurred before the split-off point which is to be charged to each joint product. There may be other costs incurred post separation which will be added to pre-separation costs to find total cost and eventually determine the profitability of the joint products. The reliability of such a measure is reduced by the arbitrary nature of the apportionment method that is used.

Example

As the result of a certain process two products X and Y are produced in the ratio 3:1. The total cost per 1000 litres of product is £2000. Product X is marketed at 50p per litre while product Y sells at £1 per litre after going through a refining process. The details of this process are as follows for each 250 litres of unrefined product Y:

Output of refined Y	200 litres
Processing cost	£100
By-product Z	20 litres
Selling price of Z	25p per litre

It is first necessary to compute the *effective value* per litre of original product Y, which is the incremental cash flow derived from product Y and its by-product.

	£	£
Sales value of 200 litres of product Y		200
Deduct: Processing cost	100	
Less: Revenue from by-product Z	5	
		95
Effective value of 250 litres of original product Y		£105
Value per litre	42p	

It is then possible to apportion the joint costs as follows:

Product	Litres	Unit Value (pence)	Total Value £	Percentage of Total Value	Apportionment of Cost £
X	750	50	375	78	1560
Y	250	42	105	22	440
	1000		£480	100	£2000

Comparing these two apportionment bases, volume and selling price, it may be said that where the raw material cost is high in relation to the processing costs it is generally preferable to use the market value method. If, however, the processing costs are high in relation to raw material cost there are considerable arguments for apportioning the cost on a volume basis. Again, on the grounds of expediency, where subsequent processing is complex it may be practically impossible to determine suitable market values and the volume method must then be used. On the other hand, if the units of product cannot be compared in like terms, as in the pig meat industry, the market value basis will be applied.

As a compromise it is suggested that pre-separation costs should be apportioned between joint products on the basis of their value at the split-off point. This may be useful for some products, but for others it may be impossible or illogical to find a market value at that stage.

The arbitrary nature of the bases used to account for joint products means that the results obtained must be used with extreme caution. These methods do not appear to produce data that can be relied upon in the context of profit measurement or pricing. The application of different bases can lead to widely differing conclusions from the same data.

Example

The cost of operating a chemical process for a one-week period is £13 700. This operating cost covers materials introduced into the process and the cost of conversion. The process produces two joint products, a household polish and an oven-cleaning fluid. During the week in question, the process produced 1800 litres of polish and 4000 litres of oven cleaner. After further independent processing, costing 50p per litre for each product, the polish sells for £5.70 per litre and the oven cleaner sells for £2 per litre.

Apportionment of Joint Costs on a Physical Basis

	Polish £	Polish £		Oven Cleaner £	Oven Cleaner £
Sales (1800 × £5.7) (4000 × £2)		10 260			8 000
Apportionment of joint costs					
1800/5800 × £13 700	4252		4000/5800 × £13 700	9448	
Post-separation costs	900			2000	
		5 152			11 448
Apparent profit		£5 108	Apparent loss		£(3 448)

The product that sells for the lower price in the market is allocated a large share of joint costs because of its volume.

Apportionment of Joint Costs on a Sales Revenue Basis

	Polish			Oven Cleaner	
	£	£		f	£
Sales		10 260			8000
Apportionment of joint costs					
10 260/18 260 × £13 700	7698		8000/18 260	6002	
			× £13 700		
Post-separation costs	900			2000	
		8 598			8002
Apparent profit		£1 662	Apparent loss		£(2)

A seemingly dramatic change in the fortunes of these two products caused by an arbitrary change in the basis of cost allocation. Clearly such analysis cannot be used as a basis for evaluation of the profitability of joint products or for making decisions about these products.

SINGLE OR OUTPUT COSTING

The term *single* or *output costing* is applied where a single article or only a few grades of similar articles are manufactured, e.g. in collieries and mining concerns, brickworks, and breweries. In general, normal process costing principles are applied but clearly less detail is required when expenditure does not have to be allocated and apportioned over a variety of different processes and products. Where single costing is used, expenditure is analysed as required in the financial ledger, and operating statements are prepared direct from the ledger totals. Thus, while in process costing the raw material is transferred from process to process at an increasing cost, this does not have to be done where there is only one product, and the material used is normally shown as a separate item at cost in the operating statement. Management will, however, wish to know the cost of each department or cost centre and conversion costs will therefore have to be broken down under a number of main headings as required. Each individual item of cost will then be shown in the form of cost per tonne, cost per 1000 units, etc. General costs of overheads will not be apportioned to departments or cost centres but will be shown separately on the operating statement.

Where several grades of product emerge, it may be necessary to apportion the expenditure to each grade. This will involve the application of joint product accounting principles at a particular stage of production, unless all the costs can be accumulated and finally apportioned on the market value basis.

The recording of raw material costs follows normal principles, but where there are a number of major materials, the separate usage of each of these will be obtained and recorded individually on the operating statement. Wages will be allocated to departments and cost centres and may be classified under appropriate headings for the purpose of control. Costs that are indirect from a cost centre point of view will still be direct to the product and these will be detailed separately on the operating statement. There is thus no need to apportion or absorb the overhead costs in the normal manner and the procedure is thereafter greatly simplified. Administration, selling, and distribution costs are also regarded as direct to the product and these will either be shown in total or be detailed in separate sections of the operating statement.

The purpose of the operating statement is to show the total cost per unit together with the separate cost per unit for each raw material and for each necessary operation or process. The statements, which will be prepared weekly, monthly, or four-weekly, will usually show the actual cost, the cost per unit, and comparative figures for previous periods.

SEMINAR EXERCISES

7.1 (a) Discuss briefly the main problem experienced in costing joint and by-products and the alternative methods available to solve that problem.   (6 marks)

(b) The Carreau Company Limited are manufacturers of decorative tiles, operating a process whereby tile blanks are produced for further decoration and treatment.

During May the process used 1500 kg of special cement at £6 per kilogram and 500 kg of hardener at £9 per kilogram. The labour-force operating the process consists of three men, each working a 40-hour week for an hourly wage of £5.80. May was a four-week costing month.

Overhead expenses are allocated to the process at the rate of 150% on direct labour.

Apart from tile blanks the process produces a quantity of grit, which is sold to a local market-garden at cost. The process expects to lose 7% in weight of the input materials during operation.

During May the process produced 12 800 blanks weighing 125 g each and 200 kg of grit.

Required:

Draft a process account for May.   (10 marks)

(c) The market-gardener does not wish to buy the by-product grit in May. It is proposed that the grit should be used to make 200 light paving-slabs for a special order at £20 each. Further processing costs for the grit would be £12 per slab.

Required:

Evaluate this proposal.   (6 marks)

(Total 22 marks)

7.2 A chemical product 'Zalpon' is made by three sequential processes: 1, 2 and 3. In process 3 a by-product arises and after further processing in a by-product process, at a cost of £4 per unit, by-product 'Zelta' is produced. Selling and distribution expenses of £3 per unit are incurred in marketing 'Zelta' at a selling price of £9 per unit.

	Process 1	Process 2	Process 3
Standards provide for:			
Normal loss in process, of input, of	10%	5%	10%
Loss in process, having a scrap value per unit, of	£2	£4	£6

For the month of June, the following data are extracted from the costing records.

	Process 1	Process 2	Process 3	By-product Process
Output (units)	17 800	17 400	15 200 of Zalpon	1420 of Zelta

	Process 1	Process 2	Process 3	Total
Costs:	£	£	£	£
Direct materials introduced (20 000 units)	40 000			40 000
Direct materials added	16 000	22 640	33 200	71 840
Direct wages	15 000	16 000	20 000	51 000
Direct expenses	14 000	16 200	14 080	44 280

Budgeted production overheads for the month were £102000. Absorption is based on a percentage of direct wages. There were no stocks at the beginning or end of the month.

Required:

Using the information given prepare accounts for:
(a) each of processes 1, 2 and 3;
(b) the by-product process;
(c) abnormal losses and abnormal gains, showing the balances to be transferred to the profit and loss statement.   (25 marks)

7.3 The information below shows, for October, the costs incurred and production for the fourth and final process in a series of operations in the manufacture of standard-sized garden gnomes.

> Work-in-Process: Opening stock: 800 units; cost £2000
> Closing stock: 1000 units

1. The opening and closing stocks were both at the same stage in their manufacture, i.e. complete for previous process costs, 80% complete for materials and 60% complete for conversion costs.
2. During October 9000 units were transferred from Process 3 at a cost of £27 000. The costs of Process 4 for October were: materials £13 140, and conversion costs £17 140.
3. The operation of Process 4 is subject to inspection when materials are 60% complete and conversion costs 30% complete. Normally no losses are expected at this stage, but during October the inspector rejected 500 units, which were later sold for scrap at £2 each.

Assume FIFO.

Required:

(i)   Prepare accounts for Process 4 and abnormal losses.   (16 marks)
(ii) Why is it important to value stocks of work-in-process?   (4 marks)

(Total 20 marks)

7.4 (a) Outline the difference between process costing and job costing with particular reference to the systems whereby cost data are accumulated.   (10 marks)

(b) What are joint costs and what difficulties arise in identifying an appropriate treatment for them in cost accounts?   (10 marks)

(Total 20 marks)

REVIEW QUESTIONS

7.1 The Good Spirits Company Limited produces two products, turpentine and methanol, by a joint process. Joint costs amount to £24 000 per batch of output. Each batch totals 10 000 litres, 25% of which is methanol and 75% turpentine.

Both products are further processed without gain or loss in volume. Further processing costs are:

(i)   methanol, 60p per litre
(ii) turpentine, 40p per litre.

Methanol sells for £4.20 per litre and turpentine sells for £2.80 per litre.

Required:

(a) What joint costs per batch should be assigned to the turpentine and methanol, assuming joint costs are assigned on a:
(i)   physical volume basis
(ii) sales value basis.   (10 marks)

(b) Prepare income statements for both products per batch on a:
(i)   physical volume basis
(ii) sales value basis.   (4 marks)

(c) The company has discovered an additional process by which methanol can be made into a consumable, pleasant-tasting, alcoholic beverage. The new selling price would be £12 per litre.
There are additional post-separation costs of £3 per litre, as well as the 60p per litre mentioned above, and the company would have to pay taxes of 15% on the new selling price. Assuming no other changes in cost:

(i)   What is the joint cost applicable to methanol using the net realisable value basis?
(ii) Should the company use the new process?   (8 marks)

(Total 22 marks)

7.2 The Sticky-bun Bakery makes cakes and uses three sequential processes: the mixing of cake ingredients, the baking of the cakes, and the packaging of the cakes. December activity was as follows:

Materials used:		£
Mixing	120 000 kg of cake mix at	10p per kilogram
Baking		–
Packaging		3000
Direct labour:		
Mixing		4500
Baking		2489
Packaging		2400
Factory overheads:		
Variable:		
Mixing		1200
Baking		4200
Packaging		2200
Fixed:		
Mixing		2400
Baking		2000
Packaging		2600

During December 100 000 cakes were produced. Fixed costs are to be allocated to processes and there are no part-completed goods in each process on 1 December or 31 December. Normal wastage is 10% of the volume of material introduced to the mixing process, but in December only 100 000 kg of mixture were passed to the baking department.

Required:

(a) Prepare process cost accounts for the month of December (work to three decimal places). (12 marks)

(b) Given that the sales manager would like to make a profit of $33\frac{1}{3}$% on sales, what price will the Sticky-bun Bakery charge for each cake? (3 marks)

(c) The production manager would like to know what the break even level of cake units is, given that the price in (b) is charged to customers. (5 marks)

(d) The 20 000 kg of cake mix lost in the mixing process are usually disposed of as worthless scrap. A dog biscuit company has offered to buy this material at a price of 8p per kilogram if it is first put through the baking process. Should the Sticky-bun Bakery accept this offer? (5 marks)

(Total 25 marks)

7.3 Gardeners Aid PLC produces three separate insecticides by passing the required chemicals through three consecutive processes, namely mixing, heating and separating.

Operating information for the month of March is shown below:

Mixing

Work-in-process opening stock: 800 litres, valued as complete for materials costing £1240, but conversion costs £320 only 50% complete.

Closing stock: 1050 litres, 100% complete for materials, but 40% complete for conversion costs.

Operating costs – materials, 4000 litres costing £6440 and conversion costs, £2182.

No losses are expected in this process. 3750 litres were transferred to the 'heating' process.

Heating

There were no opening or closing stocks of work-in-process. Operating costs consisted of materials from 'mixing' and conversion costs of £6758. It is expected that 20% of the material introduced into the process will be lost due to evaporation.

Separating

There were no opening or closing stocks of work-in-process, but during March 2800 litres of material were introduced from 'heating' and eventual production was: Product A – 1000 litres; Product B – 400 litres; and Product C – 1400 litres.
   In this process the cost of working on the three joint products can be separated, and records show, A: £3000; B: £2000; and C: £5000.
   All production was sold on 31 March at prices per litre of A – £10; B – £15 and C – £8. Alternatively, Product C can be sold at £4.50 per litre without further processing in the separating process.

Required:

(a)   Draft an operating statement for the management team responsible for this process for March, and   (16 marks)

(b)   comment to the managers on significant features revealed by the statement.   (8 marks)

(Total 24 marks)

7.4   Carlton Chemicals PLC produce an industrial sealing compound by passing material through three sequential processes. Data for July for Process 2 show: Opening stock: 6000 kg plus transfers from Process 1, 22 000 kg, less abnormal loss, 4000 kg, and closing stock, 8000 kg, to give volume passed to Process 3, 16 000 kg. Materials added during Process 2 do not increase the volume. The cost per equivalent unit is:

Process 1	Process 2	
Costs	Materials	Conversion
£2.80	£1.75	£2.50

Degree of completion:

Opening stock	100%	70%	60%
Abnormal losses	100%	60%	45%
Closing stock	100%	80%	70%

The cost of work in Process 2 on 1 July was £32 800.

Process 3 is such that there is no opening or closing stock, but for July 16 000 kg have been introduced from Process 2, 1000 kg lost and 25 000 kg put in to finished goods stores. The costs of Process 3 for the month are: materials £20 350 for 10 000 kg of a new ingredient to the mixture and conversion costs of £36 000. Any waste in this process can be sold as scrap at £3 per kilogram. Normal waste is 10% of all volume passing through the process.

Required:

Draft an account for Process 2 and for Process 3 for the month of July and an abnormal gain account. (20 marks)

8

The Costing Treatment of Service Activities

The difference between cost centres engaged in activities that are directly involved in production and those indirect cost centres providing a service to other departments in the business has been discussed in an earlier chapter. Service centre costs are often apportioned to production departments on some logical or estimated basis. However, the costing treatment of service activities within a business merits further discussion. It is important to know how much it is costing the business to support the operational departments where products are actually made. Services can form a significant proportion of total cost in an organisation that, for example, generates its own power, provides all or part of its transport (within the factory and outside for distribution), designs and prints its own packaging, organises its own marketing campaigns, and administrates its own pension fund.

As a first step in costing service activities, the service must be recognised, its limits defined, and its recipients identified. Once this is accomplished the costs of providing the service can be computed. Next, the cost of the service must be related to users, and through the users to cost units produced. This activity forms part of full absorption costing, which attempts to find a true full cost for each product to set against selling price and compute the profit made per product. The result achieved can be influenced by the apportionment basis selected. In some organisations a standard service charge is applied, but the utility of this method depends on the fairness of applying a standard charge to all production activities. Is it fair, for example, to make the same standard charge for a service provided for repetitive operations, as for individual 'one off' orders? Similarly, should the same service charge be applied to long and short production runs? Too high a charge may cause small order work to be over priced and consequently lost in a competitive market. A further complication in this analysis is that the cost of providing the service may have fixed elements that cannot be transferred to alternative operations and variable elements that fluctuate with activity. An attempt must be made to control the cost of services, perhaps within the confines of a budget, and to relate fluctuations in production activity to changes in the demand for services by user departments and the effect of such changes on service costs.

A significant factor for managerial consideration should be to evaluate the benefits derived from services provided within the firm and to judge whether those benefits are worth the cost of providing the service. It is difficult to identify all benefits and sometimes impossible to evaluate them on an objective basis. Often the value of the service is only fully acknowledged when the service is withdrawn, and by then it may be too late for re-instatement. The cost of providing a service may well be measured in a similar way, by calculating the costs that would be eliminated if the service was discontinued. It may prove complicated to cost individual services provided by a service department e.g. what it costs per month to check invoices against orders and GRNs (goods received notes) in the accounts department. The time spent by clerks must be measured and the resources of fixtures and fittings used up in this operation determined, when neither clerks nor fittings are exclusively employed on invoice checking. The appropriate amount of accounts department overhead must be allotted to the service. All this takes time and costs money, but may be worthwhile as an *ad hoc* investigation of the efficiency and cost-effectiveness of the service under investigation e.g. is the cost of invoice checking greater than the losses experienced if no check is made, or greater than the cost of paying a service sub-contractor to do the job? Are we justified in providing our own computing services, or should we sub-contract to a bureau despite the consequent loss of service flexibility? Accurate quantitative answers cannot always be provided to such questions, but at least the management accountant can attempt to formalise the decision and thus reduce the possibility of a mistake. It is difficult to compare the service provided against what should be provided, and expensive to evaluate these amounts. It may also prove difficult to measure the resources needed to provide a service, but a useful evaluation of them might be made in opportunity cost terms by estimating the profit foregone by employing the resources on the service rather than on some alternative activity. For example, the service provided by a raw material store uses space, fixtures, and funds tied up in stock, and generates running costs. Once the costs of these resources are quantified the problem arises as to whether and how to absorb them to units passing through the stores. Should these costs be absorbed on the basis of the value of stock, or the volume of stock, or the work required to handle and maintain the stock? Judgement must be exercised as to whether these resources could be put to a better use in the business by employing them, or part of them, to provide some alternative service.

OPERATING COSTS

The costs of service industries are often termed operating costs, and can be expressed per unit of service provided. Operating costs are particularly suitable for the costing of road and rail transport services and they are also used by electricity undertakings, hospitals etc. The principle is to accumulate the costs under suitable headings and to express them in terms of the unit of service rendered, e.g. the costs per unit can be compared against (i) the budgeted cost, (ii) the cost of the previous period, and (iii) the cost for the same period last year, to give an idea on the efficiency of power production. Transport undertakings express their costs in terms of the passenger-mile or kilometre for passenger traffic, or the tonne-mile or kilometre for goods transport. Hospitals use the patient-day, the number of outpatients treated, and the cost per major or minor surgical operation, etc. Electricity undertakings, hospitals, and other public services normally prepare their costs in the form of operating statements similar to those used for single or output costing, except that the cost is related to the units of service rendered rather than to the units of production achieved. West Midlands Passenger Transport Executive publish statistics showing operating costs per vehicle mile and ratios expressing load factor (passenger kilometre/bus kilometre), vehicle kilometres per employee and per licensed vehicle, passenger kilometres per employee, the peak/off-peak vehicle ratio and lost mileage as a percentage of scheduled mileage.

Operating costs are often employed in the costing of services rendered within a business even though the saleable production is dealt with on job or process costing lines. In many large businesses it is, in fact, necessary to apply the principles of costing in a variety of different ways to meet all the circumstances of each case, and in practice it is more important to know how to apply these principles than it is to memorise each particular method.

POWER HOUSE OPERATING STATEMENT		
Period No.......... ended...........		
Details	Total Cost	Cost per Therm
	£	p
Steam production costs:		
Coal–300 tonnes at £52.50	15 750.00	32.86
Water 20 000 litres at 48p per 1000 litres	9.60	0.02
Water softeners	12.40	0.03
Wages–coal handling	196.00	0.42
stoking	884.00	1.84
ash disposal	224.00	0.47
Repairs maintenance and descaling	544.00	1.13
Stores	137.20	0.29
Supervision cost	248.00	0.52
Depreciation	640.00	1.36
Total cost of steam 48 000 therms	£18 645.20	38.84
Less steam allocated to heating 12 000 therms	4 661.30	
Used for generation 36 000 therms	£13 983.90	38.84
		Cost per unit
	£	p
Electricity generation costs:		
36 000 therms steam at 38.84p	13 983.90	3.99
Operators' wages	1312.00	0.37
Stores	224.60	0.07
Repairs and renewals	568.00	0.16
Supervision	248.00	0.08
Depreciation	744.00	0.21
Total cost of electricity generated	£17 080.50	4.88
Units generated 350 000		

TRANSPORT COSTS

In costing transport undertakings the cost unit is normally the tonne-mile or tonne-kilometre-mile or passenger-mile or passenger-kilometre, but the organisation into cost centres varies according to the nature of the undertaking. As and when kilometres replace miles in common parlance, so more organisations will cost in terms of the kilometre rather than the mile. Rail transport is more complex than road transport as provision has to be made not only for the vehicles but also for the maintenance of the permanent way, the stations, signalling facilities, marshalling yards, locomotives, wagons, etc. A railway undertaking is normally split into areas and sub-areas which are analogous to the departments in a factory, and within each area separate cost centres are set up under headings such as: Stations; Engine Maintenance; Permanent Way; Carriage Maintenance; Signals; Running Costs; etc.

All costs are allocated to cost centres in the first instance, and apportionments then made as required. The fixed costs of providing stations, permanent way, etc., are absorbed on a passenger- or tonne-mile basis and from the combination of these and the actual running costs, separate costings are taken out to cover each particular service or journey.

Similar principles apply in road-haulage undertakings and in the transport departments of businesses that undertake their own transport. Separate cost centres are set up for the garages, maintenance departments, offices, administration, etc., and for each particular vehicle or group of similar vehicles. Costs are then allocated as far as possible direct to each cost centre and the fixed costs of garaging etc. are absorbed by the vehicle cost centres on a definite basis. Separate costs per mile or kilometre or per tonne-mile are then calculated for each vehicle or class of vehicle.

Each driver completes a daily log sheet on which the details of each journey are recorded e.g. mileage, weight carried, and time started and finished. In a separate section of this sheet space is provided for the entry of petrol and oil supplied, and the entries will either be initialled by the petrol-pump attendant or alternatively, he will maintain a separate record of issues. In the cost office a cost sheet will be kept for each vehicle and particulars of petrol and oil, mileage and weight carried will be entered from the daily log sheets. Other costs such as road tax, insurance, tyres, and spares will be entered direct from the purchase summary, and the wages of the drivers and assistants will be posted from the wages analysis.

When a transport undertaking carries out its own maintenance the mechanics will complete time sheets for the time they spend on each vehicle and the time will be charged up at an hourly rate inclusive of overheads. Materials issued from store will be summarised and the totals transferred to the vehicle cost sheets.

At the end of each month or other suitable period the costs will be extracted from the cost sheets, which are probably held on computer file, and entered on a vehicle operating statement. This will distinguish the running costs from the fixed cost so that a true comparison can be made of each vehicle's performance. The cost per mile or kilometre, and where appropriate cost per tonne-mile, will be calculated.

In practice there are certain variations of the straight tonne-mile – sometimes referred to as the absolute tonne-mile – and which, of course, represents the carrying of a load of one tonne over a distance of one mile. Where the material is bulky but of small weight, e.g. empty biscuit tins, it would not be profitable for a transport contractor to carry such material at the same rate per tonne as he would charge for carrying steel sections. A certain maximum volume is therefore often regarded as equivalent to one tonne. In cases where goods are being loaded and off-loaded *en route* the commercial tonne-mile is sometimes used as the cost unit. In this case the total tonnage carried is multiplied by the mileage travelled and the product is divided by two. This basis takes into account the return journey and if we take a simple case of a five-tonne load delivered 50 miles, the vehicle returning empty, the commercial tonne-miles will be computed as follows:

$$\frac{5 \times 100}{2} = 250 \text{ commercial tonne-miles}$$

In this case the same answer would be obtained on the straight tonne-mileage basis. Where, however, the above consignment requires say five deliveries, each consisting of one tonne, it will then be necessary to divide by the number of trips, as follows:

$$\frac{5 \times 500}{5 \times 2} = 250 \text{ commercial tonne-miles}$$

This method is, however, used mainly for pricing rather than costing, as where a return load is obtained the transport business normally obtains the benefit. The question of return loads is important as the costs of running a vehicle empty are not greatly different from those of running it full, and it is thus almost always profitable to obtain a return load at a cut price rather than to run the vehicle empty.

MOTOR VEHICLE LOG REPORT						

MOTOR VEHICLE LOG REPORT

Licence Holder: Type of Vehicle:

Driver: Registration No.:

Date: C Licence No.:

Periods of Work

Last Ceased Work		Commenced Work Time	Rest Intervals		Ceased Work Time	Total Time excluding rest intervals	Driver's Signature
Date	Time		From	To			

Particulars of Goods and Journeys

Goods Carried			Journey			
			Left		Arrived	
Description	Weight	Destination	Place	Time	Place	Time

Speedometer Reading		Miles Run	Petrol					Oil	Signed:
Start	Finish		At Start	Received	At Finish	Used	MPG		
									Transport Foreman Date:

Note: The lower portion of the form can be printed on the back of the sheet.

The commercial tonne-mile has the advantage that where the load is different for separate parts of the journey, it is still relatively easy to calculate the number of units. This would involve a number of calculations under the absolute tonne-mile basis. In cases where the load is fairly constant for each journey the cost is sometimes calculated on a straight cost-per-mile basis, and for the sake of simplicity this method is often used for calculating the transport cost where a business keeps a fleet of vehicles for carrying its own goods.

MOTOR VEHICLE COST SHEET

Type of Vehicle: Reg. No.:   Cost Centre:

Wages and Running Costs

Date	Ref.	Miles	Tonne-Miles	Petrol	Oil	Petrol	Oil	Wages & N.I.	Misc.	Total
				Litres	Litres	£	£	£	£	£

Maintenance and Tyres					Standing Charges			
Date	Ref.	Material	Wages	Overheads	Tyres		Annual	Monthly
		£	£	£	£		£	£
						Depreciation Insurance Licence Levy Garage Overheads		
						Notes:		

MAINTENANCE AND REPAIR WORK

Maintenance and repair work is another service activity within a business that merits a proper cost accounting treatment. Often the cost of the maintenance department is accumulated on a cost centre basis, and charged out to the user department as a preconceived apportionment, or on the basis of time spent by the maintenance and repair gang on work for each other's departments. The allocation of cost in this way may not reveal the true cost, and if maintenance and repair costs are large, a more accurate method should be used. An alternative method might be to introduce a system of job costing.

Maintenance and repair costs could then be absorbed with greater attention to the work undertaken, and an accurate cost could be charged to the department concerned. In this way, managers would be made aware of the full operating costs of equipment in their care, which might influence decisions to replace such equipment. If a large proportion of the maintenance cost of a department is due to one machine, that machine will come under careful managerial scrutiny. If managers are charged with the full cost of repairs they may be more willing to instigate programmes of preventive maintenance, and to take greater care of the plant for which they are responsible. A more realistic full absorption cost for each cost unit will be computed.

Job costing for maintenance and repair work provides the management accountant with data that cover past experience of this activity, enabling careful forecasts to be made as to what it will cost to undertake certain jobs. This information will be useful when management have to decide whether a machine should be repaired or scrapped, or whether repair or maintenance work should be sub-contracted. A forecast of repair costs facilitates control, as it provides a figure against which actual costs can be compared, so that variances are identified and remedial action can be instigated where necessary.

Job costing for maintenance and repairs requires that jobs are identified, allotted a code number, and that a job cost card is compiled for each job – the cost of materials should be entered from an analysis of stores issued; the cost of labour from time sheet analysis, and departmental overheads. This costing system will be expensive, so the benefits derived from the information it produces must be considerable to render the system cost-effective. A further difficulty with repairs and maintenance is that often a considerable part of the work is involved with small, *ad hoc* problems which need to be solved quickly and may not prove large enough to merit separate recording.

SEMINAR EXERCISES

8.1   Makers PLC operates a small fleet of five vehicles that deliver its products to customers within a local delivery area.

Maintenance records for the previous five years reveal:

Year	Mileage of Vehicles	Maintenance Cost £
1	235 000	18 250
2	250 000	19 000
3	240 000	18 500
4	220 000	17 500
5	230 000	18 000

Transport statistics reveal:

Vehicle	Number of Journeys Each Day	Average Tonnage Carried to Customers tonnes	Average Distance to Customers miles
A	6	3	15
B	5	4	25
C	3	5	35
D	2	6	40
E	1	6	60

The vehicles operate a five-day week for 50 weeks a year. Inflation can be ignored. Standard cost data include:

Drivers' wages are £170 each per week } Inclusive of
Supervisor/relief driver's wage is £220 per week } holiday pay

Depreciation, on a straight-line basis with no residual value:

	Cost	Life
Loading equipment	£120 000	4 years
Vehicles	£40 000 each	4 years
Petrol/oil costs 30p per mile		
Repairs cost 9p per mile		
Vehicle licences cost £400 p.a. for each vehicle		
Insurance costs £700 p.a. for each vehicle		
Tyres cost £3100 p.a. in total		
Miscellaneous costs £2450 p.a. in total		

Required:

(a) Calculate a standard rate per tonne-mile of operating the vehicles.

(20 marks)

(b) Comment on the use of standard rate per tonne-mile, outlining its limitations in decision making. (5 marks)

(Total 25 marks)

Section III

Cost Accounting for Planning and Control

9
Budgetary Control

The ICMA definition of budgetary control is, 'the establishment of budgets relating the responsibilities of executives to the requirements of a policy and the continuous comparison of actual budgeted results, either to secure by individual action the objectives of that policy or to provide a basis for revision'. A budget, in ICMA terminology, is 'a plan quantified in monetary terms prepared and approved prior to a defined period usually showing planned income to be generated and/or expenditure to be incurred during that period, and the capital to be employed to attain that objective'.

These two excellent definitions demonstrate that a budget is more than a mere estimate or prediction of future activity in a business; it is an agreed plan for future action, stating usually in monthly terms what the business, or other organisation, will do during the budget period. Once agreed, the budget becomes an instruction communicating to each executive in the business his role in future activity, and the levels of sales, production or expenditure that he must achieve, or the limits within which he is constrained. This achievement can be monitored by the comparison of actual results with the budgeted ones for various parts of the organisation in order to provide timely feedback on how successfully the plan is being carried out. Where any deviations occur, the need for remedial action can be identified, and such action can be organised before it is too late.

The budget itself stems from a long-term corporate plan based on the strategy of the organisation, and is one step towards the attainment of organisational goals. Although much of this chapter refers to 'the business', the technique of budgeting can be applied in all organisations. All activities in the business are fitted into the budget plan so that expenses and revenue for each budget centre can be compiled into an expected income statement for the year ahead, and a balance sheet as at the end of that period can also be drafted. These summaries of budgeted activity are known as the *master budget*. The plan for forthcoming activity involves matching sales with production in order to set attainable objectives for the various parts of the business, and planning the work to be performed and costs to be incurred by the various budget centres into which the business is divided. Each budget centre is the subject of one or more subsidiary budgets, which in turn are used to compute the summarised master budget.

The main objectives of budgetary control may be summarised as follows:

1. To provide a detailed plan of action for a business over a definite period of time.
2. To co-ordinate all the activities of the organisation in such a manner that the maximum profit will be achieved for the minimum investment of capital.
3. To provide a means of determining who is responsible for each part of the plan, to identify departures from the plan, and to supply information on the basis of which the necessary corrective action may be taken.

The budget is a co-ordinator, communicator, and motivator.

Budgetary control brings the following benefits:

1. The preparation of budgets for the various parts of the business identifies, emphasises and clarifies the responsibilities of each executive. No activity can be outside the budget, since all finance is planned, and funds can only be used for budgeted purposes. It follows that a line of responsibility is established for managers reporting upwards for their departments, and receiving reports from their subordinates.

2. An early and regular consideration of basic policies by management at all levels is part of the budgeting process since the year's plan must fit overall strategy. Executives are forced to look ahead and identify alternative courses the business might follow.

3. Planning focuses attention on the contribution made by each product or activity to the overall income of the business, and on the capital required, methods employed and costs incurred to achieve proposed goals. At this stage problems anticipated and further opportunities for profitable activity are revealed.

4. Co-ordination implies that sales, production and other activities will be geared to a common level, so that sales made can always be supplied from stock, and that production is limited to quantities intended to be sold or stocked. Managers are forced to plan in harmony.

5. The budget acts as a comparator against which actual performance can be measured, thus facilitating a detailed control of income and expenditure to highlight waste, losses and inefficiency, and identifying budget centres where prompt remedial action is required.

6. A budget acts as a constant reminder to managers of the level of performance to which they have committed themselves by accepting their part of the budget. Accepting responsibility implies commitment, and this in turn forces managers to be realistic, and express their intentions in precise figures at the planning stage.

7. Once the levels of planned sales and production are determined other requirements for stock, debtors and plant can be calculated. This enables the business to ensure that capital employed is kept to a minimum level consistent with the level of activity planned, that all resources are usefully employed and that adequate liquid funds are always available. It is possible to plan for the funds required in the business to attain budgeted levels of activity, and to identify any shortfall between funds required and funds available.

8. Top management can decentralise responsibility for parts of the business to lesser executives without losing control. The middle and junior managers can be given freedom of action to manage their department in their own ways, provided they perform according to budget.

9. Cost consciousness is increased, and an attitude of mind is encouraged in which waste and inefficiency cannot thrive. Managers come to understand the effect of their actions in terms of cost within the budget framework.

10. The budget is a communicator because, once accepted, it becomes an executive instruction, and also because it provides junior managers with detailed information on the policy of the business. Equally, during the process of setting the budget, the opinions and aspirations of junior managers must be allowed to permeate upwards through the organisation, so that all managers feel motivated as part of a team working together towards a common goal.

ESTABLISHMENT OF BUDGETS

Behind the master budget, which states the overall plan for the business in summary form, are a number of subsidiary budgets from which the master budget is built up. These include:

(a)   Sales budget
(b)   Production budget
(c)   Selling cost budget
(d)   Distribution cost budget
(e)   Administration cost budget
(f)   Development and research budget
(g)   Capital expenditure budget
(h)   Stock budgets
(i)   Cash budget.

Budgets that relate to a function of an undertaking, such as distribution, are termed *functional budgets.*

Behind these budgets are further budgets from which they in turn are constructed e.g. the production budget will show the planned production in quantity and also in terms of cost. However, it is a summary budget summarising information taken from the budgets of the departments (or to use the proper term, budget centres) that complete the work involved in production. Also, in so far as these production budget centres are served by service centres, their budgets (i.e. production budget centre budgets) will be related to the budgets of those service centres.

The production budget is thus a summary budget showing the budgeted production overheads, together with the budgeted material and direct labour costs of production, and it is built up from various budget centre budgets which show similar information on a departmental basis. Raw material costs will in turn relate to material purchasing and the material stock budget.

Parallel to the main summary budgets e.g. the selling cost budget, production budget, administration cost budget, etc., there exists another class of summary budget called a *production factor budget.* Such budgets summarise requirements and show how the necessary factor is to be procured and at what cost. They do so, not according to function, but by production factor. They are a means of gathering together, for example, total material needs, total personnel requirements, total equipment needs, etc. and thus form a basis from which the purchasing, personnel engagement and plant engineering activities can be assessed.

Finally, there exist what may be termed *capital budgets* concerned with balance sheet items such as cash, fixed assets, debtors, stocks, etc.

To show how the various subsidiary budgets are related to one another and at the same time fit together in the budget summaries, a skeleton of one is illustrated below. This shows the source of each item in the budgeted manufacturing account and trading and profit and loss accounts.

BUDGET ORGANISATION

The budget is a decision with far-reaching significance for all parts of the business, to which managers at all levels have made a contribution. Budgetary control is really two

Production Budget (or Budgeted Manufacturing Account)

for the year ending 31 December 19—

Budget Centre Budget:	Summary Budget or Other Source:		£	£
		Direct material cost:		
	Balance sheet (1 January)	Opening work-in-progress (material)		0 000
	Balance sheet (1 January)	Opening stock of raw material	0 000	
	Material procurement budget	Purchases	00 000	
			00 000	
	Raw material stock budget	Less closing stock of raw material	0 000	
Direct materials	Material requirements budget (direct section)			00 000
				00 000
	Work-in-progress budget	Deduct closing work-in-progress (material)		0 000
				00 000
		Direct wages:		
	Balance sheet (1 January)	Opening work-in-progress (wages)		0 000
Direct wages	Labour requirements budget (direct section)	Wages		00 000
				00 000
	Work-in-progress budget	Deduct closing work-in-progress (wages)		0 000
				00 000
		Production overheads:		
	Balance sheet (1 January) Material procurement budget Raw material stock budget	Overheads in progress (1 January)		0 000
Indirect materials	Material requirements budget (indirect section) – as with direct materials	Overheads incurred		00 000
				00 000
Indirect wages Indirect expense	Labour requirements budget Indirect expense summary	Deduct closing work-in-progress (overheads)		0 000
				00 000
		Budgeted production cost		£00 000

Skeleton Budgeted Trading and Profit and Loss Account

for the Year Ending 31 December 19—

Source			£	£
Sales budget	Sales			000 000
	Deduct cost of sales:			
Balance sheet (1 January)	Opening stock of finished goods		0 000	
Production budget	Production cost		00 000	
			00 000	

	Less closing stock of	£	£
Finished stock budget	finished goods	0 000	00 000
	Budgeted gross profit		000 000
Selling cost budget	Deduct: Selling costs	0 000	
Distribution cost budget	Distribution costs	0 000	
Administration cost budget	Administration costs	0 000	
Research and development			
budget	Research and development costs	0 000	00 000
	Budgeted net profit before taxation		£00 000

activities: first, the setting of the budget and then the analysis of how far the plan is achieved. The budget programme must, like any other, be the definite responsibility of some member of the undertaking. As with everything else the ultimate responsibility for budgetary control rests upon the chief executive (e.g. the managing director), but obviously much of the actual work involved must be delegated. The person who undertakes this work often bears the title of 'Budget Controller' or 'Budget Officer', even though his budgetary activities may not be sufficient to occupy his entire attention and he may also fulfil some other function.

Obviously the budget controller must have a status sufficiently high to ensure that the budgetary programme will command respect and attention throughout the organisation, but respect must be earned, and will stem from the way in which he tackles the job. Arrangements may therefore be made for the budget controller to report direct to the board, or if there is a controller (who is not also the budget controller), direct to that office. Alternatively, control over budgeting may be considered so important that it may remain in the hands of the chief executive, only the routine work of co-ordination and supervision being delegated to a staff assistant. The preparation of a budget is a task of management in which the executives must play their parts. The budget officer assists them, using his accounting skills to improve the end result. Managers must develop their own budgets, and are thus motivated to accept responsibility for them.

The managers in charge of the various functions of an undertaking will be largely responsible for preparing the budgets of their respective functions. Budgets should develop from forecasts made by managers of what is possible or likely to happen at the 'grass roots' level of the business. These people will probably be in charge at a local level when the plan unfolds, and they are expected to know more than senior centralised managers about detailed operations and local conditions. If the managers at the grass-roots level see that they can influence the budget they are more likely to adopt it as their own, thus increasing their commitment to its successful completion. Similarly, top management seek to influence the budget according to the strategic aims of the business. If grass-roots opinion of what is feasible is not in agreement with board policy, the budget controller must assist in reconciling the parties, by persuading managers to adjust their plans, or by suggesting to the board decisions required for changes of policy, e.g. if the production budget is pitched at a production level that will not meet orders anticipated by the sales budget, the factory must be persuaded to increase output through greater productivity or overtime, and the board must be sent a capital expenditure proposal to increase factory capacity. This is how co-ordination takes place. If the proposed budget seems unlikely to achieve the policy aims of the company in terms of market share, profitability etc., it may be necessary to make a fresh start based on a new set of assumptions.

The budget controller should act as a co-ordinator and adviser, working with managers and integrating the budgets prepared by the departmental heads to form the master plan, referring back to individual managers as the need arises. Under this system there may be too little emphasis on the need for co-ordination between functions, and this is likely to lead either to excessive reference back to the departments concerned, or to the adjustment of budgets by the budget controller without consulting the heads of the departments concerned. In any event, the method usually throws considerable strain upon the co-ordinating ability of the budget controller.

An alternative is to form a budget committee, composed of the managing director, the budget controller, and the heads of the main departments e.g. production, distribution, and sales. At routine meetings the chair may be taken by the budget controller, and the managing director may or may not attend. At more important meetings the managing director may take the chair, though this is not universal practice.

The budget committee first develops agreed procedures and a timetable for the budget. Meetings attempt to reconcile the forecasts of executives to board policy, by calling for revisions from managers and asking for decisions from the board. Gradually, through discussion, the various parts of the business are co-ordinated, dynamic change being effected by means of a series of small steps, known as *iteration*. During this procedure plans for alternative activities are considered and an optimum position is agreed upon. It is important to co-ordinate the timing and scale of operations, e.g. it is of little use to sell goods in the first quarter of the year if they are not scheduled for production until the third quarter. Gradually, during this iterative process, the limiting factors emerge and are dealt with where possible. The budget committee will also build into the budget the framework of responsibility, which each manager accepts before he can lead his department through the budget plan. The committee may be called on to make decisions where the budget of one department is in conflict with that of another. Eventually the finalised budget is approved and the committee will then meet throughout the year to receive reports comparing actual with budgeted performance, to consider what remedial action has been proposed, and, where necessary, to revise the budget. A useful control report will inform the manager concerned what his sales and/or costs were expected to be for a certain costing period, how far those expectations have been met or exceeded and whether attempts to attain budget performance over recent months are succeeding, together with an explanation of variances, which may help in reducing such variances in the future.

In a large organisation it is usually convenient to prepare a budget manual which sets out, *inter alia*, the responsibilities of the persons engaged in, the routine of, and the forms and records required for preparing the budget and later controlling performance. However, since there exists such a wide variation of organisational structure and methods of production, it is impossible to lay down any general procedure suitable for use in all businesses.

Some idea of the matters for which each member of a budget committee would be responsible is given by the following table:

Manager :	Responsible for :
Sales	Sales in terms of quantity.
	Selling prices, discounts, rebates, etc.
	Selling costs, including those of sales management, representation, advertising, etc.

Distribution	Distribution costs, including those of transport, storage, etc.
Production	Quantity of finished goods stocks.
	Production in terms of quantity.
	Production costs.
	Raw material stocks and work-in-progress.
Research	Research costs.
Office	Administration costs e.g., salaries, legal expenses, audit fees, etc.
Managing Director (or the Board)	Profit planning.
	Capital expenditure.
	Depreciation.
	Current assets and liabilities, e.g. level of trade debtors and the 'cash' position.
	Dividends.

In some concerns, however, the head of a department has only a restricted responsibility – final control remaining with the board or with the managing director. This is frequently the case with advertising, the amount of which is outside the control of the sales manager.

Relationship of Budgetary Control to Standard Costing

Standard costing and budgetary control have in common the establishment of pre-determined measures of performance ('budgets' and 'standards') and the comparison of actual and planned performance so as to disclose details of variations which are used for the purpose of cost control. In many instances the same standards are employed for both standard costing and budgetary control. However, in general terms, it may be said that budgetary control is wider in its conception and application than standard costing. Thus the former covers sales, capital expenditure, cash, etc., whilst the latter concentrates on standards of cost. Standards may also differ from budgets in their aim. Thus standards are sometimes set at the ideal levels to which costs *ought* to be reduced, whilst budgets are more usually based on the anticipated *actual* level of costs.

Budgetary control may be applied in such businesses as those of a jobbing nature, where the variety of the work renders standard costing almost impossible. The products in such a case will still be costed historically but income and expenditure will be controlled by means of pre-determined budgets.

Budgeting techniques are frequently employed in connection with the pre-determination of overhead absorption rates, and they are essential to the proper setting of standard overheads. Standard costing systems can exist, however, without any proper system of budgetary *control*, but while many benefits are obtainable from such systems, the introduction of budgets provides a better overall control over many of the more general factors such as sales, capital expenditure and cash.

Budget Centres

For control purposes an organisation is usually broken down into budget centres. Each budget centre must be a cost centre or group of cost centres since its costs must be accumulated separately from those of other budget centres. The main factor in setting up budget centres is one of responsibility – whatever the size of a budget centre, one person must be responsible for controlling all its costs.

To ensure the fullest cost control, attention should be given to the following matters:

1. The budget of a particular individual should specify precisely the costs controllable by him.
2. Costs for which responsibility is shared (e.g. work carried out by a maintenance department) should be kept separate from costs over which one manager has control.
3. One executive should be made responsible for controlling every cost that has subsequently to be apportioned between two or more budget centres.

Non-incorporation of Budgets in the Double Entry System

A main distinction between standard costs and budgets is that the former are normally entered in the cost accounting records, whilst the latter are not. Budgets are thus a statistical device intended to assist management in its operational control. Their use is not limited to manufacturing concerns; they are used extensively in departmental stores and similar undertakings, as well as by charitable institutions, schools, colleges, and government departments. The Chancellor of the Exchequer's annual budget is familiar to all.

THE PREPARATION OF BUDGETS

Budget Period or Horizon

Before any steps can be taken to compile budgets it is necessary to establish the period over which they are to operate. This is largely dependent upon the class of business concerned. Some firms budget for more than a year ahead, but most limit the plan to 12 months or 13 costing periods over a 52-week year. Where sales are greatly influenced by seasonal factors, budgets over short periods of from a month to a quarter are not uncommon. The period depends on how far ahead conditions in the industry can be reliably forecast. Firms in the fashion goods' and fancy goods' trades are likely to budget over short periods.

The purpose for which a budget is established has a major bearing upon the length of the budget period, and there is nothing to prevent a concern from choosing different budget periods for different purposes. Thus a capital expenditure budget will cover a period of several years, while, at the other end of the scale, circumstances may exist in which it is impracticable to prepare a cash budget for more than three to six months ahead.

Budget preparation is expensive both in time and money, so there is little to commend the adoption of too short a budget period. On the other hand, an excessively long budget period is likely to result in budgets that will cease to resemble current conditions by the end of the period. For most purposes it is found that the financial year is the most satisfactory budget period – it is normally sufficiently short for prices to remain reasonably current and at the same time long enough to present a long-term view. Furthermore, the effort required is not excessive in relation to the benefits gained. Where flexible budgeting techniques are employed, as discussed later in this chapter, provision is made for the adjustment of cost budgets to current levels of activity. It is not uncommon in some organisations to review actual progress quarterly and to show six months' actual costs and six months' budgeted costs in order to forecast a final result at the half-way stage.

The Rolling Budget

An annual budget compiled before the start of a year may well be unrealistic by the end of that year if significant inflation has taken place. Assumptions and prices that were correct a year previously may now be unrealistic. Accordingly, such a budget is not a good measure against which to set actual performance. A rolling budget is prepared for a twelve-month period, but this budget is replaced by another twelve-month budget after, say, three or four months. The frequency of the roll to update plans to reflect current prices, costs and conditions depends on the rate of inflation and the planning horizons of the business. Flexibility is essential in order to identify changes and incorporate them into the rolling budget, but so also is a systematic approach to budgeting, which permits rapid computation.

An orthodox budget based on the prices and costs ruling, say, eight months previously can restrict the ability of an organisation to react to changed conditions. In any case it is a false assumption that ongoing business operations can be expressed in discreet annual compartments. A rolling budget extends the planning horizon. Frequent budget reviews may reduce the significance of budget calculation and computation and encourage more discussion to challenge the strategy underlying the budget and develop alternatives. The annual budget produces a fairly radical change at the point where one budget period ends and another begins, but with a rolling budget more frequent but smaller changes smooth out such convulsions.

Principal Budget Factor

Reference has already been made to the value of budgets as an aid to the co-ordination of all the activities of a business, but this co-ordination does not arise automatically. Thus, if sales and production are budgeted independently, the two activities will be unlikely to match – budgeted sales of some products will exceed budgeted production, whilst budgeted production of others will exceed budgeted sales. There is always a limit to the capacity of a business to make and sell each of its products. For instance, it may not be possible to sell more of one product at the existing price because there is insufficient consumer demand. A lack of skilled labour or materials, or shortage of production facilities, may be the principal factor in the case of another product, and both these matters will need to be taken into account in balancing sales with production. The cause of such a bottleneck is termed the *principal budget factor*. The alternative terms 'governing factor' or 'limiting factor' are possibly more self-explanatory.

Limiting Factors

A limiting factor is any factor that prevents a business from extending its potential level of activity. These key, or governing, factors may have a long- or short-term effect on a business and may or may not be within the power of management to dispel. Limiting factors can arise in the following areas:

Sales. Insufficient sales can limit the ability of a business to extend profitable operations. The limit may be caused by a real or artificial ceiling to demand for the company's products. Insufficient advertising or wasteful spending of an adequate advertising budget, or the activities of an ineffective sales force contribute to this limiting factor.

Labour. A shortage of operatives with the appropriate skills, perhaps through a weak training scheme, limits the potential of the business. Poor labour relations leading to a lack of effort and co-operation and perhaps to the disruption of a strike is another dimension to labour as a limiting factor.

Materials. The possibility of a 'stock out' due to scarcity, a policy of holding too small a stock, or the failure of a sub-contractor to supply components on time, can reduce the potential of a business at the planning stage.

Plant. Insufficient capital expenditure limits the machine-hours available to production, and may mean that old machines, which suffer from frequent breakdowns, are used. Perhaps space and plant layout inhibits management's attempts to increase production.

Management. It may be a limiting factor. If it cannot introduce new ideas, or work with sufficient dynamism to reach the full potential of the business or react quickly to changed conditions.

Finance. Holding down stock levels, trade credit to back up sales campaigns and capital expenditure will inhibit a business.

During its discussions the budget committee must recognise these factors, attempt to evaluate their effect on the budget, and take steps to reduce their influence.

The following example shows in a simplified form how sales and production may be co-ordinated. It is unreal, however, in that it makes no attempt to assess the possibility of increasing sales volume by adopting a lower selling price, and in so far as it assumes that there can be no transfer of production facilities, surplus to requirements in relation to one product, to another product in respect of which there is a shortage of production facilities.

Example

The Hercules Manufacturing Company Limited manufactures five products. The company's sales and production managers have prepared the following schedule to show the quantity of each product they consider they could sell or produce, respectively, in the forthcoming year, together with details of the factor that prevents them from selling or producing more. At what level would sales match production in the case of each product?

	Production		Sales	
Product	Quantity	Limiting Factor	Quantity	Limiting Factor
A	10 000	Plant capacity	8000	Consumer demand
B	1 000	Skilled labour	5000	Policy to sell only in southern sales area
C	4 000	Restrictions on material supply	5000	Policy to export only
D	10 000	Plant capacity	9000	Consumer demand
E	5 000	Plant capacity – permission to purchase new machinery granted in principle but cash not yet available to go ahead	7500	Consumer demand

Assuming that no interchange of facilities is possible and that no arrangements can be made to extend any limiting factor, production and sales will be co-ordinated (ignoring any policy to change stock levels) at the following figures:

Product	Quantity
A	8000
B	1000
C	4000
D	9000
E	5000

Before finalising either the sales budget or the production budget in terms of quantity, it is essential that management should consider whether means are available to remove or reduce the limiting factor, and hence reduce the effect of any bottleneck. Only by so doing can profits be maximised. Where production is the principal budget factor, the following possible means of extending the limiting factor may be considered:

1. Overtime work.
2. Double or treble-shift working.
3. Incentive schemes to increase productivity.
4. Simplification of operations and/or product design.
5. Sub-contracting of work.
6. Purchase of components instead of manufacturing them.
7. Substitution of alternative materials.
8. Improvement of plant layout.
9. Improvement of production control and planning.
10. Modernisation of plant.
11. Acquisition of additional equipment, buildings, etc.

On the other hand, where ability to sell is the governing consideration, it may be possible:

1. To expand markets by selling in other parts of the country or exporting.
2. To increase sales by improving the design of the product or arrangements to service it.
3. To increase consumer demand by more extensive advertising or by the use of new or improved means of advertising or sales promotion.
4. To market new lines that will absorb surplus production capacity.
5. To increase revenue by adopting alternative or additional methods of marketing e.g. by selling direct to retailers rather than through wholesalers, or vice versa.
6. To tap new markets by finding additional uses for existing products.

Since the demand for a product tends to vary inversely with its price, the sales budget can be finally determined only when selling prices have been fixed. If selling prices are to be related to cost, which will of course vary with volume, this may mean that the sales and production budgets will each need to be revised several times before they finally agree; alternatively, the difficulty may be overcome by the preparation of a series of budgets, each showing a possible level of sales and production.

SALES BUDGET

In its final form the sales budget is a statement of planned sales in terms of quantity and value, and analysed by products. Obviously the method of arriving at the sales budget will differ widely according to the type of business. For instance, it is far more difficult to plan sales of ice cream or hotel accommodation, than it is to plan those of a staple commodity like sugar. Sales budgeting tends to involve different principles in a large business having highly trained and widely experienced managers in charge of area divisions, from those found in a small family concern, selling in a restricted area. Similarly, a new business has to face problems which no longer affect an established one. The factors which may have to be considered in forecasting sales are:

1. Past sales – which since they are matters of historical fact are not subject to exaggeration in the same way as are the assessments of salesmen etc. Where possible past sales should be so analysed as to disclose separately the long-term trend, cyclical and seasonal movements, and chance fluctuations due to such events as strikes and lock-outs, in order that a more accurate assessment of prospects may be made.
2. Forecasts of business conditions in the concern's own trade and those in related trades. For instance, a producer of margarine ought to consider the position in the butter industry, as well as that in his own.
3. Market analyses measuring the potential demand for products. In the case of a new product, a manufacturer has no past experience to guide him and is forced to depend upon market research or to fall back on mere estimates.
4. Assessments by the sales department, salesmen, etc. Since the area sales budgets represent targets for the representatives concerned, it seems reasonable that some attention should be paid in fixing them to the views of the personnel most closely concerned, i.e. those in the field. However, no general rules can be provided with regard to the weight to be attached to each factor, as this will differ according to circumstances.

Sales budgets will be prepared on an area basis, either as a step in the preparation of the summary sales budget, or as a breakdown of a main sales budget already prepared. Thus, where the assessment of sales is made on an area basis e.g. as the result of salesmen's assessments, the former will be the case. Where, on the other hand, the emphasis is on total sales e.g. as a matter of policy, analysis by sales areas will follow the preparation of the main budget.

A full assessment of the probable sales of a business can be made only after considering:

(a) the firm's own sales and those of its competitors, area by area;
(b) whether its share of business is increasing or decreasing;
(c) seasonal fluctuations;
(d) the effect of past or potential population movements;
(e) changing consumer tastes;
(f) the effect of introducing new products by the concern itself or by competitors;
(g) increases or decreases to be made in the advertising budget;
(h) the effect of sales promotion schemes planned by the firm itself or by its competitors (so far as is known);
(i) the effects of any planned improvement in existing products or of their discontinuation;
(j) The possibility of selling in new territories or of discontinuing sales in existing ones.

To obtain a conservative picture it may pay to classify forecast sales into those that result from stable business, i.e. arising from existing contracts or repeat sales to old customers, those that result from repeat orders by new customers and are thus less easy to forecast reliably, and those that are expected to stem from an expansion of business and are thus less certain than either of the foregoing classes.

It will be seen that two main forms of analysis are envisaged:

Analysis by Product Type. In order to prepare the production budget in detail, it is essential to plan sales by product type. Thus, if a company manufactures seven different models of gas cooker, it is necessary to specify in the sales budget how many of each type will be sold, so that proper arrangements can be made to plan for their manufacture. In this case a further analysis might be made by colour to ensure balanced production not only of each model but of each colour in the range. Where, however, a business manufactures largely to customer requirement, it is impossible to prepare the sales budget in quantitative terms, and whilst sales should be broken down into major product groups, they will normally be specified only on a value basis. It is obvious that the production budget cannot then show any more detailed product analysis.

Analysis by Area. Where a business has separate sales organisations covering various geographic areas, analysis of the sales budgets accordingly is important as a means of fixing a separate target for each group of representatives. Then where variations from sales targets occur, the individuals responsible can be pinpointed and action taken to award praise and reward or to train or rebuke, as is appropriate.

Analysis by areas is important too in connection with the distribution costs, as only by comparing the cost of supplying a product in a specified area (including the cost of distribution) with the corresponding revenue produced, can a manufacturer assess the profitability of trading in that area.

In its final form the sales budget of the manufacturer of stock lines is a statement in both quantitative and monetary terms, but that of a jobbing concern cannot usually be expressed quantitatively. In either case the value of sales will normally be expressed on a current basis, and must therefore take into account changes in price levels.

Example

A jobbing engineer estimates that his turnover is increasing by 10% of his Year 1 turnover per annum. This increase has in the past been largely camouflaged by falling price levels, so that sales have in fact been:

	£
Year 1	100 000 (Average price index 100)
Year 2	101 200 (Average price index 92)
Year 3	98 400 (Average price index 82)

Prices ceased to fall at the end of Year 3, and it is anticipated that the price index will remain stable in Year 4 at 80.

Sales budget for Year 4 would be:

$$\frac{[£100\,000 + (3 \times \tfrac{10}{100} \times £100\,000)] \times 80}{100} = £104\,000$$

Where the prices charged to various classes of customer differ so greatly that the use of an average selling price for each product would give inequitable results, it is necessary also to analyse the sales of each product by class of customer, applying the appropriate selling price to the quantity sold to ascertain in each case the total sales revenue from the product.

Example

The following example illustrates the building up of a typical sales budget.

The Oldfield Soap Company Limited manufactures two products, a bar-soap sold under the trade name 'Blocko', and a detergent called 'Blick'. The company's sales department has three area divisions: North, South, and Irish.

Preliminary sales budgets for the year ending 31 December 19—, based on the assessments of the sales division managers, were: Blocko – North 2 000 000; South 5 000 000; Irish 100 000; and Blick – North 3 000 000; South 4 000 000; Irish nil. Sales price (net) are 20p and 40p respectively in all areas.

Arrangements are made for the extensive advertising of Blick on the Three Ridings TV Network and it is estimated that North division sales will increase by 1 000 000. Increased production makes it possible for the company to market Blick in Ireland and arrangements are made to advertise and distribute the product there in the second half of 19—, when sales are expected to be 500 000 packets.

It is accepted that the estimated sales by South division represent an unsatisfactory target. It is agreed to increase both estimates by 10%.

Required:

Prepare a sales budget for the year to 31 December 19—

Oldfield Soap Company Limited

Sales budget for 19—

Selling price	Blocko 20p		Blick 40p		Total
	Quantity	£	Quantity	£	£
North	2 000 000	400 000	4 000 000	1 600 000	2 000 000
South	5 500 000	1 100 000	4 400 000	1 760 000	2 860 000
Irish	100 000	20 000	500 000	200 000	220 000
Total	7 600 000	£1 520 000	8 900 000	£3 560 000	£5 080 000

It is again emphasised that neither the sales budget nor the production budget can be finalised in isolation – all the various budgets must be revised, and if necessary revised again and again, until they provide for a single co-ordinated effort. This is the system of iteration in operation.

SELLING COST BUDGET

Closely associated with the sales budget is the selling cost budget, which shows the planned costs of promoting sales and retaining custom for the budget period. Included in the selling cost budget are such items as the cost of representation e.g. salesmen's salaries, commissions, and hotel expenses; depreciation and the running cost of cars, and other travelling expenses; those of sales management and of advertising. Separate subsidiary selling cost budgets are often prepared for each area and agreed with the area sales manager concerned; for sales management, in respect of costs falling directly under the control of the head office sales manager; and for advertising. Where sales management is subdivided according to product lines or product groups (one sales manager being responsible for heavy engineering products and another for precision measuring equipment, for instance) it is necessary to subdivide budgeting responsibility accordingly.

Sales Budget – Pro Forma

ELECTRICAL MANU-FACTURERS PLC Southern Area Sales Budget – Year Ending 19—	Budget This Year		Expected Actual This Year*		Budget Next Year	
	Units	£000's	Units	£000's	Units	£000's
ANALYSIS OF OUTLETS District Salesmen 1 2 3						
25 26 Agents 1 2 3						
11 12						
Total Sales						
ANALYSIS BY PRODUCT: Electric Irons Wall Heaters Fan Heaters Toasters Razor Points Sale of Rejects						
Total Sales						
ANALYSIS BY CUSTOMER: 1 2 3 4 5 Other Outlets						
Total Sales						

* The Expected Actual figure is the most recent forecast of sales for the year at the end of, say, the second or third quarter.

The total sales are analysed per outlet, product and customer. Further analysis would show the time spread of sales over the year. Note that consideration is given to the current budget and how accurately it has been achieved when setting the budget for the next year.

Before a typical selling cost budget is illustrated, the problems which arise in connection with each type of subsidiary selling cost budget will be considered separately.

Representation. Assuming that sales representation is on an area basis, there being divisional managers in charge of each sales area, each separate area will have its own representation budget either compiled by the area manager or at least agreed with him. This budget will generally be prepared in the light of past experience as modified for any known changes and in order to ensure that it presents to all concerned an acceptable indication of the costs to be incurred at a reasonably attainable state of efficiency of operation.

Past experience will have to be modified where:

1.   The sales area has been expanded or contracted, or there has been a policy change with regard to representation, e.g. a decision to adopt a wholesaler only method of distribution, thus abandoning calls on individual retailers.
2.   Changes have been made in the sales budget. For example, such changes may affect the amount of commission payable to representatives and thus influence the cost of representation generally.
3.   The basis of remuneration is changed to provide additional incentive to sell specified lines.
4.   The business is seasonal, when the 'monthly' budgets will not necessarily be straight fractions of the past year's total. Commission, for instance, will be heavy at the seasonal peak, and lower in the slack season.

Sales Management. The representation budgets are likely to vary, if not in proportion to sales, at least largely so. Any considerable increase in sales will involve the payment of additional commission, the engagement of additional staff to cover wider areas or to work existing territories more intensively, higher travelling costs, etc. A similar expansion of sales is not likely to result in a proportionally large increase in the costs of sales management since these consist largely of office salaries, building occupation costs, stationery, postage, etc., and a change in the value of sales is not necessarily accompanied by increased administrative costs. Only major variations in the volume of transactions or considerable changes in the area of representation are likely to affect the number of sales management personnel or the extent of the accommodation they need to occupy.

Publicity. The publicity or advertising budget should be developed in conjunction with the sales budget, since the latter is dependent upon the spending of the amount specified in the former.

The total expenditure on publicity is often fixed by the management as a matter of policy, on what is known as the appropriation basis. This involves the determination of how much the concern is prepared to spend during the budget period – rather than the relation of the advertising cost to revenue. In the early days of a product's existence the cost of advertising may exceed the total revenue from sales – the advertising being required to create a market for the goods. Later, when the product is firmly established, the need for advertising will persist but at a relatively lower level, although the expenditure may have to be increased subsequently to meet new competition. The volume of advertising needed is likely to vary quite widely, according to the nature of the product or service and other factors, though it is not connected in any simple way with current sales levels.

Publicity is a general term that embraces press, radio, and television advertising, posters, exhibitions, window displays, postal circulation, door-to-door distribution of samples, etc., and the publicity budget is frequently subdivided to show the manner in which the budgeted expenditure is to be applied. Where the exact manner of spending the publicity budget is not specified in advance, it is usual to analyse it on an area basis and/or by products as is shown in the illustration below.

Hardcastle PLC

Publicity Budget for the Year 19—

| | Sales Area | | | | Head Office | Total |
	North	South	Irish	Welsh		
By media:	£	£	£	£	£	£
Press	36 500	47 300	7 400	22 700	–	113 900
TV	103 900	116 100	–	212 000	–	432 000
Poster	21 200	22 300	22 100	24 300	–	89 900
Window-display	13 400	14 300	1 500	16 000	–	45 200
Exhibition	–	–	–	–	45 000	45 000
	£175 000	£200 000	£31 000	£275 000	£45 000	£726 000
By product:						
A	112 000	128 000	17 000	92 000	—	349 000
B	38 000	52 000	12 000	110 000	21 000	233 000
General	25 000	20 000	2 000	73 000	24 000	144 000
	£175 000	£200 000	£31 000	£275 000	£45 000	£726 000

DISTRIBUTION COST BUDGET

A distribution cost budget covers such items as building service costs applicable to finished goods warehouses, the handling and packing of such goods, and their transport to regional storehouses and to customers. In a large concern distribution costs are often expressed in terms of some unit of effort so that the budget can be adjusted more conveniently to varying levels of sales.

Example

The distribution cost budget of the Excelsior Chemical Company PLC includes:

	£
Boxes (per tonne of Product A packed)	126.00
Wrapping paper (per tonne of Product A packed)	214.00
Labour (packing per tonne of Product A)	78.00
Transport (per tonne-mile)	0.32

Thus, if the sales budget provides for the sales of 110 tonnes of Product A, entailing the travelling of 2400 tonne-miles, the distribution budget will include:

	£
Boxes	13 860
Wrapping paper	23 540
Labour	8 580
Transport	768

PRODUCTION BUDGET

In jobbing concerns it is difficult to budget production accurately even in terms of cost, because of its diversity. The emphasis in the following paragraphs is therefore on the simpler problems that arise where there is a range of standard articles produced for stock. The production budget in such cases is merely a summary showing the quantity and total cost of each product to be manufactured. The quantity produced is derived from quantities to be sold and stocked. Such a budget is one of the last to be finalised: it depends upon, and is built up from, numerous other budgets. In the early stages it may be a budget in quantity terms only, costs being incorporated later. Direct materials, direct labour and factory overhead budgets, for the production quantity eventually agreed, are combined and summarised as the production budget. A *machine utilisation budget* may also be produced in terms of machine-hours required to meet production targets. This amount must be reconciled to the machine time available.

Budget Centre Budgets

Once it has been decided what is to be produced, it is possible to plan the cost of its production by the construction of a separate budget centre budget for each production cost centre. This necessitates the breaking down of the effort required in production on a 'departmental' basis. It is convenient to regard the budget centre budget as consisting of three parts:

1. A statement of the budgeted prime cost of production.
2. A statement of costs within the control of the manager responsible for the centre, but which form part of the production overheads as far as the product is concerned.
3. A statement of costs allocated or apportioned to the centre but which are outside the control of the manager responsible for the centre.

Unfortunately whilst the distinction between points 1 and 2 is definite, it is not easy to determine exactly which costs should be regarded as controllable by the manager of a specified cost centre and which ought to be treated as uncontrollable. A typical case in point is power costs where a concern produces its own electricity. If apportionment is made on the basis of a fixed charge per annum, plus a variable charge per unit consumed, the former is entirely uncontrollable by a consumer department, whilst the latter is partly controllable and partly uncontrollable – the cost per unit being outside the consumer's control and the consumption within it.

The procedure for the preparation of budget centre budgets differs according to the type of production and whether or not a standard costing system is in use. The simplest case is one where only a single product is produced by a centre and there already exists a standard costing system employing current expected actual standards. Such a case will be considered first.

Direct Costs

There is no difficulty in setting standards for direct materials cost and direct wages before the completion of the production budget, since the volume of work budgeted will not normally affect these. Overhead standards, on the other hand, cannot be fixed before the production budget is completed, since the basis for the absorption of production overheads is dependent upon the volume of work laid down therein and upon the costs which it specifies.

Where a budget centre produces only one product, the standard cost card for which has already been partially prepared on the basis of the expected costs of efficient actual performance, the first section of the production budget centre budgets (that dealing with product direct material cost, wages and expense) will be prepared simply by computing:

Standard cost per unit of the element of cost concerned for the budget centre	×	Production budget in terms of quantity	=	Budget centre budget in monetary terms

Example

The Engineering Company Limited uses a system of standard costs employing standards based on the expected actual costs of efficient performance. Cost Centre 1 (which may also be termed Budget Centre 1) produces (only) Product A, the standard cost card of which has been completed as regards direct costs only, and is as follows:

STANDARD COST CARD

Period ending .... 19 ....   Product A

Cost Centre 1:

	£	£
Direct material cost:		
8 kg material 311 at 50p per kilogram	4	
15 kg material 560 at 40p per kilogram	6	
	—	
		10
Direct wages:		
4 hours at £2 per hour		8
Production overheads:		
4 labour-hours at £—		
		—
Standard production cost		£–

The production budget requires the production of 840 of Product A in the forthcoming budget period. The first section of the Budget Centre 1 budget will therefore be:

Budget Centre 1 Budget

Period ending .... 19 ......

		£	£
Product direct costs:			
Direct materials:			
	311	3360	
	560	5040	
			8400
Direct wages			6720

Earlier it was stated that the production budget centre budgets consist of three sections. It has now been shown how the first section can be prepared where a standard costing system is employed and only a single product is made by the budget centre. Similar principles are involved where there are several products. Later, when the preparation of the direct cost section of the centre budgets has been considered, attention will be given to the 'overheads' sections.

Example

Exeter Engineering Limited has partially completed the following standard product costs for the year ending 31 December 19—

<table>
<tr><td colspan="7" align="center">**STANDARD COST CARD**</td></tr>
<tr><td colspan="4">Year ending 31 December 19—</td><td colspan="3" align="right">Product A856</td></tr>
<tr><td colspan="7">Direct Material Cost:</td></tr>
<tr><td>Description</td><td>Cost Centre</td><td>Quantity</td><td>Standard Price</td><td>£</td><td>£</td></tr>
<tr><td>Casting, alloy A4, pattern 236</td><td>11</td><td>1</td><td>£ 1.850</td><td></td><td>1.850</td></tr>
<tr><td colspan="7">Direct Wages:</td></tr>
<tr><td>Oper-ation No.</td><td>Description</td><td>Cost Centre</td><td>Standard Time</td><td>Standard Rate</td><td>£</td><td>£</td></tr>
<tr><td>1
2</td><td>Turn on centre lathe
Grind</td><td>11
19</td><td>hours
2.00
1.50</td><td>£
2.35
2.30</td><td>4.70
3.45
———</td><td>8.15</td></tr>
<tr><td colspan="7">Production Overheads:</td></tr>
<tr><td></td><td></td><td>Cost Centre</td><td>Standard Time</td><td>Standard Rate</td><td>£</td><td>£</td></tr>
<tr><td></td><td></td><td>11
19</td><td>hours
2.00
1.50</td><td>£
*
–</td><td>–
–</td><td>–</td></tr>
<tr><td colspan="7" align="right">Standard Production Cost £–</td></tr>
</table>

* This section will be completed when standard overhead absorption rates have been computed on the basis of the production and budget centre budgets for the forthcoming period.

Similar standard cost cards show for product X34, materials: 4 alloy castings XX2 at 75p each and 16 bolts at 3p each, a standard cost of £3.48; labour: turning two hours at £2.35 per hour and milling one and a half hours and grinding one hour, both at a rate of £2 per hour; and for product B567, materials: 1 kg of moulded aluminium tube at 50p, and labour: 30 minutes turning and 15 minutes milling. No other lines pass through cost centre 11 (turning).

The production budget provides for the completion of the following:

Product	Quantity
A856	2000
X34	6000
B567	1900

Required:

Prepare the budget for Budget Centre 11 as regards direct product costs. Setting-up time is to be ignored as it is insignificant in comparison with total time.

Budget Centre 11 Budget: Year Ending 31 December 19—

Direct Product Costs:

	£	£
Direct material cost:		
2000 casting, alloy A4, pattern 236 at £1.850 each	3 700	
24 000 casting, alloy XX2, pattern 556 at 75p each	18 000	
96 000 bolts at 3p	2 880	
1900 kg 2 cm round alloy B65 at 50p	950	
		25 530
Direct wages: $[2000 \times 2 + 6000 \times 2 + 1900 \times 1/2]$		
1695 hours at £2.35		39 832
		£65 362

Note: only turning takes place in Cost Centre 11.

Where no standard costing system is in operation, it may still be possible to prepare the product direct cost section of the budget on these lines by establishing 'standard' prices and rates together with 'standard' methods, operation times, and material usage specifications. Since this involves much of the work of setting up a full standard costing system, without bringing any of its advantages, this method is not an efficient one. Nor is the method feasible in many cases, for production frequently cannot be standardised in the manner required. The alternative methods that exist will depend upon the circumstances of the particular business. It is sometimes possible to make each large contract the subject of a separate budget – the length of the contract determining the budget period. This method could be applied, for instance, where a company is engaged on very large civil engineering contracts. In such cases the budget would be based upon the estimates made by quantity surveyors and other experts at the time of tendering for the contract. Frequently, however, it is possible to budget direct production costs only on the basis of past experience, making any necessary adjustments for changes in price levels and in the volume or type of work.

Calculation for Production and Direct Labour Budget

Electrical Manufacturers PLC make five electrical products. This calculation would be undertaken for each product and each department and the budget for all cross cast to a total figure.

This budget has been calculated for irons and the wiring department only.

ELECTRICAL MANUFACTURERS PLC	Budgeted Production Volume					
Production Budget	*Irons*	*Wall Heaters*	*Fan Heaters*	*Toasters*	*Razor Points*	*Total*
Expected sales – colour blue	6 500					
– colour red	17 500					
	24 000					
Planned stock increase	3 000					
Less purchase from sub-contractor	(7 000)					
Quantity to be manufactured	20 000					
Direct Labour Budget						
Standard hours per product	7					
Standard hours required	140 000					
Department	*Machining*	*Assembly*	*Wiring*	*Checking*	*Packing*	*Total*
Standard hours required:						
Irons	15 000	100 000	20 000	3000	2000	140 000
Wall heaters			13 000			
Fan heaters			24 000			
Toasters			16 000			
Razor points			17 000			
Standard hours required			90 000			
Efficiency ratio			80%			
Total hours of attendance		$\left(90\,000 \times \dfrac{100}{80}\right)$	112 500			
Planned overtime hours			(12 500)			**
Normal hours required			100 000			
Normal working week (hours)			35			
Working weeks per year			49			
Number of employees required		$(100\,000 \div 35 \times 49)$	58			
Absenteeism rate			8%			
Employees to be engaged		$\left(58 \times \dfrac{100}{92}\right)$	63			
			£			
Weekly wage rate			115.5			
Direct labour cost per week			7 276.5			
* Overtime Premium		$(12\,500 \div 49 \times \text{Rate})$	1 122.0			
Gross wages per week			8 398.0			
Gross wages per year			411 502.0			
Other labour costs						
Holiday pay (3 weeks)		$(115.5 \times 3 \times 63)$	21 830.0			
National Insurance			36 608.0			
Pensions			47 904.0			
Total			106 342.0			
Total labour cost			£517 844.0			

* Overtime at £4.40 per hour (one and one third times the normal rate of £3.30 per hour).

** Limiting factor

Product Overheads

Having considered the budgeting of product direct costs, we turn to the second and third sections of the production budget centre budgets – those covering costs that are production overheads on the product. Two classes of cost are envisaged: those considered to be controllable by the cost centre concerned and those that are primarily the responsibility of some other centre and later allocated or apportioned to the centre the costs of which are under consideration. In each case the initial task is one of assessing the variability of the several costs. Having done this, it is necessary to budget the work to be completed by the centre – in terms, for example, of man-hours or machine-hours, or product units. The budget may then be developed by adding to the fixed cost component, the variable costs appropriate to the volume of work budgeted for. Service centre budgets should be apportioned to the centres concerned with the activities they serve according to the service provided.

Example

Excelsior Manufacturing PLC has prepared the following service cost centre budgets for the year 19—:

Building Service Budget

Year ending 31 December 19—

	£
Rent and Rates	17 800
Heating	33 200
Lighting	4 800
Policing and watching	9 700
Fire prevention	2 150
Insurance	3 230
Cleaning	12 320
Maintenance	2 800
	£86 000

The building is single storey with a net effective floor area (after deducting corridors, halls, lobbies, etc.) of 215 000 square metres of which 3728 square metres are occupied by the power house and 5300 by cost centre 73.

$$£86\,000 \div 215\,000 \text{ square metres} = 40p \text{ a metre.}$$

Power Service Budget

Year ending 31 December 19—

	Fixed Cost per annum	Variable Cost per 1000 Kilowatt Hours	Budget based on 400 000 Kilowatt Hours
	£	£	£
Controllable Costs:			
Wages	8 500	0.500	8 700
Fuel	–	3.000	1 200
Water	20	0.010	24
			9 924
Uncontrollable Costs:			
Building Service:			
3728 at 40p	1 491		1 491
	£10 011	£3.510	£11 415

£11 415 ÷ 400 = £28.54 per 1000 Kilowatt hours.

The estimated consumption of cost centre 73 is 40 000 kilowatt hours p.a. = £1141.
   Allocated to production budget centre 73 from other centres are the following:

	£
Salaries	11 200
Depreciation	12 400
Maintenance	4 625

These amounts are not regarded as controllable by the foreman in charge of cost centre 73, but he is considered to control:

	Fixed Cost	Variable Cost per Standard Direct Labour-Hour
	£	£
Indirect labour	–	0.080
Consumable stores	–	0.030
Tools	325	0.035
Scrap	–	0.010

Product direct costs have already been budgeted as follows:

	£
Material Cost	36 600
Wages (20 000 direct labour-hours)	45 400

Required:

Prepare the budget centre budget for centre 73, ignoring any cost not stated above.

Budget Centre Budget – Centre 73
Year ending 31 December 19—

	£	£
Product Direct Costs:		
Material Cost	36 600	
Wages (20 000 direct labour-hours)	25 400	
		62 000
Other Controllable Costs:		
Indirect labour	1 600	
Consumable stores	600	
Tools	1 025	
Scrap	200	
Power	1 141	
		4 566
		66 566
Uncontrollable Costs:		
Salaries	11 200	
Depreciation	12 400	
Maintenance	4 625	
Building service (5300 square metres at 40p)	2 120	
		30 345
		£96 911

It is impossible to lay down hard and fast rules as to which costs are, and which costs are not, controllable by particular managers. Everything depends upon the particular circumstances of the business concerned. In some concerns, therefore, costs treated in the above example as controllable may be regarded as uncontrollable by the cost centre or vice versa.

REQUIREMENT AND PROCUREMENT BUDGETS

The budget centre budgets for the various production cost centres form the foundation upon which a number of other budgets are erected. It is not sufficient, for instance, to know the budgeted costs of each section of the undertaking, as the possession of this information will not ensure the procurement of the correct materials, the engagement of the proper personnel, or the availability of the desired equipment. To this end it is necessary to summarise the material content of all budget centre budgets in order to produce a *material requirements budget* summarising material requirements, and the wages content to prepare a *labour procurement budget*, as well as the details of machine operations in order to assemble an *equipment requirements budget*. Consideration of (a) material stocks (existing and desired); (b) personnel available, and (c) equipment already on hand; and a comparison of these with the various requirements budgets will provide the material, labour, and equipment procurement budgets, respectively.

Example

It is estimated that on 1 January 19— the Ecclesall Manufacturing Company Limited will have the following raw material inventory:

Material Code	Quantity	Price	£
112	1000 kg	25p	250
113	860	£1	860
114	12 tonnes	£25	300
777	9600	0.417p	40
888	900 litres	50p	450
			£1900

The budget centre budgets of the company's five departments may be summarised as follows:

		Department				
Material		A	B	C	D	E
Code	(Quantities):					
112	(kg)	6000	8000	–	–	–
113	(number)	200	1000	700	300	–
114	(tonnes)	–	10	–	–	100
777	(number)	–	10000	9000	–	5000
888	(litres)	100	500	400	1000	600

It is estimated that all prices will remain constant. The following inventory at 31 December 19— is desired:

112	1000 kg
113	1000
114	10 tonnes
777	12000
888	1000 litres

Required:

Prepare the raw material procurement budget for the year 19— in terms of quantities and money.

Raw Material Procurement Budget

Year ending 31 December 19—

Material Code	Unit	Stock 1 Jan.	Budgeted Con- sumption	Stock 31 Dec.	To be Pro- cured	Price	Budget £
112	kg	1000	14 000	1 000	14 000	25p	3 500
113	no.	860	2 200	1 000	2 340	£1	2 340
114	tonnes	12	110	10	108	£25	2 700
777	no.	9600	24 000	12 000	26 400	0.417p	110
888	litres	900	2 600	1 000	2 700	50p	1 350
							£10 000

Wastage of labour, i.e. labour turnover, is almost inevitable and in large organisations it is necessary to provide for continuous recruitment and training. It is always the personnel officer's duty to ensure that recruitment keeps pace with losses of staff, but he will have special responsibilities in this direction when policy changes call for an increase or decrease in the establishment of a particular grade of labour, since this is likely to involve special recruitment and training programmes on the one hand, or redundancy, with negotiations likely to be needed to obtain trade union agreement to the direction in which the plan is to proceed and the possibility of redundancy payments. As it is normally in a concern's best interests to avoid labour turnover as far as possible, consideration will be given to the practicability of re-training personnel surplus to the requirements in one department, where additional labour can be used in another. This is not always feasible, of course. It is unlikely, for instance, that a labourer surplus to the planned establishment of one section, can be trained to fill a vacancy for a cost clerk. Although re-training is sometimes impossible, its possibility in other instances should not be dismissed. Security of employment is an important factor in the retention of employee goodwill, and the concern that picks up and discards staff without regard to it, is likely to experience all kinds of labour strife.

Equipment Budget

The third type of procurement budget is concerned with equipment. Just as it is necessary to compare the manpower available with that provided for by the various budget centre budgets, so it is necessary to compare the available equipment capacity with that demanded by production. The whole production budget is based on the availability of certain plant and machinery – and if it is not there, the entire budgetary programme will be frustrated. Production management must therefore match the facilities demanded with those that exist, and if necessary take appropriate steps to remedy the position. This may involve policy decisions of various kinds. It may, for instance, be possible to remove a bottleneck by purchasing a component instead of employing an already fully loaded machine to make it. Again, the working of a week-end shift for a specified period may suffice. These, and other possibilities, have already been mentioned under the heading of principal budget factor – but what happens when all these methods have been considered and either employed or rejected? There remain only two alternatives: arrangements either have to be made to purchase new equipment, which will meet the increased demand in the budget period or, alternatively, the production budget must be revised to volumes that *can* be achieved. The former involves the *capital expenditure budget*, which is discussed later. In many industries the purchase and installation of new plant and machinery is a long-term project, and increased demands for capacity cannot be met within the budget period. It would be useless, for instance, for an electricity authority to budget its plant needs on the basis of its production budget year by year, if new generating plant takes several years to plan and construct. Such a business must employ long-term forecasts of its production facility needs if it is to be able to satisfy them when the time comes to do so.

ADMINISTRATION COST BUDGET

Administration cost budgets are likely to present few problems, since the expenditure they cover consists largely of salaries and office costs, which are fixed in nature. The main budget will be subdivided into separate budgets each covering a main administration activity such as accounting, secretarial work, etc. It will be necessary to consider the existing number of administration staff, their future rates of pay, any changes in policy likely to affect the volume of work involved, the accommodation to be occupied, and so on. Changes in cost levels will also have to be taken into account, together with liabilities for outside legal and other similar expenses.

In order that the budget may provide a target for cost control purposes it is necessary to consider the reasonableness of past costs and to make adjustments to ensure that the budget presents a level of cost efficiency that is reasonably attainable and yet does not perpetuate past inefficiencies. One method of doing this is to express each item of administration cost as a unit cost, e.g. the cost of invoice typing might be expressed in terms of pence per invoice line, and that of paying dividends as a cost per shareholder. Whilst this may seem to involve a good deal of effort, there is no reason why the result of a relatively small test sample should not be employed, and the mere statement of costs in this way tends to emphasise how much it costs to dictate, type, sign, and post a letter, or to complete similar routine tasks.

OTHER INCOME BUDGET

Where a concern has considerable investments it is usual to prepare a separate budget for other income, taking into account known interest receipts and estimated dividends, after adjustment for any purchase or sale of investments planned for in the master budget.

RESEARCH AND DEVELOPMENT BUDGETS

Research and development costs may be extremely important, as they are in the aerospace industry, or they may be quite unimportant, as they are in connection with motor repair work. In the first case the cost accountant is faced with the problem of disposing of a considerable amount of such costs; in the latter he can virtually ignore them. Similarly, the research and development budget of a motor manufacturer may be very large, whilst the average department store will perhaps have none at all. It is impossible, therefore, to assess the size of a typical research budget or its ratio to sales. It will usually include payments to outside research organisations, the salaries of research staff, the costs of providing their accommodation and equipment, costs of test-runs, pilot-schemes, and the like. It is normally fixed on an appropriation basis – a definite sum being specified by management as a matter of policy. Agreement must be reached between those engaged in the research and those laying down the policy as to the precise aims of the research and the broad lines on which the appropriated sum is to be spent.

As with all budgets, emphasis will be placed on the controllability of costs, a distinction being drawn between costs controllable by the research manager and those that are beyond his control. It will also be necessary to consider which development costs, if any, are to be capitalised, since these will not form a proper charge against the revenue shown in the master budget.

CAPITAL EXPENDITURE BUDGETS

One phase of capital expenditure budgeting has already been touched upon: the need to match the equipment available with that required to fulfil the budget – the equipment requirements budget specifying the additions needed. However, capital expenditure may be incurred in many directions. Old plant wears out and must be replaced; obsolescent equipment needs to be superseded by more efficient units; new products and processes demand the acquisition of suitable machinery; all these happenings entail capital expenditure. Expansion, whether by the purchase of an existing business, or by the setting-up of new branches, also consumes capital. Few concerns possess sufficient liquid resources to be able to embark upon major capital expenditure without considerable thought, and the sums involved are often so great that it would be most imprudent to act otherwise.

It is normal, therefore, for a capital expenditure budget to be drawn up in a long-term basis, planning the amount to be spent upon each of the major projects in the process of completion. If the sums involved are large it will be necessary to consider at the same time how the required funds are to be provided. In fact, the means available often determine the size of the capital expenditure budget.

It is convenient, at this point, to consider the relationship between the capital expenditure budget and any system for authorising particular items of expenditure. Most large concerns lay down standard procedures for the consideration of all capital expenditure proposals by the controller, the board, or a 'capital expenditure committee', and whilst any such system must obviously be linked with the budgetary control of capital expenditure, the emphasis in the standard procedures is upon particular permission, whilst that in budgetary control is more general. Thus, to take a particular instance, provision may be made for the replacement of motor delivery vans at a total cost of £55 000, but this does not mean that a particular application to replace one delivery van by another will necessarily be accepted. It could be turned down for a variety of reasons e.g. that the need to replace the existing van has not been proved, or that the proposed van is too expensive in comparison with the cost of a van of another type or make.

Example

The production manager provides the following information regarding his plant requirements during the next three years:

	Year 1	Year 2	Year 3
	£	£	£
Lathes for Machine Shop A	36 000	–	–
Replacement of heavy press	–	30 000	–
Conveyors to convert Dept C to semi-automatic operation	–	42 000	–
Plant required in new Department X	–	18 000	284 000

The accounts department proposes to install a computer system in Year 1; the hardware and software are estimated to cost £48 400.

The distribution manager estimates that he will require two new vans in Year 1, costing £13 100. He estimates that in the following year eight vans having a saleable value of £4000 will be replaced by eight new vans costing a total of £46 400.

A new building to cost £510 000 will be commenced in Year 2 to house Department X. This sum will be paid as £180 000 in Year 2 and the balance of £330 000 in Year 3.

All the above-mentioned expenditure is approved in principle. Final approval of a further project, involving the purchase of land in Year 3 and costing approximately £150 000, is to be deferred until the end of Year 1.

Prepare a long-term capital expenditure budget covering the three years.

Capital Expenditure Budget

	Year 1	Year 2	Year 3
	£	£	£
Lathes for Machine Shop A	36 000	–	–
Replacement of heavy press	–	30 000	–
Conveyors	–	42 000	–
Plant for new Department X	–	18 000	284 000
Computer	48 400	–	–
Vans	13 100	42 400	–
New building	–	180 000	330 000
	£97 500	£312 400	£614 000

Note: Final approval of the purchase of land at an estimated cost of £150 000 in Year 3 is deferred until the end of Year 1.

OTHER CAPITAL BUDGETS

Stock and Work-in-Progress Budgets. The relationship of the stock budgets with those for production and sales has already been touched upon. It is important that the budget should plan for:

1. Minimum stocks consistent with the achievement of the turnover budgeted.
2. The minimum quantity of redundant stock.
3. Any seasonal build-up required to meet peak sales.
4. Changes in the volume of business, such as a rapid or gradual expansion or contraction. This matter is, of course, also the concern of stock control.

Debtors Budget. Most manufacturing concerns sell on credit terms, i.e. they do not receive immediate payment for the goods they sell but are prepared to wait for a month or other specified period after delivery. This circumstance must be taken into account in budgeting the cash receipts of a business or its debtors at a particular time. Past experience is helpful in forecasting receipts from debtors, but it needs to be modified to take into account any changes in the period of credit allowed, the strictness with which discount terms are enforced, and any special credit terms allowed on large contracts entered into. The business has no real control over the timing of receipts from debtors. If credit customers wish to delay payments, warnings etc. will not deter them. Therefore, judgement based on past experience is crucial to this budget.

The debtors budget is a reflection of the concern's credit policy, and will be changed by any variation therein. Before it is finalised, therefore, the desirability of making changes in credit policy should be considered, bearing in mind the following factors:

1.   The shortage or otherwise of cash resources.
2.   The possibility of increased business resulting from a lengthening of the credit allowed, or a loss of business consequent upon its shortening.
3.   The cost of debt collection and the incidence of bad debts.

A change in credit policy may affect the discounts allowed and could in extreme cases affect the entire balance of sales and production.

CASH BUDGETS

All entries in other budgets that are concerned with monetary transactions will affect the *cash budget*, which shows the expected flows of cash into and out of the company's bank account. This budget is compiled on a weekly or monthly basis, and can disclose how much will be in the bank, or overdrawn at the end of each month. If the bank has imposed a limit to the overdraft, it is useful to know when the limit is likely to be reached, so that further negotiations with the bank can be conducted well in advance of that date.

Management must be aware of its cash resources throughout a forthcoming budget period if it is to be able to make proper decisions on topics such as the following:

(a)   capital expenditure;
(b)   the expansion of the business;
(c)   the raising of further capital;
(d)   the investment of surpluses;
(e)   the payment of dividends etc.

Availability of cash is the limiting factor of many organisations, and a shortage of cash is the rock upon which even the most profitable of businesses can founder.

The cash budget for a budget period will begin with the opening balance of cash in hand and at the bank. To this will be added the expected cash receipts revealed by the debtors budget, cash sales, and by an *other income budget*, which covers interest and similar receipts. The date and sum receivable of other items of income such as rent, interest, and dividends can generally be predicted with reasonable accuracy. Cash from the sale of fixed assets, such as plant, premises or investments, must be included on the expected date.

Against these items will be set all payments of cash, whether on capital or revenue account, taxation or dividends, taking account of the period of credit appropriate to the payment concerned. In some circumstances it may be necessary to delay payments in order to maintain the desired cash position (or, more frequently, to prevent the lack of available cash being too apparent). Since this will normally involve not only the loss of discount for prompt payment but also possible loss of prestige, it is generally better either to arrange for overdraft facilities or to raise the required sums in some other way.

Since most of the items contained in a cash budget are only approximations, the budget cannot be regarded as an exact forecast. Many concerns, in fact, find it virtually impossible to budget cash items more than three to six months ahead, and others which attempt to budget cash a year in advance employ approximate methods.

Example

From the following information with regard to the budgets of the Ray Engineering Company Limited you are required to prepare a cash budget for the six months ending 31 December 19— on the assumption that the balance in hand on 1 July will be £96 000.

Budgeted:

19— £	Sales £	Selling and Distribu- tion Costs £	Raw Materials £	Wages £	Production Overheads £	Adminis- tration Overheads £
May	95 000	3 600	35 000	9 000	6000	2500
June	84 000	3 400	36 000	9 200	6100	2400
July	88 000	3 500	40 000	9 800	6300	2400
August	84 000	3 200	45 000	10 500	7000	2300
September	95 000	14 000	55 000	13 000	8600	2400
October	120 000	15 000	40 000	10 400	8100	3000
November	125 000	16 000	30 000	9 000	5900	2600
December	118 000	7 000	28 000	7 000	4900	2500

In addition, it is necessary to provide for the payment of £10 800 in July 19— and £86 600 in December, in respect of capital expenditure detailed in that budget. It is anticipated that a dividend of £23 000 (net) will be paid in August 19—. £10 000 5% debentures are to be redeemed at 104 on 1 July 19—. Debtors are allowed two months' credit. (Thus, May sales are paid for in July.) Creditors (for goods or overheads) grant one month's credit.

The slight time lag in payment of wages is to be disregarded, and payments in advance and accruals are to be ignored for the purpose of simplicity.

Cash Budget

For the period ended 31 December 19—

	July £	Aug. £	Sept. £	Oct. £	Nov. £	Dec. £	Total £
Receipts from debtors	95 000	84 000	88 000	84 000	95 000	120 000	566 000
Payments:							
Raw materials	36 000	40 000	45 000	55 000	40 000	30 000	246 000
Wages	9 800	10 500	13 000	10 400	9 000	7 000	59 700
Production overheads	6 100	6 300	7 000	8 600	8 100	5 900	42 000
Administration overheads	2 400	2 400	2 300	2 400	3 000	2 600	15 100
Selling and distribution costs	3 400	3 500	3 200	14 000	15 000	16 000	55 100
Capital expenditure	10 800	–	–	–	–	86 600	97 400
Redemption of debentures	10 400	–	–	–	–	–	10 400
Dividend	–	23 000	–	–	–	–	23 000
	£78 900	£85 700	£70 500	£90 400	£75 100	£148 100	£548 700

	£	£	£	£	£	£	£
Excess of receipts over payments	16 100	–	17 500	–	19 900	–	17 300
Excess of payments over receipts	–	1 700	–	6 400	–	28 100	–
Balance b/f	96 000	112 100	110 400	127 900	121 500	141 400	96 000
Balance c/f	£112 100	£110 400	£127 900	£121 500	£141 400	£113 300	£113 300

Care must be taken to exclude non-cash items from the cash budget, e.g. depreciation included in factory overheads, and to enter items in the budget on the appropriate date, e.g. insurance premium paid once a year in cash, but apportioned to give a monthly charge for overheads.

Reconciliation of Budgeted Monthly Profit with Cash Budget

The balance expected on the cash budget at the end of each month will not be the same as the budgeted profit for the month for the following reasons:

1. *Periodicity.* Sales made are credited to profit and loss but only affect the cash situation when payment is made, perhaps after the customer has taken several months' credit. If say three months' credit is given, sales made in January will be paid for before the end of April, but cash received in January will be for January cash sales and credit sales made in the previous October. The same phenomenon affects goods purchased on credit terms, which, although the cost is incurred and charged against profit, will not be paid out in cash until the period of credit allowed has expired.
2. *Non-cash costs.* Some costs set against profit are not paid out in cash, e.g. depreciation.
3. *Stocks.* Built up or run down (stockpiling or de-stocking) – the quantity of material purchased and paid for in cash may not be the same as the quantity used because of a change in stocks.
4. *Accruals and pre-payments.* Costs incurred but not yet paid will be accrued and charged against profit, e.g. electricity if the bill is not yet received, whilst some costs paid for will not yet be charged against the profit, e.g. rent in advance. Some costs paid annually will be spread over monthly cost periods for profit measurement purposes, e.g. insurance premium paid for a year.
5. *Capital items* paid in cash will not affect profit measurement, e.g. fixed assets bought and sold, loans made and repaid, dividends and taxation paid, shares and debentures issued.
6. Items collected by the company for *payment to other authorities*, e.g. Schedule E tax deductions, and pension deductions, will not affect income measurement, but will be paid out on certain dates, thereby influencing the cash budget.
7. The cash budget starts with an *opening balance* of cash or overdraft.

MASTER BUDGET

Once all the subsidiary budgets have been prepared it is possible to construct a *summary budget*, which shows the budgeted profit and loss account for the budget period and the budgeted balance sheet at its close.

The summary budget so prepared should be carefully considered by management, who must be satisfied not only that the profit planned for represents a reasonable return on the capital invested but that the forecast balance sheet shows a position of stability at which it is desirable to aim. Profit planning is the name given to techniques involving the measurement of capital and the return thereon with a view to planning its most productive use. Balance sheet planning, on the other hand, is aimed at ensuring the proper financing of the undertaking.

Before acceptance, the summary budget should be considered from many angles and may be subjected to major or minor amendments according to circumstances. Eventually, however, when management is satisfied that it is both realistic and appropriate, it will be accepted, and will then become known as the *master budget*.

SHORT-PERIOD CURRENT BUDGETS

It is usual to breakdown the main budgets into sections covering a shorter period, in order that the fullest advantages may be gained from the control information available as a result of budgeting. In the case of a concern preparing an annual budget, there will usually be a breakdown into twelve calender monthly budgets or thirteen four-weekly ones. Obviously these short-period budgets will not always be mere proportions of the annual budget; for production in some months will probably be greater than that in others; heating and lighting costs will be lower in summer months; and sales will rarely be evenly distributed over the year. All these factors need to be taken into account in drawing up short-term budgets, and it is from these that the budget controller obtains information regarding debtors, creditors, and cash in hand at the end of the budget period.

BUDGETS FOR FORWARD PLANNING v. BUDGETS FOR COST CONTROL

Planning and cost control have different aims and this may necessitate the application of different assumptions when budgeting for these distinct purposes. Budgets for the two systems might be based upon differing levels of costs and/or efficiency. There is a close connection between the standards employed in a system of standard costing and the budgets employed for purposes of cost control. The intention of each is to provide a target, and there is no reason why the same basic figures should not be employed for the two purposes – expected standards being equally appropriate in each case, i.e. those based on attainable efficient production.

However, can the same standards be employed for purposes of forward planning? Are a budgeted trading and profit and loss account and budgeted balance sheet based upon such 'standards' realistic? Everything depends upon whether the standards we have set as being based upon attainable efficient production are, in fact, attained. There is a subtle, yet considerable, difference. If a perfectly valid and absolutely fair standard is fixed for a day's work – one based on efficient attainable production – days will arise when the target is *not* attained, because of some slight hold-up or decrease in efficiency, but how often will the converse arise? Super-efficiency is far less common than inefficiency. Consider a machine operator who is required to produce 45 articles and is allowed 2 minutes for each. If he takes an extra 20 minutes over the first 20, he is faced with the task of producing the remaining 25 at the rate of 50 per hour. The loss of 20 minutes is human, but production of 50 per hour is, if the standard is correct, super-human.

Thus, careful thought is necessary before budgets based upon attainable efficient production are employed for planning purposes. It is useless to build upon such budgets a whole system of plans, i.e. sales budgets (based on productive capacity); budgeted trading and profit and loss accounts and balance sheets; if the whole edifice is going to crumble because what was attainable was not in fact attained.

In building up budgets for planning purposes, it may be necessary, therefore, to consider the possibility of variances from the standards laid down. Thus, if the standards set are not normally attainable (i.e. on an average, taking the rough with the smooth), this should be allowed for in budgeting such factors as cash, sales quantities, production costs, etc. Whether this adjustment will be necessary depends upon the precise interpretation placed upon the phrase 'attainable efficient production'. It might, for instance, be contended that it meant any of the following: (a) production attained by a single efficient employee at some past time (ensuring that there was no error in recording etc.); (b) average production attained by efficient employees (ignoring that of inefficient workers); (c) peak past performance achieved by all workers engaged in the same task; (d) average past performance achieved by all workers engaged in the same task, allowing for known inefficiency etc. Each of which will provide a slightly different standard.

Except where specifically stated otherwise, examples in this book assume the use of attainable standards, and the budgets accordingly make no provision for any failure to do so.

THE APPLICATION OF BUDGETS

The drawing up of a budget for each of the activities of a business is, in itself, an aid towards cost control as it compels managers to state their aims 'in black and white' and focuses attention upon each facet of the business in turn. The very fact that a manager is compelled, as part of the budgeting programme, to discuss his intentions with others and to explain why he considers certain expenditure inevitable will put him on his mettle and tend to ensure that his budget is realistic. Yet if budgetary control were to stop at this point, it would lose half its value, for costs are most effectively controlled by comparing them with a previously approved standard of performance, and requiring an explanation for any serious deviation from the master plan. However, the budgets we have so far discussed are not entirely suitable for this purpose, since they are based upon the assumption that each department will work at some specified level of activity, that a stated production will be achieved, and that the sales budget will be fulfilled. This rarely happens in practice, and whilst the planning budgets for certain activities provide a measure of the variation of actual costs from what they ought to have been, those for others will be quite useless for this purpose.

If the budgeted production were 100 000 units and the actual production 75 000, it would obviously be ridiculous to compare the production costs budgeted with those actually incurred, without making some adjustment for the difference in the amount of work done. In order to do this, it is necessary to construct what is termed a *flexible budget*, i.e. one which is designed to change according to the level of activity actually attained. The use of this flexible budgetary technique is confined to cost control: the planning budget is always based on a fixed level of activity, though where appropriate 'normals' are employed it may be designed in such a way that the preparation of a flexible budget from it is facilitated.

Flexible Budgets

In order to prepare a flexible budget, the cost accountant must be in a position to separate the cost under consideration into its fixed and variable components expressing his variable costs in terms of output or of man- or machine-hours, e.g. the budget for a cost centre having a budgeted output of 10 000 standard direct labour-hours in the budget period might be as follows:

Output	10 000 standard hours
	£
Direct wages	20 000
Variable departmental overheads	30 000
Fixed overheads	10 000
Indirect wages	20 000
	£80 000

Indirect wages are partly fixed cost (£5000) and partly variable (£15 000).

If in a particular period, the output of the cost centre has been 8000 standard hours, this budget may be adjusted as follows to show an allowed total cost of £67 000.

Output	8000 standard hours
	£
Direct wages	16 000 80%
Variable departmental overheads	24 000 80%
Fixed overheads	10 000 fixed
Indirect wages – fixed	5 000 fixed
– variable	12 000 (80% £15 000)
	£67 000

The adjusted budget is sometimes called a *flexed* budget. The volume of work planned for a period can be expressed in terms of 'standard hours', i.e. how long it should take to produce planned production.

The activity ratio is calculated as:

$$\frac{\text{Number of standard hours equivalent to the work produced}}{\text{Budgeted standard hours}} \times \frac{100}{1} = \frac{8000}{10\,000} \times \frac{100}{1} = 80\%$$

The activity ratio is applied as a multiplying factor to the variable costs to calculate the flexible budget. Fixed costs do not fluctuate.

Comparison of this budget cost allowance with the actual costs incurred will pinpoint any variation from the costs permitted by the budget.

Budget and Actual Comparative Statement

Cost Centre 11   May 19—

	Budget Cost Allowance	Actual	Variance Favourable/ Adverse
	£	£	£
Direct wages	16 000	18 000	2000 (A)
Variable departmental overheads	24 000	23 750	250 (F)
Fixed overheads	10 000	10 500	500 (A)
Indirect labour	17 000	16 000	1000 (A)
	£67 000	£68 250	£1250 (A)

Variable costs by their nature vary as the volume of production increases or decreases. A flexible budget will be prepared for various levels of activity, so that a fair comparison can be made between the planned cost and the actual cost for the level of production achieved.

Example

The Moulding Department is planned to produce 100 000 units in a month at an expected cost of £104 000.
   This cost is budgeted as:

> £19 000 fixed
> £85 000 variable cost (85p per unit)
> £104 000

However, actual production is 110 000 units (10% above budget) at a cost of £108 000. Clearly it would be nonsensical to compare the budgeted cost of making 100 000 units with the actual cost of making 110 000 units. The budget must be 'flexed' according to the activity ratio: 110%.

	Unit Variable Cost (pence)	Budget Costs Fixed £	Variable £	Flexed Budget £	Actual Costs £	Variances £
Materials	10	–	30 000	33 000	31 000	2000 (F)
Labour	35	8000	35 000	46 500	48 500	2000 (A)
Maintenance	5	1000	5 000	6 500	5 000	1500 (F)
Rent	–	7000	–	7 000	7 000	–
Power	15	3000	15 000	19 500	16 500	3000 (F)
		£19 000	£85 000	£12 500	£108 000	£4500 (F)

> Labour (£35 000 + 10%) + 8000   = £46 500
> [Alternatively, 110 000 units × 35p + £8000]
> Maintenance (£5000 + 10%) + 1000 = £6 500
> [110 000 units × 5p + £1000]
> Power (£15 000 + 10%) + 3000   = £19 500
> [110 000 units × 15p + 3000]

There is no definite dividing line between costs that can be controlled on fixed budget lines and those that require the application of flexible budgetary techniques. Research and development budgets, capital expenditure budgets and advertising budgets are generally treated as fixed, whilst those concerned with production, selling, or distribution costs are flexible. Others, like the building service budget, may be fixed in most circumstances, but should be regarded as flexible when considerable changes in policy arise. Consider, for instance, the effect of working an additional shift each week-end. This would involve the heating and lighting of the plant for an extra period, and would need to be accounted for if the building service budget is to be used for control purposes. Remember, the behaviour of a cost, in a fixed or variable manner, will depend on the circumstances in which the cost is incurred.
   There is a close connection between standard costing and flexible budgetary control, and it is fair to say that the latter is as much a part of modern standard costing technique as it is a part of budgetary control. In fact flexible budgets are frequently employed in connection

with standard costs even in the absence of a system of budgetary control. Furthermore, where differing cost and production normals are employed in systems of budgeting and standard costing in the same business, the flexible budgets for overheads invariably employ the same levels of costs and efficiency as the standards.

The distinction between budgets and standards is further confused by the employment of the term 'standard' to describe a flexible budget allowance which is the result of *measuring* the amount of indirect material or the quantity of indirect labour required to perform a particular task. The distinction is between costs that are estimated to behave in the manner specified in the flexible budget and those that are capable of direct measurement and expression in terms of a unit of service or product.

Despite this close connection, it must not be thought that flexible budgets exist *only* in conjunction with standard costs. Budgetary control of costs, including the employment of flexible budgets, is applicable to many concerns that would find difficulty in employing a standard costing system. It is possible, for instance, to prepare flexible budgets for the control of the costs of such widely different functions as the canteen, power house, transport section, tool room, etc., regardless of whether or not there is in existence a system of standards.

Zero Base Budgeting (ZBB)

In many organisations the usual method of budgeting is to start with the budget for the current period and update it for inflation or any forecasted changes over the next period. Any extra activity or new features of the organisation are added to form the new budget. A disadvantage of this 'incremental' method of budgeting is that managers only have to substantiate the need to spend more than the previous year. Last year's level of expenditure is considered to be acceptable, and any inefficiencies in last year's budget tend to be perpetuated by this almost automatic acceptance of that document as the starting point of the new plan.

Clearly this form of budgeting does not provide for a rigorous review of the activities and expenditure of the organisation. What is required is an examination of all budgeted activity, to see if it is necessary, and whether it should be reduced or increased. The ICMA define *zero base budgeting* as a 'method whereby all activities are re-evaluated each time a budget is formulated'. The idea is to start at zero, so that each function has to justify its existence and prove the need for all costs budgeted to be incurred, if possible relating those costs to benefits to be received. This can prove a burdensome and time-consuming procedure, but may result in cost savings if some activities, traditionally seen as being an integral part of the business, can no longer prove their worth in terms of cost/benefit, or if funds are allocated on the basis of value for money. Even with long-established departments the questions should be asked, 'Do we need this activity?', 'How much of it do we need?', 'Are we organising the activity in the right way?', and 'How much should it cost?'. It is logical that fixed costs, or plant inherited from past decisions, should be substantiated as part of the budgeting procedure to ensure that they are still worthwhile. Managers do not like to admit that any activity under their authority is not of the utmost importance, especially if it is one of their own favourite projects. Because of the executive time involved in zero base budgeting some organisations nominate a core of activities which are acceptable and do not need justification with every budget.

Zero base budgeting is a helpful technique to use in non profit-making or service organisations, such as local authorities. The various activities are identified as separate packages, to which resources are to be allocated. Each package should justify all expenditure in cost/benefit terms, but it may be difficult to quantify the benefits, or to link those benefits to certain costs, or indeed to compare very disparate services that are competing for a share of spending power in the overall budget. The questions 'How badly do we need this service?', and 'What benefits are derived from this service?' cannot be answered clearly when a proposal for an extra social worker is compared to a counter proposal to extend a mobile canteen service for pensioners. In this instance zero base budgeting requires that the package should be evaluated and ranked according to an ordinal scale. This means that executives must express an opinion in terms of 'this is preferable to that', or specify the values of alternatives to an organisation in order of priority, i.e. 1st, 2nd and 3rd. This subjective ranking provides a means whereby activities are reviewed and scarce funds allocated on the basis of the quality of service. Some organisations use complicated weighting systems for this comparison procedure. The accountant must not interfere when conflicting goals need to be reconciled in this subjective way, except to provide data to managers that will assist them in reaching a conclusion. A county treasurer may thus be instrumental in guiding the allocation of, say, £250 000, to the construction of a small home for the elderly rather than to a scheme to straighten a winding road.

PLANNING PROGRAMMING AND BUDGETING SYSTEMS (PPBS)

A non-profit organisation, e.g. a hospital or local authority, is usually concerned with the costs and expenditure of providing a service of some kind. Such organisations normally budget their expenditure down to the last detail, adjusting the previous year's costs according to the expected changes in the forthcoming year. The emphasis of such budgets is on the amount available to spend during a year in each department rather than on the overall objectives that the expenditure is intended to achieve. These budgets are usually prepared on a departmental basis and, as such, fail to show the budgeted costs of each separate activity or programme to cover the purpose of the organisation, and the efficiency or otherwise of the operation to achieve its objectives. Such short-term budgets cannot be used for long-term planning purposes, and PPBS are intended to extend the planning horizon beyond the normal budget year. Traditional departmental budgets are subordinated to a budgetary system reflecting major programmes that sometimes cut across departmental barriers to bring together specialisms required by the programme.

As a first step objectives must be defined from the long-term plan of the organisation; secondly, programmes that might achieve these objectives are drafted. Alternative methods of operation are reviewed, with costs and estimated benefits brought into account, so that the best method can be selected to carry out the programme after a reasoned judgement has been made. Funds are allocated on the basis of the cost/benefit relationship. Once again the ranking of alternatives must take place, and since benefits and sometimes costs are difficult to quantify, an ordinal scale should be employed. Spending programmes drafted to achieve objectives may involve the services of several departments, and these programmes are administered in annual slices as budgets, by a controller whose responsibility is to his programme rather than to a particular department. A department may have a role to play in several programmes, e.g. a local authority may have an objective to provide secondary education within its area, which will be achieved by a part of its education programme. This programme will cover the employment of teachers; the provision of teaching aids; education policy; the provision and maintenance of school premises and school running costs; and the employment of caretakers and cleaners. The education department administrates a major part of this programme, but departments responsible for building, premises' administration, personnel, and even parks and gardens may also be involved. The programme is judged on the basis of how worth while its objectives are when scarce resources are allocated in the budget. Alternative programme elements, or means whereby the programme can be carried out, must then be evaluated, e.g. whether to substitute sub-contract cleaning services for the Authority's own cleaning employees.

PPBS seem to remove the traditional budget emphasis on the spending requirements of each department and focus instead on the objectives of the organisation as a whole, and how these goals can be achieved most economically in order to derive the greatest benefit from the expenditure of scarce resources. Difficulties in measuring benefits and costs may prove insurmountable, and the cost/benefit trade-off built into the system may degenerate into the expression of individual executives' opinions, or the political will of dominant councillors; e.g. is secondary education of greater importance than further and higher education; or how do you allocate evening class provision between the need to educate, and the objective of providing recreation for certain sections of the community?

SEMINAR EXERCISES

9.1 Hardcastle PLC incurred the following selling costs in its last budget year:

	Sales Area				
	North	*South*	*Irish*	*Head Office*	*Total*
Representation:	£	£	£	£	£
Salesmen's salaries	127 000	133 000	75 000	–	335 000
Commission	15 000	17 000	6 500	–	38 500
Travelling and hotel expenses	28 000	21 000	13 000	–	62 000
Sales management:					
Salaries	–	–	–	41 000	41 000
Building service	–	–	–	17 000	17 000
Other costs	–	–	–	11 500	11 500
Publicity	60 000	75 000	28 000	–	163 000
	£230 000	£246 000	£122 500	£69 500	£668 000

Required:

From these figures, and the following additional information, prepare the budget for the ensuing year:

1. A new sales area 'Welsh' is to be formed to cover what is mostly virgin territory, but to take in certain areas previously covered by 'South' sales area from Bristol. Salesmen's salaries of the new area are estimated to be £78 000, which includes £12 000 to be paid to Bristol salesmen transferred to the Welsh area. Travelling expenses of Bristol representatives in the Welsh area last year were £3000. For the whole Welsh area they are expected to be £10 400 next year.
2. An additional clerk will be needed in the sales manager's office at a salary of £6000 p.a., and the building service budget shows an increase of 5%.
3. The publicity budget allows for expenditure of: North: £125 000; South: £140 000; Irish: £70 000; Welsh: £45 000 and £35 000 is budgeted as the cost of an international exhibition.

4. Commission is paid at the rate of $\frac{1}{2}\%$ of all sales. The sales budget specifies sales of: North: £6 200 000; South: £5 500 000; Irish: £2 500 000; Welsh: £1 400 000. (18 marks)

9.2 Savoury Snacks Limited has a factory in southeast England that is at present the only market for its products. It is considering setting up a factory in South Wales which will cost £50 000 for the factory and £37 000 for the required machinery.

Once established the firm expects the following revenues of expenses for a *normal year's trading.*

	£
Sales (all credit)	450 000
Raw materials	72 000
Wages	156 000
Marketing expenses	48 000
Salaries	24 000
Factory expenses	24 000
Selling expenses	18 000
Commissions	9 000

The following points are also relevant:

1. Debtors are to be allowed two months' credit, i.e. the cash for deliveries in January will be received at the beginning of April.
2. Creditors will allow one month's credit. A raw material stock of £9000 is to be purchased on the first day of the second month and maintained throughout.
3. Wages to be paid weekly in arrears. They are to commence on the second month.
4. Marketing expenses will commence from month 1 and for the first six months will be twice the normal amount. They will be paid in the month following the month they arise.
5. Salaries will be paid monthly commencing with month 1.
6. Factory expenses will be paid in the month they arise commencing with the second month.
7. The sales force is to commence operations at the beginning of the third month. Orders are to be accepted on the basis of delivery the month after order. Selling expenses are paid in the month they arise. In order to permit the building up of the necessary finished goods stock, salesmen are instructed to restrict orders to £20 000 per month for the first three months. Thereafter orders will be at the estimated level.
8. Commissions are related strictly to the level of sales and are paid the month after goods are despatched.
9. Purchase of the factory will be completed at the end of the first month and the machinery will be installed during the first month and payment made at the end of the second month.

Required:

Prepare a cash budget for the year and show what additional borrowing facilities Savoury Snacks Limited will need to negotiate in order to finance the operation.

Assume the year will commence from 1 July and that every third month is a five-week period. (22 marks)

9.3 Bunny Bowyers Limited manufacture a range of products for use by club archers. They produce two types of quiver, the De luxe and Standard models, both made from good quality leather. One grade of labour only is employed. The budget for the next three months (twelve five-day weeks) is about to be completed, and the working papers disclose the following information:

	De luxe	Standard
Budgeted sales	3600 units	6150 units
Budgeted material consumption per unit	4 kg	2 kg
Budgeted material cost £2 per kilogram		
Standard hours allowed per unit	4 hours	$2\frac{1}{2}$ hours
Budgeted wage rate for direct workers		£3.50 per hour

The company normally works a 38-hour week, and any overtime is paid at time and a half. There are 70 direct workers on the payroll.

The target productivity ratio, or efficiency ratio, for the productive hours worked by the direct workers is 90%, and it is expected that non-productive down time will be 20% of the productive hours worked.

Sales and production are expected to occur evenly throughout the period.

Stocks at the beginning of the period are expected to be 1250 De luxe units, 1600 Standard units, and 4100 kg of leather. The target closing stocks expressed in terms of anticipated activity during the budget period are: De luxe – 15 days' sales, Standard – 20 days' sales, and leather – 12 days' consumption.

Required:

(a) Calculate the material purchase budget and direct labour budget for quiver production.

(b) What additional information would you need to calculate the weekly cash payments for materials and direct labour for these two products if you also had to draft a cash budget? (22 marks)

REVIEW QUESTIONS

9.1 Hogarth commenced business on 1 January 19–1 as a supplier of feedstuffs and machinery to local farmers. His supplies are from Gilray who has agreed to allow him two months' credit. Hogarth estimates that his costs will be as follows:

1. Purchases: in January £90 000 of supplies, February £64 000 and increasing by £4000 per month thereafter.
2. Wages: £7000 each month, paid two weeks in arrears.
3. Rates: £900 for the period to 31 March 19–1 and £2200 for the half-year to 30 September 19–1, all payable on 21 April 19–1.
4. Rent: £3000 per quarter starting 1 January.
5. Sundries: £2000 per month, payable one month in arrears.
6. Carriage: £2500 per month, payable one month in arrears.

In addition, a new van costing £3000 will be bought and paid for in May 19–1. Drawings will be £1000 each month, except April, when for personal reasons Hogarth will draw £4000.

Hogarth is confident that he can sell all the goods Gilray is able to sell to him, but feels that he should maintain a good level of stocks. He plans for stocks in January to be worth £40000 at cost, increasing by £10000 per month to £90000 in June 19–1.

There is a mark-up on cost of 25% on feedstuffs and 50% on machinery. Due to seasonal fluctuations the mix of total sales (including cash sales) will alter:

	Feedstuffs	Machinery
January to March	60%	40%
April to June	50%	50%

Cash sales will be £7500 per month for the first three months and £9750 per month thereafter. Debtors will be allowed one month's credit and will also be allowed a 5% discount. It is expected that without exception they will adhere to the credit terms and avail themselves of the discount.

Hogarth brought into the business on 1 January 19–1 £3000 worth of office machinery. Depreciation of this office machinery will be 10% p.a. and depreciation of the motor van will be 25% p.a. Provision is to be made for doubtful debts in the sum of £5000.

Required:

(a) A cash budget for each of the six months to 30 June 19–1, showing the balance of the cash at bank at the end of each month.   (18 marks)

(b) The master budget, i.e. budgeted trading and profit and loss account for six months to 30 June 19–1, and budgeted balance sheet as at that date.
                                                                        (8 marks)

                                                            (Total 26 marks)

9.2 Able Bakers PLC make only two products, a sponge cake and a currant cake. The company uses one basic raw material, cake-mix, and one grade of labour. The operating statement for this year is shown below.

	£	£
Sales:		
Sponge (60p each)	96 000	
Currant (£1 each)	80 000	176 000
Cost of sales:		
Direct material	88 000	
Direct labour	32 666	
Variable overheads	12 000	
Fixed overheads	9 333	141 999
Operating Profit		£34 001

Standard material costs for production specify 0.3 kg of cake-mix for sponge and 0.5 kg for currant. Actual consumption this year was as specified in the standard. The standard wage rate is £1.20 per hour, and the labour cost of sponge is 10p and currant, 15p. The labour force has achieved standard efficiency this year, but the actual rate paid has been 20p per hour above standard. Overhead costs for the year were as specified in the standard, variable overheads varying directly with the direct labour-hours worked.

The sales forecast for next year expects 180 000 sponges to be sold, and 75 000 currant cakes. Material stocks are to be reduced by 5000 kg during the year. The material and labour standards are intended to remain the same as for this year, except the actual wage rate paid this year will be recognised as normal and a further increase of 30p per hour will be paid in recognition of a production agreement by which standard timings for each product will be reduced by 20%. Budgeted overheads will be at the same rate as for this year. Material costs are expected to rise by 5%.

Required:

(a) Calculate the budgets for material purchases and wages for next year.

(15 marks)

(b) Advise the company of the likely cost saving to be derived from the productivity scheme.

(5 marks)

(Total 20 marks)

9.3 The Winklesea Cottage Hospital (180 beds) is located in a holiday resort, the population of which doubles during the summer season of June, July and August. Outside this season Winklesea is not a very busy town. The holidaymakers cause activity at the hospital to double during June, July and August.

Hospital expenditure is carefully budgeted. The chief administrator takes the figures for the previous year and adds an amount calculated according to the expected inflation factor. This year he has added 8%. The amounts in the annual budget for each department are then divided by four, and the result is distributed as a quarterly budget for the periods ended 31 March, 30 June, 30 September and 31 December. At the end of each quarter a comparison of actual and budgeted costs is distributed to departmental managers as a control document. The hospital laundry department is one such department, and the report for the quarter ended 30 September is shown below. The overhead apportionment for occupancy cost is based on the floor area of each department, and that for administration expenses is based on expected labour costs in the department.

Winklesea Cottage Hospital **Budgetary Control Report**	*Laundry Department* 3 months ended 30 September	
	Budget	*Actual*
Patient-days	12 000	16 000
Weight processed (kg)	120 000	160 000
Costs:	£	£
Labour – Direct wages	13 200	18 415
– Overtime premium	2 100	3 150
Laundry materials	2 700	4 050
Water charges, heating and softening	3 000	3 750
Maintenance	1 500	2 250
Depreciation of plant	3 000	3 000
Manager's salary	2 500	2 750
Overhead apportionment:		
Occupancy expenses	6 000	6 500
Administration expenses	7 500	10 000

Required:

(a) Comment on the way in which the quarterly budgets have been prepared.

(b) Suggest improvements that could be made to the current system of budgeting and reporting.

(c) Flex the budget for the quarter to 30 September and suggest points that might be included in a meaningful report.   (25 marks)

10

Budgetary Control – The Behavioural Implications

Responsibility accounting according to the ICMA definition is 'a system that segregates revenues and costs into areas of personal responsibility in order to assess the performance attained by persons to whom responsibility has been assigned'. This system is an extension of budgetary control, in that the business, or whatever other type of organisation is involved, is divided up into areas of responsibility, and the budget is expressed in terms of planned performance for those areas. Responsibility centres often coincide with cost centres, but may not always do so since they are defined according to the span of control of individual managers. In so far as a manager has accepted responsibility for performance according to the budget, he should be accountable for that performance, and should organise remedial action when variance analysis focuses attention on under-achievement. Budgetary control is a system to help managers to manage, and its success or failure depends on the attitude of the managers who operate the system. Co-operation and enthusiasm as opposed to awkwardness and apathy can make or mar the success of budgetary control. Thus budgetary control must be operated with care to give consideration to the effect of parts of the system on human behaviour, and to take human reactions into account. The objective is to build a team of managers working together in harmony to achieve the goals and objectives of the organisation, but misuse of budgetary control can so influence their behaviour as to reduce the likelihood of achieving budgeted performance. Any system that sets goals for managers to achieve, evaluates their performance in a public way, and suggests that under-performance is their fault in that they must act to correct the situation, is bound to be fraught with difficulties.

MOTIVATION

When a manager receives his budget for the year, perhaps expressed in monthly instalments, this acts as an instruction to him, laying down the parameters within which he must work in the future months, and the performance he is expected to achieve. The receipt of this document alone will not be sufficient to motivate him to strive for success. If factors can be identified which will influence a manager to accept his budget and make efforts to achieve it, they can be harnessed to good effect. All managers have a set of personal aspirations and will work hard to attain them, and if they believe that it is to their own advantage to reach the targets set by the business, or that those targets are beneficial to all, they will accept the firm's goals as their own and be motivated towards their achievement.

This acceptance of the firm's goals by an executive is termed *internalisation*, and once a manager has internalised those goals, they are said to be congruent with his own. Goal congruence is important in lining up the objectives of the board with those of the managers, but incentive is also required to persuade managers to strive for goals. Goal congruence and incentive can be attained through the effect of several influences on a manager e.g. ambition, which spurs him on in the right direction once he accepts that achieving budgeted performance is a worthwhile ambition; the priority that an individual assigns to his own needs for personal achievement; and the probability that meeting the budget will provide a sense of achievement. Morale is another factor that influences personal aspirations. If a manager is proud of his past record of budget achievement he will strive to maintain his reputation and will be confident in his ability to do so. If the budget appears attainable and within the scope of what the manager deems to be possible he will again be motivated to work for the success of the business and of himself. Evaluation of performance may give an incentive to succeed. It is important, however, that goals should be clearly understood, and that confusion is diminished by not having too many sub-goals. Effort spread in too many directions may prove ineffective, and too much effort concentrated on achieving one target may reduce the resources available to work towards other equally worthwhile goals.

PARTICIPATION

The manager who has played a part in drafting a budget will identify with that budget, be more willing to accept it and to internalise its goals. During the dynamic iterative stage of the budgeting procedure, when suggestions, revisions, alternatives and limiting factors are being built into the final, acceptable master budget, if all levels of management are allowed to make a meaningful contribution to the discussion they will find it easier later to accept the compromises that may constrain them during the budget period. This part of the system underlines the importance of involving those at the grass-roots level of the organisation. If managers, on whom rests the burden of carrying out the budget plan, are allowed to suggest levels of expenditure or performance at an early stage, they will recognise that they have a realistic role to play in the budgeting procedure and goal congruence may be more easily achieved.

The opposite system to participation is to communicate the budget to managers in an authoritarian way, stifling discussion as to the reasonableness of targets set, but underlining the importance of board tactics and strategy. In this situation the budget is seen as the vehicle of top management, and if it does not work out, more junior managers will not be motivated to produce extra effort to save the situation. If participation is to be effective as a motivator, there must be genuine discussion between all parties in an effort to make a joint decision. Such discussions foster the trust and leadership required to build a good management team and enable managers to accept decisions made after arguments that they have lost. Top management must play an active leadership role in the system, but their proposals should form a basis for discussion, not instruction, so that realistic compromises can be made. Managers will then agree that objectives or performance standards are reasonable, and *intrinsic motivation* will be present, i.e. motivation because the individual believes the policy to be worth while as opposed to motivation encouraged by the hope of reward or achievement of ambition. If participation is restricted to consultation that fails to give appropriate weight to the views of line managers this will reduce the effort those managers make to ensure the successful operation of the budget plan. Clearly the activities of the budget accountant are crucial to the success of budgetary control because he is in a position to explain, encourage, and help managers to compile their budgets, thereby improving their contribution and participation in the overall budget procedure.

People are gregarious creatures and will often join a group of like-minded individuals at work or in private life, as a means of achieving their personal goals. If an individual is strongly attracted to a group, and committed to its aims, he will strive for the success of the group. A manager in a cohesive group feels that he is a member of a team, perceives the team goals as his own and works to achieve them. The term *group dynamics* is used to describe the forces operating within a group that affect an individual's commitment to the group. Participation encourages managers to feel part of a team, and if the team is in agreement with organisational policy, the dynamics of the group will assist in achieving goal congruence. An individual may accept goals that are consistent with those of his group and reject goals that conflict with the group. For example, in setting standards, the group may influence an individual to accept what he might otherwise reject and, by so doing, inspire him to devote more effort to his job. But what if the group has strong leaders who question the policy of the business or use the group to attain their own personal ambitions? In this case the group may develop into a significant disaffected force, and could reject the objectives of the organisation, leading to dysfunctional behaviour that works in the opposite direction to board policy.

Certain conditions must exist if participation is to be effective. The difference between the goals of the individual and the target of the organisation must not be so wide that they cannot be reconciled. In this situation conflict will develop. Some levels of management are more willing to accept an authoritarian budget situation, regarding the targets as an instruction that they are paid to carry out. Indeed they may feel that participation is an extra burden put on them by higher authority. Top management must be willing to give strong but constructive leadership. If they do not, the group will take over from them and sub-optimal decisions may be the result.

LEVELS OF PERFORMANCE

In order to achieve the budget target the performance required of an individual or group must be set at just the right level if subsequent difficulties are to be minimised or avoided. Standards should be set at levels that are reasonably attainable to give an incentive to attempt to achieve them, yet the standards must also reflect efficiency and lead to optimum performance. If standards are too low the business will be operating at less than optimal efficiency and managers may lose respect for the task for which they are responsible. If standards are too high managers will realise that they are unattainable, and will not attempt to achieve them. Both cases lead to a fall in morale, and less than efficient operation. The required performance should be reasonably obtainable under normal but not perfect conditions, and if accepted as such by managers, it will be internalised by them. If a manager is put under too much pressure by a budget he may react dysfunctionally, either by passing his tensions on down the line of command to his subordinates, thus spoiling relations with them and reducing co-operation, or by forming a group with his subordinates to reject responsibility for achieving the budget targets, thereby passing the pressures back up through the organisation. In this situation goal congruence is not possible, and group dynamics work against the organisation because of low morale. Unrealistic standards may cause managers to react against the budget, seeing it as a competitor in a game of bluff, or an obstacle to overcome, certainly not as an aid to good management. Levels of performance achieved in the past are a useful guide when budgeting, but the past may not reflect conditions to be experienced in the forthcoming period. Accordingly adjustments must be made based on the collective judgement of future conditions.

Some authorities on performance levels suggest that standards should be set at levels that will motivate each manager to greater efforts, even though such standards fall short of congruence with the goals of the organisation. The standard should reflect the aspiration level of the individual, i.e. what he considers to be a high level of performance, and once that target has been achieved, higher levels can be inserted into later budgets, to gradually raise performance up to a level consistent with the expectations of the business.

Thus budget standards are seen as playing a dual role, first to plan future performance in a tight and efficient way, and secondly to motivate managers. A tight budget that is not likely to be achieved fails as a co-ordinating plan and as a motivator, yet such a budget should still be drafted as an attempt to point the way to maximum performance. Perhaps there should be two budgets, one for planning and one for motivation, but this may confuse managers. It may not always be possible to set individual standards, and if an easily attainable standard is set for one manager it may be seen as discrimination in his favour by other managers who are expected to achieve more.

EXCEPTION REPORTING

It is a normal practice with responsibility accounting to report to each manager by comparing his actual performance with the level expected in the budget – without feedback there can be little control. The difference between actual cost and planned cost is termed a *variance*, and the words *favourable* and *adverse* are applied to performance that has exceeded or fallen short of the plan. Variance analysis tends to focus managerial attention on those parts of the organisation not performing according to plan, and identifies the need for remedial action. If there are no adverse variances, it means, in effect, that an executive has successfully achieved his budget objectives, but this success seems to be accepted as a matter of course, whereas adverse variances emphasise the significance of under-performance and perhaps report that under-performance to higher authorities. Exception reporting concentrates attention on the few points at which performance is below budget without giving the appropriate weight to the major part of the activity that is operating successfully, and it may thus appear to some managers as a system designed more to highlight their shortcomings than to inform of their progress. Therefore it could be resented, with the consequence that constructive remedial action may not be the result of a variance statement. Managers may question the standards and the report, offering conflict rather than constructive investigation. Teamwork towards a common goal cannot be achieved if part of the team appears to be playing against another part; this usually leads to dysfunctional behaviour, of which the following are aspects:

(a) Managers will 'build in slack' when budgets are drafted, so that variances are usually favourable and their department is cushioned against adverse conditions. They may rig their budget to delay some profitable activities until a period when adverse conditions are expected.

(b) Managers may conceal expected advantages at the planning stage, preferring them to appear as favourable (but unplanned) variances during the year.

(c) Managers may avoid risky activities that could lead to a high pay-off for the business for fear that adverse variances will blame them for failure, thus stifling enterprise. They may forego investments of benefit to the business, for fear of reducing an otherwise high return on capital employed for the department.

(d) Managers may over-budget to counteract expected cuts from their supposed opponent, the budget officer, and if the cuts are not as large as expected, they will be forced to spend up to a padded budget, thus wasting resources.

(e) Managers may accentuate short-run schemes that do long-term harm to the business, or undertake activities that are beneficial for the department, but have an adverse effect on the business as a whole. Such actions are often termed *compartmentalisation*, because the manager regards his department as more important than the rest of the business, and operates it without too much attention to the general good.

(f) Managers may filter or even falsify information to achieve the required result if short-run budget achievement is given too much weight in the evaluation of their performance.

This whole matter of budgetary standards and exception reports underlines the impact of the budget accountant on the system. His behaviour and attitude are significant for the successful operation of a budgetary control system in that he must foster the idea that responsibility accounting is a helpful managerial tool leading to improved performance, and not a device to force managers to accept impossible workloads and then to report their short-term failures to top management. A successful budget officer is seen by his managerial colleagues as an accountant who utilises his skill to assist them in their planning, and then informs them of results as quickly as possible before variances become too large. Managers too must be expected to appreciate budgetary control, to assimilate its reports, and to take a responsible positive approach to the system. A sense of balance between using the budget to spur managers on, and not using the variance analysis as a criticism of their performance is essential. Good communication between levels of management can help to achieve this balance.

CONTROLLABILITY

A further behavioural implication of budgetary control is that managerial performance should only be evaluated on the basis of matters under the control of the manager. It is unfair to expect managers to respond to adverse variances caused by factors over which they can exercise little or no control e.g. factory rent is not the responsibility of the factory manager since it was probably negotiated by the property department, perhaps even before he was appointed as factory manager. However, it is often difficult to define who is in control of a particular cost, and there are very few costs that are the sole responsibility of a single manager, since several executives may be able to influence the same cost e.g. if the volume of material budgeted to be used is exceeded, the production manager may be to blame, but the buyer may be the cause by purchasing sub-standard material (thereby achieving purchasing costs below budget), which leads to excessive amounts of scrap, and/or the personnel department by recruiting cheaper, unskilled labour, again increasing rejected work and scrap. A useful criterion to decide who controls a cost is to determine who takes the final decision about the cost. Managers should be accountable for their decisions, but should be expected to respond only to variances within their jurisdiction. A manager's definition of the limits of his authority must agree with his superiors' understanding of those limits. Managers may attempt to shift responsibility by trying to assign adverse variances to other departments in order to improve their own performance. This will increase interdepartmental conflict rather than improve co-operation, and is a further example of dysfunctional behaviour. Blame should not be in the forefront when adverse variances are considered, but rather how best to reverse misfortunes and return to budgeted performance levels.

Managers should certainly be shown costs outside their control that affect their area of responsibility to give them a full picture of what is happening to their department. Quantitative results alone are insufficient as a basis for a true judgement of managerial performance. There are many factors, which cannot be quantified yet still affect activity, that must be taken into consideration. To this end some businesses appoint product managers to co-ordinate sales, production and other functions for a single product in their range. This product manager can assimilate the inter-relationships between functions and departments, and can attempt to reconcile their conflicts. A certain amount of rivalry or competition is beneficial within an organisation to tighten up relationships and ensure all managers are working hard to be considered the most efficient, but if rivalry is allowed to develop into conflict this can be very harmful.

HARMONISATION

Sometimes a department may have more than one goal or objective, and these goals may not be congruent. The accountant must stand back when such conflict exists, leaving the reconciliation decision to the executives concerned, on the basis of their evaluation of non-quantifiable costs or benefits e.g. a policy to improve service to customers and sales by setting up local service centres, conflicts with a policy of cutting costs by centralisation. The management accountant must be ready with data to show the impact of alternative strategies, but care must be taken that quantitative factors do not dominate a decision to the exclusion of equally important non-quantitative factors. In some cases it is helpful for managers to measure non-financial aspects of conflicting alternatives e.g. listing priorities on a stated scale and/or giving weightings to certain factors. This process may substitute prejudice for judgement, and so must be used with caution. The weightings and other rules of the evaluation may become so complicated that they partially obscure the true object of the exercise, and reduce the usefulness of the result.

ATMOSPHERE

The ethos of the system is all important if budgetary control is to operate successfully. Budget accountants must not be seen by line managers as critics of their activity forecasts, investigators of variances (especially adverse ones), enforcers of budget procedures and informers with a hot line to top management. Resentment and obstruction will result from such an atmosphere. The accountant must merge into the team, helping his colleagues, drawing up variance statements with their co-operation, and participating in the search for, and evaluation of, remedial action. Communication and the discussion of feedback so that lessons are learned from it will further create the right atmosphere for teamwork to flourish. Often managers are forced to work within severe budget constraints, which impose strains on morale and co-operation. The budget accountant may be cast in the role of interferer and be blamed for an unpalatable decision when a manager relates such a decision to his staff, and the accountant in his turn may say it is the fault of top management when explaining a decision to others. Conduct of this nature is clearly counter-productive, but if the atmosphere in the organisation is conducive to harmonious relations, groups will be willing to accept responsibility for decisions and 'buck passing' will diminish.

11

Setting Standards

Pre-determined costs are those that are computed in advance of production on the basis of a specification of all the factors affecting cost. The ICMA defines a standard cost as 'a pre-determined calculation of how much costs should be under specified working conditions'.

Cost control is the guidance and regulation by executive action of the costs of operating an undertaking. It involves not only the ascertainment of current costs, but also a comparison of these with some reliable standard of measurement.

Standard costing is simply the name given to the technique whereby standard costs are pre-determined and subsequently compared with the actual costs as recorded. The difference between the standard cost and actual cost of a product or service is termed a *cost variance*, and the division of variances into their component parts for explanation purposes is known as *variance analysis*.

Past performance is not necessarily a reliable yardstick with which to compare actual costs. This procedure involves a hidden risk of comparing two uneconomic costs, neither of which provides a true measure of efficient performance, and ignores the impact on standards of change in unit prices caused by inflation and other factors, as well as the effect of organisational changes made since the previous year. For instance, the examination of a series of historical costs is not sufficient to satisfy a producer that:

(a) the best possible use has been made of raw materials, and the level of scrap has been reasonable;
(b) the right type of direct labour has been employed, and the workers have taken a reasonable time to produce an acceptable quality of product;
(c) the machines have been operated at efficient speeds to produce most economically;
(d) production has flowed satisfactorily through the various stages without unnecessary interruption;
(e) there has been no extravagance in the use of indirect materials;
(f) the right type of plant and equipment has been used;
(g) production facilities and labour have been idle for the minimum of time.

Standard costing aims to provide information regarding all these matters, but it is also a means of comparing actual cost with the budget to identify the extent of departures from plan.

Type of Performance Assumed by the Standard

Standards can be divided into two main classes: basic standards and current standards. Current standards can be further divided into ideal and expected standards.

A *basic standard* is one that is established for use unaltered for an indefinite period, which may be a long period of time, i.e. it is one that remains unchanged from year to year unless some physical feature of the relevant operations is altered. Such a standard is not revised when material prices and labour rates vary, but is maintained at its original level in order to show the trend revealed by the computed variances. A current standard can be derived from a basic standard by updating for changed conditions. An extract from a cost report of a concern using basic standard costs might appear something like this:

Cost			Basic Standard		Variance		Relative Performance	
	This month	Last month			This month	Last month	This month (%)	Last month (%)
	£	£	£		£	£		
Material	140	135	100	Material Price	10	10	90.9	90.9
				Material Usage	30	25	76.9	80.0

Calculations:

$$\frac{\text{Standard cost}}{\text{Standard} + \text{Variance}}$$

$$\frac{100}{110} = 90.9\% \qquad \frac{100}{130} = 76.9\% \qquad \frac{100}{125} = 80\%$$

By using the same basic standard for a period it is possible to readily compare the material usage at one time, with that at another. If the basic standard is changed such comparison obviously becomes more difficult. It is evident, however, that as time passes basic standards are likely to get more and more out of line with current prices and standards of efficiency, and that costs based on an obsolete cost level are of little use. It is true that trends are of interest to management, but only so over periods of, say, five to ten years, and it has rarely happened in recent years that basic standards could be retained for so long because of frequent changes in national wage rates and in world commodity prices. Furthermore, methods of manufacture have improved, labour efficiency has increased, and new materials have come into use, all of which factors have caused standards expected to remain effective for a period of years to be revised earlier than was originally intended. For this reason the basic standard finds less favour than the current standard.

The standards incorporated into a double entry accounting system are generally current standards.

A standard may be an ideal standard or an expected standard.

An *ideal standard* is one that can be attained under the most favourable conditions possible. Such standards make no allowance for accidents, defective materials, machine breakdowns, or for any other avoidable and undesirable condition. An unfavourable variance from an ideal standard reminds management of the extent to which actual performance can be improved. Performance targets are set so high that workers become discouraged, feeling that they can never attain them. Ideal standards are not commonly used because it is impossible to maintain ideal conditions at all times.

An *expected standard* is one that it is anticipated can be attained during a future specified budget period. A distinction may be drawn between a standard based on expected actual conditions, i.e. one set by reference to records of past performance modified in respect of expected changes in design, equipment, or other conditions, and a standard based on attainable efficient production.

Standards based on expected actual conditions frequently represent nothing more than estimated costs since they provide no real standard of efficiency. As has already been shown, comparison with past performance may be worse than useless, for it provides no incentive to improve upon a standard that may itself be based upon indifferent performance. Yet the phrase 'expected actual conditions' is not always used with this meaning. It sometimes serves to imply a standard in which efficiency *is* properly set, but which is based on current prices and levels of production, i.e. upon 'attainable efficient production'.

By far the most commonly used standard is the expected standard based on attainable efficient production. Such standards are set by reference to current business conditions and represent the costs anticipated if the expected prices are paid for materials and services, and if the usage of each of these factors corresponds to what is believed to be necessary to produce the planned volume of production. Such a standard is not based on the total elimination of inefficiency: rather, it allows for such waste and error as management believes to be unavoidable in practice. This is the only type of standard that will be considered in the following pages.

Standards should be reviewed frequently, for if they become unrealistic when conditions change, variances will be disclosed that do not help managers, and the system will be discredited.

SETTING STANDARD COSTS

Whether a separate standards department is organised or a standards committee is formed, the preparation of standards calls for liaison between many departments. Much of the detailed work is carried out by clerks and engineers of the purchasing, personnel, design, and production control departments. Thus, the purchasing department advises on the standard cost of materials to be used during the period under review, the production manager supplies details of routing, specifications, operation lists, etc., the personnel manager furnishes particulars of wage rates, and work study engineers set standard times for specified operations. The cost accountant collates the information and sets up his standard cost cards. Basically, this is a relatively straightforward task, as will be seen from the following simple example. In practice, however, numerous calculations are involved and sometimes difficulties arise where the departments primarily responsible for supplying information are not competent to provide it without expert guidance from the cost accountant. These problems are briefly discussed below.

Example

The Key-Way Manufacturing Company Limited produces sardine-tin keys in boxes of 1000 on long-term contract with the Mermaid Canning Company Limited, to the following specification:

```
                        SPECIFICATION                        SK646

Description:  Sardine-tin key, boxed in 1000's.        Date:  1 June 19—

Dimensions:   8 cm length from 2 mm rod, with ringed end,
              punched with slot 10 mm × 1 mm, 10 mm from
              end per drawing X172 enclosed.

Material:     Per sample (CS1364).
```

The operations involved in its production are, for purposes of simple demonstration, represented by the following flow-chart:

Mild Steel

```
2 mm diameter rod metre lengths  ———————→  Cut to length
                                               |
                                             Store
                                               |
                                             Slot
                                               |
                                           Form end
                                               |
                                         Inspect visually
                                               |
                                         Count and pack
```

Slotting, end-forming, counting and packing are undertaken on one special-purpose machine, which is treated as a single cost centre.

The standard material list is as follows:

```
                    STANDARD MATERIAL LIST                   SK646

Description:  Sardine-tin keys, 1000's boxed.          Date:  1 June 19—

                  Materials: Quantity and Description

        Alloy XM:  1 metre length, 2 mm diameter (CS1364) per 8 keys
  Box and Label:  1 box 25 cm × 10 cm × 7 cm (CB453) per 1000 keys.
```

The standard price list drawn up on the basis of the prices expected to rule during the ensuing year shows among other things:

STANDARD PRICE LIST (Extract)

Material Code	Description	Standard Price Each
		p
CB453	Cardboard box and descriptive label, 25 cm × 10 cm × 7 cm	6.00
CS1364	Alloy XM – metre length 2 mm diameter	3.44

The standard operation list appears as follows:

STANDARD OPERATION LIST			
Description: Sardine-tin keys SK646, boxed 1000's.			Date: 1 June 19—
Operation No.	Operation Name and Description	Machine	Standard Time per 1000
1	Cut 10 cm lengths from metre rod	Rod cutter	10 minutes
2	Slot	Special purpose key-producing machine	
3	Form end		15 minutes
4	Output counted and packed automatically in cartons of 1000		

The rod cutter is operated by an operator of grade C2, and the special purpose key-producing machine by an operator-inspector grade B1 and a material-handler grade D. The wages manual gives the following information regarding the remuneration of such operatives:

WAGES MANUAL (Extract)

Grade	Basic Hourly Rate (£)	Overtime	Holidays	Pension
B1	2.80	Time-and-a-quarter	10 working days	None
C2	3.60	Time-and-a-quarter	10 working days	None
D	3.48	Time-and-a-quarter	10 working days	None

The premium element of overtime pay together with holiday pay and provision for pensions are regarded as overheads — the appropriate amounts being included in the budget. The personnel officer anticipates that wages' rates will remain unchanged throughout the year to come.

Inspection of the 'overhead' estimates for the forthcoming year provides the following information:

	Rod Cutters (Cost Centre 45)	Special Purpose Key-producing Machine (Cost Centre 98)
Estimated cost for the year	£8 400	£4160
Estimated hours of operation	10 000	2000

From this information the standard cost card can be drawn up and will appear as follows:

STANDARD COST CARD		SK646
Description: Sardine-tin keys – boxed in 1000's.		1 June 19—

	Standard Cost Per Box	
	P	P
Material Cost:		
Alloy XM (125 at 3.44p)	430	
Box and descriptive label	6	436
Wages:		
Cutting to length (C2)	60	
Slot, form end, inspect, count and pack (B1: 70p, plus D: 87p)	1.57	217
Overheads:		
Rod cutting (cost centre 45–84p per hour)	14	
Slot, form end, etc. (cost centre 98–208p per hour)	52	66
Total Cost Per Box		719

Prepared by	Checked
GH	RES

SETTING MATERIAL STANDARDS

In order to fix material standards it is necessary to specify (a) the quantity; and (b) the price, per unit of product, of each kind of direct material to be used. Although neither of these factors is the direct concern of the cost accountant, it is important that he should understand the methods adopted in setting these standards.

Standard Quantity

In the simplest case it is possible to set standards for the proper usage of materials by direct measurement of the product. For instance, where lemonade is made to a fixed formula without loss in mixing or bottling, input and output are simply related.

Often it is necessary to consider carefully the method of using the material before fixing a standard that will represent the most economical method of arranging the pattern on the material in order to reduce waste to the minimum. Consider the care involved in laying out a dress pattern before cutting. Without such care the quantity of dress material specified by the pattern manufacturer will prove quite inadequate.

In many cases a certain amount of waste is unavoidable. For instance, however careful a cutter may be, some waste of cloth in cutting out a man's suit is inevitable. In other trades a percentage of breakage is bound to occur. It is impossible, for example, to cut glass for the glazing of greenhouses and sheds without some loss. Even an expert glass-cutter is not infallible. The problem in setting standards in cases like this is to determine what is a realistic allowance to make for defective materials and minor errors, in order to set workers a standard that they realise they can attain if they are careful, whilst ensuring that the allowance is low enough to minimise all losses that can reasonably be avoided. It is important at this stage to inject into the standard what is normal and unavoidable. Spoilage may depend on the skill and motivation of the workers. A bonus or the effect of the learning curve can affect their performance. The setting of such standards demands the co-operation of supervisors, production engineers, the cost accountant, and possibly that of the workers themselves.

Example

In the manufacture of brass ash-trays, a trained operator should be able to cut out blanks with a spacing of 2 mm. Thus if the standard method is to employ a sheet of brass, size 52 cm × 32 cm, such a sheet will produce 15 ash-trays 10 cm in diameter (i.e. 5 ash-trays along the length of the sheet and 3 rows across).

   If such a sheet costs £1.65, the standard material cost of each ash-tray (ignoring scrap) will be 11p.

Whilst the use of standard costs is more common in industries that produce standard products for stock, they can also be applied for jobbing work, particularly where there is an element of standardisation in the components or sub-assemblies employed or in the methods adopted. It will still be necessary to prepare a standard cost card, but there will now be a separate card for each job. The standard cost of materials in such cases is set on the basis of the engineering specifications that will show the quantity of each material required for the job, allowance being made for such normal losses and breakage as is appropriate on the basis of past experience of using the materials for similar jobs. Special orders of this type frequently consist largely of specially assembled standard parts or components, the standard cost of which can be obtained in the same way as that for any other standard product made for stock. It may be thought that the preparation of standard cost cards for a number of separate jobs, and the accumulation of costs in respect of each, will entail excessive clerical work, but this is not necessarily so: everything depends upon whether the proportion of estimates accepted is high or low, and upon the difficulty of estimating with a degree of accuracy, which may suitably be termed the fixing of a 'standard'.

   Less satisfactory methods of fixing material usage standards are: to take the average standard of all similar jobs for a given period (e.g. a month); to use an average of the best and poorest performances in such a period; or to take the best previous performance. It is possible, however, to base reasonably accurate standards on the results of a properly supervised test run, or a series of such runs. This type of method is frequently employed where it is difficult to employ any other, e.g. to assess how much adhesive is required for the side seam of a plastic paint container, or how much tar should be mixed with a particular grade of stone to give a good road surface.

   It will be recognised that standard costs are not limited to production costs. There is nothing to prevent the fixing of standards for packing and distribution. In fact it is frequently quite easy to include the cost of all packing materials and wages in the standard cost of a product.

Standard Price

As already suggested, material price standards may be based on ideal prices or expected prices; current standards being usually based on the latter. Current expected price standards are generally set by the purchasing department and agreed to by top management after considering:

(a) prices specified in long-term contracts;
(b) forecasts of commodity price trends; and
(c) purchase prices on recent orders.

Account should be taken of price advantages obtainable by purchasing in the most economical manner, i.e. in the most economic quantity (in relation to the demand), with the least cost (e.g. in respect of carriage) and on normally accepted credit terms. Unavoidable losses in store through breaking bulk, evaporation and similar causes are normally taken into account by the use of an inflated issue price. It is a matter of policy whether to regard carriage inwards as a part of the material cost or as an overhead, but whichever method is adopted in fixing standards it must also be adopted in computing actual costs. To regard carriage inwards as an item of overhead is inadvisable if such a course can be avoided, as materials from one source may be supplied carriage paid, whereas those from another may be charged at a price that does not include the carriage, which has to be paid for separately by the buyer.

Example

The Cough Candy Company produces a standard line of cough candy, made to the following recipe:

Sugar	75 kg
Syrup	30 kg
Fats	10 kg
Flavouring	3 kg

A loss of 18 kg is expected in boiling, pouring and cutting, assuming normally efficient production.

The company has a long-term contract for sugar at 14p per kilogram. The average price of syrup has been 20p per kilogram during the past year but is expected to fall by 5%. Fats have cost 32p per kilogram and no change in price is likely. Flavouring costs have fluctuated considerably during the past year, but the purchasing officer estimates that they will average 180p per kilogram.

Prepare the standard cost card for the ensuing year in so far as it relates to material costs.

STANDARD COST CARD

Cough Candy ....19.......

	Standard Price per kilogram	Per 100 kilograms of Output		Standard Cost per kilogram of Output
		Standard Quantity	Standard Cost	
	p	kg	£	p
Sugar	14	75	10.50	10.50
Syrup	19	30	5.70	5.70
Fats	32	10	3.20	3.20
Flavouring	180	3	5.40	5.40
		118		
Less loss in boiling, pouring, and cutting		18		
Standard Material		100	£24.80	24.80

The traditional recipe should be reviewed in order to discover whether a less expensive mixture can be used without loss of customer demand.

SETTING DIRECT WAGES STANDARDS

Labour-time Standards

The most scientific method of determining labour-time standards is that of work study, using the technique of method study to ensure that the work is carried out in the most effective way, and that of work measurement to determine the amount of work involved. Work measurement is a task for the specialist, the cost accountant is concerned only with its results and not with either the way in which the work involved is broken down into elements that are separately rated and timed to build up a standardised cycle time, or with the relaxation and other allowances made in establishing the target time.

The alternatives to scientific work study in setting labour-time standards are records of past performance, estimates based on personal experience, and the making of test-runs of the operations involved under expected normal conditions. Where a better basis is not available one or other of these methods must be adopted, but they are not entirely satisfactory because they do not provide an assessment of what the standard performance ought to be. This means that there is no incentive from this source to improve plant layout, to develop planning, routing, or materials handling, and to provide a smooth flow of production without unnecessary delays and bottlenecks. Nor is management encouraged to improve operation instructions or the training of workers so that operations will be performed in the best possible manner. Skill and motivation must be taken into account. The manager should try to recruit good workers and get the best from them. The difference between standard hours allowed for certain work and actual hours taken is evidence of his success.

Rates of Pay

The method of computing standard wages cost is influenced by the type of wages system in operation e.g. by day rates, piece rates, multiple piece rates, or a premium bonus system.

Where workers are paid on time rates it is necessary to establish:

(a)   the labour time standard for each operation;
(b)   the grade of labour to be employed on each operation; and
(c)   the wages rate for each grade of labour.

The establishment of the labour-time standard has already been considered. The grade of labour to be employed will be specified by the production manager (possibly via the production control department) in an operating instruction, and the rate of remuneration will be a matter of policy under the general authority of the personnel manager.

Where workers are paid on piece rates the problem is simpler, it being necessary only to apply the piece rate to find the standard cost. It will be seen later, however, that time is still important in connection with the absorption of overheads.

The rate to be regarded as the standard where multiple piece rates or bonus systems are in operation, and the setting of standard costs in such cases, are to an extent matters of management policy.

Basically, all that needs be done is to divide total earnings at the normal rate of production either by the number of units produced (to get the standard cost per unit), or by the number of hours taken (to get the standard rate per hour). The principal source of difficulty is the estimate of the normal rate of production, since this may considerably influence the cost per unit especially where a differential piece rate system is employed.

Basic pay does not represent the total cost of a worker's services to his employer, who has to defray, in addition, the cost of his share of National Insurance contributions, holiday pay, and perhaps pension contributions. It is not suggested that these additional costs constitute part of the direct wages for the purpose of standard setting, though it could be contended that they should. The alternative is to regard them as production overheads and this is preferable as a means of reducing clerical labour. The main point to observe is that whatever method is followed in the fixing of standards, this must also be adopted in the allocation of actual costs: it would be manifestly wrong to regard the employer's share of National Insurance as part of the standard direct wages, but to treat it as an overhead in computing actual costs. An allowance for normal idle time must be built into the standard time, and a bonus, if regularly paid, is part of the standard labour cost. Abnormal bonuses and overtime premiums are best excluded from standard labour costs.

Example

In a preserve factory a team of three girls is engaged in the bottling of jam. Their hourly rates are as follows:

	p
Senior Operator	280
Junior Operators (two)	220 each

Production is 960 jars per standard hour.

Required:

Prepare the standard cost card in so far as it relates to wages. Express costs to three decimals of a penny, showing the cost per 1000 jars and the cost per jar.

STANDARD COST CARD (Extract)	Standard Cost per 1000 Jars		Standard Cost per Jar
	p	p	p
Wages:			
Senior Operator: 1 hour 12 mins. at 280p per hour, per 1000	336.0		
Junior Operator (two): 1 hour 12 mins. at 220p per hour each, per 1000	528.0		
		864.0	0.864

The Learning Curve

Practice makes perfect, so when new methods or new products are introduced it is only to be expected that the time taken to complete certain operations will be progressively reduced as the operatives become more skilled or competent. Labour cost per unit will fall as learning proceeds, but soon the 'start up' phase gives way to a 'steady state' phase when no further skill advantages can be derived and the unit cost will stabilise. Obviously the learning curve has considerable significance for standard setting, since if timings are taken during the start up phase and laid down as standards, favourable variances will be experienced thereafter as operatives increase their work rate. Therefore, bonuses based on such early timings become permanent features of the remuneration system and are easily attainable. Conversely, if the standard is set at the steady state level, adverse variances will appear during the learning phase, which could affect employee earnings, morale and the overall acceptance of the new methods. Standards should be set with caution in the early stages and tightened by negotiation as learning proceeds. The impact of learning will not be restricted to direct labour, since it may influence the cost of supervision, material (since scrap will be reduced as experience increases) and overheads charged to production on a time basis. The learning curve, or cost experience curve, demonstrates this phenomenon graphically.

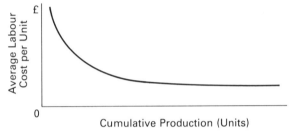

At first the curve falls steeply, but then levels off as operatives become fully experienced and no further cost savings can be made. Units produced in January may well cost more than units produced in June, so the value of units in stock will be influenced by the learning phenomenon. Decisions must take learning into effect, e.g. a company may tender for a contract to supply components, but not on the basis of a labour cost of say £5 a unit derived from time trials at its factory, but on the basis of perhaps £4 a unit, which will be the labour cost after the learning phase has been completed.

SETTING DIRECT EXPENSE STANDARDS

Direct expenses are not very common but where they arise it is normally easy to establish standards. Typical examples of direct expenses are sub-contractors' charges and royalties on production. A firm estimate given by a sub-contractor should prove an accurate standard, as would the amount of royalty formally agreed upon by the parties concerned. It is only in such cases as travelling expenses chargeable direct to a particular contract that it will be necessary to rely upon reasonable estimates.

SETTING STANDARD OVERHEAD ABSORPTION RATES

To set standard overhead absorption rates it is first necessary to determine:

(a)   the overhead to be incurred in the forthcoming period;
(b)   the base of absorption; and
(c)   the quantity of that base in the forthcoming period.

Where standard costing is employed in conjunction with a system of budgetary control, (a) and (c) are ascertainable from the budget centre budgets. Where separate budgets are not available it is necessary to relate all the costs to a definite level of activity known as the normal activity. The normal activity of each cost centre is stated in terms of the base of absorption, which may be expressed in standard hours (or minutes) or alternatively in units of output. The output of each cost centre is usually based on expected standards at attainable efficient production. Having determined the standards of output it is necessary to ascertain what overhead costs should be incurred at these levels and the standards will be set accordingly. These standards will cover indirect materials, indirect wages, and indirect expense and should be calculated from the information available, e.g. if a time study standard has been set for movement labour, allowing one hour at £2.20 per hour per 1000 packets handled from A to B, the overhead standard for 100 000 packets a period will be £220. Similarly the cost of electricity might be calculated from the number of hours run by each machine at normal activity, multiplied by the standard usage per hour and the standard rate per unit. The most satisfactory results will be obtained only where the standards are set objectively, i.e. when it is decided what the costs *ought* to be at the selected level of output, and not what they have been in the past when inefficiencies may have occurred and output have been at a different level. The standard costs of general overheads and services must be determined in a similar manner and these will be apportioned to the individual cost centres as explained above. The total standard cost for each cost centre is then divided by the number of hours or units to obtain the standard overhead absorption rates.

The determination of (b), the base of absorption, follows principles already discussed in Chapter 4.

Normally a separate standard cost centre overhead absorption rate is pre-determined for each separate production cost centre, but in appropriate cases it may be possible to compute standard cost rates for selling and distribution overheads also. In appropriate circumstances it is possible also to fix standard cost apportionment rates in respect of service centre costs, e.g. those of steam and power.

Since standard overhead absorption rates are frequently expressed in the form of cost centre hourly rates, i.e. either as machine-hour rates, or labour-hour rates, it is generally necessary to ascertain the time involved in each operation. Where payment is at time rates, attention will in any event have been paid to the fixing of standard operation times, but this need is not so obvious where workers are paid by the piece.

Where setting-up time is involved the cost of this should, as far as possible, be included in the overheads, regardless of whether or not the set up is carried out by the operator or by a full-time machine setter. Where the setting time is large in relation to the operating time it may be necessary to determine standard batch quantities for each product, and to prepare the standard cost card on the basis of this size of batch. As the cost varies with the batch size it is necessary in this case to extract a batch variance whenever the normal quantity is departed from. In some cases separate standard costs are computed for setting up and for production, the former being fixed and the latter being expressed in the normal way as a standard cost per unit. The valuation of inventories is then a matter of policy, for the standard unit cost includes no element for setting up.

ADVANTAGES OF STANDARD COSTS

Standard costs have all the general advantages of pre-determined costs, plus a number of advantages of their own. Pre-determined costs may be said to provide:

(a)   Economy of calculation.
(b)   Early availability of cost information.
(c)   The ability to anticipate changed conditions.

Standard costs give the following additional advantages:

(d)   The mere preparation of standards involves such a consideration of methods that sources of inefficiency are likely to be disclosed. This leads to the introduction of improved methods even before the standard costing system is put into operation. The setting of standards may, for instance, disclose that materials are being purchased in uneconomic lots, and that less frequent orders for a larger quantity would produce a significant saving through quantity discounts.
(e)   By watching for deviations of actual performance from standard, management observes inefficiencies and is able to correct them. Similarly, it can detect and reward exceptional efficiency. Thus, a plumber engaged on sub-contract work for a builder constructing a housing estate for a local authority may find his costs rising and his profits falling. Upon installing a simple standard costing system he may find that whilst each house has exactly one bath, one pedestal basin, one sink, and one water closet, the quantity of these items supplied to a typical group of 20 houses was: 28 baths, 27 pedestal basins, 27 sinks, and 23 water closets. Increased material control would close this opening for loss.
(f)   The use of standard costs in pricing inventories for balance sheet purposes eliminates from such valuations any unnecessary or excessive expenditure.
(g)   By confining its attention to deviations from the plan (i.e. to variances), management can use its energies in the most profitable directions.
(h)   Standard costs adjusted in line with current conditions provide an excellent basis for the preparation of estimates and may be used in preparing tenders or in fixing selling prices etc.

SEMINAR EXERCISES

11.1   (a)   What is a standard cost?
(b)   What benefits are derived by a business from a system of standard costing?
(c)   What problems are encountered in developing a standard costing system?

(18 marks)

11.2   (a)   What is a standard hour?   (3 marks)

(b)   Gamston Garments PLC manufacture woollen, knitted goods – pullovers, jumpers and scarves. During November they were budgeted to produce 2800 pullovers, 5500 jumpers and 3700 scarves. In one standard hour an operative is expected to complete either 6 pullovers, 8 jumpers or 15 scarves.
   Actual production during November was: 2400 pullovers, 5000 jumpers, 3600 scarves, and 1300 hours were worked.

Required:

Calculate ratios for November to reflect:

(i)   productivity of labour force;

(ii)   activity of the department – actual production relative to budget;

(iii) capacity – actual utilisation of budgeted resources.   (9 marks)

(c)   If productivity increases then profitability will increase. Do you agree? Relate your answer to Gamston Garments above.   (6 marks)

(Total 18 marks)

12

Variance Analysis

The difference between a standard cost and the comparable actual cost incurred during a period, is known as a *cost variance*. Where the actual cost incurred exceeds the standard cost, the difference is referred to as an *unfavourable variance*, or *adverse variance*. Where actual cost is less than standard, the variance is *favourable*.

Variances focus managerial attention on deviations from expected cost, but the variances must be analysed if management is to take appropriate action. Failure to make this analysis leads to the presentation of information that is misleading or less helpful than it should be. Consider, for instance, the case of a favourable variance being offset by an adverse one, as may happen when material purchasing is very efficient but material usage is excessive.

Variances occur for four major reasons:

1. *Direct materials cost variance*: the difference between the standard cost of direct materials specified for the output achieved and the actual cost of direct materials used.
2. *Direct wages cost variance*: the difference between the standard direct wages specified for the activity achieved and the actual direct wages paid.
3. *Overhead cost variance*: the difference between the standard cost of overheads absorbed in the output achieved and the actual overhead cost – this includes fixed and variable overheads.
4. *Sales margin variance*: the difference between the standard profit margin on budgeted sales and the actual profit margin on actual sales.

Each of these variances, however, may be analysed into two or more components.

Sales margin may vary from standard because more or less has been sold than was expected, or because sales have been made at prices that differ from standard. Material cost variances occur because materials are purchased at prices different from standard or because more or less material is used than should have been used for what has been produced. Labour costs vary from standard because a non-standard wage rate has been paid, or because the labour force has worked more or less than the standard hours for actual production.

Variances are not confined to sales or production costs, but can be calculated wherever a standard is set, e.g. transport costs, administration costs etc. The diagram on page 281 shows the interconnection of the major variances and the following example demonstrates how they are calculated.

Some authorities no longer recognise the fixed overhead capacity variance, but as is shown below, this variance can be useful if a situation is to be clearly analysed.

Example

Tissington Tubes PLC make cycle frames for sale to other bicycle manufacturers, or direct to the public. The standard production cost of a Tissington frame is as follows:

		£
Direct materials:	5 kg at £1 per kilogram	5
Direct labour:	2 hours at £3	6
Variable overheads:	50p per direct labour-hour	1
Fixed overheads:	Recovery rate £2 per direct labour-hour	4
Total cost		£16

Variable overheads are expected to fluctuate with direct labour-hours. Fixed overheads are budgeted for the year at £60 000 and on forecasted direct labour-hours of 30 000 they are absorbed to production at a rate of £2 per hour. This calculation implies that 2500 direct labour-hours are budgeted as production capacity to be used each month, and £5000 of fixed overheads is to be charged to production each month. Therefore production is budgeted at maximum capacity of 1250 frames per month. During June 1000 frames were produced at an actual cost of:

		£
Direct materials:	5324 kg purchased at 91p per kilogram	4 845
Direct labour:	1848 hours paid at a rate of £3.29 per hour	6 080
Variance overheads:	expenditure	1 100
Fixed overheads:	expenditure	5 300
Total cost		£17 325

Comparison of a flexed budget for 1000 frames with actual cost shows the following variances:

		Flexed Budget £	Actual Cost £	Variance £
Direct materials:	1000 frames × £5	5 000	4 845	155 (F)
Direct labour:	1000 frames × £6	6 000	6 080	80 (A)
Variable overheads:	1000 frames × £1	1 000	1 100	100 (A)
Fixed overheads:	allocated	5 000	5 300	300 (A)
		£17 000	£17 325	£325 (A)

A total variance of £325 from a budget of £17 000 seems only a small deviation from plan, but adverse variances can compensate for favourable variances. These variances must now be analysed in an attempt to isolate their causes if realistic remedial action is to be planned. Note that the company uses a full absorption costing system and fixed overheads are treated accordingly.

MATERIAL COST VARIANCES

The material cost variance can be separated into two components:

1. Direct materials price variance, which is caused by the payment of more or less than the standard price of materials.
2. Direct materials usage variance, which arises from the use of more or less materials than specified in the standard for the product.

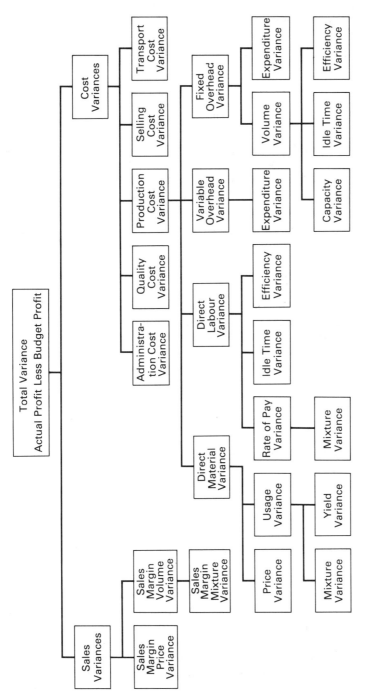

Variance Analysis Chart. This chart shows the variances that can be calculated for a full absorption costing system. For standard marginal costing, the fixed overheads for production, selling costs and administration would be shown as expenditure variances only, whilst sales and variable cost variance would influence a total contribution variance.

Direct Materials Price Variance

This variance isolates cost savings or increases caused by buying at non-standard prices. The formula for calculating the materials price variance may be expressed as:

(Actual quantity purchased × Actual price) − (Actual quantity purchased × Standard price)

or alternatively:

(Actual price − Standard price) × Quantity purchased

This variance is adverse when the actual price paid for material exceeds the standard price, and favourable when the actual price is less than the standard price. In computation, variances are shown as (F) for favourable and (A) for adverse.

In cases where more than one material is used the variance will be computed for each material. Once the price variance is recognised it is charged to costing profit and loss account, as a cost or benefit derived from purchasing activity in that period, and the materials are dealt with at standard cost from then on. They are entered in the stores' records at standard and issued to production at standard, and shown in the balance sheet as stocks at standard if they are not all used up by the end of the period.

An alternative method is to stock the materials at actual price and charge them out of stores to production at standard price. This method recognises the price variance only when materials are used and charges it to income on a usage basis.

The material price variance in the example above is calculated at:

$$(AQ \times AP) \quad - \quad (AQ \times St\,P)$$
$$(5324\,\text{kg} \times 91\text{p}) - (5234\,\text{kg} \times £1)$$
$$£4845 \quad - \quad £5234 \quad = \underline{£479}\ (\text{F})$$

Material has been purchased at less than standard cost, so actual cost is less than the amount which should have been incurred to buy this quantity. The existence of an adverse material price variance does not always indicate inefficiency by the purchasing office or the responsibility of the buyer. Market factors beyond the control of the buyer may change prices, but it is also a fair comment that an experienced buyer should have foreseen these changes, and built them into his standard price. Random market fluctuations may cause monthly variances which even out over a year.

A favourable price variance does not always indicate efficient buying; it may mean that inferior materials have been purchased, which can cause other adverse variances, e.g. material usage, and labour efficiency. The buyer may therefore be responsible for waste and excess costs in parts of the business that do not appear to be under his management. A miscalculation by the accountant as to the re-order point could lead to a stock-out, which in turn would force the buyer to procure materials at short notice, for which he may have to pay prices in excess of the standard. An adverse price variance may mean that materials of superior quality than those specified in the standard have been purchased, and this factor could influence labour efficiency or even the price charged for the completed product. Constraints within the stock budget may prevent the buyer from negotiating large purchases at favourable discounts, but this fact may not emerge from normal variance analysis.

Direct Materials Usage Variance

This variance highlights the difference between the amount that should have been used and the actual amount used, in order to calculate the actual number of units produced. The formula for calculating the material usage variance is:

(Actual quantity at standard price*) – (Standard quantity at standard price)

or:

(Actual quantity – Standard quantity) at Standard price

This variance should be calculated individually for each material used, often showing a favourable result for one material, which may compensate and hide adverse variances for other materials.

The material price variance in the example above is:

$$(AQ \times StP) \quad - \quad (StQ \times StP)$$
$$(5324 \text{ kg} \times £1) - (5000 \text{ kg} \times £1)$$
$$£5324 \quad - \quad £5000 \quad = \underline{£324} \text{ (A)}$$

The extra cost incurred at standard price of using 324 kg more than was planned for producing 1000 frames is £324. Note how the adverse usage variance and favourable price variance compensate to conceal the true extent of the departure from standard, if only a single material cost variance of £155 favourable is calculated.

	£
Price variance	479 (F)
Usage variance	324 (A)
Overall variance	£155 (F)

The benefits derived from an efficient buying department seem to have been lost in part by waste in the factory.

The causes of these two variances must now be established. In the first instance investigation will be made with the buyer concerning the price variance, and with the production manager for the usage variance. The reason may not, however, be so easy to track down, since if the buyer has purchased cheaper materials, this could be the cause of excessive wastage in the factory resulting in the adverse usage variance. There may be a number of factors that contribute to a usage variance e.g. defective non-standard material, improperly adjusted machinery, or work undertaken by an apprentice in order to reduce the labour cost.

If materials are wasted, the factory manager or departmental foreman is most likely to be held responsible, and it is fair that he should account for the amount of extra material used at standard price. However, if the extra material used must be purchased at more than standard price, is it fair to hold the buyer responsible for the adverse price variance? He has performed his task according to standard, apart from buying the extra material necessary to compensate for production errors. The buyer would argue that the price variance is, in this case, the fault of the production manager, and that remedial action should be organised by that department to prevent its re-occurrence.

---

* An alternative term for actual quantity at standard price is standard cost of actual output.

DIRECT WAGES VARIANCE

Direct wages variance can be separated into two components:

1. Direct wages rate variance, caused by the payment of more or less than the rate specified in the standard.
2. Direct labour efficiency variance, which arises when the work takes more or less hours than are specified in the standard for the product.

Direct Wages Rate Variance

In certain cases it is possible to extract the wages rate variance on the payroll itself by providing separate columns for the wages earned at the actual rate paid, and also for those that would have been earned if the standard rate had been paid. However, wages rate variances frequently arise, not because a particular man is paid more than was expected, but because a grade of labour different from that appointed is used. Where this happens it is possible to extract the variance by employing job time cards ruled to show the:

(a) actual time taken for the operation;
(b) standard time specified for it;
(c) standard rate per hour; and
(d) actual rate per hour paid.

Alternatively, the actual wages paid relating to each cost centre may be compared with the sum of the actual hours worked multiplied by the standard hourly rate for each of the various grades of labour.

Yet another way of obtaining the wages rate variance in respect of a cost centre is to extract from the total direct wages paid the labour efficiency variance of the centre and the standard cost of its output. The balance is the wages rate variance.

However the wages rate variance is extracted, the formula for its calculation is:

$$(\text{Actual hours paid} \times \text{Actual rate}) - (\text{Actual hours paid} \times \text{Standard rate})$$

or alternatively:

$$(\text{Actual rate per hour} - \text{Standard rate per hour}) \times \text{Hours paid}$$

The labour rate variance calculated in the example above would be:

$$(\text{Actual hours paid} \times \text{Actual rate}) - (\text{Actual hours paid} \times \text{Standard rate})$$

$$1848 \text{ hours} \times £3.29 \quad - \quad 1848 \text{ hours} \times £3$$

$$£6080 \quad - \quad £5544 \quad = £536 \text{ (A)}$$

Proper accounting demands that the wages rate variance included in any wages accrued be reported; it is not sufficient to state only the variance on the wages paid. The variance may be caused because a rate increase negotiated with the union has not yet been incorporated into the standard. This variance is beyond the control of the managers and likely to appear month after month until the standard cost is adjusted. An example of mismanagement that is controllable is a rate of pay variance caused by the work being allocated to skilled operatives whose wage rate is above that of the labour grade planned to be used on the job.

Where necessary, the wages rate variance may be analysed in order to show separately the effect of:

(i) using skilled workers to perform unskilled operations where there is a shortage of skilled work;
(ii) using unskilled workers to perform skilled work;
(iii) service increments paid to long-service employees, which result in variations in the rate paid for the same skill of operation;
(iv) wage awards in excess of those provided for in the standard, or standard not yet adjusted for recent negotiations;
(v) overtime otherwise than as provided for in the standard.

The degree of analysis provided for in the system will depend upon the circumstances – it is not necessarily profitable to analyse wages rate variances in full detail, though this may sometimes be advisable. In the example above, cost has increased above standard because wages in excess of standard rate have been paid, and the reason should be investigated.

Direct Labour Efficiency Variance

A direct labour efficiency variance to some degree fills a position corresponding to material usage variance in connection with materials, just as the wages rate variance fills that corresponding to the material price variance.

Having isolated the variance from standard caused by the price paid for labour, the next consideration must be to investigate the impact on cost of the way in which that labour has been employed. The direct labour efficiency variance compares the amount of work achieved in the hours paid for, with the production that should have been achieved in that time if the labour force had been working according to standard timings. This variance attempts to answer the question, 'Have they performed as efficiently as they were expected to perform?', and could be calculated as:

(Actual hours at standard rate)   –   (Standard hours for actual production at standard rate)

1848 hours × £3   –   2000 hours × £3

£5544   –   £6000   = £456 (F)

Total labour variance is £80 adverse, but it comprises rate of pay £536 adverse and efficiency £456 favourable. Once again a favourable variance masks an adverse variance until further analysis is undertaken. The efficiency variance shows the cost saved because work equivalent to 2000 standard hours was accomplished in only 1848 hours paid for by the business.

Idle Time Variance

Further analysis may define efficiency more accurately. Normal idle time is usually built into the standard timings, but let us assume that in this problem abnormal idle time was experienced, caused by a machine breakdown, or a material stock-out, or a power failure, equivalent to 200 labour-hours. The operatives were paid during this time, but there was no production. Accordingly an adverse idle time variance can be calculated, which may or may not be controllable by management.

$$\text{(Hours paid at standard rate)} \quad - \quad \text{(Hours worked} \times \text{Standard rate)}$$

$$\text{(1848 hours} \times £3) \quad - \quad \text{(1648 hours} \times £3)$$

$$£5544 \quad - \quad £4944 \quad = \underline{£600} \text{ (A)}$$

The intervention of this variance shows efficiency in a new light. The operatives have now completed 2000 standard hours of work in only 1648 hours.

The efficiency variance may now be calculated as follows:

$$\text{(Hours worked at standard rate)} \quad - \quad \text{(Standard hours for actual production at standard rate)}$$

$$1648 \times £3 \quad - \quad 2000 \times £3$$

$$£4944 \quad - \quad £6000 \quad = \underline{£1056} \text{ (F)}$$

This is a true measure of their efficiency.

An adverse efficiency variance may be caused by the use of inferior materials that take longer to turn into completed products, and increase the incidence of wastage, or the use of cheaper but less skilled labour, or even poor morale among the labour force. It is important to differentiate between production time wasted in abnormal idle time, whether the fault of management or not, and the time lost because inefficient operatives have failed to complete a job in the standard time. The efficiency variance may also be influenced by absenteeism in excess of the level included in the budget on which the standard is based.

VARIABLE OVERHEAD EXPENDITURE VARIANCE

Variable overheads by definition fluctuate with changes in the volume of production. They can be budgeted according to some variable factor which will express that fluctuation, e.g. per product, per direct labour-hour or per machine-hour. In the example above, direct labour-hours (DLH) are used. The variance is calculated according to the formula:

$$\text{(Budgeted expenditure for actual production)} \quad - \quad \text{Actual expenditure}$$

$$\text{(1000 units} \times £1) \quad - \quad £1100 \quad = \underline{£100} \text{ (A)}$$

This variance merely informs management that overspending has taken place, and could be further analysed to disclose the reasons for that overspending, e.g. purchases above standard price or purchases in excess of standard quantity. Stepped costs could influence this variance if the cost per unit is decreased or increased when a certain volume is achieved. In cases where variable overhead costs fluctuate with or are linked to direct labour-hours, it is possible to calculate an efficiency variance if hours worked are more or less than standard for the volume of production, so that variable overheads charged to production differ from standard.

FIXED OVERHEAD VARIANCE

The overhead variance may be broken down into:

1. Overhead expenditure variance caused by incurring more or less overheads than was provided for in the fixed budget on which the standard overhead absorption rate was based. More or less has been spent.

2. Volume variance, which arises when more or less output is achieved than was specified in the budget on which the standard overhead absorption rate was based, so more or less fixed overheads are absorbed as a charge to production cost. The variance in the volume of output achieved is caused by any or all of the factors, 'capacity usage', 'efficiency', 'idle time' and 'calendar', differing from the standards set and for which variances will be extracted. As these sub-variances fully explain the reasons for the variance in volume, they replace it in the final summary, as shown in the following pages.

Overhead Expenditure Variance

The overhead expenditure variance is computed by applying the formula:

Actual overheads incurred − Overheads budgeted for period

£5300   −   £5000   = £300 (A)

More was spent than was intended.

Calendar Variance

This variance is now little used, but is nevertheless worthy of mention. Where the overhead budget is in terms of, say, twelve months a further variance – calendar variance – arises where the number of working days in the current month differs from, say, one twelfth of those in the budgeted period.

Overheads budgeted per calendar   Overheads for appropriate length
month (*one-twelfth year*)   −   of month (*working days*)   = Calendar variance

The occurrence of a public holiday during a costing period will reduce the number of working days available in that period. A company may work with twelve calendar months in a year, or with thirteen four-week costing periods. A four-week period contains twenty working days, and if there is a public holiday on one of those days, the capacity available for production, and therefore the fixed overheads that can be absorbed by that production, is reduced by $\frac{1}{20}$ or 5%.

Capacity Usage or Utilisation Variance

Capacity usage variance shows the effect of working above or below the capacity (measured in labour/machine-hours) assumed in the budget upon the basis of which the standard overhead absorption rate was fixed. The formula for computing it is:

(Budgeted hours − Actual hours) × Standard overhead per hour = Capacity usage variance
2500   −   1848   ×   £2   =   £1304 (A)

Overhead Efficiency Variance

This is a companion variance to the direct labour efficiency variance and represents the effect of labour efficiency upon overheads. It may be analysed in the same way as that variance, i.e. by jobs, departments, processes, or operations. Where appropriate, the two variances may be shown on the same report and aggregated, for any action that corrects a variance in one tends also to correct that in the other. Furthermore, the true cost of inefficiency and the true worth of efficiency can be found only by aggregating these variances. It would be wrong, for instance, to suggest out of hand that increased speed that showed a favourable labour efficiency variance of £50 was unprofitable if it resulted in an increased material usage variance (unfavourable) of £60, as the favourable effect upon the overhead efficiency variance might very well be far more than £10.

An overhead efficiency variance is computed by applying the formula:

$$\left(\begin{array}{c} \text{Actual hours} \\ \text{worked} \end{array} - \begin{array}{c} \text{Standard hours} \\ \text{for work done} \end{array}\right) \times \begin{array}{c} \text{Standard overhead} \\ \text{absorption rate} \end{array} = \begin{array}{c} \text{Overhead efficiency} \\ \text{variance} \end{array}$$

This variance may also be analysed as an idle time variance, showing the fixed overheads not absorbed because abnormal idle time was experienced, and as an efficiency variance, showing the amount of overheads absorbed to production, above or below standard, through the ability of the labour force to work above or below standard speed.

Idle Time Variance

(Actual hours paid − Actual hours worked) × Standard absorption rate

(1848   − 1648)   ×£2   = £400 (A)

This means that production was lost and the overheads budgeted to be charged to that production were not so charged.

Efficiency Variance

(Actual hours worked − Standard hours for actual production) × Standard absorption rate

(1648   −   2000)   ×   £2   = £704 (F)

This means that an extra £704 of fixed overheads were absorbed by the production of units in excess of what should have been produced on a time basis. The analysis of fixed overhead costs in the example above can be explained as follows:

	Hours	£
Actual expenditure		5300
Expenditure variance		300(A)
Fixed budgeted expenditure	2500	5000
Capacity not used − Capacity usage variance	652	1304(A)
Hours paid for	1848	
Capacity wasted − Idle time variance	200	400(A)
Hours worked	1648	
(Extra overheads absorbed because production was more than should have been produced in the hours worked)		
Efficiency variance	352	704(F)
Standard hours for actual production	2000	
Fixed overheads absorbed by actual production		£4000

Capacity variance discloses the fixed overheads that were not absorbed to production because certain capacity was not used. The idle time variance shows the overheads not charged to production because capacity stood idle, even though it was intended to use that capacity.

Reports may be prepared to explain the idle time variance, comparing the budgeted hours with the actual hours worked for each department, process, operation, or machine. In this example the budgeted hours are equal to the capacity that was intended to be used and the report investigates reasons why it was not used.

IDLE MACHINE REPORT

Machine Shop 1   Period: to 30 June 19—

Section A   Foreman: H. E. Johnson

Machine	Budgeted Hours	Actual Hours	Overtime Hours	Idle Hours	No operator	No Material	Awaiting Set-up	Awaiting Tools	Under Repair	No Work	Machine-Hour Rate	Idle Time Variance Favourable/ (Adverse)
					|| Analysis of Idle Hours by Cause							
											£	£
1 A 1	156	152		4	4						2.60	(10.40)
1 A 2	156	120		36						36	1.96	(70.56)
1 A 3	156	168	12								1.50	18.00
1 A 4	156	156	8	8			8				2.10	–
	624	596	20	48	4	0	8	0	0	36		£(62.96)

Note: no work available for machine 1 A 2 in week 4. Efforts being made to obtain work.

The standard cost variances can of course be employed as part of a double-entry cost accounting system. The appropriate accounts would appear as on the following page.

Materials Control Account

	£		£
Purchases	4845	Costing p/l account:	
Costing p/l account:		Usage variance	324
Price variance	479	Work-in-progress	
		(1000 units × £5)	5000
	£5324		£5324

Direct Labour Control Account

	£		£
Cash paid	6080	Costing p/l account:	
Costing p/l account:		Idle time variance	600
Efficiency variance	1056	Rate of pay variance	536
		Work-in-progress	
		(1000 units × £6)	6000
	£7136		£7136

Variable Overheads Control Account

	£		£
Cost incurred	1100	Costing p/l account:	
		Expenditure variance	100
		Work-in-progress	
		(1000 units × £1)	1000
	£1100		£1100

Work-in-Progress Account

	£		£
Materials	5 000	Finished goods store	16 000
Labour	6 000	(1000 units × £16)	
Variable overheads	1 000		
Fixed overheads	4 000		
	£16 000		£16 000

Fixed Overhead Control Account

	£		£
Cost incurred	5300	Costing p/l account	
Costing p/l account		Expenditure variance	300
Efficiency variance	704	Idle time variance	400
		Capacity variance	1304
		Work-in-progress	
		(1000 units × £4)	4000
	£6004		£6004

Production Cost Variance Statement

	Adverse	Favourable	£
Actual cost of actual production			17 325
Material variances:			
Price		479	
Usage	324		
Labour variances:			
Rate of pay	536		
Idle time	600		
Efficiency		1056	
Variable overheads:			
Expenditure	100		
Fixed overheads:			
Expenditure	300		
Capacity	1304		
Idle time	400		
Efficiency		704	
	3564	2239	(1325)(A)
Standard cost of 1000 units transferred to finished goods store			£16 000

Alternatively variances may be posted from the control accounts to variance accounts and from there to costing profit and loss account.

STANDARD COSTING RATIOS

Further interpretation of the results derived from a standard costing system can be achieved by the use of simple ratio analysis. Output is expressed in terms of standard hours (the amount of work expected to be produced in one hour). The following ratios can be calculated for the example above as follows:

Efficiency Ratio

The standard hours equivalent to the work produced is expressed as a percentage of the actual hours spent in producing that work.

$$\frac{\text{Standard hours for actual production}}{\text{Actual hours worked}} \times \frac{100}{1} = \frac{2000}{1648} \times \frac{100}{1} = 121.3\%$$

Clearly the labour force have worked much less than the standard time expected for the production of 1000 frames.

As an alternative, the hours paid may be used in this ratio instead of hours worked, but this will confuse a comment on managerial efficiency with labour efficiency, and conceals the effect of 200 hours of abnormal idle time.

Activity or Volume Ratio

The standard hours equivalent to actual production is expressed as a percentage of the standard hours equivalent to budgeted production.

$$\frac{\text{Standard hours for actual production}}{\text{Standard hours for budgeted production}} \times \frac{100}{1} = \frac{2000}{2500} \times \frac{100}{1} = 80\%$$

The business has achieved 80% of the target that it planned to achieve – 20% of budgeted production has been lost, in spite of very efficient work by the labour force.

Capacity Ratio

The full capacity production for a period is expressed in standard hours, and this amount is compared with the actual amount of capacity utilised, which is usually taken to be hours worked.

$$\frac{\text{Actual hours worked}}{\text{Total hours available}} \times \frac{100}{1} = \frac{1648}{2500} \times \frac{100}{1} = 65.9\%$$

Under-utilisation of capacity available has not been compensated for by labour efficiency.

Alternatively this ratio can be calculated as the proportion of total hours available, which are budgeted to be used. In the example above the business is budgeted to work at full capacity of 2500 hours.

The situation of abnormal idle time is far from clear. If 'hours paid' rather than 'hours worked' is used in the efficiency ratio, then 'hours paid' must be used in the capacity ratio.

QUALITY COST VARIANCE

The quality of planned production may be specified in the standard for that product. If a production department fails to produce goods of the required quality, some units will be rejected and these units will be scrapped, sold at reduced prices, or reworked to rectify their faults. The standards will include an allowance for an acceptable or normal level of rejected production. The difference between the allowance for normal rejects and the actual cost of scrap or rectification is the quality cost variance.

A formula to assist in its calculation is:

(Units of actual production + Standard allowance for rejects) – (Cost of rejected units + Rectification cost less disposal value)

A further investigation into the cause will analyse the total variance to its constituent parts e.g. returns from customers, rejects from the factory production line.

REVISION VARIANCE

Standards are set but there is no guarantee that the conditions forecast in the standard will in fact be experienced. As the budget period unfolds, and month succeeds month, differences may emerge which reflect a permanent change in say material prices, or labour timings caused by the introduction of new methods. Differences of this nature will recur each month and form part of a variance which is quite outside the control of the management. In this situation it is best to recognise the change and revise the standard to accommodate it, so that the variances then disclosed will represent controllable factors for which remedial action is required. The difference between budgeted performance and the new revised standard is a revision variance.

Example

The standard overhead absorption rate for Cost Centre 34 ($33\frac{1}{3}$p per machine-hour) is based on the following budgets:

Overheads (Cost Centre 34)	£130 000
Machine-hours	390 000

During the year budgeted overheads are increased to £156 000, but the standard cost rate is not changed.

The concern's year is divided into thirteen 28-day accounting periods, for one of which the actual results are:

Overheads (Cost Centre 34)	£16 000
Machine-hours (actual)	27 000
Machine-hours of work produced	24 000

Show the analysis of the overheads variance.

Analysis of Overhead Variance – Cost Centre 34

Period Ended...........19—

	Adverse £	Favourable £
Revision variance:		
$\dfrac{156\,000 - 130\,000}{13}$	2000	–
Overhead expenditure variance:		
$£160\,000 - \dfrac{£156\,000}{13}$	4000	–
Overhead efficiency variance:		
$270\,000 - 240\,000 \times 33\frac{1}{3}$p	1000	–
Capacity usage variance:		
$\dfrac{390\,000}{13} - 270\,000 \times 33\frac{1}{3}$p	1000	–
Overhead variance $[£160 - (240 \times 33\frac{1}{3}p)]$	£8000	

DIRECT MATERIALS YIELD VARIANCE

In process industries where a standard process yield can be specified, it is possible to distinguish a further variance, yield variance, which is part of the materials usage variance; the formula for which is:

(Actual yield – Standard yield specified for actual input) × Standard cost per unit = Yield variance

The yield variance isolates the differences between the expected and actual outputs from a given quantity of inputs.

Example

A chemical process expects to lose 5% of volume in process. 2000 kg of material is put into the process during the month of June, so 1900 kg should be produced. Process costs for materials etc. are £5700, so a cost of £3 per kilogram is the average cost. Any production above or below the expected yield is multiplied by £3 per kilogram to give a favourable or adverse yield variance. If 1850 kg are produced, the yield variance will be:

$$\text{Actual yield} - \text{Expected yield} \times \text{Standard cost}$$
$$1850 \text{ kg} \quad - \quad 1900 \text{ kg} \quad \times \quad £3 \quad = £150 \text{ (A)}$$

DIRECT MATERIALS MIXTURE VARIANCE

Where a standard mixture is specified, a material mixture variance will arise whenever there is a departure from the standard formula. Material mixture variance forms part of the material usage variance and is computed as follows:

$$\begin{array}{c} \text{Standard cost of actual quantity} \\ \text{of the standard mixture} \end{array} - \begin{array}{c} \text{Standard cost of actual quantity} \\ \text{of the actual mixture} \end{array} = \begin{array}{c} \text{Material mixture} \\ \text{variance} \end{array}$$

Example

A standard mixture consists of 80% (by weight) of metal A and 20% of metal B. The standard cost of the metals is: A, £48 per tonne; B, £480 per tonne.

The mixture actually produced consisted of 390 tonnes of metal A, and 110 tonnes of metal B; 500 tonnes in total.

Compute the material mixture variance.

	£	£
Standard cost of the actual quantity of the standard mixture:		
Metal A: $500 \times \dfrac{80}{100}$ tonnes at £48 per tonne	19 200	
Metal B: $500 \times \dfrac{20}{100}$ tonnes at £480 per tonne	48 000	
		67 200
Standard cost of the actual quantity of the actual mixture:		
Metal A: 390 tonnes at £48	18 720	
Metal B: 110 tonnes at £480	52 800	
		71 520
Material mixture variance		£4 320 (A)

The following example, based on a typical examination question, demonstrates the extraction of the several variances involved in a simple process.

Example

The standard cost card for the production of a coloured bathroom tile appears as follows:

Standard material mixture:

		£
Material A	50 kg at 12p	6.00
Material B	40 kg at 2p	.80
Material C	10 kg at 8.8p	.88
	100 kg	7.68

		£
Wages: 2 hours at £3		6.00
Production overheads: 2 hours at 46p		.92
		£14.60

Standard yield: 200 tiles
Standard cost per tile: 7.3p
Standard time: 120 minutes ÷ 200 tiles = 0.6 minutes each tile

The following are the actual costs of production for the week ended . . . . 19 . . .
during which 20 800 tiles were made:

	£
4 800 kg Material A at 12p	576
4 200 kg Material B at 2p	84
1 000 kg Material C at 9.6p	96
10 000 kg	756
Wages 240 hours at £3.20	768
Production overheads absorbed:	
240 hours at 46p	110.4
	£1634.4

Prepare a statement showing the standard cost of production, and the actual cost of
production, and the analysis of the variances disclosed above.

Statement of Actual and Standard Costs of Production

Process . . . .   Week ending . . . . . . .19 . . . . .

	£	£
Standard cost of 20 800 tiles at 7.3p each		1518.4
Yield variance (800 tiles at 7.3p each)		58.4
Standard cost of 20 000 tiles at 7.3p		1460.0
Material price variance (Material C):		
1000 × (9.6p − 8.8p)	(80.00)	
Material mixture variance:		
* £676 − (100 × £7.68)	92.00	
Wage rate variance:		
240 hours at 20p (i.e. £3.20 − £3)	(48.00)	
Labour efficiency variance:		
(240 − 2000 × 0.6 minutes) × £3	(120.00)	
Overhead efficiency variance:		
(240 − 2000 × 0.6 minutes) × 46p	(18.40)	
		174.4
Actual cost		£1634.4

* Standard cost of actual mixture is £756, less price variance £80. Adverse variances are shown in brackets.

Note: it has been assumed that the standard yield specified is unaffected by any slight change in material
mixture. In practice a changed input mix might give rise to a known variation in standard yield, which ought then
to be taken into account in computing variances. It is also assumed that the labour required is unaffected by the
yield and depends entirely upon the quantity of the input. If this is not the case, it is not proper to employ a yield
variance, and calculations must be based on the material usage and the labour and process time required for the
stated *output* and not by reference to a standard *input*.

A DIFFICULTY EXPERIENCED IN INTERPRETING MIX AND YIELD VARIANCE

It is normal practice to calculate material variances by taking out the price variance first, and thereafter treating the materials at standard price, so that the impact of price fluctuations on the mix and yield variances is not considered. This may be harmful when a decision to substitute one material for another comes to be made.

Example

Reverting to our example concerning cycle frames, let us assume that the 5 kg of material used to make each frame comprise of 2 kg of nickel alloy casting and 3 kg of steel tubing. The nickel costs £3 per kilogram and the steel £1 per kilogram.

Standard direct material cost: 2 kg nickel alloy casting at £3 = £6
3 kg steel tubing at £1   = £3
5 kg   £9

(Standard mixture = Nickel 40%; Steel 60%)

Let us suppose that the price of nickel rises sharply on the world market to £5 per kilogram and, in response, the management adjust the mixture using 1.5 kg of nickel and 4 kg of steel for each frame – a weight of 5.5 kg for each frame.

A batch of 1000 frames is made and the following variances are calculated:

	£	£
Price variance:		
Nickel 1500 kg (£5 − £3)		3000 (A)
Mixture variance:		
Nickel £3 (1500 kg − 2200 kg)	2100 (A)	
Steel £1 (4000 kg − 3300 kg)	700 (A)	
5500 kg		1400 (A)
40% or ⅖ of 5500 kg = 2200 kg 60% or ⅗ of 5500 kg = 3300 kg		
Yield variance:		
Nickel £3 (2200 kg − 2000 kg)	600 (A)	
Steel £1 (3300 kg − 3000 kg)	300 (A)	
		900 (A)
		£2500 (A)

This analysis does not help managers to judge the true benefits resulting from their decision. The total variance is £2500 adverse, but if the change to the mixture had not been made the only variance would have been an adverse price variance of 2000 × £5 − £3 = £4000. When there is a change of standard mix the assumption that one material can be substituted for the same quantity of another does not always prove true, and thus yield variance will be affected by the change of mixture.

THE SALES MARGIN VARIANCES

The difference between standard selling price and standard cost per unit is the standard profit margin and this amount multiplied by the volume expected to be sold is the budgeted profit. Cost variances explain the difference between actual cost and standard cost, and sales margin variances analyse the difference between actual quantity sold at actual selling price and standard quantity at standard price. Basically there are two reasons for this difference – selling price varies from standard, or volume varies from standard – but a third variance is sometimes present if a range of products have been sold in a different combination than the mixture specified in the budget. An adverse sales variance occurs when actual performance is less than standard. This is the opposite of the situation that exists with cost variances, where a favourable situation exists if actual cost is less than standard. The sales margin variances are primarily the responsibility of the managers organising the sales force.

Reverting to the main example in this chapter concerning cycle frames, the standard cost was £16, so if they are planned to be sold at £20, the standard profit per unit will be £4, and if the sales budget plans 5000 sales in the forthcoming period the budgeted profit will be £20 000. However, actual sales are recorded as 4800 units sold at £21, so the actual profit is £24 000, and the total variance is £4000 favourable.

Sales Margin Price Variance

This variance measures the effect on profit of making sales at prices that are more or less than standard price; it is the difference between actual price per unit and standard price per unit for the volume sold.

The formula for this variance calculation is as follows:

(Actual sales volume at actual profit margin)	–	(Actual sales volume at standard profit margin)	
(4800 × £5)	–	(4800 × £4)	
£24 000	–	£19 200	= £4800 (F)

Alternatively: Actual margin – Standard margin × Actual volume will calculate this variance.

Sales Margin Volume Variance

This variance measures the effect on profit of selling more or less than the expected quantity of units; it is the difference between the actual volume sold and the standard volume at the standard profit margin.

The formula for the calculation of this variance is as follows:

(Actual sales volume at standard profit margin)	–	(Standard sales volume at standard profit margin)	
(4800 × £4)	–	(5000 × £4)	
£19 200	–	£20 000	= £800 (A)

Alternatively: Actual volume – Standard volume × Standard margin will calculate this variance.

These two variances are interdependent in so far as an adverse price variance should mean a favourable volume variance and vice versa. The extent of the connection depends on the elasticity of demand for the product. Often external market factors influence the price or volume variance, e.g. a recession, or a change in tastes to other goods.

Sales Margin Mixture Variance

If a company is selling more than one product a sales margin mixture variance will occur if actual sales are not made in exactly the same proportion as the mixture planned in the budget. This is an extension of the volume variance in that if all products in the range increase or decrease by the same proportion the actual mixture sold for the actual volume will be the same as the standard mixture applied to the actual volume. However, sales of products in a range do not fluctuate in sympathy, so the variance of profit must be calculated as:

(Standard mixture for actual volume) − (Actual mixture for actual volume) × Standard profit margin

The classic case is where more of the high profit margin goods and less of the low profit margin goods are sold, so that even with a drop in total sales, the profit is increased.

Extending the main example in this chapter, assume that three types of frame are sold, namely red, blue and silver. The budget contains the following information:

Frames	Standard Price £	Standard Cost £	Standard Margin £	Standard Mix Units	Standard Proportion	Standard Profit £	Standard Sales £
Red	18	16	2	2000	40%	4 000	36 000
Blue	20	16	4	1000	20%	4 000	20 000
Silver	22	16	6	2000	40%	12 000	44 000
				5000		£20 000	£100 000

Actual sales were:

Frames	Actual Price £	Standard Cost £	Actual Margin £	Actual Volumes Units	Actual Profit £	Actual Revenue £
Red	18.5	16	2.5	3000	7 500	55 500
Blue	19	16	3	1500	4 500	28 500
Silver	23	16	7	1500	10 500	34 500
				6000	£22 500	£118 500

Sales revenue has exceeded budget by 18.5%, but profit is only 12.5% above budget.

Price Variance = (Actual margin − Standard margin) × Actual volume

Frames	Actual Margin £		Standard Margin £		Difference £		Actual Volume		Variance £
Red	2.5	−	2	=	+0.5	×	3000	=	1500 (F)
Blue	3	−	4	=	−1	×	1500	=	1500 (A)
Silver	7	−	6	=	+1	×	1500	=	1500 (F)
									£1500 (F)

Volume and Mixture Variance

This occurs when more units have been sold than was planned but sales have also been made in a different mixture from standard. The volume variance calculates the profit that would have been made if sales of all produces had increased in the same proportion. The volume variance assumes such an increase and is calculated by finding the average standard margin for all units in the budget and applying that figure to the extra units produced above standard.

Five thousand units were expected to make a profit of £20 000, an average of £4 each. Six thousand units have been sold, so if the extra thousand sales are proportionate to the standard mixture, a favourable variance of £4000 is derived. To calculate the mixture variance the proportions of the standard mix must first be applied to the total actual sales to find the volumes that should have been achieved if the extra sales had been made in accordance with the standard mix.

Frame	Standard Proportion		Total Actual Sales Units		Standard Mix for Actual Sales		Actual Mix for Actual Sales		Difference		Standard Profit Margin £		Variance £
Red	40%	×	6000	=	2400	−	3000	=	+600	×	2	=	1200 (F)
Blue	20%	×	6000	=	1200	−	1500	=	+300	×	4	=	1200 (F)
Silver	40%	×	6000	=	2400	−	1500	=	−900	×	6	=	5400 (A)
					6000		6000						£3000 (A)

A greater proportion of low profit margin products has been sold resulting in an adverse mixture variance.

Alternatively, the variance can be calculated as:

Actual units sold at standard profit — Total units sold at average standard profit

$$(3000 \times £2 + £1500 \times £4 + £1500 \times £6 = £21\,000) - (6000 \text{ units at } £4 = £24\,000)$$
$$= £3000 \text{ (A)}$$

A management statement to reflect these variances might be drafted as follows:

	£	£	£	£	£
Standard profit					20 000
Frames	Red	Blue	Silver	Total	
Price variance	1500 (F)	1500 (A)	1500 (F)	1500 (F)	
Mixture variance	1200 (F)	1200 (F)	5400 (A)	3000 (A)	
Volume variance				4000 (F)	
				1000 (F)	
Total sales variances					2 500 (F)
Actual profit					£22 500

The impact on profit of sales made at prices other than standard is clearly demonstrated. Sales have increased, but the extra profit that should have resulted from this increase has been reduced because a less profitable mixture of products was sold.

ANALYSIS OF SALES BUDGET VARIANCES

Often a study of variances thrown up in main budget/actual comparative statements, will show a need for further analysis before the underlying causes of a variation can be pinpointed. Assume, for example, that the sales director of a large nationwide organisation receives the following summary sales report:

Sales Report

By sales districts—February 19—

	\multicolumn{4}{c}{District}	Total
	North	South	Welsh	Irish	
	£	£	£	£	£
Sales budget	350 000	545 000	125 000	98 000	1 118 000
Actual sales	354 000	540 000	131 000	54 000	1 079 000
Sales variance (Brackets = Adverse)	£4 000	£(5000)	£6 000	£(44 000)	£(39 000)

This result immediately suggests the need to enquire into the position in the Irish district, and one form of analysis which ought to suggest itself straightaway is one by product, such as the following:

Sales Report

Irish district—by product—February 19—

	\multicolumn{3}{c}{Product}	Total
	Blocko	Blick	Scrubbo	
	£	£	£	£
Sales budget	40 000	40 000	18 000	98 000
Actual sales	21 000	16 000	17 000	54 000
Sales variance	£(19 000)	£(24 000)	£(1 000)	£(44 000)

This, in turn, suggests a need to investigate sales of Blocko and Blick in the Irish sales district, as a result of which the following analyses might be prepared:

Sales Report

Irish district—Blocko—February 19—

	Quantity	Price	£
Sales Budget	1 600 000	2.5p	40 000
Actual Sales	720 000	2.92p*	21 000
Variance	(880 000)	0.42p	£(19 000)

* Increased price with effect from 15 February 19—, to take into account increased freight rates.

Sales Report

Irish district—Blick—February 19—

	Quantity	Price	£
Sales budget	800 000	5.0p	40 000
Actual sales	384 000	4.17p*	16 000
Variance	(416 000)	0.83p	£(24 000)

* Selling price reduced by means of 1p off scheme as from 6 February 19—, in view of competition from 'Murky' selling at 4p throughout Ireland.

Considering each report in turn, it will be seen that despite the increased selling price of Blocko, revenue from its sale has dropped by £19 000. As it seems likely that the fall in revenue results directly from the price increase, it is perhaps profitless to analyse the position further, but if this were not the case it would be possible to assess separately the effect of price change and the effect of the change in demand:

Sales volume variance:

	£
Actual sales at budgeted price (720 000 at 2.5p)	18 000
Sales budget at budgeted price (1 600 000 at 2.5p)	40 000
	£(22 000)

Sales price variance:

	£
Actual sales at actual price (720 000 at 2.92p)	21 000
Actual sales at budgeted price (720 000 at 2.5p)	18 000
	£3 000

In the case of Blick, the position is somewhat different: it is not increasing prices and increasing costs that are at the heart of the trouble, but competition. Even in this case the analysis of the sales variance into two components is not particularly profitable since it does not provide any measure of the fall in demand, and hence of the fall in revenue, which would have occurred had there been no decision to lower the price. Nor on the other hand does it indicate the cost of such a price reduction had there been no change in other factors, i.e. no additional competition.

Having studied one case in which top management was able by a process of analysis to locate the cause of the trouble – though in this example the difficulties should have been obvious to the district sales manager in Ireland whose duty it was to have communicated them to his superiors – it is interesting to consider a case in which the summary sales report (by districts) leaves top management quite unaware of the situation which is developing.

Suppose the sales report by districts to be as follows:

Sales Report

By districts—February, 19—

	District			Total
	North	South	East	
	£	£	£	£
Sales budget	30 000	70 000	45 000	145 000
Actual sales	32 000	70 000	45 500	147 500
Sales variance	£2 000	£—	£500	£2 500

It is unlikely that the sales director will be dissatisfied with the position, yet, below the surface may lurk the following figures (expressed in the form of a sales report—south district—by products):

Sales Report

South district—February, 19—

	Product			Total
	A	B	C	
	£	£	£	£
Sales budget	40 000	20 000	10 000	70 000
Actual sales	8 000	18 000	44 000	70 000
Sales variance	£(32 000)	£(2 000)	£34 000	£—

If we imagine that the profit to volume ratio of the various products is: A, 50%; B, 40%; and C, 6%; it will be seen how disastrous such a state of affairs could be, for with no variation in volume, profits earned will drop by £14 760, computed as follows:

	£
50% of £32 000	16 000
40% of £2000	800
	16 800
Less: 6% of £34 000	2 040
	£14 760

This fall in profit arises simply because there has been a change of sales mixture. The example emphasises the need for all aspects of a problem to be considered, as this state of affairs would be disclosed by a report giving the sales budget less budgeted production cost of sales, in comparison with actual sales less standard production cost of actual sales, as shown below:

Sales Report

Comparison of actual gross profit with that budgeted
South District—February 19—

	Budget £	Actual £
Sales	70 000	70 000
Less: Standard production cost of sales	49 000	63 760
Gross profit (at standard cost)	£21 000	£6 240
Profit variance		£(14 760)

It is a common misapprehension that the adverse variances are the important ones, and that favourable variances can be more or less ignored. This conception frequently leads to missed opportunities – the possibilities that were present having been grasped by another concern. This is particularly the case in connection with sales budgets. Any increase in sales over the budget should be subject to just as careful scrutiny as a deficiency; for something must be causing people to buy more. The questions are 'What?' 'Are consumer tastes changing?' 'Is it something we have done?' 'Have we improved our product?' 'Or is some other producer losing ground? If so, why?' 'And how can we profit by the position?' Unless the sales manager asks questions such as these, he will always be a step behind the market and liable to be caught out by any change.

It is not enough merely to ascertain the sales variance. The next step is to determine its cause. A mere request for reasons is not sufficient; those advanced must be diligently considered in the light of all relevant factors before being confirmed or rejected. Also, when the proffered reasons for a variance are rejected, further search must be made until the true cause can be established.

DISADVANTAGES OF STANDARD COSTING

Clearly no system is perfect, and the traditional method of setting standards and analysing variances is not without its critics. The objects of the system are: to draw attention to operations that are not following the budgeted plan; to give management a norm against which performance can be evaluated; and to provide data to assist with future planning.

Variances occur for a number of reasons other than the efficiency or inefficiency of the manager concerned. The standards themselves may have been set in error, or changes may have taken place since the setting date, which invalidate the standard as a comparator. Managerial performance should only be judged against a standard adjusted to relevant current conditions, hence the importance of the revision variance. Controllable and uncontrollable causes of variances must be identified if managerial performance is to be evaluated on a fair basis.

A standard is an expected quantity or cost level, and as such is really an average of what is forecast. Actual costs may fluctuate around that mean and cause adverse and favourable variances, which ought to cancel themselves out over time. Some variances occur in the area of responsibility of an executive, but may be caused by action or decisions made in other departments. Unless variance analysis recognises that departments are dependent upon one another, and that a variance can be influenced by activity elsewhere in the business, e.g. the buyers' cheap material can cause an adverse usage variance in the factory, the true benefit of the analysis to the business will be lost. Indeed if the factory manager is called to account for the result of activity for which the buyer is being praised, resentment may flourish and future co-operation will suffer. Perhaps considering the poor quality material used, the factory did very well to waste so little, and the adverse usage variance masks the high standard of work undertaken in that department.

Variances must be judged in the light of conditions external to the business. Adverse sales variances mean that the sales force have failed to meet their targets, but if their performance has been accomplished in a contracting market, and if they have maintained market share, whereas other companies have lost customers, then the sales force have performed well and should be congratulated. Conversely, if they have exceeded their targets, and have still not taken full advantage of conditions in the market-place, the favourable variance does not show the difference between actual sales and potential sales, which may be adverse.

Investigation of variances can be expensive, and managers must be assured of benefits in excess of that cost before investigation is authorised. The relative size of the variance when compared to the total cost of that factor of production could act as a criterion for this decision. Managerial time spent on investigating past variances may reduce the efficiency with which current production is organised. The investigation is only really worthwhile if it uncovers these hidden causes of variances and results in a change to an original decision.

Standard costs may not be appropriate for use in decision making. The term *relevant cost* will be explained in Chapter 14, but it means that in certain circumstances the actual or standard cost of, say, a material used may be misleading if it is applied in a decision context. Suppose a business uses a scarce material; if that material is wasted perhaps it cannot be replaced, and the profit that could be derived from its use is foregone. An adverse usage variance calculated at standard cost does not take into account the profit margin that could be made on the scrapped material. The same reasoning holds good for scarce labour. An adverse efficiency variance means that the labour force has taken longer than the standard time to complete its work, i.e. that time has been wasted. If the operatives concerned are highly skilled, and that skill is in short supply, the wasted hours cannot be replaced. Thus the profit that could have been made from production not undertaken because of this wasted time has been foregone and represents the true relevant cost of mismanaging the use of scarce labour. This aspect of the situation is ignored by the normal standard costing efficiency variance. If the standard time for actual production is

2000 hours, and actual hours worked are 2200, then the adverse efficiency variance is 200 hours wasted at, say, £5 per hour = £1000. However, if during those 200 wasted hours the labour could have made 100 further units of production, which cannot now be made because this grade of labour cannot be replaced, the profit of, say, £3 per unit is lost, a further £300, consequent upon the inefficiency demonstrated by the variance.

WORKING PAPERS AND OPERATING STATEMENTS

In view of the somewhat troublesome computations involved in preparing operating statements in connection with a system of standard costing and flexible budgetary control, it is normal to employ a standard pre-printed or duplicated skeleton working paper which may be termed a *cost and variance analysis sheet*. A typical example of such a sheet is illustrated below.

COST AND VARIANCE ANALYSIS SHEET

Department: Assembly   Period 4: Ended 28 February 19—

DIRECT WAGES	A Budgeted Standard Hours	B Standard Hours of Work Achieved	C Actual Hours	D Activity Ratio	E Efficiency Ratio	F Standard Rate per Hour	G Standard Cost of Standard Hours Achieved	H Standard Cost of Actual Hours	J Actual Cost	K Total Variance	L Labour Efficiency	M Wages Rate	N Allowed Cost
				B÷A	B÷C		B×F	C×F		G−J	G−H	H−J	G+M
				%	%	£	£	£	£	£	£	£	£
Assembly Line: 1	2400	1800	2000	75	90	1.25	2250	2500	2540	(290)	(250)	(40)	2290
2	1600	2400	3000	150	80	2.20	5280	6600	6650	(1370)	(1320)	(50)	5330
	4000	4200	5000	105	84		£7530	£9100	£9190	£(1660)	£(1570)	£(90)	£7620

DIRECT MATERIALS	O Standard Quantity Allowed	P Actual Quantity Consumed	Q Standard Price	R Standard Cost of Actual Quantity	S Standard Cost of Quantity Allowed	T Actual Cost	U Total Variance	V Price	W Usage	X Allowed Cost
				P×Q	O×Q		S−T	R−T	S−R	S+V
				£	£	£	£	£	£	£
M 101	400	410	10	4100	4000	4350	(350)	(250)	(100)	4250
M 102	360	380	2	760	720	730	(10)	30	(40)	690
M 108	1000	1110	1	1110	1000	1060	(60)	50	(110)	950
	1760	1900		£5970	£5720	£6140	£(420)	£(170)	£(250)	£5890

OVERHEADS	a	b	c	d	e	f	g	h	j	k	Remarks
	Fixed	Variable per Standard Hour of Work Achieved	Budget Cost Allowance a + B.b	Overhead Absorbed	Actual Cost	Total Variance d − e	Volume d − c	Controllable c − e	Uncontrollable (other than Volume) c − e	Allowed Cost c + j	
	£	£	£	£	£	£	£	£	£	£	
Supervision	100	–	100	–	104	–	–	–	(4)	104	Salary increase.
Service labour	20	0.050	230	–	242	–	–	(12)	–	230	Excess hours.
Setters	50	0.010	92	–	90	–	–	2	–	92	–
Maintenance labour	40	0.020	124	–	135	–	–	–	(11)	135	Controllable by maintenance foreman.
Lost time	–	0.010	41	–	54	–	–	–	(12)	54	No materials.
Cleaning	25	0.015	82	–	95	–	–	(7)	–	88	–
Overtime premium	–	0.005	28	–	58	–	–	–	(37)	58	Overtime worked by authority of planning dept. in view of breakdown of line 1 in week 3 of period.
Consumable materials	38	0.025	143	–	138	–	–	5	–	143	–
Total departmental overheads	£273	£0.135	£840	–	£916	–	–	£(12)	£(64)	£904	
Service centre costs apportioned	–	–	410	–	426	–	–	–	(16)	426	
Total overheads	–	–	£1250	£1239	£1342	£(103)	£(11)	£(12)	£(80)	£1330	

SUMMARY					Variance Analysis							
						Controllable			Uncontrollable			
	Actual Cost	Standard Cost	Total Variance	Uncontrollable	Controllable	Labour Efficiency	Material Usage	Overhead	Wages Rate	Material Price	Overhead	Volume	Allowed Cost
	£	£	£	£	£	£	£	£	£	£	£	£	£
Direct wages	9190	7530	(1660)	(90)	(1570)	(1570)	–	–	(90)	–	–	–	7620
Direct material	6140	5720	(420)	(170)	(250)	–	(250)	–	–	(170)	–	–	5890
Overheads	1342	1239	(103)	(91)	(12)	–	–	(12)	–	–	(80)	(11)	1330
	£16672	£14489	£(2183)	£(351)	£(1832)	£(1570)	£(250)	£(12)	£(90)	£(170)	£(80)	£(11)	£14840

Column A is completed by reference to the production budget; Columns B and C are prepared from job time records and production records; Column F may be taken direct from the standard cost card; while Column J is taken from the payroll. All other entries in the direct wages section of the form are obtained by calculation as shown in the sheet headings.

Columns O and P are taken from material requisitions and excess material requisitions or similar documents; the standard price (Column Q) may either appear on the pre-printed issue documents or be taken from the standard cost card, whilst the actual cost (Column T) will be taken from the stock record cards (which are assumed to be maintained at actual price). All other entries relating to direct materials are the result of calculations shown on the sheet.

A flexible budget is employed, taking the form:

$$F + (S_h \times V_{sh})$$

where F represents fixed costs, S_h represents the number of standard hours of work completed, and V_{sh} represents the variable costs allowed per standard hour of work completed.

The basis of this flexible budget is supplied in columns (a) and (b). The overheads absorbed, taken from records of production and the standard cost cards, are stated in Column (d), whilst the actual costs incurred are stated in column (e). All other figures, except that for apportioned costs, which is assumed, are computable from this information. Reasons assigned for variances are, however, assumed for purposes of illustration, and show without discussing the matter, some of the difficulties faced by management in assigning controllability. Thus, wages rate variance is assumed to be uncontrollable, i.e. the result of action (or inaction) by some other department, which has not resulted in the revision of the standard.

Whilst operating statements can be, and sometimes are, presented in a form similar to that employed in the cost and variance analysis sheet above, this is likely to bewilder most managers who have not had the benefit of training in accounting. As has already been stated a number of times, a simple form of accounting statement is frequently the most effective. These figures could therefore be condensed into an operating statement on the lines of that illustrated opposite.

DEPARTMENTAL OPERATING STATEMENT
Period 4: Ended 28 February 19—
Department: Assembly
Departmental Manager: Mr H. W. Jones

	Whole Department	Assembly Line 1	Assembly Line 2
Ratios:			
Activity	105%	75%	150%
Efficiency	84%	90%	80%

COST CLASSIFICATION	Allowed Cost £	Actual Cost £	Controllable Variance £
Direct Wages:			Labour Efficiency
Assembly Line:			
1	2290	2540	(250)
2	5330	6650	(1320)
Total	£7620	£9190	£(1570)
Direct Materials:			Material Usage
M 101	4250	4350	(100)
M 102	690	730	(40)
M 108	950	1060	(110)
Total	£5890	£6140	£(250)
Overheads Allocated to Department:			Controllable Overheads
Supervision	104	104	–
Service labour	230	242	(12)
Setters	92	90	2
Maintenance labour	135	135	–
Lost time	54	54	–
Cleaning	88	95	(7)
Overtime premium	58	58	–
Consumable materials	143	138	5
Total overheads allocated to department	£904	£916	£(12)
Total Cost of Department	£14414	£16246	Total Controllable £(1832)
Apportioned Service Centre Costs	£426	£426	Remarks:
TOTAL COST	£14840	£16672	

SEMINAR EXERCISES

12.1 (a)   What factors are significant when a standard is being set for the direct labour cost of a product?

(b)   Maxwell Manufacturers PLC make two products, De Luxe and King Size, by passing them through two workshops – the casting department and the assembly department.

Budgeted production for June:

	Casting	Assembly
De Luxe	3000 units	2500 units
King Size	4000 units	4500 units

Standard labour cost per unit:

	Casting	Assembly
De Luxe	£3	£8
King Size	£6	£6
Standard wage rate per hour:	£3	£4

The operating statement for June showed actual performance as:

	Casting	Assembly
De Luxe	2000 units	3000 units
King Size	3900 units	4300 units
Gross wages paid to direct labour	£31 000	£47 000

June is a four-week costing month, the standard working week being 40 hours. There are 67 direct workers employed in the casting department and 72 in the assembly department. A power failure caused all employees in the assembly department to stand idle for three hours during the month.

Required:

Calculate the direct labour variances for June.   (15 marks)

12.2   Ayebee PLC manufactures two products, A and B. Information taken from the standard cost cards and the budget for the three months up to 30 June is as follows:

	Standard Cost Details per Unit	
Variable Product Costs	A	B
	£	£
Direct material X £3.10 per kg	6.20	9.30
Direct material Y £2.10 per kg	8.40	4.20
Direct labour (Assembly) £4.50 per hour	13.50	11.25
Direct labour (Finishing) £3.60 per hour	7.20	3.60
Variable overheads (Assembly) £2.50 per hour	7.50	6.25
Variable overheads (Finishing) £2.60 per hour	5.20	2.60
	£48.00	£34.00
Selling price	£71.00	£60.20

Fixed production overheads for the quarter are £78 000 and charged to products using budgeted direct labour hours and finished goods are valued at standard cost.

	Budget for Period 1	
Product	A	B
Production (units)	5000	4000
Sales (units)	4600	4400

Actual information for period 1 is as follows:

Direct materials issued to production X 24 200 kg at £2.90 per kg
                                       Y 30 600 kg at £2.20 per kg

Direct labour (Assembly) 27 000 hours–wages paid £113 400
Direct labour (Finishing) 15 700 hours–wages paid £54 950
Variable overheads (Assembly) £66 000
Variable overheads (Finishing) £39 000
Fixed overheads £83 000

Production:	A 5600 Units	Sales:	A 4800 units for £344 000
	B 4200 Units		B 4400 units for £260 000

Required:

(a) Prepare a statement reconciling budgeted profit with actual profit for the three months up to 30 June. (20 marks)

(b) Explain what is meant by 'interdependence' of variances, illustrating your answer by references to the statement you have prepared for (a) above. (5 marks)

(Total 25 marks)

12.3 Data for overhead expenditure and activity for the assembly department during June are shown below:

	Budget	Actual
Activity (standard hours)	16 000	16 900
	£	£
Fixed overheads:		
Salaries	13 500	12 700
Maintenance	6 500	6 650
Variable overheads:		
Power	35 200	40 300
Consumable stores	12 000	11 840
Indirect labour	8 800	9 000

Budgeted activity is 16 000 standard hours.
Variable overheads vary with standard hours produced.
Overheads are absorbed by means of a standard hour rate.

Required:

(a) Calculate:
  (i) Fixed overhead volume variance
  (ii) Fixed overhead expenditure variance
  (iii) Variable overhead expenditure variance.

(b) Draft an operating statement for the assembly department overhead costs. (20 marks)

12.4   The assembly department of a company employs 120 operatives on a 40-hour week and produces two products, A and B. The standard direct labour cost of A is £15 and of product B, £2.50. The standard rate for labour in the assembly department is £5 per hour with a guaranteed wage per week of £200. Overtime is paid at a premium of one third on direct labour rates.

Data for the last two months are as follows:

	April	May
Production: A	4 400	4 700
Production: B	10 500	9 300
Gross wages paid to direct operatives	£112 000	£99 400
Hours paid for:		
Normal time	19 200	19 200
Overtime	2 400	–
Hours worked	21 600	18 600

Required:

(a)   Calculate an efficiency or productivity ratio for the assembly department in April.

(b)   Calculate direct labour variance for the department for April and May.

(c)   Draft entries to the wages control account and work-in-progress account for direct labour in April.

(d)   How far do the efficiency variances compiled in (b) measure the effect of employee efficiency on profit?   (20 marks)

REVIEW QUESTIONS

12.1   Woodhouse Weavers Limited are manufacturers of fabric used in the tent-making trade. They produce two grades of fabric:

'Economy' – a light material used for frame tents.

'Super' – a heavy-duty material used for marquees.

The budget for the month of June shows the following figures for the weaving department:

	Economy	Super
Production volume – standard width	40 000 m	32 000 m
Standard cost per metre:		
Nylon (£3 per kilogram)	0.2 kg	0.2 kg
Jute (£4 per kilogram)	0.2 kg	0.3 kg
Direct labour (£2 per hour)	12 mins	15 mins
Departmental overheads:		
Variable £24 000		
Fixed £20 000		

Fixed overheads are absorbed on the basis of standard hours produced. Variable overheads vary directly with fluctuations in standard hours. June actual costs were:

Production:	Economy	35 000 m; Super	34 000
Material usage:	Nylon	13 000 kg costing	£40 500
	Jute	19 000 kg costing	£72 000
Direct labour worked:		15 800 hours; paid	£30 500
Overheads:	Variable cost	£24 750	
	Fixed cost	£21 050	

Required:

Calculate the standard costing variances for materials, labour and overheads.

(18 marks)

12.2 Buffo PLC, which manufactures a detergent for industrial use, operates a system of standard costing. The budgeted profit and loss account for a month, based on normal production and sales of 20 000 litres, is shown below:

		£
Sales		120 000
Production cost of sales:		
Materials	40 000	
Labour	20 000	
Variable overheads	8 000	
Fixed overheads	12 000	80 000
Selling and administration costs		8 000
		88 000
Net profit		£32 000

The detergent is packed in 20-litre drums. Only one material is used in production and no material loss occurs – the finished volume is the same as the input. Labour is paid at a standard rate of £3 per hour.

Actual results for the month of April were:

Production and sales	21 000 litres
	£
Sales	130 800
Materials (22 900 litres)	44 000
Labour (7 100 hours)	22 200
Variable overheads	8 500
Fixed overheads	12 300
Selling and administration costs	8 000
Total costs	95 000
Profit	£35 800

Required:

(a) Prepare a standard cost sheet for a 20-litre drum of the detergent.

(5 marks)

(b) Prepare a statement reconciling budgeted and actual profits for April.

(15 marks)

(Total 20 marks)

12.3 Alco Limited manufactures and markets a single product and operates a standard costing system within a budgetary control framework.

The actual information for Period 1 is summarised as follows:

Production. 6600 units, including 400 units that were found to be faulty on inspection and were rectified.

Sales. 6000 units, sales value £306 000.

Direct Labour. 23 000 hours were spent on production; 350 hours spent on rectification is included in this time. However, 23 400 hours, which included 2200 hours overtime at one and a half times standard rate, were paid. Wages paid amounted to £73 500. Your variance analysis should show the effect on standard profit of overtime, rectification, and idle time.

Direct Material. 24 000 kg were purchased at £50 600 and 19 500 kg of material were issued to production, including 250 kg of material used on rectification. There was no opening stock of material, but closing stock was the difference between purchases and the amount issued.

Variable Factory Overheads. For the period amounted to £61 200. This cost varies in proportion to hours paid, thus variances for overheads incurred during idle time and rectification time can be computed.

Fixed Factory Overheads. For the period amounted to £26 600. These costs are absorbed by a direct labour-hour rate.

Selling Overheads. For the period amounted to £19 400 and this includes an expense of £1500 that was not included in the budget for this period.

It is the company's policy to value direct material stocks at standard price and finished goods' stocks at standard factory cost and write off all variances in a period against the profit for that period.

The budget for Period 1 was as follows:

	£	£	£
Sales (5600 units at £50)			280 000
Production (6000 units)			
Direct material (18 000 kg)	36 000		
Direct labour (24 000 hours)	72 000		
Variable factory overheads	60 000		
Fixed factory overheads	30 000		
Budgeted factory cost	198 000		
Less closing stock (400 units)	13 200	184 800	
Other overheads		17 000	
Total cost			201 800
Profit			£78 200

Required:

(a) Draft a standard cost card for one unit of production.

(b) Prepare a statement explaining the difference between the budgeted profit and actual profit for Period 1 in a form that brings out clearly the reasons for the cost and sales margin variances. (25 marks)

12.4 Sorb PLC launched a new product on 1 January and set the following budget for the trading activity for the first six months:

	£	£
Sales (10 000 units at £20)		200 000
Production 12 000 units:		
Material 37 500 square metres × £1.3	48 750	
Labour 16 000 hours × £3	48 000	
Variable overheads (16 000 hours × £2.4)	38 400	
135 150 ÷ 12 000 = £11.2625 at standard cost		
per unit	135 150	
Less stock of finished goods:		
2000 units × £11.2625	22 535	
		112 625
		87 375
Less fixed overheads:	34 000	
Start-up costs (adverts for product)		
Launch (spent in January)	30 000	64 000
Budgeted profit		£23 375

The following information is relevant:

1. The budget was drafted on the understanding that production would be spread evenly over the six months, but as January passed it became apparent a 'learning period' was necessary during which standards set in the budget would not be achieved. The learning period was considered to be over by the end of March.
2. During the budget period it became apparent that the material usage of 3.125 square metres was too optimistic and that a more realistic amount of 3.5 square metres would cover actual normal wastage.
3. Negotiation with a trade union changed the standard wage rate from 1 June to £3.51.
4. The selling price of £20 had been set too high for the product to compete in the market and it was sold at £19 from 1 April onwards.

Actual Data

	Jan–March	April–June	Total
Units produced	4 000	6 500	10 500
Units sold	3 000	5 500	8 500
Hours worked	7 900	9 100	17 000
Wages paid	£24 590	£28 410	£53 000
Material used (square metres)	17 620	22 620	40 240
Cost of material used	£26 430	£31 668	£58 098
Variable overheads	£18 000	£23 000	£41 000
Fixed overheads	£17 000	£18 000	£35 000
Start-up costs	£28 000	–	£28 000

Required:

Draft a statement for management, which reconciles actual performance to budget, distinguishing operating, planning and learning variances.   (35 marks)

Section IV

Costs and Decision Making in the Short Term

13

Marginal Costing and Cost–Volume–Profit Analysis

A marginal cost is the cost of producing a marginal unit of production, i.e. one extra unit of production. Accordingly marginal cost is the amount by which total costs increase when one unit more is manufactured, or the amount of cost that will be avoided if one unit less is made. Marginal cost thus concerns variable costs, because fixed costs by definition do not change with the volume produced. In marginal costing, variable costs are charged to cost units, and the surplus derived from setting variable cost of production against sales revenue is termed *contribution*. This surplus is the contribution made by products sold towards the fixed overhead costs of the period.

The behaviour of costs is important in marginal costing, since costs classed as variable will form part of the calculation of contribution, and fixed costs will be written off against contribution for the period. Thus marginal cost differs from full absorption costing, in that fixed overheads are not absorbed to production and thus not carried forward as part of the cost of the stock of work-in-progress or finished goods. Whilst these two methods will show a different profit from the same series of transactions, they are not truly alternatives. Full absorption costing is often used as a costing system in a business, but marginal costing is more likely to be used as a method whereby costs can be analysed for the purpose of decision making, although standard marginal costing may be used as a costing system.

FIXED AND VARIABLE COSTS

Some costs will not vary if the volume of production or sales fluctuates, because by their nature they are fixed for a certain time period e.g. rent, or salaries can be forecast fairly accurately for a year ahead. However, it cannot be assumed that such costs will always behave in a fixed way. If the time scale is extended far enough, no cost will remain the same, so it is fair to say that all costs vary in the long run. If conditions change (e.g. a lease is sold) then a fixed cost may change (as rent is no longer payable). Direct costs, such as materials and labour concerned with each production unit, will normally vary in direct proportion to volume. Between these two classes of fixed and variable costs are semi-variable costs, which vary in sympathy with but not in proportion to changes in volume. Such costs may contain a fixed and variable element (e.g. electricity with a standing charge and a cost per unit used), or may increase in a stepped progression as volume increases (e.g. an extra supervisor employed when the labour force reaches a certain number). The behaviour of costs cannot be expected to remain as fixed or variable under all circumstances and for all time periods. Thus, when contribution is computed, a careful appraisal of cost behaviour under present conditions should be made.

ABSORPTION COSTING AND MARGINAL COSTING

SSAP 9 affirms that for published financial accounts, stocks of work-in-progress and finished goods should be carried forward from one accounting period to another at the lower of cost or net realisable value. The term cost in this context means all the costs involved in bringing the stock to its present location and condition and this includes a fair share of related production overhead expenses. The standard therefore appears to support full absorption costing, by encouraging a proportion of the fixed costs of one accounting period to be carried forward to the next period as part of the cost of stock. Marginal costing values stock at variable cost, and writes off all fixed costs to the period in which they are incurred. For the purposes of reporting performance to managers on a monthly basis, or the results of individual products, this method can prove very useful, since contribution rather than profit is disclosed.

Example

A company manufactures and sells a single product at £15 per unit. Unit production costs are: materials £6, labour £3 and variable overheads £2. Variable selling expenses are 5% of sales revenue. Fixed costs are: production £25 000, selling £15 000 and administration £12 000 spent each month. Production overheads are absorbed on the basis of a normal production of 20 000 units a month, i.e. £1.25 per unit. Sales for the months of January to April were (in units): 20 000, 22 000, 20 000 and 21 000 respectively, but production was 23 000, 20 000, 20 000 and 20 000 for those months.

Full Absorption Costing

	£	Jan. £	£	Feb. £	£	Mar. £	£	Apr. £
Sales (units)		20 000		22 000		20 000		21 000
Production (units)		23 000		20 000		20 000		20 000
Sales		300 000		330 000		300 000		315 000
Opening stock		–		36 750		12 250		12 250
Production costs (£12.25)	281 750		245 000		245 000		245 000	
	281 750		281 750		257 250		257 250	
Closing stock	36 750		12 250		12 250		–	
		245 000		269 500		245 000		257 250
Gross profit		55 000		60 500		55 000		57 750
Variable selling costs	15 000		16 500		15 000		15 750	
Fixed selling costs	15 000		15 000		15 000		15 000	
Fixed administration costs	12 000		12 000		12 000		12 000	
		42 000		43 500		42 000		42 750
		13 000		17 000		13 000		15 000
Fixed production overheads over-absorbed		3 750		–		–		–
Net profit		£16 750		£17 000		£13 000		£15 000

Marginal costing

	Jan.		Feb.		March		April
Sales	300 000		330 000		300 000		315 000
Opening stock	–		33 000		11 000		11 000
Variable production cost	253 000		220 000		220 000		220 000
	253 000		253 000		231 000		231 000
Closing stock	33 000		11 000		11 000		–
	220 000		242 000		220 000		231 000
Variable selling costs	15 000		16 500		15 000		15 750
		235 000		258 500		235 000		246 750
Contribution		65 000		71 500		65 000		68 250
Fixed costs:							
Production	£25 000						
Selling	£15 000						
Administration	£12 000						
		52 000		52 000		52 000		52 000
Net profit		£13 000		£19 500		£13 000		£16 250

The difference in profit between the two methods concerns the amount of fixed production overheads carried forward as part of the cost of stock under full absorption costing. The difference in January is £3750, in favour of full absorption costing (or fixed overheads charged to a closing stock of 3000 units at £1.25 each). Under marginal costing all fixed overheads are written off in the period. In February marginal costing shows £2500 more profit than the full absorption method, because fixed overheads of £1.25 on 2000 units de-stocked would, under marginal costing, be charged against profit in January, whereas, under full absorption costing, they form part of the cost of sales in February. In April, marginal costing again shows more profit than full absorption costing, because fixed overheads at £1.25 each on 1000 units of stock sold in April, but not produced in that month, are not set against sales revenue in April under this system, since these fixed overheads were written off against sales in January when the stock was originally built up.

Clearly where volume produced and sold are the same, both methods will show the same profit (March); if production exceeds sales and stocks are built up, marginal costing shows a smaller profit than full absorption costing (January); but if sales exceed production and stocks are run down, marginal costing shows a greater profit than full absorption costing (February and April). The management will be surprised when they evaluate their performance for January and February by using full absorption costing, because sales have increased by 10% in February, but profit is only £250 up on January. The fixed production overheads are over-absorbed in January because production exceeds the 20 000 units on which the absorption rates are based. This over-absorption, when added back to profit, has contributed to the discrepancy.

Advantages of Marginal Costing

1. The use of marginal costing avoids the necessity to allocate, apportion and absorb fixed overhead costs to products or departments. Chapter 4 has already demonstrated the sometimes doubtful logic behind apportionment and absorption and the cost of these activities.

2. The use of contribution as a measure of performance removes the doubts about the fairness of fixed overhead allotment and provides a more reliable measure for decision making. Decisions should be based on costs that vary, since fixed costs will not change as a result of a decision.
3. Stocks are valued at direct or variable cost, and fixed overheads, which are usually related to time, are written off to the period in which they are incurred. Thus the impact on profit of fluctuations in the volume of stock is reduced, especially where monthly cost statements are produced, and the fixed costs of one period are not carried forward into the next period as part of the cost of stock, which may eventually be unsaleable.
4. Marginal costing shows more clearly the impact on profit of fluctuations in the volume of sales.

In spite of these advantages there is still much to be said for full absorption costing. Fixed overheads over or under-absorbed each month disclose the effect of fluctuations in the volume of production and the cost of production capacity underutilised, i.e. fully employed. Fixed costs must be covered in the long run, and this important factor may be forgotten in a marginal costing system that emphasises variable costs. In a seasonal business where production is to build up stocks during some months of the year in preparation for the busy season, the fixed overheads of those months will, under marginal costing, be charged against the small sales revenue of the 'out of season' period, thus disclosing a loss. In these circumstances it seems wiser to carry forward the fixed overhead cost as part of the stock and match it with revenue when sales are made in the busy season. Much depends on whether fixed factory overheads are considered to be part of the cost of making a unit of production, or whether they are viewed as time costs, related strictly to an accounting period.

COST–VOLUME–PROFIT ANALYSIS

The idea of marginal costing and the interplay of fixed and variable costs can be used to advantage to interpret or forecast profit at different volumes of production. Investigation of the relationship that exists between costs and profits at different points on the volume scale discloses some factors of great significance for managers.

Example

Extending the example used above, the costs and revenues can be expressed as follows:

	£	£
Selling price		15.00
Variable costs:		
Direct materials	6.00	
Direct labour	3.00	
Variable overheads	2.00	
Variable selling costs	0.75	
		11.75
Contribution per unit sold		£ 3.25

Fixed costs are £52 000. Maximum production capacity 30 000 units. The facts in tabular form are:

Volume (units)	Fixed Cost £	Variable Cost £	Total Cost £	Sales Revenue £	Loss £	Profit £
Nil	52 000	–	52 000	–	52 000	
5000	52 000	58 750	110 750	75 000	35 750	
10 000	52 000	117 500	169 500	150 000	19 500	
15 000	52 000	176 250	228 250	225 000	3 250	
20 000	52 000	235 000	287 000	300 000		13 000
25 000	52 000	293 750	345 750	375 000		29 250
30 000	52 000	352 500	404 500	450 000		45 500

The table is constructed in steps of 500 units for simplicity. It could have been computed for each individual additional unit produced. Marginal cost is variable cost in this example.

At volumes up to 15 000 units, losses are made, but at volumes above 20 000 units, profits are made. The point at which losses cease and profits begin is called the break even point and at this volume total cost equals total revenue. If price less variable cost equals contribution per unit, the number of contributions required to cover fixed cost will be the volume of production at the break even point. The following formula is used to calculate the break even point:

$$\frac{\text{Fixed cost}}{\text{Contribution per unit}} = \text{Break even volume}$$

$$\frac{£52\,000}{£3.25} = 16000 \text{ units}$$

Proof:

$$£52\,000 + (16\,000 \times £11.75) = £240\,000 \text{ (Cost)}$$
$$16\,000 \times £15 = £240\,000 \text{ (Revenue)}$$

$$16\,000 \text{ contributions of } £3.25 = £52\,000 \text{ (Fixed cost)}$$

It is also possible to calculate quickly the profit that will be made at a certain volume of sales – say, 22 000 units. The formula is:

$$\text{Contribution} - \text{Fixed cost} = \text{Profit at that volume}$$
$$(22\,000 \times £3.25) - £52\,000 = £19\,500$$

Alternatively, the volume of sales required to give a certain required profit (say, £35 750) can be rapidly computed. The formula is:

$$\frac{\text{Fixed cost and required profit}}{\text{Contribution per unit}} = \text{Volume of sales that must be achieved}$$

$$\frac{£52\,000 + £35\,750}{£3.25} = 27\,000 \text{ units}$$

The profit to volume ratio (p/v) expresses the relationship of contribution to selling price:

$$\frac{\text{Contribution}}{\text{Selling price}} \times \frac{100}{1} = \%$$

$$\frac{£3.25}{£15} \times \frac{100}{1} = 21.6667\%$$

This means that 21.67% of every sale is a contribution towards the fixed costs of the business. The p/v ratio can be used to answer the following questions:

(a)   How much turnover or sales revenue is required to break even? Remember break even is when contribution equals fixed cost.

$$21.6667\% \text{ of break even turnover} = \text{Fixed costs of } £52\,000$$

$$\text{Therefore break even turnover} = £52\,000 \times \frac{100}{21.6667} = £240\,000$$

(b)   How much profit would be made at a turnover of say £350 000? Remember 21.6667% of revenue is contribution, and contribution less fixed cost is profit.

$$\left(£350\,000 \times \frac{21.6667}{100}\right) - £52\,000 = £23\,835$$

Another factor of importance to management is the margin of safety. This is defined as the difference between the level of capacity budgeted to be used and the break even point.

If the budget plans to work the factory at 80% of full capacity, 80% of 30 000 maximum production, i.e. 24 000 units, are planned to be made and sold. If the break even point is at 16 000 units, a margin of safety of 8000 units or 33% of budget capacity is calculated. This means that the budget must be under-achieved by one third before losses are experienced.

All contribution above the break even point is profit so:

$$\text{p/v ratio} \times \text{Margin of safety} = \text{Budgeted profit}$$

$$21.667\% \times 8000 \text{ units at } £15 = £26\,000$$

This amount is the profit if budgeted sales of 24 000 units are achieved.

The cost–volume–profit relationship can be expressed in diagrammatic form as a break even chart or graph. Volume of units produced or capacity used is shown on the horizontal axis and cost or revenue is shown in pounds on the vertical axis. The fixed and variable costs and sales revenue for the example above are shown on individual graphs illustrated below.

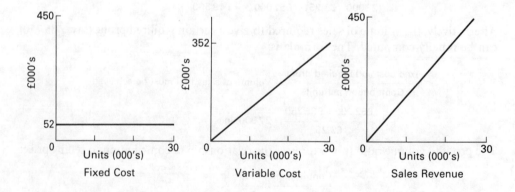

The three elements can be combined on a break even chart. Fixed cost plus variable cost equals total cost. The distance AB measures budgeted profit.

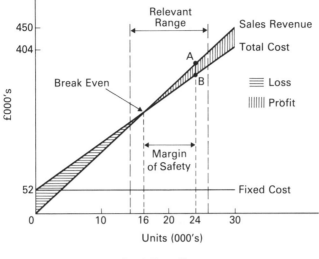

Break Even Chart

An alternative method of drawing a break even chart emphasises contribution as the difference between sales revenue and variable cost. The distance AC measures contribution when 20 000 units are produced; the distance AB measures the profit when 20 000 units are produced.

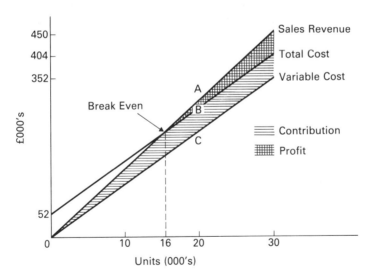

Alternative Break Even Chart

The data in the example can also be shown on a profit graph, which discloses the profits or losses made at different volumes. When no goods are produced a loss equal to fixed cost (£52 000) is made. This graph enables a comparison between the performance of Product A (in our example) and Product B, an alternative open to the company. Although B breaks even at a smaller volume, and has lower fixed costs, it is not as profitable as A once high

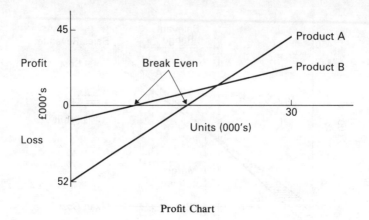

Profit Chart

volume production is reached. If a recession is forecast it might be wise to produce B, but if a boom is expected with high sales volumes, A should be produced.

LIMITATIONS OF BREAK EVEN ANALYSIS

It is apparent that the break even chart is constructed by drawing straight lines. A major flaw in break even analysis, which restricts its utility as a management tool, is the assumption of linearity. In the real world costs and revenues do not behave in a strict linear relationship to volumes produced. Selling price per unit may not be the same for all amounts across the range of volumes, since if demand is flexible prices must be reduced in order to sell a greater volume of product. Variable cost per unit may not be the same at all volumes across the range; as production increases unit costs may fall if suppliers cut prices to gain large orders for materials, but eventually at higher volumes unit costs may increase as one product competes with another for scarce resources. In these two cases a curvilinear relationship is probable, perhaps with more than one break even point. The optimum volume of production where profit is maximised is at the point where the distance AB is maximised. As illustrated, the total revenue curve becomes less steep as the price is reduced to sell more goods. The cost curve starts at the point equal to the fixed cost and rises as unit costs increase with higher volume sales.

On the two graphs illustrated, graph *A* shows raw material costs against the volume produced if the supplier gives a trade discount on all purchases when total purchases

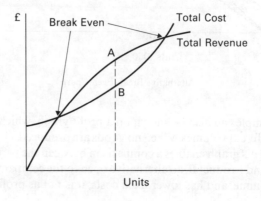

exceed a certain volume, and graph *B* shows labour cost if a bonus is paid per unit after a certain volume has been produced and a guaranteed weekly wage (xy) is paid.

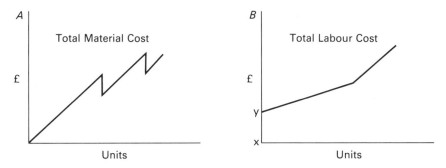

Clearly volume alone is not the only factor to influence cost. Managers may not be very interested in costs and revenues at the extremes of low or high volume, but prefer analysis of a range of volumes relevant to their operations. Break even analysis can assume linearity for certain parts of the volume range – the *relevant range*, which restricts analysis to a section of the graph that is pertinent to forecast volumes. In our example the relevant range might extend from, say, 15 000 to 25 000 units (see page 323).

A further doubtful assumption that limits the credibility of break even analysis is that fixed cost will remain the same at all points on the volume scale. This is unlikely since as more units are produced, extra facilities (plant, premises, and working capital) must be provided, so fixed cost is likely to increase in a stepped fashion once available production capacity is used up. A break even chart drawn for stepped fixed costs will show more than one break even point.

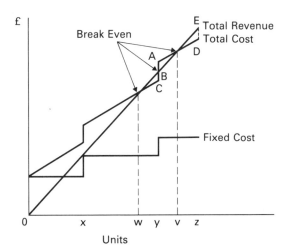

If each step of the fixed cost represents the cost of additional production facilities, certain interesting conclusions can be drawn from this graph:

(i)   It is not viable to use only one set of production resources, which will produce OX units, since a loss is made at that volume.

(ii) If two sets of production resources are committed, a volume of OW must be sold to break even and at maximum production OY, a profit of BC will result.

(iii) If a third set of production resources is used, a loss AB will immediately arise unless sales can be increased beyond OY. This increase must be at least up to OV in order to break even, or up to OZ, since only then is the profit DE as great as BC, the profit made when the original organisation was working at full capacity. The inference is that unless sales are forecast beyond OZ units, it is not worthwhile to commit a third set of resources.

Another assumption that reduces the validity of break even analysis is that costs can be easily identified as fixed or variable in nature and that they will retain their classification at all points on the volume scale and in all circumstances. This is just not so as will be seen in the section on cost behaviour. Semi-variable costs comprising a fixed and variable element need to be fitted into the break even chart.

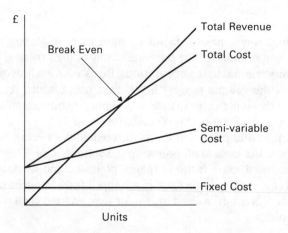

Total Cost = Fixed Cost + Semi-variable Cost + Variable Cost

In spite of these doubtful assumptions concerning linearity and cost behaviour, break even analysis seems to be useful in a one-product firm or when forecasting the results of individual products. The technique is difficult to apply to a business that makes more than one product, unless the product mix remains the same across the volume range.

A further disadvantage of break even analysis is that it assumes that production and sales are co-ordinated at the same volume. If a change in stock levels takes place during the period of analysis, the costs and revenue will not be comparable and conclusions reached from the graph will be false. The sales value of production can be compared with costs, but this tactic removes the analysis from a consideration of what is really going to happen.

THE APPLICATION OF COST–VOLUME–PROFIT ANALYSIS

Martin is the proprietor of a garage and filling station. To extend his business he is considering a plan to borrow £10 000 from a bank and to use the funds to purchase a car, which he can hire out to customers on a daily or weekend basis. He calculates that interest at 15% will cost him £125 per month, that road tax and insurance will cost a further £50 per month and maintenance undertaken in the garage will amount to £25 per month. Variable running costs of the car are 9p a mile and Martin thinks that if he charges 15p a mile for the use of the vehicle, customers will drive the car for 4000 miles each month.

Advise Martin:

1. Fixed cost = £200 per month.
   Contribution = 15p − 9p = 6p a mile.
   Break even point £200 ÷ £0.06 = 3333 miles per month.
2. Profit on expected mileage 4000 × 6p − Fixed cost (£200) = £40.
   Remember that no element of depreciation or capital repayment has been included in the calculation. If all the profit were used to repay the loan it would take 20 years to complete repayment.
3. Margin of safety − break even is at 3333 miles per month. Actual performance would have to be 667 miles below budget, an error of 16%, before the service made a loss. (4000 expected miles − 3333 = 667).
4. How much must Martin charge if he wishes to make a profit of at least £100 per month?

$$\frac{\text{Fixed cost} + \text{Required profit}}{\text{Contribution on 4000 miles}} = 0$$

£200 + £100 = Contribution required on 4000 miles
£300 ÷ 4000 = Contribution on 1 mile = 7p

If costs remain at 9p a mile, add contribution of 7p to get 16p a mile. Alternatively, the required profit could be made if the customer drove the car (£300 ÷ 6p of present contribution) 5000 miles per month.
5. What will be the effect on Martin's business if petrol prices rise by 10p a litre, or the rate of interest increases to 20%. The car is expected to travel 20 miles per litre of petrol.

   (a) A price rise of 10p will be equivalent to 0.5p per mile and this will reduce contribution to 5.5p per mile. A new break even point of (£200 ÷ £0.055) 3636 miles will be established and profit on budgeted volume of activity will be (4000 × £0.055 − £200) = £20. If profit is to be maintained at £40 per month, an extra (£20 ÷ £0.055) 363 miles must be driven by customers.
   (b) An extra 5% p.a. interest on a loan of £10 000 increases fixed cost by £500 p.a., or £42 per month. This cost increase would turn the expected monthly profit of £40 into a loss of £2. To counteract this cost increase, prices to customers must rise by (£42 ÷ 4000) 1p a mile to give the extra contribution required to new fixed cost. Alternatively, increased business could provide this contribution (£42 − £0.06) if 700 more miles were driven by customers each month.

COST BEHAVIOUR

Cost accountants are frequently faced with the problem of predicting the behaviour of costs. Managers pose questions such as:

1. How will our costs be affected if we cut production of article A by 25% and increase that of article B by 30%?
2. Would it be worth our while to operate a system of two-shift working?
3. Is it really profitable to work overtime to meet sales demands if we have to pay time-and-a-half for it? Would it still pay if workers received double time?

4.   If we could cut the selling price of this model by £5, the sales department believe we could sell another 10 000. Would it pay us to do this?
5.   Would it be a profitable proposition to replace this machine with another, capable of producing twice as many articles per hour?

All these problems demand an ability to assess the manner in which costs are likely to behave in certain circumstances. Similar questions confront the cost accountant when he assists in the preparation of budgets, and also when he attempts to assess what costs should have been in given circumstances.

A cost may be fixed in the short run and variable in the long run, or it may change from fixed to variable if conditions change e.g. if a branch office is closed the fixed cost of the premises will no longer be incurred.

Across the relevant range a cost can be assumed to behave in a linear manner. In the diagram on fixed, variable and semi-variable costs, line A represents a typical fixed cost such as rent, rates, insurance or depreciation calculated on a time basis; while line C shows the behaviour of a typical variable cost such as direct wages, or direct material cost. Line B shows a semi-variable cost, i.e. one which, whilst having a fixed element, tends to increase with output. The cost of cleaning is semi-variable, since some cleaning is required even if no production takes place, but the total cost will increase as production increases.

Line B shows a cost which rises from £4000 at zero production to £8000 at 100% and £12 000 at 150% of present capacity.

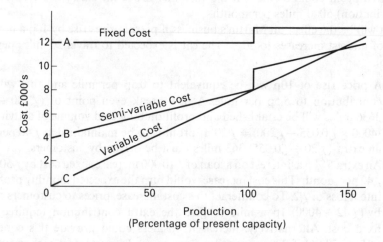

Fixed, Variable and Semi-variable Costs

Another way of expressing this is to state that the cost consists of a fixed component of £4000 and a variable element equal to £40 per per cent of capacity. Note the step in the progression at 100%, when premises are extended and fixed cost and semi-variable cost increase. All semi-variable costs are capable of being broken down into fixed and variable components in this manner, so for many purposes it is sufficient to consider only two types of cost – fixed cost and variable cost – the semi-variable costs being subdivided on their merits.

Fixed and variable are only relative terms. For instance, in many circumstances production wages are considered to be a variable cost; yet it is very difficult to reduce wages proportionately to production at low levels, perhaps because of agreements with a trade union concerning a minimum wage, a guaranteed working week, or a pledge of no redundancy. A time comes when the minimum labour force – one man from each trade – cannot be fully employed and yet cannot be discharged if any production is to be achieved. In such conditions piece-workers insist on being paid time wages for the period in which they are idle, regardless of whether their remuneration is normally subject to such a guarantee. Even the rate of variation is likely to change in time. Acceptance of a wage claim, for example, would provide a new rate of variation as shown in the graph below. Payment of a bonus has a similar effect after the bonus earning level is achieved.

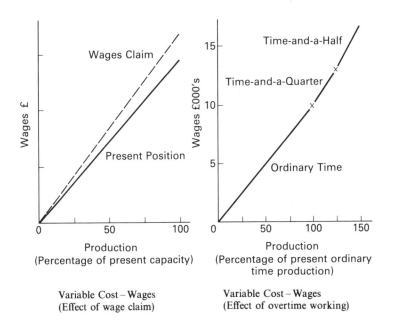

Variable Cost – Wages
(Effect of wage claim)

Variable Cost – Wages
(Effect of overtime working)

Even the suggestion that wages vary in proportion to output except at low production levels is not entirely correct. If production is to be pushed past what can be achieved iɪ. ordinary time, overtime must be worked. The illustration shows how labour cost might vary in a concern working a 40-hour week, where the first ten hours overtime (worked in the evening) are paid for at time-and-a-quarter and the next ten hours (worked at the weekend) are paid for at time-and-a-half.

In industries where labour is not the controlling factor in output, production wages cannot really be regarded as freely variable with production, e.g. where the process or plant controls the output, the shortage of one or two people may make little difference to the output and the wages cost per unit will fall. Also, over a short period productive wages of workers on time work, or whose time wages are guaranteed, are virtually fixed, since few businesses are prepared to lay off labour in proportion to falling production in a recession until they are convinced that it would be a protracted one.

Material cost, too, is not a perfectly variable cost. The hurried work at high levels of output may give rise to excessive usage, while the greater ease of working at low pressure may bring abnormally low spoilage. Quantity discounts available at high outputs may be lost when production is lower. These two factors may tend to compensate, but they will rarely cancel each other exactly – there will be some lack of linearity somewhere. For most purposes, however, it is sufficiently accurate to assume that such costs do vary in a linear way, and this greatly simplifies working.

Just as variable costs are not fully variable, so fixed costs too do not remain so indefinitely. Most fixed costs are capable of variation as a matter of policy and many are liable to change eventually because of external factors. One of the illustrations below shows how the cost of providing a building (rent, rates and insurance) might vary. Alternative A shows the effect of increases in rent, rates, and insurance of the present building, the result of external pressures. In other words it shows the variation of a 'fixed' cost in relation to time. Alternative B, on the other hand, shows the effect of a change of policy. As a result of moving to other accommodation, costs have risen from £10 000 p.a. to £18 000, but this has been accompanied by a 50% increase in available capacity. Mostly, however, since the cost accountant wishes to compare the result of doing one thing now, with that of doing something else, now, long-term changes caused by external factors or resulting from other policy decisions have no relevance to many of the decisions with which he is faced. The simple division of costs into fixed and variable costs is therefore quite adequate.

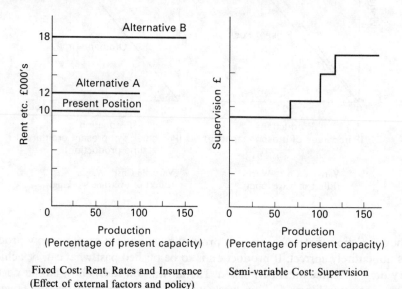

Fixed Cost: Rent, Rates and Insurance   Semi-variable Cost: Supervision
(Effect of external factors and policy)

Another cost that has a fixed component but that does not strictly follow the semi-variable pattern is plant maintenance cost. Maintenance policy has a considerable effect here, but the illustration opposite gives some idea of how maintenance cost might vary in a particular case. Maintenance cost in this context means the cost of maintaining machinery in good order, whether as preventive maintenance intended to avoid plant breakdown or on the repair of such breakdowns and the renewal of defective parts when they occur. In the illustration it is assumed that basic preventive maintenance is provided even at zero production, and that this is relatively high in proportion to the additional cost of maintenance required because of actual production. There is therefore a relatively small increase in cost between zero production and that achieved in a single shift. Thereafter the cost of maintenance will tend to increase because preventive maintenance will have to be carried out in the evening or early morning, probably at overtime rates. This becomes particularly noticeable as treble shift working is approached. Once the machine works round the clock, there will be no real opportunity or preventive maintenance. Accordingly maintenance costs will fall, but will be replaced either by the cost of major breakdowns brought about by insufficient maintenance or by the additional fatigue placed upon machinery that never rests. Costly major overhauls will be necessary in these circumstances from time to time.

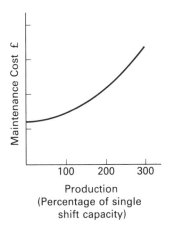

Semi-variable Cost: Maintenance (Effect of single, double and treble shift working)

In practice, of course, it would be difficult to prepare a graph such as that illustrated, for breakdowns are rarely predictable, and unless the average cost of a very large number of machines is adopted it is usually found that maintenance cost varies widely from period to period. One cannot even say that this is how maintenance cost will vary in a typical case – the maintenance needs of different classes of machine are so varied and the results of treble shift working so unpredictable in the short term, that the graph might take some entirely different form. Only one thing is certain: it will rarely be a straight line.

The variable costs we have considered so far have been production costs, but obviously not all costs are related to production. Salesmen's commission, for instance, clearly has a connection, not with production, but with sales. Other costs are entirely a matter of policy, e.g. neither research costs nor advertising varies automatically with sales or production. Admittedly many concerns allocate funds to advertising on the basis of their future sales plans, but there is no direct connection: advertising allocations only follow sales as a matter of policy, and there may even be positions in which the opposite ought to be the case. Falling sales may, for instance, indicate the need not for less advertising but for more. In the same way, where a new competitor appears, there may be a need for high-pressure advertising, quite regardless of the sales trend.

Where sales depend on advertising, an increase in advertising will, all things being equal, bring increased sales. Frequently, however, so many other factors are involved that the final result is a matter for conjecture. For instance, much of the force of an advertising scheme may be lost if a competitor introduces a more attractive scheme simultaneously. In many trades the weather has a considerable effect: winter overcoats will not sell well in a warm winter, despite increased advertising.

Another feature of costs to be considered is their behaviour in times of increasing or falling production – that is while the change is taking place rather than when conditions have settled down to the new level. Consider the next illustration. Rather than taking the

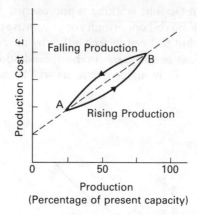

Production Cost in Times of Rising and Falling Production

straight line AB, which assumes that the variable elements of cost will be perfectly variable, the tendency will be for costs to follow the lower curve when production is increasing, i.e. costs will increase rather less rapidly than might be expected because of the tendency of employees to work a little harder when business is brisk and because the new workers needed cannot be recruited immediately. Conversely, when production is falling there is a tendency to follow the upper curve because of the employers' reluctance to dismiss workers until sure that the recession is more than a temporary one. When work is short, employees tend to make it last, fearing dismissal if they are found idle, so there is a general decrease in efficiency, which results in somewhat higher costs.

It will be apparent that the division of costs into those fixed in relation to output and those which vary therewith, is far from being entirely reliable. For many purposes, however, it is sufficiently accurate, particularly over the limited range of variation of output likely to be experienced, i.e. the relevant range. Few concerns have to contend with wide variations in output as changes are usually relatively gradual, but some cost accountants deem it desirable to draw attention to the fact that their predictions are reliable only between certain limits. Methods of doing this on a diagram are:

1. To confine the diagram to the area in which a reliable prediction can be made.
2. To shade the area in which predictions are considered accurate, whilst leaving the remainder of the chart unshaded.
3. To use dotted lines in unreliable areas of the diagram and solid lines where the estimate is considered to be reliable.

Consider, for instance, the supervision chart on page 330. If production will lie between 75 and 100% of capacity, the cost of supervision can be regarded as fixed at the second level shown in the graph. Outside these limits this will not be true – but that is beside the point if production is to be within them. Similarly, unless production exceeds 100%, wages will vary as shown by the 'ordinary time' line on the wages graph on page 329, and can be regarded as truly variable inside that limit. If production were to lie in the range 100 to 125% of capacity, the

$$\text{Wages cost would be: } £10\,000 + \left\{ \begin{array}{l} \text{Production} \\ \text{(per cent of capacity} - 100) \times £100 \times \dfrac{125}{100} \end{array} \right\}$$

Another way of expressing this is:

$$\text{Wages cost} = \left\{ \begin{array}{l} \text{Production} \\ \text{per cent of capacity} \times \text{\pounds}125 \end{array} \right\} - \text{\pounds}2500$$

In other words, the resultant total cost is the same as if there were a variable cost of £125 for each 1 % of capacity used, reduced by a negative fixed cost of £2500. This is the formula that the cost accountant could adopt for wages if he knew production would lie within the range 100 to 125 % of capacity. Similarly, if production were expected to lie in the range 125 to 150%, the formula to be adopted would be:

$$\text{Wages cost} = \frac{\text{Production}}{(\text{per cent of capacity} \times \text{\pounds}150) - \text{\pounds}5625}$$

In making a prediction or budget the cost accountant must have regard to this fundamental point: the degree to which costs are fixed or variable can be determined only in relation to a particular range of activities. No form of prediction, whether based upon budgeting or marginal costing techniques or upon break even analysis, can be valid if this fact is neglected.

EFFECT OF SHIFT WORKING

In times of expanding trade many concerns cannot fulfil customers' demands by current production and are therefore compelled to consider the practicability of working additional shifts. It may be possible to attract married women to work a three or four-hour evening shift five days a week, and so meet increased demand. The cost accountant may be asked whether this is a profitable proposition or otherwise. To prepare the necessary estimates he must consider each item of cost separately, studying the manner in which it is likely to behave under the changed circumstances. The following may be his possible line of thought:

Building Service Costs. Rent, rates, and insurance will remain unchanged under the proposed scheme. Heating and lighting are likely to increase out of proportion to the time involved, it being both darker and colder in the evening than in the day. Building maintenance is likely to increase slightly, since most building maintenance is dependent more on outside factors (e.g. the elements) than upon use. Cleaning costs may increase slightly, but if the building is still cleaned once a day they will not rise in proportion to output.

Equipment Service Costs. Depreciation of equipment due to wear and tear is likely to increase in proportion to use, though there will be no increase in the possibility of obsolescence. Not only may more maintenance be required, but this may be more difficult to undertake. Work previously completed by the maintenance staff during the evening will now have to be done at weekends when time will be more highly paid. The heavy increase in maintenance costs, which arises with triple shift working – because even urgently needed preventive repairs are difficult to fit in – should not, however, occur.

Personnel Service Costs. The behaviour of personnel service costs will depend on a number of factors, e.g. many costs will increase if the personnel on evening shift are workers not employed by the concern on day work, for this involves the preparation of additional personnel records, time cards, payroll entries, and the separate payment of wages. It may in fact involve the calculation of pay-as-you-earn and even holiday pay and/or pensions. Additional shifts worked by existing employees involve far less work and cost. It is a matter of policy whether canteen, sports club, and similar facilities are open to evening shift workers, but if they are, increased costs will be involved. Since labour turnover is likely to be relatively high in connection with evening shift workers, and as the cost of engaging and training workers may therefore have to be spread over a fairly short period, its effect on unit costs could be considerable. Evening shift schemes will not therefore generally be considered where skilled work is necessary or where there is any great difficulty in obtaining shift workers.

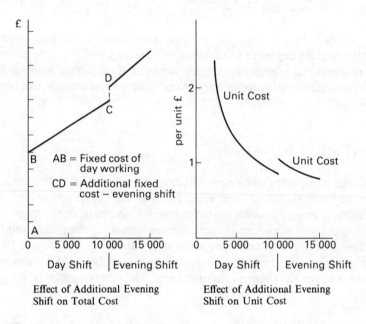

Effect of Additional Evening
Shift on Total Cost

Effect of Additional Evening
Shift on Unit Cost

Material Service Costs. Since most materials will arrive in normal working hours, the costs of receiving and inspecting are likely to increase only because of the increased volume. Overtime premiums may have to be paid, however, to storekeepers and personnel engaged on material handling during the evening, and these costs are thus likely to increase faster than they would with increased daytime volume.

Production Services. Whilst some production service costs may increase, most will remain fixed. There is not likely, for instance, to be any increase in the number of work studies required.

Production Costs. Variable production costs should not differ greatly from those of daytime work, apart from any difference in operator grade or any need to pay overtime rates or shift bonuses. There may, however, be variations in material cost brought about by the increased difficulty of accurate working in artificial light or after a day's work elsewhere, on the one hand, and savings on quantity purchases, on the other. Efficiency on evening work is unlikely to reach the daytime level but much depends upon the type of work involved and the class of personnel engaged. The illustrations opposite show the possible effect of evening shift working on total cost and unit cost respectively.

THE USE OF SCATTER DIAGRAMS

Fixed and variable costs present the cost accountant with far fewer problems than do semi-variable ones. In estimating or planning fixed costs, all he has to do is to consider the effect on past figures of changes in circumstances and policies. Thus it may have been decided to increase the production manager's salary by £3000 a year, and this will have to be taken into account when computing the fixed costs for the current year. Similarly, new machinery may have been acquired, rents may have been increased, and so on, all of which changes affect fixed costs. Variable costs are also simple to deal with. All the cost accountant needs to do to compute the variable cost per unit is to divide the variable cost for the past period (adjusted for changed conditions) by production in that period.

Semi-variable costs are not quite such a simple matter, however. Before a cost accountant can estimate them he must split them into their fixed and variable components, and he has no means of doing this on the basis of the results of only one period. If, however, he has a number of past results and has converted these so that they refer to a common price level – that existing currently – he can work like this:

1. Plot each of the results available on a diagram, the horizontal axis of which relates to production in terms of quantity and the vertical axis of which relates to the cost in pounds.
2. Draw the straight line which appears to be the 'best fit' to the scatter diagram just drawn. (The line of best fit will leave roughly as many points on one side of the line as on the other.)
3. The point where this line of best fit cuts the vertical axis marks the fixed cost. The variable cost per unit can be computed by comparing the cost shown by the best fit line to be appropriate to one unit with that appropriate to two, or if the scale does not permit this by using some other multiple, say, 100, to find the cost of a number of units.

Example

The cost accountant of the Acmo Manufacturing Company Limited wishes to analyse power costs into fixed and variable components. Figures for the last six years, after adjustment for changes in price, have been as follows:

Year	Power Costs £	Machine-Hours
1	13 000	20 000
2	13 000	22 000
3	9 600	14 000
4	11 000	18 000
5	11 000	21 000
6	9 400	16 000

Plotting these figures in a scatter diagram, he is able to insert a line of best fit as illustrated below.

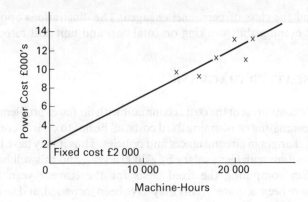

Scatter Diagram Showing Power Costs, including Line of 'Best Fit'

From this it can be found that the fixed cost of power is approximately £2000, and since the total power cost rises from £2000 at zero machine-hours to, say, £12 000 at 20 000 machine-hours, it is a simple matter to calculate that the variable element is:

$$\frac{£12\,000 - £2000}{20\,000} \quad \text{(i.e. 50p) per machine-hour}$$

As has been shown earlier, few costs behave in a linear manner throughout all possible volumes of production, so it will be necessary to consider carefully the range for which this formula is likely to be valid.

Alternatively the cost accountant may:

1. Estimate the cost at two volumes and so establish a straight line that supplies the same information as the line of best fit in the scatter diagram.
2. Build up separate estimates of the behaviour of every item of cost.
3. Estimate the cost at one volume and estimate the effect of changes in that volume. The effect of changes in volume is simply another way of expressing the variable element, and it is merely a matter of arithmetic to work back to the fixed component.

SEMINAR EXERCISES

13.1 (a) Ernest Rust is in charge of student catering facilities at a large college in the east Midlands. Adverse comment has been received as to the service provided in some campus buildings, which are far from the central restaurant. Mr Rust must soon decide whether to lease food vending machines for installation in these buildings. The machines would work for a 39-week year but can only be hired on an annual basis. The following cost information has been quoted to Mr Rust by the vending machine company.

Average selling price per unit sold	60p
Average direct cost per unit sold	48p
Lease rental per machine p.a.	£12 000
Casual labour for replenishing machines	Two operatives at £90 per week
Charge for annual service agreement	£360
Electricity	£20 per week
Proportion of college administration expenses	£750

Ernest Rust has budgeted for sales of £117 000 p.a. for each machine.

Required:

Advise Ernest Rust. (10 marks)

(b) (i) The chief administrative officer later notifies Mr Rust that the college authorities require a profit of at least £50 per week from each machine.

(ii) Mr Rust fears that as well as the alteration in (b) (i) above, the vending machine company may raise the rental by 50% once the machines are installed and the college is committed. Alternatively, he fears that the company may raise the average direct cost per unit sold to 53p.

Required:

Further advise Ernest Rust. (8 marks)

(c) Discuss briefly the limiting assumptions that reduce the usefulness of break even analysis as a management tool. (7 marks)

(Total 25 marks)

13.2 Korstat Limited, a manufacturer of stationery supplies, has always sold its products through wholesalers. Last year its sales turnover was £4 million and a net profit of 10% on sales was reported in its published accounts.

Due to an increase in stationery sales in department stores and supermarkets, Korstat Limited is considering eliminating its wholesalers and selling direct to retailers. A feasibility study was carried out and it was estimated that the change-over would result in a 40% drop in sales, but net profit would be £300 000 as a result of eliminating the middleman. Fixed expenses would increase from the present figure of £600 000 to £660 000 owing to the additional warehouses and distribution facilities required.

Required:

(a) Would the proposed change raise or lower the break even point in pounds? If so, by how much? (9 marks)

(b) What sales volume, in pounds, must Korstat obtain under the proposed plan to make as much profit as it made last year? (6 marks)

(Total 15 marks)

13.3 (a) Using the information below prepare profit statements for the months of June and July using:

(i) marginal costing
(ii) full absorption costing. (16 marks)

(b) Suggest reasons why the two methods in (a) disclose different amounts of profit for May and June. (6 marks)

Data per unit:	£
Selling price	50
Direct material cost	18
Direct labour cost	4
Variable production overheads	3

Monthly costs:	
Fixed production overheads	99 000
Fixed selling expenses	15 000
Fixed administration expenses	25 000

Variable selling costs are 10% of sales revenue and normal production capacity is 11 000 units per month.

	Sales (units)	Production (units)
June	10 000	12 000
July	12 000	10 000

(Total 22 marks)

REVIEW QUESTIONS

13.1 (a) 'Fixed costs are really variable; the more you produce the less they become.' Do you agree with this statement? (10 marks)

(b) Sketch a separate graph to show the behaviour of the following costs as production volumes increase:

(i) supervisory labour;
(ii) depreciation of plant on a machine-hour basis;
(iii) planned preventive maintenance plus unexpected maintenance;
(iv) monthly pay of a salesman who receives £15 000 p.a. plus a commission of 1% paid on his previous month's sales *when they exceed* £30 000;
(v) as for (iv) but the wording in italics to read *sales in excess of* £30 000.

(15 marks)

(Total 25 marks)

13.2 The following are the unit costs of manufacturing and selling a given item at a level of 20 000 per month for Johnson Limited:

		£
Direct materials		2.00
Direct labour		2.40
Factory overheads:	variable	1.60
	fixed	1.00
Selling overheads:	variable	3.00
	fixed	1.70

The company's normal selling price is £12 per unit.

Required:

(a) (i) Calculate the company's break even point in terms of numbers of units sold.
(ii) Draw a break even graph to depict the company's situation, identifying the break even point. (10 marks)

(b) Determine the optimal policy for the company in each of the situations depicted below, supporting your answer with calculations and/or explanations as necessary.

(i) The company is preparing its annual financial accounts. At what amount should the company value each unit in stock at the year-end for inclusion in the balance sheet in order to comply with normal accounting practice?

(ii) The company can hire automated machinery for a rental charge of £20 000 per month, which will enable it to halve its workforce. However, the remaining employees will require a 25% pay increase to gain their acceptance of this change. Should the company hire the machinery?

(iii) The company has 1000 units of this item left over from last year's model, which must be sold through regular channels at reduced prices. If unsold, the units will be completely valueless, and the company will have to pay 20p per unit to a scrap merchant to remove them. What is the minimum price the company should be prepared to accept for these units?

(iv) A proposal is received from an outside supplier who will make and deliver this item directly to the customers of Johnson Limited, as sales orders are forwarded from Johnson's sales staff. Johnson's fixed selling costs will be unaffected, but its variable selling expense will be cut by 20%. Johnson's plant will be idle, but its fixed production overheads would continue at 50% of present levels.

What is the maximum price Johnson can afford to pay this supplier to leave its present total profit unchanged? (12 marks)

(Total 22 marks)

13.3 Kesterjon Press Limited plans to launch a new monthly magazine to sell at £1 per copy, with expected sales of 600 000 copies a month, but the managers do not know how reliable this estimate will prove to be. Two different methods of producing the magazine are under consideration with estimated costs of:

	Method A	Method B
Variable costs	60p a copy	53p a copy
Specific fixed costs	£105 000 per month	£159 500 per month
Semi-variable costs:		
Production of 450 000	£60 000	£55 000
Production of 550 000	£70 000	£60 000
Production of 650 000	£80 000	£65 000

The fixed costs' content of the semi-variable costs does not change throughout the range of activity shown. The managers anticipate that the new magazine will adversely affect sales of their existing magazine to the extent that for every 12 copies of the new magazine that are sold, sales of the existing magazine will fall by one copy.

The existing magazine sells 300 000 copies a month at a price of 75p. Variable costs are 39p a copy and fixed costs are £85 000 per month.

Required:

(a) Calculate for each production method the impact on company profits the new magazine will make if monthly sales are 500 000, 600 000, or 700 000 copies.

(b) Calculate for each production method the amount by which actual sales could be below planned expected sales before the new magazine ceases to be profitable to the company.

(c) What advice would you give the management?   (20 marks)

14

Short-term Decision Making

One principle underlying successful decision making in the short term is the recognition of costs and revenues that are relevant to the decision and the exclusion of other non-relevant data. Cost behaviour may alter as circumstances change, so the correct identification of the real effect of a decision on the overall profit of a business is important. Contribution, which is the net result of revenue less variable cost, is a relevant figure to use as a comparator for alternatives, or as a means by which to measure the success of projected schemes. Fixed costs that do not vary as a result of the decision are outside the calculation of contribution; thus only relevant costs can influence the decision. It is also important to realise that costs are not the only factors to be taken into account. Other factors that cannot be accurately measured in monetary terms should also have an influence on decisions. Such factors are referred to as *qualitative factors*, e.g. the effect a decision may have on the morale and subsequent performance of the labour force will have an unquantifiable effect on future costs. The significance of qualitative factors is enhanced if analysis by quantitative factors does not give a clear-cut answer to the decision.

RELEVANT COSTS

To ascertain costs or revenues that are relevant to a decision, it is necessary to measure the difference in cash flow to be experienced as a result of the decision. Relevant costs are sometimes termed *incremental* or *differential costs* to emphasise that the cost of a proposed course of action is best defined as the extra cost incurred thereby, and this amount can be measured as the extra cash paid out consequent upon that decision. Costs that are not affected by a decision are not relevant to that decision, but remember that cost behaviour may change with circumstances and what was considered a fixed cost may become variable, that revenue lost counts as a cost, and that costs saved count as a revenue. Only costs to be experienced in the future are relevant to a decision. Money spent already is sunk and gone, and as a 'sunk cost' should be ignored at decision time, e.g. the cost of a feasibility study or market surveys already undertaken cannot be considered when deciding if a project should be developed further, since, whether the decision is positive or negative, that cost has been incurred. It is quite illogical to argue that the loss on disposal of a machine is part of the cost of replacing that machine. The loss represents past profits overstated because depreciation was inadequate, but the cash received from the sale of the old machine would certainly be a differential cash flow caused by the replacement decision and should be included in that decision. It is wrong to try to include 'committed costs' in decision making, since such costs are already contracted for or paid. Non-cash costs such as depreciation or writing off old plant should also be ignored.

Past costs can be used to predict future costs, but care must be taken to update the past for changes that will affect the future. Any fixed overhead costs to be absorbed by a project should be ignored when deciding about that project, because the overhead charge is merely a share of a central cost, which will not itself increase or decrease because of the new project. Contribution is well suited to such analysis; any project that shows a positive contribution should theoretically be accepted. However, it is harmful to commit resources to a portfolio of projects whose contribution, considered in aggregate, will not cover the fixed overheads. The use of scarce resources must be planned in such a way as to maximise contribution.

A decision concerns the selection of a course of action from two or more alternatives, one of which may be to do nothing. The differential cash flow to be received by acceptance or rejection is the criterion to use when the decision is made. By choosing one course of action, the cash flow from the alternative is foregone, so this is the 'opportunity cost' attached to the decision. Sometimes it is difficult, if not impossible, to define the next best alternative or to compute the cash flow expected from it. If a number of projects are competing for scarce resources, they can be ranked in order of cash flow, so that the opportunity cost of choosing one project is displayed as the return for the next best project in the queue.

Materials are held in stock at historic cost, but the situation of materials to be used in a project can seriously affect their cost, which will be counted against the project. Materials that are in regular use will need to be replaced, so the cost of using them is the cash outflow to replace the stock used up. Materials that are surplus and about to be sold off will cost the project the cash flow from the sale that is foregone, if, instead, they are used in production (net realisable value). Materials that did cost money in the past but that are now to be scrapped as worthless cost nothing in incremental terms if they are used on a project. Scarce materials used should be costed at opportunity cost, or the profit that is foregone by not using them on an alternative scheme. A special purchase of material for a project will cost the actual cash paid out.

A similar logic can be applied to the cost of labour. If a manager is asked to postpone his retirement in order to work on a project, the cost to the company is his salary, less the pension that would otherwise have been paid to him. The labour cost of a job is the amount paid out for its completion. If overtime is to be worked the cash outlay is the cost to use when evaluating the project, but if the job is to be undertaken in idle time no extra payment is involved and the labour cost is nil. If labour is diverted from one job to another, any penalties paid for late delivery on the original job are part of the cost of this diversion. The cost of skilled labour of a scarce type is the income foregone by not using that labour on an alternative project.

Relevant costs for machinery must be defined. The use of a machine does not cause a cash outflow, but by wearing out the machine it brings closer the date of replacement of that machine so some part of its capital cost should be charged against the project. The fall in value of plant whilst employed on a certain project is another method of calculating its cost to the project, this being the loss sustained by postponing the retirement of the machine, instead of selling it at once. Historic cost based depreciation has no place in costs for decision making; to be at all realistic, depreciation should be based on current replacement cost. Overhead expenses are only included in analysing a decision if they are incremental and stem directly from the project under consideration.

A significant factor that must be considered in short-term decisions is the ripple effect of the decision. Just as a child throws a pebble into a still pool and watches the ripples spread across the surface, so projects or decisions that bring changes to a business, permeate through the organisation and affect other matters. The publisher of a new magazine must take into account the effect it will have on existing publications owned by the company, in case the business as a whole is worse off as a result of an otherwise profitable project.

Example

Polymix PLC manufactures chemical compounds and has been offered the opportunity to produce under licence 4000 drums of a car polishing agent 'Gradex' at a price of £100 per drum.

The specification of each drum of Gradex is as follows:

Direct materials:	
Waxing agent	20 kg
Mixer	10 litres
Polymer sealant	1 litre
Direct labour:	
Skilled	2 hours at £4 per hour
Unskilled	6 hours at £2 per hour

Investigation reveals the following information: skilled labour is under-utilised at Polymix just now, but it is company policy not to shed skilled labour. Acceptance of the contract for Gradex would reduce the idle time paid to skilled operatives, which is now treated as a non-production overhead expense. Unskilled labour is considered to be a variable cost.

Material required for the Gradex contract would be drawn from stock. The wax is used by Polymix in several production processes and would need to be replaced. The mixture is in stock, having been purchased for another contract, which has been cancelled, and is now awaiting sale. 10 000 litres of sealant is currently in stock but is considered obsolete and toxic. Polymix has made arrangements to dispose of this sealant at a cost of £5000 to the company.

Material cost data	Wax	Mixer	Sealant
Book value per kilogram/litre in stock	£0.80	£3.00	£40
Replacement cost	£1.00	£3.20	No longer made
Net realisable value	£0.90	£2.50	–

Variable production overheads are estimated at £3 per direct labour-hour for all products. The Gradex project requires supervision by an experienced chemist and Mr J. Sope has been persuaded by a fee of £26 000 to defer his early retirement for six months to complete the Gradex contract. He normally earns £40 000 a year and had hoped to retire on a pension of 50% of his salary.

Fixed factory overheads are absorbed by a single recovery rate applied to all departments based on productive labour-hours. Estimates for next year's activity, which exclude the Gradex contract, show overheads of £600 000 and hours of 300 000. These fixed costs would increase by £32 000 if the contract is accepted. Polymix already produce a car polish under the trade name 'Polydip'. If the Gradex contract is accepted, sales of Polydip would be reduced by 5000 drums, and the consequent reduction in production would reduce budgeted fixed overheads by £28 000 in the forthcoming year. The specification for Polydip per drum is: price, £40; material, 12 kg of wax; and labour, four hours of unskilled operative-time.

Required:

Advise the management of Polymix.

Polymix Solution

The relevant costs are:

Materials:	
Wax	Replacement cost
Mixer	Net realisable value
Sealant	A cost saving $\frac{4}{10} \times £5000$
Labour:	
Skilled labour is not an incremental cost	

Supervision	Fee	£26 000
	Pension saved	£10 000
Extra cash outflow		£16 000

Variable overheads	Varies with direct labour-hours ($8 \times £3$)
Ripple effect	A cost of making Gradex is the profit foregone on lost sales of Polydip.

Incremental Profit from Acceptance of Gradex contract

	Drum £	Batch of 4000 £000's	Total £000's
Sales revenue (4000 drums × £100)			400
Material costs:			
Wax (20 kg × £1)	20	80	
Mixer (10 litres × £2.5)	25	100	
Sealant (no value)	–	–	
Labour costs:			
Skilled	–	–	
Unskilled (6 hours × £2)	12	48	
Variable overheads (8 hours × £3)	24	96	
Supervision (£16 000 ÷ 4000)	4	16	
	£85		340
Surplus			60
Less: fixed cost increase			(32)
Plus: disposal cost of sealant avoided			2
Gross return on Gradex			30
Loss on Polydip:		£000's	
Sales revenue (5000 × £40)		200	
Costs:			
Materials (12 kg wax at £1 × 5000)		(60)	
Labour (4 hours × £2 × 5000)		(40)	
Variable overheads (4 hours × £3 × 5000)		(60)	
		40	
Less fixed cost avoided		(28)	(12)
Net incremental benefit of producing Gradex			£18

Advice:

The contract is worthwhile, since it shows an incremental profit of £18 000. Care must be taken to insure that the estimate of the ripple effect of Gradex on Polydip is accurately forecasted.

Uncertainty

All decisions are based on forecasts of future costs and revenues, yet data concerning the future may not prove to be accurate. The expected accuracy of information used to formulate a decision is expressed as the confidence with which managers can rely on that data or the probability that what is forecast will actually happen. There may be several possible results and the probability that each one will take place can be expressed as a percentage of total probability, e.g. in forecasting revenue, sales are most likely to be £250 000, but there is a slight chance that they will reach £280 000 and a greater possibility that only £230 000 of goods will be sold. Management, using judgement and their experience of the market, estimate that there is a 60% chance or probability of revenue of £250 000, only a 10% probability of revenue of £280 000, but a 30% probability that revenue of £230 000 will be achieved. It would be wrong to base a decision on any one of these possibilities, so they are all built into a combined figure of 'expected revenue'. The figure is really an average, weighted for the probability of each alternative.

Revenue	×	Probability	=	Expected revenue
£				£
230 000	×	0.3	=	69 000
250 000	×	0.6	=	150 000
280 000	×	0.1	=	28 000
		Expected revenue		£247 000

SENSITIVITY

There is a measure of uncertainty attached to all forecasted figures built into a decision, so it is logical to assess the impact on the expected result of an estimate that is subsequently proved wrong. If a proportionally small change in one factor can have a much greater impact on the final outcome of the project, perhaps turning it from a profitable result to a loss, the project is said to be sensitive to a change in this factor. Alternatively, if it takes a proportionally large difference between the forecasted amount and the actual amount, for a factor to affect the result of the project, then the project is insensitive to fluctuations in the amount of this factor. Sensitivity measures how far the forecasted figures can be wrong before the project ceases to be viable.

Example

Planned sales of Product X are 50 000 units at £25 each. Each Product X costs £24 to make: £20 for materials and £4 for labour. Fixed costs attributed to Product X are £30 000.

The break even point is the contribution of £1 per product divided into fixed costs of £30 000, which equals a sales volume of 30 000 units, which in turn shows a margin of safety of 20 000 units, or 40% of planned sales. Thus the sales forecast must be wrong by 40% before losses are made, so sales volume is not a sensitive factor bearing on the success of Product X. Contribution at planned sales is £50 000, with a profit of (£50 000 minus £30 000 fixed cost) £20 000. Therefore fixed cost could rise by as much as £20 000 (or 66% of forecast) before that profit was turned into a loss. Thus this factor is also not sensitive for the success of the project. However, variable costs and price show much more sensitivity. If the price falls by only £1, the contribution is reduced to nil, and a loss of £30 000 would be made because the fixed overheads would not be covered by revenue.

A price reduction of only 40p on a price of £25 (1.6%) would reduce contribution to 60p per unit, and at planned volume of sales (50 000 × £0.6), the product would break even since contribution equals fixed cost at that volume. Thus price is a very sensitive figure for the evaluation of this product, and only a small mistake in forecasting the price will nullify the expected profit.

Similarly variable cost is also sensitive. An increase in material cost of 40p (on £20 this is only 2%) will reduce contribution and can negate the expected profit on Product X. Great care must be taken to ensure that the forecast of this sensitive factor is correct. An increase of 40p per unit on the labour cost of each product (on £4 this is 10%) will also reduce contribution to 60p per unit and shows that labour costs are less sensitive than price or material cost for the ultimate viability of the product.

A weakness of sensitivity analysis is that although it computes the sensitivity of individual factors for the ultimate success of the project, the actual amount of the factors may not fluctuate from forecast discretely, i.e. one at a time. The actual figures experienced for price, labour cost and fixed cost may all differ from the amounts used in the computation on which the decision was based; these fluctuations may all move in the same direction, or they may compensate each other, e.g. a labour-cost increase may be compensated by a reduction of fixed cost or a price increase.

BASIC RULES FOR SHORT-TERM DECISION MAKING

It is difficult to lay down rules for decision making because the circumstances vary for each decision. It may be necessary to choose between two alternatives or to rank a number of projects in order of acceptability. Contribution is a useful comparator, since it combines the differential factors of revenue and variable cost. Fixed costs that do not change are outside the calculation, so that any mistakes made through an arbitrary allocation of fixed costs are avoided.

Closure of Part of the Business. Decisions of this type concern the evaluation of a factory, a product, a geographical region, a type of customer or any other sector of the business that can be reviewed as an individual entity and compared with similar parts of the business. The object of the analysis is to increase profits by dropping loss-makers and perhaps replacing them with alternatives. The contribution of each outlet, department or product to the pool that will cover fixed overheads and profit is the best measure of viability in the context of closure. In calculating the contribution, cost behaviour in the changed circumstances of potential closure must be considered with care. Costs that might normally be considered as fixed may, in the context of the decision, become variable and vice versa, e.g. rent of a branch office is no longer paid if the office is closed.

Departments or products that show a negative contribution should be closed if there is no possibility of an improvement. Negative contribution means that the variable cost per unit exceeds price, so the business would be better off without this activity. Where a positive contribution is disclosed, there is no case for closure since the department or product is making some contribution to fixed cost, and closure would mean the loss of this contribution, and so reduce profit.

The application of these two rules is not absolute and is moderated by maintaining activities with a negative contribution if the business is prepared to take the loss. This may only be temporary in order to avoid breaking up a well-organised part of the business, which it is hoped will revive, or for strategic reasons to gain some other benefit. Activities that make a positive contribution are sometimes discontinued if the contribution is deemed insufficient and the resources tied up in the activity could be disinvested to earn a higher return elsewhere. Qualitative factors are significant at this stage. The ripple effect of closure must also be considered, since benefits or disadvantages could be felt in other parts of the business consequent upon closure of a seemingly unrelated activity.

Example

Plumtree Publications PLC controls four local newspapers. Each paper has its own editorial staff and local office, but the four papers are printed at a central printing plant in Plumtree. The profitability of each paper is under investigation and, on the basis of the budgeted cost statement for the next half-year shown below, the board are considering the closure of three of the four papers.

	Kirkby Chronicle		Hucknall Herald		Ratcliffe Reporter		Trumpton Times	
	£	£	£	£	£	£	£	£
Sales		400 000		800 000		600 000		200 000
Production costs								
Direct materials	110 000		120 000		110 000		80 000	
Direct labour	175 000		220 000		190 000		125 000	
Fixed factory over-								
heads absorbed	40 000		80 000		60 000		20 000	
Editorial staff	45 000		90 000		135 000		10 000	
Local office costs	35 000		80 000		170 000		10 000	
		405 000		590 000		665 000		245 000
Profit*/(loss)		£(5000)		£210 000		£(65 000)		£(45 000)

* Profit is £95 000

Further investigation reveals that £40 000 of advertising revenue at present earned by the *Trumpton Times* in a half-year could be transferred to the *Ratcliffe Reporter* if the *Trumpton Times* were to cease publication. There is no possibility of economy in editorial staff or local office costs for any paper.

Advise management!

It is clear the management intend to close the *Chronicle*, *Reporter* and *Times* because they expect them to make losses, but the closure decision should be made in terms of contribution, as follows:

£000's	Kirkby Chronicle		Hucknall Herald		Ratcliffe Reporter		Trumpton Times		Total
	£	£	£	£	£	£	£	£	£
Sales		400		800		600		200	
Variable cost									
Materials	110		120		110		80		
Labour	175		220		190		125		
Editorial staff	45		90		135		10		
Local office costs	35		80		170		10		

£000's	Kirkby Chronicle £	£	Hucknall Herald £	£	Ratcliffe Reporter £	£	Trumpton Times £	£	Total £
		365		510		605		225	
Contribution		35		290		(5)		(25)	295
Fixed factory overheads									200
Net profit									£ 95

Note: In the context of closure the editorial and local office costs become variable rather than fixed. It is wrong to close a paper that is making a positive contribution, so the management's plan to close the *Chronicle* would lose a positive contribution of £35 000. The original plan to close the *Chronicle, Reporter* and *Times* would leave only the *Herald* with a contribution of £290 000 to cover fixed costs of £200 000, so expected profit would fall to £90 000.

If the *Reporter* and *Times* are closed because they show a negative contribution, the *Chronicle* and *Herald* together will provide a contribution of £325 000 towards fixed costs of £200 000, so that profit will increase to £125 000. The ripple effect is that closure of the *Times* transfers advertising revenue of £40 000 to the *Reporter*, which, when added to sales, changes the negative contribution of that paper to a positive £35 000, thus preventing closure. Therefore, if only the *Trumpton Times* is closed, the contribution will be £360 000 towards fixed costs of £200 000 and at net profit of £160 000.

THE MAKE OR BUY DECISION

A company is often in a position where it has to decide whether it should make a component in its own factory or whether it should 'buy out' the component from another manufacturer. Cost is only one factor that contributes to this decision, since qualitative factors may also be significant. Following the basic tenets of relevant costing, the sub-contractor's bought out price (the future cash outflow of the alternative) should be compared with the variable cost of producing the component 'in house'. If fixed cost does not change as a result of the decision, it is not relevant. Any cost incurred up to the time when the decision is made, e.g. testing a sample of the bought out product for quality, is a sunk cost and should be ignored, since whichever way the decision goes, that cost will not be affected.

If variable cost exceeds bought out price, the components production should be sub-contracted, since this will reduce the cash overflow to a minimum.

Example

A company needs 10 000 coil springs to build into its main product. The alternatives available are to make the component for £15 each (materials £6, labour £4, variable overheads £2, fixed overheads absorbed £3), or to buy it from a specialist manufacturer for £14 each.

At £14 the bought out price is less than the full absorption cost of £15 but greater than the more relevant variable cost of £12. Thus other things being equal, the product should be produced in the factory rather than bought from a sub-contractor. The fixed overheads absorbed are a proportion of general factory costs allocated to the component, and they will still have to be covered whether or not the spring is manufactured in the factory.

This example is set in the context of freely available production resources. If capacity is fully utilised then the cost of making a component is the contribution foregone by diverting resources from some other product, i.e. opportunity cost.

The Qualitative Factors Influencing a Make or Buy Decision

If a component is made in the main factory the producer can check to ensure that it is well made, but if it is sub-contracted then there is less immediate control over the standard of the output. The main manufacturer must assure himself that the components bought out maintain the desired quality, especially if the component has an exacting specification. Faulty components built into the main product can cause breakdowns after sale, thus adversely affecting the reputation of the main product, and increasing the cost of after sales service. These costs cannot be easily quantified.

With bought out components there is always the fear that the supplier will not meet the scheduled delivery dates. Factors outside the control of the main manufacturer, such as a strike or machine breakdown at the sub-contractor's factory, can interrupt supplies and disrupt production schedules at the main factory. When a component is made in the main factory it is easier to improve quality control, and co-ordinate production to usage, to avoid stock outs, keep stocks to a minimum, and also utilise idle capacity.

There are strategic arguments against buying out components. If a company comes to depend on its suppliers they may be able to increase their price by negotiation for further orders; or the company could find itself cut off from supplies if a rival takes over the sub-contractor, or offers more for the use of his production capacity. Production in the main factory facilitates the design and introduction of improvements to the component. Security is improved since there is no need to inform another company of plans for improvement to the product, which might be passed on to rival producers.

If components are bought out, part of a skilled workforce may become redundant at the main producer's factory, which could cause a fall in morale and perhaps even a strike. The company is more confident of its ability if it can demonstrate that it can provide components for itself; such a demonstration will keep other component suppliers 'on their toes' and may prevent them from attempting to take advantage of the main company when quoting for future orders. Management may wish to place the company in a position of self-sufficiency and growth, thus adopting a policy of not buying out components as a means of achieving this objective.

OPTIMUM USE OF A LIMITING FACTOR

Limiting factors have been explained in a previous chapter and defined as any factor that prevents a business from expanding its potential. Contribution analysis can be used to maximise profit where a limiting factor is in operation by concentrating activity on those parts of the business that make the greatest contribution per unit of limiting factor. In this way the business is planned to use the factor that is curbing its operations in the best possible way, e.g. to concentrate production on a product mix which maximises profit within the limits imposed. It is illogical to allot fixed cost to products in the context of this decision, since whichever mix of products is selected, the fixed cost will not change – so contribution is the proper comparator to use.

Example

A company manufactures two products: A and B. The products use the same material and grade of labour and their cost structures are as follows:

	Product A		Product B
	£		£
Direct material (5 kg × £5)	25	10 kg × £5	50
Direct labour (8 hours × £2)	16	4 hours × £2	8
Variable cost	41		58
Price	61		73
Contribution	£20		£15

If there were no limiting factors other than production capacity it would be preferable to concentrate production on A rather than B. One thousand A's produced in a week make a contribution of £20 000 to fixed overheads and profit, but the contribution derived from production of one thousand B's is only £15 000. If, however, a limiting factor affects production, then contribution per unit of limiting factor will point the way to the most profitable use of available resources:

$$\frac{\text{Contribution}}{\text{Units of limited factor used}}$$

Contribution per Unit of Limiting Factor

	Product A	Product B
If material is the limiting factor:	$\dfrac{£20}{5\,kg} = £4$	$\dfrac{£15}{10\,kg} = £1.50$

To maximise profit, production should be concentrated on A rather than B.

	Product A	Product B
If labour is the limiting factor:	$\dfrac{£20}{8\ hours} = £2.50$	$\dfrac{£15}{4\ hours} = £3.75$

To maximise profit, production should be concentrated on B rather than A. As a proof of this conclusion, calculate the production budget if only 150 000 kg of material are available, i.e. material is the limiting factor, and forecast sales are 10 000 A's and 14 000 B's.

Material required to make what can be sold would be:

A:	10 000 units × 5 kg	50 000 kg
B:	14 000 units × 10 kg	140 000 kg
Material required		190 000 kg
Material available		150 000 kg
Shortfall		40 000 kg

A production budget concentrating on A, which gives the greatest contribution per unit of limiting factor, would show:

				£
Production of A:	10 000 units—material used	50 000 kg;	contribution	200 000
Production of B:	10 000 units—material used	100 000 kg;	contribution	150 000
Limiting factor		150 000 kg		£350 000

Material not used to produce A has been used to produce B. Alternatively, suppose that B is budgeted as the dominant product:

			£
Production of B: 14 000 units—material used	140 000 kg;	contribution	210 000
Production of A: 2 000 units—material used	10 000 kg;	contribution	40 000
Limiting factor	150 000 kg		£250 000

Contribution (and therefore profit earned) is significantly smaller if the rule is ignored and the wrong plan is adopted. Maximum profit is achieved within the constraints of limited materials' supply by concentrating on production of A, making some B's and contracting out the production of 4000 B's, using the logic and qualitative factors explained above.

The example can be extended to consider the optimum production budget if labour is the limiting factor with, say, 110 000 hours available. Labour required for production to meet the sales forecast would be:

	Hours
Product A: 10 000 units × 8 hours	80 000
Product B: 14 000 units × 4 hours	56 000
Hours required	136 000
Hours available	110 000
Shortfall	26 000

Product B has a greater contribution per unit of limiting factor than A and should therefore be selected as the dominant product. If 14 000 B's are made, 56 000 hours will be used up, leaving 54 000 hours available for product A, so that $(54 000 \div 8)$ 6750 A's can be made. The production budget would be as follows:

		£
Product B: 14 000 units, using	56 000 hours, gives contribution	210 000
Product A: 6 750 units, using	54 000 hours, gives contribution	135 000
Limiting factor	110 000 hours	£345 000

If product A is selected as the dominant product, the budget shows a smaller contribution:

		£
Production of A: 10 000 units, using	40 000 hours, gives contribution	200 000
Production of B: 8 750 units, using	70 000 hours, gives contribution	131 250
Limiting factor	110 000 hours	331 250

PRICING

As with all short-term decisions, the management accountant does not make the decision; his role is to offer advice to management, often in the form of a cost statement, which summarises the financial implications of the decision. This is well illustrated in the case of pricing where the profit to volume (p/v) ratio can be used to set parameters for a decision and leave the marketing expert to decide how far sales will change under certain circumstances.

Example

A product sells for £2 with variable cost of production 80p. Fixed costs are £28 000 and budgeted sales are 32 000 units. A disagreement has developed between two executives in the business. The marketing director suggests that a price reduction of 10% will so increase sales that profit will increase, but the production director, mindful of the wear and tear on his factory machinery, is arguing for a price increase of 10% to slightly reduce the volume sold but to increase the profit.

Advise management.

The key to this problem is the profit to volume (p/v) ratio. This ratio shows the proportion of each sale which is a contribution towards fixed costs and overheads. It is important to discover the budgeted profit and to see how the two alternative plans compare with that result.

	Present Budget	Reduce Price 10%	Increase Price 10%
	£	£	£
Selling price	2.00	1.80	2.20
Variable cost	.80	.80	.80
Contribution	1.20	1.00	1.40
Percentage contribution to price	$\frac{120}{200}\times\frac{100}{1}$	$\frac{100}{180}\times\frac{100}{1}$	$\frac{140}{220}\times\frac{100}{1}$
	$= 60\%$	$= 55.5\%$	$= 63.6\%$
	£		
Contribution on 32 000 sales	38 400		
Less fixed costs	28 000		
Required profit	£10 400		
Sales required to give a contribution of		$\frac{£38\,400}{1}\times\frac{100}{55.5}$	$\frac{£38\,400}{1}\times\frac{100}{63.6}$
		$= £69\,189$	$= £60\,377$
		or 38 438 units at	or 27 444 units at
		a price of £1.80	a price of £2.20
An increase/(decrease) of		6438 units	(4556 units)
		or 20% volume	or 14% volume

The management accountant is able to inform his managerial colleagues that if the price is reduced by 10%, demand must be so elastic as to cause sales to increase by 20% or more in volume terms if profit is to be increased by this strategy. Alternatively, if the price is increased by 10%, sales must not fall by more than 14% in volume terms if more profit is to be made than is planned by the current budget. The guidelines have been set, it is then up to the marketing experts to estimate future sales.

Pricing Strategy

The marketing specialists estimate demand for a product at a range of prices and work out their approach to the market. Price influences the volume sold, but it is not the only factor to influence volume, nor does it affect all products in the same way. The normal rule is that the lower price is set, the greater will be the volume demanded. The response of total demand to a change in price is termed *price elasticity of demand*. If price is cut by 5% and the volume sold increases by more than 5%, then demand is said to be elastic. When a new product is launched there is a tendency to set a relatively high price to compensate for errors in cost forecasting and to *skim* off large profits per unit associated with demand for a 'new product'. This strategy soon gives way to *penetration pricing*, which sets a lower price to compete with rival goods and establish a market share for the product. The point at which the change from skimming to penetration is made depends on how soon the novelty of the product wears off and how difficult it is for competitors to enter the market. As price is reduced, the volume of sales will increase and allow the economies of large-scale production to be exploited so that unit costs fall until there are no further opportunities for cost reduction and the market settles into its long-run pattern. A business will attempt to maximise profits by setting sales targets at the volume where the difference between total revenue and total cost is at a maximum. This will be the point at which the marginal cost of producing one extra unit is equal to the marginal revenue derived from the sale of that unit. The best possible, or optimum, volume of sales is 70 000 units because profit AB is maximised at that volume. In order to boost sales from 50 000 to 70 000 units, price must be reduced from £10 to £9.

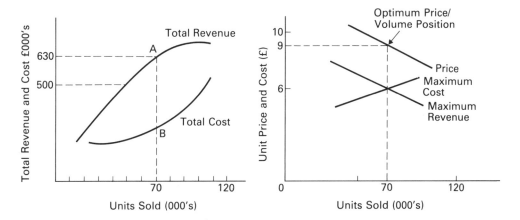

The extra revenue earned per unit over this range is marginal revenue.

50 000 units sold at £10 give total revenue of £500 000.
60 000 units sold at £9.50 give total revenue of £570 000 = £70 000 increase.
70 000 units sold at £9 give total revenue of £630 000 = £60 000 increase.

From £10 to £9.50, revenue increases by £70 000 for 10 000 extra units or £7 per unit. From £9.50 to £9, revenue increases by £60 000 or £6 per unit. If the cost of making one unit is £6 at a volume of 70 000, it is not worthwhile to expand beyond this point because revenue earned by making extra units is falling and the cost of making those units is rising. An economist would attempt to make this analysis by adjusting volume one unit at a time until MR = MC. In practice the full range from nought to 120 000 units is of little value, since a realistic analysis can be made over a relatively narrow band.

Pricing Based on Costs

In the long run it is wrong to sell at a price less than the full absorption cost of the product, but in the short run, and in certain special situations, a price in excess of marginal cost can be adopted. Price may be determined by adding a required mark up or profit margin to unit cost. Rate of return pricing adds to the cost a mark up that will provide a required rate of return on the capital employed.

Example

Budgeted production is 100 000 units with a variable cost of £20 each and fixed costs of £800 000. Fixed assets are valued at £2 800 000 and working capital at £12 per unit. A return of 18% on capital employed is required.

Fixed assets	£2 800 000
Working capital 100 000 × £12	£1 200 000

$$£4\,000\,000 \times \frac{18}{100} = £720\,000$$

This equals £7.20 per product and price is:

	£
Variable cost	20.00
Fixed cost	8.00
Mark up	7.20
	35.20

The percentage mark up on cost can be calculated as:

$$\frac{\text{Capital employed}}{\text{Total cost}} \times \text{Required rate} = \frac{£4\,000\,000}{£8\,000\,000 + £2\,000\,000} \times \frac{18}{100} = 25.7\%$$

$$\text{Total cost is £28 so mark up will be } £28 \times \frac{25.7}{100} = £7.20$$

Apart from the difficulties of defining capital employed and fixed cost per unit, or the mark up required in a multi-product firm, rate of return pricing suffers from the disadvantage of ignoring demand and the activities of competitors. Fixed costs are included in the calculation, so the principle of using incremental costs on the basis that they are relevant to decisions is abandoned. Selling price is only one factor in the marketing decision and must be merged with such items as advertising, packaging, sales tactics and market strategy.

Marginal Cost Pricing

Pricing based on marginal cost and contribution avoids the need to allocate fixed costs to units and enables the cost–volume–profit relationship to influence the decision. A minimum price per unit can be established as the amount that covers variable or incremental cost, so that any increase in price beyond this amount makes some contribution to overheads. Whilst in the long run fixed costs must be covered, in the short run price can be allowed to fall below full absorption cost to 'beat off' competition, survive in a period of depression, or to establish a product in a new market. Once the volume sold of a product reaches the break even point, fixed costs are covered by contribution and any contribution on sales beyond that point is profit. Thus production can be expanded so long as goods can be 'dumped' in a different segment of the market at artificially low prices, which, so long as they cover variable cost, will increase profits. Special orders and the utilisation of surplus capacity should be viewed from the standpoint of marginal cost, provided they do not reduce sales at normal prices in established markets. It is not unknown for a company to sell at a loss to break into a lucrative market, with the expectation that it will recoup these initial losses at a later date.

Prices based on marginal costs circumvent the difficulties of over or under-absorption of fixed overheads, which can lead to quotations for orders that either price a company out of the market or offer prices that do not cover costs adequately. Using marginal cost it is easier to compute the optimum position, which balances volume and cost, and in a segmented market it is easier to take decisions using costs relevant to that part of the market alone. Where technological change move quickly, the life of a product may be short so that the long run for a product is rarely experienced, being replaced by a series of short runs as the product is developed and changed. A producer of micro-computers cannot hope for the market to settle since new development regularly changes the whole situation.

SEMINAR EXERCISES

14.1 Part Finished Limited is a publishing and printing company that specialises in the production of paperback books. The stock is kept in an unbound and unfinished state until it is ordered by customers. The cost of a single publication is as follows:

i)   Preparation costs, and costs incurred from commissioning authors, photographs, composition, etc. for whatever quantity of publication produced, will be £12 000.

ii) Printing costs are £100 per thousand up to 50 000 and then £60 per thousand for any further copies.

iii) Binding and other finishing costs are £60 per thousand whatever quantity is produced.

The book is to be sold direct to retailers at 40p per copy.

Required:

(a) Prepare a table showing the production costs for 40 000, 50 000, 60 000, 70 000 and 80 000 copies of the finished publication, together with the average cost per copy for each of these quantities. Also show the marginal cost per copy for each increment of 10 000 copies, in the range 40 000 to 80 000 copies.
At the proposed selling price to retailers:
(i)   State the break even quantity.
(ii) What would be the profit if the company produced and sold 70 000 copies?

(b) Part Finished Limited has printed 70 000 copies of the publication, but it has not sold as well as expected and 10 000 copies are left unsold. A dealer has offered to buy these for £1100. Using the information given state whether you would advise the company to accept this offer. What additional factors might also influence your recommendation?   (22 marks)

14.2 (a) Explain with examples what you understand by the term *limiting factor*.
                                                                                                                              (7 marks)

(b)   The Carreau Company Limited are manufacturers of decorative tiles. The business produces four major patterns of tile, namely Willow, Nautical, Floribunda and Cuboid. These tiles sell at prices of £23, £31, £25 and £20 respectively. The tiles are produced in the finishing department.

The factory plans to work for four 40-hour weeks in June. Production is automated as far as kiln time is concerned, but skilled labour is employed to prepare the blanks for the kiln. The ten craftsmen are paid £6 per hour, under an agreement that restricts operations to a 40-hour week.

Fixed costs are £6000.

	Willow	Nautical	Floribunda	Cuboid
Other cost information:				
Sales potential – volume	600	500	400	1000
Material costs – blanks, plus other decorating materials	£14	£16	£14	£13
Direct labour time per product	45 minutes	90 minutes	60 minutes	30 minutes
Machine time per product	3 hours	1 hour	2 hours	2 hours

Required:

(i)   Draft a production plan for the finishing department whereby profit is maximised and show the expected profit. Assume that adequate material and machine time are available.

(ii) Redraft your production plan on the assumption that machine time is limited to 2140 hours.   (15 marks)

(Total 22 marks)

14.3   The Carreau Company Limited is employed in the manufacture of decorative tiles. Their manufacturing range covers four patterns: Willow, Cuboid, Floribunda and Nautical. Budgeted production quantities at full capacity are: Willow 30 000, Cuboid 10 000, Floribunda 8000, and Nautical 10 000, with prices set at £3.00, £3.50, £2.50 and £2.00 respectively for each tile.

The cost accountant has produced a budgeted full absorption costing statement, as a result of which the managing director plans to cease production of the Floribunda, Cuboid and Nautical tiles. You have been contacted as a consultant to advise on the validity of this decision.

Your investigations reveal the following information:

Raw material costs per tile are: Willow 90p, Cuboid £1, Floribunda 90p, Nautical 85p.

Willow and Floribunda use the same material, and if Floribunda ceases production, then the company will lose a quantity rebate of 10% of the price of that raw material.

Direct labour is paid at £5 per hour and production times for tiles are: Willow, 7 minutes 12 seconds; Cuboid, 6 minutes; Floribunda, 6 minutes; and Nautical, 9 minutes.

Factory overheads are budgeted at £29 000 and are apportioned to products according to volume of production.

Separate transport facilities are maintained for each product. The cost is budgeted to be £3000 per product at full capacity, but will not be incurred if a product is no longer made.

Administration costs are apportioned equally to the four products. The total is budgeted at £8000.

Selling costs are considered to be fixed in nature since a pre-determined amount is set aside in the budget for this activity. The amounts are: Willow £14 000, Cuboid £10 000, Floribunda £4800 and Nautical £5000. The cost will not be incurred if a product is no longer made.

Required:

(a) Compute a budgeted full absorption costing statement to explain the managing director's planned decision. (10 marks)

(b) Compute an alternative statement and advise the managing director. (15 marks)

(Total 25 marks)

14.4 The Spinnaker is a washing machine produced by Front Sales Limited and sold exclusively by mail order. Last year 10 000 machines were produced and sold at a selling price of £190 each. The cost of each machine was:

	£
Direct materials	60
Direct labour	60
Other direct costs	6
Variable overheads	8
Variable cost	134
Fixed overheads	24
Total cost	£158

During the coming year it is expected that costs will increase by the following:

	%
Direct material	30
Direct labour	15
Other direct costs	20
Variable overheads	10
Fixed overheads	5

Market research has shown that the company could increase the selling price of the machine to £210 and still sell 8000 units; alternatively, if the price was reduced to £175 it would be possible to double sales to 20 000 units.

You are required, for the coming year, to:

(a) Determine the selling price of the machine if the number sold and the annual profits are to remain unchanged.

(b) Determine how many machines the company would have to sell if it did not change the price charged but maintained the profit level achieved last year.

(c) Evaluate the market research information and give your advice on the price that should be charged for the Spinnaker in the coming year. In giving your advice you should take into account the results of parts (a) and (b) above. (18 marks)

REVIEW QUESTIONS

14.1 Sparks PLC produce goods for the electrical trade. Each year they buy in a certain component, an electronically programmed switch to build into various product lines. They buy 100 000 switches each year for £1 each.

Last year calculations as to the cost of making the switches showed:

> Materials (100 000 switches):   £35 000
> Direct labour: £60 000 at a standard rate of £3 per hour
> Overhead expenses: an increase from £110 000 to £114 000

The standard recovery rate for £114 000 of overheads would be 60p per direct labour-hour. The standard cost based on these figures was £1.07 for each switch, and purchasing saved £5000 over the cost of making the switches. However, the suppliers now suggest a price increase to £1.21 each. Further investigations reveal that material costs have risen by 10% and wages by 20% since the previous calculations. Overheads now cost £133 000 p.a. and would rise to £137 000 p.a. if the switch were manufactured. A costing based on this information showed an increase of 17.5p per component over the previous figure, so the management concluded that it was still preferable to purchase rather than manufacture.

Required:

(a) Show calculations to substantiate the standard costs of £1.07 and £1.245 for the switches.   (10 marks)

(b) Rethink the decisions using relevant costs.   (12 marks)

(Total 22 marks)

14.2 Cropston Castings Limited produce aluminium castings for components in the motor trade. The company makes all of the parts that it uses, but the budget forecasts for next year indicate a shortfall of machine time as a limiting factor. There is a difference of 15 000 machine-hours between capacity available and capacity required. Consequently, the management have asked a sub-contractor to tender for the supply of certain parts. The cost structure of those parts is:

	Part A £	Part B £
Material	2.75	3.45
Labour	1.00	0.80
Fixed overhead expenses	3.00	2.00
	£6.75	£6.25
Quantity required	40 000	30 000
Tenders received from suppliers	£5.50	£6.00

Fixed overhead expenses are absorbed to production at a rate of £6.00 per machine-hour.

Required:

(a) Advise the management of Cropston Castings Limited as to its best course of action in the circumstances outlined above and support your advice with a costing statement. (12 marks)

(b) Summarise the qualitative factors that might influence a company to make a component rather than buy it. (13 marks)

(Total 25 marks)

14.3 Quotation Limited has been invited to tender for the supply of 500 weighing machines.

Information by the estimating department for the manufacture of one weighing machine is as follows:

Direct Material:

Bearings	2 units at £5.50 each
Gear wheels	2 units at £4.50 each
Circuits	3 units at £11 each
Plastic panels	5 units at £3 each
Finishing materials	2 kg at £2 per kg
Packing material	1 set at £4 per set

Direct Labour:

Machining	2 hours at £6 per hour
Assembly	3 hours at £3 per hour
Finishing	2 hours at £5 per hour
Packing	1 hour at £2 per hour

Information dealing with the costing policies of the company is as follows:

(i) Production variable overhead costs in the machining and finishing departments are closely related to the direct labour costs and, accordingly, a rate of 50% of direct labour costs is applied to charge this cost, while those of the assembly and packing departments are closely related to direct labour-hours and, accordingly, a rate of £2 per hour is used to charge this cost.

(ii) All other costs are fixed and are charged to products at 20% of production variable costs. However, in order to complete the order, existing plant needs to be adapted at a cost of £1800 and a further £1000 is required to remove the adaptations and return the plant to its current use.

(iii) The FIFO method is used in pricing materials and the estimating department has used this method.

(iv) Direct labour is charged to products using the normal rate of pay, and overtime premium is 50% of the normal rate. The estimating department uses the normal rate in preparing direct labour specifications.

You have, in addition, independently verified the following information:

(a) The current market price of bearings is £4 each.

(b) The gear wheels in stock are reserved for a contract and any use would require replacement at £3 each.

(c) The circuits are assembled by the electrical division of the company and the book value is based on the transfer price to the stores, calculated as follows:

Direct variable cost	4.00
Indirect variable cost	2.00
Apportioned fixed costs	2.00
Division profit	2.00
Transfer price	£10.00

(d) The company has 2500 plastic panels in stock. These are now obsolete and have no resale value and will be disposed at a cost of £200 if not used on this order.

(e) The finishing and packing materials are used on other products and can be replaced at the prices shown.

(f) Assembly labour is presently working at full capacity and any additional work will result in overtime.

(g) Machine labour is currently under-utilised and this order will reduce the idle time.

(h) Labour in the packing and finishing departments is paid only for the hours worked.

Required:

(a) Prepare a statement to show the minimum price the company should charge for the 500 machines.   (18 marks)

(b) What factors besides 'costs' would be taken into account in determining selling prices?   (7 marks)

(Total 25 marks)

14.4 General Engineers PLC is a manufacturing company making and selling engineering components and assemblies to the trade. Due to general depression in the engineering industry, the company is operating below capacity and the sales manager, with the view to utilising the spare capacity, has secured an enquiry from a customer. The estimating department has prepared the following schedule of material, labour and manufacturing resources required to meet the order, together with explanatory notes.

Schedule Prepared by the Estimating Department

(i) Required: 1500 units of Material A.
     Note: Material A is in stock at £4 per unit. This material is now obsolete and can be sold to a scrap merchant at £0.50 per unit.

(ii) Required: 800 units of Material B.

Note: Material B was purchased a few weeks ago at £6 per unit to complete another order and is in stock. The resale price of this material is £5 per unit, but any use of this material would require replacement at £6 per unit.

(iii) Required: 1600 kg of Material C.

Note: 1100 kg of Material C is in stock at £4 per kg. This material is obsolete, toxic and unsaleable and arrangements are going to be made to dispose this material at a cost of £200. However, Material C could be imported at an all-inclusive price of £4.50 per kg.

(iv) Required: 300 kg of Material D.

Note: Material D is in very short supply and 1400 kg are in stock at £2.50 per kg. This material is used in a popular engineering component that has the following details:

		Per Component (£)
Selling price		60
Material 5 kg at £2.50	12.50	
Other variable costs	22.50	35
Contribution		£25

(v) Required: 100 hours of machine labour. Rate £6 per hour.

Note: 300 hours of machine labour are presently unutilised.

(vi) Required: 400 hours of welding labour. Rate £8 per hour.

Note: The welding labour is presently fully utilised and any additional work would necessitate overtime working at time-and-a-half.

(vii) Required: 500 hours of assembly labour. Rate £4 per hour.

Note: The company has assembly labour in excess of present requirements. Plans are under way to lay off assembly labour at a cost of £900. However, this could be avoided if an order results from this enquiry.

(viii) Required: 400 hours of finishing labour. Rate £6.50 per hour.

Note: The company's finishing labour is in excess of present and foreseeable future requirements. The company has decided to make a part of the finishing labour redundant at a cost of £1000.

(ix) Required: Manufacturing variable overheads.

Note: The manufacturing variable overheads have been found to be closely related to labour-hours and a rate of £2.50 per labour-hour has been established to reflect this cost.

(x) Required: Gear-cutting machine – 25 hours.

Note: The company does not have a suitable gear-cutting machine to meet the requirements. A suitable machine could be hired at a cost of £10 per hour with a minimum hire charge of £350.

(xi) Required: Fixed overheads.

Note: It is the company's practice to charge 50% of the variable manufacturing overheads to recover the fixed costs of the company.

(xii) Required: Profit.

Note: The company's selling prices are determined to yield a profit of 20% of the selling price.

Required:

Prepare a quotation to show the relevant costs that should be attributed to this enquiry and append brief notes explaining the reasoning underlying the computation of the costs.   (20 marks)

Section V
Long-term Decision Making

15

Introduction to Capital Budgeting

Capital budgeting concerns the investment of resources in long-term projects. Investments made during the current year will provide benefits extending more than one year into the future. Investment opportunities usually exceed resources available, so it is necessary to investigate projects in depth and select the ones that, in the long run, will prove most beneficial to the business. Hence capital budgeting is also loosely known as 'Investment Appraisal' or 'Capital Project Evaluation', and is closely connected to the financial management of the business. The funds available for long-term projects and the cost to the business of those funds are the result of three important and interconnecting decisions, namely: What is to be the total gross investment in the business? What sources of capital are to provide the funds? How are those funds to be invested in fixed and current assets? Capital budgeting decides how available funds are to be committed, and this implies the appraisal and evaluation of capital expenditure projects.

A matter so important as capital budgeting should be the subject of a systematic approach: to seek out and generate projects for investment; to fit these proposals into the long-term objectives of the business; to budget the short-term supply of investment funds within the business and to co-ordinate it with those funds needed to finance projects; to evaluate projects according to a trustworthy criterion, which enables management to form a realistic opinion of their worth; to select worthwhile projects; to control the development of projects after the decision to invest; to audit the success of projects during operation and when terminated; and, to re-appraise projects and decide whether they are ripe for disposal.

Capital budgeting covers a range of investments from large-scale activities, such as the construction of a new factory or the development of additional products, to smaller investments, such as the installation of new machinery. The importance of capital budgeting is that immediate and long-term profit is the direct consequence of investment. Large sums of money are involved and will be committed for long periods into the future. Successful decisions concerning these investments will improve the wealth of shareholders in the long run, but if a mistake is made the company will have to live with that mistake or disinvest and suffer the losses inherent to the disposal of second-hand plant. A wrong decision can mean the development of products with little market appeal. Competitors can then bring the good ideas to the market, leaving the company at a disadvantage, which may take years to overcome. The evaluation and selection of projects is a complicated matter involving the balancing of many factors, quantitative and qualitative, and a decision should only be taken on the basis of careful analysis. The decision, once made, will set the pattern for the business, the operations, the earnings and the growth into the future and influence the long-term success or failure of the enterprise.

BASIC DATA REQUIRED FOR CAPITAL PROJECT EVALUATION

A reliable decision on such an important matter can only be made after the accumulation of sufficient relevant information, which, when sifted, will give a full picture of the scheme.

Capital Cost and the Time Profile of the Expenditure

It is important to be quite certain of the full amount of capital to be sunk into a project before the decision is made, since this avoids budgetary overspend during the installation stage and financial difficulty if all the funds required are not available, e.g. a well-versed computer salesman may quote the price for his machine, but this is not the only cost involved in computerising the records of a business. The system may need to be re-designed, software programs written, appropriate stationery printed, staff re-trained and air-conditioned premises constructed – amounting to considerable extra costs to set against the benefits to be derived from the scheme. The phasing of the expenditure is also significant because the project may not all be paid for at one point in time. Progress payments may be called for before the project is complete and in operation, and part of the price may be retained for a period to ensure that machinery etc. is properly installed. The use of idle funds awaiting completion of the project must also be planned. Some projects may even require the expenditure of funds at the end of the project, perhaps to make good damage or dilapidations under a lease agreement. Data as to how soon the project could commence, the length of the development period before cash inflow begins and the likely cost of the project if it is deferred for a year or for five years are useful at the decision stage.

Life and Scrap Value

It is important to know, though difficult to forecast, the time period during which a project may be operational. Obsolescence may shorten the period during which a machine or product makes a contribution to the profit of the business. The residual or scrap value of a machine, or the assets tied up in a project, is the amount expected to be received at the end of the economic life. If economic life itself is hard to forecast with accuracy, scrap value is an estimate of even greater uncertainty.

Net Cash Flow

If an investment commits funds for a period of years, it is important to ascertain the extent of the return to be expected from that investment over its full life. Financial accounting carves business activity into annual slices, which are reported in terms of profit and financial position at the end of each financial year. To evaluate say a five-year project, the net return over its whole economic life should be set against the capital cost. As was shown in Chapter 14, the cash flowing in to a project, net of cash flowing out from a project, is the best way to measure such income and avoids difficulties associated with drafting annual accounts, such as accruals, prepayments, stock valuation and depreciation. Depreciation is a non-cash cost that spreads the capital cost of a machine over the years of its useful economic life, according to an accounting policy, but if that cost is accounted for in project evaluation as the cash outflow at the beginning, depreciation merely charges it out again.

Accordingly, cash flow is usually computed by adding back to net profit, any depreciation or other non-cash costs that have been deducted in the profit computation.

Incidence of Income

Cash flow from a project is spread over a number of years, but the return received in successive years cannot be given equal weighting when the project is evaluated. Ask yourself the simple question – would you rather receive £10 000 now or £10 000 in a year's time? The choice is always for immediate payment, since delay introduces an element of risk or uncertainty that the payment a year hence may not be forthcoming, that cash received in a year's time will buy less because inflation will have raised prices by then, or that £10 000 received now can be invested to grow with interest to more than £10 000 after one year. The value now, or present value (PV), of £10 000 to be received in a year's time is not £10 000, but it is the amount that must be invested now to grow to £10 000 after twelve months. Assuming a rate of interest of 10% p.a. £9091 is the PV of £10 000 to be received after a year.

	·£
Principal	9 091
Interest at 10%	909
Accumulated sum	£10 000

If the £10 000 is to be received after two years the PV would be £8263.

	£
Principal	8 263
Interest at 10%: first year	826
Accumulated sum	9 089
Interest at 10%: second year	909
Accumulated sum (adjusted for rounding)	£10 000

The PV of an amount can be found by calculation, but it is easier to use an actuarial table, showing the PV of £1 at various rates for various periods, and to multiply the cash flow by the appropriate PV of £1 to calculate *discounted cash flow* (DCF).

$$\text{PV of £10 000 in one year at 10\%} = 10\,000 \times \frac{1}{1.1} = £9091$$

$$\text{PV of £10 000 in two years at 10\%} = 10\,000 \times \frac{1}{(1.1)^2} = £8263$$

The same calculation can be made for any discount rate or any number of years, e.g. 15% at:

$$\frac{1}{1.15} \quad \text{or} \quad \frac{1}{(1.15)^2} \quad \text{or} \quad \frac{1}{(1.15)^3} \quad \text{or} \quad \frac{1}{(1.15)^n}$$

or 25%:

$$\frac{1}{1.25} \quad \text{or} \quad \frac{1}{(1.25)^2} \quad \text{for two years} \quad \text{or} \quad \frac{1}{(1.25)^3} \quad \text{for three years} \quad \text{or} \quad \frac{1}{(1.25)^n} \text{for } n \text{ years}$$

Incidence is the term used to express the point in time when the impact of cash flow is felt by a project. In the light of discounted cash flow analysis, cash flow in the earlier years will be more significant for the final result – the PV of the stream of cash flows – than cash flow in later years. This phenomenon is sometimes referred to as 'the time value of money', and underpins the need to determine the timings of revenue from a project.

Example

Project A returns £20 000 immediately but Project B returns £10 000 at the end of each of the next two years. If the cost of capital is at 10% p.a. the cash flows of the two projects could be compared as follows:

| | Project A | | | Project B | | |
	Cash Flow	Discount Factor	PV	Cash Flow	Discount Factor	PV
	£		£	£		£
Now	20 000	1.0000	20 000	–	× 1.0000	–
End of year 1	–	–	–	10 000	× 0.9091	9 091
End of year 2	–	–	–	10 000	× 0.8265	8 265
Present value of income stream			£20 000			£17 356

The cash flow profile experienced by Project B is worth less than that of Project A in PV terms even though both projects show a gross return of £20 000.

Working Capital

A common mistake with capital project evaluation is to include only capital expenditure on the project, and to ignore the working capital invested in stocks and debtors without which the project would not be capable of operation. These assets are as important to the project as the fixed assets purchased for it. Working capital operates as a cycle if cash is used to buy stocks that are then built into finished goods, sold to debtors and turned back into cash. At any point in time there will be an amount of working capital invested in a project and it should thus be counted in the evaluation, not forgetting that working capital is disinvested at the end of the project as stocks are run down and debts are collected. Working capital is gradually increased as the project develops and stocks and debtors less trade credit received increases, until a normal level for the project is reached.

Ripple Effect

As with short-term decisions the effect of a new project on the profit made by the rest of the business must be identified and brought into the evaluation.

Cost of Capital to be Committed to a Project

It is usually impossible to link funds borrowed to individual investments, so some more general measure is required. Capital is recruited from many different sources – shareholders, ploughed-back profits, long-term lenders, trade creditors, bank overdraft etc. – and each source has a cost or rate of its own. It would be incorrect to select one source, to set the cost of capital to a company and to argue that all funds invested had cost, say, the rate charged for the most recent borrowing, or the most expensive borrowing, or the largest individual source. Accordingly, an average cost of capital from all sources of funds, weighted for the amount from each source is often used as the *hurdle rate*, or return on capital invested, which must be covered before a project is considered profitable. In a perfect market a business is held to continue recruiting fresh funds for investment up to the point at which the return on the next investment is less than the cost of capital. Thus the cost of capital is used as the discount factor when cash flows are discounted.

Risk

An estimate must be made of the risks involved in each planned investment. There is no scale by which this can be measured, but a careful consideration of the circumstances will reveal uncertainties and perils to be overcome. A high-risk project will demand a high return to compensate for the risk. Techniques have been derived to reduce the significance of uncertainty on a project.

Tax and Government Grants

Profitable projects must bear the burden of taxation, but to encourage investment the government eases that burden by giving certain investment grants or allowances for capital expenditure that can be set off against corporation tax. Often the tax likely to be paid and the timing of such payments has considerable influence on the cash flow of a project and is thus influential in deciding the viability of a project or the ranking of rival projects. Costs saved by a project increase profit, and that profit is liable to corporation tax. The tax will not normally be paid until the year after the profit has been made, so in terms of the incidence of the cash outflow, tax is usually one year in arrear of the profit from which it is derived.

Alternatives

It is rare for one project to be considered in isolation. Usually a list of projects is drawn up, each project competing for a share of scarce investment funds. The task of the accountant is to rank them in order of preference and find the best combination for the use of those funds. Sometimes projects are mutually exclusive and a choice must be made between alternatives. Clearly a dependable method of evaluation is needed in order to make comparisons of this type.

METHODS OF EVALUATION

Managers consider a wide range of potential projects for investment and a number of evaluation methods have been developed, which can be applied when best suited to the circumstances of the case. These methods have their strengths and weaknesses.

Necessity

Sometimes an investment must be made to comply with a change in the law or to ensure the survival of the business. In this case cost/benefit analysis is less important, since if the investment is not made the company may be forced to pay fines or even cease operations, e.g. the installation of fire doors, warning devices and fire escapes in a hotel may be necessary to meet the new fire regulations. However, the existence of the alternative 'not to invest' must not be forgotten in such circumstances, since all investment must show a sufficient return to compensate for the use of funds, and managers must consider whether it is worthwhile to continue to operate under new conditions, or whether it is preferable to disinvest and move capital to some other venture.

Pay Back Method

This is a well tried, widely used and simple method of evaluation, which computes the time taken by a project to pay back from its cash flow the amount of capital invested. The project that pays back soonest is the preferred investment. Projects that cannot repay within a certain time, say three years, are rejected, e.g. two projects, A and B, are under consideration:

	Project A	*Project B*
Life	5 years	9 years
Cost	£160 000	£150 000
Cash flow p.a.	£40 000	£30 000
Pay back period	160 ÷ 40	150 ÷ 30
	= 4 years	= 5 years

Therefore, Project A is preferred to Project B since the capital expenditure is returned in a shorter time.

This method suffers from two important disadvantages in that it treats cash flow in successive years with equal significance, and thus fails to take account of the time value of money, and it ignores all cash flow after the point at which pay back is reached. This crude and simplistic method cannot consider working capital in the computation. In the example above, management must decide whether it prefers A with a total cash flow of £200 000 over five years and the flexibility to reinvest at that point, or B, which earns £270 000 over nine years.

The pay back method fails to focus attention on this aspect of the problem since it does not consider the return over the full life of the rival projects. Pay back is still widely used in industry, often as a 'coarse screen' to reject weak projects from the range of opportunities available to a firm, and derive a short list for more detailed analysis. In a situation where technological change can dramatically reduce the economic life of projects, or where cash shortages in a business promote the need for cash flow in early years, the pay back method can still be a useful method of capital project evaluation, since it favours projects that cover their cost as quickly as possible. By the same token it may also reject sound long-term projects, because of the failure to consider the overall return on the capital invested.

Rate of Return Method

This method computes the rate of return on invested funds over the full life of a project and selects for investment the project with the higher rate of return, or those projects whose return is in excess of a minimum or hurdle rate. The result of the computation is expressed as a rate, which managers can understand and link to the cost of capital. This is suggested as a further advantage of this method. However, the multiplicity of rates can lead to confusion, and the equal treatment of all cash flows denies the principle of the time value of money and the incidence of income, since the rate calculated is just an average.

Reverting to the example above, and introducing a hurdle rate of 25 % p.a., rates can be computed as follows:

(i) Gross return:

$$\textit{Project A} \quad \text{£40 000 p.a. for five years} = \text{£200 000}$$

$$\frac{\text{Gross return}}{\text{Funds invested}} \times \frac{100}{1} = \frac{\text{£200 000}}{\text{£160 000}} \times \frac{100}{1} = 125\%$$

$$\textit{Project B} \quad \text{£30 000 p.a. for nine years} = \text{£270 000}$$

$$\frac{\text{£270 000}}{\text{£150 000}} \times \frac{100}{1} = 180\%$$

Project B is preferable.

(ii) Annual return:

$$\textit{Project A} \quad \frac{\text{Annual return}}{\text{Funds invested}} \times \frac{100}{1} = \frac{\text{£40 000}}{\text{£160 000}} \times \frac{100}{1} = 25\%$$

$$\textit{Project B} \quad = \frac{\text{£30 000}}{\text{£150 000}} \times \frac{100}{1} = 20\%$$

Now Project A is preferable, and Project B does not exceed the hurdle rate of 25 %. If working capital had been included with the funds invested, neither project would have been viable at a required rate of return of 25 %.

(iii) Annual return on average funds invested. If £160 000 is sunk in a project, part of the amount can be deemed to be repaid each year from cash flow, so that at the end of the project's life the whole has been disinvested. The average capital employed over the life of the project, assuming disinvestment at a steady rate, would be half the amount invested at the beginning of the project. A return expressed as a rate on this amount gives yet another solution:

$$\textit{Project A} \quad \frac{-\text{£160 000}}{2} = \text{£80 000 average investment}$$

$$\frac{\text{Annual return}}{\text{Funds invested}} \times \frac{100}{1} = \frac{\text{£40 000}}{\text{£80 000}} \times \frac{100}{1} = 50\%$$

$$\textit{Project B} \quad \frac{\text{£150 000}}{2} = \text{£75 000 average investment}$$

$$\frac{\text{Annual return}}{\text{Funds invested}} \times \frac{100}{1} = \frac{\text{£30 000}}{\text{£75 000}} \times \frac{100}{1} = 40\%$$

Project A is still preferable, but using this rate both projects are in excess of the hurdle rate and thus considered to be viable.

Clearly this method of project evaluation should not be used unless one rate is selected and used consistently and unless all managers fully understand the results of the computation.

Discounted Cash Flow (DCF)

This method bases the decision on cash flowing in and out from a project, over its full life, and reflects the incidence of those flows by discounting them to their present value. Thus flows at different times can reflect the impact of tax payments, allowances and government grants. After discounting, these flows can be readily compared because they are all expressed in a common denominator – present value. The computation can be adjusted to account for risk and uncertainty. Perhaps the most difficult feature of DCF is the selection of the discount rate to be applied, but, as shown above, the rate should reflect the cost of capital, yet could be raised or lowered according to the management's perception of the riskiness of the project under review. DCF can be applied in various ways, but there are two major variants of this method:

(i) *Net Present Value* (NPV) discounts inflows and outflows to their present value (PV) at the appropriate cost of capital and sets the PV of cash inflow against the PV of cash outflow to calculate NPV. If a project has a positive NPV it is considered to be viable, because the PV of the inflow exceeds the PV of the outflow. If projects are to be ranked or the decision is to select one or another, the project with the greatest NPV would be chosen.

Example

Two mutually exclusive projects, C and D, are to be evaluated. They both have three-year lives, capital costs of £150 000 payable immediately, and total cash inflows of £200 000, but the incidence of these cash flows shows a very different profile for C and D. The projects would be discounted at the cost of capital, say 10%, but for this example they will be discounted at 15% and 20% as well in order to investigate the effect on the computation of increasing the discount rate.

	Discount Factors				Project C				Project D		
	PV of	PV of	PV of	Net Cash	PV	PV	PV	Net Cash	PV	PV	PV
	£1 at	£1 at	£1 at	Flow	10%	15%	20%	Flow	10%	15%	20%
Year	10%	15%	20%	£	£	£	£	£	£	£	£
1	0.9091	0.8696	0.8333	100 000	90 910	86 960	83 330	25 000	22 720	21 740	20 832
2	0.8263	0.7561	0.6944	75 000	61 980	56 710	52 080	75 000	61 980	56 710	52 080
3	0.7513	0.6575	0.5787	25 000	18 780	16 440	14 470	100 000	75 130	65 750	57 870
				200 000				200 000			
PV of inflow					171 650	160 110	149 880		159 830	144 200	130 762
PV of outflow (spent now)					150 000	150 000	150 000		150 000	150 000	150 000
NPV					21 670	10 110	(120)		9 830*	(5 800)*	(19 238)

At a cost of capital of 10% both projects have a positive NPV and are therefore viable. If a choice must be made between C and D, Project C would be chosen because it has the greater NPV. The cash flow profile of C concentrates inflow in the early years, which suffers less by discounting than D, whose heavier flow is in later years of the economic life.

If the cost of capital is considered to be 15%, Project C is still a viable project, but D now shows a negative NPV and will not be undertaken. At a cost of capital of 20% neither C nor D show a positive NPV.

Note how the NPV is reduced as the rate of discount is increased, and that at a discount factor somewhere between 10% and 15% D ceases to be positive and becomes negative, and that at a discount factor somewhere between 15% and 20% C ceases to be viable. The NPV of the projects at different rates of discount can be plotted on a graph as follows:

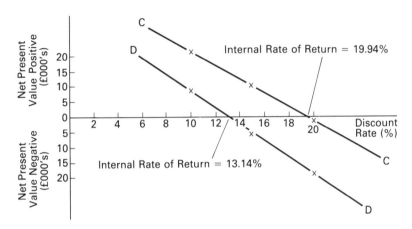

(ii) *Internal Rate of Return* (IRR). This method uses discounting to determine the rate which, if applied to inflows and outflows, will bring them to equality. In the example above the net cash flows (which are the result of deducting running costs flowing out from revenue flowing in) were discounted at 10%, 15% and 20%. Project D showed a positive NPV at 10% but was negative at 15%. This means that at a rate of discount somewhere between 10% and 15%, the net cash flows from the three years of working life will be reduced to a PV £150 000, equalling the PV of immediate cash outflow to set up the project. This rate is called the *internal rate of return*, and can be calculated by extrapolation. The formula is:

$$\text{Bottom of class} + \left[\left(\frac{\text{Position in class}}{\text{Range of class}}\right) \times \left(\frac{\text{Class interval}}{1}\right)\right]$$

Project D:

$$10\% + \left(\frac{9830}{9850 + 5800} \times \frac{5\%}{1}\right) = 13.14\%$$

Thus if the cash inflows of Project D above are discounted at 13.14% their PV will be £150 000, just equal to the PV of the cash outflow.

The IRR for Project C above can be calculated as:

$$15\% + \left(\frac{10110}{10110 + 120} \times \frac{5\%}{1}\right) = 19.94\%$$

This method of evaluation is sometimes referred to as the *trial and error yield method*, since it is trial and error that locates the range in which the IRR is set. The IRR implies that

Project D gives an overall return of 13.1% and Project C a return of 19.9%. Thus C would be preferred to D if the projects are mutually exclusive, and both would be viable if the business used a hurdle rate of 12% return required from investment projects.

Example

The examples above illustrate the principles of DCF, but in fact the computation is much more complicated if taxation and working capital are included. Project E has a four-year life with projected net profits of £17 000 each year after charging depreciation of £7000 p.a. to write off the capital cost of £28 000, which is payable as £20 000 at once and £8000 during year one. It is expected that the machinery will be sold for its residual value of £2000 at the end of year four. Corporation tax is payable at 40% and the depreciation charge equals the taxation writing down allowances of 25% p.a. Corporation tax is paid nine months after the end of the year in which the profit is made. The residual value of £2000 is received on an asset, which is fully written down for tax purposes, and will itself bear tax at 40% for year four, thus increasing the tax paid in year five by £800. Stock of £6000 will be required throughout the project and debtors of a further £8000 will be financed in year one. Note that a four-year project requires a five-year computation for tax payments and working capital realisations in year five.

Year	Discount Factor 10%	Capital Expenditure £	Working Capital £	Net Profit £	Depreciation £	Tax £	Net Cash Flow	Discounted Cash Flow
0	–	(20 000)	(6 000)	–	–	–	(26 000)	(26 000)
1	0.9091	(8 000)	(8 000)	17 000	7000	–	8 000	7 273
2	0.8264	–	–	17 000	7000	(6800)	17 200	14 214
3	0.7513	–	–	17 000	7000	(6800)	17 200	12 922
4	0.6830	2 000	–	17 000	7000	(6800)	19 200	13 114
5	0.6209	–	14 000	–	–	(7600)	6 400	3 974

NPV £25 497 positive

Outflows are in brackets.

The project shows a handsome surplus when the PV of inflows is set against the PV of outflows.

Net profit and depreciation are added together to calculate cash flow. They have been shown in separate columns above, but a single column headed 'Cash Inflows', with £24 000 each year could be used instead.

QUALITATIVE FACTORS AFFECTING THE EVALUATION OF PROJECTS

If a project shows only a small NPV after discounting, the effect of non-quantifiable factors not brought into the computation may be significant and may induce managers to ignore a purely figure-oriented solution to the decision. A project to replace existing plant with more modern machinery may provide extra capacity if the new machines can complete the present task in say 80% of their working week, or if they can undertake extra or more sophisticated operations. A project to replace three machines by one larger machine will increase the risk, because if the single machine breaks down all production will cease, whereas under the present system even if two machines are out of commission there will at least be some production from the third, perhaps to provide parts for other departments in the business and to avoid disruption to production. Replacement or mechanisation decisions can cause redundancy and consequent poor labour relations unless retraining can maintain employment prospects within the company.

The short-term decision rules concerning relevant costs apply to long-term decisions. Sunk costs and apportionments of fixed overheads should be ignored, whilst costs saved or tax payments reduced by capital allowances act as cash inflows.

NPV versus IRR

These two methods use discounting to evaluate capital projects and are often used in conjunction by managers – IRR being calculated to check the findings of the NPV analysis. Unfortunately under certain conditions these two methods can give conflicting solutions to a decision problem. The two methods can be expressed in formula terms as:

$$NPV$$

$$\sum_{t=1}^{N} \frac{Ft}{(1+K)^t} - I$$

$$IRR$$

$$\sum_{t=1}^{N} \frac{Ft}{(1+r)^t} - I = 0$$

Solve the equation for r

The symbols mean:

F	Annual cash flows	K	Cost of capital or other discount rate
Ft	Cash flow over life of project		
I	Initial cost	$t=1$	Take one year at a time up to N
		$\sum\limits^{N}$	
N	Project life		Sigma N, i.e. find the aggregate of N profit periods

The main reasons for conflict between the solutions derived from NPV and IRR is that many projects are not strictly comparable and their differences are not treated in the same way by the two methods. If the capital cost of the two projects is different the IRR yielded by the smaller project may be high, but because of its size the NPV may be small, e.g. Project E invests £100 now to receive £150 in a year's time. This project has an IRR of 50%, but, discounted at a cost of capital of 10% (£150 × 0.9091 – £100), the NPV is £36. Project F, however, invests £1000 now to receive £1250 in a year's time. This project has an IRR of 25% and a NPV, discounted at 10% (£1250 × 0.9091 – £1000), of £136. Project E is preferable under an IRR evaluation, but Project F would be chosen under an NPV evaluation because of its size. Clearly these projects should not be compared, because of the differences in their capital cost. The proper course in this event is to compare one investment plan for the use of £1000 with another, so that Project F would be compared with Project E plus other projects to use the remaining £900 for a year.

Another reason for conflicting answers derived from the NPV and IRR methods is that one project may have a longer life than another and its cash flow in later years will suffer from high rates of discount and reduce the NPV of the project. The proper course in this situation is to work to the extent of the longer period, e.g. to compare Project G whose economic life is ten years to Project H with a life of five years is unfair, so G should be compared to H *plus* some other project to use the funds from Project H in the last five years of the ten-year cycle.

Example

Two projects, I and J, require funds of £200 000 each if they are to proceed, but investment funds are limited so that only £200 000 are available. Thus a choice must be made between

I and J. Project I will return cash flow of £240 000 after one year, but Project J returns £362 122 in four years' time. Cost of capital is 10%.

	Project I	Project J
Cash outflow	£200 000	£200 000
Cash inflow	£240 000 in one year	£362 122 after four years
NPV	£240 000 × 0.9091 − £200 000	£362 122 × 0.6830 − £200 000
J is preferable	= £18 184	= £47 329
IRR	£24 000 × 0.8333 = £200 000	£362 122 × 0.5523 = £200 000
I is preferable	= 20%	= 16%

Note   £0.6830 is PV of £1 to be received in four years' time at 10%
£0.5523 is PV of £1 to be received in four years' time at 16%
£0.8333 is PV of £1 to be received in one years' time at 20%

The projects have different lives. If they are to be compared, Project J must be compared with the amount to which £200 000 invested in I will grow by the end of the fourth year. Project I provides £240 000 at the end of year one, and the solution to the problem depends on the rate at which these funds can be reinvested during years two, three and four. This is the *reinvestment rate*.

Project I has an IRR in excess of that of Project J for only one year. It would be wrong to assume that the funds flowing from Project I could be invested at 20% (the IRR) for a further three years just because Project I earns this rate during year one. The IRR of Project I has no connection with the market return on capital invested, since it is merely the return earned on one project. A safer assumption would be that the £200 000 from Project I could be reinvested at the cost of capital (10%) and that those funds would accumulate to:

$$£240 000 + 10\% = £284 000 + 10\% = £312 400 + 10\% = £343 640$$

by the end of year four, and hence Project J is preferable.

Comparison of projects can be made in terms of what they accumulate to at the end of their life, which is known as *terminal value*. It would appear that the logic behind the IRR method is flawed, as to assume that all flows from a project can be reinvested at the IRR for that project confuses the market rate for funds with the return from a single project. If the cost of capital is 12%, this should be the rate at which funds can be borrowed or invested in the market. Cash flows derived from a project with an IRR of, say, 18% cannot be reinvested at 18%, but at the market rate of 12%. For this reason NPV is held to be a more reliable method for capital project evaluation than IRR.

Two investments with different cash flow profiles may also show conflicting solutions when appraised by the NPV and IRR methods, e.g. Projects K and L are mutually exclusive and they both require an investment of £70 848 over a four-year life. The cash flow profile for these projects is however quite different.

Project K

Year	Cash Flow	Discount Factor 10%	PV	Discount Factor 25%	PV
0	(70 848)	–	(70 848)	–	(70 848)
1	30 000	0.9091	27 273	0.8000	24 000
2	30 000	0.8264	24 792	0.6400	19 200
3	30 000	0.7513	22 539	0.5120	15 360
4	30 000	0.6830	20 490	0.4096	12 288
NPV			£24 246		Nil

IRR is 25%

Project L

Year	Cash Flow	Discount Factor 10%	PV	Discount Factor 22%	PV
0	(70 848)	–	(70 848)	–	(70 848)
1	–	0.9091	–	0.8197	–
2	15 000	0.8264	12 396	0.6719	10 079
3	30 000	0.7513	22 539	0.5507	16 521
4	98 025	0.6830	66 951	0.4514	44 248
NPV			£31 038		Nil

IRR is 22%

Project K has a regular cash flow throughout its life, whereas Project L has greater cash flows later in its economic life. At higher rates of discount these flows are significantly reduced, thus causing L to have a lower IRR than K. Project K is preferable when an IRR evaluation is undertaken. Project L is preferable when an NPV evaluation is undertaken.

These projects are mutually exclusive, so which one is to be selected for investment? The answer to this problem depends on the investment opportunities that are available for the difference in funds flowing from the projects. Incremental analysis will identify the difference between K and L. Project L has the greater NPV, so the cash flow of K is subtracted from L.

Year	Cash Flow K £	Cash Flow L £	L − K £	Discount Factor 16%	PV of Differential Flows £	Discount Factor 17%	PV of Differential Flows £
0	(70 848)	(70 848)	Nil	–	–	–	–
1	30 000	–	− 30 000	0.8621	− 25 863	0.8547	− 25 641
2	30 000	15 000	− 15 000	0.7432	− 11 148	0.7305	− 10 958
3	30 000	30 000	Nil	0.6407	–	0.6243	–
4	30 000	98 025	+ 68 025	0.5523	+ 37 570	0.5336	+ 36 298
			£23 025	NPV	£559	NPV	− £301

The IRR of the differential cash flow is 16.6%.

Project L has a NPV of £6792 in excess of Project K and provides a gross cash flow of £23 025 more than K. Project K is only preferable to L if it can be combined with another project to earn more than 16.6% on these differential funds. The decision between projects K and L depends on the rate at which the differential cash flows can be invested – the reinvestment rate.

Further examples of the application of DCF techniques are as follows:

Example

You are acting as financial consultant to a large public company in the United Kingdom, which is organised as three autonomous divisions, each making its own investment decisions.

The Exeter and West Division is at present considering two independent investment projects and is uncertain, on the basis of analysis to date, as to how to proceed. Project M is a normal investment in machinery to increase production, but because of marketing difficulties it will pay back more heavily towards the end of its four-year life. Project N is to purchase the lease of an old warehouse, which has three years to run. Whilst considerable profit can be made during those three years by sub-leasing the building as working areas for newly established small businesses, a considerable bill for dilapidations will be payable at the end of the lease. Both projects are considered to be risky, so the local managerial staff have discounted them at 25% and 20% to give the following results:

	M	N
Cash flows (£000's)		
Year 0	(500)	(900)
Year 1	100	1269
Year 2	200	864
Year 3	200	(1305)
Year 4	250	Nil
NPV at 25%	(87.2)	Nil
NPV at 20%	(41.5)	1.095

The cost of capital for this division is 15%.

Required:

(a) Evaluate the two projects by NPV and IRR methods, using hurdle rates of 15% and 20%.

(b) Advise local management, and explain the NPV and IRR methods to them, so far as their application to independent projects is concerned.

Solution for the Exeter and West Division

		Project M						Project N				
Year	Flow	15%	PV	20%	PV	Flow	15%	PV	20%	PV	25%	PV
0	(500)		(500)		(500)	(900)	–	(900)	–	(900)	–	(900)
1	100	0.870	87.0	0.833	83.4	1269	0.870	1104.03	0.833	1057.080	0.800	1015.2
2	200	0.756	151.2	0.694	138.8	864	0.756	653.18	0.694	599.620	0.640	552.9
3	200	0.658	131.6	0.579	115.8	(1305)	0.658	(858.69)	0.579	(755.595)	0.512	(668.16)
4	250	0.572	43.0	0.482	120.5	–	0.572	–	0.482	–	0.410	–
NPV			12.8		(41.5)	NPV		(1.48)		1.095		Nil

Using the IRR method:

$$\text{M}\quad 15\% + \left(\frac{12.8}{12.8 + 41.5} \times 5\% \right) = 16.18\%, \text{ say } 16\%$$

$$\text{N}\quad 15\% + \left(\frac{1.48}{1.48 + 1.095} \times 5\% \right) = 17.87\%, \text{ say } 18\% \text{ and } 25\%$$

Advice

M   Acceptable at 15% cost of capital by NPV and IRR.
     Rejected at 20% cost of capital by NPV and IRR.

N   Is a special case, with an uncommon cash flow profile. Rejected by NPV at 15%, positive at 20%, and negative at 25%. The project has an IRR of 18% and 25%.

The cash flow profile with large outflows at beginning and end of its life causes N to have two IRRs. The project only appears positive at a cost of capital between 18% and 25%. Therefore, take qualitative factors into account – marginal case – risky – reject.

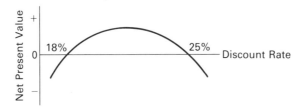

Example

The Wyvern Division is considering two mutually exclusive projects, with risk characteristics identical to the other assets employed in the division. The division has a cost of capital of 8 %, but these two projects are the only schemes likely to be available over the next five years which give a positive return. Local management has appraised the projects as follows:

Expected cash flows £000's	O	P
Year 0	(100)	(100)
Year 1	16	110
Year 2	44	4
Year 3	46	6
Year 4	42	2
Year 5	2	2
IRR	16.05%	19.7%
NPV at 8% £000's	£21 280	£12 884

There is concern that a correct decision should be made. At a meeting with the local managers, the factory manager urges acceptance of O since it has the highest NPV when the post-tax cash flows are discounted at the cost of capital, but the managing director supports P because it has the higher IRR, 'A yield of nearly 20 % on an investment of £100 000 must be superior to a return of 16 % on a similar outlay when both projects have equal lives', is his comment. The marketing manager, a business studies graduate who once read a book on this subject, argues that P should be chosen as its pay back period is shorter and the early cash flows can be reinvested elsewhere to earn a further return.

Required:

Explain the inconsistency in ranking these mutually exclusive projects, and suggest how the problem can be resolved.

Solution for the Wyvern Division

Projects O and P have the same initial investment but a different cash flow profile. P pays back in year 1, whereas O has flows spread over years 2, 3 and 4. With a low rate of discount (8 %) these late flows would not be heavily penalised, so O would have an advantage over P, apart from the fact that they are greater in total (150 to 124). P has a higher IRR because its early inflows need a higher rate of discount to reduce them to parity with the PV of cash outflows. P has paid back a significant amount of the capital sum by the end of year one and after that its apparently low flows give a high return on the outstanding investment.

The inconsistency can be resolved by appraising the incremental project made up of cash flow differences between the two projects.

Year	O	P	O − P	8%		15%	
0	(100)	(100)	Nil				
1	16	110	(94)	0.926	(87.044)	0.870	(81.780)
2	44	4	40	0.857	34.280	0.756	30.240
3	46	6	40	0.794	31.760	0.658	26.320
4	42	2	40	0.735	29.400	0.572	22.880
	2	3	Nil				
					£8.396		£(2.340)

The IRR or the differential cash flow is:

$$\text{IRR} \quad 8\% + \left(\frac{8.396}{8.396 + 2.340} \times 7\% \right) = 13.5\%$$

The incremental flows are positive at a cost of capital of 8%, with an IRR of 13.5%, therefore Project O should be selected. Therefore P would only be better than O if it could be combined with another project, Q, which would give a return in excess of 13.5% on the incremental funds. This analysis focuses attention on the reinvestment rate.

Executive comments: agree with factory manager; NPV selects best project based on overall return to maximise cash flow.

Managing Director: Yes, 20% is better than 16% on the same investment, but O and P only have the same investment in year 1. After that the investment in P becomes much lower and the rate of return thereon higher. In these circumstances O, which has a lower but acceptable rate of return on a large investment, is preferable, unless the surplus funds flowing from P in year 1 can be reinvested at a rate in excess of 13.5% – the *differential return*. If this is not so, as the cost of capital rate of 8% implies, then O should be selected. This argument also answers the comment of the marketing director.

Example

The Mercian Division is considering a suggestion to make and sell a single model of calculator/computer for household use. The plant required for this project could be purchased for £240000 and would attract 25% capital allowances for four years. The divisional accountant has analysed the project as follows:

Year	1	2	3	4
Sales (£000's)	400	600	800	600
Costs (£000's)				
Materials:				
Opening stock	40	80	80	60
Plus purchases	200	240	300	180
	240	320	380	240
Less closing stock	80	80	60	–
Cost of material used	160	240	320	240
Labour	80	120	120	80
Production expenses	80	90	92	100
Depreciation	40	40	40	40
Group administration charge	54	76	74	74
Interest	22	22	22	22
	436	588	668	556
Net profit	(36)	12	132	44
Corporation tax at 50%	(18)	6	66	22
Profit after tax	(18)	6	66	22

The product development manager provides the following additional information:

(i) The plant used for this product is highly specialised and is unlikely to have any residual value after meeting dismantling costs at the end of its four-year working life. Depreciation is based on a six-year life using the straight line method.

(ii) The opening stock will be purchased before the project starts.

(iii) Production expenses include a proportion of fixed factory overheads charged out as 25% of labour costs. The remaining production expenses are all incremental cash costs.

(iv) Adoption of this proposal will make existing machinery redundant, since the new plant can do the work of the old machinery in otherwise idle time at a cost saving of £12 000 p.a. The old machinery which is completely written down for tax purposes has a book value of £60 000 but could be sold at once for only £20 000, which would be subject to tax. If the proposal is not adopted, the old machinery would be sold in four years' time for £8000. These cost savings are ignored in the above analysis except that the disposal proceeds have been deducted from the envisaged external incremental borrowings and are reflected in a reduced interest charge.

(v) The board requires a return of 14% on capital projects to equal the cost of capital for the division. They work to three decimal places.

The marketing director has expressed the following reservations to the scheme on the grounds that the calculation excludes:

(i) An advertising campaign to launch the product, costing an estimated £40 000 before production commences, with supplementary expenditure of £10 000 in the first three years of the project.

(ii) The new product will compete with a typewriter attachment already marketed by the division and will force a revision of budgeted sales.

	Original Forecast	Revised Forecast
Year 1	5000 × £160	5000 × £150
Year 2	4000 × £120	3000 × £100
Year 3	2000 × £80	–
Year 4	–	–

Production costs of the typewriter attachment are budgeted as:

	Year 1	Year 2	Year 3
Variable costs	£120	£90	£60
Fixed costs: apportionment of factory	£20	£20	£20
overheads	£140	£110	£80

Required:

Appraise the project (specifying your assumptions) and discuss major factors that should be given further consideration. Assume corporation tax will be at 40% for the next five years.

Solution for the Mercian Division

Ripple Effect – Reduction in Cash Flow of Typewriter Attachment

Original forecast	Year 1	Year 2	Year 3
Selling price	160	120	80
Variable cost	120	90	60
Contribution per unit	40	30	20
Volume	5 000	4 000	2 000
Cash contribution	£200 000	£120 000	£40 000
Revised forecast:			
Contribution	30	10	–
Volume	5 000	3 000	–
	£150 000	£30 000	
Reduction	£50 000	£90 000	£40 000

Incremental Profit (£000's)

	Year 1	Year 2	Year 3	Year 4
Sales	400	600	800	600
Cost savings	12	12	12	12
	412	612	812	612
Purchases	200	240	300	180
Labour	80	120	120	80
Production expenses	60	60	62	80
Advertising	10	10	10	–
Reduction in cash flow	50	90	40	–
	400	520	532	340
Net incremental cash flow	12	92	280	272
Adjustment to convert cash flow to profit:				
difference between material purchased and used	40	–	(20)	(60)
Incremental profit	52	92	260	212
Corporation tax at 40%	20.8	36.8	104	84.8
Payable in year	2	3	4	5

Cash Flows (£000's)

Years	0	1	2	3	4	5
Cost of machinery	240	–	–	–	–	–
Tax allowance (25% × 40%)		(24)	(24)	(24)	(24)	–
Old machine	(20)				8	
Tax balancing charge		8	–	–	–	(3.2)
Initial advertising	40					
Stock build up	40					
Operating flows		(12)	(92)	(280)	(272)	–
Corporation tax			20.8	36.8	104	84.8
	300	(28)	(95.2)	(267.2)	(184)	81.6
PV factor	1.0	0.877	0.796	0.675	0.592	0.519
PV	300	(24.556)	(73.209)	(180.36)	(108.928)	42.35

NPV is £44 703, therefore project is viable.

THE CONTROL AND AUDIT OF CAPITAL PROJECTS

Once a decision has been made to invest a large sum of money, it is essential to monitor the development of the project and to check on its commercial success. A systematic approach to post audit will ensure that all the appropriate questions are asked and that all the answers are considered with care. The decision to invest is made on the basis of estimates, and it is often at the development stage that the extent of this uncertainty is revealed when actual costs are incurred. Actual expenditure may exceed the amount authorised, and it is imperative that such circumstances must be reported back to the decision makers so that they can re-appraise the decision in the light of fresh evidence, and decide whether to abort the project, or how to provide the extra funds. The twin of cost overrun is delay in completion of a project. This too must be reported back to the decision team since it will affect the cash, production and sales budgets. Delay in completion of part of a project can ruin a carefully co-ordinated plan, and such delay must be recognised at an early stage to allow remedial action to be effective, e.g. an advertising campaign to launch a new product will lose its impact on the market if production delays at the factory prevent goods arriving in the shops.

Data for reports on the development of large schemes might include:

1. Budgeted cost and the cost to date.
2. Over/under-expenditure to date – estimate of extra finance required.
3. Estimated cost to completion – estimated total over/under expenditure on budget.
4. Start date and scheduled completion date.
5. Estimated completion date.
6. Details of penalty clauses, and effect of delay on other parts of the business.
7. Percentage complete in terms of time and cost.
8. Comment on the quality of the work.
9. Analysis of factors causing delay or increasing the cost.
10. Suggested remedial action.

It is also important to follow up capital projects once they are operational, to check on their success and test the validity of the estimates made and criteria used when the project was evaluated. An understanding of past mistakes increases the 'know-how' and experience of the decision-making team and improves their performance in the future.

Illustrated below is the present value table to be used with the exercises.

	PRESENT VALUE OF £1											
						Rate						
Year	10%	11%	12%	13%	14%	15%	16%	17%	18%	19%	20%	25%
1	0.909	0.901	0.893	0.885	0.877	0.870	0.862	0.855	0.847	0.840	0.833	0.800
2	0.826	0.812	0.797	0.783	0.770	0.756	0.743	0.731	0.718	0.706	0.694	0.640
3	0.751	0.731	0.712	0.693	0.675	0.658	0.641	0.624	0.609	0.593	0.579	0.512
4	0.683	0.659	0.636	0.613	0.592	0.572	0.552	0.534	0.516	0.499	0.482	0.410
5	0.621	0.594	0.567	0.543	0.519	0.497	0.476	0.456	0.437	0.419	0.402	0.328
6	0.565	0.535	0.507	0.480	0.456	0.432	0.410	0.390	0.370	0.352	0.335	0.262

SEMINAR EXERCISES

15.1 Glapton Glassworks Limited are investigating the suggestion that they should manufacture an artistic, moulded, glass statuette for the luxury end of the tourist trade. They have spent £25 660 on a market survey which has forecast a life of four years for the product before cheaper competitors make it unsaleable. The survey states that if price is set at £130 for each unit, the best estimate of demand is 4000 units in Year 1, 6000 each in Years 2 and 3, and then falling to 2000 in Year 4. Pre-launch advertisements will cost £20 000.

Management has undertaken a costing exercise, which shows a profit per unit as follows:

	£	£
Selling price		130.00
Less:		
Costs:		
Materials	30	
Labour (10 hours at £7)	70	
Variable production		
overheads	10	
Direct fixed costs	12.51	
Head office costs	5	
		127.51
Profit per product		£2.49

Information revealed during the costing exercise is as follows:

1. Factory space is worked to full capacity at present, so extra premises would need to be rented at £14 600 p.a. on a short lease to house the production process.
2. Artwork on the master moulds for the statuette would cost £20 000. Production moulds made from the master would cost £5000 per set, and would last for 5000 units of production. This cost can be written off for tax purposes as a revenue expense.
3. Machinery used in the production process could be transferred from a redundant process in the main factory. This machinery cost £135 000 and is three years into an expected useful life of nine years. It would cost £6220 to refurbish this machinery.
4. The manager of the redundant process is paid a salary of £10 000 p.a. He is about to be dismissed with a compensation payment of £7000, but could be employed to organise production of the new product.
5. Head office fixed costs are allocated to production by Glapton Glassworks Limited at a rate of 50p per hour.
6. The machinery to be transferred was recently the subject of an offer from another glassworks who wished to purchase it for £80 000. This machinery is expected to be valueless in four years' time and is written down to nil for tax purposes.

Direct fixed costs:	£
Rent (4 years at £14 600)	58 400
Depreciation of moulds	35 000
Depreciation of plant (£135 000 ÷ 9) × 4	60 000
Refurbishing machines	6 220
Supervision (Manager: 4 years × £10 000)	40 000
Feasibility study	25 660
	£225 280

£225 280 ÷ 18 000 = £12.51

The management approach you for advice as to whether they should proceed with this project. They have doubts as to the reliability of their estimates concerning the life of the project and the cost of capital, which they suggest is 15%.

Required:

(a) List the points of principle that affect this decision and advise management as to whether to proceed with the project. (15 marks)

(b) Comment on the sensitivity of the project to fluctuations in the estimates of the cost of capital, and (4 marks)

(c) warn management as to the limitations of your calculations, and suggest other factors that might clarify this decision. (6 marks)

Assume corporation tax at 40%. All cash flows arise at the end of each year.

(Total 25 marks)

15.2 The following passage is an extract from the minutes of a management meeting held recently at Quandary Limited, a middle-sized manufacturing company in Nottingham. The managing director was in the chair, and the meeting was attended by directors responsible for marketing, production and finance and the company secretary.

Managing Director: This meeting has been called to discuss the alternatives open to us for the investment of a sum of £40 000, which appears as a surplus on the cash budget. Provision has been made for dividend, taxation and the replacement of plant, but there still remains a sum of £40 000, which will otherwise lie idle in our bank account from January next unless we can put it to work.

Finance Director: The sum is only available for a two-year period, since part of our long-term strategy is to extend the factory in two years' time, and we shall need all the surplus funds at our disposal at that time to help to finance this investment. Whatever project we choose must pay for itself in two years.

Production Director: I propose that the whole £40 000 is spent on the provision of a new stacking system in the factory. We are very short of space at the moment, and improved stacking would reduce costs by £30 000 each year, as well as provide us with some much needed elbow room.

Company Secretary: The need for this improved equipment will be over in two years' time when the factory extension will give you all the extra space you need. Have you thought of what you could do with the stacking equipment then? It is designed to customers' individual specifications and, as such, would be worthless on the second-hand market.

Marketing Director: I think my suggestion is a better one. In my view we should spend £4000 to purchase the trademark under which we now market one of our products. This is the only trademark we use that is not owned by us, and we would save royalties of £3200 p.a. which we now pay for its use. We would need to spend a further £300 on entertainment expenses to pursuade the owner to sell and this would not be tax allowable.

Production Director: That does not sound a very good suggestion, since it does not guarantee an income. What if demand falls and there is no need to use the trademark? Why pay in advance for royalties one may never need to pay?

Marketing Director: I disagree. What if your stacking machinery should break down? Just think of the bottleneck in the factory.

Production Director: That is not likely to happen and even if it did, we could go back to our present system until repairs were carried out.

Managing Director: Now gentlemen, enough of this bickering, I want to determine which of your ideas will maximise our return on capital employed.

Finance Director: We have an after tax target rate of return of 10% for all our projects, as this is our cost of capital, but it does not follow that we can invest funds at that rate (net of tax) in the short-term money market. I will compare these projects, but it seems to me that the answer given will depend on the criterion used for evaluation.

Required:

Analyse and comment on the significant features of this conversation with a view to advising the Finance Director.

Assume corporation tax at 40%. DCF tables are to three decimal places and there is a 25% writing down allowance on both projects. Any unused allowances are set off against profits in Year 2. (25 marks)

15.3 The Hendon Cot Company Limited is a badly organised, old-fashioned business, which finds difficulty in continuing to operate under current conditions. The company's only product is a wooden cot selling at £20. A market survey taken recently showed that the market potential of this product was in decline. The survey suggested that sales would be 8000 units in 19–3, 5000 in 19–4 and 19–5 and only 4000 in 19–6. A further decline to 1500 in 19–7 was forecast, after which no further sales would be practicable.

The prime cost of each cot is £12–£4 for materials and £8 for labour. Material prices are expected to remain stable over the next five years, but labour rates will rise by 12.5% in 19–4 and a further 15% in 19–7. The fixed overhead expenses of the business are £25 000. Machinery with a current book value of £80 000 is used to make the product, and the annual depreciation thereon of £8000 is included in the fixed overhead expenses. The current market value of this machinery is £40 000 and it is expected to be worth £10 000 in three years' time so far as resale is concerned and valueless at the end of 19–7.

The factory buildings are held under a lease that has ten years to run. The lease could be sold at once for £30 000, but since it is near the end of the term, this value is expected to decline at the rate of £2000 p.a. for the next three years, and £4000 p.a. thereafter.

If the factory is closed down immediately, cost incurred as a result of closure would be £7000. Closure in three years' time is forecast as costing £9000 and in five years' time it is expected to cost £11 000.

The cost of capital in the company is considered to be 10%. The board have discussed the situation at some length but, as yet, have reached no decision.

Required:

(a) Compute a statement for the board to show the optimum date for closure of the factory.
(b) Discuss other factors that could be significant in this decision.

Ignore taxation.   (25 marks)

REVIEW QUESTIONS

15.1 The management committee of Alternative Ventures Limited have recently completed their medium-term planning operation. The plan indicates that an immediate cash surplus of £200 000 will be available for investment over the next four years, but that it is earmarked for a specific purpose after that date. News of this surplus has spread rapidly throughout the organisation and various executives have made suggestions as to its best method of employment during the next four-year period. Three of these schemes have been passed by the management committee as being feasible.

Scheme 1

The finance director has suggested that the funds should be used to buy the company's own debentures on the market. As the coupon rate on these stocks is 10%, he argues that this would reduce the interest burden borne by the company each year. At the end of the four-year period the debentures could be re-issued to raise the £200 000 required.

Scheme 2

The sales manager of a subsidiary company suggests that the funds should be used to improve facilities in 20 shops operated by his company. He argues that with better shop fronts, lighting, and display cabinets, sales will increase. A survey of the situation suggests an increase in net cash flow after tax of £30 000, £40 000, £60 000 and £35 000 for the next four years respectively. Only £150 000 will be required at once; a further £50 000 will be needed after nine months. It is not expected that capital allowances will be claimable on any of this expenditure since it is viewed by the Inland Revenue as replacement rather than innovation and will be written off against taxable profit at the earliest opportunity.

Scheme 3

The production director of Alternative Ventures Limited has an acquaintance who is an inventor, and he suggests that the surplus funds should be used in a joint venture to finance the commercial development of a new product designed by this acquaintance. The full sum would be required at once to pay for a share stake in the new company, but the inventor would be able to pay £20 000 at the end of the second year and £100 000 at the end of Year 4 to buy back the shares when full rights in the project would revert to him. No cash flow is expected in the first year, but subsequent flows net of tax are estimated at £14 000, £38 000 and £56 000 for the second, third and fourth years respectively. It is proposed that the flows from the last two years of the project should be divided equally between the inventor and the company, but the flow from Year 2 is to belong to the company entirely.

Required:

Evaluate the three schemes detailed above and comment upon other factors arising from them that are significant for this decision.

Assume corporation tax at 40%.   (25 marks)

15.2 You are asked to review a major expansion project proposal, intended to commence operations immediately after the installation of plant on 1 January 19–2. The plant is to be installed in an already existing but unused building owned by Notts Engineering Limited. The plant cost will represent 65% of the capital expenditure budget for the year.

NOTTS ENGINEERING LIMITED				CAPITAL PROPOSAL

Date of Proposal: 15 May 19–1
Proposed Project Commencement
Date: 1 January 19–2; plant to be purchased on 31 December 19–1
Location: Disused warehouse

Capital Costs	Cost £	Life	Residual Value	Tax Allowance
Building	Nil	–	–	–
Plant	£600 000	5 years	Nil	25% p.a.
Working Capital	Nil	–	–	–

Year	Cash Flow Benefits £	Tax Flows at 40% £	Net £	Discount Factor 10%	Present Value of Cash Flows £
19–2	75 000	60 000	135 000	0.91	122 850
19–3	120 000	30 000	150 000	0.83	124 500
19–4	320 000	–	320 000	0.75	240 000
19–5	200 000	(68 000)	132 000	0.68	89 760
19–6	100 000	(20 000)	80 000	0.62	49 600
19–7	–	(40 000)	(40 000)	0.56	(22 400)
					604 310
Investment Cost					600 000
					4 310

	Yes	No		
Approval	☐	☐	Date	

Further enquiries establish that major projects in Notts Engineering Limited are required to:

(a) be profitable, in meeting an after tax 10% DCF return, and
(b) meet a simple pay back criterion of three years maximum.

You are provided with the file, which includes the proposal in respect of the project concerned, as it was presented to the board. The taxation year-end for the company is 31 December.

Required:

(a) Since you only have the file copy of the proposal, there is no indication of what the board decision has been, nor indeed if a decision has yet been made. For the benefit of a senior production manager who is assisting you with the review, but whose appreciation of financial matters is not as strong as your own – explain whether board approval is likely, given the criteria outlined earlier. Your reasons must be fully explained and relevant calculations shown.

(b) State, with reasons, whether you agree with the treatment of the buildings in this appraisal. What additional information would you like in this area?

(c) In your view, recently produced economic forecasts suggest that project cash flow benefits as stated are likely to prove optimistic in terms of their timing. Would the following revised pre-tax cash flow projections lead to any different a conclusion by the board?

	£
19–2	25 000
19–3	70 000
19–4	150 000
19–5	380 000
19–6	200 000

(25 marks)

15.3 Soft Centre PLC has incurred development costs of £200 000 to produce a new software system and it has received an offer of £150 000 from another company for the rights to manufacture and market the product. Alternatively, it can manufacture and market the product itself.

It is estimated that an additional immediate investment will be required to commence production and the marketing manager has given the following sales forecast:

Sales Volumes	Years	1	2	3	4
Units		1000	4000	2800	2200

At the end of four years it is anticipated that new technology will take over and that the system will be obsolete.

The selling price of the product in the first year is expected to be £200 per program and the unit cost £140. In future years, due to inflation, costs are expected to rise by 10% compound, but because of competition, selling prices are expected to rise by only 5% p.a. The return required for projects of this risk class is 15% and all receipts and payments can be deemed to be made at the end of each year. Taxation may be ignored.

Required:

(a)   Use the NPV method to advise Soft Centre on the maximum amount it can afford to spend on the immediate production investment if the company is to make and sell the product rather than sell its rights.

(b)   Describe two other non-discounting methods used to appraise capital projects and briefly contrast them with discounting methods.   (25 marks)

16

Uncertainty and Business Decisions

Previous chapters illustrate that the accountant has a significant role to play when business decisions are taken, in that he is the member of the decision team who produces and arranges the figures on which the decision is based. A decision will have an impact on the future operations and profitability of the business, and thus these figures should reflect future conditions. Forecasts of such items as demand at different prices, rates of interest, costs, government action, and the general state of the economy, cannot be made with absolute accuracy, so an unavoidable element of uncertainty must be present when an accountant provides data for the decision-making team. Uncertainty increases the risk associated with the decision. Some mathematical techniques can be used to reduce the impact of this uncertainty on decisions.

In the final analysis, however, much depends on the psychological outlook of the decision team and their attitude to risk. They may be what are termed *risk seekers* willing to take a chance, or risk averters, who react with greater caution in circumstances where uncertainty is present.

PROBABILITY

A major difficulty occurs when figures are produced for inclusion in a decision computation. Suppose, for example, that demand next year for product A is forecast as 12 000 units at a price of £5 each, and for an alternative product, B as 15 000 units at £5 each. These forecasts are usually the 'most likely' or 'best' estimates of future demand, but the question must be asked as to how confident is the forecaster that his most likely result will in fact take place, and, conversely, what are the chances that some alternative level of demand will prevail.

It is possible to tabulate different levels of future demand for products A and B, analysed as to an optimistic view, a most likely view, and a pessimistic view of future trading conditions, by projecting levels of demand if the economy picks up, or if normal conditions prevail, or if there is a slump.

Product A (sales next year at £5 each)		*Product B* (sales next year at £5 each)	
Boom:	14 000 units	Boom:	20 000 units
Normal:	12 000 units	Normal:	15 000 units
Slump:	8 000 units	Slump:	Nil

The first step is to estimate the likelihood (probability) that boom, normal or slump conditions will take place. If you assume that one of the three must happen, the probability or chance of each one happening can be expressed as a percentage, say, for example, boom 10%, normal 60% and slump 30%. These amounts can then be applied to the levels of demand forecast above. In this way an expected demand (a form of average weighted for probability) will be produced. Note that we are assuming the same probabilities for A and B, and also that there are only three alternatives. These assumptions may not be sophisticated enough in real life, in which case the analysis becomes more complicated.

Product A		
Probability × Demand	= Expectation	
Boom: 10% × 14 000 =	1 400	
Normal: 60% × 12 000 =	7 200	
Slump: 30% × 8 000 =	2 400	
Expected demand	11 000	

Product B		
Probability × Demand	= Expectation	
Boom: 10% × 20 000 =	2 000	
Normal: 60% × 15 000 =	9 000	
Slump: 30% × nil	=	–
Expected demand	11 000	

Probabilities can be expressed as decimals, e.g. 0.1, 0.6, 0.3, but they will always total one. Already, by applying this technique, product A has caught up with its rival, and in terms of 'expected demand' there seems to be nothing to choose between them. Although an arithmetical answer has been produced, it must be realised that the accuracy of that answer depends on a man-made estimate of the probabilities.

The next step is to try to differentiate between these two alternative products, which now have the same expected demand. If a graph is drawn to represent the results in the table above and probability against demand is set, the range of demand for each product can be seen.

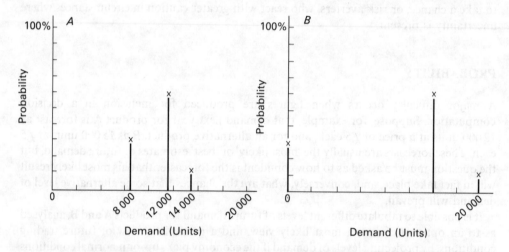

Let us now change the assumptions a little and suppose that there are many more possible outcomes than the ones used in the examples. We can thus calculate more expectations, so that when they are graphed they will appear as a continuous curve rather than three points. Under this assumption the probability distribution is no longer seen as the series of discrete values shown on the bar chart, but instead as a continuous function or graph drawn as a smooth curve. It is argued that the product with the wider range will suffer under this analysis, since the wider the range the more likely it is that the higher probabilities will be reduced, because the total probability spread over the entire range must add to 100%.

Assuming a zero probability that demand for A will exceed 14 000 and be less than 8000 and that demand for B will exceed 20 000, the probability distributions when graphed and

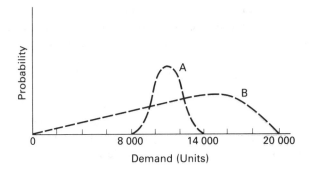

superimposed one upon the other might appear as illustrated. The general rule is that the tighter the probability distribution (when the alternatives in the range are not far from the mean) then the lower the risk on the project, since the more likely it is that the actual result will be close to the expected value. A convenient measure of dispersion that sets a value for tightness of a probability distribution about its mean is the *standard deviation*. If this is calculated for products A and B, it will be possible to differentiate between these two alternatives where expected demand is the same for both products.

Product A

Possible Demand	Expected Demand	Deviation	Squared	Probability	Related Outcome
14	11	+3	9	0.1	0.9
12	11	+1	1	0.6	0.6
8	11	−3	9	0.3	2.7
		Variance of probability distribution			4.2

Standard deviation = $\sqrt{\text{Variance}}$ = $\sqrt{4.2}$ = 2.049

Product B

2	11	−9	81	0.1	8.1
15	11	+4	16	0.6	9.6
0	11	−11	121	0.3	36.3
		Variance of probability distribution			54.0

Standard deviation = $\sqrt{\text{Variance}}$ = $\sqrt{54}$ = 7.349

The possible demand levels for B are spread over a wider range than those for A, so that if the most likely event does not take place, the next most likely event could be farther from the expected demand, e.g. for B there is a 30% chance of selling no units, so that B appears more risky than A.

DISCOUNT RATES ADJUSTED FOR RISK

Probability techniques can be applied to short and long-term business decisions. The greatest uncertainty, however, is experienced when estimates are made far into the future for the evaluation of capital projects. The projected cash flows are discounted and it is quite feasible to discount one project at a higher rate, to take account of its greater riskiness, so that a fair comparison can be made of the NPV of the project with its alternatives.

Some accountants will suggest that as forecasts are made farther into the future, they are more uncertain and less likely to be accurate, and on this premise they argue that cash flows in the later years of a project should be discounted at higher rates, to reduce the impact of these uncertain figures on the final NPV. Once again, the extra degree of discount to be applied for the extra risk encountered, or the year in which a higher discount factor is to be applied, are matters for discussion and subjective decision.

COEFFICIENT OF VARIATION

Standard deviation is a convenient measure of dispersion with which to compare the uncertainty associated with competing projects. However, some difficulties can occur when risk is measured in this way. Projects may have the same standard deviation above and below the mean expected return, but the mean expected return or cash flow may not be the same for the two projects. For example, Project C may have a standard deviation of £4000 on a mean expected return of £20 000, but Project D has a standard deviation of £4000 on a mean expected return of £50 000. The coefficient of variation highlights this difference by calculating the likely percentage deviation from the mean.
The formula is:

$$\frac{\text{Standard deviation}}{\text{Mean expectation}} \times \frac{100}{1}$$

Project C shows a coefficient of variation of: $\dfrac{4000}{20\,000} \times \dfrac{100}{1} = 20\%$

and

Project D shows a coefficient of variation of: $\dfrac{4000}{50\,000} \times \dfrac{100}{1} = 8\%$

The significance of this calculation is that C has more risk per £1 of expected return than D and thus would seem to be more risky even though the two projects have the same

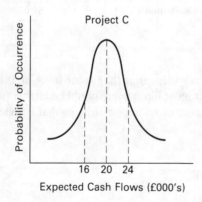

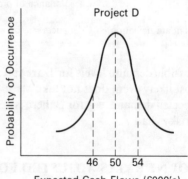

Probability Distribution of Projects C and D to Illustrate Different Expected Returns with the Same Standard Deviation

standard deviation from the expected mean. Coefficient of variation is a useful comparator in this situation, where comparison of standard deviation is misleading.

UNCERTAINTY OVER TIME

To assume that the uncertainty attached to the expected cash flows from a project will remain the same all the years of the life of the project is an over simplification. Standard deviation as a measure of dispersion can be used to illustrate how risk increases over time.

Example

Project E has a five-year life. The probabilities associated with likely cash flows in Years 1 and 5 are as follows:

	Year 1			*Year 5*		
Cash Flow	*Probability*		*Cash Flow*	*Probability*	
£		£	£		£
4000	0.2	800	1666	0.3	500
5000	0.6	3000	7500	0.4	3000
6000	0.2	1200	5000	0.3	1500
Expected cash flow		£5000	Expected cash flow		£5000

Year 1

Possible	*Expected*	*Deviation*	*Squared*	*Probability*	*Related Outcome*
4000	5000	+1000	10 000	0.2	2000
5000	5000	nil	–	0.6	–
6000	5000	–1000	10 000	0.2	2000
					4000

Standard deviation $= \sqrt{4000} = 63.25$ Coefficient of variation $\dfrac{63.25}{5000} \times \dfrac{100}{1} = 1.26\%$

Year 5

1666	5000	–3334	11 115 556	0.3	3 334 669
7500	5000	+2500	6 250 000	0.4	2 500 000
5000	5000	nil	–	0.3	–
					5 834 669

Standard deviation $= \sqrt{5 834 669} = 2415$ Coefficient of variation $\dfrac{2415}{5000} \times \dfrac{100}{1} = 48.3\%$

The expected cash flow for Year 5 is the same as for Year 1, but it is computed from a wider spread of alternatives, and thus the probability of experiencing actual cash flows that are different from the expected cash flow is increased. This increase means that in Year 5 expectations are more uncertain than for Year 1, the degree of risk having increased over time. The coefficient of variation is larger for Year 5 so risk is increasing over time.

THE NORMAL PROBABILITY DISTRIBUTION

Earlier in this chapter probability was expressed as a continuous function, instead of a bar chart. On the bar chart, probability at each point was measured by the height of the bar. However, with a continuous probability distribution, probabilities are found by calculating the area under the curve between the points of interest. The total area under the curve represents all probabilities, or 100. The shape of the curve is perfectly bell-shaped, i.e. the profile on either side of the arithmetic mean is the same. The probability of a return in the range from 40 000 to 70 000 can be found by calculating the proportion of the total area under the curve that lies within the shaded area. This calculation can be undertaken by integrating the curve over this interval, but if the curve is normal or perfectly bell-shaped with the same profile on either side of the arithmetic mean, a mathematical table of areas under the normal curve, the Z table, can be used for this calculation.

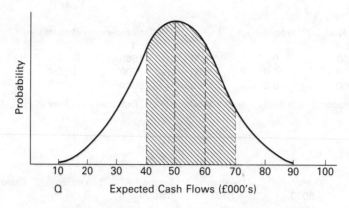

Arithmetic Mean: 50 000
Standard Deviation: 10 000 on either side of that mean

It is an inherent property of the normal probability distribution that 68.26 % of the area under the curve is within one standard deviation on either side of the mean, and that 95.46 % of the area under the curve is within two standard deviations on either side of this mean. This information applied to the Z table can be used to calculate the probability that the outcome will fall between two stated points, or that the actual outcome will exceed a stated minimum. It follows that if Z has a power of 1.0, i.e. one standard deviation from the mean, 34.13 % of the area under the normal curve will be in the sector between Z and the arithmetic mean and that, therefore, there is a 34.13 % probability of a result in the range from Z to the arithmetic mean.

Z Table

The Z table defines the area under the normal distribution function. The value of Z is the number of standard deviations of a selected point from the mean; the table discloses the area under the curve, from the mean to each value for Z.

Values from a Z Table

Z	Percentage of Total Area Area from Mean to Z
0.0	0.0000
0.5	0.1915
0.75	0.2734
1.0	0.3413
1.5	0.4332
2.0	0.4773
2.5	0.4938
3.0	0.4987

The power of Z for a particular distribution is found by the formula:

$$\frac{\text{Point of interest} - \text{Arithmetic mean}}{\text{Standard deviation}}$$

Therefore Z is the number of standard deviations from the mean. From the Z table, the probability of an expected cash flow in the range £40 000 – £70 000 on the graph above can be calculated:

$$Z_1 = \frac{40 - 50}{10} = 1.0 = 0.3413$$

$$Z_2 = \frac{70 - 50}{10} = 2.0 = 0.4773$$

$$\underline{0.8186} \text{ of the total area}$$

0.8186 of the total area lies between these two points, so there is a 81.86 % probability of an outcome in the range £40 000–£70 000.

To determine the probability that the actual outcome would be greater than £70 000, the formula is re-arranged: the proportion of area under the curve from Point Q on the graph up to £70 000 to the total area must be calculated.

From Q up to 50 the arithmetic mean is 50% = 0.5000
From 50 up to 70 the arithmetic mean is:

$$Z = \frac{70 - 50}{10} = 2, \text{ so from the table} = 0.4773$$

Probability of a result up to £70 000	0.9773
Total area	1.0000
Probability of a result in excess of £70 000	0.0227

or 2.27 % (a slender chance of such a result.)

Example

S. A. Vitt & Company Limited are a medium-sized firm in the knitting industry with a leasehold factory in the east Midlands. As financial manager of the company you have recently reviewed for the board the costs of heating the factory during the winter months, and as a result they have invited several firms of specialists in the trade to tender for the insulation of the factory. They have selected a tender in the sum of £24 000 from Wysall

Warmers Ltd., the terms of the contract to include payment on completion of the work except for 15 % retention money, which is to be released twelve months after completion if the work proves satisfactory. The experts from the installation company estimate that work covered by the tender will result in an annual saving of 20 000 litres of fuel oil. An independent heating consultant has charged you £1400 for a report that substantiates this claim. Your auditors, when consulted on this matter, suggested depreciation on a reducing balance at 25 % p.a. over the remaining four-year life of the factory lease.

Your own enquiries from fuel oil suppliers reveal a lack of certainty in the trade with projected fuel oil prices as follows:

	Per litre	Probability
19–1	30p	5%
	40p	90%
	50p	5%
19–2	40p	10%
	50p	80%
	60p	10%
19–3	50p	20%
	60p	60%
	70p	20%

The figures for 19–4 show a normal distribution with a mean price of 70p and a standard deviation of 10p.

Required:

(a)   Evaluate the proposal to insulate the factory – assume a cost of capital of 15 %, corporation tax at 40 % and capital allowances at 25 % p.a.

(b)   Demonstrate how the uncertainty attached to the forecast of fuel oil cost savings has changed during the period under review by applying a suitable measure of uncertainty to the figures for 19–1 and 19–3.

(c)   A director of the company, who is not convinced by the expected values on which your evaluation is based, asks you what is the likelihood that your projected cost savings for 19–4 will be right, give or take £1000, and also wishes to know what chance there is of a cost saving of at least £12 500 in that year. Compute an answer to his questions.

Solution

(a)   *Expected Cost Savings*

			£
19–1	20 000 litres × 30p × 5% (0.05) probability	=	300
	20 000 litres × 40p × 90% (0.9) probability	=	7 200
	20 000 litres × 50p × 5% (0.05) probability	=	500
			£8 000
19–2	20 000 litres × 40p × 10% probability		800
	20 000 litres × 50p × 80% probability		8 000
	20 000 litres × 60p × 10% probability		1 200
			£10 000

19–3	20 000 litres × 50p × 20% probability	2 000
	20 000 litres × 60p × 60% probability	7 200
	20 000 litres × 70p × 20% probability	2 800
		£12 000

19–4 A mean of 70p gives an expected cost saving of
£14 000 (20 000 litres × 70p)

Corporation tax is paid in the year after the costs are saved and capital allowances claimed.

Year 1 receive 40% of £6000 capital allowances = £2400.
Year 2 pay 40% on £8000 less £6000 capital allowances = £800.
Year 5 pay 40% on £14 000 = £5600.

Computation of NPV

		Inflow			Discount	
Year	Expenditure	Cost Saved	Tax	Net	Factor	PV
0	(20 400)	–	–	(20 400)	–	(20 400)
1	(3 600)	8 000	2400	6 800	0.870	5 916
2	–	10 000	(800)	9 800	0.756	7 409
3	–	12 000	(1600)	10 400	0.658	6 843
4	–	14 000	(2400)	11 600	0.572	6 635
5	–	–	(5600)	(5 600)	0.497	(2 783)
					NPV	£3 620

Note: Outflows are in brackets
A positive NPV denotes a viable project.
Basic assumptions noted:

(i)   Ignore consultant's fees – sunk cost.
(ii) Ignore depreciation – not relevant to whole life appraisal.
(iii) Assume sufficient profit to take up capital allowances at earliest opportunity, and
      that allowances are credited in full against tax.

(b)   The basic rule is that the tighter the probability distribution, the lower is the risk. A
      convenient measure of dispersion to set a value for the tightness of the probability
      distribution about its mean is the standard deviation. A further measure is the
      coefficient of variation.

		Possible Saving	Expected Saving	Deviation	Squared	Probability	Related Outcome
20 000 litres at 30p	=	6 000	8 000	– 2000	4 000 000	0.05	200 000
20 000 litres at 40p	=	8 000	8 000	Nil	Nil	0.90	Nil
20 000 litres at 50p	=	10 000	8 000	+ 2000	4 000 000	0.05	200 000
				Variance of probability distribution			400 000

Standard deviation $= \sqrt{\text{Variance}} = \sqrt{400\,000} = 632.5$

Coefficient of variation $= \dfrac{632.5}{8000} \times \dfrac{100}{1} = 7.9\%$

	Possible Saving £	Expected Saving £	Deviation	Squared	Probability	Related Outcome
20 000 litres × 50p =	10 000	12 000	− 2000	4 000 000	0.2	800 000
20 000 litres × 60p =	12 000	12 000	Nil	Nil	0.6	Nil
20 000 litres × 70p =	14 000	12 000	+ 2000	4 000 000	0.2	800 000
			Variance of probability distribution			1 600 000

Standard deviation $= \sqrt{1\,600\,000} = 1254.9$

Coefficient of variance $= \dfrac{1254.9}{12\,000} = 10.5\%$

(c)　What is the probability of a cost saving of £1000 on either side of the arithmetic mean. The formula is:

$$\frac{\text{Point of interest} - \text{Arithmetic mean}}{\text{Standard deviation}}$$

$$Z_1 = \frac{\pounds13\,000 - \pounds14\,000}{20\,000 \text{ litres at } 10p} = \frac{-\pounds1000}{\pounds2000} = 0.5 = \text{on the Z table } 0.1915$$

The minus sign above merely shows that the first of the two parameters lies to the left of the mean.

$$Z_2 = \frac{\pounds15\,000 - \pounds14\,000}{20\,000 \text{ litres at } 10p} = \frac{\pounds1000}{\pounds2000} = 0.5 = \text{on the Z table} \quad \frac{0.1915}{0.3830}$$

38.3% of the area under the normal distribution is in the range required, so there is a 38.3% (0.383) chance or probability of a saving of £13 000 to £15 000.

What is the probability of a cost saving of *at least* £12 500? To answer this question, the area under the curve to the right of the point at which the expected return is £12 500 must be calculated, since this shows the probability of a result beyond that point.

$$Z_1 = \frac{\pounds12\,500 - \pounds14\,000}{\pounds2000} = 0.75 = \text{on the Z table} \quad 0.2734$$

$$Z_2 = \text{Half the total area to the right of the mean} \quad \frac{0.5000}{0.7734}$$

This indicates a 77.34% probability of a result in excess of £12 500 saved, and thus only a (100%–77.34%) 22.66% chance of a saving of less than £12 500.

DECISION TREES

Many decisions cannot be made at one point in time, but are instead the result of a sequence of decisions, made at different decision points as the project develops. At these various stages alternatives are available, and the accountant must follow these alternatives in order to calculate which is the most profitable option open to the business. Varying degrees of uncertainty can be attached to the alternatives and built into the calculation, and as each decision point is reached, fresh information may change the probabilities of certain results.

The accountant must first lay out the options available, in a map or plan showing the decision points and the options associated with those decisions, and the chance events, the probabilities of which affect the decisions. The eventual diagram resembles a tree lying on its side, and it is possible to work from the main decision through the chance events down each branch of the tree to find other points in the sequence where decisions have to be made, and to associate these alternatives with further probabilities.

Once the tree has been mapped out, the accountant can fill in likely outcomes at the end of each branch, and working from right to left down the branches calculate, with probabilities and discounting, the choices that show the highest NPV. This is known as the *roll back technique*, because an eventual result is found by rolling back across the diagram from the branch ends to the base.

Example

Trent Search Limited is a research organisation in the East Midlands that plans to build a conference centre with residential accommodation on land adjoining the site of its workshops and laboratories. There is a difference of opinion among the members of the management board as to whether the venture should be implemented on a grand scale or whether the scheme should be allowed to develop from a small beginning. The enthusiasts on the board foresee a large centre, fully booked from its inception; the pessimists argue that demand for the services of a conference centre in that area will always be small; whilst the cynics see an initial high demand that will fall away after two years, as soon as the novelty of the idea has worn off.

Market researchers have been recruited to assess the market. They report that there is a 60% chance that a large centre would sustain full bookings (90% of capacity) over the next ten years, a 30% chance that demand for its services would be small (25% of capacity), and a 10% chance that an initial high demand would fall away after two years.

Computations of likely costs and cash flows produced the following data:

1. A large conference centre would cost £6 million to build, but would return an annual cash flow of £2 million when operating at high capacity. Operations at 25% of capacity would produce a cash flow of £200 000 p.a., since the impact of overhead expenses would reduce the return.
2. A small conference centre would cost £2.6 million to build, and would return a cash flow of £800 000 p.a. when operating at demand levels equal to 25% of the capacity of the large centre. If demand is high, however, a cash flow of £900 000 p.a. can be expected, which will later fall to £600 000 p.a. as the limited size and the presence of competition combine to reduce bookings.
3. The cost of expanding a small centre after a two-year delay is estimated at £4.4 million, and it is calculated that the large centre would return an annual cash flow of £1.4 million for a further eight years if operating at 90% capacity. It is also calculated that an expanded centre working at 25% capacity would earn only £100 000 p.a. in cash flow.

It is the normal practice of this organisation to discount capital projects at 10%.

Required:

Analyse the situation and advise the management as to the best course of action, and first, consider the situation carefully to find the decision points and alternatives available. Next, draft a decision tree based on your first step and enter probabilities on the alternative branches. Enter costs and likely cash flows at the appropriate points on the diagram. Last, roll back from the branch ends to the base, calculating a value for each alternative at the decision points, discounting at the cost of capital and applying probabilities to the calculation.

Solution

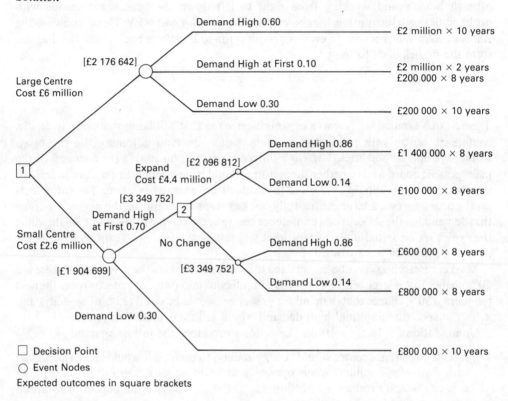

☐ Decision Point
◯ Event Nodes
Expected outcomes in square brackets

$60\% + 10\% = 70\%$ probability of high demand for the first two years; 60/70 chance that initial demand will stay high = 86%, and a 14% probability of low demand in later years.

Present Value of Cash Flows – Rolling Back from Right to Left

Decision 2 (PV as at the time Decision 2 is made)

Expand high demand £1 400 000 for 8 years × 5.334	PV = £7 467 600
Expand low demand £100 000 for 8 years × 5.334	PV = £533 400
No change high demand £600 000 for 8 years × 5.334	PV = £3 200 400
No change low demand £800 000 for 8 years × 5.334	PV = £4 267 200

Note: Multiplying the same cash flow to be experienced in each of the next eight years by 5.334, is the same as discounting it at 10% for eight years in succession, i.e. 0.909 + 0.826 + 0.751 + 0.683 + 0.621 + 0.564 + 0.513 + 0.467 = 5.334.

Discounted Expected Value for Decision 2

Expand:	$(0.86 \times £7\,467\,600) + (0.14 \times 533\,400)$	£6 496 812
	Less extra investment	£4 400 000
	PV of that branch at decision point 2.	£2 096 812
No change:	$(0.86 \times £3\,200\,400) + (0.14 \times £4\,267\,200)$	= £3 349 752

Thus 'no change' is the best alternative.

Decision 1. Decision point 2 value is treated as though it were a lump sum received at the end of 2 years.

Calculations

Large Centre

High demand £2 million $\times 6.144$ (PV of ten-year income stream) = £12 288 000
High demand at first £2 million $\times 1.735$ (the first 2 years)
         $+ £200\,000 \times 4.410$ (from years 3 to 10)
Low demand £200 000 $\times 6.144$ = £1 228 800   = 4 352 000
Note: Reading from the 10% discount table: $0.909 + 0.826 + 0.751 + 0.683 + 0.621 + 0.564 + 0.513$
$+ 0.467 + 0.424 + 0.386 = 6.144$

Small Centre

High demand at first £3 349 792 $\times 0.826$ (PV of lump sum)	£2 766 928
£900 000 $\times 1.735$ (first 2 years)	£1 561 500
	£4 328 428
Low demand £800 000 $\times 6.145$	£4 916 000

Discounted Expected Value for Decision 1

Large Centre

$(0.60 \times £12\,288\,000) + (0.10 \times £4\,352\,000) + (0.30 \times £1\,228\,800)$	=	£8 176 640
Less investment		£6 000 000
		£2 176 642

Small Centre

$0.70 \times £4\,328\,428 + 0.30 \times £4\,916\,000$	=	£4 504 699
Less investment		£2 600 000
		£1 904 699

Thus the large centre is the best alternative.

SEMINAR EXERCISES

16.1 The Lenton Engineering Company Limited recently sent their chief designer to the USA to review developments in the American market. He has now returned with details of a new type of food mixer that is being developed over there. Lenton are considering the design and manufacture of a liquidizer attachment to be used as an extra fitment for the new mixer when it is sold in the UK. The chief designer's notes show that 10% of the experts he questioned in the USA believed the new mixer would reach the UK market in a year's time, whereas 30% thought it would be launched in four years' time, and the remainder suggested a five-year delay before it reached us. The PV of net cash flows from making and selling the liquidizer are estimated by the company to be £400 000 if the market develops one year from now, £250 000 if it develops four years from now and £160 000 if it develops five years from now.

Lenton have not developed a liquidizer before, and whilst its immediate development would cost £100 000, they feel they have only a 50% chance of a successful development at present. A number of alternative courses of action present themselves. The company could abandon the whole project, or wait for one year to see if the mixer has penetrated the UK market. They could then abandon or develop the liquidiser at a PV cost of £90 000, with a 70% chance of success, but they would be late into the market and the PV of their receipts they estimate at £240 000. A further alternative is that the company could delay a decision for a second year, and then abandon or develop the project. Development costs at that stage would have a PV of £70 000, including the expenditure of £20 000 on acquiring extra product data during the second year of delay, and the chance of a successful development would be 90%. At this point, however, the mixer could only come on the market at the four or five year point from now.

Required:

A decision tree to indicate the best course of action for the company to adopt. Note that no discounting is required because the information in the question is given in PV terms.   (20 marks)

16.2 Executive Models PLC manufactures high-quality desk-top ornaments, which are sold by mail order and through major stores.

Auto Miniatures Limited is prepared to sell the design and manufacturing rights for three models of vintage motor cars. However, it will only sell the rights to *one* product, not two or three. The costs of the rights are:

Stutz Bearcat	£62 500
Bugatti	£75 000
Bentley 4½ litre	£52 500

The directors of Executive models are agreed that any of these products (which would have a sales life of only one year) would make an attractive addition to its range and now wish to select the best of the three products.

The management accountant has provided the following information:

	Stutz Bearcat	Bugatti	Bentley 4½ litre
	£	£	£
Selling price per unit	199	140	115
Variable cost per unit	98	75	65
	£000's	£000's	£000's
Fixed production costs	70	95	60
Advertising	55	40	20

These figures are considered to be very accurate. Sales volumes for each product are, however, a much greater problem and the sales manager has provided the following analysis of possibilities:

Stutz Bearcat		Bugatti		Bentley 4½ litre	
Volume (units)	Probability	Volume (units)	Probability	Volume (units)	Probability
2000	0.7	Nil	0.1	2500	0.1
3000	0.2	3000	0.4	3000	0.3
4000	0.1	6000	0.5	4000	0.4
				5000	0.2

Required:

(a) Advise Executive Models of the best course of action based on the information given above.
(b) Discuss three other factors that may be relevant to the choice.
(c) In the case of the Bugatti, it is suggested that Executive Models should commission a market research study costing £20 000, which would be able to determine precisely whether the sales would be nil, 3000 or 6000 units. Is it worthwhile to undertake the study? Assume all costs are avoidable.

(25 marks)

Section VI

Performance Evaluation Within Divisions

17
Measuring Performance for Divisions

The modern trend is towards larger and larger businesses as companies merge together to improve their competitive ability in the market-place. As size increases so does the problem of control, and senior management is forced to delegate more and more decisions to local management as parts of the organisation become increasingly remote from the central administrative core of the group and increasingly specialised in their activities. The solution to this problem is to organise the business in the form of a 'division' for each of the natural parts into which the group can be divided. Divisional management must be responsible to top management for the performance of that segment of the business that is under its control.

A group may be divided into segments or divisions on a number of different bases, e.g. regional, or according to their activities. Thus a group of companies in the building industry may have divisions for civil engineering, house building, mechanical installations, and plant hire and supply. Each division may contain a number of companies in the same trade, all reporting to divisional management, rather than top or central management. There is no rule to decide whether a divisional form of organisation exists, since companies operate in different ways, and divisional managers are given various degrees of autonomy and responsibility. At one end of the scale there is the profit centre, which is a division given profit objectives by central management but where divisional managers may have the responsibility to decide on markets, pricing, suppliers and the level of working capital to be used. Such managers are very independent, answering to central management only for the achievement of profit targets and requiring central authority for decisions affecting group strategic policy and capital investment decisions concerning capital to be raised and long-term investments to be made.

This type of division often manufactures and sells its own product, but it must co-ordinate with other parts of the group, even though it is free to sell to whom it pleases outside the group and choose its suppliers. If a division is an investment centre the management may have the right to make investment decisions concerning the levels of stocks and debtors or small capital purchases, but must refer large capital schemes to central management for group approval. The system is that divisional managements are provided with a certain amount of capital and their success is judged according to whether they meet their profit targets, but how they achieve this is left to them to decide. At the other end of the scale there are some sub-groups of companies within a large organisation that bear the name 'division' but that are subject to comprehensive organisation from head office. Some other 'divisions' are allowed limited autonomy, perhaps to decide pricing and market strategy, volume of output, number of employees etc.

Independence of management and autonomy in decision making is the key to the existence of a divisionalised form of management. There is no clear-cut dividing line to say when part of a business qualifies as a division, but the level of constraints within which a divisional manager operates sets the limit, e.g. a detailed budget imposed by a central planning department reduces autonomy, but guidelines, advice, or goals set for the manager, will still allow him some freedom of action.

A workable system to generate congruent plans and yet maintain divisional independence might be constructed as follows:

1. The central planning division constructs a provisional scheme to allocate scarce resources, based on information supplied by the divisions. Proposals for divisional profit targets and the adjustment of transfer prices will be generated at this stage.
2. Discussion and negotiation take place between each division and the central planners on making alterations to the scheme for such matters as resource allocation, transfer prices etc.
3. Each division drafts its own budget within the constraints of the central overall scheme for the group.
4. The central planners monitor divisional performance and prepare for the next overall scheme.

This system may not produce optimal budgets but the benefits of divisionalisation probably outweigh this disadvantage.

THE CASES FOR AND AGAINST DIVISIONAL FORMS OF ORGANISATION

Decentralisation means that decisions can be taken at local level without the delay of an application to head office, and by the use of local knowledge concerning the situation, product or region, as the case may be. Senior managers are thus free to concentrate on group strategy rather than utilising their time making local operating decisions. Autonomy is beneficial for the morale and motivation of local managers, who feel free to make decisions and accept responsibility for their own decisions. This system works so long as managers are profit oriented, perhaps by a bonus payment on results. Divisionalisation allows managers to use initiative and grooms them for further promotion to the highest grades in the business. This system is not perfect and may lead to costly mistakes being made by junior managers, who are allowed too much freedom of responsibility before their experience is sufficiently developed to cope with decisions at a certain level. Divisional managers tend to decide on the basis of what is of most benefit for their division rather than for the business as a whole. Such decisions can prove harmful to the group. Equally harmful is the situation where a divisional manager may see his position as a stepping stone to promotion and therefore be tempted to concentrate his efforts on demonstrating good short-term profits at the expense of future operations or non-financial factors, which may damage the division after he has moved on. His successor may inherit old, worn-out plant, disgruntled customers, long-term investments whose expected returns do not develop as planned, and large stocks of unsold goods priced at full absorption cost in order to pass on overheads to a later period. Divisional organisation often seems to require a large and expensive central administrative staff, even though the divisions are autonomous and employ their own administrative staff, so duplication of work may occur. Unless central management lay down clear guidelines, divisions may compete with one another and the atmosphere of co-operation, so essential to success, will be dissipated.

SERVICE DIVISION

Some business organisations use a service division to support the productive divisions with central services, perhaps by operating group transport, by undertaking administrative services or printing for all parts of the group. Such a division may operate in a situation where it is removed from the pressures of the economy, e.g. the demand for its product is determined by the operating divisions in the group. Perhaps the object of a service division is to supply its service to other divisions at the lowest possible cost, or at a certain quality, so that the success of the service division should be measured by the standard of achievement of this objective rather than its profitability. Some service divisions have to compete with external suppliers for the work they undertake within the group, or, alternatively, they may not be allowed to price a job higher than the lowest external quote that the user division can find. Profit versus the standard of service, and protection within the group versus the efficiency from a competitive situation are the two major problems that a service division must face.

EVALUATING DIVISIONAL PERFORMANCE

The basic rules are that:

1. Activities that increase divisional profit but that reduce overall group profit should be discouraged.
2. Divisional profits should be uninfluenced, wherever possible, by efficiency or inefficiency elsewhere in the group (transfer pricing, see Chapter 18); and
3. factors under the control of divisional managers should influence divisional profits.

The performance of a division can be measured in various ways according to the criteria for success. Good operating performance is demonstrated by increasing profitability, when compared with the budget or plan, or with the performance of competitors. Performance ratios, such as net profit to turnover, material stock to usage, work-in-progress stock to cost of production, finished goods to cost of sales, and expenses to sales, give an indication of success or failure when compared with a norm. Other factors, such as market share, days lost through strikes, and working capital used, are also significant, but an unscrupulous divisional manager can in the short run improve these indicators at the expense of customer goodwill, labour morale, plant modernisation and new product development, all of which are not susceptible to easy measurement.

The economic performance of the division is measured to answer the basic question: 'Should investment in this segment be increased or maintained, or should the division be closed down?' Measurement should be more in terms of whether the division can produce enough profit to give a sufficient return on the funds invested and to compensate for the risk taken with those funds, e.g. return on investment. If the divisional return is insufficient and action to improve the return has failed, disinvestment should follow, with group funds being transferred to some more profitable alternative. In present value, or PV, terms the aggregate PV of the future expected income stream must exceed the PV of the capital released by a liquidation of the division, or the division should be closed.

The performance of the managers of a division should be measured according to yet another set of rules. Comparison with other divisions within the group may be misleading, unless they are operating under similar conditions as regards market conditions – competition, volume, plant facilities, labour relations and material supplies, e.g. how do you compare a division that owns its own plant and a factory purchased 15 years ago with another division owning a new factory built and equipped last year with yet another division that rents its premises and leases its plant. Such comparisons depend for credibility on artificial means, whereby the cost accountant attempts to remove the differences either by charging a notional rent for property owned or by valuing property not owned and ignoring rent paid.

The most important rule for the evaluation of divisional management is that factors outside the control of the managers should not be allowed to count against them. The budget is a useful comparator for actual performance, but adjustment must be made for extraordinary items that were not foreseen when the budget was drafted. The same standard of performance cannot be applied to divisions that are trading in different circumstances, e.g. if division A is budgeted to make a return of 8 % on its capital employed and actually makes 10 %, this is good and its management should be congratulated, but if division B, which should have made a return of 18 %, can only show 15 %, it reveals a disappointing performance when measured against its potential and plan, even though its performance is 50 % better than that of division A. This is the difference between the evaluation of the performance of divisional management and the economic performance of the division, in which case the required return on investment can be applied equally to all divisions.

CHOOSING A MEANS TO MEASURE DIVISIONAL PERFORMANCE

A number of methods can be applied, but for the majority of businesses the choice is narrowed down to four:

Contribution. This is the contribution made by the division towards the central costs and profit of the business as a whole. All divisional costs, whether fixed or variable, are considered as direct costs in this context, and the surplus of revenue above all divisional costs is contribution, which can be used as a means of comparing one division with another, or one division with itself, over a certain period of time. This is a simple method, which avoids the false and often arbitrary allocation of central costs to divisions, but its weakness is that it fails to include an element of the funds invested in the division and the cost to the group of those funds. It is interesting to discover the comparative size of the contribution made by a division, but of little use if it is not known whether the contribution is sufficient to service the funds used in earning that contribution. It is possible for a divisional manager to increase divisional contribution by investing central funds in low-yielding projects without any penalty for using those funds in this way.

Divisional Profit. This is defined as contribution less a proportion of group central administrative expenses. This method demonstrates whether a division can pay for its share of group costs, but its relevance depends on the fair and proper allocation of these costs. Since the allocation is outside the control of divisional management, this method should not be used to evaluate managerial performance and as divisional profit does not reflect the funds invested in the division it can hardly be used to evaluate economic performance.

Divisional profit may be computed on a consistent accounting basis for all divisions, but the result shown may be biased if one division fails to receive an appropriate price for goods and services it provides for other divisions (transfer prices). As mentioned, divisional profit is not properly applicable to service divisions. Whilst it is true that group central costs are outside the control of divisional managers, they should nevertheless recognise that their operations must provide sufficient profit to cover these costs. Joint costs for facilities shared by divisions and, in some cases, joint revenue must be allocated on a basis acknowledged to be equitable by the managers concerned.

Divisional Return on Investment. (ROI) or Net Profit to Capital Employed. Earnings are set against invested funds with this method, which gives a return that can be ranked against the return of other divisions or compared with the cost of capital for the group. Divisional managers are made aware that if they waste capital by holding it in the form of idle funds, under-utilised plant or high levels of stock and debtors, their return will fall, so this method acts as a spur to efficiency. ROI must, however, be applied with caution, because profit and investment can both be measured in ways that may bias the result, e.g. capital invested in fixed assets measured in a period of inflation at historic cost instead of replacement cost, or profit boosted in the short run by inadequate provisions for future events. The elements of both net profit and capital employed may not all be under the control of divisional management, so it may be unfair to judge the performance of a manager who is forced to pay rent under a lease negotiated by his predecessor on buildings that he would not use if the senior management gave him the chance to transfer the division to other premises. Managerial responsibility can hardly be measured by ROI if central group assets are allocated to divisions and inappropriate values used. Assets shared by divisions or assets lying idle can cause difficulties for ROI.

Although ROI can be a useful measure of performance, it can also lead to problems, in that it is quite possible for a divisional manager to adopt a policy that he considers will maintain or raise his rate of return even if the policy is irrational from the company's point of view. For example, if a rate of 20% is at present being earned on the divisional investment, the management may decide not to urge the acceptance of an investment proposal that promises 15% p.a. (even though it has a substantial positive NPV), since this would pull down the division's average rate of return, despite the fact that it would be well above the group requirement as a return on investment. This is known as a *sub-optimal decision*. To remedy problems of this type, residual income has been developed.

Residual Income. This measure is defined as the net profit of the division less an investment carrying charge on group funds used by the division (Divisional investment from the group × Cost of capital rate). A useful result is derived from the question: 'How much surplus has the division made above the cost of funds required to finance its operations?' Earnings and investment both influence the result of this measuring device, and changes in the various elements that make up earnings and investment are measured on the same scale, e.g. if, by efficient management, stocks are reduced by £120 000, the interest carrying charge for a year (at 10%) is reduced by £12 000, and this is equivalent in the calculation to a cost increase of £1000 a month.

This measure suffers from the same defects as the ROI, i.e. it mixes together controllable and non-controllable items and some elements in the calculation can be manipulated by divisional managers. Once again autonomy is the key to divisional performance. If a divisional manager is informed by the group of the amount of group funds he must use, he cannot control the investment in the division, but if he is at liberty to draw down central funds on demand, then the responsibility for over or under-investment in the division must be his.

PROBLEMS OF MEASURING DIVISIONAL PERFORMANCE

A division is by definition part of a group, and the problems of measuring its performance are mainly caused through difficulties in separating the division from the rest of the group and defining the costs of common processes and group assets used by the division.

The true measure of divisional income is confused by the allocation of the costs of support activities provided by the group and used in common by all divisions. Such costs should not count in the economic evaluation of a division's performance, unless the divisional manager can influence the cost or amount of the service used by the division. Non-controllable costs allocated to a division should be shown either as a separate item after the divisional profit is struck, or should be charged as the amount agreed in the budget, so that no cost savings or cost over-run at head office can influence divisional performance.

Interest paid by the group on finance that is raised centrally should not be allocated to divisions. This does not remove the need for divisional performance to cover the cost of funds invested in divisional operations. Group interest represents only the debt proportion of those funds. Residual income measures the surplus above the required return on group finance after allowing for interest on short-term borrowings made locally by the divisional manager.

The interdependence of divisions leads to the awkward problem of transfer pricing. If one division buys from another, the price set for this intra-group transaction will influence the profitability of the two divisions. Taxation may be borne by the group or by companies in the divisions, but capital grants are specific to assets acquired by individual divisions, and divisional managers can affect profit after tax by making their capital purchases at the most advantageous moments.

It is difficult to define with certainty the capital employed in a division. Traceable assets are easy to measure, but assets shared with other divisions, perhaps outside the control of the divisional management, are difficult to attribute to divisions. Managerial performance could be measured in terms of controllable assets, but economic evaluation needs to set the profit against all group funds invested in the division. This does not mean total assets, since they are in part financed by creditors, who are outside the group. If divisions share the use of assets held centrally, some arbitrary basis of allocation must be employed to allocate these assets to divisions, e.g. the research laboratory or idle cash balances. Statistical methods of allocation based on use seem fair if divisional management has some control over the use it makes of such assets.

Example

Comparator PLC is a company with well-diversified interests. It is organised on a divisional basis. The divisions are autonomous, having complete discretion as to selling prices and trading terms. Finance is available from a central fund operated by the financial director at head office. Interest on these funds is charged at 15% p.a., which is considered to be the cost of capital for the group. Each division is allowed to draw down up to £400 000 to finance its operation, but must finance expansion beyond this point from its own resources.

The balance of the head office loan account with each division will fluctuate as funds are drawn or repaid at the end of each month. The interest paid on these funds to the group head office is calculated on a monthly basis. At the year-end the balance of the account is settled by a cash movement to return to the opening figure. Net profit for the year is then added to the balance of the account or remitted to head office.

The board wish to compare the profitability of two divisions that are operating in similar markets but in different geographical areas.

Required:

Compare the performance and position of the two divisions and make any recommendations you consider necessary to improve their financial situation. The following information is provided:

	£	Southern Division £	£	Northern Division £
Operating Statement (year to 31.12.–9)				
Sales		500 000		2 360 000
Cost of sales		360 000		1 920 000
Gross profit		140 000		440 000
Expenses:				
Wages and salaries	28 000		146 000	
Bank interest			14 000	
Interest to group	30 600		40 000	
Expenses	16 400		192 000	
		84 000		392 000
Net profit		£56 000		£48 000
Balance sheet (as at 31.12.–9)				
Initial investment		396 000		272 000
Profit for the year		56 000		48 000
Head office loan account		£452 000		£320 000
Fixed assets:				
Plant (net of depreciation)		152 000		232 000
Vehicles (net of depreciation)		124 000		60 000
		276 000		292 000
Current assets:				
Stock	132 000		292 000	
Debtors	100 000		152 000	
Cash	24 000			
	256 000		444 000	
Less current liabilities:				
Trade creditors	80 000		332 000	
Overdraft	–	176 000	84 000	28 000
Net assets		£452 000		£320 000

Solution

Comparator PLC – Ratio Analysis

		South (S)		North (N)	
Return on group funds at year-end		56:452	12.4%	48:320	15%
Return on average group funds		56:424	13.2%	48:296	16.2%
Net profit + interest: Net assets + overdraft		96:452	21.2%	102:404	25%
Net profit to gross capital employed at year-end		56:532	10.5%	48:736	6.5%
* Sales to gross capital employed at year-end		500:532	0.94 times	2360:736	3.2 times
Net profit to sales		56:500	11.2%	48:2360	2%
Gross profit to sales		140:500	28%	440:2360	18.6%
Expenses to sales			16.8%		16.6%
Current ratio (current assets to current liabilities)		256:80	3.2:1	444:416	1.06:1
Acid test or Quick asset ratio (debtors and cash to current liabilities)		124:80	1.5:1	152:416	0.37:1
Debtors to sales (days)			73		23
Creditors to cost of goods sold (days)			81		63
Stock to cost of goods sold (days)			134		55
Fixed assets to sales		276:500	1.8 times	292:2360	8.1 times
Current assets to sales		256:500	1.9 times	444:2360	5.3 times
Fixed assets to current assets		276:256	1.1:1	292:444	0.66:1

* This is known as the *turnover ratio*.

Comments would include the following points:

Profitability

S is more profitable than N on gross capital employed.
N is more profitable than S on group funds.
  This reflects the use by N of funds outside the group, e.g. trade credit and overdraft.
S has drawn down more than its quota of group funds and is holding an idle cash balance.
N has not yet drawn down its quota from group but has recruited external finance, some of
it cheap, e.g. trade credit, and some of it expensive, e.g. overdraft.

Activity

N uses capital employed more intensively than S as shown by the turnover ratio.
S has a higher profit margin on sales than N, e.g. gross profit ratio.
Expenses to sales are the same for both, but the net profit to sales margin of N is
dangerously low.
Perhaps N tries for a low return on a high volume – narrow margin and quick turnover.
S tries for a high return on a low volume.

Liquidity

S is better than N in terms of current and quick ratios. This reflects the policy of N to
finance extra turnover by current liabilities. S has cash whilst N is overdrawn – the safety
margin is a matter of managerial policy.

Is N approaching an overtrading situation, i.e. over-dependence on external short-term funds to finance expansion? If so more group finance is needed to correct the situation. Using cheap trade credit to the full is an advantage to the group.

Management of Short-term Funds

N is giving less trade credit than S – it is collecting its debts more quickly and holds lower stocks. This fits with the idea of a narrow profit margin on a rapid turnover of assets.

S manages to obtain a longer period of credit from suppliers than N. This may reflect the adverse liquidity position of N.

Capacity

The turnover ratios for both fixed and current assets show a more intensive use of assets by N. The balance between fixed and current assets between the divisions is not the same. N uses less fixed assets to current assets than S.

N has a greater turnover but fewer vehicles than S. This could mean that it has a different distribution policy. An alternative explanation is that N is leasing both plant and vans and thus using assets that do not appear on the balance sheet.

Residual Income

This is an alternative comparator for divisional performance.

	South (£)	North (£)
Group funds drawn down	452 000	320 000
Group cost of capital applied to group funds (15%)	67 800	48 000
Net profit and group interest charge	95 600	88 000
Residual income	£27 800	£40 000

By this test N is the more efficient.

The comparator can be applied if divisions are autonomous as to the amount of group funds they use.

Remedial Action for Divisions

To improve liquidity N should draw down more group funds as a safety margin. This action will improve credit worthiness and avert the suggestion of overtrading. If discounts are available from suppliers for early payment at an annual rate in excess of group cost of capital, then group funds should be used for early payment.

S should investigate the reasons for holding large stocks and should review stock and debtor policies. It must trade off the advantages of large stocks and credit lines to support sales effort against the cost of these facilities.

SEMINAR EXERCISES

17.1   Interbisk PLC is an international company specialising in the production and sale of biscuits and cookies. The dog biscuit division of this group is Roverbix. The divisional profit statement for the month of December 19–5 is:

	£	£	Budget £
Sales (50% on credit terms)		1 140 000	1 200 000
Divisional expenses:			
Materials	700 000		
Manufacturing costs	70 000		
Marketing	93 000		
Divisional administration	58 000		
		1 021 000	1 000 000
Divisional contribution		119 000	200 000
Proportion of head office expenses		100 000	100 000
Net profit		£19 000	£100 000

The balance sheet for the division analyses the divisional net investment as follows:

	£	£
Traceable assets:		
Premises		600 000
Plant		510 000
Vehicles		30 000
		1 140 000
Stock:		
Material	900 000	
Finished goods	160 000	
Debtors	900 000	
Current liabilities	(320 000)	1 640 000
Net traceable assets		2 780 000
Proportion of centrally administered assets:		
Cash	10 000	
Other	60 000	70 000
Divisional net investment		£2 850 000

The dog biscuit industry does not experience seasonal fluctuations. The month of December is typical of all the other months in the year so far as performance is concerned. The cost of capital for the group is 15%.

Required:

(a) Evaluate the performance of the management of the Roverbix division using four methods. Note the limitations of the methods you have employed.

(21 marks)

(b) How would your method of evaluation of the performance of this division differ if the evaluation were made to check economic rather than managerial performance?

(4 marks)

(Total 25 marks)

18
Transfer Prices

Divisions within a group often trade together, a manufacturer buying raw materials or components from other group companies, or selling finished goods to a group distribution company in a discrete geographical market. These transactions within a group may not be subject to the competitive pressures of market forces, so difficulties can be encountered in fixing the price at which goods will pass from one part of the group to another. A *transfer price* can be defined as an administered or notional price at which a division receiving services or products from a fellow division in the group is charged and at which the selling division is compensated for its activities. The extent to which cost and profit are covered by the price is often a matter of group policy and negotiation and whether market forces outside the group are allowed to influence transfer prices.

There are sound reasons why a transfer-pricing system is needed in a group of companies, if only to set an amount at which inter-company transfers can be recorded and year-end stocks valued. The profitability of an individual division cannot be measured unless a charge is made for goods received from or sold to other group companies and it follows that the level of divisional profit may be seriously affected by such transfer prices. Scarce resources can be allocated to divisions by a pricing system that will cause managers to use such resources with great economy. Transfer prices should be used to motivate divisional managers to act in the best interests of the group, whilst at the same time encouraging them to the maximum advantage for their own division. The transfer price sets the amount for which the management of the receiving division has accepted responsibility. International groups manipulate transfer prices to transfer profit from one country to another in order to minimise the impact of local taxation rules. This reason is at variance with the other objectives of transfer pricing, which can be summarised as: the encouragement of autonomy within divisions, the clarification of problems of measuring divisional performance and the promotion of goal congruence between divisional managers pursuing local aims and the goals of the group as a whole.

In a way transfer pricing is a form of cost allocation with important behavioural implications for divisional managers. The fairness of prices at which inter-group transfers are made will affect the morale of managers, especially if the performance of their division is evaluated on the basis of such transfer prices. A manager forced to sell to another division at below market rate may be forgiven for believing that his division is disadvantaged by such a system and a true measure of the division's performance is not disclosed. A system of transfer prices that motivates managers to take divisional decisions for the greater benefit of the group as a whole may conflict with a system that encourages decisions that will optimise the performance of the division. Negotiation and compromise are necessary to reconcile these differences and produce a system that is both simple to operate and acceptable to all parties as being fair. Transfer prices may have far-reaching effects in a group. They will influence the profitability of divisions and will also be an important component in the decision of a supplying division as to its volume of output and whether it should supply other divisions. The final pricing decision of a receiving division and the decision as to whether to 'buy out' a component are also influenced by the transfer price from a division within the group.

It is no surprise that in a matter of such great practical importance to a group, many methods of transfer pricing have been developed, and that these have been extended by academic debate and research. There are basically two systems to use: transfer prices based on cost and transfer prices based on the open market. However, a third system of negotiated prices is usually adopted in practice.

The options available can be analysed as follows:

Full Absorbed Cost. This is calculated as direct production costs and an apportionment of the supplying division's fixed overhead expenses. Standard rather than actual costs should be used so that adverse variances experienced by the supplying division are not passed on to the receiving division.

Cost Plus. This is calculated as full cost plus an agreed profit margin for the supplying division, to give some incentive to sell within the group. One should be wary of the cost plus system, since it perpetuates inefficiency by the supplying division if costs are not competitive; the greater the cost, the larger the profit margin enjoyed by the supplying division will be if an agreed percentage is added to the cost.

Variable Cost. This is calculated as the direct costs only of the supplying division. This method seems to punish the supplying division by not allowing even a contribution towards its overheads. Conversely, there is no check to see that the direct costs represent efficient operation.

Variable Cost Plus a Lump Sum. This is calculated as variable cost with the addition of a payment once a year to cover the fixed costs and perhaps the profit margin of the supplying division. In this case the receiving division is charged for part of the supplying division's infrastructure, which it maintains to meet the need for sales within the group.

Opportunity Cost. This is calculated as the direct costs of production plus any contribution foregone by the supplying division if scarce resources are diverted to intra-group work. This element may be very difficult to identify, let alone quantify.

Obviously there is much room for negotiation in the five cost-oriented, price-fixing methods itemised above. The market-based approaches described below are equally fertile areas of negotiation, sometimes leading to conflict within a group, which can only be settled by centrally imposed prices. These are:

Market Price: the price at which the receiving division acquires the goods or services in an open market transaction, if such a price can be easily found. In an industry where prices fluctuate rapidly this basis will cause constant change in the transfer price.

Net Market Price: the market price less the selling expenses of the supplying division, since no selling effort is deemed to be required for sales within the group.

Average Market Price: the price at which the goods or services are supplied to the market in the long run. The average market price ignores short-term temporary fluctuations in supply and demand.

Distress Price: a low market price set at a time of slump when over-production and falling demand depress prices. In time, market forces will adjust to this situation. It seems unfair to expect the supplying division to make and supply goods at a price governed by low-priced bargains and sales of bankrupt stocks. Conversely, the receiving division may argue that it could buy at the distress price if it was not forced to buy within the group.

Substitute Price: the market price of an equivalent or similar unit to that transferred between divisions. Identification of substitutes is difficult, and adjustments to the price to compensate for details of non-equivalence are a matter for negotiation.

Pro-rated Contribution: the direct cost of the supplying division plus a share of the overall contribution made by the product to group profit. The obvious difficulty here is to measure the contribution to the group and then agree on how that contribution is to be divided between the interested divisions.

A transfer price must be set in advance of a transaction and if a market price can be established this will form a convenient point at which negotiations can commence, bringing in cost, opportunity cost, volumes concerned and the extent to which the respective parties to the transaction are keen to strike a bargain. Often during negotiations the strength of the personalities of managers on either side or the political support they can muster among the senior management of the group prove to be significant in setting a transfer price.

If sub-optimisation is to be avoided the transfer price should be fixed at a point at which a manager at group head office, realising the needs of both the supplying and receiving divisions and bearing in mind the overall benefit of the transaction to the group, would not wish to make any adjustments. The price should not be below the opportunity cost of the supplying division to sell elsewhere or above the market price at which the receiving division can buy outside the group. Alternatively, the price should be set at the incremental cost to the supplier or the net market cost, whichever is the greater. If divisional performance is to be measured in order to evaluate managerial talent the market price should be used for transfers, but since this may not lead to the optimum overall situation for the group, then perhaps a dual-price system might be applied, depending on the purpose for which analysis is required. This suggestion, however, leads away from the important criteria expressed at the beginning of this chapter, that transfer prices should be simple to operate and easy to understand.

PROBLEMS OF TRANSFER PRICING

The problems associated with setting transfer prices and their significance for divisional performance often lead to the establishment of a price by negotiation or by dictation from senior management at group level. Where full cost is to be used, this should be the average cost experienced over a period of time covering the fixed costs of the supplying division, but if prices are to cover these costs there is no spur to improve efficiency in the supplying division if this division is paid cost plus a percentage for goods supplied to another division. This is an impetus to inefficiency, because the higher the cost the larger the percentage thereof will be, which constitutes the profit of the supplying division. There is no market test of efficiency with the cost-based methods.

If full cost means the cost per unit for standard efficiency at normal volume, in the long run difficulties may emerge if the volume fluctuates from standard in a particular year, e.g.

fixed costs for the division are set at £150 000 and production at 30 000 units. Thus fixed cost per unit is £5, and if variable cost is £10, then a full cost transfer price of £15 would be set. Suppose, however, that in one year volume fell to 18 750 units, fixed cost per unit would then be £8, and with variable cost at £10, the total cost of £18 would exceed the transfer price by £3 a unit and the supplying division would make a loss. It would be unfair to evaluate managerial performance on the basis of that loss outside the control of managers at the supplying division. If transfer pricing irons out such fluctuations in the long run it clearly does not show the current cost in a particular year.

Group strategy must be considered. If a supplying division has a full cost transfer price of say £20 a unit, but the receiving division can buy outside for £18 a unit, it would appear to be more beneficial for the group if outside suppliers are used. However, if the supplying division has a marginal cost of £15, and is operating at 70% of capacity, the selling division will lose a contribution to its overheads of £5 a unit, so that the receiving division can reduce its cost by £2 a unit. Therefore, in group terms, a net contribution of £3 a unit is foregone, unless divisional interests are subordinated to those of the whole group. In this case senior management might need to enter into the negotiation and dictate a price, thereby reducing divisional autonomy.

Marginal cost is the incremental cost of production per unit, for the supplying division. Theoretically the receiving division should buy at this transfer price up to the point where marginal revenue from the sale of one extra unit equals marginal cost, plus any process costs added by the receiving division. But how is marginal cost to be determined if the supplying division sells outside the group to other customers? Will the marginal unit be based on the units sold within, or outside the group?

What if marginal cost of production is less than the market value. If this is so, the supplying division should increase its production until marginal revenue falls to equal marginal cost. If, however, the quantity demanded by the receiving division is limited this expansion cannot occur, and senior management must intervene to allow a transfer price in excess of marginal cost (thereby recognising the inadequacy of marginal cost), or they must force the division to accept marginal cost at the expense of their autonomy.

Unless there is the independence that autonomy produces, the divisional managers cannot be held responsible for results achieved from decisions taken without their agreement. Truly autonomous divisions should be allowed to trade *inter se* at open market prices, if a market exists, and prices can be identified. In the market-place buyers with large orders can expect to negotiate favourable prices, below the market price, and a receiving division may be forced to forego such discounts. Divisional managers should be free to negotiate with each other to establish the transfer price so long as they are not constrained by a requirement to buy or sell within the group, there is full market information available to both parties and they act in the best interests of the group. Unfortunately negotiations are time-consuming, and therefore costly, and may cause some conflict amongst divisional managers where instead co-operation should be present. If the parties are unable to agree a price, then senior management may be forced to mediate, perhaps generating charges of favouritism, which would merely exacerbate the situation.

Example

General Manufacturing PLC has organised its operations along divisional lines; Audio Visual (AV), Computer Communications (CC), and Specialised Engineering (SE). The SE division has a fibre optics machine, which both of the other divisions wish to use for certain of their products. The specialised machinery can only be used for 48 working hours each week, and the SE division works for 50 weeks per year.

Details of the products to be processed on the fibre optics machine are:

Division	AV	CC
Product	F39	T16
Selling price	£3995	£960
Variable cost per unit (including fibre optic time)	£2500	£850
Allocated fixed cost	£98 450	£62 800
Fibre optic processing time	1 hour	30 minutes
Annual demand	800 units	2400 units

The user divisions have calculated a transfer price for the use of the fibre optics machinery based on full absorption cost and an appropriate profit margin.

Variable cost per hour	£150
Fixed cost	50
Profit	30
Hourly rate	£230

The SE division is not in agreement with this transfer price. Several rival companies possess fibre optics equipment and are willing to sell processing time at £300 per hour. The SE division has also sold some processing time outside the group at this rate, but the cost of re-setting, adjusting and monitoring the equipment for such rentals is estimated to be £10 per processing hour.

Group management are called in to mediate in this dispute and suggest a transfer price equal to 'variable cost plus opportunity cost'.

Required:

Calculate the alternative transfer price and suggest a production schedule for the optimum use of the fibre optics machinery.

Solution

Note that fixed costs play no part in this analysis.

Contribution per hour of fibre optics processing time:

	F 39	*T 16*	*External Rental*
	£	£	£
Variable unit cost	2500	850	160
Less fixed cost and profit element in transfer price	80	40	–
	2420	810	160
Unit selling price	3995	960	300
Contribution per unit	1575	150	140
Contribution per hour of fibre optics machinery time	1575	300	140
Ranking of alternatives	1	2	3

Optimal use of fibre optics machinery time:

	Hours
800 units of F 39	800
2400 units of T 16	1200
Rental outside the group	400
Hours available 50 × 48	2400

Transfer price calculation:

	£
External rental 300 − 10	290
Variable cost	150
Opportunity cost	140

The transfer price is based on market price outside the group, with a reduction for direct cost of re-setting etc. In group terms, if variable cost is £150, the opportunity cost element in the transfer price would be £140, or contribution foregone if outside sales are not made.

Of course the SE division was not satisfied at a proposed transfer price of £230 per hour, since if allowed to make its own decision it would not rent its plant to AV or CC at that price, because it could maximise its return by renting outside at £300 per hour. If the transfer price is £300 per hour, the SE division would be indifferent as to whether the machinery was rented inside or outside the group, and the AV or CC division could not object at being asked to pay the market price without a subsidy from the SE division. If either of the user divisions find that it is not worthwhile to use the fibre optics machinery at this price, then the situation should be carefully reviewed, as indeed should any activity where unit price does not cover direct costs.

To extend this example, assume that the AV division plan to introduce a new product, F40, which will also require the use of the fibre optics machinery of the SE division. Details are as follows:

Variable cost per unit	£680
(including the charge from SE division for fibre optics machinery at £230 per hour)	
Apportioned share of annual divisional fixed production overheads	£53 000
Fibre optics machinery processing time: four units completed every hour	

Demand for F40 is considered to be price elastic:

Selling price	£1040	£1000	£950
Expected sales units	2600	3200	3900

The difficulty is in determining the best selling price at which to launch the product, how best to use the fibre optics machinery, and how a transfer price based on variable cost plus opportunity cost will promote the optimum use of scarce resources.

F 40: Unit variable cost (£680) less fixed cost and profit element in transfer price (£80 ÷ 4 units per hour) = £680 − £20 = £660

Best selling price of F40:

Alternative prices	£1040	£1000	£950
Demand	2600	3200	3900
Fibre optics time	650 hours	800 hours	975 hours
Contribution per unit (price less variable cost) £380		£340	£290
Total contribution	£988 000	£1 088 000	£1 131 000

Contribution per hour of fibre optics machinery: £988 000 ÷ 650 hours = £1520 for the first 650 hours, but thereafter
Marginal contribution is that an extra £100 000 of contribution (£1 088 000 – £988 000) is earned by the next 150 hours (800 – 650), so the
Incremental contribution for the next 150 hours is £100 000 – 150 hours = £666 per hour
Incremental contribution per hour for the following 175 hours (975 – 800) is £43 000 (£1 131 000 – £1 088 000) ÷ 175 hours = £246 per hour

Ranking of products to maximise contribution per hour for the use of fibre optics machinery:

Product F 39	800 hours at £1575	800 units
Product F 40	650 hours at £1520	
	150 hours at £666	3200 units
	1600	
Product T 16	800 hours at £300	1600 units
Total hours available	2400	

Production of T16 will be limited to 66 % of demand and there will be no capacity available for rental outside the group.

A transfer price calculated as variable cost (£150) plus opportunity cost (contribution from marginal hour used = £300) shows a total of £450 per hour for the use of the machinery. This will certainly remove all demands for rental outside the group, but it may also discourage the CC division, which makes product T16 and, as shown above, earns a contribution of only £300 per fibre optic machine-hour. At a transfer price of £450 per hour, it is cheaper for CC division to buy on the open market at £310 per hour, but if this occurs the group machinery will lie idle for 800 hours each year. Clearly, group central management must intervene to negotiate a settlement that is agreeable to all the parties concerned.

SEMINAR EXERCISES

18.1 (a) What are the major objectives for developing transfer prices?

(b) AYE PLC has a decentralised organisational structure – each division operating as a separate profit centre and delegated full authority on all decisions involving the sale of the division's output to both outsiders and other divisions. Division A has in the past always purchased its requirements of Component Q 439 from Division B. However, when informed that Division B was increasing its price to £3, Division A's management decided to purchase its annual requirements of 10 000 components Q 439 from outside suppliers. The component can be purchased for £2.50 on the open market. Division B insists that owing to the recent installation of some highly specialised equipment and the resulting high depreciation charges, Division B would not be able to make an adequate profit on its investment unless it raised its price. Division B's management appealed to the head office for support in its dispute with Division A and supplied the following budget information:

Product: Component Q439

Practical capacity: 50 000 components
Expected level of activity: 45 000 components
Expected sales to Division A: 10 000 components
Expected sales to external customers: 35 000 components

Level of activity (units)	40 000	45 000	50 000
	£000's	£000's	£000's
Cost of production:			
Direct materials and labour	60.0	67.5	75.0
Variable production overheads			
Supplies	8.0	9.0	10.0
Indirect wages	12.0	13.5	15.0
Handling costs	4.0	4.5	5.0
Fixed production overheads			
Building occupancy	25.0	25.0	25.0
Indirect wages	10.0	10.0	10.0
Depreciation	62.0	62.0	62.0
Handling	11.0	11.0	11.0
	£212.0	£225.0	£238.0

Required:

(i) Assume that there are no alternative uses for B's internal facilities. Determine whether the company as a whole will benefit if Division A purchased the components from outside suppliers for £2 per component.

(ii) Assume that there are no alternative uses for B's internal facilities and that the open market price for the component drops to £1.80. Should Division A purchase from outside suppliers?

(c) What reasons might top management have for employing this cost plus pricing arrangement? Outline the objections to this basis.   (25 marks)

Section VII
The System and the Ledgers

19

Management Information Systems and Cost Book-keeping

MANAGEMENT INFORMATION SYSTEMS

The task of the manager is to plan, communicate, motivate, organise and control the part of the business that is his responsibility. These activities are undertaken in a climate of uncertainty, but the difficulties are eased if management information supplies reliable data concerning what is actually taking place. The management information system must provide the right information to the right person at the right time and in the right form.

To be useful, information must be relevant to the tasks and problems of the manager who receives it. This implies that the information concerns aspects of the business that the manager can influence or control and that the information will be put to use because it is recognised by the manager as relevant to his task, and therefore beneficial. The cost of the information must not exceed that benefit, but both cost and benefit are often difficult to measure. Management information must be disclosed in good time if it is to be influential in changing plans or prompting remedial action. Management reports can be made on a regular basis, e.g. monthly, but it is necessary to ensure that they are not treated in a routine manner, so that any message they contain is overlooked or ignored, or no longer seen as important. An audit of management information reports may indicate the fact that managers could work just as effectively without certain expensive cost statements. Sometimes a manager will need information on an *ad hoc* basis to assist him to solve a non-routine problem. The adequacy of the database and the retrieval facilities available to the accountant will determine how much helpful information he can supply in these circumstances.

Management information should be provided in a form that is easily assimilated and understood by the recipient, which reduces the possibility that it will be misunderstood and increases the likelihood that it will lead to prompt action. Managers should not be overloaded with figures; a well-ordered statement should make its point and lead to a conclusion, highlighting salient features and cutting out unnecessary data. The management accountant should edit the information that is provided to managers at various levels in the business, including the appropriate level of detail or summary, to fit the requirements of the recipient. Reports to management must be designed to reveal information that will help the managers, and such information is best defined after discussion with each manager. Comparison with a norm, or with expected results drawn from a budget, will add perspective to the information, which may be in monetary or non-monetary form, e.g. units of production or standard hours.

The management information system must be designed to recognise all transactions and collect and record raw data, to arrange and analyse the data, thereby converting it all to information, if necessary to store information and include a retrieval system, and, finally, to evaluate information and report appropriately. It is important that no transaction should evade the system. The accountant is faced with a set of interrelated events in an organisation that he must fit into a pattern. He must interpret the events and derive some meaning from the information they generate, drawing the relevant part of that pattern to the attention of managers whose duty and responsibility it is to administrate segments of the organisation. Reports should follow through the flow of resources in a business and identify waste and inefficiency. The success and value of a system of management information can be measured by the impact it has on the organisation, and this impact will be increased according to the accuracy, reliability, selectivity, flexibility and response time associated with the system. If internal checks are built into the system, all concerned will place greater reliance on the accuracy of the information the system provides. Once again, the cost/benefit relationship of such accuracy is a key factor in the design of the system.

When a cost book-keeping or recording system is installed these basic principles must be considered whether or not the records form part of an integrated system, which operates for financial accounting purposes as well.

As organisations become more complex it is important to apply a systematic approach to the provision of management information. As the volume of transactions increases, electronic methods are applied to data processing, and in these circumstances the existence of a reliable routine is vital to success. The human brain should apply a logic check to data as it is processed, which must be replaced by checks built into the computer program or whatever other system is used. Internal check comprises the routine checks on day-to-day transactions, which operate as part of the system. If the work of one person is proved to be independent of or is complementary to the work of another, errors will be found, fraud made more difficult and management information will become more reliable. If individual responsibilities are arranged so that no one individual can undertake all the activities involved with a single transaction, then collusion must take place before fraud can be accomplished. It is often wise to rotate the duties of an individual to prevent the development of such collusion.

Much can be achieved if forms are designed in such a way as to highlight key information, or if routines are organised to ensure a check is made at significant points in the system, e.g. an invoice cannot be passed for payment until it is agreed with the order and GRN and it must be initialled by the checker to indicate that all checks have been made. If a clerk has to take responsibility for a check it will ensure that care will be taken with this work. Strict rules concerning the recording of transactions as soon as they take place help to ensure that no item is missed, whilst control of documentation, e.g. serial numbers on order pads, may prevent their use for illicit purposes. Colour coding and multi-set stationary will assist in the correct routing of documents to various parts of the organisation.

Management information must be cost-effective. The system must be such that efficiency is increased by the information it provides, and every attempt must be made to cut out procedures that do not increase efficiency. It is the task of managers who use the information, as much as that of the accountant, to suggest improvements and to ensure that the system as specified is properly operated by their subordinates. The use of cheap but low-calibre employees to operate the system is a false economy, since mistakes may reduce the reliability of the management information. Internal audit of management reports is a costly remedy, and the expense of an extra check on the information, even on a sample basis, may not be worth the saving from those mistakes discovered.

It is difficult to set a boundary beyond which no further information be provided to management. Too much data in a report may confuse the issue and cloud judgement. A decision should be more accurate if based on ample management information, but individual circumstances will determine the point at which the benefit or pay-off from extra information is exceeded by the cost of providing that information. This situation could at best be expressed as the potential loss avoided if managers could be better informed when they make the decision, set against the cost of providing extra information. Management information should be scrutinised according to its usefulness, perhaps in terms of the difference it could make to a decision and the cost of a potential error if the decision is made without the benefit of certain facts.

COST BOOK-KEEPING

In its simplest form costing consists of memoranda, which vary from mere jottings on scraps of paper to formal documents, books, or cards that are not part of a set of accounts maintained on double-entry principles. There is no doubt that valuable information can be so obtained, e.g. a small shopkeeper, who already has an adequate financial accounting system, may not need to maintain a set of cost accounts as well. Any costs he wishes to compute, from time to time, can be computed outside his accounting system when the occasion arises. He need not, for example, set up as a separate cost centre each of his delivery vans, for if he wants to know the running costs of a particular vehicle he can analyse his invoices etc. and make an analysis of the vehicle's journeys to compute his running cost per kilometre run, or per tonne-mile. The main disadvantage of such a procedure is the likelihood of the required memorandum records not being available when wanted, and the absence of general control.

Memorandum records are not always uncontrolled. The share register and plant register of a large company are usually regarded as memorandum records outside the financial accounting system, but they are not permitted to get out of step with the share capital and plant accounts which, in effect, control them. Similar control accounts can be operated with a costing system maintained on memorandum lines and there is no valid reason why this should not operate satisfactorily. Mere cost ascertainment, however, is not sufficient. The modern manager demands information that will enable him to control costs, and is not content that costs incurred should merely be accounted for. This usually involves the maintenance of a formal system of cost accounting, either as part of an integrated cost and financial accounting system, or closely linked with an independent system of financial accounting. It is with such systems that this chapter is mainly concerned.

Even when there is a formal system of cost accounting, *ad hoc* reports and analyses in memorandum form will be called for, since it is not practicable to make every possible analysis in the accounting records themselves because of the volume of work involved. Formal cost accounting may bring the benefits of standardisation and of increased accuracy, but it cannot entirely displace memorandum analyses even in the largest concern. There will always be some form of analysis that is not available and that needs to be extracted 'by hand'.

Integrated Accounts

A single book-keeping system that contains both financial and cost accounts is termed an integrated accounting system. Such a system has been envisaged throughout the earlier chapters of this work.

The hub around which an integrated accounting system revolves is the *general ledger*. This contains two basic types of account: simple accounts and control accounts. The former represent assets, liabilities, etc. in their own right, whereas each of the latter forms a connecting link with a subsidiary ledger in which the detailed composition of the control account balance is recorded. No distinction need be made between accounts that are 'cost accounts' and those that are 'financial accounts'. The fact that such a system tends to merge cost and financial accounting to form one inseparable accounting function, and thus to cause the loss of the independence otherwise enjoyed by cost accounting, reduces the cost of accounting by avoiding duplication in processing and recording business transactions.

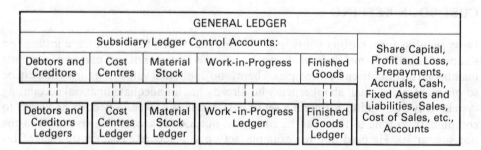

Main Accounts and Subsidiary Ledgers in a Completely Integrated System

Another barrier to the ready acceptance of integrated accounts is the 'need' to supply management with accounts in which the items are classified according to their nature. Financial accountants supply information in the form of a manufacturing account, trading account, profit and loss account and a balance sheet, and they produce this information perhaps at quarterly intervals. As business organisations have grown in size, managers have developed a requirement for up-to-date information concerning only parts of the business under their control and separate cost accounts have replaced the former system.

It is extremely difficult to interpret figures presented without any departmental (or functional) analysis. Consider the item salaries shown in the profit and loss account; this may represent the salaries of personnel engaged in administration, e.g. on accounting and secretarial work; selling, e.g. on representation and sales management; distribution, e.g. packing and delivering; research; advertising; etc. Only a manager who is already well aware of the entire position could assess the significance of any change in the total charge for salaries.

An integrated system can produce operating statements for individual managers, analysing at frequent intervals performance for the sector of a business under the control of each manager, yet these statements are produced from the same accounting system that provides the trial balance from which the year-end financial accounts are drafted. It follows that the cumulative costing figures for the year can be reconciled to these financial accounts, usually through the aggregate of the figures on the monthly *costing profit and loss account*.

The control accounts for material (stocks), labour and overheads hold totals for the many lesser accounts that record individual costs in these sectors. Each material has a stock record card to show purchases, returns and requisitions issued to the factory for various jobs, processes or departments. The total of wages paid is analysed, first between direct and indirect labour cost, and the direct labour is further analysed to production

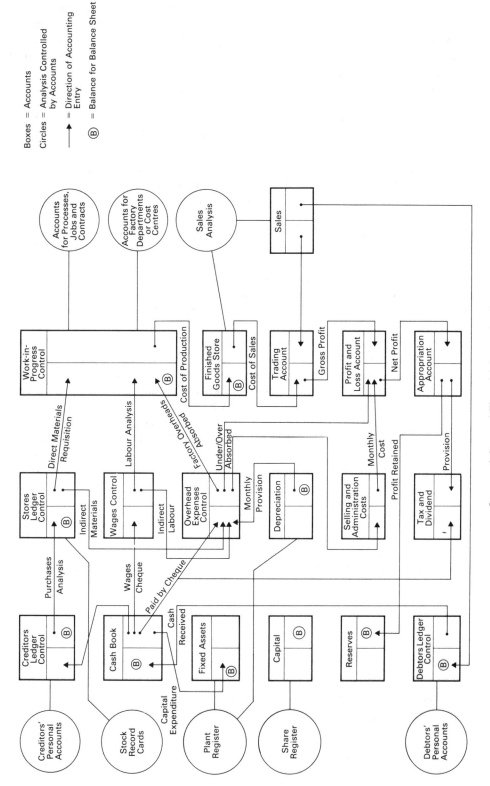

Boxes = Accounts

Circles = Analysis Controlled by Accounts

→ = Direction of Accounting Entry

Ⓑ = Balance for Balance Sheet

Integrated Cost and Financial Accounting System

departments in the factory. Indirect labour is treated as an overhead expense and forms part of the overhead control account. Other overheads with individual accounts (rent, rates, light and heat) are controlled in total through the overhead control account and analysed to departments or other segments of the business. Any over or under-absorption of overheads is written off direct to the profit and loss account.

Work-in-progress control is maintained through the factory or manufacturing account, in which the costs of completed production transferred to finished goods store are built up. This form of control may cover the activity of one factory, but the materials, labour and overhead costs of the factory may be analysed to various batches, processes, jobs or departments, so that detailed operating statements for the cost centres analyse the situation for the management concerned in the operation of these centres. Selling and administrative overheads are accumulated in one account and charged to profit and loss, but the figures can be analysed for detailed departmental reports. For a further explanation of integrated accounts the reader should follow the direction of the accounting entries in the diagram of accounts for an integrated system.

This system allows for a monthly profit and loss account and balance sheet and, at the same time, detailed segmental reports to managers. Business activity cannot be expected to finalise itself neatly at the end of each month of the year, so there will be balances carried forward from one period to another, and these balances will also require careful analysis if managers are to control them, whether they are items in the plant register, the stock record cards or debtors' personal accounts.

To introduce standard costing into this system all that is required is to transfer the costs of direct materials, direct labour and overheads from the control accounts for stores, wages and overheads into work-in-progress control at standard amounts and to transfer the corresponding variances to variance accounts where they are in turn written off to costing profit and loss account. This account is credited with the standard net profit and the variances then increase or decrease this amount until the actual profit is computed.

If marginal or direct costing is to be used as a recording system the transfers to work-in-progress concern only direct materials, direct labour and direct overheads. Fixed overheads are written off on a time basis to the profit and loss account.

Example

In the absence of the accountant you have been asked to prepare a month's cost accounts for a company that operates a batch costing system fully integrated with the financial accounts. The cost clerk has provided you with the following information, which he thinks is relevant.

	£
Balance at beginning of month:	
Stores ledger control account	25 175
Work-in-progress control account	18 210
Finished goods control account	36 164
Prepayments of production overheads b/f from previous month	3 100
Transactions during the month:	£
Materials purchased	78 150
Materials issued: to production	28 350
for factory maintenance	5 280
Materials transferred between batches	2 450

	Direct Workers £	Indirect Workers £
Total wages paid – Net	18 646	4 342
Employees' deductions	4 264	790
Employers' deductions	1 200	500

	£
Direct wages charged to batches from work tickets	16 236
Recorded non-productive time of direct workers	4 230
Direct wages incurred on production of capital equipment, for use in the factory	2 570
Selling and distribution overheads incurred	6 240
Other production overheads incurred	11 200
Sales	78 400
Cost of finished goods sold	60 830
Cost of goods completed and transferred into finished goods store during the month	63 130
Physical stock value of work-in-progress at end of month	25 360

The production overhead absorption rate is 150% of direct wages and it is the policy of the company to include a share of production overheads in the cost of capital equipment constructed in the factory.

Required:

(a) Prepare the following accounts for the month:
Stores Ledger Control Account
Work-in-Progress Control Account
Wages Control Account
Finished Goods Control Account
Production Overhead Control Account
Profit and Loss Account.
(b) Itemise aspects of the accounts that should be investigated.

(a)

Stores Ledger Control Account

	£		£
Opening balance b/f	25 175	Work-in-progress control account	28 350
Creditors	78 150	Production overhead control account	5 280
		Closing balance c/f	69 695
	£103 325		£103 325

Work-in-Progress Control Account

	£		£
Opening balance b/f	18 210	Finished goods control account	63 130
Stores ledger control account	28 350	Closing stock c/f	25 360
Wages control account	16 236		
Production overhead control account	23 854		
Profit and loss account: Stock gain	1 840		
	£88 490		£88 490

Finished Goods Control Account

	£		£
Opening balance b/f	36 164	Cost of goods sold account	60 830
Work-in-progress control			
account	63 130	Closing stock c/f	38 464
	£99 294		£99 294

Production Overhead Control Account

	£		£
Prepayments b/f	3 100	Work-in-progress control	
		account*	24 354
Stores ledger control account	5 280	Capital under construction	
		account*	3 855
Wages control account:		Profit and loss account:	
Direct	4 230	Under-absorbed overheads	2 833
Indirect	5 232		
Employers' deduction	2 000		
Cash/Creditors	11 200		
	£31 042		£31 042

Profit and Loss Account

	£		£
Cost of goods sold account	60 830	Sales	78 400
Selling & distribution		Work-in-progress account:	
overhead account	6 240	Stock gain	1 840
Production overheads under-			
absorbed	2 833		
Profit c/f	10 337		
	£80 240		£80 240

* Production overheads absorbed, by production £16 236×150% = £24 354
by capital work £2570×150% = £3855

Wages Control Account

	£		£
Wages paid (cash):		Work-in-progress control	16 236
Direct	18 646	Production overhead control:	
Indirect	4 342	Direct	4 230
Employees' deductions:			
Direct	4 264	Indirect	5 232
Indirect	790	Employers' deductions	2 000
Employers' deductions:	2 000	Unexplained balance	2 344
	£30 042		£30 042

(b) Some items disclosed by these accounts merit further investigation. The unexplained balance on the wages control account seems to concern direct workers. Amounts of £16 236 and £4230 have been charged to the work-in-progress and overhead accounts, but the amount paid or deducted totals £22 910 (£18 646 + £4264), so presumably the wage analysis is in error.

It is difficult to imagine how a stock gain could arise on the work-in-progress control unless the stock figures are incorrect or a gain in process has been ignored. Certainly the closing stock figure of the stores ledger control should be checked, since it shows an increase of £44 520 or 176% of the opening figure. Either the stock figure is wrong, or purchasing has not been co-ordinated to the requirements of the factory for raw materials.

Non-integrated Cost Accounting

Where the cost and financial accounting systems are non-integrated there is no means of 'communication' between the two systems, though they obviously relate to the same facts and are largely based upon identical sources of information. Both systems must record wages, for instance, though the emphasis will be in different directions. Financial accounting will be concerned with the general nature of the item whereas cost accounting will look to the function performed by the labour; to the responsibility for incurring the cost; to the efficiency with which the work was done, etc. In order to prove that the cost and financial accounts are 'in step' it is usual to reconcile the profit shown by the costing records with that disclosed in the financial accounts, as will be described later in this chapter. In the meantime it is necessary to consider the source of the entries in the cost ledger under such a system and also the nature of the entries themselves.

In an integrated system, once an invoice is entered in the books as an item awaiting payment, its inclusion in costs is almost automatic. In fact, action would normally need to be taken to prevent the charge of such an item being made in costs. No such check is present in a non-integrated system: the inclusion of an item for financial accounting purposes does not, of itself, ensure that it will appear in costs, but only a measure of co-operation is needed to ensure that a satisfactory procedure is followed. Once each invoice has been recorded in the financial records its safe delivery to the cost accounting section must be ensured and this is usually done by supplying a run-list of the invoices transferred together with details of the total invoices transferred in the period to date. Similar principles should be adopted with regard to invoices for expenses and to payments for salaries, wages, etc. Wherever details of the analysis employed for financial accounting purposes can assist the costing section, they should be supplied too. Co-operation is even more essential where there is a non-integrated system than where there is an integrated one. Its absence will lead to chaos when the time comes for the two sets of accounts to be reconciled.

Obviously the financial accountant must provide the cost accountant with details of accruals and prepayments and with information that will enable him to compute overhead absorption rates where this is not already available to him. The charges for depreciation, for example, must be known to the cost accountant, as he must employ them in his machine-hour rates.

The entries in a non-integrated system are much the same as those in an integrated one, except that no asset or liability accounts appear in the cost ledger apart from those concerned with stocks and work-in-progress. In their place is a *cost control* account. All entries bringing items into costs are debited to the appropriate accounts in the cost ledger (e.g. raw material stock, cost centres, etc.), the corresponding credit being to the cost control account. Sales, on the other hand, are debited to the cost control account and credited to a sales account. The cost of sales and sales accounts are closed to a trading and profit and loss account in the cost ledger, to which are debited any period costs, such as research costs, together with exceptional losses, such as idle time, storage losses, etc. The balance of the trading and profit and loss account is transferred to the cost control account. If this latter account is thought of as the cost accountant's 'capital account' the similarity with financial accounting will be apparent. As with previously discussed systems there are a number of variants. Sometimes, for example, the costing records are confined to production and administration costs and no attempt is made to compute a 'costing' profit or loss.

Example

The following balances are extracted from a cost ledger as at 1 January 19   :

	£	£
Raw material stock ledger control	18 350	
Work-in-progress ledger control	23 450	
Production overheads	105	
Administration overheads		125
Finished goods ledger control	13 450	
Cost ledger control		55 230
	£ 55 355	£ 55 355

The following transactions took place during January.

	£
Goods finished (at cost)	85 250
Production overheads incurred (including indirect materials £ 2350)	4 320
Administration overheads absorbed by production	3 310
Salaries and wages:	
Direct labour	12 550
Production salaries	5 250
Office salaries	1 525
Raw materials purchased	52 550
Administration overheads incurred (including indirect materials £ 540)	1 200
Goods sold (at cost exclusive of selling and distribution overheads)	85 590
Raw materials issued to production (direct)	60 550
Production overheads absorbed	8 880

Required:

(a)   Construct the accounts in the cost ledger from the above information.
(b)   Schedule the remaining balances at 31 January.

Selling and distribution costs do not appear in the cost ledger.

(a)   Raw Materials Stock Ledger Control

19—		£	19—		£
Jan. 1	Balance b/f	18 350	Jan. 31	Production overheads	2 350
Jan. 31	Cost ledger control:			Administration overhead	540
	Purchases	52 550		Work-in-progrees	60 550
				Balance c/d	7 460
		£ 70 900			£ 70 900
Apr. 1	Balance b/d	7 460			

Work-in-progress Ledger Control

19—		£	19—		£
Jan. 1	Balance b/f	23 450	Jan. 31	Finished goods	
Jan. 31	Direct labour	12 550		ledger control	85 250
	Direct materials	60 550		Balance c/d	23 490
	Production overheads				
	absorbed	8 880			
	Administration				
	overheads				
	absorbed	3 310			
		£ 108 740			£ 108 740
Feb. 1	Balance b/d	23 490			

Production Overheads

19—		£	19—		£
Jan. 1	Balance b/f	105	Jan. 31	Work-in-progress	
Jan. 31	Production overheads			ledger control:	
	incurred (expense			Overheads absorbed	8 880
	and material)	4 320		Balance c/d – under-	
	Salaries	5 250		absorbed	795
		£ 9675			£ 9675
Feb. 1	Balance b/d	795			

Administration Overheads

19—		£	19—		£
Jan. 31	Administration over-		Jan. 1	Balance b/f	125
	heads (expense and		Jan. 31	Work-in-progress	
	material)	1200		ledger control:	
	Office salaries	1525		Overheads absorbed	3310
	Balance c/d – over-				
	absorbed	710			
		£ 3435			£ 3435
			Feb. 1	Balance b/d	710

Finished Goods Ledger Control

19—		£	19—		£
Jan. 1	Balance b/f	13 450	Jan. 31	Cost ledger control	85 590
Jan. 31	Work-in-progress			Balance c/d	13 110
	ledger control	85 250			
		£ 98 700			£ 98 700
Feb. 1	Balance b/d	13 110			

Cost Ledger Control

19—		£	19—			£
Jan. 31	Finished goods	85 590	Jan. 1	Balance b/f		55 230
			Jan. 31	Production overheads		1 970
				Salaries and wages		19 325
				Raw material purchases		52 550
	Balance c/d	44 145		Administration overheads		660
		£ 129 735				£ 129 735
			Feb. 1	Balance b/d		44 145

(b)

Trial Balance

31 January

	£	£
Raw material stock ledger control	7 460	
Work-in-progress ledger control	23 490	
Production overheads	795	
Administration overheads		710
Finished goods ledger control	13 110	
Cost ledger control		44 145
	£ 44 855	£ 44 855

Reconciliation of Cost and Financial Accounts

Where cost and financial accounts are separate, it is necessary to reconcile the results disclosed by the former with those shown by the latter. Otherwise the two sets of accounts may get out of step and so provide conflicting information on the basis of which unwise policy decisions can easily be made. A cross-check is useful to confirm the accuracy of both systems. In theory, reconciliation merely involves the making of such adjustments to the results shown by the cost records as will take account of the slightly different bases upon which the two sets of accounts are drawn up.

The major causes of differences between cost and financial accounts can be classified as follows:

Entries appearing only in the cost accounts. Notional costs may be set against profit to charge for the use of assets owned by the group and to ensure that the costing profit disclosed for each department or product measures the true return earned by that part of the business as though it were independent and received no hidden benefit from group resources. A notional rent is often charged for the use of property owned by the business or a notional interest is charged on group funds used to finance a department or activity as part of its capital employed. The financial accounts will show no such charges, interest being confined to amounts paid out to debenture holders and not extended to share capital or reserves.

Appropriations. After the profit figure has been measured, that profit is appropriated for a number of different purposes, e.g. to pay taxation or dividends, or to be retained in the business. Such items can play no part in the costing system and must be eliminated when the costing and financial profit is reconciled.

Matters of policy. Certain costs may be derived from a board decision rather than a business expense. As such these artificial extras, or provisions, will affect the financial accounts but may not be included in the cost accounts. The board may, for example, decide to write down stocks or goodwill, provide an extra amount to cover doubtful debts, or top up the company's pension fund. If the result of these decisions has not been included in the cost accounts, then the amounts must be adjusted in the reconciliation.

Items excluded from cost accounts. In some companies miscellaneous income from investments or bank deposits or rent received from sub-let properties is excluded from the costing system because it cannot easily be allotted to a particular department or product. Capital items, such as profits on the sale of an investment, stamp duty on share issues, damages and costs from legal actions and penalties payable under certain contracts, will appear in the financial accounts but may be excluded from the cost accounts.

Items where the costing treatment is different from the financial accounting treatment. Accounting policies pursued in the financial and cost accounts may differ, so that those differences must be recognised, measured and included in the reconciliation, e.g. the basis on which stocks are valued – if the cost accountant applies LIFO, whilst the financial accountant is constrained from using that method by the rules enshrined in SSAP 9. Different methods or rates of depreciation are unlikely to be used by cost and financial accounts, but may be present and thus form part of the reconciliation.

Example

The following is a summary of the trading and profit and loss account of Octopus Limited for the quarter ended 31 December 19—:

	£		£	£
Materials consumed (direct)	69 800	Sales (60 000 units)		150 000
Wages (direct)	38 100	Finished stock (2000 units)		4 000
Production overheads	21 300	Work-in-progress:	£	
Administration overheads	9 550	Materials	1600	
Selling and distribution overheads	11 350	Wages	900	
Preliminary expenses written off	1 000	Production overheads	500	
Goodwill written off	2 350		——	3 000
Dividend	2 500	Dividends received (gross)		13 500
Taxation	5 000			
Net profit	9 550			
	£170 500			£170 500

The company manufactures a standard unit.

In the cost accounts, production overheads have been absorbed by production at 20% of prime cost, administration overheads at 15p per unit produced, and selling and distribution overheads at 20p per unit sold. The net profit shown by the cost accounts was £6600.

Prepare:

(a) Control accounts for production overheads, administration overheads and selling and distribution overheads;
(b) A statement reconciling the profit disclosed by the cost records with that shown in the financial accounts.

(a)   Production Overheads

19—		£	19—		£
Dec. 31	Cost ledger control	21 300	Dec. 31	Work-in-progress	21 580
	Balance c/d	280			
		£ 21 580			£ 21 580
			Jan. 1	Balance b/d	280

Administration Overheads

19—		£	19—		£
Dec. 31	Cost ledger control	9 550	Dec. 31	Finished goods	9 300
				Balance c/d	250
		£ 9 550			£ 9 550
Jan. 1	Balance b/d	250			

Selling and Distribution Overheads

19—		£	19—		£
Dec. 31	Cost ledger control	11 350	Dec. 31	Cost of slaes	12 000
	Balance c/d	650			
		£ 12 000			£ 12 000
			Jan. 1	Balance b/d	650

(b)   **Reconciliation Statement**

			£
Profit per cost accounts			6 600
Overheads under/over-absorbed:			
	Under	*Over*	
	£	£	
Production		280	
Administration	250		
Selling and distribution		650	
	£250	£930	
			680
Profit per cost accounts after adjustment for under- or over-absorption of overheads			7 280
Deduct: Write-down of finished stock			
(£ 4380 – £ 4000)			380
Trading profit for the quarter after adjustment			6 900
Add: Dividends received			13 500
Profit for the quarter available for appropriation			20 400
Deduct: Preliminary expenses		1000	
Goodwill written off		2350	
Dividend		2500	
Taxation		5000	
			10 850
Profit for quarter per financial accounts			£ 9 550

Note: The cost of the finished goods stock is computed as follows:

		Per Unit £
Materials:		
	$\dfrac{£\,69\,800 - £\,1600}{62\,000}$	1.100
Wages:		
	$\dfrac{£\,38\,100 - £\,900}{62\,000}$	0.600
		1.700
Production overheads:		
20% of £1.700		0.340
Administration overheads		0.150
		£2.190

$$2000 \text{ at } £\,2.190 = £\,4380$$

In practice, reconciliation will prove tedious and difficult, if not impossible, unless active steps are taken to prepare for it by making the financial and cost accounting classifications compatible. The employment of control accounts through which main groups of costs such as wages, materials, selling and distribution costs, administration costs, depreciation, etc. are passed, materially lessens the difficulties of reconciliation since it facilitates sub-reconciliations of each main group of costs, and so confines any difference to a relatively small area.

SEMINAR EXERCISES

19.1 Seepower Limited, a company engaged in the manufacture of specialist marine engines, operates a historic job cost accounting system that is *not* integrated with the financial accounts.

At the beginning of May the opening balances in the cost ledger were:

	£
Stores ledger control account	86 400
Work-in-progress control account	168 350
Finished goods control account	50 250
Cost ledger control account	305 000

During the month the following transactions took place:

		£
Materials:	Purchases	41 700
	Issues — to production	64 400
	— to general maintenance	2 450
	— to construction of manufacturing equipment	8 650
Factory wages: Total gross wages paid		126 000

£13 500 of the above gross wages were incurred on the construction of manufacturing equipment, £37 750 were indirect wages and the balance were direct.

Production overheads:

Actual amount incurred, excluding items shown above, was £151 350; £32 000 was absorbed by the manufacturing equipment under construction and under-absorbed overheads written off at the end of the month amounted to £6550.

Royalty payments:

One of the engines produced is manufactured under licence. £3150 is the amount that will be paid to the inventor for the month's production of that particular engine.

Selling overheads: £21 000.

Sales: £415 000.

The company's gross profit margin is 25% on factory cost.

At the end of May stocks of work-in-progress had increased by £13 000. The manufacturing equipment under construction was completed within the month, and transferred out of the cost ledger at the end of the month.

Required:

Prepare the relevant control accounts, costing profit and loss account, and any other accounts you consider necessary to record the above transactions in the cost ledger for May.   (25 marks)

SOLUTIONS TO SEMINAR EXERCISES

1.1 1. Cost information to help management control business activity: a monthly profit statement, showing the gross profit made by each type of work, or class of vehicle, less selling and administration costs to give a net profit figure. This data could be compared with the budget for the period, or with similar information for the same month the previous year.

2. Operating cost per vehicle: analysed between fixed and variable costs, e.g. fixed – licence, insurance, depreciation, maintenance; variable – fuel, tyres, drivers' wages and expenses – cost per tonne-mile or kilometre could be produced.

   This information would help management to estimate a price for future loads, judge the relative efficiency of various types of vehicles and thus influence replacement policy.

3. Activity: a log could show the miles run each month per vehicle, the amount of idle time, and the incidence of empty return journeys. This data would reveal idle capacity, and overworked capacity, to help decide whether the combination of large and small vehicles is correct.

4. Maintenance costs: a comparison of in-house maintenance costs with the sub-contract maintenance would show up the relative efficiency of the maintenance department. A plant register with details of each vehicle will reveal those with heavy repair costs, and those on which major overhauls have taken place, so that a correct choice is made when vehicles are scrapped.

5. Costs of selling and administration: to compare rigorously with budget and costs for a previous comparable period to detect any unwarranted increase in overheads at an early stage.

1.2 (a) The purpose of cost accounting is to provide information to management, either at regular intervals or when a request is made, to facilitate planning, controlling, evaluating and decision making. In Sparks Stores PLC there are four groups of managers who can benefit from this information, i.e. shop managers, warehouse managers, transport managers, and senior managers at head office. The level of detail provided for each manager would depend on the circumstances.

   (i) Planning or budgeting requires expected cost and revenue information for alternative courses of action, and controlling requires a speedy comparison of actual performance with budget. A monthly analysis of gross and net profit for each shop, data on the profitability of various product lines, details of stock levels, and rapid warning of slow-selling lines are required. The wages and overhead expenses could be analysed for each shop, and compared across all shops, perhaps as a percentage of sales achieved.

   (ii) Cost data on the operation of the transport fleet, to ensure that the alternative to outside contractors really is more expensive, and that van capacity does not lie idle.

   (iii)   At the warehouse, stock holding costs could be set against the benefits of large stocks to derive an amount for the most economic holding quantity for each product.

   (iv)   At head office, analysis of overhead expense to ensure that it does not exceed budgeted levels.

   (v)   For *ad hoc* decisions, reports will be made on request for such matters as pricing decisions, continuing the sale of various lines, product mix, opening new shops, etc.

(b)   To meet these requirements costs would need to be classified:

    (i)   by period
   (ii)   by cost centre – shop/depot/vehicle/head office functions
   (iii)   by product
   (iv)   by behaviour – fixed, variable, semi-variable
   (v)   by controllability and
   (vi)   by relevance to a particular decision.

2.1

Date	Receipts		Issues		Stock	
		£		£		£
1/10					200	200
4/10	10/417 1800 × £1	1800			2000	2000
10/10			D127 1000 × £1	1000	1000	1000
25/10	10/649 1600 × £1.20	1920			1000 }	} 1000
					1600 }	} 1920
1/11			D460 1000 × £1	1000	1600	1920
20/11			D512 1000 × £1.20	1200	600	720
6/12	12/131 1400 × £1.60	2240			600 }	} 720
					1400 }	} 2240
20/12			D720 600 × £1.20	720		
			400 × £1.60	640	1000	1600*
			Charge to Production	£4560		

Table title: Stock Record Card – Component 437Q (FIFO)

	Stock Record Card – Component 437Q (LIFO)					
Date	Receipts		Issues		Stock	
		£		£		£
1/10					200	200
4/10	10/417 1800 × £1	1800			2000	2000
10/10			D127 1000 × £1	1000	1000	1000
25/10	10/649 1600 × £1.20	1920			1000 }	} 1000
					1600 }	} 1920
1/11			D460 1000 × £1.20	1200	1000 }	} 1000
					600 }	} 720
30/11			D512 600 × £1.20	720	600	600
			400 × £1.00	400		
6/12	12/131 1400 × £1.60	2240			600 }	} 600
					1400 }	} 2240
20/12			D720 1000 × £1.60	1600	600 }	} 600
					400 }	} 640
			Charge to Production	———— £4920		£1240*

	Stock Record Card – Component 437Q (Weighted Average Cost)					
Date	Receipts		Issues		Stock	
		£		£		£
1/10					200	200
4/10	10/417 1800 × £1	1800			2000	2000
10/10			D127 1000 × £1	1000	1000	1000
25/10	10/649 1600 × £1.20	1920			2600	2920
1/11			D460 1000 × £1.12	1120	1600	1800
20/11			D512 1000 × £1.12	1120	600	680†
6/12	12/131 1400 × £1.60	2240			2000	2920†
20/12			D720 1000 × £1.46	1460	1000	1460*
			Charge to Production	£4700		

* Closing stock
† Slight differences due to rounding in average calculation.

Calculations:

$$\frac{£2920}{2600 \text{ units}} = £1.12$$

$$\frac{£2920}{2000 \text{ units}} = £1.46$$

2.2

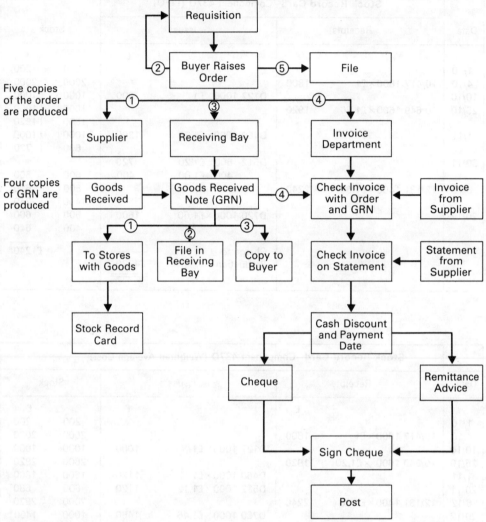

Flow Chart to Illustrate a System for the Purchase of and Payment for Materials

2.3 (a) *Economic order quantity* (EOQ) is that size of purchase order which minimizes the combined annual cost of placing orders and holding stock. Stock holding costs rise as the order size increases following the rise in the average annual stock level. Ordering costs fall as fewer orders are placed during the year. (See graph on opposite page.)

			Units
(b)	(i)	Re-order level:	
		Maximum use in maximum lead time (4000 × 3)	12 000
		Normal use in normal lead time (3200 ÷ 2)	6 400
	(ii)	Minimum stock level	5 600
	(iii)	Re-order quantity	58 400
		Maximum storage space	64 000
	(iv)	Average stock (64 000 + 5600) ÷ 2	34 800

(c)

		1	2	3	4	5	6
(i)	Number of orders	1	2	3	4	5	6
(ii)	Order size (based on 18 000 total)	18 000	9 000	6 000	4 500	3 600	3 000
(iii)	Average stock (ii ÷ 2)	9 000	4 500	3 000	2 250	1 800	1 500
(iv)	Average stock value (£4.80)	£43 200	£21 600	£14 400	£10 800	£8 640	£7 200
(v)	Average annual stock holding cost (iv × 1 %)	£432	£216	£144	£108	£86.40	£72
(vi)	Annual ordering cost	£30	£60	£90	£120	£150	£180
		£462	£276	£234	£228	£236.40	£252

The lowest total cost is with four orders p.a., so EOQ is 4500 units. Note that in the range from 3600 units to 6000 units the difference in total cost is small. This suggests that the total cost curve flattens off in this range. Using the EOQ formula:

$$Q = \sqrt{\frac{2 \times \text{Annual quantity} \times \text{Cost per order}}{\text{Annual cost of carrying one unit}}}$$

Annual cost of carrying one unit:

$$£432 \div 9000 = £0.048$$
$$\text{or } £72 \div 1500 = £0.048$$

$$Q = \sqrt{\frac{2 \times 18\,000 \times 30}{0.048}}$$

$$Q = 4743 \text{ units}$$

Therefore 4500 units is the EOQ.

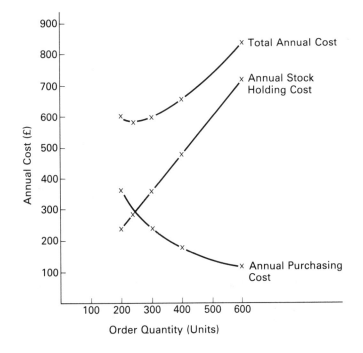

3.1   (a)

Wages Control Account

	£		£
Cash (*Note* 1) – direct	3875	Work-in-progress account	3518
indirect	1945	(*Note* 2)	
Income tax account – direct	470	Production overhead account	3192
indirect	200	(*Note* 2)	
National Insurance account – direct	150		
indirect	70		
	£6710		£6710

Production Overhead Control Account

	£		
National Insurance account	360		
(employer's contribution)			
Wages control account (*Note* 2)	3192		

Work-in-Progress Account

	£		
Wages control account (*Note* 2)	3518		

Cash and Bank Account

			£
		Wages control account – direct	3875
		indirect	1945

Income Tax Account

	£		£
Balance c/f	670	Wages control account – direct	470
		indirect	200
	£670		£670

National Insurance Account

	£		£
		Wages control account – direct	150
		indirect	70
Balance c/f	580	Production overhead account	
		(employer's contribution)	360
	£580		£580

(b)   *Employer's National Insurance contributions* cannot be attributed to individual batches of production, so will be debited to production overheads and charged to products by means of an absorption rate. An alternative is to gross up the hourly wage rates to include this cost.

Group Bonus. The bonus should be charged either to the work-in-progress account if the earnings can be traced to individual batches and if that degree of detail is considered worthwhile, or to the production overhead account where it will be charged evenly to all products via the overhead absorption rate.

Overtime Earnings. For direct workers, the actual hours can be traced to a particular batch, so the basic rate element should be charged direct to that batch. The overtime premium, worked to increase production generally, should be charged, via the overhead absorption rate, to all production. If overtime is worked at the request of a customer, it would be legitimate to charge the premium direct to the batch.

For indirect workers, all earnings are indirect and charged to production through the absorption rate unless there is a specific chargeable request for overtime by a customer.

Workings

Note 1 – Calculation of Wages

Direct Workers	£	Indirect Workers	£
Attendance time 1600 × £2.50	4000	1350 × £1.50	2025
Overtime premium 100 × £1.25	125	40 × £0.75	30
Shift premium	180		70
Bonus	190		90
Gross wage	4495		2215
Employees' deductions:			
Income tax	(470)		(200)
National Insurance	(150)		(70)
Net wage	£3875		£1945

Note 2 – Analysis of Direct Workers' Gross Wage

	Direct £		Indirect £
Productive time 1390 × 2.5	3475	210 × £2.50	525
Overtime premium 20 × 1.25	25	80 × £1.25	100
Shift premium & bonus	–		370
	£3500		£995

Analysis of Indirect Workers' Gross Wage

	Direct £		Indirect £
Attendance time 8 × £1.50	12	1342 × £1.50	2013
Overtime premium 8 × £0.75	6	32 × £0.75	24
Shift premium & bonus	–		160
	£18		£2197
Total debit to work-in-progress account	£3518	Production overhead account	£3192

3.2 (a)　Labour turnover is normally measured as the ratio of the number of persons leaving in a period to the average number on the payroll. Some authorities calculate labour turnover by the formula:

$$\frac{\text{New employees} + \text{Leavers}}{\text{Average number of employees}} \times \frac{100}{1} = \%$$

The cost implications are:
Cost of leaver – paperwork – disruption if sudden.
Advertise post.
Interview and recruitment of replacement.
Training new employees.
Spoilt work while learner improves.
Accidents and damage to machines by unskilled learners.
Production lost when skilled person replaced by learner.
Investment in staff development wasted.

(b)　Period　1　6%
　　　　　　2　10%
　　　　　　3　9%
　　　　　　4　10%
　　　　　　5　11%
　　　　　　6　13%

Extra information:
Number of new employees joining the firm.
Departments involved – is one department the cause?
Skill ratings of leavers – do they come for training?
Length of service of leavers – did they stay long?
Numbers dismissed as opposed to leaving.
Numbers leaving through natural wastage.
Seasonality of business – trough in period 6.
Statistics for same period last year – to ascertain extent of change.
Particulars of new employers in region, attracting good workers.

(c)　　(i)　Trade associated with casual labour.
　　　(ii)　Lack of employee facilities, e.g. canteen, sports club, crèche, etc.
　　(iii)　Wage rates below norm.
　　(iv)　Attitude of certain managers.
　　　(v)　Poor recruitment techniques – wrong people employed.
　　(vi)　Poor working conditions.
　　(vii)　Lack of job security or promotional prospects.
　(viii)　Ageing workforce – retirements.

3.3

Moulding Department

Wages Control Account

	£		£
Cash account (*Note 1*)	60 230	Work-in-progress control account (*Note 2*)	50 760
Employees' duductions account (*Note 1*)	11 322	Production overhead control account (*Note 3*)	20 792
	£71 552		£71 552

Note 1   Gross Wages Paid

	Direct Workers £	Indirect Workers £
Ordinary time (7200 × £7.20)	51 840	1600 × £4.20 6720
Overtime (1260 × £9.60)	12 096	160 + £5.60 896
	£63 936 +	£7616 = £71 552

	£
Total gross wages	71 552
Net wages paid (per question)	60 230
∴ employees' deductions	£11 322

Note 2   Debit to work-in-progress control account:

Direct workers' productive time 7050 hours × £7.20   £50 760

Note 3   Debit to production overhead control account:

Direct workers' non-productive time	1410 hours × £7.20	10 152
Direct workers' overtime premium	1260 hours × £2.40	3 024
Indirect workers' gross wages (see above)		7 616
		£20 792

(b)   (i)   One acceptable method would be to compare the previous week's actual earnings of the direct operatives with the amount they would have earned if the proposed scheme had been in operation.

	£	£
Existing remuneration scheme (*Note 1*)		63 936
Proposed scheme:		
Puss Cat (480 units × £80)	38 400	
Go Cat (150 units × £125)	18 750	
Non-productive down time 5640 hours (*Note 4*) × 20% × £5	5 640	
		62 790

It would appear that the proposed incentive scheme would reduce the labour cost in the moulding department.

An alternative method, although less accurate, of examining the effect of the proposed incentive scheme would be to compare unit labour costs, i.e.

	Puss Cat	Go Cat
	£	£
Existing method of remuneration:		
4800 hours ÷ 480 units × £7.20	72.0	–
2250 hours ÷ 150 units × £7.20	–	108.0
Plus 20% down time	14.4	21.6
	86.4	129.6

Hours required for previous week's production under proposed scheme would be:

480 × 8 hours	3840
150 × 12 hours	1800
	5640

plus allowance for non-productive time:

5640 × 20%	1128
	6768
Ordinary time (180 operatives)	7200
Ordinary time surplus to requirements	432 hours × £5 = £2160

If the surplus hours are not paid for, then operatives will either be working for less than a basic 40-hour week, or redundancies/transfers will occur. If the ordinary time surplus of 432 hours is paid for, the proposed scheme is not cheaper.

It has been assumed so far in this solution that workers will respond as estimated. However, if targets are not achieved (a 20% increase in efficiency is called for), there will be more down time if this remains at 20% of hours required, consequently increasing costs and perhaps generating potential unrest amongst the operatives.

Note 4   Calculation of allowed hours for previous week's production

Puss Cat	(480 units × 8 hours)	3840
Go Cat	(150 units × 12 hours)	1800
		5640 hours

(b) (ii)   432 labour-hours will be saved on a normal week's work, so ten employees will be redundant. Can they be redeployed, or will their redundancy affect labour relations?

Less idle time is allowed by the scheme. What if idle time is caused by factors unaffected by labour? Should the scheme include a guaranteed minimum weekly wage.

How will the scheme affect the indirect workers? They may lose overtime payments as a result, and this could provoke discord among the labour force.

Will the extra speed of production reduce quality or increase waste? What is the cost of inspection likely to be?

With less hours worked, will factory overhead costs be saved?

4.1 (a) *Redistributive Service Department Costs*

	Blank Making £	Decorating £	Finishing £	Power House £	Maintenance £
Overhead incurred	28 300	16 400	15 700	19 600	12 700
Maintenance redistributed	5 080	3 175	2 540	1 905	(12 700)
Power house redistributed	9 677	5 376	4 301	(21 505)	2 151
Maintenance redistributed	860	538	430	323	(2 151)
Power house redistributed	145	81	65	(323)	32
Maintenance redistributed	13	8	6	5	(32)
Power house redistributed	3	1	1	(5)	–
Overheads redistributed	£44 078	£25 579	£23 043		

Blank Making Overheads

	£		£
Incurred	44 078	Absorbed	45 000
Under-absorbed to profit and loss	922		
	£45 000		£45 000

Decorating Overheads

	£		£
Incurred	25 579	Absorbed	22 580
		Under-absorbed to profit and loss	2 999
	£25 579		£25 579

Finishing Overheads

	£		£
Incurred	23 043	Absorbed	19 732
		Under-absorbed to profit and loss	3 311
	£23 043		£23 043

Absorption Rates

Blank making: $\dfrac{£50\,000}{10\,000} = £5.000$

Decorating: $\dfrac{£25\,000}{6\,000} = £4.166$

Finishing: $\dfrac{£16\,000}{3\,000} = £5.333$

Amount Absorbed

Blank making 9000 hours × £5.000 = £45 000

Decorating 5420 hours × £4.166 = £22 580

Finishing 3700 hours × £5.333 = £19 732

(b) Blank making department		£
	Hours worked 1000 less than budget × £5	5000 (A)
	Cost incurred less than forecast	5922 (F)
	Favourable variance from budget	£922 (F)
Decorating	Hours worked 580 less than budget × £4.17	2419 (A)
	Cost incurred greater than forecast	579 (A)
	Adverse variance from budget	£2998 (A)
Finishing	Hours worked 700 greater than budget × £6.33	3733 (F)
	Cost incurred greater than budget	7043 (A)
	Adverse variance from budget	£3310 (A)

4.2 (a)

$$\frac{\text{Production overheads}}{\text{Direct wages}} \times \frac{100}{1} = \frac{450}{300} \times \frac{100}{1} = 150\%$$

Job 2843:

	£
Material	380
Direct wages	340
Production overheads	510
	1230
Gross profit	410
Price	£1640

(b) The casting department incurs significant overhead costs in the form of depreciation and machine maintenance. However, assembly, with five times as much labour, incurs only a quarter of the overhead attributed to casting.

A blanket rate means that the overheads of the casting department are averaged with those of other departments. Jobs may not pass through all departments and it is unfair to burden a job in the assembly department with the overheads of the casting department and to undercharge production in the casting department. A time rate can distort product costs.

Separate absorption rates, based on a significant activity for each department, would give a more reasonable cost.

Casting department – machine-hours	$\frac{240}{80} = £3$ per hour
Assembly department – direct labour-hours	$\frac{60}{100} = 60\text{p}$ per hour
Finishing department – direct labour cost percentage	$\frac{150}{50} \times \frac{100}{1} = 300\%$

(c) Job 2843:

Casting: 80 machine-hours × £3	=	240
Assembly: 80 direct labour-hours × 0.6	=	48
Finishing: £20 × 300%	=	60
		£348

(d)

	Absorbed £000's	Actual £000's	Over/(Under)- absorbed £000's
Current rates:			
Casting (150% labour)	90	260	(170)
Assembly	240	56	184
Finishing	90	160	(70)
	£420	£476	£(56)
Suggested rates:			
Casting (90 × £3)	270	260	10
Assembly (90 × 0.6)	54	56	(2)
Finishing 300%	180	160	20
	£504	£476	£28

4.3 (a)

	Machine Shop £	Assembly Department £	Canteen £	Total £
Allocated overheads	74 000	39 000	16 000	129 000
Apportionment of canteen costs (based on number of employees)	10 000	6 000	(16 000)	–
	£84 000	£45 000	–	£129 000

	Machine Shop	Assembly Department
Absorption bases	Machine-hours	Direct labour-hours
Budgeted hours (*Note 1*)	28 000	18 000
Budgeted overhead absorption rate	£3 per machine-hour	£2.50 per labour-hour

Total Budgeted Cost per Unit

	Product A £	Product B £
Materials	9	6
Labour:		
Machine Shop	20	24
Assembly Department	12	12
	32	36
Overheads:		
Machine Shop	12	24
Assembly Department	10	10
	22*	34
	£63	£76

Comment re Absorption Methods Used

Most overheads vary with time and, therefore, time-based absorption methods reflect actual conditions. In the Assembly Department, time expended on products is mainly labour based. Consequently a labour-hour rate of absorption would provide an equitable base. As wage rates are constant in the Assembly Department, overheads could equally equitably be absorbed as a percentage of direct wages.

In the Machine Shop a considerable proportion of overheads will be incurred as a result of machine running time, and machine-hours would therefore provide an equitable basis for absorbing overheads.

(b)   Variable overhead absorption rates (*Note* 2):

Machine Shop	£1 per machine-hour
Assembly Department	£0.50 per labour-hour

Variable overheads per unit of A

	£
Machine Shop (four machine-hours at £1)	4
Assembly Department (four labour-hours at 50p)	2
Total	£6

* Therefore fixed overheads per unit equal £16 (if total overheads are £22)

300 units extra sales and production will result in extra contribution of:

	£	
300 × 16 =	4800	(Fixed overheads over-absorbed)
300 × 5 =	1500	(Profit £68 − £63 = £5)
	£6300	increase in profit

Workings

Note 1 – Calculation of Budgeted Hours

Product	A		B		
Budgeted production	2000 units		2500 units		
Machine Shop hours per unit	4		8		
Total Machine Shop hours	8000	+	20 000	=	28 000 hours
Assembly Department labour-hours per unit	4		4		
Total Assembly Department labour-hours	8000	+	10 000	=	18 000 hours

Note 2 – Calculation of Variable Overhead Rates

	Machine Shop	Assembly Department
Variable overheads (all allocated)	£28 000	£9000
Absorption base	28 000 machine-hours	18 000 labour-hours
Variable overhead rate	£1 per machine-hour	£0.50 per labour-hour

5.1 (a) Job costing system accumulates data on a job cost card, which acts as an instrument of control. The costs to date can be seen at any time. Materials are requisitioned from the stores and entered on the job card. The price is determined by stores' records. Materials returned are similarly recorded.

Labour is analysed monthly, and a charge is made to each job based on time sheets completed by operatives.

Overheads are assessed to jobs on a direct labour-hour rate basis. The use of such a rate implies that overheads are related to time and/or labour, or that skilled manual work is more significant to production than machine time. Miscellaneous costs are directly attributable to the job. The job card facilitates the calculation of stocks of work-in-progress at the end of each month, e.g. July £2040 + £1120 + £560 = £3720, and allows a comparison of actual cost with estimate.

(b) At first glance the job shows a profit of £213, or 3.3 % on price. Estimated costs totalled £4760, so a profit of £1740 should have been made, 26.7 % on price.
Material cost exceeds estimate by £357, or 17.85 %.
Labour cost exceeds estimate by £460, or 25.55 %.
Overheads exceed estimate by £180, or 20 %.
Miscellaneous costs exceed estimate by £539, or 89.83 %.

It is apparent that the job started three weeks later than schedule (21/7), that much of the first materials ordered were returned to stores (24/7), that total materials used exceeded the estimate, and that progress was held up until the delivery of bought-out components (15/9), which were not estimated for when the job was priced.

Overheads of £900 on a direct labour-hour rate of £2 implies that 450 labour-hours were estimated for the job. An estimated labour cost of £1800 for 450 hours work means a rate of pay of £4 per hour. The total hours worked were 540, and the wage rate in September exceeded £4 an hour, suggesting that some overtime was worked to complete the job once the components had been received.

The job absorbed more overheads than estimated, because more labour-hours were worked to complete it.

(c) Control action should be taken before the job is completed if it is to be effective. Investigations should cover the following:

(i) Over-use of materials and return to stores of faulty material (MRN7/13).
(ii) Delay whilst waiting for delivery of unscheduled component parts.
(iii) Need for component parts not covered by estimate.
(iv) Late start on job.
(v) Labour time exceeded estimate by 20 % and some overtime was worked.
(vi) Delivery 1 October; invoice 4 December. Why this delay, since it also holds up receipt of the price and can contribute to a cash-flow problem?

(d) (i) The summary should show a comparison of actual and estimated costs with differences (or variances) shown in terms of pounds and percentages.

6.1   (a)   (i)

Contract Account

31/3/–5	£	31/3/–5	£	£
Materials from stores	94 110	Balances carried forward:		
Materials purchased	284 700	Materials		31 640
SDLO wages	184 930	Plant and machinery		
Hired lorries, plant and machinery	61 490	less depreciation		104 000
Plant and machinery purchased	130 000	Work-in-progress:		
Tools and consumable items	1 800	Cost of work	647 350	
Accruals c/f:		Profit	41 790	689 140
SDLO wages	4 000			
Hired expenses	500			
Administration (Rate Fund) charge	21 460			
Revenue account	41 790			
	£824 780			£824 780

1/4/–5	£
Materials b/f	31 640
Plant and machinery b/f	104 000
Work-in-progress b/f	689 140

Note: Depreciation calculation	£
Cost	130 000
Depreciation 20%	26 000
Written-down value c/f	£104 000

(ii)   *Calculation of SDLO Profit to be taken to Revenue Account*

	£
Cash received (value of work certified less retentions)	641 700
Add 10% retention (1/9 × £641 700)	71 300
Value of work certified	£713 000

	£	£
Cost of work certified:		
Expenditure to date		782 990
Less Work not certified	4 000	
Materials and book value	31 640	
Plant c/f at book value	104 000	(139 640)
Cost of work certified		£643 350

	£
Notional profit/loss:	
Value of work certified	713 000
Cost of work certified	643 350
Profit	£69 650

Profit to be taken to the SDLO revenue account:

$$\frac{2}{3} \times \frac{641\,700}{713\,000} \times £69\,650 \qquad £41\,790$$

(iii)	Work-in-progress:		£
	Cost of work certified		643 350
	Cost of work not certified		4 000
	Profit taken to date		41 790
			£689 140

(iv)			£
	Fixed assets:		
	Plant and machinery – cost		130 000
	Less depreciation		26 000
			104 000
	Current assets:	£	
	Stock of raw materials		31 640
	Work-in-progress	689 140	
	Less payments in advance	(641 700)	47 440

(b) To take profit only at the end of a long-term contract will distort the measurement of profit, not only in the year of termination but also in the years of production. Therefore it is appropriate to take credit for ascertainable profit (profit made on parts of the job that are satisfactorily completed) while the contract is still in progress. Such profit must reflect the proportion of the total contract that has been completed to date, inequalities of profitability in the various stages of the contract, and conservatism in the form of prudent estimates of costs, to the completion contingencies and rectification work that may be necessary. Profit can be taken before completion, as long as a favourable outcome to the contract can be predicted with reasonable certainty.

6.2 Contract A

	£	£
Contract price		300 000
Costs to 31 March (£248 612 – £14 850)	233 762	
Costs incurred in quarter	29 415	
Costs to completion	8 600	
Plant depreciation (£1 509 + £3 720)	5 229	
Total costs to completion		277 006
Total estimated profit on contract		£22 994

$$\frac{\text{Cash}}{\text{Certificate}} \times \frac{\text{Certificate}}{\text{Price}} \times \text{Estimated Profit}$$

	£
$\dfrac{25}{28} \times \dfrac{28}{30} \times £22\,994$	19 162
Less profit taken up to 31 March	14 850
Profit for quarter to 30 June	£4 312

This job is so near to completion that it is possible to project forward to the final result. An element of caution is injected into the calculation to reflect cash received and certificated work as well as the basis of estimate on which future costs are calculated.

Contract B

	£	£
Value of work certified		180 000
Cost of work certified:		
Work-in-progress 31 March	62 345	
Costs incurred in quarter	93 931	
Depreciation	10 755	
	167 031	
Less Costs not certified	4 396	162 635
Estimated profit		£17 365

$$\frac{2}{3} \times \frac{15}{18} \times £17\,365 = £9647$$

A conservative formula is applied to the estimated profit to reflect cash received from the client and the fact that the job appears to be half finished at this state. Profit is only taken on work covered by a certificate, but much could yet go wrong with this job before it is completed.

Contract C

This contract is at an early stage in its completion and it is too soon to assume that a profit has been made.

6.3

		Hospital £000's	Power Plant £000's	Dam £000's
Plant wdv at 1 January 19–6		450	1200	1050
Purchases		1087	600	187
Less wdv at 31 December 19–6		(900)	(787)	(262)
Depreciation		£637	£1013	£975
Work-in-progress at 1 January 19–6		–	3600	10 050
Less profit		–	–	1 725
				8 325
Cost for the year:	Materials	1650	2400	1 575
	Labour	1050	1725	1 462
	Expense	525	712	1 162
	Depreciation	637	1013	975
Total cost to date		£3862	£9450	£13 499

Hospital:	Value of work certified		3525
	Total cost to date	3862	
	Less cost not certified	112	3750
	Loss		£(225)

A loss has been made and must be included in the profit and loss account. It is against the principle of conservatism to ignore this loss and carry forward the work-in-progress at cost.

		£000's
Power plant:	Value of work certified	11 250
	Cost of work certified	9 450
	Profit to date	£1 800

$$\frac{2}{3} \times \frac{\text{Cash received}}{\text{Work certified}} \left(\frac{£10\,125}{£11\,250}\right) \times £1800 = £1080$$

Presumably the traditional formula has been applied to the profit to date to compute a prudent profit figure to be recognised this year.

		£000's	£000's
Dam:	Price		18 000
	Cost to date	13 499	
	Cost to completion	637	
	Extra depreciation	262	14 398
	Total estimated profit on contract		£3 602

$$£3602 \times \frac{\text{Cash}}{\text{Certificate}} \left(\frac{£14\,850}{£16\,500}\right) \times \frac{\text{Certificate}}{\text{Price}} \left(\frac{£16\,500}{£18\,000}\right) = 2972$$

Less profit taken to date	1 725
Profit to be taken this year	£1247

The company proposes to take this year as profit, the total estimated profit on the contract. This is a bad mistake since the contract is not yet completed, and £1 725 000 of the profit has already been taken. It should be noted that work still to be certified in the sum of £1 500 000, will cost £1 200 000 + £637 000 + £262 000 to complete. These figures underline the need for prudence in taking profit on this job.

(b)

	Hospital £000's	Power Plant £000's	Dam £000's
(i) Work-in-progress = Cost	3862	9 450	13 499
Plus profit or minus (loss)	(225)	1 080	1247
Plus profit already taken	–	–	1 725
	3 737	10 530	16 471
Less Progress payments received or receivable	(352)	(1 125)	(1 650)
	£3385	£9 405	£14 821

(ii) Debtors – progress payments in arrears (3525 – 352) – 3000 = 173

(iii) Fixed assets – plant at wdv   900   787   262

7.1 (a) The main problem experienced in costing joint and by-products concerns the apportionment of joint costs up to the point of separation.

Methods:

(i) physical measurement

(ii)   market value at point of separation
(iii)   market value when eventually sold.

The physical basis is simple to apply and seems logical if the same effort and cost are used to produce a unit of each product. In a complex process it is reasonable to assume that non-allocatable cost accrues in proportion to the quantity processed. Selling price may bear little relation to joint process costs.

(b)

Process Account

	kg	£		kg	£
Cement	1500	9000	Blanks	1600	17600
Hardener	500	4500	Grit	200	2200
Labour		2784	Normal loss	140	–
Overheads		4176	Abnormal loss to p/l	60	660
	2000	£20460		2000	£20460

$$\frac{£20460}{1860} = £11$$

(c)   Special order:

Revenue	£4000
Extra cost	£2400
Surplus	£1600

Yes the order is worthwhile since it shows a contribution of £1600. The processing costs of the grit must not be set against the revenue since it will not be affected by the order.

7.2

Process 1

	Units	£		Units	£
Material	20000	40000	Output to Process 2	17800	109767
Material	–	16000	Normal loss	2000	4000
Wages	–	15000	Abnormal loss	200	1233
Expenses	–	14000			
Overheads (200%)	–	30000			
	20000	£115000		20000	£115000

$$\frac{£115000 - £4000}{18000 \text{ units}} = £6.167$$

Process 2

	Units	£		Units	£
From Process 1	17 800	109 767	Output to Process 3	17 400	198 640
Material	–	22 640	Normal loss	890	3 560
Wages	–	16 000			
Expenses	–	16 200			
Overheads (200%)	–	32 000			
Abnormal gain	490	5 593			
	18 290	£202 200		18 290	£202 200

$$\frac{£196\,607 - £3560}{17\,800 - 890} = £11.416$$

Process 3

	Units	£		Units	£
From Process 2	17 400	198 640	Normal loss	1 740	10 440
Materials	–	33 200	By-product Zelta	–	–
Wages	–	20 000	Finished goods store	15 200	286 801
Expenses	–	14 080	Abnormal loss	460	8 679
Overheads (200%)	–	40 000			
	17 400	£305 920		17 400	£305 920

$$\frac{£305\,920 - £10\,440}{17\,400 - 1740} = £18.868$$

Abnormal Loss

	Units	£		£
Process 1	200	1233	Scrap sales 200 × £2	400
Process 3	460	8679	Scrap sales 460 × £6	2760
			p/l account	6752
		£9912		£9912

Abnormal Gain

	£		£
Normal loss account:		Process 2 490 units	5 593
Scrap sales foregone 490 × £4	1960		
p/l account	3633		
	£9912		£5593

Normal Loss

	£		£
Process 1 2000 units	4 000	Cash from scrap sales	4 000
Process 2 890 units	3 560	Abnormal gain − (490 × £4)	1 960
Process 3 1940 units	10 440	Cash from actual scrap sales	
		(890 − 490 × £4)	1 600
		Cash from scrap sales	10 440
	£18 000		£18 000

By-product Zelta

	£		£
From Process 3	–	Sales 1420 × £9	12 780
Processing costs 1420 × £4	5 680		
Selling costs 1420 × £3	4 260		
p/l account	2 840		
	£12 780		£12 780

7.3　　*Calculation of Equivalent Units*

	Units	Process 3 Costs		Materials		Conversion Costs
Opening stock	800					
Costs to completion		—	20%	160	40%	320
Transferred from Process 3 and completed	7500	100%	7 500	100%	7 500	100%	7 500
Closing stock	1000	100%	1 000	80%	800	60%	600
Abnormal loss	500	100%	500	60%	300	30%	150
			9 000		8 760		8 570
			£27 000		£13 140		£17 140
			9000		8760		8570
			= £3		= £1.5		= £2

The abnormal loss is discovered on inspection at a point that all opening stocks have passed. Therefore abnormal loss is found entirely from the units introduced from Process 3 in October.

Closing stock:

	£
Process 3 (1000 × £3.0)	3000
Materials (800 × £1.5)	1200
Conversion costs (600 × £2.0)	1200
	£5400

Transferred to stores

		£
(i)	Opening stock completed:	
	Process 3 costs b/d	2 000
	Materials (160 × £1.5)	240
	Conversion costs (320 × £2.0)	640
		2 880
(ii)	In and out (Units into process and completed):	£
	Process 3 (7500 × £3.0)	22 500
	Materials (7500 × £1.5)	11 250
	Conversion costs (7500 × £2.0)	15 000
		48 750
		£51 630

Abnormal loss:

	£
Process 3 (500 × £3.0)	1 500
Materials (300 × £1.5)	450
Conversion costs (150 × £2.0)	300
	£2 250

Process 4

	Units	£		Units	£
Opening stock	800	2 000	Abnormal loss	500	2 250
From Process 3	9 000	27 000	Transfer to stores	8300	51 630
Materials	–	13 140	Closing stock	1000	5 400*
Conversion costs	–	17 140			
	9 800	£59 280		9800	£59 280

Abnormal Loss Account

	£		£
Process 4	2 250	Cash from scrap sales (500 × £2)	1 000
		Profit and loss a/c	1 250
	£2 250		£2 250

* 1000 × £3 + 800 × £1.5 + 600 × £2 = 5400

(b) It is important to value stocks of work-in-progress because:

  (i) Costs must be accurately apportioned between finished goods and stocks in process in order to find the true cost of finished goods and the costs of this month to be carried forward.

  (ii) A valuation of stock is required for balance sheet purposes.

  (iii) A true cost leads to accurate profit measurement.

7.4 (a) Process costing occurs where a quantity of an homogenous product is passed through one or more processes in a continuous flow during the course of its manufacture. Individual cost units are not identified, but, instead, costs are analysed to processes as cost centres and absorbed to cost units or batches on an average basis as they pass through each cost centre, e.g. in a bakery with mixing, baking and packing processes. Job costing occurs where cost units are of such individual significance as to be capable of separate identification, so that as the job is completed (perhaps by passing through separate departments or processes) an individual cost is compiled for each job, e.g. the building of a piece of switchgear in an electrical machinery factory.

Process Costing: allocate and apportion direct costs and overheads to process cost centres by means of requisitions, labour analysis and overhead apportionment. Then average this cost to units of throughput, working on the expected volume result, so that abnormal losses or gains can be identified.

Job Costing: individual job cost card to act as a cumulative record of materials, labour and overheads as the job progresses to completion, compiled from requisitions, labour analysis by time sheet and overheads charged per direct labour-hour or machine-hour according to whichever cost centre is used.

(b)   A process may produce more than one product from a common input of materials, labour and overheads. Whether these products are joint products or by-products depends on their individual significance. Joint costs are those process costs incurred up to the point of separation. The joint products may be sold at once or processed further, but the difficulty encountered concerns how the joint costs are to be apportioned to the joint products. One of three methods is usually used: apportionment per volume, per eventual sales value and per value at the point of separation. All give an arbitrary apportionment, so that any profit figure derived from them will be suspect.

8.1 (a)   Maintenance costs are semi-variable – use high/low point method to determine the variable and fixed costs:

	Miles	Cost £
High	250 000	19 000
Low	220 000	17 500
Variable element	30 000	£1500 or 5p per mile
Total cost for	220 000	17 500
Less variable cost at 5p per mile		11 000
Therefore fixed cost		£6 500

Vehicle statistics:

Vehicle	Journeys per Day	Average Tonnes	Average Miles	Tonne-mile	Miles Run
A	6	3	15	270	90
B	5	4	25	500	125
C	3	5	35	525	105
D	2	6	40	480	80
E	1	6	60	360	60
			Daily:	2 135	460
			Weekly:	10 675	2 300
			Annually:	533 750	115 000

	£	£
Variable costs for 115 000 miles:		
Maintenance at 5p	5 750	
Petrol/oil at 30p	34 500	
Repairs at 9p	10 350	50 600
Fixed costs:		
Maintenance	6 500	
Tyres	3 100	
Vehicle licences (£400 × 5 vehicles)	2 000	
Insurance (£700 × 5 vehicles)	3 500	

	£	£
Depreciation of vehicles: $\dfrac{£40\,000 \times 5 \text{ vehicles}}{4 \text{ years}}$	50 000	
Depreciation of equipment: $\dfrac{£120\,000}{4 \text{ years}}$	30 000	
Drivers' wages (£170 × 5 drivers × 50 weeks)	42 500	
Supervisor/relief driver (£220 × 50 weeks)	11 000	
Miscellaneous	2 450	
		151 050
		£201 650

$$\text{Standard cost per tonne-mile} = \frac{£201\,650}{533\,750} \text{ tonne-mile}$$

$$= 38\text{p}$$

(b) The standard cost per tonne-mile is compiled by adding together variable costs, semi-variable costs and fixed costs. So long as only five vehicles are used, fixed costs are unlikely to change, but extra vehicles or vehicles of different types added to the fleet will render the standard unworkable. Fixed costs form a major part of the rate. For decision making, such as whether to take on additional business or hire out a vehicle that is under-utilised, it is essential to base the decision on the variable cost element within the standard rate per tonne-mile, which is:

$$\frac{£50\,600}{533\,750} = 9.48\text{p}$$

The standard rate is based on estimates of mileage and tonnes carried as well as budgeted costs. Should the mileage or the actual weight carried be significantly different, there are bound to be variance, but, provided the causes of these variances are identifiable, it need not be a serious limitation of the standard.

Other limitations concern the type of goods carried, e.g. some goods are bulky but light in weight; others may be small in size but heavy. Efficiency is best controlled by exercising control over the costs of each expense heading and ensuring journeys are planned to effect high utilisation of the vehicle capacity. Therefore, as a comparative standard or yardstick, the standar rate per tonne-mile may not be suitable for all transport fleets.

9.1 Selling Cost Budget for the year to .... 19......

	North £	South £	Irish £	Welsh £	Head Office £	Total £
Representation:						
Salaries	127 000	121 000	75 000	78 000	–	401 000
Commission	31 000	27 500	12 500	7 000	–	78 000
Travel and subsistence	28 000	18 000	13 000	10 400	–	69 400
Sales management:						
Salaries					47 000	47 000
Building services					17 850	17 850
Other costs					11 500	11 500
Publicity	125 000	140 000	70 000	45 000	35 000	415 000
	£311 000	£306 500	£170 500	£140 400	£111 350	£1 039 750

9.2

Savoury Snacks – Cash Budget

Weeks	4 July £	4 Aug. £	5 Sept. £	4 Oct. £	4 Nov. £	5 Dec. £	4 Jan. £	4 Feb. £	5 Mar. £	4 Apr. £	4 May £	5 June £
Receipts												
Sales							20 000	20 000	20 000	37 500	37 500	37 500
Total receipts							20 000	20 000	20 000	37 500	37 500	37 500
Payments:												
Raw materials		9 000	6 000	6 000	6 000	6 000	6 000	6 000	6 000	6 000	6 000	6 000
Stock		8 000	9 000									
Wages			15 000	12 000	12 000	15 000	12 000	12 000	15 000	12 000	12 000	15 000
Marketing			8 000	8 000	8 000	8 000	8 000	4 000	4 000	4 000	4 000	4 000
Salaries		2 000	2 000	2 000	2 000	2 000	2 000	2 000	2 000	2 000	2 000	2 000
Factory	2 000	2 000	2 000	2 000	2 000	2 000	2 000	2 000	2 000	2 000	2 000	2 000
Machinery	50 000	37 000										
Selling			1 500	1 500	1 500	1 500	1 500	1 500	1 500	1 500	1 500	1 500
Commissions					400	400	400	750	750	750	750	750
Total payments	52 000	58 000	43 500	31 500	31 900	34 900	31 900	28 250	31 250	28 250	28 250	31 250
Excess payments	52 000	58 000	43 500	31 500	31 900	34 900	11 900	8 250	11 250	+9 250	+9 250	+6 250
Cumulative	52 000	110 000	153 500	185 000	216 900	251 800	263 700	271 950	283 200	273 950	264 700	258 450

The maximum amount the company would need to finance is = £283 200

9.3 (a)

Production Budget

	De luxe	Standard
Budgeted sales	3 600 units	6 150 units
Add expected closing stock	900	2 050
	4 500	8 200
Less opening stock	1 250	1 600
	3 250	6 600
	4 kg	2 kg
	13 000 kg	13 200 kg

Material Purchase Budget

Total material consumption	26 200 kg
Add closing stock	5 240 kg
	31 440 kg
Less opening stock	4 100 kg
Amount to be purchased	27 340 kg
Budgeted price per kilogram	£2
Budgeted material purchases	£54 680

Direct Labour Budget

	De luxe	Standard
Budgeted production	3 250 units	6 600 units
Standard time per unit	4 hours	$2\frac{1}{2}$ hours
Standard hours for production	13 000 hours	16 500 hours

Total hours	29 500
Convert to budgeted productive man-hours ($29 500 \times 10/9$)	32 778
Add budgeted down time at 20%	6 556
	39 334
Less ordinary time available: 70 workers × 38 hours × 12 weeks	31 920
Overtime required	7 414

Total wages budget will be:

31 920 hours at £3.50	111 720
7414 hours at £5.25	38 924
	£150 644

(b) Information required would be:

(i) Expected stock movements each week and the time intervals at which replacement orders are placed.

(ii) The credit period taken from suppliers.

(iii) Amounts outstanding with suppliers at the beginning of the period. (i), (ii) and (iii) will help to identify likely payments to suppliers.

(iv) Intervals at which wages are paid.

(v) Any arrears of wages brought forward from a previous period.

(vi) Any deductions from wages that must be paid to third parties, e.g. Schedule E Tax, National Insurance, pensions contributions, with dates.

Workings:

$$\text{Budgeted closing stock } \frac{15 \text{ days}}{60 \text{ days}} \times 3600 = 900 \text{ units}$$

$$\frac{20 \text{ days}}{60 \text{ days}} \times 6150 = 2050 \text{ units}$$

$$\text{Budgeted closing stock materials } \frac{12 \text{ days}}{60 \text{ days}} \times 26\,200 = 5240 \text{ kg}$$

11.1 (a) A *standard cost* is a pre-determined calculation of how much costs *should* be under specified working conditions. The amount specified is determined by the standard setter depending on whether he is setting an 'ideal' standard or an 'attainable' standard. The standard is compiled from estimates of the various elements of cost that should be incurred for a specific task – technical specification gives quantities of materials, time study shows labour and machine time required, material prices and wage rates expected to apply during the period convert quantities to cost.

(b) *Benefits*. Standards provide a scale against which the success of actual operations can be measured, in fine detail. Variances show the extent of the difference between what a certain activity should have cost and what it has cost and identify areas for further investigation and remedial action. Control of this nature improves managerial understanding of what is happening, and thus increases efficiency. Standards assist in planning (alternatives can easily be costed if they are reduced to standard operations), motivation (standards provide targets for managers to achieve), and simplification (operations are expressed in terms of standard cost). Also, standard times can be used when plant utilisation is planned.

(c) *Setting standards*. The difference between ideal and attainable standards should be understood. Ideal standards can harm morale if managers believe that they cannot be attained, yet attainable standards may fail to stretch the organisation to full efficiency and may build in mistakes from a previous period. *Forecasting*, on which standards are based, must be realistic. If mistakes are made the tempo of the business may be wrong, so errors must be recognised and the appropriate standards reviewed. *Installing the system*. Standard cost cards must be compiled. This means a lot of clerical work, as well as work spent on measuring and pricing materials and components, and measuring labour times. Forecasting material prices is difficult during a period of inflation.

11.2 (a) A standard hour is the quantity of work achievable at standard performance, expressed as a standard unit of work in a standard period of time. It is the amount of work that an average worker could achieve if working under normal conditions for one hour.

(b) *Standard Hours Equivalent to Work Done*

Pullovers: 10 minutes × Actual quantity 2400 = Standard time 400 hours
Jumpers: 7.5 minutes × Actual quantity 5000 = Standard time 625 hours
Scarves: 4 minutes × Actual quantity 3600 = Standard time 240 hours

$$1265$$

Standard Hours equivalent to Budgeted Production

Pullovers: 10 minutes × Budgeted quantity 2800 = Standard time 467 hours
Jumpers: 7.5 minutes × Budgeted quantity 5500 = Standard time 688 hours
Scarves: 4 minutes × Budgeted quantity 3700 = Standard time 247 hours

$$1402$$

Productivity of Direct Operatives – Efficiency Ratio

$$\frac{\text{Standard hours for actual production}}{\text{Actual hours worked}} = \frac{1265}{1300} \times \frac{100}{1} = 97\%$$

Actual Production Relative to Budget – Volume Ratio or Activity Ratio

$$\frac{\text{Standard hours for actual production}}{\text{Standard hours for budgeted production}} = \frac{1265}{1402} \times \frac{100}{1} = 90\%$$

Capacity Ratio – Actual Utilisation of Budgeted Resources

$$\frac{\text{Actual hours}}{\text{Standard hours for budgeted production}} = \frac{1300}{1402} \times \frac{100}{1} = 93\%$$

(c) In general, if the labour force produce more at a reducing labour cost per unit then profit will increase, especially if such extra production takes advantage of fixed costs, which do not change. However, fixed costs may increase in stepped progression and variable costs of materials and overheads may also increase per unit, thus reducing profits. Cost behaviour is significant in this situation.

Extra production must be sold, and productivity leading to increased stocks will cause further storage costs to arise. Only if fewer workers produce the previous volume of production – and this means redundancy – will costs fall and profit increase. Any change in the mixture of goods produced and sold could also affect profit.

12.1 (a) Significant factors in setting a direct labour standard are:

(i) The levels of attainment that are to be built into the standard. Some businesses set 'ideal' standards, which can only be achieved by constant effort at maximum efficiency. Such standards may show what is expected by top management, but they may be so far ahead of what is reasonably attainable that morale suffers and managers will not try to achieve them. Some standards are based on past performance, but this is likely to perpetuate past mistakes, encourage complacency and ignore future conditions. The best standards are carefully planned to reflect future conditions and are kept at tight but attainable levels.

(ii)   Specification of the standard tasks to be undertaken.

(iii)   Standard timings for these tasks, based on time and motion study, past experience and test runs. The test runs will establish an attainable time for the average employee working at a normal expected rate, allowing for fatigue, normal idle time, etc.

(iv)   Labour grades required to bring the appropriate skill to the task.

(v)   Hourly rates of pay, and bonuses.

(b)   Direct Labour Variances for June

	Casting		Assembly		Total
		£		£	£
A. Standard cost or actual production:					
De Luxe	2000 × £3	6 000	3000 × £8	24 000	30 000
King Size	3900 × £6	23 400	4300 × £6	25 800	49 200
		£29 400		£49 800	£79 200
B. Actual hours worked at standard rate:					
67 × 40 × 4 × £3		£32 160	72 × 3 × 40 × £4	34 560	
			72 × 37 × £4	10 656	
				£45 216	£77 376
C. Actual hours attended at standard rate:					
67 × 40 × 4 × £3		£32 160	72 × 4 × 40 × £4	£46 080	£78 240
D. Gross wages paid		£31 000		£47 000	£78 000
Labour rate of pay variance C − D		£1160 (F)		£920 (A)	240 (F)
Labour idle time variance B − C		Nil		864 (A)	864 (A)
Labour efficiency variance A − B		2760 (A)		4584 (F)	1824 (F)
Total direct labour variance A − D		1600 (A)		2800 (F)	1200 (F)

12.2   (a)

		A	B	
Budgeted profit A	(4600 × 13.00)	59 800		
Budgeted profit B	(4400 × 19.20)	84 480		£
				144 280
Margin price variance		3200 (F)	4880 (A)	
Margin volume variance		2600 (F)	–	
		£5800 (F)	£4880 (A)	
				920 (F)
Profit at standard cost				145 200

Cost Variances

	X	Y	
Material price	4840 (F)	3060 (A)	
Material usage	1240 (A)	420 (F)	
	£3600 (F)	£2640 (A)	960 (F)

£

	Assembly	Finishing		
Labour rate	8100 (F)	1570 (F)		
Labour efficiency	1350 (F)	1080 (A)		
	£9450 (F)	£490 (F)		

			9940 (F)	
	Assembly	Finishing		
Variable overhead expenditure	2250 (F)	1040 (F)		
			3290 (F)	
Fixed overheads:				
Expenditure	–	5000 (A)		
Capacity	–	7400 (F)		
Efficiency	–	–	2400 (F)	16 590 (F)
Actual profit				£161 790

(b) Interdependence refers to the influence one variance has on another. This may arise within one element of cost or may cover other elements. A favourable price variance caused by the purchase of cheap material may influence an adverse usage variance if the cheap material increases the scrap in production. An adverse sales margin price variance means that sales are made below standard price. This may affect the sales volume variance as more products are sold at a lower price. A favourable labour rate of pay variance may mean that a lower grade of labour has been used, and this, in turn, could increase material usage as scrap exceeds standard allowances.

12.3 (a)

Overhead Absorption Rates

	Fixed	Variable	Total
Budgeted overheads	£20 000	£56 000	£76 000
Budgeted standard hours	16 000	16 000	16 000
Absorption rate	£1.25	£3.50	£4.75
A: Standard cost of actual production	16 900 × £1.25	16 900 × £3.50	
	£21 125	£59 150	£80 275
B: Fixed budget	£20 000	–	–
C: Actual expenditure	£19 350	£61 140	£80 490
Total variance			£215
Volume variance A – B	1125 (F)		1125 (F)
Expenditure variance:			
Fixed (B – C)	650 (F)		650 (F)
Variable (A – C)		1990 (A)	1990 (A)
	£1775 (F)	£1990 (A)	£215 (A)

(b)

Operating statement

	Flexed Budget £	Actual Cost £	Variance £
Fixed overheads:			
Salaries	13 500	12 700	800 (F)
Maintenance	6 500	6 650	150 (A)
Variable overheads:			
Power	37 180	40 300	3120 (A)
Consumables	12 675	11 840	835 (F)
Indirect labour	9 295	9 000	295 (F)
	£79 150	£80 490	£1340 (A)

The flexed budget is derived by applying the fraction to the variable overheads in the fixed budget:

$$\frac{\text{Actual standard hours}}{\text{Budget standard hours}} \left(\frac{16\,900}{16\,000}\right) = 1.05625$$

12.4 Workings

Product A – Standard cost £15 ÷ £5 = 3 hours standard time

Product B – Standard cost £2.50 ÷ 30 minutes standard time

Standard Direct Labour Cost:

Product A	4 400 units × £15.00 = 66 000	4700 units × £15.00 = 70 500	
Product B	10 500 units × £2.50 = 26 250	9300 units × £2.50 = 23 250	
	April £92 250	May £93 750	

(a) *Efficiency ratio*

$$\frac{\text{Standard hours for actual production}}{\text{Actual hours worked}} \times \frac{100}{1}$$

$$\frac{(4400 \text{ units} \times 3 \text{ hours}) + (10\,500 \text{ units} \times 30 \text{ minutes})}{21\,600 \text{ hours}} \times \frac{100}{1}$$

$$\frac{18\,450 \text{ hours}}{21\,600 \text{ hours}} \times \frac{100}{1} = 85.4\%$$

(b)

		April	May
A	Standard cost for actual production	£92 250	£93 750
B	Hours worked at standard rate	21 600 × £5	18 600 × £5
		£108 000	£93 000
C	Hours paid at standard rate	21 600 × £5	19 200 × £5
		£108 000	£96 000
D	Actual wages paid	£112 000	£99 400
	Rate of pay variance (C − D)	£4000 (A)	£3400 (A)
	Idle time (B − C)	Nil	£3000 (A)
	Efficiency (A − B)	£15 750 (A)	£750 (F)

(c)

Wages Control Account (April)

	£		£
Cash (wages paid)	112 000	Work-in-progress account	92 250
		(standard cost of actual production)	
		Direct labour efficiency variance	15 750
		Direct labour rate of pay variance	4 000
	£112 000		£112 000

Work-in-progress Control Account (April)

	£		£
Wages control account	92 250		

Alternatively, wages of £112 000 paid could be debited to work-in-progress account and the variances written off from work-in-progress account.

(d) (i) The guaranteed weekly wage obscures a true view of the situation. In April, if the workforce had achieved 100% efficiency, it could have produced 4400 A's and 10 500 B's in 18 450 hours, but they would have been paid for 19 200 hours, the difference presumably being idle time of 750 hours. There is no idle time variance for April, however, and yet overtime has been paid. In this case the adverse efficiency variance seems to be overstated.

(ii) The rate of pay variance in April is caused by the payment of overtime $(2400 \div 3 \times £5 = £4000)$ and presumably the reason for this is inefficiency, but it does not show up in the efficiency variance. In May the labour force has worked efficiently, thus avoiding the need to pay overtime. The adverse rate of pay variance without overtime points to the use of higher grade labour.

(iii) Labour efficiency can affect other aspects of production, e.g. a reduction of waste materials.

13.1 (a) *Workings*

Contribution 60p – 48p = 12p or 20% of selling price

Fixed Costs:	£	
Rent	12 000 p.a.	
Labour	7 020 p.a.	$(2 \times £90 \times 39$ weeks$)$
Service	360 p.a.	
Electricity	780 p.a.	$(£20 \times 39$ weeks$)$
	£20 160	

College administration costs are not incremental to this decision and so can be ignored.

Advice

Expected profit:

Contribution (£117 000 × 0.2) − Fixed cost

£23 400　　　　− £20 160 = £3240

Break even point:

$$\frac{£20\,160}{12p} = 168\,000 \text{ sales p.a.}$$

or　　4 308 sales per week

or　　£2 585 average turnover per week

Margin of safety:

Expected sales £3000 less break even sales £2585 = £415

$$\frac{£415}{£3000} \times \frac{100}{1} = 13.8\%$$

At the expected volume of sales, a profit of £3240 would be made. The estimate of expected sales would have to be over-optimistic by 13.8 % before a loss is experienced.

(b) (i) Profit margin of £50 per week for 39 weeks = £1950 of extra contribution required. The new break even point is:

$$\frac{£20\,160 + £1950}{12p} = 184\,250 \text{ sales p.a.}$$

4 724 sales per week
£2 834 average weekly takings

This amount is less than expected sales, so the proposition remains viable.

(ii) *New break even point for change in rental*

Fixed costs of £22 110 + extra fixed costs of £6000 = $\dfrac{£28\,110}{12p}$ = 234 250 annual sales

6 006 weekly sales
£3 603 average weekly takings

This amount is 20 % above expected sales. If the budgeted sales are achieved, a loss of £28 110 − £23 400 (£4710) would be made, but the loss includes payment of £50 × 39 (£1950) to college authorities. The true loss would be £2760.

New break even point for a change in direct cost

60p − 53p = 7p contribution

$$\frac{£22\,110}{7p} = 315\,857 \text{ sales p.a.}$$

8 099 average sales per week
£4 859 average takings per week

If budgeted sales are achieved a loss would be made:

$$£22\,110 - (117\,000 \times \tfrac{7}{60}) = £8460 \text{ loss}$$

$$195\,000 \text{ contributions of 7p} = £13\,650 - £22\,110 = £8460 \text{ loss.}$$

(c) Points to be covered would include:

   (i) relevant range;
   (ii) linearity – some costs behave in a curvilinear manner;
   (iii) fixed and variable costs are not clearly defined and do not behave in the same way throughout the range, e.g. stepped costs;
   (iv) sales of one product only or sales mix stays the same.

13.2 (a) *Old situation*

$$\text{Sales} = \text{Variable cost} + \text{Fixed cost} + \text{Profit}$$
$$£4\,000\,000 = \text{Variable cost} + £600\,000 + £400\,000$$
$$\text{Variable cost} = £3\,000\,000, \text{ which is 0.75 of sales.}$$

New situation

$$£2\,400\,000 = \text{Variable cost} + £660\,000 + £300\,000$$
$$\text{Variable cost} = £1\,440\,000, \text{ which is 0.6 of sales.}$$

Old break even point:

Let S = break even sales
$$S = 0.75S + £600\,000$$
$$0.25S = £600\,000$$

$$S = £600\,000 \times \tfrac{100}{25}$$

$$S = £2\,400\,000$$

New break even point:

Let S = break even sales
$$S = 0.6S + 660\,000$$
$$0.4S = £660\,000$$

$$S = £660\,000 \times \tfrac{10}{4}$$

$$S = £1\,650\,000$$

The break even point is lowered by £750 000.

(b)   Let S = required sales
$$S = 0.6S + £660\,000 + £400\,000$$
$$0.4S = £1\,060\,000$$
$$S = £1\,060\,000 \times \tfrac{10}{4}$$
$$S = £2\,650\,000$$

13.3   (a)   *Profit Statement – Marginal Costing*

		June		July
Sales units		10 000		12 000
Production units		12 000		10 000
	£	£	£	£
Sales at £50		500 000		600 000
Less variable production costs at £25*	300 000		250 000	
Add opening stock	–		50 000	
	300 000		300 000	
Less closing stock	50 000		–	
	250 000		300 000	
Add variable selling expenses	50 000		60 000	
		300 000		360 000
Contribution		200 000		240 000
Less: fixed costs:				
production overheads	99 000		99 000	
selling expenses	15 000		15 000	
administration expenses	25 000		25 000	
		139 000		139 000
Net profit		£61 000		£101 000

*

	£
Direct material cost	18
Direct wages	4
Variable production overheads	3
	£25

Profit Statement – Full Absorption Costing

		June		July
Sales units		10 000		12 000
Production units		12 000		10 000
	£	£	£	£
Sales at £50		500 000		600 000
Less production costs absorbed at £34*	408 000		340 000	
Add opening stock	–		68 000	
	408 000		408 000	
Less closing stock	68 000		–	
	340 000		408 000	
apply (over)/under-absorbed fixed				
production overheads at £9	(9 000)		9 000	
		331 000		417 000
Gross profit		169 000		183 000
Less: variable selling expenses	50 000		60 000	
fixed selling expenses	15 000		15 000	
fixed administration expenses	25 000		25 000	
		90 000		100 000
Net profit		£79 000		£83 000

*

Direct material cost	18	
Direct wages	4	
Variable production overheads	3	
Fixed production overheads	9	(£99 000 ÷ 11 000 units)
	£34	

(b) Taken together, the two bases disclose the same total profit for the two months.

In June marginal costing discloses £18 000 less profit than full absorption costing. This difference is caused by a build up of 2000 units in stock. Under full absorption costing, the fixed production overheads absorbed by these units cost £18 000 (2000 × £9), and this amount is carried forward in the cost of stock rather than being written off against profit in June as with the marginal costing system.

In July, sales exceed production by 2000 units, and the £18 000 of fixed production overheads is charged against revenue, as the stocks created in June have been sold.

14.1 (a)

Volume		40 000	50 000	60 000	70 000	80 000
		£	£	£	£	£
Revenue		16 000	20 000	24 000	28 000	32 000
Direct cost: printing	4000		5000	5600	6200	6800
binding	2400		3000	3600	4200	4800
		6 400	8 000	9 200	10 400	11 600
Contribution		9 600	12 000	14 800	17 600	20 400
Fixed costs		12 000	12 000	12 000	12 000	12 000
Profit/(loss)		£(2 400)	–	£2 800	£5 600	£8 400

Break even

	40 000	50 000	60 000	70 000	80 000
Average cost per copy	£0.46	£0.40	£0.35	£0.32	£0.296
Marginal cost per copy			£0.16	£0.12	£0.12

(b) 10 000 copies remain unsold and £1100 has been offered for them. The books are not yet bound and so have cost £600 in direct production cost. It would cost an extra £600 to bind them, and this cost must be incurred to earn the £1100, thus showing a profit on the deal of £500. The cost of production so far (£600) is irrelevant to this decision since it will not change whether or not the deal is completed. The offer should be accepted unless:

(i) The scrap value of the book is greater than £500 – opportunity cost.

(ii) The deal affects relations with customers who have already bought the book – the ripple effect.

(iii) Holding costs are less than the extra revenue above £1100 expected from future offers.

14.2 (a) A limiting factor is any factor in a business that limits the volume of production at any particular moment or that otherwise prevents the business from performing at maximum capacity. Examples would include:

1. Labour: hours
              grade
2. Machine time: manufacturing capacity
3. Raw materials and components: quantity
                                    quality
4. Financial resources

5. Managerial ability
6. Sales: volume
        price.

(b)

	Willow		Nautical		Floribunda		Cuboid	
	£	£	£	£	£	£	£	£
Selling price		23.0		31.0		25.0		20.0
Direct cost:								
Material	14.0		16.0		14.0		13.0	
Labour	4.5		9.0		6.0		3.0	
		18.5		25.0		20		16.0
Contribution		£4.5		£6.0		£5.0		£4.0
Contribution per labour- hour		6.0		4.0		5.0		8.0
Contribution per machine-hour		1.5		6.0		2.5		2.0

Ranking with labour as limiting factor: Cuboid, Willow, Floribunda, Nautical
Ranking with machine time as limiting factor: Nautical, Floribunda, Cuboid, Willow

Labour time required to manufacture sales potential = 2100 hours
Labour time available (10 × 40 × 4) = 1600 hours

(i)   *Production Plan* (Labour as limiting factor)

	Willow	Nautical	Floribunda	Cuboid	Total
Volume produced	600	166	400	1000	
Contribution	£2700	£996	£2000	£4000	£9696
Fixed costs					£6000
Profit					£3696

(ii)   *Production Plan* (Machine times as limiting factor)

	Willow	Nautical	Floribunda	Cuboid	Total
Volume produced	–	500	400	420	
Contribution	–	£3000	£2000	£1680	£6680
Fixed cost					£6000
Profit					£680

14.3 (a)   *Budgeted Production Statement*

	Willow	Cuboid	Floribunda	Nautical	Total
Volume	30 000	10 000	8 000	10 000	
Price	£3.00	£3.50	£2.50	£2.00	
	£	£	£	£	£
Revenue	90 000	35 000	20 000	20 000	
Costs:					
Material	27 000	10 000	7 200	8 500	
Labour	18 000	5 000	4 000	7 500	
Factory overheads	15 000	5 000	4 000	5 000	
Transport	3 000	3 000	3 000	3 000	
Administration	2 000	2 000	2 000	2 000	
Selling	14 000	10 000	4 800	5 000	
	79 000	35 000	25 000	31 000	
Profit (loss)	11 000	–	(5000)	(11 000)	£(5000)

(b)

Statement in Contribution Terms

	Willow	Cuboid	Floribunda	Nautical	Total
	£	£	£	£	£
Revenue	90 000	35 000	20 000	20 000	
Direct costs:					
Material	27 000	10 000	7 200	8 500	
Labour	18 000	5 000	4 000	7 500	
	45 000	15 000	11 200	16 000	
Contribution	45 000	20 000	8 800	4 000	
Less: Other variable costs in context of closure:					
Transport	3 000	3 000	3 000	3 000	
Selling	14 000	10 000	4 800	5 000	
Contribution	28 000	7 000	1 000	(4000)	32 000
Fixed overheads					(29 000)
Administration					(8 000)
					Loss £5 (000)

Advice to Managing Director:

1. If his decision is implemented, positive contributions of Cuboid and Floribunda are lost, and contribution of Willow is reduced by £3000 (being a quarter of material cost as rebate is lost), so loss increases to £12 000.
2. Retain products with positive contribution.
   Drop products with negative contribution.
   Loss reduced to £1000.
3. Seek means to improve contribution of Floribunda by cutting costs, increasing sales, or transferring demand from Nautical.

14.4   *Workings*

	Last Year £ (per unit)	10 000 units		Next Year £ (per unit)
Selling price	190.0			
Material	60.0		+30%	78.0
Labour	60.0		+15%	69.0
Direct cost etc.	6.0		+20%	7.2
Variable overheads	8.0		+10%	8.8
	£134.0			£163.0
Contribution	56.0	560 000		
Fixed overheads	24.0	240 000	+5%	£252 000
Profit		£320 000		

(a)

		£
Profit required		320 000
Fixed costs to cover		252 000
Contribution required		£572 000
Number of units		10 000
Contribution per unit		47.2
Variable cost		163.0
Selling price		£220.2

(b)

		£
Selling price		190.0
Variable cost		163.0
Contribution per unit		£27.0
Contribution required		£572 000
At £27 per unit		21 185 units

(c)

	£	£
Selling price	210.0	175.0
Variable cost	163.0	163.0
Contribution per unit	47.0	12.0
Units	8 000	20 000
Contribution	376 000	240 000
Fixed cost	252 000	252 000
Profit/(Loss)	£124 000	£(12 000)

Data provided are incomplete as we do not know what happens at intermediate prices. However, we do know (see part [a]) that simply to maintain profit at last year's level, 10 000 units would need to be sold at £220.2. Could 10 000 units be sold at this price? In the light of the market research, part (b) presents an unrealistic option – only 20 000 would be sold at £175. The best available result, therefore, comes from a price of £220, which gives a reduced profit.

15.1 (a) *Points of principle*
1. Depreciation is excluded from NPV calculation.
2. Plant transferred is accounted for at exit value – opportunity cost.
3. Redundancy payment to manager is saved – the rule for incremental costs is applied – but will there be a redundancy payment at the end of the project?
4. Head office costs are ignored, not incremental costs.
5. Feasibility study is a sunk cost and should be excluded.
6. An alternative is to sell the machinery at once for £80 000, thus attracting a tax balancing charge of £32 000.

The calculation of cash flow is based on a contribution per product of £20.

	Year 1	Year 2	Year 3	Year 4
Volume	4 000	6 000	6 000	2 000
	£	£	£	£
Contribution	80 000	120 000	120 000	40 000
Direct costs	17 600	24 600	24 600	24 600
	62 400	95 400	95 400	15 400
Tax at 40%	24 960	38 160	38 160	6 160

£25 000 + £6 200 = £31 220 written off against taxable profit reduces tax paid by 40% × £31 220 = £12 488 + (40% of £20 000 for advertising) £8000 = £20 488

Year	Cash Flow £	Capital Expenditure £	Tax £	Net £	Discount Factor 15% £	PV £
		(80 000)				
0	(20 000)	(6 220)	–	(131 220)	1.0000	(131 220)
		(25 000)				
1	62 400	–	20 488	82 888	0.8696	72 079
2	95 400	(5 000)	(24 960)	65 440	0.7561	49 479
3	95 400	(10 000)	(38 160)	49 240	0.6572	32 360
			2 000			
4	15 400	–	(38 160)	(18 760)	0.5718	(10 727)
			4 000			
5	–	–	(6 160)	(6 160)	0.4972	(3 063)
					NPV	£ 8 908

Outflows are in brackets

There is a positive NPV so the project is viable

(b)

Year	Discount Factor 25% £	Cash Flow £	PV £
0	1.000	(131 220)	(131 220)
1	0.8000	82 888	66 310
2	0.6400	65 440	41 881
3	0.5120	49 240	25 211
4	0.4096	(18 760)	(7 684)
5	0.3277	(6 160)	(2 019)
			(7 522)

$$15 + \left(\frac{8908}{8908 + 7522} \times 10 \right) = 20.4\%$$

IRR of project

$$20 - 15 = 5 \qquad \frac{5}{15} = 33\%$$

An error of 33% of the cost of capital figure used in the calculations would be needed before the project ceases to be viable.

(c)

1. The volume changes over 4 years: will variable costs behave in proportion to this
    fluctuation and will fixed costs show a tendency to be semi-variable? For
    example, with labour, there is no estimate for recruitment, training or
    redundancy costs.

2. A project such as this will require servicing by working capital in order to fund
    stocks and debtors. This aspect of capital employed in the project has been
    omitted from the analysis. A significant amount applied in Year 1 and disinvested
    in Years 3 and 4 after the application of the discount factor could affect the NPV
    calculation.

3. Uncertainty – the calculations above depend on a single estimate for factors such
    as materials, labour, overheads and revenues. The probability that alternative
    cost levels may apply should be taken into account, as should the possibility that
    changes in costs may cancel each other out or may all tend in the same direction.
    The market survey should have produced information as to the probability of
    various sales volumes that may be experienced.

15.2   Tax

Capital allowance is 25% of £40 000 = £10 000 in Year 1 and the remaining cost of
£30 000 in Year 2.

Cash flow Year 1 is £28 000 less capital allowance £10 000 gives taxable profit of
£18 000, so 40% thereof (£7200) is paid out in Year 2 as tax.

Cash flow Year 2 is £28 000 less capital allowances of £30 000, which means that taxable
profit is reduced by £2000 and tax paid is £800 **less** in Year 3.

Production Project

Year	Cash Flow	Tax	Net	PV(10%)	PV(15%)	PV(20%)
	£	£	£	£	£	£
0	(40 000)	–	(40 000)	(40 000)	(40 000)	(40 000)
1	28 000	–	28 000	25 452	24 360	23 324
2	28 000	(7200)	20 800	17 180	15 725	14 435
3	–	800	800	600	526	463
			NPV	£3 232	£611	£(1 778)

Outflows are in brackets

$$\text{IRR} = 15 + \left(\frac{611}{2389} \times 5\right) = 16.28\%$$

Marketing Project

Year	Cash Flow	Tax	Net	PV(10%)	PV(20%)	PV(25%)
	£	£	£	£	£	£
0	(4300)	–	(4300)	(4300)	(4300)	(4300)
1	3200	–	3200	2909	2666	2560
2	3200	320	3520	2908	2443	2253
3		(1280)	(1280)	(961)	(741)	(655)
			NPV	£556	£68	£(142)

$$\text{IRR} = 20 + \left(\frac{68}{210} \times 5\right) = 21.62\%$$

Cash flow Year 1 is £3200 less £4000 expenditure written off, therefore taxable profit is reduced by £800 and tax paid is 40% thereof (£320) **less**.

Differential Analysis

Year	P	M	P − M	PV(15%)	PV(20%)
	£	£	£	£	£
0	(40 000)	(4300)	(35 700)	(35 700)	(35 700)
1	28 000	3200	24 800	21 576	20 658
2	20 800	3520	17 280	13 064	11 992
3	800	(1280)	2 080	1 369	1 204
				£309	£(1 846)

$$\text{IRR} = 15 + \left(\frac{309}{2155} \times 5 \right) = 15.72\%$$

Significant Features

1. The marketing suggestion is open-ended since it will give benefits after Year 2. When comparing the alternatives, the total returns from each scheme should be considered.

2. The production suggestion uses all the funds, but the marketing suggestion does not. A meaningful comparison must compare one scheme for the investment of £40 000 with another for the use of that amount. The marketing suggestion needs to be combined with a third suggestion to use up all the funds available.

3. The IRR of the incremental cash flows of the production scheme over the marketing scheme is 15.72%. Thus, unless the surplus funds not taken up by the marketing scheme can be invested at a rate in excess of this, then the production scheme will be the best alternative.

4. The production scheme is best when the NPV is computed using a 10% discount rate, but the marketing suggestion wins if the IRR criterion is used. The size of the production scheme accounts for its victory under the NPV system. The IRR, or yield method, is only significant if there is a certainty that funds can be reinvested at the yield rate. No such certainty exists here.

5. The alternatives may not have the same degree of risk. Clearly opinions as to comparative riskiness differ within the management team.

6. The cost of capital used to evaluate the projects is 10% after tax. This does not represent what can be earned on short-term investments. Quandary Limited may be willing to invest below the cost of capital in the short run, in order to have funds available when they are needed for the factory extension. Liquidity is more important in this case than profitability.

15.3 (a) *Close Now*

		£
Sell lease		30 000
Sell plant		40 000
Less closure cost		(7 000)
		£63 000

Close in Three Years

Year	Inflow £	Lease Sale £	Plant Sale £	Closure Cost £	Net £	Discount Factor £	
1	47 000				47 000	0.909	42 723
2	18 000				18 000	0.826	14 860
3	18 000	24 000	10 000	(9000)	43 000	0.751	32 293

PV of net cash flow   **£89 876**

Close in Five Years

Year	Inflow £	Lease Sale £	Plant Sale £	Closure Cost £	Net £	Discount Factor	£
1	47 000				47 000	0.909	42 723
2	18 000				18 000	0.826	14 868
3	18 000				18 000	0.751	13 518
4	11 000				11 000	0.683	7 513
5	(8 525)	16 000	–	(11 000)	(3 525)	0.621	(2 189)

PV of net cash flow   **£76 433**

Workings

		19–3 £		19–4 £		19–5 £		19–6 £		19–7 £
	£		£		£		£		£		
Selling price		20		20		20		20		20
Cost:										
Material	4		4		4		4		4	
Labour	8		9		9		9		10.35	
		12		13		13		13		14.35
Contribution		8		7		7		7		5.65
Volume		8 000		5 000		5 000		4 000		1 500
		£		£		£		£		£
Total contribution		64 000		35 000		35 000		28 000		8 475
Less fixed overheads		25 000		25 000		25 000		25 000		25 000
Net profit		39 000		10 000		10 000		3 000		(16 525)
Add back depreciation		8 000		8 000		8 000		8 000		8 000
Cash inflow		£47 000		£18 000		£18 000		£11 000		(£8 525)

(b) Other significant factors:

    (i) Working capital should be brought into the calculation. This will favour immediate closure. Over a five-year scheme, a run-down of sales leads to a gradual disinvestment. The effect of discounting reduces the significance of inflows in later years.

    (ii) Can we find an alternative to closure, to:
      (a) stimulate demand
      (b) cut prices
      (c) find a new market
      (d) find a different product?

    (iii) Is the machinery so specific that it can only make cots? There seems to be too much machinery for our needs – can we sell some now and still keep going? Will maintenance costs increase in future years?

    (iv) What alternatives may appear during the next few years that are not available now? If we close at once we cannot take advantage of them.

    (v) How dependable is the market survey demand profile and other estimates of future costs and receipts?

    (vi) What alternative employment will be available for our capital if it is disinvested in two years' time?

    (vii) Capital loss on machines – this is a red herring, since it represents past profits overstated and can have no impact on the disinvestment position.

    (viii) Extra £27 000 if we wait to close for three years at 9000 p.a. – is it worth the risk?

    (ix) The validity of 10% cost of capital as discounting factor.

16.1 Market Develops in One Year: probability 0.1 (10%)
Market Develops in Four Years: probability 0.3 (30%)
Market Develops in Five Years: probability 0.6 (60%)

Alternatives

Develop now; wait one year; abandon. If they wait one year they must then decide in the light of new market information whether to develop, abandon, or wait one more year. If they delay a second year they must then decide whether to develop or abandon.

Decision

Wait one year because a likely cash flow of £179 457 is better than £55 500 or nil from the alternatives.

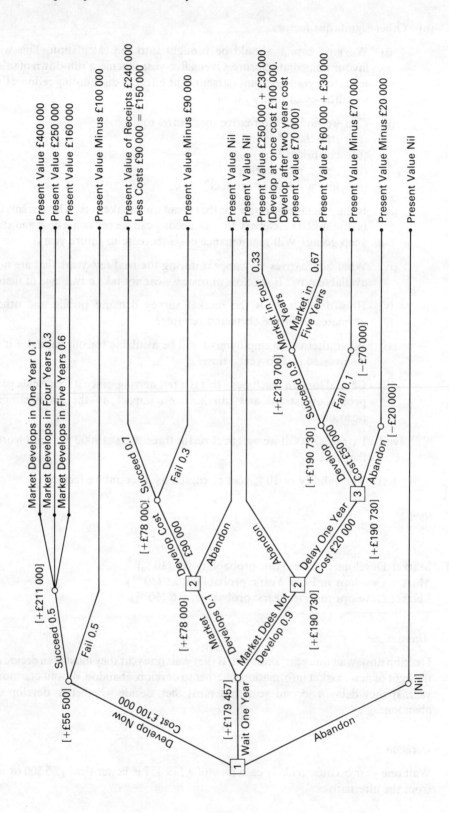

16.2 (a)

		Stutz Bearcat		Bugatti		Bentley 4½ litre
Expected sales (units)	2000×0.7	1400	3000×0.4	1200	2500×0.1	250
	3000×0.2	600	6000×0.5	3000	3000×0.3	900
	4000×0.1	400			4000×0.4	1600
			Nil×0.1	–	5000×0.2	1000
		2400		4200		3750
Contribution per unit		£101		£65		£50
		£		£		£
Total contribution		242 400		273 000		187 500
Rights	62 500		75 000		52 500	
Fixed production costs	70 000		95 000		60 000	
Advertising	55 000		40 000		20 000	
Fixed costs		187 500		210 000		132 500
Expected profit		£54 900		£63 000		£55 000

The highest expected profit arises from acquiring the rights to the Bugatti.

(b) Many other factors may need to be considered. These could include:

    i) Attitude to risk. Many managements are conservative and averse to risk, whilst others are more aggressive and willing to take higher risks.

    ii) Accuracy of estimates of costs and selling prices. An under-estimate of £15 on selling price or variable costs would wipe out the profit on the Bugatti.

    iii) Accuracy of probabilities. These are clearly crucial to the outcome.

    iv) Possibility of competition using different designs or imitation.

    v) Production capacity. Could an additional line be produced using existing capacity, or would new capacity be required?

    vi) Size of venture/profit relative to total turnover and profit.

(c)

Sales (units)	Contribution £		Fixed Costs £	Profit £	Profit × Probability £
0	0	less	210 000	(210 000) ×0.1	(21 000)
3000×65 =	195 000	less	210 000	(15 000) ×0.4	(6 000)
6000×65 =	390 000	less	210 000	180 000 ×0.5	90 000
				Expected profit	£63 000

The possible outcomes show that there are equal chances of profit or loss. If sales are 0 to 3000 (combined probability of 0.5 or 50%) then losses will occur. If sales are 6000 (probability 0.5 or 50%) then there will be a substantial profit.

Since all costs are avoidable, it would be worthwhile to spend £20 000 on the market research study. This would have the effect, should this product prove unsuitable, of reducing by £20 000 the expected profit on the next best product – the Bentley – but would avoid the situation where a loss is made, e.g. cost of survey £20 000 less loss avoided, say £6000 = cost of being certain, £14 000, to deduct from profit on the Bentley of £55 000. A potential loss of £6000 is transformed into a likely profit of £41 000.

17.1   Evaluation of managerial performance should include all elements in the division that management can control. The degree of autonomy enjoyed by a division will determine the control that managers maintain over pricing, investment and other factors that affect profit.

Profit Contribution

The division has contributed £119 000 to the central costs and profit of the group, but this is well below budget. The responsibility of management for this deficit depends on the influence that divisional managers can exercise over sales, marketing and costs, and whether the budget used as a yardstick was attainable in realistic terms. Contribution does not take into account the assets under the control of divisional management and cannot comment on the return on investment needed to earn that return. Management at Roverbix division could increase contribution by the wasteful investment of group funds at returns below the cost of capital without suffering any penalty if this method were used to evaluate their performance.

Net Income

This measure of performance shows only a small net profit for the division. As a performance evaluator it fails to set return against investment and also includes head office charges, which, presumably, are outside the control of divisional management.

Return on Investment (ROI)

$$\frac{\text{Net income}}{\text{Investment}} \times \frac{100}{1} = \frac{12 \times £19\,000}{£2\,850\,000} \times \frac{100}{1} = 8\%$$

Whether this performance is good or bad depends on the expected return and the cost of capital for the group (15%). It certainly sets the return against investment, but for evaluation of managerial performance perhaps centrally administered assets and allocated head office costs should not be included in the analysis. Perhaps the following could be used as an alternative.

$$\frac{£119\,000 \times 12}{£2\,780\,000} \times \frac{100}{1} = 51\%$$

The measurement of profit and investment may be made in ways that lead to unreliable conclusions from ROI, e.g. historic cost of assets set against current cost revenue. Decisions that maximise divisional ROI may not necessarily be best for the group as a whole.

Residual Income

Residual income is the income remaining after deducting a charge for the use of funds invested in the division based on the cost of capital.

	Net profit	£19 000
(2 850 000 × 0.15 ÷ 12)	Investment charge	£35 625
	Residual income	£(16 625)

Management are not making sufficient return to service group funds allocated to the division at the group cost of capital. However, if head office expenses and centrally administered assets are excluded, a divisional residual income can be calculated relating to factors that divisional managers can influence. Residual income can be calculated as follows:

		£
Net profit		119 000
Investment charge	2 780 000 × 0.15 ÷ 12	34 750
Residual income		£84 250

Other measures of managerial performance:

Stock control

$$\frac{\text{Closing stock materials}}{\text{Usage of materials}} \times \frac{365}{1} = \frac{£900\,000}{£800\,000 \times 12} \times \frac{365}{1} = 34 \text{ days}$$

Debtor control

$$\frac{\text{Debtors}}{\text{Credit sales}} \times \frac{365}{1} = \frac{£900\,000}{(\frac{1}{2} \times 1\,140\,000 \times 12)} \times \frac{365}{1} = 48 \text{ days}$$

(b) *Economic Performance.* This is to decide whether the division produces enough income to support the capital invested in it. Does invested capital produce more than it costs? To this end, all costs of the division, whether controllable by divisional management or not, and all traceable and centrally administered assets should be taken into account. All divisions are compared according to a single standard.

18.1 (a) (i) Motivation: to promote goal congruence between divisions in order to attain top management goals.
   (ii) Motivation: to promote a healthy, competitive spirit between divisions, without causing needless arguments, in a manner conducive to the success of the company as a whole.
   (iii) Performance evaluation.
   (iv) To aid policy decisions, e.g. resource allocation.
   (v) To preserve the autonomy of decision making within divisions.
   (vi) To enable the transfer of profit between countries by international groups in order to minimise overall tax, reduce import duties, move funds etc.

(b) *Division B*

Variable cost per unit = £75 000 + £10 000 + £15 000 + £5000 = £105 000 ÷ 50 000 units = £2.10

   (i) The company as a whole will not benefit if Division A buys from outside suppliers:

Purchase cost	10 000 × £2.50	25 000
Divisions B's saving in variable costs	10 000 × £2.10	21 000
		£4 000 (A)

(ii) The company as a whole will benefit if Division A buys from outside suppliers:

Purchase cost	10 000 × £1.80	18 000
Division B's saving in variable costs	10 000 × £2.10	21 000
		£3 000 (F)

(c)   *Main Reasons for Cost Plus Pricing*

(i) Risk sharing: if productive returns are uncertain, interdivisional risk sharing may be facilitated by the cost plus arrangement. Of course, this presumes some insurance or risk-sharing market imperfection.

(ii) The variable costs may underestimate the marginal cost because of competing products; if the form uses full costing plus the proper allowance as a substitute for the opportunity cost of production.

Reasons against:

(i) The use of full cost is widespread. The performance of the recovering division will bear the accumulated efficiencies or inefficiencies of other divisions not subject to their control. Transfer prices that ensure recovery of the selling division's actual costs often fail to provide an incentive to control costs.

(ii) Full cost pricing is dangerous, as prices contain the cost of under-utilised capacity and a profit mark-up. The use of such prices may tend to hide inefficiency, since any excess cost incurred by a transferral division are passed on to the transferees in the transfer prices.

19.1

Cost Ledger Control Account

	£		£
Sales account	415 000	1.5. – Balance b/f	305 000
Capital under construction account	54 150	Stores ledger account:	
		Purchases	41 700
Balance c/f	234 500	Wages control account	126 000
		Production overhead account	151 350
		Work-in-progress account:	
		Royalty	3 150
		Selling overhead account	21 000
		Profit	55 450
	£703 650		£703 650

Stores Ledger Control Account

	£		£
1.5.–Balance b/f	86 400	Work-in-progress account:	
Cost ledger control account:		Issues	64 400
		Production overhead account:	
Purchases	41 700	Issues	2 450
		Capital account:	
		Issues	8 650
		31.5.–Balance c/f	52 600
	£128 100		£128 100

Wages Control Account

	£		£
Cost ledger control account	126 000	Capital account	13 500
		Production overhead account	37 750
		Work-in-progress account	74 750
	£126 000		£126 000

Production Overhead Control Account

	£		£
Stores Ledger account:			
Issues	2 450	Capital account	32 000
Wages control account	37 750	Work-in-progress account:	
		Absorption (*Note* 1)	153 000
Cost ledger control account	151 350	Costing p/l account	6 550
	£191 550		£191 550

Work-in-Progress Control Account

	£		£
1.5. – Balance b/f	168 350	Finished goods control account (*Note* 3)	282 300
Stores ledger account:			
Issues	64 400	31.5. – Balance c/f (*Note* 2)	181 350
Wages control account	74 750		
Production overheads absorbed	153 000		
Cost ledger control account:			
Royalty	3 150		
	£463 650		£463 650

Finished Goods Control Account

	£		£
1.5.–Balance b/f	50 250	Cost of sales account (*Note 4*)	332 000
Work-in-progress account	282 300	31.5. – Balance c/f	550
	£332 550		£332 550

Capital under Construction Account

	£		£
Stores ledger account	8 650	Cost ledger control account	54 150
Wages control account	13 500		
Production overheads absorbed	32 000		
	£54 150		£54 150

Sales Account

	£		£
Costing p/l account	£415 000	Cost ledger control account	£415 000

Cost of Sales Account

	£		£
Finished goods account (*Note 4*)	£332 000	Costing p/l account	£332 000

Selling Overhead Account

	£		£
Costing ledger control account	£21 000	Costing p/l account	£21 000

Costing Profit and Loss Account

	£		£
Selling overhead account	21 000	Sales account	415 000
Production overheads under-absorbed	6 550		
Cost of sales account	332 000		
Profit:			
Cost ledger control account	55 450		
	£415 000		£415 000

Note 1   Balancing figure.

Note 2   Closing balance of work-in-progress = £168 350 (opening balance)

$$+ \text{£ 13 000 (increase per question)}$$
$$\underline{\underline{\text{£181 350}}}$$

Note 3   Balancing figure.

Note 4   Transfer from finished goods stocks to cost of sales $= £415\,000 \times \dfrac{100}{125} = £332\,000$

A simple trial balance will agree at £234 500.

Index